About the
Author

D1365828

About the Author

The Passionate Reader's Guide
to the Authors You Love, Including Things
You Never Knew, Juicy Bits You'll
Want to Know, and Hundreds of Ideas
for What to Read Next

Alfred Glossbrenner and Emily Glossbrenner

CADER BOOKS

A HARVEST ORIGINAL • HARCOURT, INC.

SAN DIEGO   NEW YORK   LONDON

Copyright © 2000 by Alfred Glossbrenner and Emily Glossbrenner and Cader Company Inc.

All rights reserved. No part of this publication may be reproduced or transmitted in any form or by any means, electronic or mechanical, including photocopy, recording, or any information storage and retrieval system, without permission in writing from the publisher.

Requests for permission to make copies of any part of the work should be mailed to the following address: Permissions Department, Harcourt, Inc., 6277 Sea Harbor Drive, Orlando, Florida 32887-6777.

Produced by Cader Books
38 E. 29 Street
New York, NY 10016
www.caderbooks.com

Library of Congress Cataloging-in-Publication Data
Glossbrenner, Alfred.
About the author: the passionate reader's guide to the authors you love, including things you never knew, juicy bits you'll want to know, and hundreds of ideas for what to read next / Alfred and Emily Glossbrenner with Cader Books.—1st ed.
p.   cm.
Includes index
ISBN 0-15-601302-9
1. Literature—Bio-bibliography—Dictionaries.
I. Glossbrenner, Emily.   II. Title.
PN451.G56   2000
809".003—dc21   99-086206
[B]

Designed by Charles Kreloff
Text set in ITC Century Condensed
Printed in the United States of America
First edition 2000

K J I H G F E D C B A

PHOTO CREDITS

p. 4: Frank Capri/SAGA/Archive Photos; p. 6: Frank Capri/SAGA/Archive Photos; p. 8: Reuters/Gary Hershorn/Archive Photos; p. 10: Steven Wassen/SAGA/Archive Photos; p. 12: Corbis/Hulton-Deutsch Collection; p. 14: Library of Congress, Prints & Photographs Division, Carl Van Vechten Collection; p. 16: Marion Ettlinger/Corbis Outline; p. 18: Corbis/Hulton-Deutsch Collection; p.22: AP Photo/Michel Lipchitz; p.24: AP Photo/Steve Castillo; p. 28: Corbis/Bettmann; p. 30: Corbis/Caroline Penn; p. 32: Library of Congress, Prints & Photographs Division, Carl Van Vechten Collection; p. 34: David Barry/Corbis Outline; p. 36: Popperfoto/Archive Photos; p. 38: Corbis/Bettmann; p. 40: Bernard Gotfryd/Archive Photos; p. 42: Hulton Deutsch Collection; p. 44: Corbis/Matthew Mendelsohn; p. 46: Frank Capri/SAGA/Archive Photos; p. 48: Archive Photos; p. 50: Frank Capri/SAGA/Archive Photos; p. 52: Corbis/© John M. Mantel; p. 54: Corbis/AFP; p. 56: Bernard Gotfryd/ Archive Photos; p. 58: Hulton Deutsch Collection; p. 60: Corbis/Bettmann; p. 62: Hulton Deutsch Collection; p. 64: Hulton Deutsch Collection; p. 66: Bernard Gotfryd/Archive Photos; p. 68: Christopher Little/Corbis Outline; p. 70: Library of Congress, Prints & Photographs Division, Carl Van Vechten Collection; p. 72: Library of Congress, Prints & Photographs Division, Carl Van Vechten Collection; p. 76: AP Photo/HO, Columbia University; p. 78: Corbis/E.O Hoppe; p. 80: Corbis/Hulton-Deutsch Collection; p. 82: Frank Capri/SAGA/Archive Photos; p. 84: Corbis/Bettmann; p. 86: Frank Capri/SAGA/Archive Photos; p. 88: Bernard Gotfryd/Archive Photos; p. 90: Frank Capri/SAGA/Archive Photos; p. 92: AP Photo/File; p. 94: Corbis/Bettmann; p. 98: AP/Wide World Photos; p. 100: Frank Capri/SAGA/Archive Photos; p. 102: Frank Capri/SAGA/Archive Photos; p. 104: Hulton Deutsch Collection; p. 106: AP Photo/Natasha Lane; p. 108: AP Photo/Patricia McDonnell; p. 110: Library of Congress, Prints & Photographs Division, Carl Van Vechten Collection; p. 112: AP Photo/Craig Line, File; p. 114: Archive Photos; p. 116: Sarah Hood/SAGA/Archive Photos; p. 118: John Petter Reinertsen, Samfoto AS; p. 120: Hulton Deutsch Collection; p. 122: Jim Foreman; p. 124: AP Photo/G. Paul Burnett; p. 126: Corbis/AFP; p. 128: AP/Wide World Photos; p. 130: Corbis/Bettmann-UPI; p. 132: Corbis/© John M. Mantel; p. 134: Corbis/Roger Ressmeyer; p. 136: Hulton Deutsch Collection; p. 138: Sarah Hood/SAGA/ Archive Photos; p. 140: Frank Capri/SAGA/Archive Photos; p. 142: Corbis/Bettmann; p. 144: Corbis/Roger Ressmeyer; p. 146: Archive Photos; p. 148: Library of Congress, Prints & Photographs Division, Carl Van Vechten Collection; p. 150: Archive Photos/David Lees; p. 152: AP/Wide World Photos; p. 154: Anthony Browell; p. 156: Frank Capri/SAGA/ Archive Photos; p. 158: Corbis/Mitch Gerber; p. 160: Lee/Archive Photos; p. 162: Corbis/Bettmann; p. 164: Frank Capri/SAGA/Archive Photos; p. 166: AP/Wide World Photos; p. 168: Archive Photos; p. 170: Horst Tappe/Archive Photos; p. 172: Archive Photos; p. 174: © 1980 John Marmaras; p. 176: Frank Capri/SAGA/ Archive Photos; p. 180: courtesy St. Martin's Press; p. 182: Corbis/© Veronica Herndon/LGI Photo Agency; p. 184: Bernard Gotfryd/Archive Photos; p. 188: Corbis/Oscar White; p. 190: Mitchell Gerber/Corbis; p. 192: Archive Photos; p. 194: courtesy of Scholastic, Inc.; p. 196: Corbis/Bettmann-UPI; p. 198: Corbis/Hulton-Deutsch Collection; p. 200: Roddy McDowall; p. 202: Frank Capri/SAGA/Archive Photos; p. 204: AP/Wide World Photos; p. 206: AP Photo/Str/Tom Keller; p. 208: Bernard Fallon/Corbis Outline; p. 210: Corbis/Alex Gotfryd-Peter C. Jones; p. 212: Archive Photos; p. 214: Peter Simon; p. 216: Frank Capri/SAGA/Archive Photos; p. 218: Archive Photos/Express Newspapers; p. 220: Hulton Deutsch Collection; p. 222: SAGA/Archive Photos; p. 224: Hulton Deutsch Collection; p. 226: Diana Walker; p. 228: SAGA/ Archive Photos; p. 230: Library of Congress, Prints & Photographs Division, Carl Van Vechten Collection; p. 232: Frank Capri/SAGA/Archive Photos; p. 234: © Renato Rotolo/Corbis; p. 236: Library of Congress, Prints & Photographs Division, Carl Van Vechten Collection; p. 238: AP/Wide World Photos; p. 240: Archive Photos; p. 242: AP/Wide World Photos; p. 244: Library of Congress, Prints & Photographs Division, Carl Van Vechten Collection; p. 246: Reuters/Jacky Naegelen/Archive Photos; p. 248: Hulton Deutsch Collection; p. 250: Library of Congress, Prints & Photographs Division, Carl Van Vechten Collection;

Contents

Acknowledgments

There are more elegant ways to convey the thought, but the fact is, this book is the product of a heck of a lot of work on the part of a heck of a lot of people. Starting with Michael Cader, who helped us shape our original idea, designed the book, and found the perfect editor, Jane Isay at Harcourt. Passionate readers themselves, Michael and Jane offered countless ideas and suggestions for making the book informative, lively, and fun. We couldn't have done it without them.

We'd also like to thank Chris O'Connell for his careful copyediting and fact checking of the manuscript, as well as Alison Pavia. And a special thanks as well to Camille N. Cline, an editor with whom we had worked on other projects at Cader Books. Now a senior editor at Taylor Publishing, Camille generously shared her list of freelancers with us. Without these talented people, and one or two others we found on our own, we might still be writing. Thus we gratefully acknowledge the invaluable assistance and contributions of Josh Boak, Cristine Grace, Amy Lemley, Shelley Lewis, Timothy A. Meis, Nicholas Montemarano, Jennifer Nauss, Eileen Smith, Susan Steinberg, Phil Stockwell, Joel Weinstein, and Kathleen Valenzi.

Finally, we'd like to thank the many bookstore owners and bookstore clerks we've encountered over the years who are so skilled at "hand selling"—taking a customer aside and personally explaining the appeal of a particular author or book. Their efforts have certainly broadened our reading lives, just as we hope this book will broaden yours.

About the Authors

Alfred and Emily Glossbrenner have been delighting readers for over 25 years. Alfred began writing shortly after graduating from Princeton in 1972. Emily joined him in 1990, leaving a successful career at IBM for the vagaries of the writing trade. Known for their in-depth research and uncanny ability to identify and present the essence of a topic, the Glossbrenners are the authors of over 60 books, with combined sales of over one million copies. Their work has been consistently praised by publications as diverse as *Booklist*, *Forbes*, *Esquire*, *Wired*, and the *New York Times*. Passionate readers for as long as they can remember, Alfred and Emily live and write in a book-filled 1790s farmhouse in Bucks County, Pennsylvania.

Introduction

Has a novel ever left you breathless? Have you ever found yourself sitting in stunned silence after reading the last line, the totality of the experience resonating within? At odd moments, do unforgettable characters and striking scenes float unbidden into your brain? Is talking about books and exchanging tips on what to read next one of the great pleasures of your life?

If so, you are definitely a *passionate reader*. You're someone who has discovered that, in Emily Dickinson's famous line, "There is no frigate like a book to take us lands away." Nor is there any movie, TV show, or interactive multimedia computer game that can match the experience of reading a novel. You are someone for whom reading is as essential as oxygen—some part of you would die if you were denied access to fiction. Well, as immodest as it sounds, if you like to read, you will love this book.

You'll find it is packed with the kind of information that will enhance the pleasure you can derive from a favorite author while telling you what you need to know about authors you have not yet read. And there are tons of suggestions on what to read next.

That's the broad overview. Which may be all you need. Frankly, we don't usually read introductions, at least not past the first four paragraphs. So go ahead. Thumb through the book. Dip in anywhere. Then, if you can pull yourself away, come back here for a briefing on how *About the Author* was designed and the features it includes.

The Juicy Bits and More

Many have argued that a work of art stands on its own and that details about the person who created it are irrelevant. They may be right. But we still want to know those details! Somehow, knowing that William Faulkner faked a war-injury limp and walked with a cane when returning from World War I—which he had spent as a trainee in the Canadian Royal Air Force, never seeing combat of any kind—makes this Nobel Laureate more approachable. As has often been said, all writers are liars, but few have demonstrated such audacity. Yet this was never mentioned when we studied Faulkner in school.

Similarly, we think it's charming that Sue Grafton's father wrote mystery novels in his spare time—some of which were published to good reviews—and we love the fact that she has a grandchild named Kinsey. We like knowing that both Amy Tan and Barbara Kingsolver are talented musicians who perform in a band called the Rock Bottom Remainders with Dave Barry, Stephen King, and Matt Groening. No professor ever told us that Henry James felt that criticism was intellectually superior to creative writing, and that he saw himself primarily as a critic. And we were shocked—shocked, mind you—to learn that a particularly randy author claimed she had to have sex with her lover at least twice a week to combat writer's block.

That's what we mean by "juicy bits" in the subtitle of this book. The facts are well documented. But they never appear in academically oriented reference works, most of which are designed to provide critical commentary, and many of which limit themselves to writers of serious literature. We don't do that here.

Instead, we assume that you have access to the *Encyclopedia Britannica* (available at www.britannica.com free of charge), *Benét's Reader's Encyclopedia,* and other reference works of comparable quality. (See our "Catalogs and References" section for additional suggestions.) If you need term-paper-style information, there are plenty of other places to turn, including the many companion volumes and leading critical studies cited in most of our author write-ups.

We are also aware that passionate readers—recognizing that good stories are being told by talented writers in every genre—read fiction of all stripes and types. Sometimes you crave the exquisite prose of a John Updike or the piercing insights of an Ann Beattie, but at other times nothing but the fast-paced plotting of a Dick Francis or a John Grisham will do. *About the Author* is a book that speaks to these and many similar urges, while tempting you to expand your boundaries further still.

The Selection Process

About now, you're sure to be asking yourself, "How did they decide which 125 writers to profile?" We began with the stipulation that only writers of fiction would be considered.

Then, with input from academics, booksellers, editors, and other passionate readers, we began to develop a preliminary list. We consulted bestseller lists, lists of prize winners, and lists of memorable films based on novels. We also looked for authors whose work has had an impact on our culture, and we tried to identify the leaders in every major genre. We looked for writers from different eras and for newer writers with rapidly expanding audiences and growing acclaim from fans.

The result was a list of over 500 authors, each of whom deserves to be read for one reason or another. In winnowing that number to a manageable 125, we looked first to see if a "corona of interest" had developed around the author. Is there a fan club? Is there a Web site? Are there companion volumes and biographies? In effect, are there resources we can direct you to that will enhance your enjoyment of the author? We make no claim that these 125 authors were chosen because they are somehow better or more talented than the hundreds not included. Indeed, it was never our goal to make critical judgements. Instead, we set out to capture the essence of each author's work and to convey what it is that fans love about it.

Of course, the "corona" criterion did not leave us with a neat list of 125. As we worked to develop our final list, we made an effort to include all major styles and types of writing, with special emphasis on the most enduring, popular, and important novelists. But our main concern was always to supply the kind of information that would lead you to a really good read.

In keeping with that goal, we made a point of including as many authors as possible from our original list of 500 in the "If You Like…" recommendations of the write-ups. If you like V. S. Naipaul, for example, you might also like Nadine Gordimer and Michael Kundera, neither of whom has a main entry. If you like Joyce Carol Oates, you might also like Anita Brookner and Cormac McCarthy. And so on.

What the Author Write-ups Include

For each of the 125 featured authors, we've organized and presented the information in a standard format, designed to be lively and fun to read. Here's what's included in each author write-up:

Photograph. For those of us who've ever wondered what Jane Austen looked like, or whether J. K. Rowling is a man or a woman.

Biographical Highlights. Brief snippets of biographical information—date and place of birth, education, family, and so forth. This may seem like boilerplate, but you won't want to skip it because we've used the space to wedge in significant details on every author.

Fan Mail/Publisher Contacts. How to contact the author, either directly, or through his or her publisher. Many times in our lives, we have seen a movie, heard a song, or read a book and wanted to tell its creator how much we enjoyed it. But we've been stymied by not knowing where to send such a letter. In this book, we were determined to make it as easy as possible for readers to contact authors who publicize a "Fan Mail" address. For others, you can look up the publisher in the "Publisher and Author Contacts" section of the book and write to the address given there.

Quick Take. The opening paragraphs. Designed to introduce, characterize, and position the author in the grand scheme of things. What's the author known for? What have the critics said? What are the author's major themes?

Good to Know. Interesting nuggets about the writer, his or her works, life, etc. "Juicy bits," anecdotes, family information, and anything else that reveals the author's personality or offers some insight into his or her work.

Treatises and Treats. Outstanding companion volumes, biographies, reader's guides, and audiotapes. Also fan clubs, societies, newsletters, and annual celebrations and readings. We also made a special effort to search out and direct you to the best Web sites devoted to each author. These are marvelous resources that will add immeasurably to your reading life.

Best Reads/Reading List. Whenever possible, we've listed all of an author's novels, including any prizes the books have won. When there isn't space, we list the titles that most readers and critics agree are among the author's best.

If You Like … A tricky section, to be sure, since opinions vary so. But then, these are merely suggestions. If they lead you to read and enjoy even one author or novel you might otherwise not have encountered, they will have done their job.

Best Book to Read First. Should you start with the first book in a series that didn't hit its stride until the third title, or begin with that third book? Do you start with the novel that won all the prizes, or with an earlier book that most critics agree established the author's reputation? We have done our best to offer well-reasoned suggestions and guidance to get you started with unfamiliar authors.

Sidebars and Quotes. Most author write-ups also include a sidebar and a quote. The sidebars typically contribute an anecdote or story about the author. The quotes appear in the far-right column and may be from the author, an admirer, or a critic. All of which, we hope, will contribute to your pleasure when reading an author.

More Great Stuff for Passionate Readers

Following the 125 author write-ups, you'll find a veritable gold mine of information for passionate readers, organized into three sections: "Prize Winners and Prized Books," "Readers' Resources," and "Special Events and Publishers." Here's a quick tour of what you'll find in each one.

PRIZE WINNERS AND PRIZED BOOKS

This section takes a different approach to answering the question "What should I read next?" It begins with "Major Literary Fiction Awards," offering a comprehensive listing of hundreds upon hundreds of prize-winning books. From the Booker Prize to the National Book Award, from the Nobel Prize and Pulitzer Prize to the PEN/Faulkner Awards—they're all here! Plus the Web sites to check for updates. For the curious, we also made a point of explaining how the winners are selected in each case.

Next is a similarly comprehensive treatment of genre fiction. Here are the Bram Stoker Award winners for horror, the RITA Award winners for romance, the Hugo and Nebula winners for science fiction, the Spur Award winners for Westerns, the Mythopoeic Awards for novels of the land of faerie, and, of course, for mystery lovers, the Edgars, Agathas, Macavitys, and Gold and Silver Dagger Awards. Also included are lists of authors who have been voted "Grand Masters" of each genre by their peers. Our thought is that if you've always wanted to try some genre, it just makes good sense to start with the best.

But wait! There's more. We couldn't resist including the controversial Modern Library "100 Best Novels" list—and a counterlist prepared by students enrolled in the Radcliffe Publishing Course. Plus the "50 Most Frequently Banned Books in the 1990s." Oprah's Book Club selections are here, too, as is information on how to quickly summon to your computer screen the bestseller lists prepared by leading newspapers and magazines.

READERS' RESOURCES

If you've ever considered joining one of the 500,000 reading groups that exist across the country or forming one of your own, this is the place to begin. You'll be amazed at the quantity and quality of help that's available—how-to books for group leaders, guides on what to read, printed and electronic guides to specific authors (courtesy of their publishers), and much more.

Then it's on to a short guide to audiobooks—what to look for, where to buy or borrow them, and how to find reviews—followed by a selected list of special book catalogs and recommended reference works. You'll also discover how easy it is these days to get your hands on an out-of-print book and how to tap into the growing field of "e-books" that you download from the Net and read on a Palm Pilot or other computer-like device.

And how about this: You hear an author interviewed on the radio and, seconds later, you can have a review of his or her book from one of the leading newspapers or magazines on your screen. You may even be able to read the book's first chapter! The "Featured Authors" portion of the *New York Times* Web site makes this especially easy, so you may want to read about it here, even before turning to the author write-ups.

SPECIAL EVENTS AND PUBLISHERS

The final section presents a directory of literary events like the National Storytelling Festival in Jonesborough, Tennessee, and the various genre-oriented conventions that are held each year. But we have also identified local and regional book festivals and fairs. Literary events of this sort take place annually in dozens of states, and many include author readings, lectures and panel discussions, vendors, and, of course, passionate readers.

The book concludes with a list of all the publishers for the authors featured in the first part of the book. We've provided the phone numbers, Web sites, and the best address to use when sending author fan mail.

Contacting Us

In nearly 25 years of book writing, we have never enjoyed a project as much as this one. We found it an absolute delight. That's why we can be so certain that, if you read fiction of any sort, even just a book or two a year, you will find something here that will increase your enjoyment. And if you're a passionate reader, you have untold pleasures in store.

We're equally certain that our selection of authors will be controversial. So don't be shy. Let us know what you think. Is there an author you'd like to recommend for the next edition? Are there some additional "If You Likes" that you would suggest for one of the authors in this book? Do you know of a truly wonderful companion volume, Web site, or other resource that we should tell readers about? Bring them to light! Your comments will not be in vain. In a word, come join your fellow passionate readers in the dance. And please feel free to contact us:

Alfred and Emily Glossbrenner
699 River Road
Yardley, PA 19067
E-mail: gloss@gloss.com

About the
Author

Margery Allingham

Born
May 20, 1904, in London, England, to Herbert Allingham and Emily Hughes Allingham, both writers

Pseudonyms
Maxwell March, Margery Allingham Carter, and Margery Allingham Youngman-Carter

Education
Attended Endsleigh House School, Colchester; the Perse School, Cambridge; and the Regent Street Polytechnic, London, where she studied drama and speech.

Family
Married in 1927 to Philip Youngman Carter, the artist who four years earlier—when they were both just 19 years old—had designed the cover for her first book, *Blackkerchief Dick*. Carter later became editor of the *Tatler*.

Home
D'Arcy House, in the village of Tolleshunt D'Arcy, Essex, England, and a flat in London's Bloomsbury district

Died
June 30, 1966, of cancer, in Colchester, Essex, England

Publishers
Amereon Ltd.
Carroll & Graf

Margery Allingham—along with Agatha Christie, Dorothy L. Sayers, and Ngaio Marsh—was part of what is now known as the Golden Age of British detective fiction. A prolific writer who sold her first story at age eight and published her first novel before turning 20, Allingham went on to become one of the preeminent writers who helped bring the detective story to maturity in the 1920s and 1930s.

Her most enduring contribution to the genre is Albert Campion, the aristocratic, self-effacing detective who lives with his valet, ex-burglar Magersfontein Lugg, in a private flat above a police station off Piccadilly Lane. Written in the style of the "cozy mystery," her stories are marked by a lack of gore and gratuitous violence or sex but are stocked with wit, intelligence, ingenuity of plot, and a love of language. Allingham's range grew with her years, and by the time she wrote *Fashion in Shrouds* (1938), a reviewer for the *Observer* remarked that to Albert Campion "has fallen the honor of being the first detective to feature in a story which is by any standard a distinguished novel."

Good to Know

❖ Margery Allingham claimed (at age 19) that her first novel, a pirate story called *Blackkerchief Dick*, was true and had been dictated to her by 17th-century pirates through seances. Her husband later explained to the world that the story was just the product of his wife's fertile imagination.

❖ Actress Allingham: While a student at Regent Street Polytechnic, she wrote a verse play called *Dido and Aeneas*. It was later performed in London, featuring Allingham in the starring role.

❖ During World War II, she was prepared to be an agent of the British Resistance if England had been invaded. Her estate at that time was stocked with caches of weapons, explosives, and emergency food supplies.

❖ Allingham's detective novels often reflect the English country-estate environment she knew from living on the edge of the Essex marshlands in the village of Tolleshunt D'Arcy. She also wrote about contemporary life in this area in her only work of nonfiction, *The Oaken Heart* (1941).

❖ The best-known media adaptations of her work are the two four-episode "Campion" series produced by the BBC and aired in the U.S. as part of the PBS television show *Mystery*. Starring Peter Davison (*Dr. Who* and *All Creatures Great and Small*) as Campion and the late Brian Glover as Lugg, the series first aired during the 1989–90 and 1990–91 TV seasons. (The episodes are not yet available on videotape.)

Treatises and Treats

MARGERY ALLINGHAM SOCIETY

Meets at various locations twice a year, with gatherings typically taking the form of a dinner in London and an all-day excursion to "Allingham Country" in East Anglia. Annual membership is $10.00 and includes two issues of *The Bottle Green Gazette*, the society's journal. For more information, contact:

Pamela Bruxner
c/o 2B Hiham Green
Winchelsea, East Sussex TN36 4HB
England
www.author.co.uk/circles/allingham.htm

COMPANIONS

Ink in Her Blood: The Life and Crime Fiction of Margery Allingham by Richard Martin (UMI Research Press, 1988).

Margery Allingham: A Biography by Julia Thorogood (Heinemann, 1991).

Campion's Career: A Study of the Novels of Margery Allingham by B. A. Pike (Bowling Green State University Popular Press, 1987).

(Note: All three of these books are currently out of print, but you can probably find them in your local library or from used book sources.)

BEST OF THE NET

Margery Allingham Archive
www.grapevine.net/~nedblake/
    allingham_01.html
A fan page devoted to the life and work of Margery Allingham—worth a visit for its comprehensive bibliography, reviews of her novels and the BBC's "Campion" TV series, and information about the Margery Allingham Society.

Best of the "Campion" Novels

Flowers for the Judge, 1936
The Fashion in Shrouds, 1938
Pearls Before Swine, 1945
The Tiger in the Smoke, 1952
Cargo of Eagles, 1968

If You Like Margery Allingham . . .

For more classic English mysteries in the Allingham mold, try Agatha Christie, Ngaio Marsh (her first name is pronounced "ny-oh"), and Dorothy L. Sayers. You might also like John Dickson Carr, Edmund Crispin, Martha Grimes, and Josephine Tey.

Best Book to Read First

The Tiger in the Smoke, described by one reviewer as a "chilling story of a killer adrift in the London fog, and one of the books which, in its excellence, seems to surpass the limits of the detective genre." The tension is almost too great to bear.

The Inimitable Mr. Campion

Margery Allingham's sleuth is the aristocratic Albert Campion. Featured in 19 novels and many short stories, he had an inauspicious beginning in "The Black Dudley Murder," where he was "pretty much of a caricature, a cleverly updated version of Baroness Orczy's Scarlet Pimpernel, the indolent man-about-town," according to H. R. F. Keating in the *St. James Guide to Crime and Mystery Writers*.

But he was soon upgraded to protagonist and appeared in several short stories published in periodicals of the 1920s and 1930s, many of which appeared in *Mr. Campion and Others* (1939). "We do know that 'Campion' is not his real name," says actor Peter Davison, who played the detective in the BBC/*Mystery* series. "I am pretty sure that he is the black sheep, probably the youngest son, of an aristocratic family. . . . I think it's significant that his manservant is an ex-convict."

After Allingham's involvement in the war effort, her books were characterized by critics as "deeper, richer, and more subtle," and Campion matured with them. Allingham described Albert Campion as enigmatic, and as one critic notes, "the detective seems to delight in his own quicksilver nature, adopting pseudonyms, if not outright disguises, for his various adventures . . . consorting with both aristocrats and gypsies."

The short stories and novels in which Campion appears are among the most distinguished in the genre—vivacious, stylish, observant, shapely, intricate, and witty. They are unfailingly intelligent and imaginative.

—B. A. Pike,
Campion's Career: A Study of the Novels of Margery Allingham

Born
April 15, 1940, in
Mark, Somerset,
England

Education
Attended Brasenose
College, Oxford,
1963–66. Received a
diploma in sports
education from Oxford
Institute.

Family
Married Mary Weeden,
a chemist, in 1966.
Two sons.

Home
London and The Old
Vicarage, Grantchester
(a structure and village
celebrated by Rupert
Brooke in the 1912
poem of the same
name)

Fan Mail
Jeffrey Archer
The House of Lords
Westminster
London, England SW1

Publisher
HarperCollins

Jeffrey Archer

I'm a storyteller," Lord Jeffrey Archer once said to an interviewer. "I never know what's going to be in the next line, the next paragraph, or the next page." Archer has applied this talent to numerous novels and short stories in various genres, earning himself a great deal of money and a position as one of the bestselling writers in his native England and in the United States. His books have sold more than 100 million copies worldwide.

Whether it's a political novel, an international thriller, or a novel of revenge, most reviewers agree that Archer always spins a good yarn. There are twists and turns and interesting characters, combined with satisfying conclusions in which good is rewarded and evil is punished. And thanks to his political service and connections, Archer is well qualified to tell a tale of political intrigue from the inside.

Good to Know

❖ Archer founded the public relations firm of Arrow Enterprises, Ltd. at age 28. He worked tirelessly and made a small fortune.

❖ In 1969 he won a seat in Parliament (Conservative Party) and became, at 29, that body's youngest member. He lost everything five years later when a company he had invested in collapsed due to management fraud and embezzlement.

❖ Feeling obligated to repay debts amounting to some $620,000, Archer left Parliament, took a room in Oxford, and began writing a novel based on his experiences. The book, *Not a Penny More, Not a Penny Less*, became an instant bestseller in the U.S. and launched Archer's writing career.

❖ Archer often bases his novels on public figures: Ted Kennedy (the target of an assassination attempt in *Shall We Tell the President?*), Margaret Thatcher (the main character in *First Among Equals*), Saddam Hussein (*Honor Among Thieves*), and Rupert Murdoch and the late Robert Maxwell (*The Fourth Estate*).

❖ In 1992 he was created Life Peer (a British Lord) as part of the Queen's Birthday Honors.

❖ Archer owns the Playhouse, a theater in London's West End. He's also an avid art collector. In 1998 he bought Andy Warhol's 1982 portrait of Princess Diana, who had been a personal friend. Valued at more than $8.5 million, the portrait depicts the Princess with green and black hair. "Earl Spencer saw it at a private showing," Archer says, "and he was delighted."

Treatises and Treats

BIOGRAPHY
Jeffrey Archer: Stranger than Fiction by Michael Crick (Hamish Hamilton, 1995). This biography draws heavily on a decade's worth of newspaper columns written in the 1950s by Lord Archer's mother, Lola. Appearing in the *Weston Mercury*, the column was called "Over the Teacups: News and Jottings for Women." Mrs. Archer always called her son Tuppence in the column, never once using his real name. Based on excerpts we've read, Archer was a truly remarkable little boy. Though this book is currently out of print, it's offered for sale online at the British-based Internet Bookshop (www.bookshop.co.uk).

BEST OF THE NET
HarperCollins Web Site
www.harpercollins.com

For such a popular author, there is surprisingly little available on the Internet. Your best bet is to go to the HarperCollins site and do an author or title search. You'll find book summaries, reviewers' comments, and biographical information.

Jeffrey Archer's Greater London Forum
www.london-forum.co.uk

Of interest primarily to Londoners and Archer fans interested in his political views on local issues like "traffic and transport." The discussion area includes notices of occasional online chats with Archer, and information on where to find transcripts of past sessions. Keep in mind, though, that the conversations at this site are meant to be political rather than literary. Visitors who post fan-mail messages and queries about Archer's books are encouraged to contact him at his House of Lords address.

The Lord's Work

ALL THE NOVELS

Not a Penny More, Not a Penny Less, 1976
 (adapted as a 1990 British TV movie)
Shall We Tell the President?, 1977
Kane & Abel, 1980
 (adapted as a 1985 TV miniseries with an all-star cast)
The Prodigal Daughter, 1982
 (a sequel to *Kane & Abel*)
First Among Equals, 1984
A Matter of Honor, 1986
 (Steven Spielberg bought the film rights)
As the Crow Flies, 1991
Honor Among Thieves, 1993
The Fourth Estate, 1996
The Eleventh Commandment, 1998

SHORT FICTION

A Quiver Full of Arrows, 1982
A Twist in the Tale, 1989
The Collected Short Stories, 1998

If You Like Jeffrey Archer...

You might also like books by the late Alan Drury, who invented the political thriller with *Advise and Consent*. The Cold War is long gone, but while the issues have changed, Alan Drury's Washington, DC–based political novels ring true to this day. Other authors you may want to consider include: Eric Ambler; David Baldacci; Stephen Coonts; Clive Cussler; Len Deighton; Nelson DeMille; Ken Follett; Frederick Forsyth; Jack Higgins; Robert Ludlum; Lawrence Sanders; Trevanian; Morris West.

Best Book to Read First

Offering all the style and wit that made Archer famous, *Not a Penny More, Not a Penny Less* was sparked by the author's personal experience of being defrauded of over $500,000. The book's characters include an Oxford don, an English lord, a society physician, and a French art dealer who team up to seek revenge against Harvey Metcalf, an expert in international stock fraud who took their money. Sounds delicious, and it is.

Sex, Lies, and Audiotape

The great contradiction of Jeffrey Archer's life," said Bill Bryson in the *New York Times Magazine* (November 25, 1990), "is that the one thing he has tried hardest to do—become a successful politician—is the one thing he has most signally failed to accomplish." His latest failure reverberated throughout the country when, after spending over $1 million of his own money to become the Tory nominee in the first direct election for Mayor of London, Archer had to abandon the campaign in late 1999 after a 1986 sex scandal resurfaced. (After the original scandal, Archer had collected a record-setting $800,000 award in a libel case against the *Daily Star*, one of two London tabloids that alleged an encounter between Archer and a prostitute.)

But in November of 1999, Ted Francis, a television producer and former close friend, secretly taped a phone conversation with Archer. Allegations then surfaced that Archer had asked Francis to provide a false alibi during the 1987 trial, and compensated him for the testimony. Soon thereafter, Archer's former literary agent, Richard Cohen, was reported as telling Scotland Yard that he, too, was asked to give an inaccurate alibi at the trial.

As a result, the Conservative Party expelled Archer, and the *Daily Star* is seeking $4.8 million in costs, interest, and damages. Mary Archer, his wife of 35 years, has said that she is "cross" with her husband but that "we are all human and Jeffrey manages to be more human than most—I believe his virtues and talents are also on a larger scale."

Isaac Asimov

Born
January 20, 1920, in Petrovichi, Russia. In 1923, he moved to New York City with his parents, who owned and operated a Brooklyn candy store for some 40 years.

Education
Columbia University, B.S. in chemistry, 1939; M.A. in chemistry, 1941; Ph.D. in biochemistry, 1948.

Family
Sister Marcia and brother Stanley (father of Eric, who writes for the *New York Times*). Married Gertrude Blugerman in 1942 and had two children. Divorced in 1973. Married Janet Jeppson, a psychiatrist he had met in 1956 while signing books at a science fiction convention, in 1973.

Home
New York City, for many years in the West 70s between Central Park West and Columbus Avenue

Died
April 6, 1992, in New York City, of heart and kidney failure

Publisher
(one of several) Doubleday

Compulsive. That's the only way to describe a writer whose normal routine was to rise at 6:00 A.M. and work from 7:30 in the morning until 10:00 at night. Over the years, this routine produced nearly 500 books on subjects ranging from a line-by-line analysis of all of Shakespeare's plays, *Paradise Lost*, and *Gulliver's Travels;* to chemistry, astronomy, and atomic physics; to histories of Greece, Rome, England, and France.

What Asimov is best known for, however, is science fiction—in particular his *Foundation* and *I, Robot* series. Under the guidance of legendary editor John W. Campbell Jr., Asimov (along with Heinlein, Sturgeon, Van Vogt, Pohl, and Williamson), contributed mightily to converting science fiction from the space-opera pulp-fiction genre it had been into a genre of strong stories based on ideas and logical extrapolations from known or postulated facts.

And with Asimov, that's what you get: mind-opening ideas, logic, and strong plots. What you don't get are richly developed characters or a distinctive literary style. But, then, if your ideas and speculations are compelling enough—and Asimov's always are—a serviceable, workmanlike style is really all you need.

Good to Know

❖ Asimov taught himself to read before he was five and skipped several grades, graduating from high school at 15. After getting his Ph.D., he worked at the Boston University School of Medicine, starting as an instructor and eventually becoming a full professor of biochemistry. During World War II, he served as a civilian chemist (1942–45) at the now-defunct Navy Air Experimental Station near Philadelphia.

❖ The science fiction magazines on the newsstand at the family's candy store were what first piqued Asimov's interest in the genre. His father disapproved of young Isaac reading such "junk," but he persisted, playing on the word "science" in the names of magazines like *Science Wonder Stories* to convince his father to let him read them. He first tried writing stories at age 11.

❖ At 18, Asimov hand-delivered a story to John W. Campbell at *Astounding Stories* in Manhattan. (Roundtrip subway fare was 10 cents, while postage would have cost 12 cents.) Campbell met with him for over an hour, ultimately rejected the story, but offered copious suggestions and lots of encouragement to try again. Asimov took his advice, and his first published story, "Marooned Off Vesta," ran in the October 1938 issue of *Amazing Stories*.

❖ Three years later, in 1941, he sold "Nightfall" to Campbell at *Astounding Science Fiction*. The original agreement was for a penny a word, but Campbell upped the rate by 25 percent because the story was so good. Nearly 30 years later, the Science Fiction Writers of America voted "Nightfall" the best SF short story ever written.

❖ *Pebble in the Sky*, his first SF novel, appeared in 1950, followed shortly thereafter by *I, Robot* (1950) and *Foundation* (1951). His "Lucky Starr" novels were written under the pen name Paul French. By 1958, he was so popular that he could quit teaching and write full-time.

❖ Asimov suffered a heart attack in 1977 and had triple-bypass surgery in 1983. Yet he continued to produce ten or more books per year. No agent, no researchers, no typist, no one to answer mail. "This way there are no arguments, no instructions, no misunderstandings. I work every day.... Writing is my only interest. Even speaking is an interruption."

Treatises and Treats

AUTOBIOGRAPHIES AND LETTERS

In Memory Yet Green (Doubleday, 1979). An autobiography covering the years 1920–54.

In Joy Still Felt (Doubleday, 1980). Covers the years 1954–78.

I. Asimov: A Memoir (Doubleday, 1994). Winner of the Hugo Award for Best Nonfiction in 1995. Presents, in 166 brief chapters, Asimov's opinions, observations, and history, along with a fairly thorough catalogue of his books and story collections.

Yours, Isaac Asimov, edited by Stanley Asimov (Doubleday, 1995). A collection of excerpts from letters that Isaac Asimov wrote over the years.

BEST OF THE NET

Isaac Asimov Home Page

www.clark.net/pub/edseiler/WWW/
    asimov_home_page.html

Maintained by Asimov fan Edward Seiler, this is the Internet mother lode for information and links devoted to Isaac Asimov and his works.

Isaac Asimov Newsgroup

alt.books.isaac-asimov

A good place to pose questions and exchange opinions about Asimov. But check out Seiler's Web page first, where you'll find the extraordinarily detailed and well-written Isaac Asimov FAQ (frequently asked questions) file.

Asimov Life and Times

www.nytimes.com/books/97/03/23/
    lifetimes/asimov.html

A long Web address, but worth the keystrokes. Articles and reviews dating from 1961 about the "Good Doctor," including his 1992 *New York Times* obituary and much more.

Asimov Classics

Original Foundation Trilogy: *Foundation*,
    Foundation and Empire, and *Second
    Foundation*, 1951–53
    (Hugo Award for Best All-Time Series)
Foundation's Edge, 1982
    (Hugo Award)
The Gods Themselves, 1972
    (Hugo and Nebula Awards)
The Complete Robot, 1983
The Martian Way and Other Stories, 1982

If You Like
Isaac Asimov...

You will probably also like these other "Grand Masters of Science Fiction": Arthur C. Clarke, Lester del Rey, Robert A. Heinlein, Frederik Pohl, and Clifford Simak.

All Work and No Play?

Asimov was a P. G. Wodehouse fan and an active member of the Wodehouse Society. He also loved Gilbert and Sullivan operas—so much so that he joined the Gilbert and Sullivan Society, attended most of their meetings, learned the songs, and occasionally served as toastmaster at benefit shows in Manhattan.

Best Book to Read First

Start with *Foundation*. (You can read its prequel, *Forward the Foundation*, later.) Or try the story collection, *I, Robot*. If you like these titles, you have years of pleasure ahead, since each is the basis for a multi-book series.

"I make no effort to write poetically or in a high literary style. I try only to write clearly and I have the very good fortune to think clearly so that the writing comes out as I think, in satisfactory shape."

— Isaac Asimov, in a 1984 interview

Born
November 18, 1939, in Ottawa, Ontario, Canada. Raised in a cabin in the Canadian wilderness, where her father, a forest entomologist, researched and drew pictures of bugs.

Full Name
Margaret Eleanor Atwood, known to her friends and family as Peggy

Education
Victoria College, University of Toronto, B.A., 1961. Master's from Radcliffe College, 1962. Went on to Harvard for a Ph.D, but never finished her dissertation on "The English Metaphysical Romance."

Family
Married to novelist Graeme Gibson for close to three decades. They have, altogether, "three children—mostly grown up now—and a cat."

Home
Toronto, Canada

Fan Mail
O. W. Toad, Ltd.
c/o McClelland & Stewart
481 University Avenue, #900
Toronto, Ontario
 M5E 2E9
CANADA

Publisher
Doubleday

Margaret Atwood

Margaret Atwood is a Canadian who, unlike many "American" authors, newscasters, actors, and celebrities, is proud to proclaim her true nationality. Ranked with Robertson Davies as one of Canada's foremost writers, she is a first-rate poet, storyteller, and novelist who writes intelligently and passionately about women in difficult situations. Her female characters often suffer, but they are never passive victims. And the books and stories they populate are exquisitely written page-turners that also deliver a powerful political message.

A committed feminist and a member of Amnesty International, PEN International, and other organizations devoted to a vision of social justice, Atwood traces her political activism all the way back to her childhood. "I should never have been a Brownie," she says. "I was told to go out and sell those cookies. It was a good cause, but it ruined me for life."

Good to Know

❖ Atwood began writing as a child, producing poems, morality plays, comic books, and an unfinished novel about an ant—all by the age of six. As a teenager, she decided she wanted to write for a living, but her parents discouraged her, fearing she'd starve to death. (They wanted her to be a botanist.)

❖ Undaunted, she self-published her first volume of poetry, *Double Persephone*, and won her first writing award (the E. J. Pratt Medal) in 1961, the year she graduated from college. The print run was 200 copies. Cover price, 50 cents. (One of the books sold recently for $1,800.)

❖ Atwood has contributed poems, essays, short stories, book reviews, and literary criticism to many magazines. She has also written several children's books, including *Princess Prunella and the Purple Peanut*, which mocks traditional fairy tales.

❖ As further proof that a feminist *can* have a sense of humor, Atwood has composed a poem to send in reply to the many requests she receives for "blurbing" books by fellow authors. Posted at her Web site (www.web.net/owtoad), it ends like this:

So I wish you Good Luck, and your author,
*   and book,*
Which I hope to read later, with glee.
Long may you publish, and search out the
*   blurbs,*
Though you will not get any from me.

Treatises and Treats

MARGARET ATWOOD SOCIETY

A professional association of educators, students, and researchers. Dues are $10 a year ($5 for students), and membership includes the group's semiannual newsletter with information on Atwood's public appearances, news about forthcoming books, and more. For additional information, contact:
Ms. Mary Kirtz
Department of English
University of Akron
Akron, OH 44325
mkirtz@uakron.edu
www.cariboo.bc.ca/atwood

BIOGRAPHIES
Margaret Atwood: A Biography by Nathalie Cooke (ECW Press, 1998) and **The Red Shoes: Margaret Atwood Starting Out** by

Rosemary Sullivan (HarperCollins, 1998). At her Web site, Atwood tells visitors that two unauthorized biographies about her were published in late 1998. Though she doesn't mention the books by name, she states emphatically that, contrary to media reports, neither book was authorized, fact-checked, or in any way supported by her. ("I don't think biographies of living people should be written," says Atwood, and "I am not dead yet.") We don't know for sure, but it's a good guess that these are the two offending titles.

READING GUIDES

Margaret Atwood by Coral Ann Howells (St. Martin's Press, 1996). Many books have been written about Atwood's poetry and novels, but most of them are scholarly dissertations published by university presses. This book, in contrast, has earned praise for its accessible style.

Doubleday Reading Group Guides are available for most of Atwood's novels—in some cases bound right into the book. To order a reading guide for a specific Atwood novel, call Doubleday (800-605-3406). Or visit the Doubleday/Random House Web site (www.randomhouse.com), where you can download the reading guides for free.

BEST OF THE NET

Official Margaret Atwood Site

www.web.net/owtoad
The author's own Web site (*owtoad* is an anagram for Atwood), with biographical information, awards, insights on writing, books about the author, and more. All of it Atwood-approved.

Atwood Society Information Page

www.cariboo.bc.ca/atwood
A must-visit site for any Margaret Atwood fan. In addition to information about the society, the site includes the most exhaustive bibliography of publications by and about the author that you're likely to find anywhere. Plus information on subscribing to the ATWOOD-L mailing list.

Atwood At Her Best

NOVELS

The Edible Woman, 1969
Surfacing, 1972
Lady Oracle, 1976
Life Before Man, 1979
Bodily Harm, 1981
The Handmaid's Tale, 1985
Cat's Eye, 1988
The Robber Bride, 1993
Alias Grace, 1996

SHORT FICTION

Dancing Girls, 1977
Murder in the Dark, 1983
Bluebeard's Egg, 1983
Wilderness Tips, 1991
Good Bones, 1992

If You Like Margaret Atwood...

You might also like books by these authors, all of whom write with a distinct feminist/female viewpoint: Barbara Kingsolver, Alice McDermott, Toni Morrison, Naomi Wolf, and Virginia Woolf.

Best Book to Read First

The Handmaid's Tale, a book that postulates a future world controlled by fundamentalist Christians in which few women can bear children and those who can are forced to do so for the rulers. The book received a Governor General's Award (Canada's top literary prize). The *New York Times* hailed it as "Margaret Atwood's best novel to date." (It was made into a movie scripted by Harold Pinter, starring Robert Duvall, Faye Dunaway, and Natasha Richardson.)

Fertile Words

Toronto Life Gardens commissioned Margaret Atwood to write a piece called "A Garden Memoir," the first paragraph of which is presented here. It captures something that will resonate with many busy people, while offering some small insight into Atwood herself:

I'm not a very good gardener, for the same reason I wouldn't make a very good poisoner: both activities benefit from advance planning. I get seduced by catalogues, with their glossy photos and adjectives, and by pictures of rose-covered trellises and beds of mature perennials; but somehow you can't just throw all that into the ground on the first Sunday in May. Then there's the upkeep. Over the years, my various gardens have shared a certain improvised look, which on closer inspection may turn out to be weeds. I have taken to calling these "native wildflowers."

Jean Auel

Born
February 18, 1936, in
Chicago, Illinois, the
second of Neil and
Martha Untinen's five
children. Her father
was a house painter.

Full Name
Jean Marie Untinen
Auel (pronounced
"owl")

Education
Attended Portland
State University and
earned an M.B.A. in
1976 from the Univer-
sity of Portland, taking
classes at night while
working for an elec-
tronics firm.

Family
Married Ray Bernard
Auel in 1954, shortly
after graduating from
high school. They have
five children.

Home
Sherwood, Oregon, a
small town southwest
of Portland

Fan Mail
Jean M. Auel
P.O. Box 430
Sherwood, OR 97140

Publisher
Crown

Incongruous as it may sound, Jean Auel writes warm, passionate novels about the Ice Age, a period in Earth's history that occurred over 20,000 years ago. It's a time usually referred to as "prehistory" due to the lack of written records. But Auel's in-depth research and creative imagination provide the next best thing to documentation of the times—engrossing novels that tell real stories. The success of her "Earth's Children" series of books, beginning with *The Clan of the Cave Bear* in 1980, opened a still-flourishing literary genre, the Prehistorical Novel.

That Auel was a pathfinder is fitting, given the similar characteristics of the protagonist of her series. Ayla, for example, is a Cro-Magnon woman living among the more primitive Neanderthals. Ayla not only discovered how to make fire using flint, she also improved weaponry, sewing, and medicine. Her physical appearance, however, made her an outsider, and her "modern" ways caused friction with the less advanced Neanderthals.

Auel is known for her painstaking research on prehistoric cultures and survival techniques. Critics praise her insight into gender roles, cave life, and the differences between our Neanderthal and Cro-Magnon ancestors. She also gets high marks for her imagination and the timeless nature of her stories. Her characters are rounded portrayals of people who, although they lived 20,000 years ago, experienced the same problems, conflicts, and emotional complexities of today. Though garbed in animal skins and armed with flint-tipped spears, they are nonetheless modern men and women.

"I found myself with an idea for, I thought, a short story," Auel says. That was in 1977. "Because it nagged at me all day—just wouldn't go away—I decided to try to write this story of a young woman who was living with people who were different." After researching life in prehistoric times, Auel produced a one-page outline of the story in about half an hour. Then came 12-hour and 16-hour days at the typewriter. "I'd fall into bed, and as soon as I got up, I'd be right back at it." Within six months, she had produced a manuscript of 450,000 words!

Good to Know

❖ Crown Publishers offered Jean Auel $130,000 for *The Clan of the Cave Bear* (1980), a breathtaking amount for a first novel at the time. For her fourth book, *The Plains of Passage* (1990), and the two proposed books that would complete the Earth's Children series, Crown reportedly offered Auel a total of $25 million.

❖ At 1.6 million copies, *The Plains of Passage* broke the record for the largest first printing of a hardcover book of fiction. The novel went into a second printing before the first copies were available in stores and broke the record for first-day sales—selling over 15,000 copies on October 3, 1990. Soon after, *Entertainment Weekly* included Jean Auel in its list of the 101 most influential people in the entertainment business.

❖ *The Clan of the Cave Bear* earned Auel a place as finalist for Best First Novel in the 1981 American Book Awards. Other awards pay tribute to the caliber of her research in history and science: the Silver Trowel Award from the Sacramento Archeology Society, the Contribution Award from the Department of the Interior and Society for American Archaeology, and the Centennial Medal from the Smithsonian Institution.

❖ Auel's college studies included science, math, and business subjects. Later, to learn about writing, she turned to books such as Leon Surmelian's *Techniques of Fiction Writing: Measure and Madness* and Lajos Egri's *The Art of Dramatic Writing*.

❖ As part of her research into prehistoric life, Jean Auel learned from survivalists how to make fire using flint. Traveling to the Dordogne region of France to research the final books in her series, she explored caves, viewed cave paintings, and participated in an archeological dig.

❖ John Sayles did the screenplay for the film version of *The Clan of the Cave Bear* (1986), starring Daryl Hannah. Although the movie got lousy reviews, Auel would like to see more of the Earth's Children series adapted for the big screen. But she may delay future film negotiations until all six books in the Earth's Children series are completed.

❖ Before turning to writing, Auel worked as a circuit board designer, technical writer, and credit manager of an electronics company. She once wrote a pamphlet called *So You Want to Design Circuit Boards*.

❖ Her literary favorites include the fairy tale *East of the Sun and West of the Moon*, Tolkien's *Lord of the Rings* trilogy, Robert Heinlein's *Universe*, and Ursula K. Le Guin's *The Left Hand of Darkness*. She became interested in historical fiction through James Michener's *The Source* and *Hawaii*, and Mike Waltari's *The Adventurer*, *The Wanderer*, and *The Egyptian*.

Treatises and Treats

BEST OF THE NET
Jean Auel Page
www.geocities.com/Athens/6293/auel.html
A comprehensive and well organized fan page, with news and chat, message board, book recommendations "to help you through the wait for Jean's next book," and advice on the best Internet newsgroups and mailing lists for Auel aficionados.

Book List

THE EARTH'S CHILDREN SERIES
The Clan of the Cave Bear, 1980
The Valley of Horses, 1982
The Mammoth Hunters, 1985
The Plains of Passage, 1990

If You Like Jean Auel . . .

Try some of these books while waiting for book five of the Earth's Children series:

Reindeer Moon by Elizabeth Marshall Thomas
She Who Remembers by Linda Lay Shuler
The Moon and the Sun by Vonda McIntyre
Children of the Ice by Charlotte Prentiss
Beyond the Sea of Ice by William Sarabande
Mother Earth, Father Sky by Sue Harrison
Daughter of the Red Deer by Joan Wolf

Best Book to Read First

Start with *The Clan of the Cave Bear*, the first book in the Earth's Children series.

The Long-Awaited Fifth

Since the 1990 publication of *The Plains of Passage*, fans have been eagerly, almost desperately, awaiting book five in Jean Auel's proposed six-volume series. With each passing year, the intensity grows. Rumors abound—especially on the Internet—about Auel's health, her relations with her publisher, and what the title of the fifth volume will be.

Her family reports that she is indeed working on the fifth book, as well as the sixth and final volume. Son Kendall says there are no problems or distractions. In fact, aware of all the buzz in chat rooms and concerned that getting drawn into it might interfere with her work, his mother "steadfastly refuses to look at the Internet."

The real power of a novel over all other forms of writing is its ability to reach in and grab you, wrench your gut, and make you feel. . . . That's probably why I don't care very much for intellectual novels. It's wasting the medium. I'd rather do my intellectual reading in nonfiction.

—Jean Auel, in an interview for *Contemporary Authors*

Jane Austen

Born
December 16, 1775, in the village of Steventon in Hampshire, England, to the Reverend George and Cassandra Austen

Education
Studied at home under the tutelage of her father.

Family
The second daughter and seventh child in a family of eight: six boys and two girls. Never married, although she had a number of suitors and several offers of marriage. Closest companion: her unmarried sister, Cassandra, who, with misguided protectiveness, destroyed many of Austen's letters after her death.

Home
Hampshire, England

Died
July 18, 1817, in Winchester, Hampshire, England, at the age of 41, probably of Addison's disease

Publishers
Modern Library
Oxford University Press
Penguin

In the language of university English professors, Jane Austen wrote "novels of manners." That simply means she wrote about how people actually behaved—their customs, values, mores (both private and public), and the conventions of their society, and how their actions conformed to or defied those conventions. Duty, honor, lust, love, longing, property, and propriety—and every other base and higher element of human nature—all played out in a society of rigidly enforced public standards unlike anything Americans have seen in over 100 years. That is what Austen is about. And she presents it all with finely detailed observations, nicely turned phrases, and a wit as subtle and sharp as a rapier's point.

Hers are small stories of little apparent import. The contemporaneous outside concerns of war, politics, and Napoleon never obtrude. Yet within the narrow confines of geography and class that Jane Austen chronicled so skillfully, readers will find the entire world.

Good to Know

❖ Thanks to a father who encouraged his children's intellectual pursuits, Austen began writing at age 12. Earliest known works include light-hearted plays, verses, short novels, and parodies contained in three surviving manuscript notebooks.

❖ Austen started her first serious novel, *Susan*, when she was 18. She sold it in 1794 for £10, but it wasn't published until 1817 as *Northanger Abbey*.

❖ She experienced a major disruption in 1801 when her father retired to Bath. Owning no home, the family lived with relatives and in a succession of temporary lodgings until Rev. Austen died in 1805.

❖ Austen returned "home" at last in 1809 when brother Edward was able to provide his mother and sisters with a large cottage in the village of Chawton, within his Hampshire estate and not far from Steventon.

❖ Stability led to renewed energy, and Austen began preparing *Sense and Sensibility* for publication. The title page read simply "By a Lady," and the book was advertised as an "Interesting Novel"—meaning that it was a love story. Austen promised to cover her publisher's losses if necessary, but she made a £140 profit. (Her father's annual salary as rector had been £600.)

❖ *Sense and Sensibility* received very positive reviews, and Austen went on to publish *Pride and Prejudice*, *Mansfield Park*, and *Emma*. Sir Walter Scott, writing about *Emma* in the *Quarterly Review* in 1816, praised "this nameless author" as a master of "the modern novel."

❖ At the time of her death, Austen was working on *Sanditon*, a novel satirizing health resorts. *Persuasion*, completed before she became ill, was published posthumously with *Northanger Abbey* in December 1817. That's when her brother Henry announced to the world her authorship of all six published novels.

Treatises and Treats

JANE AUSTEN SOCIETY OF NORTH AMERICA

Describing itself as "serious but not stuffy," this group's annual meetings include not only presentations of scholarly papers but also lessons in 18th- and 19th-century card games and dancing, spirited debates over favorite characters, and discussions of all aspects of Jane Austen's life and times. For more information, call 800-836-3911 or visit www.jasna.org.

COMPANIONS AND BIOGRAPHIES

What Jane Austen Ate and Charles Dickens Knew: From Fox Hunting to Whist–the Facts of Daily Life in 19th-Century England by Daniel Pool (Simon & Schuster, 1993). A delightful book, with an extensive glossary and sections devoted to topics like "The Country House Visit," "How the English Kept Clean," and "Drink and the Evils Thereof."

The Jane Austen Companion: With a Dictionary of Jane Austen's Life and Works, edited by J. David Grey (Macmillan, 1986). Lively and informative essays on Austen's life and work by scholars and enthusiastic amateurs.

Jane Austen: A Family Record by William Austen-Leigh and Richard Arthur Austen-Leigh (G. K. Hall, 1989). Considered the standard biography. First published in 1913 as *Jane Austen: Her Life and Letters*, this version has been revised and expanded by editor Deirdre Le Faye.

MUSIC AND RECIPES

Piano Classics from the World of Jane Austen, an audio CD by Karlyn Bond. The music Jane Austen heard, drawn from her personal library, social sphere, and time period. Send $19 ($21 for shipment outside the U.S.) to Karlyn Bond, P.O. Box 522403, Salt Lake City, UT 84152-2403.

The Jane Austen Cookbook by Maggie Black (Chicago Review Press, 1995). A "celebration of the meals and manners" of Jane Austen and her fictional characters, with updated recipes for vegetable pie, gooseberry vinegar, ginger beer, and other 19th-century fare.

BEST OF THE NET

Jane Austen Information Page
www.pemberley.com/janeinfo/janeinfo.html
The premiere Jane Austen resource, created by Henry Churchyard and hosted by a site named for Mr. Darcy's home in *Pride and Prejudice*. Annotated, full-text versions of Austen's novels, plot summaries, lists of characters and genealogy charts, reviews and commentary, biographical information, and an extensive bibliography. Also, a search feature for locating words and phrases in Austen's writings, and information about subscribing to the Austen-L mailing list.

Jane Austen Society Web Site
www.jasna.org
Another excellent online source. In addition to information about the Society, you'll learn about tours of Jane Austen's England, film and TV adaptations of her novels, and the Jane Austen Rare Book Collection at Goucher College.

All the Novels

Sense and Sensibility, 1811
Pride and Prejudice, 1813
Mansfield Park, 1814
Emma, 1815
Northanger Abbey, 1817
Persuasion, 1817

If You Like Jane Austen . . .

Try the Regency romances of Georgette Heyer, the top choice of Austen fans according to the authoritative Austen-L mailing list. Favorites in the 29-book series include *A Civil Contract, The Grand Sophy,* and *The Reluctant Widow*. Another possibility: Stephanie Barron's "Jane Austen Mystery Series" from Bantam Books.

Best Book to Read First

Pride and Prejudice or *Emma,* either of which will give you a wonderful introduction to the world of Jane Austen. Even if you read them in high school, give them another try.

Pride and Prejudice . . . is the book that makes me most feel that everything is going to be all right, that the world is a hospitable place, and that, as Anne Frank once said, people are really good at heart. . . . I never tire of Elizabeth Bennett or her family, even her silly mother. One summer my family moved to West Virginia. . . . The Bennetts saved my life. They moved with me, and I spent all my time with them until, finally, I made some friends. The only thing I don't like about Pride and Prejudice is the ending, because then it's over.

—Anna Quindlen, *New York Times*

An Austen Atlas

I f you're planning a trip to Great Britain, be sure to arrange beforehand for a free copy of the Vauxhall Movie Map featuring dozens of film and TV locations. Emma Thompson's *Sense and Sensibility,* for example, used Saltram House near Plymouth for the Dashwood family home, while Montacute House in Somerset served as the Palmer estate. To order, call 800-462-2748 or visit www.bta.org.uk.

James Baldwin

Born
August 2, 1924, in New York City. Did not know his father. He and eight brothers and sisters were raised by their mother, Berdis Emma Jones, a house cleaner, and stepfather, David Baldwin, a storefront preacher and factory worker.

Full Name
James Arthur Baldwin

Education
DeWitt Clinton High School, New York City

Home
Grew up in Harlem. Lived for a while in Greenwich Village before departing for France at age 24. Returned to the U.S. periodically until his death.

Died
December 1, 1987, of stomach cancer, in St. Paul de Vence, Franc

Publishers
Modern Library
Library of America

James Baldwin's swift, international rise to success as a novelist and essayist was also his undoing. By the age of 21 he was writing on issues of race and society for leading intellectual journals, and although he left the United States to live in France before the civil rights movement swelled in this country, his early works were regarded as literary documents of the era.

To social activists of the 1950s and 60s, and especially to disaffected white youth, Baldwin was an appealing, consummate outsider: black, homosexual, an artist, and an exile. He wrote for both black and white readers about the moral bankruptcy of a society that refused to acknowledge its racist past—he called it "a fatal bewilderment"—and about the redemptive power of love, which fit well with the integrationist tenor of the times.

Baldwin came to be as much a speaker as a writer, and was looked upon as a representative of the black viewpoint on racial issues. He later complained that his transformation into a celebrity robbed him of his authentic voice. As positions hardened along the racial divide, especially after the murders of respected public figures like Medgar Evers, Martin Luther King, and Malcolm X, he was harshly repudiated by a new generation of African-American writers who believed that black authors should write for black audiences.

Toward the end of a career that had started so luminously, Baldwin suffered health problems and writer's block, and critics were unenthusiastic about what he did produce.

Good to Know

❖ Following in the footsteps of his tyrannical stepfather, James Baldwin became a Pentecostal preacher at the age of 14. His preaching experience and his stepfather's harsh and domineering nature served as the catalysts for his first and most famous novel, *Go Tell It on the Mountain.*

❖ Baldwin's unique contribution to literature was a transcendently novelistic portrayal of the country's explosive racial frictions, addressed to both blacks and whites in personal terms. His arrival on the scene was, as one critic put it, "a major breakthrough for the American imagination."

❖ Though he spent most of his adult life abroad, Baldwin refused to think of himself as an exile. He preferred the term "commuter," and saw the distinction as essential to his development as a writer. "Once I found myself on the other side of the ocean, I could see where I came from very clearly…. I am the grandson of a slave, and I am a writer. I must deal with both."

❖ Baldwin's homosexuality was as much the stuff of his literary scrutiny as his African heritage. In fact, his second novel, *Giovanni's Room*, forsakes the confusions of race in America for those of sexual identity in the Parisian countryside. In the straight-laced 1960s, it was a book that even admirers found hard to take.

Treatises and Treats

COMPANIONS

James Baldwin: A Biography, by David Adams Leeming (Henry Holt, 1995). Written by a friend and colleague who had access to Baldwin's papers, this is more a memoir than a critical interpretation, but it is a believable portrayal.

Talking at the Gates: A Life of James Baldwin, by James Campbell (Viking, 1991). An exploration of Baldwin's complicated, often angry relationships with the important writers in his life, from the older generation that influenced him to those who became his peers.

Conversations with James Baldwin, edited by Fred L. Standley and Louis H. Pratt (University Press of Mississippi, 1989). Interviews with a master conversationalist by some of America's best talkers, including Studs Terkel, Nat Hentoff, and Ben Sahn.

BEST OF THE NET

The New York Times Featured Authors

www.nytimes.com/books/specials/author/html The *New York Times* archives offers a rich lode of material on James Baldwin. There are reviews of his books by Irving Howe, Langston Hughes, Joyce Carol Oates, Mario Puzo, and others; elegaic commentary by William Styron, Toni Morrison, and Amiri Baraka; and articles that Baldwin wrote for the *Times*, such as his piece on black English. You can also enjoy Baldwin's rich, resonant voice as he discusses his life and work in a 1986 interview with National Public Radio's Terry Gross.

Go Read It

ALL THE NOVELS

Go Tell It on the Mountain, 1953
Giovanni's Room, 1956
Another Country, 1962
Tell Me How Long the Train's Been Gone, 1968
If Beale Street Could Talk, 1974
Just Above My Head, 1979
Harlem Quartet, 1987

SELECTED ESSAY COLLECTIONS

Notes of a Native Son, 1955
Nobody Knows My Name: More Notes of a Native Son, 1961
The Fire Next Time, 1963

If You Like James Baldwin...

A key to understanding Baldwin's artistic milieu lies in the figures who inspired him: the writers of the Harlem Renaissance and those who came after. Langston Hughes's *Weary Blues* and Richard Wright's *Native Son* are two excellent works from that era. A fine contemporary novel like Toni Morrison's *Beloved* reveals both the distance that literature has traveled since midcentury and the full-bodied timeliness of Baldwin's prose. Finally, for an ageless, lush account of the black experience in the rural American South, nothing can top Zora Neale Hurston's *Their Eyes Were Watching God*.

Go Rent It

In 1984, as part of an effort to generate enthusiasm for reading or rereading the original novel, James Baldwin's *Go Tell It on the Mountain* was adapted for the highly acclaimed PBS television series *American Playhouse*. Praised for its terrific dialogue and stellar cast—including Emmy Award–winners Ruby Dee, Paul Winfield, and Alfre Woodard—the film version is now available on videotape, so you can probably find it at your local video rental store. Or you can order it from Amazon.com, Reel.com, and other online sources.

Best Book to Read First

Go Tell It on the Mountain, Baldwin's first novel, caused a sensation for its eloquent portrayal of a black youth's coming of age in midcentury urban America. It describes the teenager's turbulent family life and his religious awakening. And, more so than in the increasingly polemical work that followed, it is a highly personal story that plays out with the greater social drama of racial strife as a persistent backdrop. Baldwin regarded *Go Tell It on the Mountain* as an exorcism of what hurt him the most in his life. It was, he said, the book he had to write before he could write anything else.

At his peak he had the beautiful fervor of Camus or Kafka. Like them he revealed to me the core of his soul's savage distress and thus helped me shape and define my own work and its moral contours.

—William Styron, a remembrance in the *New York Times* (December 20, 1987)

Ann Beattie

Born
September 8, 1947, in
Washington, DC, to
James A. Beattie, a
government bureau-
crat, and Charlotte
Crosby Beattie

Education
American University,
B.A., 1969; University
of Connecticut, M.A.,
1970; further graduate
study, 1970–72

Family
Married twice, most
recently to Lincoln
Perry, an artist.

Home
She and her husband
divide their time
between homes in
Maine and Key West,
Florida.

Fan Mail
Ann Beattie
c/o Janklow & Nesbit
598 Madison Avenue
New York, NY 10022

Publisher
Knopf

Ann Beattie has been called the voice of her generation and is often compared to authors like John Updike, J. D. Salinger, Joseph Heller, and John Cheever. Her novels and short stories chronicle the lives of the flower children of the 1960s who floundered into the 1970s, feeling disillusioned and purposeless. (This was not her goal, she says. She simply wrote about the people who surrounded her.) Her characters, consumed by self-pity and the emptiness of their own lives, inevitably fail at interpersonal relationships, both familial and sexual. In novels such as *Chilly Scenes of Winter*, *Falling into Place*, and *Picturing Will*, Beattie artfully and painfully depicts the lives of this Woodstock generation in devastating detail.

Though Beattie has written six novels, it is her short fiction, with its understated, deadpan, ironic style, that first earned her critical attention. In fact, short fiction is the form she prefers. Jonathan Yardley of the *Washington Post Book World* has described Beattie as a "miniaturist," and it is precisely this quality of her fiction that writers such as T. Coraghessan Boyle praise in her novels. Of her bestselling fourth novel, *Picturing Will*, Boyle observes, "Her style has never been better suited to a longer work, and she writes out of a wisdom and maturity that are timeless. But look to the details, the small things. They are everything here."

Good to Know

❖ Beattie received 22 rejection slips from the *New Yorker* before selling them a story. But not to worry—she never set out to be a writer. J. D. O'Hara, one of her professors at the University of Connecticut, prodded her along, read and critiqued her drafts, and then, with her permission, mailed the stories out for her. The *New Yorker* finally accepted "A Platonic Relationship" when Beattie was 25.

❖ She typically writes her short stories in a few hours of concentrated effort. Novels take a bit longer: *Falling in Place* (1980) required seven weeks, during which Beattie burned up two typewriters.

❖ After writing the initial 350 pages of her fifth novel, *Another You*, Beattie discarded the manuscript because she discovered she didn't care deeply about the characters. She began again and finished the novel on time, but it took her five months to recover from the false start: "I had to admit to myself that there was no other skill I had, and that I couldn't just get into a snit and change careers, because it just wasn't going to happen. I mean, you just hope that there's mercy."

❖ Recalling her high-school years, Beattie says, "I became self-destructive." Graduating with a D-minus average, she would never have gotten into college were it not for her father's connections at American University. She can't remember what she had in mind in going to graduate school, except for the fact that a personnel agency had told her she wouldn't get a job unless she cut her nails, something she had no intention of doing.

❖ While interviewing Beattie for a *New York Times* article some years ago, Joyce Maynard told the author: "I get the feeling—looking at your friends' photographs on the refrigerator—that I must know some of their stories." "Well, you do," Beattie replied. "And I've had friends actually pick up the *New Yorker* and throw it across the room. But I never expose something that is a real bitter wound in some person. And I give nice dinner parties to make up for it."

❖ Known for her practical jokes, Beattie once called *Esquire* editor Rust Hills to announce her impending arrival at his office with her "personal trainer." When she showed up accompanied by an obese friend posing as her trainer, the unwitting Hills was rendered speechless, much to Beattie's delight. Moments passed, during which Hills stuttered some polite comments, before Beattie finally let him in on the joke.

Treatises and Treats

COMPANIONS

The Critical Response to Ann Beattie, edited by Jaye Berman Montresor (Greenwood Press, 1993) and **Ann Beattie** by Christina Murphy (Twayne, 1986), both of which are out of print, but you can probably find them at the library or from used book sources.

BEST OF THE NET

New York Times Featured Authors

www.nytimes.com/books/specials/author.html
Check here for reviews of Ann Beattie's novels and story collections, including ones written by fellow authors Margaret Atwood, T. C. Boyle, and Alice Hoffman. You'll also find the complete text of Joyce Maynard's 1980 interview with Beattie, and several more recent articles about her from the *New York Times* archives.

"My Life" Reading Guide

www.randomhouse.com/resources
So far, only one of Ann Beattie's books, *My Life, Starring Dara Falcon*, is among the reading guides offered by Random House, but you'll find it here. The guide includes a one-page description of the book, discussion questions, and suggestions for further reading—just the thing for your next book group meeting.

A Generation's Voices

ALL THE NOVELS

Chilly Scenes of Winter, 1976
Falling in Place, 1980
Love Always, 1985
Picturing Will, 1989
Another You, 1995
My Life, Starring Dara Falcon, 1997

SHORT-STORY COLLECTIONS

Distortions, 1976
Secrets and Surprises, 1979
The Burning House, 1982
Where You'll Find Me and Other Stories, 1986
What Was Mine, 1991
Convergences, 1998
Park City: New and Selected Stories, 1998

If You Like Ann Beattie...

You might also like John Cheever, J. D. Salinger, and John Updike, fellow *New Yorker* writers with whom she's often compared.

Best Book to Read First

Chilly Scenes of Winter, Beattie's first novel. Her mentor, J. D. O'Hara, writing for the *New York Times* described it as "the funniest novel of unhappy yearning that one could imagine. Funnier."

Miss Beattie's power and influence . . . arise from her seemingly resistless immersion in the stoic bewilderment of a generation without a cause. . . . In the now swollen chorus of minimalist fiction, it was she who first found the tone for the post-Vietnam, post-engagé mood, much as Hemingway found the tone for his own generation's disenchantment.

—John Updike,
New Yorker

Kid Stuff

Beattie and her husband have no children of their own. But whenever friends' children come to visit, they invariably ask where her kids are. "They can't believe that an adult would have all this stuff," Beattie once told an interviewer. The "stuff" she's referring: a giant cardboard Land O'Lakes Butter sign, a large head of Richard Nixon, a tin kangaroo wind-up toy, a set of toy appliances still in the box labeled "My Dream Kitchen," a bull-dog face mask, tiny celluloid baby dolls, and more. It's no wonder the kids are confused.

Saul Bellow

Born
June 10, 1915, in
Lachine, Quebec,
Canada. Parents were
Russian Jews who got
out of St. Petersburg in
1913. One of several
children, he grew up
speaking Yiddish,
Russian, French, and,
finally, English. Moved
to Chicago at age nine.

Real Name
Solomon Bellow

Education
Attended University of
Chicago, 1933–35.
Graduated from North-
western University in
1937, B.S. with honors
in sociology and
anthropology. Began
graduate study in
anthropology at Univer-
sity of Wisconsin but
quit because he found
his thesis kept turning
into a story. North-
western later gave him
an honorary doctorate.

Family
Four marriages and
four divorces before
marrying fifth wife
Janis Freedman, a
professor, in 1989.
Four children from
marriages one, two,
three, and five.

Home
Boston and Vermont,
where he has a studio
in the woods.

Publisher
Viking

Winner of the 1976 Nobel Prize, the 1975 Pulitzer, and numerous National Book Awards, Saul Bellow—along with Malamud, Roth, Mailer, and others—is part of a group of writers whose focus on the Jewish-American experience had such resonance and influence after World War II, particularly as the details of the Holocaust gradually became known. Alienation and accommodation are important themes with Bellow. But even more universal is the theme: "How do we as human beings make sense of the chaos?" Bellow's characters learn to find what they need in the quiet of their deepest souls. And, far from being dark and depressing, the outlook is almost always guardedly optimistic.

As he has demonstrated many times, in creating his fiction, Bellow has the knowledge and power to draw upon any element of any culture in the world. Careful readers will discover resonant symbols, recurring motifs and themes, and characters who wrestle with the elemental questions of life, death, moral responsibility, and existence. The depths are there, should you care to plumb them. But fundamentally, people love Bellow for his real-life characters and dialogue, his sense of place, his wry humor, and his sheer humanity. Whichever book you select (we recommend starting with *Herzog*), you are sure to encounter some part of yourself in every Bellow novel.

Good to Know

❖ Saul Bellow grew up in Chicago during the Roaring '20s, a time of urban chaos, close-knit communities, and the rise of organized crime.

This was no doubt an exciting and frightening time. The urban environment certainly had a major influence on his fiction.

❖ After working as a teacher and serving in the Merchant Marine, Bellow worked in the Editorial Department of the *Encyclopedia Britannica* from 1943 to 1946.

❖ He held faculty appointments at the University of Minnesota, Yale, New York University, Princeton, and Bard. Guggenheim Fellowships and other stipends helped finance his travel and writing.

❖ Bellow is the only author to receive three National Book Awards, for *Herzog*, *Mr. Sammler's Planet* and *The Adventures of Augie March*. He was awarded the Pulitzer for *Humboldt's Gift* in 1975.

❖ He won the Nobel Prize in Literature in 1976, the first American to do so since Steinbeck in 1962. Meeting the press after the announcement of his prize, Bellow expressed a real fear of becoming a celebrity. "Being a writer is a rather dreamy thing. And nobody likes to have the diaphanous tissues torn. One has to protect one's dream space."

Treatises and Treats

COMPANIONS
Author/journalist James Atlas has been working on a biography of Saul Bellow for quite some time. Such a long time, in fact, that the delivery date has become something of a smirk in New York literary circles. (A writer for *Salon* magazine quipped that Atlas has been "famously at work" on the biography "since he was in short pants.") But Atlas is too

good a writer not to deliver. And when he does, the book will be worth the wait.

In the meantime, there's **Handsome Is: Adventures with Saul Bellow** by Harriet Wasserman (Fromm International, 1997). Wasserman was Bellow's one-time lover (*literally* one time) and long-time literary agent (30 years). Their business relationship ended in 1995 when Bellow signed with Andrew Wylie, the "Dark Prince" (black tie, black shirt, black coat) super-agent of New York. Wasserman used to type Bellow's novels and note his editorial changes in seven-hour phone calls, so she was less than pleased when he decided to jump ship.

You might also consider **Conversations with Saul Bellow**, edited by Gloria L. Cronin and Ben Siegel (University Press of Mississippi, 1994). It's a collection of interviews with the author spanning the years from 1953 through 1992.

BEST OF THE NET

Saul Bellow Society and Journal Web Site
english.byu.edu/cronin/saulb
A good starting point for information about Saul Bellow and his work, this site features descriptions of all of his books and plays, the press release for his 1976 Nobel Prize, and an extensive bibliography. You can also read a sample newsletter and find out about joining the Saul Bellow Society and subscribing to its newsletter and journal.

New York Times Featured Authors
www.nytimes.com/books/specials/
    author.html
Click on "Saul Bellow" for a wonderful collection of book reviews, articles, and interviews from the *New York Times* archives.

Prized Prose

NOVELS

Dangling Man, 1944
The Victim, 1947
The Adventures of Augie March, 1953
    (National Book Award)
Seize the Day, 1956
Henderson the Rain King, 1959
Herzog, 1964
    (National Book Award)
Mr. Sammler's Planet, 1970
    (National Book Award)
Humboldt's Gift, 1975
    (Pulitzer Prize)
The Dean's December, 1982
More Die of Heartbreak, 1987
Ravelstein, 2000

NOVELLAS

A Theft: A Novella, 1989
The Bellarosa Connection, 1989
Something to Remember Me By, 1991
The Actual, 1997

Best Book to Read First

Start with *Herzog*, considered by many critics to be Bellow's finest novel. Then try *Henderson the Rain King*, his funniest novel and a perennial favorite among college students. (Singer Joni Mitchell supposedly got the idea for "Both Sides Now" from a line in this novel.)

In His Own Words

Saul Bellow is a passionate believer in the healing power of art and in man's need for same. In his 1976 Nobel Prize acceptance speech, he reaffirmed his conviction that art is more important than science:

"Only art penetrates what pride, passion, intelligence, and habit erect on all sides—the seeming realities of this world. There is another reality, the genuine one, which we lose sight of. This other reality is always sending us hints, which, without art, we can't receive. Proust calls these hints our 'true impressions' . . . The value of literature lies in these intermittent true impressions . . . What Conrad said was true: Art attempts to find in the universe, in matter as well as in the facts of life, what is fundamental, enduring, essential."

If Bellow were referring to a pile of scrap metal and old tires welded together and offered as art, you'd say, "I don't think so." But he is talking about his own work, which all of us can read, contemplate, and enjoy. With Bellow there really is a "there" there.

[E]ven those readers who consider themselves well-adjusted will recognize in the comic-pathetic-heroic Herzog not a stranger but a part of their very selves.

— Clifton Fadiman, commenting on *Herzog* in *The New Lifetime Reading Plan* (HarperCollins)

Maeve Binchy

Born
May 28, 1940, in Dalkey, a small village outside Dublin, Ireland. Daughter of William T. Binchy, a lawyer, and Maureen Blackmore Binchy, a nurse

Education
Holy Child Convent in Killiney (considered a progressive school at the time); University College, Dublin, B.A. in history, 1960

Family
Married Gordon Thomas Snell (a BBC presenter and, later, a writer of children's books) in 1977.

Homes
Dublin, Ireland, and London, England

Fan Mail
Maeve Binchy
P.O. Box 6737
Dun Laoghaire
County Dublin, Ireland

Publisher
Delacorte

Maeve Binchy is one of the most beloved writers of contemporary Irish literature. True to her Irish heritage, she is a great storyteller, setting her tales in rural Irish villages or small neighborhoods. Her fiction is characterized by a strong sense of place, a good story, and interesting, largely sympathetic true-to-life characters. Michele Slung, writing for the *New York Times Book Review*, said Binchy "gives us rural Ireland, a frequently maddening yet ultimately seductive place that can render problems only in contrasting shades of old and new, past and present, strange and familiar."

Most of Binchy's novels take place in the 1940s, '50s, and '60s and focus on the predicaments of talented, capable, and spirited female protagonists who try to take control of their lives while dealing with such problems as unreliable men, adultery, divorce, and alcoholism. There is honesty—and empathy— in Binchy's explorations of the parent-child relationship, the illusion of romance, the shattering of innocence, close and often unlikely friendships, societal roles, families, and the routines and little details of small-town life.

Susan Isaacs summed up the reason for Binchy's popularity in a review for the *New York Times Book Review* when she said, "the author doesn't daze the reader with narrative bombshells (or, for that matter, with brilliant language), but recounts ordinary events... with extraordinary straightforwardness and insight." In short, Binchy makes readers care about her characters' lives and troubles, no matter how mundane those troubles may seem.

Good to Know

❖ Though raised a Catholic, after becoming a teacher at a Jewish school and visiting Israel once on vacation, Maeve Binchy decided she'd like to work on a kibbutz. While abroad, she wrote letters home to her father, detailing life in the strife-ridden country. Binchy's father sent one of these letters to the *Irish Times*, which published it and paid £18 (not bad, considering Binchy was making only £16 a month on the kibbutz). The piece launched her career as a professional writer. Binchy continues to be a beloved columnist, publishing amusing, offbeat articles twice a week.

❖ Binchy did not become a bestselling author until she was 43 years old. She once told an interviewer, "I started everything in life a little bit later than everybody else—to be a cub journalist at 28 was very old. I felt, okay, maybe at 35, 36, 37 I could start to write plays as well."

❖ Commenting on the impact of her status as a bestselling author, Binchy told the *Daily Telegraph*, "I was already happy then, married to a man I love....We had a very good life with not quite enough money to pay the bills. But we didn't buy a new house, we just did up the old one and made it more comfortable, and it's wonderful not to have to worry about providing for our old age anymore."

❖ Her current project is *Avoid Disappointment*, a book of linked short stories.

Treatises and Treats

MEDIA ADAPTATIONS

Echoes was made into a TV miniseries that aired in Great Britain in 1988 and in the U.S. on PBS in 1990. And a film version of *Circle of Friends*, starring Minnie Driver and Chris O'Donnell, was released in 1995 to rave reviews from Binchy fans.

AUDIOBOOKS

Evening Class (BDD Audio Publishing; abridged), *Circle of Friends* (BDD Audio Publishing), and *The Lilac Bus* (abridged; Chivers) are all read by the author's cousin, Kate Binchy, who does a fabulous job of bringing each individual character to life with sensitive, on-target portrayals.

BEST OF THE NET

Official Maeve Binchy Web Site

www.randomhouse.com/features/binchy
Check here for an author bio, interview, book descriptions, periodic contests for fans, and a RealAudio greeting by Maeve Binchy.

Oprah's Book Club

www.oprah.com/bookclub/bookclub.html
Binchy's latest novel, *Tara Road*, was featured on Oprah's Book Club in September 1999, so you'll find excerpts, reviewer comments, and an author interview at this site, under "Previous Book Club Selections."

Visiting Ireland

NOVELS

Light a Penny Candle, 1982
Echoes, 1985
Firefly Summer, 1987
Silver Wedding, 1988
Circle of Friends, 1990
The Glass Lake, 1995
Evening Class, 1996
Tara Road, 1999

SHORT-STORY COLLECTIONS

The Central Line: Stories of Big City Life, 1978
Victoria Lane, 1980
Maeve Binchy's Dublin Four, 1982
London Transports, 1983
The Lilac Bus: Stories, 1991
The Copper Beech, 1992
This Year It Will Be Different: A Christmas Treasury, 1996
The Return Journey, 1998

If You Like Maeve Binchy . . .

Try *The Shell Seekers* by Rosamunde Pilcher and *The Rector's Wife* by Joanna Trollope. Also books by Edna O'Brien and Belva Plain.

Best Book to Read First

Circle of Friends. Widely considered to be Maeve Binchy's best novel, it revolves around the friendship of two girls and juxtaposes the world of professional upper-middle-class Dublin with that of a small country town.

We have a lovely room with a long, long desk and two word processors. We get on perfectly well sitting beside each other. Just the sound of the keyboard and the printer is all we hear. If one of us doesn't like what the other has said, the rule is ten minutes of sulking time. . . . After that the sulks can be constructed as being moody or difficult. . . . xWe're not perfect in our judgment of each other's work, but at least we're honest. And normally we're praising—but if we don't like something, we say it straight out.

—Maeve Binchy, commenting on what it's like to live—and work—with her husband and fellow writer, in an interview for *Contemporary Authors*

Maeve's Magic

I n an article for *USA Today* (March 4, 1999), book reviewer Ann O'Donnell Prichard relates a conversation with her mother-in-law about Maeve Binchy's latest book: "Why are you eyeing my advance copy of Maeve Binchy's new novel so lustfully?" asks Prichard.

"Well, she tells such a good story, you never want it to end," replies her mother-in-law.

"Therein lies the secret of Binchy's immensely popular Irish romances, from *Circle of Friends* to *Evening Class* to the latest, *Tara Road*," says Prichard. "Readers, mainly female, can't get enough. Binchy's books are big, her boys are backsliders, her heroines are spirited, and virtually everybody has dancing eyes and healthy hair. Unlike Frank McCourt's Ireland of malnutrition, grinding poverty, and tenements in *Angela's Ashes*, Binchy talks of treacle tarts and prams, polished silver, and soap-opera-esque scandals in Dublin's emerging smart set. Goodbye, cockles; hello, Green Tiger economy."

T. Coraghessan Boyle

Born
December 2, 1948, in Peekskill, New York

Real Name
Thomas John Boyle. Changed his middle name to Coraghessan (pronounced "kuh-RAGG-issun") when he was 17. The name is from his mother's side of the family.

Education
State University of New York at Potsdam, music major, 1970; Iowa University, Ph.D. in 19th-century British literature, 1977

Family
Married to Karen Kvashay in 1974. Three children.

Home
Santa Barbara, California

Fan Mail
T. C. Boyle
c/o Georges Borchardt
136 East 57th Street
New York, NY 10022

Publisher
Viking

T. Coraghessan Boyle is one of the best known, most imaginative novelists writing today. His often absurd, quirky, satirical style has been compared to William Faulkner, Gabriel García Márquez, and Evelyn Waugh. Often beginning with historical events, Boyle goes on to alter them, blurring the boundary between fact and invention. "I'm not writing historical novels—in the conventional sense," he says. "I don't think the traditional historical novel works, because the historical impulse—the research—overwhelms the aesthetic vision. I'd say instead that I'm writing contemporary novels with historical settings. I'm more interested in how the past is reflected in the present than I am with replicating history."

George Kearns of the *Hudson Review* calls Boyle's first novel, *Water Music* (1981), "a historical novel unlike any other, for the language is simultaneously that of its period (circa 1800) and that of streetwise America (circa 1980)." A tale of two men—Mungo Park, a real-life Scottish explorer, and Ned Rise, a (fictional) drunken con man from London—this novel allowed Boyle to further strengthen his reputation as a prominent American humorist.

With the publication of *World's End* in 1987, Boyle's fame began to increase. A complex and intricate novel, it describes the intertwining of three families over ten generations. John Calvin Batchelor of the *Washington Post Book World* says Boyle "displays a talent so effortlessly satirical and fluid that it suggests an image of the author at a crowded inn of wicked wits in a tale-telling fight for best space at the hearth."

And speaking of satire, Robert Cohen of the *Los Angeles Times* compared Boyle's *The Road to Wellville* (1993)—the story of Dr. John Harvey Kellogg and his Battle Creek Sanitarium with its emphasis on corn flakes and colonic irrigation—to a "Marx Brothers farce...minus Groucho, Chico, and Harpo." Read the book first, but then check for the 1994 movie of the same name, with Anthony Hopkins, Bridget Fonda, Matthew Broderick, and many other stars. (Fans of TV producer David E. Kelley will be interested to know that Camryn Manheim and Lara Flynn Boyle—now costars on *The Practice*—met on the *Road to Wellville* set.)

Good to Know

❖ T. C. Boyle never intended to become a writer. While studying music at SUNY Potsdam, he enrolled in a creative-writing course on a whim and soon began composing plays and short stories. He went on to apply to the University of Iowa Writers' Workshop: "The only one I'd ever heard of was 'Iowa'...so I wrote to them, and they accepted me, because they accept you just on the basis of the work. I could have never gotten in on my record." The record Boyle is referring to: a 2.0 undergraduate grade-point average. But he left Iowa with a 4.0 and a Ph.D.

❖ After college, Boyle accepted a position as a high school teacher in order to avoid serving in Vietnam. His main interests at the time were "hanging out" and "taking a lot of drugs." He was, he confesses, "a dilettante of heroin."

❖ He's been a professor of English at the University of Southern California since 1977, but also writes methodically from 9 A.M. to 1 P.M., seven days a week.

❖ A lean, six-foot-three "Ichabod Crane" of a man, T. C. Boyle is difficult to miss in a crowd. Particularly considering his "protopunk" image: spiked hair (said to resemble "strained apricots" or "steel wool"), Van Dyke beard, earrings, colorful sneakers, a loud jacket over a T-shirt (bearing the name of his latest book), and a scowl. Says Russell Banks: "This hipster that we greet and interview is really a total invention of his. It will be interesting to watch him in the coming years, because it's a hard persona to project when you're 65 and bald."

❖ Bad behavior: Boyle has been known to drink with buddies, wake up on strangers' floors, burn dolls' heads in fireplaces, abscond with "jacket required" jackets, and blast Springsteen. In high school, he and his friends stole a three-foot-high statue of Jesus and set it up on Peekskill's main street so it appeared to be directing traffic.

Treatises and Treats

BEST OF THE NET

T. Coraghessan Boyle Home Page
www.tcboyle.com
Created for T. C. Boyle by his son, Milo, this is a work in progress. The best feature to date is "What's New," Boyle's somewhat sporadic short-entry journal of what he's been up to of late. The site also includes book excerpts, reviews, and reader's guides for his novels and short-story collections.

New York Times Featured Authors
www.nytimes.com/books/specials/
   author.html
Click on "T. Coraghessan Boyle" for a collection of book reviews and articles that have appeared in the *New York Times*, along with the complete first chapter of *Riven Rock* and the story "Modern Love" from *T. C. Boyle Stories*.

Live, in Concert

Boyle loves to perform and shock. He often tells absurd stories to warm up the crowd at public readings, making his selections based on what he thinks will procure the biggest rise from an audience, rather than promoting his latest work.

Frank Conroy of the University of Iowa Writers' Workshop says of Boyle, "He wants to be a rock star and win the Nobel Prize." Boyle's response: "That's the old school, where a [public] reading is a dignified sharing of new work. . . . I don't care if the audience is 600 Saul Bellows, I'm going to knock them dead with a comedy routine. I'm out there as a missionary for literature, because if people laugh and enjoy themselves, they might actually do something as bizarre as reading the book."

History Unleashed

NOVELS
Water Music, 1981
Budding Prospects: A Pastoral, 1984
World's End, 1987
East Is East, 1991
The Road to Wellville, 1993
The Tortilla Curtain, 1995
Riven Rock, 1998
A Friend of the Earth, 2000

SHORT-STORY COLLECTIONS
Descent of Man, 1979
Greasy Lake and Other Stories, 1985
If the River Was Whiskey, 1990
Without a Hero, 1994
T. C. Boyle Stories, 1998

If You Like
T. C. Boyle . . .

You might also like the novels and short stories of E. L. Doctorow and Mark Helprin. Or try some of these authors, with whom he is often compared: Donald Barthelme, Don DeLillo, Flannery O'Connor, William Faulkner, Gabriel García Márquez, and Evelyn Waugh.

Best Book to Read First

Most critics agree that *World's End* is Boyle's most ambitious work. Cynthia Cotts of the *Village Voice* praises the novel for "juggling a thousand gems with kaleidoscopic control," while Benjamin De Mott from the *New York Times Book Review* deems it a "smashing good book, the peak achievement thus far in a career that seems now to have no clear limits."

It is hard to think of writers to compare [T. C. Boyle] with. In his sheer energy and mercilessness, his exuberantly jaundiced view, he resembles perhaps a middlebrow Donald Barthelme, or Don DeLillo crossed with Dr. Seuss, or Flannery O'Connor with a television and no church.

—Lorrie Moore,
New York Times

Ray Bradbury

Born
August 22, 1920, in
Waukegan, Illinois, the
third son of Leonard
Spaulding Bradbury,
a telephone lineman,
and Esther Moberg
Bradbury

Full Name
Raymond Douglas
Bradbury

Education
Attended schools in
Waukegan, Illinois, and
Los Angeles, Cali-
fornia.

Family
Married Marguerite
Susan McClure in
1947. They have four
daughters.

Home
Los Angeles, California

Hobbies
Painting in oil and
watercolors and
collecting Mexican arti-
facts.

Fan Mail
Ray Bradbury
c/o Don Congdon
156 Fifth Avenue,
 #625
New York, NY 10010

Publisher
Avon

Although his books are usually shelved in the science fiction section, Ray Bradbury is anything but a science fiction writer. When Heinlein and Asimov did science fiction, the science was at least plausible. With Bradbury, the details of the science never matter. What matters is the situation and the characters.

Bradbury's literary soulmate is, in fact, the late Rod Serling, creator of *The Twilight Zone*. Bradbury's stories can take place anywhere—on Mars in the distant future, on a spaceship headed toward the sun, or on a planet where it rains constantly, driving the colonists insane. And like Serling, Bradbury has the ability to present characters, incidents, plots, and descriptions that you remember decades after first encountering them.

For example, few images in literature of any sort can match Bradbury's in the short story "There Will Come Soft Rains" when he presents a fully automated house that continues to operate long after its owners have been vaporized in a nuclear attack. His description of the silhouettes burned into the exterior walls by the bodies of the children playing outside when the bomb exploded will stay with you forever.

His dialogue isn't nearly as sharp as Serling's, and he does tend to strip-mine an idyllic Midwestern childhood to excess. But the poetic impact of his best images—like the scene in *Fahrenheit 451* (the temperature at which paper burns) that describes the scores of individuals who have each memorized a book to preserve it from the depredations of the "firemen"—is incomparable. Images and concepts like these reach you on a non-intellectual level, but they are incredibly powerful, and they are most definitely the essence of Ray Bradbury's work.

Good to Know

❖ Bradbury started in 1940 as a newsboy in Los Angeles. He began writing full-time in 1943 and since then has published more than 500 works—novels, short stories, plays, screenplays, television scripts, and poetry.

❖ Movie credits include the screenplay for John Huston's highly acclaimed 1956 film of Melville's *Moby-Dick*. Several of his own books and stories have been made into movies, including François Truffaut's celebrated *Fahrenheit 451*. In the late eighties, Bradbury adapted 65 of his short stories for *The Ray Bradbury Television Theater*.

❖ He has won many awards, including the O. Henry Memorial Award, the Benjamin Franklin Award, the World Fantasy Award for Lifetime Achievement, and the Grand Master Award from the Science Fiction Writers of America.

Treatises and Treats

COMPANIONS AND GUIDES

The Ray Bradbury Companion by William F. Nolan (Gale, 1975). A great reference book for Bradbury's early work, with criticism, biography, bibliography, and facsimiles of unpublished writings. No longer in print, but you can probably find it in the library or from a used-book dealer like Bibliofind (www.bibliofind.com). Nolan, a close personal friend of Bradbury's, is himself an award-winning science fiction and mystery writer.

For a more recently published book of criticism and interpretation, look for *Ray Bradbury and the Poetics of Reverie* by William F. Touponce (Borgo Press, 1998).

BEST OF THE NET

The Ray Bradbury Page

www.brookingsbook.com/bradbury

Created and maintained by a pair of Bradbury enthusiasts, this is an excellent starting point for scholars, researchers, students, and fans—well-organized, informative, and regularly updated with new information about upcoming books, public appearances, awards, and so forth. Don't miss the "Ray Bradbury Links" page, where you'll find a good collection of interviews, articles, reading guides, and advice on tracking down signed first editions of Bradbury's books. (Best Bet: The Phantom Bookshop in Ventura, California, www.phantoms.com.)

Avon Books Web Site

www.avonbooks.com

Check here if you need help deciding which Bradbury book to read next. In addition to descriptions of each title, Avon often provides multipage excerpts.

Ray Bradbury Newsgroup

alt.books.ray-bradbury

If you have a question that isn't answered at either of the above Web sites, try posting it to this newsgroup.

Unscientific Favorites

NOVELS

Fahrenheit 451, 1953
Dandelion Wine, 1957
Something Wicked This Way Comes, 1962
Death Is a Lonely Business, 1985
A Graveyard for Lunatics, 1990
Quicker Than the Eye, 1996

SELECTED STORY COLLECTIONS

Presented here with original publication dates, though most are available in more recent editions.

The Martian Chronicles, 1950
The Illustrated Man, 1951
The Golden Apples of the Sun, 1953
The October Country, 1955
The Vintage Bradbury, 1965
I Sing the Body Electric!, 1969
The Best of Bradbury, 1976
The Stories of Ray Bradbury, 1980

A Memory of Murder, 1984
Driving Blind, 1997

If You Like Ray Bradbury...

You'll be pleased to know that you can find his work in over 700 anthologies and in back issues of *Playboy*, *Saturday Review*, *Weird Tales*, *Magazine of Fantasy and Science Fiction*, *Omni*, *Life*, and other publications. Trouble is, a lot of his early stories and articles were published under pseudonyms. For details on how the names were chosen and when and where he used them, visit The Ray Bradbury Page (www.brookingsbook.com/bradbury).

Ray Bradbury Pseudonyms

Guy Amory
D. R. Banet
Edward Banks
Anthony Corvais
Cecil Claybourne Cunningham
E. Cunningham
Leonard Douglas
Brian Eldred
William Elliott
Omega
Ron Reynolds
Doug Rogers
Douglas Spaulding
Leonard Spaulding
Brett Sterling
D. Lerium Tremaine

Best Book to Read First

Fahrenheit 451 or *The Martian Chronicles*. Or choose a story at random from *Vintage Bradbury*, the author's personal selection of his 22 best short stories.

Everything of mine is permeated with my love of ideas—both big and small.... I have fun with ideas. I play with them.... If my work sparks serious thought, fine. But I don't write with that in mind.... My goal is to entertain myself and others.

—Ray Bradbury, in an interview for *Future* magazine, October 1978

Bradbury Reads Bradbury

To experience first-hand why Bradbury is considered one of the world's master storytellers, treat yourself to the four-tape audio-cassette package, *Ray Bradbury Himself Reads 19 Complete Stories*, including all-time favorites like "There Will Come Soft Rains" and "The Illustrated Man." The tapes are available through bookstores. Or you can buy them directly from Audio Partners Publishing (800-231-4261, www.audiopartners.com).

Lilian Jackson Braun

Born
1916 or thereabouts, in Massachusetts. She declines to give her age, saying, "I tell people that psychologically I'm 35, physically I'm about 55, and chronological age I don't believe in."

Education
Graduated from high school at age 16.

Family
Married her second husband, former actor Earl Bettinger, in 1979.

Home
North Carolina

Publisher
Putnam

Lilian Jackson Braun is the author of the phenomenally successful *The Cat Who...* mystery series. Her stories of crime-solving cats include neither violence nor profane language, and certainly no graphic sex. Nevertheless, they have sold over 10 million copies in the last 30 years.

When the first book, *The Cat Who Could Read Backwards*, hit the bookstores in 1966, *New York Times* mystery-fiction reviewer Anthony Boucher declared that Koko the cat was "probably the New Detective of the Year." Other critics have praised Braun for her descriptive powers and for successfully "characterizing cats without relying solely on corny, cutesy feline antics." (*Booklist*)

The main human character in the series is Jim "Qwill" Qwilleran, a newspaper writer, recovering alcoholic, and, following an earlier divorce, a confirmed bachelor. The main love interest is Polly Duncan, the town librarian in Pickax City, Moose County (population 3,000). Cats of every sort appear in each book, but the four main cats are those owned by Qwill and Polly:

K'ao Ko Kung (Koko). A seal point, blue-eyed Siamese named for a 13th-century Chinese painter and poet. Sleek, smart, and definitely psychic, he is a very picky eater, with a preference for top-grade red sockeye salmon and catawba white-grape juice. Koko loves to read (backwards), and is the one who discovers all the clues and communicates them to Qwill, often through "tail language" or by knocking a particular book off a shelf.

Yum-Yum. Sometimes known as "Yum-Yum, the Paw" because her infamous right paw could "steal the nose off your face," according to Qwill. (Fascinated by shiny objects, Braun's real-life Yum-Yum used to take her gold pencil and hide it under a rug.) Like Koko, Yum-Yum will not eat anything but freshly prepared food.

Brutus. Not the brightest Siamese in the litter. Originally known as Bootsie, but renamed Brutus by owner Polly Duncan, a change that caused him to become more dignified in his behavior. More than a tad overweight, Brutus is on a strict diet, but he'll steal the food right off your fork.

Catta. Polly's female Siamese, acquired as a companion for Brutus. The two do not have a tension-free relationship, but they are faithful friends despite a significant age difference.

Qwill and his cats got off to a promising start in the 1960s. But as the hard-boiled detective mystery style became increasingly popular, Braun was abandoned by her publisher. For the next 18 years, she focused on her career at the *Detroit Free Press,* where she covered decorating, antiques, art, architecture, preservation, and the like.

After retiring from the paper, she eventually revived the series with *The Cat Who Saw Red* (1986). *The Cat Who Robbed a Bank* (2000) is the latest installment, but Braun says she can't wait to wrap up one book and get started on the next. Which is great news for her fans, all of whom enjoy the books as much for their witty and entertaining characters and cat antics as for the mysteries.

Good to Know

❖ At age 17, Braun was selling articles to *Baseball Magazine* and *The Sporting News* under the pseudonym Ward Jackson. She also wrote "spoems" (sport poems) for the *Detroit Times*—six per week for the entire baseball season and part of the football season.

❖ Known as LJB to her fans, she avoids publicity. You might spot her at the occasional book signing or cat show, but her promotional efforts are mostly confined to the letters she sends to readers with an enclosed greeting from Koko.

❖ She chose a male protagonist for her series to discourage readers from assuming that the stories are autobiographical—though she and Qwill do have some things in common. Both, for example, have a favorite chair where they can recline and write their stories with a standard lead pencil and pad of paper.

Treatises and Treats

COMPANIONS

The Cat Who ... Companion by Sharon Feaster (Prime Crime, 1998). A comprehensive reference guide to the series, covering everything from the amusing habits of Koko and Yum-Yum to dining in Moose County. Also featured are summaries of the crimes and clues, an alphabetical listing of characters, and various interesting tidbits about Qwilleran.

BEST OF THE NET

The Cat Who ... Web Site
members.tripod.com/~KaterinaB69/
    catwho/catwho.html
This excellent fan page features a bio on Qwill, an annotated listing of all the characters in the series, personal and professional background information on Braun, and links to other LJB resources on the Web.

Unofficial Lilian Jackson Braun Fan Club
www.geocities.com/Heartland/
    Estates/6371/lillian.htm
Over 100 LJB fans visit here regularly to participate in everything from book-group discussions to a cookbook project. (Note that the last part of the Web address includes two *l*'s, though the author's name does not.)

All the Cats Who ...

The Cat Who Could Read Backwards, 1966
The Cat Who Ate Danish Modern, 1967
The Cat Who Turned On and Off, 1968
The Cat Who Saw Red, 1986
The Cat Who Played Brahms, 1987
The Cat Who Played Post Office, 1987
The Cat Who Knew Shakespeare, 1988
The Cat Who Sniffed Glue, 1988
The Cat Who Went Underground, 1989
The Cat Who Talked to Ghosts, 1990
The Cat Who Lived High, 1990
The Cat Who Knew a Cardinal, 1991
The Cat Who Wasn't There, 1992
The Cat Who Moved a Mountain, 1992
The Cat Who Went into the Closet, 1993
The Cat Who Came to Breakfast, 1994
The Cat Who Blew the Whistle, 1995
The Cat Who Said Cheese, 1996
The Cat Who Tailed a Thief, 1997
The Cat Who Sang for the Birds, 1998
The Cat Who Saw Stars, 1998
The Cat Who Came to Breakfast, 1999
The Cat Who Robbed a Bank, 2000

If You Like Lilian Jackson Braun ...

Try Rita Mae Brown's mystery series (written in collaboration with her tiger cat, Sneaky Pie) or Carole Nelson Douglas's "Midnight Louis" books. You might also like books by Lydia Adamson, who writes the "Alice Nestleton" series of mysteries involving cats, the "Lucy Wayles" mysteries about birdwatching, and the "Dr. Nightingale" series featuring a veterinarian.

Susan Conant writes a series for dog lovers featuring Holly Winter, a Cambridge, Massachusetts-based dog columnist.

Best Book to Read First
The Cat Who Saw Red garnered an Edgar Award nomination in 1986 and is highly regarded among fans. But the book *Publishers Weekly* called the best of the series is *The Cat Who Blew the Whistle*. There's "enough background information to make new readers feel at home, and devotees of the series will applaud the added interest of railroading language and lore."

The best thing about writing is that you don't have to go anywhere to do it. I don't travel to promote my books, I don't give lectures, I just live quietly and write my kitty-cat stories.

—Lilian Jackson Braun, in a 1998 interview for *Publishers Weekly*

Catastrophic Inspiration

The original Koko was a Siamese kitten that Lilian Jackson Braun received as a fortieth birthday present from her husband. Koko was the author's first pet, and she and the cat adored one another. Tragically, just two years later Koko fell from a tenth-floor window and was killed. To deal with Koko's death, Braun wrote a short story, "The Sin of Madame Phloi," inspired by Koko's fatal fall. The story eventually led to the creation of *The Cat Who...*series, which Braun considers a memorial to her dear Koko.

William S. Burroughs

Born
February 4, 1914, in
St. Louis, Missouri, to
Mortimer P. Burroughs,
the owner of a plate-
glass company, and
Laura Lee Burroughs

Full Name
William Seward
Burroughs

Pseudonyms
William Lee and Willie
Lee

Education
Los Alamos Ranch
School (then the most
expensive school in
America); Harvard
University, A.B., 1936,
graduate study, 1938.
Also studied medicine
at the University of
Vienna (1937) and
Aztec and Mayan
history at Mexico City
College (1949–50).

Family
Married Ilse Herzfeld
Klapper, a German Jew,
in 1937, to allow her to
escape Nazi Germany
(divorced, 1946);
married Joan Vollmer,
1946 (died 1951). One
son from his second
marriage.

Died
August 2, 1997, in
Lawrence, Kansas, of
a heart attack

Publishers
Grove/Atlantic
Viking Penguin

A drug addict turned experimental novelist, William S. Burroughs has been called "one of the most controversial and influential writers of the past decades" (Bob Halliday, *Washington Post Book World*). He represents for many readers and critics the artist as outsider and rebel. He has had a tremendous influence as an avant-garde theorist and as a counterculture forerunner, and was well known for his "cut-up" writing technique, which he used in an attempt to destroy language systems and thereby liberate the mind.

Concerned throughout his life with issues of personal freedom, the control systems of society, and ways of freeing oneself from social restrictions, Burroughs viewed writing as his most powerful tool in fighting such restrictions. In doing so, he makes liberal use of what Norman Mailer has referred to as "gutter talk," though, says Mailer, Burroughs "captures speech like no American writer I know."

Burroughs helped to inspire the hippie and punk movements of the 1960s and 1970s. The publication of *Naked Lunch* effectively ended America's last obscenity laws, paving the way for greater freedom in the arts and allowing explicit sexual material to be published legally in this country. Burroughs "has had considerably greater cultural impact than the extent of his present readership might indicate," writes Bruce Cook in the *Detroit News*. "It would not be an overstatement to say that he is one of the secret shapers of American culture—such as it is today."

Good to Know

❖ Burroughs came from a distinguished family. His mother was a descendent of Robert E. Lee, and his paternal grandfather invented the adding machine and founded the Burroughs Corporation. His parents sold their shares in the company shortly before the stock market crash of 1929, and the $200,000 they received saw them through the Depression. (Burroughs always maintained that he lived almost entirely on the royalties from his books, not from family money.)

❖ He served in the army for several months before being discharged for psychological reasons: he had deliberately cut off the first joint of a finger to impress a friend.

❖ Police pressure due to his drug addiction forced him to move from New York to Texas to Louisiana. In 1949, he and his second wife, Joan, fled to Mexico—which they liked because morphine could be easily obtained by prescription, and Benzedrine, which Joan used, was sold over-the-counter.

❖ In 1951, while living in Mexico, Burroughs killed Joan in what he described as an accidental shooting. As he relates in *Burroughs*, a documentary film about his life, his wife balanced a glass on her head at a drinking party and dared Burroughs to shoot it off, William-Tell style. His bullet struck her in the head and she died instantly. Burroughs was released without charges.

❖ He lived in Tangier, Morocco, from 1953 to 1958, writing in seclusion and filling more than 1,000 pages with social satire and fragmentary notes about his travels and drug use. From these notes, with the help of Jack Kerouac and Allen Ginsberg, he produced four novels: *Naked Lunch*, *The Soft Machine*, *The Ticket That Exploded*, and *Nova Express*.

❖ In 1954, he sold his typewriter to buy heroin, though he kept working in longhand. "I had not taken a bath in a year nor changed my clothes or removed them except to stick a needle every hour in the fibrous grey wooden flesh of terminal addiction…. I did absolutely nothing. I could look at the end of my shoe for eight hours."

❖ Musical connections: The term "heavy metal" comes from *Naked Lunch*. And the group Steely Dan borrowed its name from Burroughs's writings. The Rolling Stones have written songs about his characters, while David Bowie and Patti Smith have used Burroughs's famous "cut-up" technique to compose their songs. Burroughs himself even hit the British record charts with *Nothing Here but the Recordings,* an album containing readings from his work and some cut-up tape-recorder experiments.

Treatises and Treats

COMPANIONS

Gentleman Junkie: The Life and Legacy of William S. Burroughs by Graham Caveney (Little, Brown, 1998). Concentrates on Burroughs as a cultural phenomenon and his legend in avant-garde circles for epic drug use and adventurous prose. The book's design reflects Burroughs's cut-up technique: text is superimposed over art (reproductions of photos, newspaper clippings, and other documents), all of it laid out on pages colored red, orange, yellow, and blue.

Word Virus: The William S. Burroughs Reader, edited by James Grauerholz and Ira Silverberg (Grove/Atlantic, 1999). The essential writings of Burroughs, collected in one volume, including a chapter from his and Jack Kerouac's never-before-published collaborative novel.

MAGAZINE

Beat Scene Magazine. The only Beat specialist magazine in the world. Includes stories, photos, news, reviews, and events about the Beat generation of writers, including Burroughs. Five-issue subscription is $35. Write to: D. Hsu, P.O. Box 105, Cabin John, MD 20818

BEST OF THE NET
William S. Burroughs Files
www.hyperreal.org/wsb
An electronic reference guide to Burroughs, including information about his literary works, recordings, film and video appearances, and related publications.

More than Random Reads

NOVELS USING CUT-UP TECHNIQUE
Naked Lunch, 1962
    (originally published in 1959 as *The Naked Lunch*)
The Soft Machine, 1961
The Ticket That Exploded, 1962
Nova Express, 1964
Exterminator!, 1973

OTHER NOVELS
Junkie, 1953 (reissued as *Junky*, 1977)
Port of Saints, 1973
Blade Runner: A Movie, 1979
    (*not* the 1982 Ridley Scott movie; Scott borrowed the title for his screen adaptation of a Philip K. Dick novel)
Cities of the Red Night, 1981
The Place of Dead Roads, 1983
Queer, 1985 (a continuation of *Junkie*)
The Western Lands, 1987

NONFICTION
My Education: A Book of Dreams, 1994
    (a memoir)

If You Like William S. Burroughs …

You might also like Jack Kerouac. Or try *Candy* by Terry Southern and *Last Exit to Brooklyn*, by Hubert Selby Jr., both of which ran into legal trouble concerning their graphic content.

Best Book to Read First

Naked Lunch, the bestseller that made Burroughs's literary reputation, remains his most widely known book. It consists of a series of sketches arranged in random order. In fact, Burroughs randomly stacked the pages on a table at his publisher's office, a procedure that he declared would create as good an ordering of the contents as any other.

Burroughs's voice is hard, derisive, inventive, free, funny, serious, poetic, indelibly American, a voice in which one hears transistor radios and old movies and all the clichés and all the cons and all the newspapers, all the peculiar optimism, all the failure.

—Joan Didion

A. S. Byatt

Born
August 24, 1936, in Sheffield, England, to John Frederick Drabble, a judge, and Kathleen Marie Bloor Drabble. Younger sister Margaret Drabble is a formidable author, critic, and intellect.

Full Name
Antonia Susan Drabble Byatt

Education
Newnham College, Cambridge, B.A. (first class honors), 1957; graduate study at Bryn Mawr College, 1957–58, and Somerville College, Oxford, 1958–59

Family
Married in 1959 to Ian Byatt, an economist, with whom she had two children: Antonia and Charles (killed by a drunk driver at 11). Divorced 1969. Married Peter Duffy, a financial specialist, in 1969; two daughters from this marriage: Isabel and Miranda.

Home
London, England, and a country home in France

Fan Mail
A. S. Byatt
37 Rusholme Road
London SW15 3LF
England

Publisher
Random House

A. S. Byatt, whose reputation as an important 20th-century author has come late in her career, is known for novels that find intellectual passions as vibrant and all-consuming as emotional ones. Indeed, she has long been a pillar of the British intellectual establishment, producing not only thought-provoking novels but also reviews and insightful works of criticism. Byatt's work frequently combines compelling stories with literary scholarship or historical inquiry.

Her early novels alerted critics to her talents. But it was her fifth novel, *Possession: A Romance* (1990), that brought her the acclaim and the wider audience she now enjoys. The book tells the story of two literary scholars whose investigation into the lives of two poets leads to their own love affair. Writing in *Spectator*, Anita Brookner called *Possession* "capacious, ambitious…marvelous," and said it was "teeming with more ideas than a year's worth of ordinary novels." Readers and critics alike have praised Byatt's skill at inventing 19th-century-style letters, poems, and diaries for inclusion in *Possession* and other novels.

The publication of *Angels and Insects* in 1992 did not disappoint the new legions of Byatt fans. The *Times Literary Supplement* declared the book "more fully assured and satisfying than *Possession*" and called it Byatt's "best work to date." But the book had the bad luck of coming out just as its publisher's imprint, Turtle Bay Books, was imploding, so it got no publisher support. Fortunately, the movie adaptation starring Kristin Scott Thomas generated the much-needed buzz to sell the book.

Byatt's latest novel *Babel Tower* (1996) is part of a series that includes *The Virgin in the Garden* (1978) and *Still Life* (1986), portraying England after World War II and featuring a character named Frederica Potter. The forthcoming final installment in the tetralogy will be called *A Whistling Woman*.

Good to Know

❖ Prolonged bouts with asthma and a near-fatal ovarian infection when she was ten gave Byatt plenty of time for reading. Her favorites as a child: Coleridge, Tennyson, Sir Walter Scott, Jane Austen, and Charles Dickens. Today's favorites: Wallace Stevens ("the greatest modern poet"), Willa Cather, George Eliot, Walter Moseley, Martin Cruz Smith, and Iris Murdoch (her literary idol).

❖ Language, says Byatt, is "the one thing I really understand more than I care about sex or cooking or families or anything…. My best relationships are with other writers. In many ways, I know George Eliot better than I know my husband."

❖ The idea for *Possession* came to her one day in the British Museum Library when Byatt saw a Coleridge scholar hard at work. "It started with the idea of 'possession.' Does the scholar possess the poet or does the poet possess the scholar?"

❖ American publishers were not interested in *Possession*. Eventually, Turtle Bay Books, a now-defunct Random House imprint, offered to publish it. But the editor, Susan Kamil, wanted to delete much of the poetry and many of the letters. As Kamil was detailing her requested changes over tea at the Ritz in London, Byatt fainted. When she came to, she told Kamil she would not make any changes at all. *Possession* was soon published in England (initial print run: 7,000 copies) and won the prestigious Booker Prize. So Turtle Bay gave in and agreed to publish the book just the way it was.

❖ When asked why she calls herself "A. S." instead of "Antonia Susan," she replies that it has something to do with T. S. Eliot and P. D. James, other writers who initialized their names.

❖ Byatt writes anything she regards as "serious" with a pen, slowly. But she writes journalism on her word processor. "I skipped the typewriter phase completely," she says. "I hate them. I still have to think with my fingers." She tries to write every day from 9:00 A.M. to 7:00 P.M., stopping in the middle for a swim.

❖ Her three pieces of advice for would-be writers: Read everybody. Always stop writing in the middle of something, when you know where you will start the next day. Carry a notebook everywhere.

Treatises and Treats

COMPANIONS

A. S. Byatt by Richard Todd (University Press of Mississippi, 1997) and *A. S. Byatt* by Kathleen Coyne Kelly (Twayne, 1996) both offer biographical information, critical commentary on the author's novels and stories, and well-researched bibliographies.

BEST OF THE NET

New York Times Featured Authors
www.nytimes.com/books/specials/
    author.html
Click on "A. S. Byatt" for a collection of book reviews, interviews, and articles by and about Byatt. You can also hear the author read from some of her work.

A. S. Byatt Home Page
www.asbyatt.com
Check here for details of forthcoming events and publications, a number of essays on the author's work, and an extensive bibliography.

Books for Thought

FREDERICA POTTER SERIES
The Virgin in the Garden, 1978
Still Life, 1986
Babel Tower, 1996
A Whistling Woman (not yet published)

ALL THE OTHER NOVELS
The Shadow of the Sun, 1964
The Game, 1967
Possession: A Romance, 1990 (Booker Prize, *Irish Times*/Aer Lingus International Fiction Prize)
Angels and Insects: Two Novellas, 1992

SHORT-STORY COLLECTIONS
Sugar and Other Stories, 1987
The Matisse Stories, 1995
The Djinn in the Nightingale's Eye: Five Fairy Tales, 1995
Elementals: Stories of Fire and Ice, 1999

If You Like A. S. Byatt . . .

You might also enjoy John Fowles's *The Magus* and Umberto Eco's *The Name of the Rose*.

Best Book to Read First

Possession: A Romance, which the *New York Times* called "A *tour de force* that opens every narrative device of English fiction to inspection without, for a moment, ceasing to delight."

Perhaps the most important thing to say about my books is that they try to be about the life of the mind as well as of society and the relations between people. I admire—am excited by—intellectual curiosity of any kind (scientific, linguistic, psychological) and also by literature as a complicated, huge interrelating pattern.

—A. S. Byatt

Literary Rivals

A. S. Byatt and her younger sister, Margaret Drabble, have been intense competitors throughout their lives. In fact, they have a reputation as the Joan Fontaine and Olivia de Havilland of British literature. "There was too much competition," Byatt says about her childhood relationship with her sister. "We didn't get on."

Though Byatt resents it when critics and interviewers draw comparisons to her more famous sister, perhaps her true literary rival is Martin Amis. She wasn't pleased when Amis was paid an $800,000 advance for his novel *The Information*. "I don't see why I should subsidize his greed simply because he has a divorce to pay for and has just had his teeth redone," groused Byatt. Amis has admitted that he hasn't gotten around to reading Byatt's work yet, though he said that he thinks she's pretty.

Truman Capote

Born
September 30, 1924,
in New Orleans, to
Lillie Mae Faulk
Persons, a former Miss
Alabama, and Archulus
Persons, whose family
owned the Streckfus
Steam Boat Line. They
named their son
Truman Streckfus
Persons.

Childhood
His mother decided
that she was unsuited
to raising a child, so
Truman was packed off
to live with relatives in
Monroeville, Alabama.
When he was four, his
parents divorced. His
mother married Cuban-
born businessman
Joseph G. Capote, and
sent for Truman, then
nine years old. He was
adopted by Capote and
took his name.

Education
Attended Trinity School
and St. John's
Academy (military
school) in New York
City and Greenwich
High School in
Connecticut. Gradu-
ated from Franklin High
School in NYC.

Died
August 25, 1984, in
Los Angeles, of liver
disease complicated
by phlebitis and
multiple-drug intoxica-
tion

Publisher
Random House

With the possible exception of Oscar Wilde, Truman Capote was the most flamboyantly gay famous writer in modern memory. The provocative photos on the backs of Capote's books were no accident. Nor was his television-talk-show image of an effete, limp-wristed author with an acid tongue and a knack for the outrageous statement.

In the end, however, like Wilde, Capote delivered the goods. Norman Mailer once said that Capote "wrote the best sentences of anyone in our generation." And when you read those sentences, you don't hear Capote's real-life lispy, high-pitched voice. You hear a master craftsman who almost always knows what to leave in and what to leave out. At his very best, as with *In Cold Blood*, Truman Capote can be absolutely spellbinding. But even when he is presenting New York socialite gossip (as in "La Côte Basque, 1965"), he never fails to fascinate.

Technically, drugs and alcohol did him in. but they were really just the facilitators of his self-destructive urges. He had to know that publishing the "La Côte Basque" excerpt from his never-finished novel *Answered Prayers* in a 1975 edition of *Esquire* would destroy the relationships he had cultivated with New York's high society. But he did it anyway. He was shunned as a result and spent the last nine years of his life in an ever-deepening narcotic haze.

According to the refrain from the Don McLean song, "Vincent," the world was never meant for one as beautiful as Vincent van Gogh. Much the same could be said of Truman Capote. By all accounts, he was a delicate soul, but the writings he left behind rank with the very best.

Good to Know

❖ Capote began writing at age eight and did so continuously throughout his childhood. "Actually, I never did any homework. My literary tasks kept me fully occupied...," he says in the preface to *Music for Chameleons*.

❖ During his early "motherless" years in Monroeville, Alabama, one of his closest friends was an elderly cousin, Miss Sook Faulk, to whom he paid loving tribute in "A Christmas Memory." Another was a young tomboy named Harper Lee, who later wrote *To Kill a Mockingbird*. Truman appears in the novel as Dill Harris, the pale, blond child who had an imagination as big as the universe.

❖ Capote was determined never to set foot inside a college classroom. "If I was a writer, fine. If I wasn't, no professor on earth was going to make me one," he told *Playboy* (March 1968). After high school, he got a clerical job with the *New Yorker*.

❖ While at the *New Yorker*, he began submitting short stories to magazines, many of which won awards. In 1948, *Other Voices, Other Rooms*, his only work centered on a gay-related subject, launched him as an up-and-coming novelist.

❖ On November 16, 1959, the newswires carried a story about the murder of an entire family in a small Kansas town. Three days later, Capote and Harper Lee arrived in Holcomb, Kansas. After six years of exacting research, *In Cold Blood* appeared in 1965. The book would earned Capote more than $2 million in royalties and movie rights. But the extreme, extended stress of the project led him to begin taking tranquilizers and other drugs.

❖ In November 1966, Capote created and hosted his famous "Black and White Ball" at the Plaza Hotel in New York City. It was attended by 540 of his "closest friends."

❖ Capote's literary acclaim, success, and innate wit paved his way into New York society. As a homosexual, Capote posed no threat to any of the monied males. He became a confidante of the ladies—whom he subsequently betrayed in the excerpts from his roman à clef, *Answered Prayers*.

Treatises and Treats

BIOGRAPHIES AND PAPERS

Truman Capote: In Which Various Friends, Enemies, Acquaintances, and Detractors Recall His Turbulent Career by George Plimpton (Doubleday, 1997). A must-read for Capote fans. The book is filled with gossip and firsthand accounts by family members, socialites, fellow authors, and Hollywood stars.

Capote: A Biography by Gerald Clarke (Simon and Schuster, 1988). Based on hundreds of hours of interviews with Capote and with everyone who knew him, plus access to his personal papers, this is the definitive biography.

Truman Capote Papers, c. 1924–1984. Housed at the New York Public Library, Center for the Humanities, Manuscripts and Archives Division. Holograph manuscripts and typescripts of Capote's published and unpublished work, notes, photographs, scrapbooks, and other materials. For more information, call 212-930-0801 or visit the library's Web site (www.nypl.org/research/chss).

BEST OF THE NET

New York Times Featured Authors
www.nytimes.com/books/specials/author.html Click on "Truman Capote" for book reviews and his 1984 obituary in the *New York Times*. Also, the original chilling news story, "Wealthy Farmer, 3 of Family Slain," that caught Capote's eye and inspired him to write *In Cold Blood*.

Acclaimed Works

Other Voices, Other Rooms, 1948
The Grass Harp, and A Tree of Night, and Other Stories, 1956
Breakfast at Tiffany's: A Short Novel and Three Stories, 1958 (The book that inspired the Audrey Hepburn/George Peppard movie. Also includes "A Christmas Memory.")
In Cold Blood, 1965
Music for Chameleons, 1983
Answered Prayers, 1987

Best Book to Read First

In Cold Blood, Capote's "nonfiction novel," is unquestionably his masterpiece. But for an accurate taste, without a novel-length commitment, dip into *Music for Chameleons*, a collection of 14 short pieces, both fiction and nonfiction, including "Mojave," originally published in *Esquire* as part of *Answered Prayers*, and "A Beautiful Child," a fascinating portrait of Marilyn Monroe.

To me, the greatest pleasure of writing is not what it's about, but the music the words make.

—Truman Capote

A Christmas Memory

No one familiar with Truman Capote's life and work can avoid a pang of sorrow at the way things turned out. Somehow you just ache for the tender soul who became a media clown and died of drug intoxication, yet almost until the end could write passages like this one from "A Christmas Memory," published in *Mademoiselle* magazine in 1956:
Imagine a morning in late November. . . . A woman with shorn white hair is standing at the kitchen window. She is wearing tennis shoes and a shapeless gray sweater over a summery calico dress. She is small and sprightly, like a bantam hen; but, due to a long youthful illness, her shoulders are pitifully hunched. Her face is remarkable—not unlike Lincoln's, craggy like that, and tinted by sun and wind; but it is delicate too, finely boned, and her eyes are sherry-colored and timid. "Oh my," she exclaims, her breath smoking the windowpane, "It's fruitcake weather!"
This utterly charming story was made into an Emmy Award–winning TV film in 1966, starring Geraldine Page and narrated by Truman Capote. Though not yet available on video, it is often rebroadcast at Christmas time.

Caleb Carr

Born
August 2, 1955, in
New York City, to
Francesca von Hartz
Carr, a social worker,
and Lucien Carr, an
editor at United Press
International, former
Beat poet, and friend
of Kerouac, Ginsberg,
and Burroughs. He was
the second of their
three sons.

Family
Parents divorced when
he was eight and his
mother later married
novelist John Speicher.
Ancestor Dabney Carr
was Thomas
Jefferson's school-
mate, good friend, and
brother-in-law. He is
buried next to
Jefferson under a great
oak tree at Monticello.

Education
Attended Kenyon
College, 1973–75;
New York University,
B.A. in history, 1977.

Home
New York City, in an
apartment on the
Lower West Side of
Manhattan

Fan Mail
Caleb Carr
c/o Suzanne Gluck
International Creative
    Management
40 West 57th Street
New York, NY 10019

Publisher
Random House

Storytelling comes naturally to Caleb Carr. His career began as a journalist and military historian writing for publications such as *World Policy Journal*, the *New York Times*, and *Military History Quarterly*. His 1991 military biography of Frederick Townsend Ward, *The Devil Soldier: The American Soldier of Fortune Who Became a God in China*, was well received by critics. But as *Los Angeles Times* critic Jonathan Kirsch observed, *The Devil Soldier* "often reads more like a historical thriller than the serious work of history that it is."

Kirsch's comment was a foreshadowing of things to come, for Carr's next book was the bestselling historical thriller, *The Alienist* (1994). He had made a stab at fiction some years earlier with a coming-of-age novel, *Casing the Promised Land* (1980). But it was with *The Alienist* that he found his niche. In the book, psychologist Dr. Laszlo Kreizler leads a manhunt to find a serial killer who is mutilating young male prostitutes. *The Alienist* is distinguished for its historical detail and includes cameo appearances by Teddy Roosevelt, Lincoln Steffens, and J. P. Morgan. Capturing the essence of life in New York City in the 1890s, the book struck a chord with both history buffs and fans of crime fiction and remained on the bestseller lists for months.

Carr plans to write a number of sequels, each focusing on a different crime and narrated by a different member of Dr. Kreizler's group. In the first of the sequels, *Angel of Darkness* (1997), the story is told by Stevie Taggert, a reformed teenage street tough whom the doctor has taken under his wing. A hefty volume of 600 pages, *Angel of Darkness* provides readers once again with exquisite historical details, along with a thought-provoking plot dealing with an aberration of the maternal instinct: a mother who kidnaps and kills children, even her own. Like its predecessor, the book became a bestseller, reaching the number-two position on the *Publishers Weekly* hardcover fiction list.

The futuristic novella *Killing Time* is Carr's most recent project, the first half of which was published in serial form in *Time* magazine in November and December of 1999.

Good to Know

❖ While a student at Columbia University in the 1940s, Carr's handsome father Lucien pleaded guilty to manslaughter in the stabbing death of Frank Kammerer, a homosexual who had relentlessly pursued him. Lucien Carr, who was not gay and repeatedly spurned Kammerer's advances, was eventually pushed over the edge. After killing the man, he dumped his body in the Hudson River and enlisted the help of Jack Kerouac to dispose of the murder weapon. The next day, however, Lucien turned himself in to the police. He served two years in prison.

❖ Carr originally presented his book proposal for *The Alienist* as a true story. "There wasn't a lot of enthusiasm for me to do fiction just at that point." After convincing his editor and agent of the significance of the historical gem he had uncovered, he confessed that it was entirely made up. His ruse earned him a contract and a modest advance. Once the book became a bestseller, he sold the film rights for half a million dollars.

❖ Despite his publishing successes, Carr still lives in the same apartment in a five-floor walkup on Manhattan's Lower West Side. He likes the fact that, when he goes out his door, he always finds something that outrages him. This anger "fuels his writing," he maintains.

❖ The Filipino pygmy in *Angel of Darkness* is often singled out as a ridiculous character. Carr created him as "a little tip of the hat to Conan Doyle and the pygmy in 'The Sign of Four,'" as well as a tribute to a time when eccentricity was appreciated and celebrated.

❖ Contemporary fiction is "very self-indulgent, very unentertaining, very dreary," says Carr. "If you were to say, 'Do you consider yourself a novelist in a Dickensian sense?' I would say, 'Oh, yes, absolutely.'" Substitute Philip Roth or Norman Mailer, however, and Carr replies, "No, no, no. I don't do that. I'm something else. I'm an historian."

Treatises and Treats

AUDIO

The Alienist, read by Edward Hermann (Simon & Schuster Audio). This superb abridged version won *Audiofile* magazine's Audiofile Earphones Award. Hermann moves easily between narrator and characters, and employs accents ranging from New York to Eastern Europe with eerie authenticity. You'll be on the edge of your seat.

The Devil Soldier, read by George Wilson (Recorded Books). This 11-cassette unabridged recording of Carr's highly acclaimed biography of Frederick Townsend Ward is available for rental or purchase (800-638-1304, www.recordedbooks.com).

All the Novels

Casing the Promised Land, 1980
The Alienist, 1994
The Angel of Darkness, 1997
Killing Time, 2000

If You Like Caleb Carr . . .

Read Jack Finney's *Time and Again*, a time-travel novel blending science fiction and romance against the backdrop of New York City in the 1880s. Originally published in 1970, the book has become a cult classic and led to a 1995 sequel, *From Time to Time*.

If your interest runs more toward crime and the psychology of killers, try Thomas Harris's *Silence of the Lambs*, Jonathan Kellerman's *Monster*, and Andrew Vachss's *A Choice of Evil*.

Best Book to Read First

The Alienist. The setting is New York City in 1896. A deranged psychopath is stalking and murdering young male prostitutes, and police chief Theodore Roosevelt enlists the help of Dr. Laszlo Kreizler to catch the killer. Kreizler, an "alienist" (the term used at the time for practitioners of the new science of psychology), creates a psychological profile of the killer, and he and his motley investigative team set about tracking the person down.

What The Alienist gave me was the ability to live the lifestyle I've always lived and not worry about the future. So rather than go out and spend all the money and change my lifestyle radically, I decided, wait a minute, let's just assume this never happens again, that this is a fluke. Let's just look at this book as a kind of security blanket. If you are fortunate enough to write other successful books, then let's start to play around a little.

—Caleb Carr, in *Newsday* (September 16, 1997)

Back to the Future

Caleb Carr bid a temporary farewell to turn-of-the-century New York for his project, *Killing Time*, set in central Africa in the year 2024. Curiously, though the story is set in the future, it will initially be published as a serialized novel, a form popularized in the mid-1800s by writers such as Charles Dickens.

Henry Luce, founder of Time/Life, is probably spinning in his grave, but the first half of the novel appeared in five installments in *Time* magazine during November and December 1999. On the other hand, Luce always had a sense of what people wanted, and clearly, people no longer want to read the traditional news-oriented weekly magazine. So perhaps it really is a small step from *covering* entertainment to *carrying* it. Random House will publish the complete novel in late 2000.

Is this novel really such a departure from Carr's previous work? Carr says, "I hope people will remember that I am not trying to write science fiction. I am trying to write future history. I'm not trying so much to look forward as to step forward and look back—a historical look on the future." Uh, okay.

Lewis Carroll

Born
January 27, 1832, in
Daresbury, Cheshire,
England, to the
Reverend Charles
Dodgson, rector of
Daresbury, and Francis
Jane Lutwidge
Dodgson

Real Name
Charles Lutwidge
Dodgson (pronounced
"DOD-son")

Education
Richmond School,
Christ Church College,
Oxford University, B.A.,
1854; M.A., 1857

Died
January 14, 1898, of
bronchitis (after being
ill with influenza), in
Guildford, Surrey,
England

Publisher
(one of many)
W. W. Norton

Why would *anyone* today read Lewis Carroll (a.k.a. Charles Dodgson)? We've all seen the cartoon and live-action versions of *Alice's Adventures in Wonderland*. We may have experienced the Mad Hatter's Tea Party Ride—a Tilt-O-Whirl in giant teacups—at a Disney theme park. Why bother with the books, most of which were written in the 1860s and 1870s?

The answer, for children and adults alike, is "sheer delight." Forget about the fact that, next to the Bible and Shakespeare, Lewis Carroll is probably the most quoted author in the English language. His books are "filled with zany characters, slapstick humor, and clever wordplay" that can never be captured completely in a cartoon or movie (*Dictionary of British Children's Fiction*). You really do have to "read the book," and in doing so, you will encounter a remarkable mind and a remarkable wit that operates on many levels.

At their most superficial, Carroll's stories are enormously entertaining to children and to the child in each of us. But there is a lot more going on beneath the surface. Carroll was a well-read Oxford mathematics professor with a special love for games and puzzles—and for magic tricks and puns. So you need to know, for example, that the English dormouse is a small squirrel that takes its name from the Latin word for "to sleep." (Think "dormitory," and you'll have it.) Naturally, the dormouse at the Mad Hatter's May tea party would have trouble staying awake. And who else is at the party—the March Hare (as in "mad as a March hare," a reference to the frenzy of male rabbits during their March mating season) and the Mad Hatter (a reference to the "madness" that infected many hat makers as a result of using mercury to cure felt).

If you think you know Lewis Carroll, you may want to read him again. (We recommend Martin Gardner's *Annotated Alice*, as you'll see.) If you've never actually read an "Alice" book, you have a tremendous treat in store. Listen to the language and give yourself over to the fantasy. You can analyze everything later. For now, revel in the fact that at age seven, Alice is sensible, logical, and yet open to any new experience life throws her way. She is "childlike" with an innocence and openness that appeals to readers of all ages.

Good to Know

❖ Recollections of the participants differ, but all agree that the "Alice" stories began with a boat trip up the Thames by Charles Dodgson, the Reverend Robinson Duckworth, and the three daughters of Henry George Liddell, dean of Christ Church, Oxford. Duckworth later wrote that he and Dodgson rowed as Alice Liddell steered. And that "the story was actually composed over my shoulder…I remember turning round and saying 'Dodgson, is this an extempore romance of yours?' And he replied, 'Yes, I'm inventing as we go along.'" The date was Friday, July 4, 1862, "as memorable a day in the history of literature," according to W. H. Auden, "as it is in American history."

❖ Lewis Carroll once arrived at what he thought was a children's party and entered the parlor on his hands and knees, trying to affect the attitude of a bear. Unfortunately, he had the wrong address and found himself in the middle of a gathering of women reformers. "The embarrassed [Carroll] suddenly rose to his feet," his nephew recalled, "and, without attempting any explanation, fled from the house with a celerity considerably more equine than ursine."

❖ Carroll invented the idea of dust jackets, suggesting to his publisher that *The Hunting of the Snark* (1876) be produced with a printed paper cover showing the title of the book. The rest is publishing history.

❖ In 1998 Carroll's own copy of *Alice's Adventures in Wonderland*—one of six known original 1865 editions—was sold at a Christie's auction for $1.54 million, a record for a children's book and 19th-century literature.

❖ *Alice in Wonderland* has been filmed many times. The most recent version is a delightful 1999 three-hour TV special with an all-star cast that incorporates high-tech special effects while preserving the flavor of the famous John Tenniel illustrations. The Mad Hatter's tea party alone (with Martin Short as the Mad Hatter) makes it well worth renting.

Treatises and Treats

LEWIS CARROLL SOCIETY

A nonprofit organization dedicated to furthering Carroll studies and making research materials more accessible. The Society meets twice a year, and members receive a subscription to the group's newsletter and discounts on books as they are issued. Annual dues are $20. For more information, contact: Ellie Luchinsky, Secretary
18 Fitzharding Place
Owings Mills, MD 21117
www.lewiscarroll.org/lcsna.html

COMPANIONS

The Annotated Alice: The Definitive Edition by Martin Gardner (1960, repr. W. W. Norton, 1999). This book includes both *Wonderland* and *Through the Looking Glass*, with the original Tenniel illustrations and detailed explanatory notes by mathematician, puzzle-master, professional explainer, and *Scientific American* columnist Martin Gardner. The "Alice" books have always stood on their own, but Gardner's work reveals many wonderful, additional levels of meaning.

Lewis Carroll: A Biography by Morton N. Cohen (Vintage Books, 1996). Includes newly found letters, diaries, and Carroll's photographs and drawings—all in an attempt to provide insight into the life of the famous children's author. According to *Booklist*, "Every lover of Carroll and of Victoriana should consider this a must-read book."

Lewis Carroll in Wonderland: The Life and Times of Alice and Her Creator by Stephanie Lovett Stoffel (Harry N. Abrams, 1997). A short introduction to the life of Carroll, with 130 illustrations (nearly 100 of them in color).

BEST OF THE NET
Lewis Carroll Home Page
www.lewiscarroll.org/carroll.html
Lots of good information for the Carroll enthusiast, including a discussion board, some of Carroll's photographs and mathematical games, information about Lewis Carroll societies and mailing lists, and links to other Internet resources.

Carroll's Adventures

Alice's Adventures in Wonderland, 1865
Through the Looking Glass and What Alice Found There, 1872
The Hunting of the Snark: An Agony in Eight Fits, 1876
Sylvie and Bruno, 1889
Sylvie and Bruno Concluded, 1893

Best Book to Read First

His most famous book, *Alice's Adventures in Wonderland*. It's available in many editions, but look for one with the original Tenniel illustrations—like W. W. Norton's *The Annotated Alice: The Definitive Edition* (1999), which also includes detailed explanatory notes by Martin Gardner.

Sometimes an idea comes at night, when I have to get up and strike a light to note it down—sometimes when out on a lonely winter walk, when I have had to stop, and with half-frozen fingers jot down a few words which should keep the new-born idea from perishing—but whenever or however it comes, it comes of itself.

—Lewis Carroll, 1887

An Innocent Love of Children

Noting Lewis Carroll's inordinate fondness for Alice Liddell (rhymes with "fiddle"), the little girl who inspired the "Alice" books, and emphasizing Carroll's hobby of photographing partially clothed or naked young girls (something we would never stand for today—unless, of course, the photos were part of an ad for T-shirts, jeans, or designer underwear), some have suggested over the years that the famous children's author was in fact a pederast.

But Martin Gardner thinks otherwise. Pointing out that, to many Victorians, little girls were the embodiment of virtue and idealized beauty, he writes in his introduction to *The Annotated Alice*, "There is no indication that Carroll was conscious of anything but the purest innocence in his relations with little girls, nor is there a hint of impropriety in any of the fond recollections that dozens of them later wrote about him.... Carroll's little girls appealed to him precisely because he felt sexually safe with them."

Raymond Chandler

Born
July 23, 1888, in Chicago Illinois, to Maurice Benjamin Chandler, a railway engineer, and Irish-born Florence Thornton Chandler

Education
Went to London with his mother at age seven when his parents divorced. Educated in England, France, and Germany.

Family
Married to Californian Cissy Pascal, who was 18 years his senior, for 30 years, from 1924 until her death in 1954.

Died
March 26, 1959, in La Jolla, California

Publishers
Library of America
Modern Library

The publication of Raymond Chandler's first short story in *Black Mask* magazine in 1933 was the start of a beautiful friendship. The magazine altered the face of crime fiction, publishing authors of what became known as the "hard-boiled school" of the detective genre, such as Erle Stanley Gardner, Carroll John Daly, and Dashiell Hammett. While Hammett has been credited as one of the inventors of the hard-boiled school, Chandler raised the lowly crime story to a new level of intensity with his crackling dialogue, poetic prose, and colorful imagery. He is one of the most quotable fiction writers of our time and has been acclaimed as the finest writer of American crime fiction.

Chandler's Los Angeles is a character unto itself, a provocative temptress, beckoning the hero into its seamy, steamy "mean streets." Philip Marlowe, protector of these streets, is a latter-day knight bound by a code of honor to right the wrongs and expose the corruption. Chandler deliberately sets up his detective as an underdog—a character often despised by the very people he is trying to help. Marlowe's quest is impeded at every turn by clients who lie to him and law officers who harass him, threatening to yank his license for the slightest impropriety. Far from glamorous, he is underpaid, underloved, and undervalued. It's no wonder that he finds himself constantly struggling to maintain his own moral compass.

Chandler's first book featuring Detective Philip Marlowe, *The Big Sleep*, is his best known and most successful. (Humphrey Bogart played Marlowe in the 1946 film adaptation.) Chandler mined his previously published short fiction to create several more Marlowe novels, including *Farewell My Lovely* (the author's personal favorite), and *The Long Goodbye*. With these novels he began transforming what had hitherto been regarded as mere escapist literature to works of greater social criticism.

Good to Know

❖ After taking the British Civil Service Exam and working for six months as an Admiralty clerk, Chandler resigned to become a writer. His family was not pleased. Failing at both poetry and journalism, he returned to America, held a variety of odd jobs, then enlisted with the Canadian Army in 1917 and fought in France.

❖ Following the Great War, Chandler experienced success at last, working with a California oil company until 1932, when he was fired after a bout of depression and heavy drinking. So at age 44, it was back to his true love—writing. "Blackmailers Don't Shoot," the story that launched his career, appeared in *Black Mask* magazine the following year.

❖ Chandler originally considered naming his detective Malory, in honor of Sir Thomas Malory, author of *Le Morte d'Arthur*. Ultimately he settled on "Marlowe," after the poet, dramatist, and Shakespeare contemporary. There is a building named after Christopher "Kit" Marlowe on the Dulwich College campus in England, where Chandler attended classes between 1900 and 1904.

❖ At the time of his death in 1959, Chandler was at work on a novel in which Marlowe is married and living in Palm Springs. The book was completed by Robert B. Parker and published in 1989 as *Poodle Springs*. (Parker's own detective character, Spenser, was named after Renaissance dramatist Sir Edmund Spenser, in the Chandler tradition.)

Treatises and Treats

COMPANIONS

Raymond Chandler: A Biography by Tom Hiney (Atlantic Monthly Press, 1997). *New York Times* critic R. W. Lewis calls Hiney's account of Chandler's life a "thoughtful and finely rounded biography." An English journalist, Hiney takes us from the author's childhood beginnings up until his final years of drinking and womanizing. His discussion of the Marlowe novels is quite illuminating.

The Life of Raymond Chandler by Frank McShane (Dutton, 1976). Another informative and insightful portrait, by the editor of Chandler's notebooks and correspondence as well as the two-volume Chandler collection published by the Library of America in 1995.

Raymond Chandler's Los Angeles by Elizabeth Ward with Alain Silver (Overlook Press, 1989). Illustrated with 100 black-and-white photos juxtaposed with excerpts from Chandler's fiction, this elegant volume evokes the atmosphere of the city that Chandler describes as both "rich and vigorous and full of pride" and "lost and beaten and full of emptiness." Reissued to commemorate the 50th anniversary of Chandler's *The Big Sleep*.

BEST OF THE NET

Twists, Slugs, and Roscoes
www.miskatonic.org/slang.html
"The flim-flammer jumped in the flivver and faded." Something lost in translation? You need to consult this swell online glossary compiled by William Denton for fans of the detective genre. Denton has excavated terms from the works of Raymond Chandler and Dashiell Hammett, and plans to do the same for other hard-boiled writers, whose characters are famous for saying things like "I jammed the roscoe in his button and said, 'Close your yap, bo, or I squirt metal!'"

Hard-Boiled Tales

The Big Sleep, 1939
Farewell, My Lovely, 1940
The High Window, 1942
The Lady in the Lake, 1943
The Little Sister, 1949
The Simple Art of Murder, 1950
  (includes the stories "Trouble Is My Business" and "Pick-Up on Noon Street," and the essay "The Simple Art of Murder")
The Long Goodbye, 1953
Playback, 1958
Poodle Springs, 1989
  (with Robert B. Parker)

If You Like Raymond Chandler . . .

You might try Ross Macdonald, who continued the tradition of Raymond Chandler and Dashiell Hammett with his Lew Archer series. Robert B. Parker picked up the baton in the 1970s with a more contemporary tough-guy, Spenser, who sees a psychotherapist and works out at the gym regularly. Another possibility: James M. Cain, whose book *Double Indemnity* was adapted for the big screen by Chandler.

Best Book to Read First

Start with *The Big Sleep*, the first of the Philip Marlowe novels. Set in Los Angeles in the 1930s, it's a classic case filled with blackmail, murder and deception—not to mention the wonderfully direct prose style that made Chandler famous: "She was trouble. She was tall and rangy and strong-looking. Her hair was black and wiry and parted in the middle. She had a good mouth and a good chin. There was a sulky droop to her lips and the lower lip was full."

When in doubt, have a man come through the door with a gun in his hand.

—Raymond Chandler

Bogart *Is* Marlowe

Most of Chandler's Philip Marlowe novels have been made into movies, but none more successfully than *The Big Sleep*. The 1946 version starring Humphrey Bogart and Lauren Bacall was directed by Howard Hawks and scripted by, among others, William Faulkner.

But Cary Grant was actually Chandler's first choice for the role of Marlowe. Once the film was released, though, Chandler wrote to his publisher, "Bogart . . . is so much better than any other tough-guy actor that he makes bums of the Ladds and the Powells. . . . Bogart is the genuine article."

Later film adaptations starred Alan Ladd, Robert Mitchum, Dick Powell, James Garner, and Elliott Gould as Marlowe. But it was Bogart's performance that set the standard against which they were all judged.

John Cheever

Born
May 27, 1912, in
Quincy, Massachu-
setts, to Frederick
Cheever, a prosperous
manufacturer who lost
his fortune in the stock
market collapse of
1929, and Mary Liley
Cheever, a gift-shop
owner

Education
Attended Thayer
Academy. (Expelled at
age 17.)

Family
Married Mary M.
Winternitz, a poet and
teacher, in 1941.
Three children: Susan
and Benjamin (both
writers), and Frederico.

Died
June 18, 1982, in
Ossining, New York, of
cancer

Publisher
Knopf

John Cheever is considered by many to be one of the most important short-story writers of this century. He has been aptly called "the Chekhov of the suburbs" for his ability to capture the drama and sadness of his characters' lives by revealing the trauma hidden beneath seemingly insignificant events. Perhaps more than any other writer, Cheever created the genre that came to be known as "the *New Yorker* story," in which characterization, acute observation, and consummate literary skill are far more important than plot.

Many of his stories and novels are set in what has become known as "Cheever country"—the wealthy suburban communities of New York's Westchester County and Connecticut, the towns the author called Shady Hill, St. Botolphs, and Bullet Park. Most of Cheever's characters are white and Protestant. And most are bored with their jobs and dissatisfied with their marriages and their lives in general. These are people who are quite well-off but have to keep working at their spirit-crushing jobs to maintain their lifestyles—people who spend their nights staggering around high on alcohol and tranquilizers, only to get up the next day (hung over), commute into Manhattan, and come home from work to get drunk again.

Cheever's fiction focuses on the complexity and the ultimate loneliness of the human condition, sometimes with a sense of absurdity or irony, but always with a sense of compassion. "Mr. Cheever's account of life in suburbia makes one's soul ache," wrote Guy Davenport in the *National Review*. His novels have been labeled by some critics as competent, if not sub-par, especially when compared with his stories. But *The Wapshot Chronicle* (1957) is certainly an exception. It won the National Book Award and made the Modern Library's list of the 100 Best Novels of the 20th century.

Good to Know

❖ Cheever's expulsion at age 17 from the Thayer Academy in Massachusetts provided the theme for his first published story, which he sold to the *New Republic* in 1930 for $87. Five years later he became a regular contributor to the *New Yorker*, the magazine that published the majority of his stories.

❖ His social drinking began during the 1950s, and during the next 20 years progressed to full-blown alcoholism. In 1975, he checked himself into a rehabilitation clinic and managed to end his addiction. Unlike many other authors, he was able to continue writing successfully after he became sober.

❖ As a child, Cheever was considered effeminate. Friends and family suspected that he was gay, but he managed to hide this fact from them and from himself for many years. It was not until he had been with several male lovers that he became more open about his bisexuality. He spent most of his life with two selves—the public John Cheever who wore Brooks Brothers suits and went to church, and the private John Cheever who tried unsuccessfully to resist his attractions outside his marriage.

❖ Before he was able to write full-time, Cheever supported himself writing synopses for MGM and teaching in Sing-Sing prison. He worked briefly in the 1960s as a Hollywood scriptwriter on a film version of D. H. Lawrence's *The Lost Girl*. Cheever's own story "The Swimmer"—by far his most anthologized short story—was made into a 1968 film starring Burt Lancaster. Three other stories—"The Sorrows of Gin," "The Five Forty-Eight," and "O Youth and Beauty!"—were made into films broadcast by PBS in 1979.

❖ Two of Cheever's three children, Susan and Benjamin, are writers. Benjamin Cheever's novel *The Plagiarist* (1992) contains a portrait of an alcoholic, aging man of letters. Susan Cheever has published two memoirs about her father.

Treatises and Treats

COMPANIONS

Conversations with John Cheever, edited by Scott Donaldson (University Press of Mississippi, 1987). A compilation of interviews with the author.

The Letters of John Cheever, edited by Benjamin Cheever (Simon & Schuster, 1988).

John Cheever: A Biography by Scott Donaldson (Random House, 1988). The standard biography, which relies heavily on Cheever's own writings to tell the story of his life.

The Journals of John Cheever by John Cheever (Knopf, 1991). Written during a period of 35 years in 29 loose-leaf notebooks, Cheever's journals were edited by Robert Gottlieb for this 400-page book. (Ex–*New Yorker* editor Gottlieb worked with Cheever on his last five books.) It includes many of Cheever's darker reflections on life, in particular his alcoholism and his growing dissatisfaction with his marriage.

The Critical Response to John Cheever, edited by Francis J. Bosha (Greenwood Press, 1993). Collects the major criticism of Cheever's fiction, from 1943 to the present. Also includes, for the first time, a long interview given by the author less than a year before his death—most likely his last interview publicly heard.

Home Before Dark: A Biographical Memoir of John Cheever by Susan Cheever (Washington Square Press, 1999). Cheever's daughter uses previously unpublished letters, journals, and personal stories to create an honest portrait of her father.

Treetops: A Family Memoir by Susan Cheever (Washington Square Press, reprint, 1999). The companion volume to *Home Before Dark*.

Best Reads

ALL THE NOVELS

The Wapshot Chronicle, 1957
  (National Book Award)
The Wapshot Scandal, 1964
Bullet Park, 1987
Falconer, 1977
Oh, What a Paradise It Seems, 1982

SHORT-STORY COLLECTIONS

The Way Some People Live: A Book of Stories, 1943
The Enormous Radio and Other Stories, 1953
The Housebreaker of Shady Hill and Other Stories, 1958
Some People, Places and Things That Will Not Appear in My Next Novel, 1961
The World of Apples, 1973
The Stories of John Cheever, 1978
  (Pulitzer Prize, National Book Critics Circle Award, and American Book Award)

If You Like John Cheever . . .

Try the novels and short stories of fellow *New Yorker* contributors John O'Hara and John Updike. You might also like Raymond Carver, one of the grand masters of short fiction.

Best Book to Read First

Cheever is better known for his short stories than for his novels. The best place to start is thus his award-winning *The Stories of John Cheever* (1978). According to *Time* magazine's Paul Gray, the publication of this volume of stories "revived single-handed publishers' and readers' interest in the American short story."

Fiction is our most intimate and acute means of communication, at a profound level, about our deepest apprehension and intuitions on the meaning of life and death.

—John Cheever

A Seinfeld Legacy

Late in life, Cheever declared: "I don't anticipate that my work will be read. I might be forgotten tomorrow; it wouldn't disconcert me in the least." Little did he know that ten years after his death, he would be immortalized in "The Cheever Letters," episode 46 of the popular Seinfeld television show. As fans will recall, it's the one in which George and Susan lay two bombshells on her father: they've accidentally burned down his cabin, and they've discovered a packet of love letters from her secret paramour, author John Cheever.

Agatha Christie

Born
September 15, 1890,
in Torquay, Devon,
England, to Frederick
and Clarissa Miller

Full Name
Agatha Mary Clarissa
Miller Christie

Pseudonym
Mary Westmacott
(used for her romantic
fiction)

Education
Tutored at home by her
mother until age 16,
when she was sent off
to Paris to study
music.

Family
Married Royal Air
Corps Colonel
Archibald Christie in
1914. Divorced 14
years later. One child:
Rosalind. Married
archaeologist Max
Edgar Lucien Mallowan
in 1930.

Died
January 12, 1976

Publishers
Berkley
HarperCollins
St. Martin's

Dame Agatha Christie, the self-styled "Duchess of Death," produced her first mystery when her sister dared her to "write a good detective story." *The Mysterious Affair at Styles* (1920) sold only 2,000 copies. But writing turned out to be Agatha Christie's forte, eventually earning her the rank of third place worldwide in overall sales, behind the Bible and Shakespeare, at over 2 billion copies. Decades after her death, her titles continue to sell nearly 25 million copies a year.

Her writing style is considered workmanlike—"I don't enjoy writing detective stories," she once said. "I enjoy thinking of a detective story, planning it, but when the time comes to write it, it is like going to work everyday, like having a job." It was those plans and plots, however, that set the standard for the genre. At her best, Christie's novels are able to distract the reader from the most important clues, creating intricate puzzles that, when revealed, seem entirely logical.

The characters from her novels were quite often from the middle class or upper-middle class. Her two most famous fictional creations, the spinsterish Miss Jane Marple and the slightly ridiculous Belgian, Hercule Poirot, display her adept characterization.

Good to Know

❖ In World War I, Agatha Christie was a volunteer dispensary nurse, a position that gave her special knowledge of drugs and poisons. Assisting her second husband's excavations in the Middle East also provided useful material, particularly for *Death on the Nile*.

❖ Christie's play *The Mousetrap* was written in 1947 as an 80th birthday present for Queen Mary, the mother of King George VI. Its title was derived from *Hamlet*. The play has since become the longest-running play in theatrical history, earning over £15 million (roughly $24 million) for Christie's grandson, to whom she gave the rights when he was nine.

❖ The immensely popular character Hercule Poirot (the name comes from the word *poireau*, which is French for "leek") has been played by such notable actors as Albert Finney and Peter Ustinov on film and David Suchet on TV. Christie wrote of this amusingly pompous Belgian in *The Mysterious Affair at Styles*; "I believe a speck of dust would have caused him more pain than a bullet wound."

❖ In 1971, Agatha Christie was named Dame Commander, Order of the British Empire, by Queen Elizabeth II.

Treatises and Treats

AGATHA CHRISTIE SOCIETY

One of the best ways to stay on top of news and information is to join the Agatha Christie Society. Chaired by the author's grandson, the group's stated purpose is to foster communication between Christie's countless loyal fans worldwide and "the various media who strive to bring her works to the public." Members receive a quarterly newsletter with all the latest on Christie-related books, movies, videos, and plays; letters from fans; information about awards and competitions, and so forth. To join, contact:
Agatha Christie Society (USA)
P.O. Box 1896
Radio City Station
New York, NY 10101-1896
E-mail: AgathaUS@aol.com

COMPANIONS

Agatha Christie A to Z: The Essential Reference to Her Life and Writings by Dawn B. Sova (Facts on File, Inc., 1997). An impressive, scholarly, and near comprehensive work on the life and novels of the famed detective novelist. One drawback is that Sova uses the British titles for the books, which may be confusing for U.S. readers who know their favorites by different titles.

Agatha Christie: An Autobiography by Agatha Christie (Boulevard, 1996. Originally published as *Come Tell Me How You Live*, 1975). An engrossing look behind the secretive life, marriages, and early years in Victorian England of the most widely translated author in English. One glaring omission: the author fails to provide a satisfying explanation of what she was doing when she disappeared for 11 days in 1926. For more on that, look for ***Agatha Christie and the Eleven Missing Days*** by Jared Cade (Dufour, 1999).

What's Your Agatha Christie I.Q.?: 1,001 Puzzling Questions About the World's Most Beloved Mystery Writer by Kathleen Kaska (Carol Publishing Group, 1996). The ultimate trivia test for dyed-in-the-wool Christie fans.

In the Footsteps of Agatha Christie by François Rivière, with photographs by Jean-Bernard Naudin (Trafalgar Square, 1997). Sumptuous photos of the cliffs and countryside, hotels and stone cottages, in Agatha Christie's home county of Devon, England.

BEST OF THE NET

Agatha Christie Icelandic Homepage
www.hi.is/~ragnaj/eac.htm
Christie fans around the world have created Web sites in her honor, but this is one of the most interesting and informative, with listings of films and television series, best books, quotations, trivia, a link to the Agatha Christie Society, and more.

Dame Agatha's Personal Favorites

The Murder of Roger Ackroyd, 1926
The Mysterious Mr. Quin, 1930
   (also published as *The Passing of Mr. Quin*)
Miss Marple and the 13 Problems, 1932
Mr. Parker Pyne, Detective, 1934
   (also published as *Parker Pyne Investigates*)
Death on the Nile, 1937
The Moving Finger, 1942
The Body in the Library, 1942
Death Comes as the End, 1944
The Labours of Hercules, 1947
The Crooked House, 1949

If You Like Agatha Christie...

You might also like classic British mystery writers Margery Allingham, Ngaio Marsh, and Dorothy L. Sayers.

Best Book to Read First

The Murder of Roger Ackroyd is considered her most ingenious and original novel. Or try *The A. B. C. Murders, Ten Little Indians,* or *Murder on the Orient Express.*

Her skill was not in the tight construction of plot, nor in the locked-room mystery, nor did she often make assumptions about the scientific and medical knowledge of readers. The deception in these Christie stories is much more like the conjurer's sleight-of-hand. She shows us the ace of spades face up. Then she turns it over, but we still know where it is, so how has it been transformed into the five of diamonds?

—Julian Symons, *Bloody Murder, from the Detective Story to the Crime Novel: A History*

A Real Christie Mystery

By far the most intriguing episode of Agatha Christie's life is her still largely unexplained disappearance for 11 days in 1926. Rumored to have faked her own death to implicate her cheating husband, Christie eventually reappeared, claiming amnesia, after a huge manhunt. The events of those 11 days were made into the fictionalized 1979 film *Agatha*, starring Vanessa Redgrave, Dustin Hoffman, and Timothy Dalton. More recently, they were the subject of a 1997 BBC documentary and a book, *Agatha Christie and the Eleven Missing Days*, by Jared Cade, one of the research consultants for the documentary.

Tom Clancy

Born
April 12, 1947, in Baltimore, Maryland. His father was a mail carrier.

Education
Graduated in 1965 from Loyola High School in Towson, Maryland. Continued his Jesuit education at Loyola College in Baltimore, Maryland, graduating in 1969 with a degree in English literature. ("I wasn't smart enough to do physics," says Clancy.)

Family
Married for 30 years (1969–99) to Wanda Thomas, with whom he has four children. After their divorce, he married Alexandra Llewellyn, a cousin of his friend, General Colin Powell.

Home
A large, gated estate called Peregrine on the Chesapeake Bay in Huntingtown, Maryland

Fan Mail
Tom Clancy
P.O. Box 800
Huntingtown, MD
  20639

Publisher
Putnam

Tom Clancy singlehandedly invented the techno-thriller genre with *The Hunt for Red October* in 1984. But the real-life story of how he did it—and how he has managed to keep turning out bestsellers after the collapse of the Soviet Union's "Evil Empire"—is almost as intriguing as one of his own page-turners.

Stuck in a boring job at an insurance agency owned by his wife's family, Clancy wrote *Red October* in his spare time, drawing solely on publicly available information and his own inspired educated guesses and extrapolations. The latest submarine and intelligence technologies of the day play a pivotal role in the story, and there are many well-informed explanations of how it all works. In many cases they are as captivating as the story itself, a Tom Clancy hallmark.

Clancy has earned tens of millions of dollars a year since the success of *Red October*. But what's *really* impressive is that he has found a way to continue to produce techno-military bestsellers long after the disappearance of the Soviet Union and the threat of nuclear annihilation that has been the engine of so many Cold War novels. He's done it by focusing on other antagonists: the Irish Republican Army, South American drug cartels, forces in the Middle East, terrorists, and revenge-seekers who crash a Boeing 747 into the U. S. Capitol.

Tom Clancy clearly has a great gift for storytelling. As outlandish as his plots may sometimes seem, when you read Clancy's books, you *believe*. And you cannot wait to find out what happens next. Since weapons and intelligence technologies continue to advance, fans can count on the fact that there will always be some new weapon to explain—and deploy!—in a future Tom Clancy thriller.

Good to Know

❖ Clancy wanted to serve in Vietnam, but poor eyesight prevented him from entering the military. So, rather like Stephen Crane, who had never been to war when he wrote *The Red Badge of Courage*, Clancy had never set foot in a submarine when he wrote a book that by all accounts perfectly captures life underwater.

❖ His manuscript for *The Hunt for Red October* was rejected by dozens of publishers before he submitted it to the U. S. Naval Institute Press (www.nip.org), a very small Annapolis-based company which, after 100 years of concentrating exclusively on nonfiction, had decided to experiment with novels. They paid Clancy $5,000 and subsequently auctioned the paperback rights for close to $50,000. The initial print run was 14,000 copies—quite a vote of confidence for a first novel!

❖ *Red October* didn't really take off until President Reagan called it "the perfect yarn." Then, as when President Kennedy praised Ian Fleming's James Bond novels, sales went through the roof!

❖ *The Hunt for Red October* contains such accurate descriptions of high-tech military hardware that former Navy Secretary John Lehman once joked that had Clancy been in the navy, he would have had him court-martialed for security violations.

❖ Clancy's Huntingtown, Maryland, estate includes a pool, football field, tennis court, indoor pistol range, and a World War II–vintage tank as a lawn ornament. Visitors approaching the house will encounter an official-looking road sign reading "Tank Crossing."

Treatises and Treats

COMPANIONS

The Tom Clancy Companion edited by Martin H. Greenberg (Berkley Books, 1992). Although in need of an update, this is a must-have book for Clancy fans. It includes a 200-page alphabetical guide to the characters, weapons, ships, tanks, and hardware in the first six novels (up to and including *The Sum of All Fears*). Also an in-depth interview with Clancy, and 12 of his essays on issues such as nuclear proliferation and gun control.

Tom Clancy: A Critical Companion by Helen S. Garson (Greenwood Press, 1996). Discussion and commentary on plot development, characters, writing style, and themes in Tom Clancy's novels. Written by a professor of English and American Studies at George Mason University, the book devotes a chapter to each of the first eight novels. The author also presents biographical information about Clancy, and a bibliography of critical sources and reviews of his work.

BEST OF THE NET

Tom Clancy FAQ
www.cosbyassoc.com/clancyfaq
This site covers all things Clancy—books, movies, games, and general information. Site owner Stephen Cosby does an excellent job of harvesting and organizing information posted to the two main Clancy newsgroups (alt.fan.tom-clancy and alt.books.tom-clancy). He has even culled some of the posts Clancy himself has made to these groups. You'll also find links to nearly a dozen other Clancy Web sites and information on subscribing to a fan-sponsored mailing list.

Official Tom Clancy Site
www.penguinputnam.com/clancy
Check here for excerpts and sample chapters from Tom Clancy's latest books. You can also sign up to receive an e-mail newsletter that the publisher sends out from time to time with news and information about the author and his work.

Real Fiction

The Hunt for Red October, 1984
> Neighbor Edward I. Beach, former sub commander and author of *Run Silent, Run Deep,* helped with the details.

Red Storm Rising, 1986
> Assisted by Larry Bond, who was a naval analyst at the time and is now a best-selling writer.

Patriot Games, 1987
The Cardinal of the Kremlin, 1988
Clear and Present Danger, 1989
The Sum of All Fears, 1991
Without Remorse, 1994
Debt of Honor, 1994
Executive Orders, 1996
Rainbow Six, 1998

You will also find Clancy's name on the Op-Center series (created with Steve Pieczenik) and the Power Plays series (created with Martin Greenberg). According to *Publishers Weekly*, the Op-Center books were written by Jeff Rovin, and the Power Play books may have been written by Jerome Priesler, each of whom has published novels under his own name. Clancy has also lent his name to numerous nonfiction books devoted to various aspects of the military.

If You Like Tom Clancy...

You might also like these authors:
Larry Bond
Dale Brown
Stephen Coonts
Harold Coyle
Len Deighton
Ken Follett
W. E. B. Griffin
Robert Ludlum

Best Book to Read First

The Hunt for Red October. Critics agree that Clancy's mastery of the writing craft has improved since this initial sortie, but if you want to see what all the shouting's about, this is the book to start with. If it doesn't make you stay up past your bedtime, you will never be a Clancy fan.

[My readers] are people who want to know how the world really works. My covenant with my readers is that I tell them the way things really are. If I say it, it's real.

—Tom Clancy

Thinking Caps

Clancy writes at the computer in the library of his home. The room contains over 3,000 books—and 200 military hats. He begins each morning at 8:00 A.M. by editing his previous day's output. Then he writes until lunchtime. He averages ten manuscript pages a day and does *not* work from an outline!

Mary Higgins Clark

Born
December 24, 1929,
in New York City to
Luke Higgins, a Bronx
pub owner who died
when she was ten, and
Nora Durkin Higgins

Education
Attended New York
University. Graduated
summa cum laude
from Fordham Univer-
sity with a B.A. in
philosophy, 1979.

Family
Married in 1949 to
Warren F. Clark. He
died in 1964, leaving
her with five children.
Second marriage in
1978 to attorney
Raymond C. Ploetz was
annulled six years later.
Third marriage in 1996
to John Conheeney, a
retired Merrill Lynch
Futures CEO. Between
them they have 15
grandchildren.

Homes
Saddle River, New
Jersey, and a pied-à-
terre overlooking
Central Park in New
York. Summer homes
in Spring Lake, New
Jersey, and Dennis,
Massachusetts

Fan Mail
c/o Eugene H. Winick
Macintosh & Otis
475 Fifth Avenue
New York, NY 10017

Publisher
Simon & Schuster

Just as Alfred Hitchcock specialized in films about ordinary people suddenly caught up in extraordinary events, Mary Higgins Clark writes about "terror lurking beneath the surface of everyday life" (*Washington Post*). A smart, sophisticated investment banker treats herself to a luxury cruise and meets a captivating man, but something is not right. A mother looks out into the backyard where her little boy and girl were playing just moments earlier and sees only one red mitten. Two friends make a habit of dating men through the personal ads—until one is found dead on a Manhattan pier wearing one of her own shoes and one dancing slipper.

A smart, entertaining storyteller with a gift for creating strong, believable female characters (who she then puts in jeopardy), Mary Higgins Clark is possessed of some writerly magic that makes it all work. "What's amazing," wrote the *Detroit News*, "is how expertly she manages to keep us hooked time after time, and even better, create new plots, each fresh as a mountain stream."

"I write for the mainstream," says the Queen of Suspense. "I write about nice people not looking for trouble. They find evil in their own car, home, everyday life." Although Clark's more recent novels are often set in glamorous locations, each offers yet another demonstration of her skill as a master manipulator—one who can build the tension and suspense to an often shattering (and always satisfying) conclusion.

Good to Know

❖ Mary Higgins Clark (MHC for short) sold her first story to *Extension* magazine in 1956 for $100—after six years and 40 rejection slips. Widowed at 35 with five children, she also wrote four-minute radio scripts. ("It taught me to write tightly," she says.). Jobs in radio and advertising followed.

❖ Her first book, a biography of George Washington called *Aspire to the Heavens* (1969), was a colossal failure—due at least in part to the fact that bookstores mistakenly thought it was a prayer book and shelved it in the religion section.

❖ Success came six years later when her first novel, *Where Are the Children?* (1975), became an instant bestseller, and four-figure advances became a thing of the past. She was paid just $3,000 to write *Where Are the Children?*, but when it came time to sell the paperback rights to her second novel, *A Stranger Is Watching* (1978), she asked for and got over a million dollars. The story was filmed by MGM in 1982.

❖ When she's in the midst of a book, MHC usually begins work at 5 A.M.—a habit she developed when her children were small and she had no choice but to do most of her writing at the kitchen table between 5 A.M. and 7 A.M. Under deadline pressure, she may work until midnight. The walls of her home office are painted deep crimson. "Red keeps you awake, don't you think?" she told the *Wall Street Journal*.

❖ Two other Clarks you may encounter on the mystery shelves: MHC's daughter Carol Higgins Clark, author of *Twanged* and several other titles featuring detective Regan Reilly, and former daughter-in-law Mary Jane Clark, a CBS news producer who recently published her first mystery novel, *Do You Want to Know a Secret?*.

Treatises and Treats

COMPANIONS AND SPECIAL PUBLICATIONS

Mary Higgins Clark: A Critical Companion (Greenwood Publishing, 1995) by Linda Claycomb Pelzer, associate professor of English at Wesley College in Dover, Delaware. Covers Clark's first 14 books (through *Let Me Call You Sweetheart*), revealing "the serious intent of a popular writer of popular fiction." The book examines common themes, explores Clark's treatment of social issues, and highlights the "surprising depth of Clark's work."

MHC Library of Suspense, a special "collector's edition" of Mary Higgins Clark novels, with matching hardcover bindings and new forewords by the author. Available from the Mystery Guild mail-order book club. For more information, write to MHC Library of Suspense, Mystery Guild, P.O. Box 5249, Clifton, NJ 07015-9421.

Mary Higgins Clark Mystery Magazine, published by *Family Circle* as a periodic "special issue." In addition to MHC, contributors have included Elmore Leonard, P. D. James, Edna Buchanan, and other notable authors. For subscription information, write to Mary Higgins Clark Mystery Magazine, Family Circle, P.O. Box 5172, Harlan, IA 51593-2672.

BEST OF THE NET

Mary Higgins Clark Home Page
www.maryhigginsclark.com
MHC publisher Simon & Schuster has done a wonderful job with this Web site. Part of its main www.simonsays.com site, the MHC home page offers summaries of all the author's books and their corresponding audio versions and TV and movie adaptations, as well as text excerpts and reader reviews. S&S even offers a mailing list to inform subscribers of the latest MHC news and novels and a bulletin board for exchanging comments with other fans. You'll also find a great deal of information about Mary Higgins Clark herself, including her answers to a list of fan questions.

Suspense, Inc.

NOVELS

Where Are the Children?, 1975
A Stranger Is Watching, 1978
The Cradle Will Fall, 1980
A Cry in the Night, 1982
Stillwatch, 1984
Weep No More, My Lady, 1987
While My Pretty One Sleeps, 1989
Loves Music, Loves to Dance, 1991
All Around the Town, 1992
I'll Be Seeing You, 1993
Remember Me, 1994
Let Me Call You Sweetheart, 1995
Silent Night: A Novel, 1995
Moonlight Becomes You, 1996
Pretend You Don't See Her, 1997
All Through the Night, 1998
You Belong to Me, 1998
We'll Meet Again, 1999

STORY COLLECTIONS

The Anastasia Syndrome and Other Stories, 1989
The Lottery Winner: Alvirah and Willy Stories, 1994
My Gal Sunday, 1996

If You Like Mary Higgins Clark . . .

Try some of these "novelists of suspense" recommended by Jean Swanson and Dean James in their book, *By a Woman's Hand: A Guide to Mystery Fiction by Women* (Berkley Prime Crime, 1996):
Patricia Cornwell
Kate Green
Nancy Baker Jacobs
Judith Kelman
Rochelle Mager Krich
T. J. MacGregor
D. F. Mills

Best Book to Read First

You can really start anywhere with Mary Higgins Clark, since each of her books introduces a new set of characters. So pick up a copy of her latest book, *We'll Meet Again*, or try *Loves Music, Loves to Dance* or *Pretend You Don't See Her*, two of her longest-running bestsellers.

I feel a good suspense novel can and should hold a mirror up to society and make a social comment. I would like to get across a sense of values. I like nice, strong, people confronting the forces of evil and vanquishing them.

—Mary Higgins Clark, *Cosmopolitan* (May 1989)

Joseph Conrad

Born
December 3, 1857, in Berdiczew, Podolia, Russia. His nobleman father, Apollo Korzeniowski, was a poet and writer, and, along with his mother, Ewa Bobrowski Korzeniowski, a political activist.

Real Name
Jósef Teodor Konrad Walecz Korzeniowski

Education
Tutored in Switzerland. Self-taught in classical literature. Attended maritime school in Marseilles, France.

Family
Married Jessie George in 1896. Two children, Alfred Borys and John Alexander.

Died
August 3, 1924, of a heart attack, in Bishopsbourne, Kent, England

Publishers
Penguin
Random House

Joseph Conrad's life and literary career are filled with amazements. He did not hear English spoken, much less learn it, until he went to sea at the age of 21. Yet he became one of the language's most accomplished writers. Much of his early work dealt with the high seas, where he spent roughly 15 years. For a time he was thought of as an author of sailing adventures. Now, however, his reputation is that of a pre-eminent modernist whose innovations helped transform the novel from entertainment into high art.

A Conradian narrative typically subjects its leading characters to physical, psychological, and moral extremes. Danger and alienation prevail. Conrad's descriptive powers and his technical accomplishments—flashbacks and flash forwards, differing points-of-view, stories within stories—often make the *telling* of his stories as compelling as his dark scheme of things.

The Conrad canon is varied, divided by critics into three phases: stories of the sea, political novels that often have urban settings, and the miscellaneous works of his later years—considered by many to be inferior to his previous work. The diversity of his writing was upsetting to a lot of readers, including his esteemed literary contemporaries. He collaborated on books with Ford Madox Ford, who spoke highly of him. But Virginia Woolf, Ernest Hemingway, and D. H. Lawrence were among his detractors.

Good to Know

❖ Conrad went to sea after four years of training in Marseilles. Much has been made of a gunshot wound he suffered during that time, with the speculation centering on whether it was the result of a suicide attempt or a duel. He was leading the high life, gunrunning for the Carlists in Spain, and gambling with the sizable allowance that his uncle had given him to live in France.

❖ Conrad became a dedicated sailor, rising through the ranks to captain his own ship, the *Otago*, in 1888. By then he had traveled most of the world's seas, and in 1890 he was given the command of a Congo River steamboat for a fateful journey into the African heartland. That trip was the basis for his classic, *Heart of Darkness*, an indictment of Western imperialism and a blistering satire of bourgeois European ideals. He described what he saw in the Belgian-occupied region as "the vilest scramble for loot that ever disfigured the history of human conscience and geographical exploration."

❖ This turn to the darker chambers of his characters' inner life is what sets Conrad apart. His concern with the unsteadiness of our psychological and moral bearings prefigured the works of Henry James, D. H. Lawrence, and other modernists, and his technical suppleness echoed throughout the 20th century, in the novels of innovators like Virginia Woolf, William Faulkner, and John Fowles.

❖ In his own time, Conrad was met with high praise, faint praise, and outright raspberries. But by the late 20th century he was so highly regarded that four of his works—*The Secret Agent*, *Nostromo*, *Heart of Darkness*, and *Lord Jim*—made the Modern Library's list of the 100 Best Novels of the 20th century. No other author has as many.

Treatises and Treats

COMPANIONS

Joseph Conrad: A Critical Biography by Jocelyn Baines (Greenwood Publishing Group, 1960) and *Joseph Conrad: The Three Lives* by Frederick R. Karl (Farrar, Straus, and Giroux, 1979) are the standard Conrad biographies.

The Collected Letters of Joseph Conrad, edited by Frederick R. Karl and Laurence Davies (Cambridge University Press, Volume III, 1988 and Volume IV, 1991). Conrad's letters offer a panorama of the difficulties in the writer's life. They also reveal a persona that is considerably less pleasant than reading his books would lead you to believe. These two volumes are considered essential for an understanding of Conrad and his writing.

CONRAD AT THE MOVIES

At least 30 films have been made of Conrad's works, starting with *Victory* (1919) and running through *Swept from the Sea* (1997). The most stunning of all, however, is *Apocalypse Now* (1979), Francis Ford Coppola's resetting of *Heart of Darkness* in Vietnam during the war. It features Marlon Brando, Robert Duvall, Martin Sheen, a very young Laurence Fishburne, Harrison Ford, Dennis Hopper, Frederic Forrest, and Albert Hall. For a behind-the-scenes look at the tumults and obstacles encountered during the making of this masterpiece, see the 1991 documentary *Hearts of Darkness: A Filmmaker's Apocalypse*.

BEST OF THE NET
Joseph Conrad Pages
www.stfrancis.edu/en/student/kurtzweb/
  conrad.htm
Start your Web search for Conrad information at this site prepared by students in the English department at the University of St. Francis in Joliet, Illinois. Lots of excellent links, including many to sites offering the full text of Conrad's books online.

High Seas, High Art

SELECTED WORKS
*Almayer's Folly: A Story of an Eastern
  River*, 1895
The Children of the Sea, 1897
  (later published as *The Nigger of the
  Narcissus*)
Lord Jim: A Romance, 1900
Heart of Darkness, 1902
Typhoon, 1903
Nostromo: A Tale of the Seaboard, 1904
The Secret Agent: A Simple Tale, 1907
Under Western Eyes, 1911
Chance: A Tale in Two Parts, 1913
Victory: An Island Tale, 1915
The Rescue: A Romance of the Shallows, 1920

If You Like
Joseph Conrad . . .

You might also like Rudyard Kipling's tales of the British in India, P. C. Wren's *Beau Geste* about the French Foreign Legion in North Africa, Jack London's sea stories, and, for period spy stories, G. K. Chesterton's *The Man Who Was Thursday* and John Buchan's *The Thirty-Nine Steps*.

Best Book to Read First

The short novel, *Heart of Darkness*, has everything that made Conrad great: a harrowing, heartbreaking test of human character, vivid descriptions of an exotic locale, and a savagely critical regard for Western colonialism, all unfurled with breathtaking technical virtuosity.

I'd rather dream a novel than write it, for the dream of the work is always much more lovely than the reality of the thing in print.

—Joseph Conrad, in a letter written in 1907

One Could Always Baffle Conrad . . .

In the midst of modernism's uproar at the turn of the 20th century, a lot of eminent voices made a lot of noise about the writing of Joseph Conrad. "We would pardon his cheerless themes were it not for the imperturbable solemnity with which he piles the unnecessary on the commonplace," ran an anonymous but widely shared sentiment early on, in 1898. This may have been a wounded traditional sensibility speaking in the face of innovations it did not recognize, but H. G. Wells remarked years later, "One could always baffle Conrad by saying 'humour.' It was one of our damned English tricks he never learned to tackle."

Pat Conroy

Born
October 26, 1945, in
Atlanta, Georgia, to
Colonel Donald
Conroy, a Marine
Corps pilot, and
Frances Dorothy
Conroy. He was the
first of their seven
children.

Full Name
Donald Patrick Conroy

Education
Earned a B.A. in 1967
from The Citadel in
Charleston, South
Carolina (fictionalized
by Conroy as the
Carolina Military Insti-
tute in *The Lords of
Discipline*).

Family
Married three times,
most recently in 1998
to novelist Sandra
King Ray, who has
given him a new appre-
ciation for the
"extraordinary beauty
of older women . . . I
had no idea that a
man in his fifties could
fall in love with a
woman in her fifties."
Two daughters, one
from each of his first
two marriages.

Homes
San Francisco and
South Carolina

Publisher
Doubleday

Pat Conroy is part of a long tradition of American writers whose fiction is ultimately molded and informed by and rooted in the South—with all that that implies about a strong military tradition, relations between blacks and whites, a sense of history and family, and "over-real" characters. Writing in the *Los Angeles Times*, Garry Abrams notes that "misfortune has been good to novelist Pat Conroy. It gave him a family of disciplinarians, misfits, eccentrics, liars, and loudmouths. It gave him a Southern childhood in which the bizarre competed with the merely strange. It gave him a military school education apparently imported from Sparta by way of Prussia. It gave him a divorce and a breakdown followed by intensive therapy. It gave him everything he needed to write bestsellers, make millions, and live in Rome."

There is little question that most of Pat Conroy's fiction is quasi-autobiographical. But that in no way diminishes its power. Filtering his life through his prodigious storytelling talents enables Conroy to produce lyrical, imaginative, even poetic stories that undoubtedly have a much greater impact because they owe so much to real-life experiences and characters. Conroy doesn't write thinly veiled romans à clef. Instead, he uses real people and situations as catalysts to produce entertaining fiction that manages to capture their essential truths.

Good to Know

❖ Pat Conroy's father was a nuke-carrying Marine Corps pilot whose job was to "clear the air of MiGs" in the event of a war with Cuba. His mother, Frances Dorothy Conroy, a gracious Southern lady with a spine of steel, was called "Peggy" all her life in honor of Margaret Mitchell. Her death prompted Conroy to write *Beach Music*, during which he discovered that he had been raised by "one of the most beautiful, Machiavellian and craftiest women ever to come out of the South, a woman who had a family history she continuously lied about. My mother was the first fiction writer in the family."

❖ Conroy's first job was teaching English at a Beaufort, SC high school. He then tried to get into the Peace Corps. But the position he wanted failed to materialize, so he took a job teaching illiterate black children in a one-room schoolhouse on remote Daufuskie Island off the South Carolina coast. His account of the experience, *The Water Is Wide*, became the movie *Conrack* starring Jon Voight.

❖ His poet sister hasn't spoken to him since the publication of *The Prince of Tides*, a novel featuring a female poet who has a breakdown similar to the one his sister experienced. When *The Great Santini* appeared, with its unlikable main character modeled on Conroy's father, his paternal grandparents told him they never wanted to see him or his children again. On the other hand, Conroy's mother submitted a copy of the book to the judge as evidence during her divorce proceedings.

❖ An early manuscript of *Beach Music* included a scene in which a character based on Conroy's brother Tom commits suicide. In August 1994, Tom Conroy, a diagnosed paranoid schizophrenic, did indeed commit suicide. Pat Conroy was devastated and removed the scene from his book.

❖ After writing the preface for the 60th anniversary edition of *Gone With the Wind* in 1996, Conroy became the leading candidate to write the sequel to Alexandra Ripley's hugely successful 1991 *GWTW* sequel, *Scarlett*. But instead of a sequel, Conroy proposed to write a companion novel called *The Rules of Pride: The Autobiography of Capt. Rhett Butler, C.S.A.*, for which he was to have been paid $4.5 million. The deal fell through in early 1999, a victim of disagreements over royalty percentages, fees, and ultimate editorial control.

Treatises and Treats

COMPANIONS

Pat Conroy: A Critical Companion by Landon C. Burns (Greenwood Press, 1996). According to the publisher, this is the first book-length study of Conroy's work. It explores "the recurring motifs in his fiction and his special writing talents as a prose stylist of uncommon distinction." There are chapters on his two nonfiction books and on each novel, except *Beach Music*, which was published after this volume was written. (For a guide to *Beach Music*, visit the Random House Web site "Book Group Corner" described below, or call 800-605-3406 to order the printed version.)

BEST OF THE NET

Random House Book Group Corner
www.randomhouse.com/resources/
    bookgroup
Pat Conroy is just one of many authors fea-

tured here, and for most of his books, all the site offers is the conventional publisher's catalog write-up and ordering information. But for *Beach Music*, you'll find the *Reader's Companion to Beach Music*, a well-written and informative guide that includes an author bio, suggested questions for reading group discussions, and an excerpt from the book.

Misfits, Liars, and More

NOVELS
The Great Santini, 1976
The Lords of Discipline, 1980
The Prince of Tides, 1986
Beach Music, 1995

NONFICTION
The Boo, 1970
The Water Is Wide, 1972

If You Like Pat Conroy...

You might also like Larry McMurtry, Anne Rivers Siddons, and Anne Tyler. Consider as well the novels and poems of Reynolds Price, Olive Ann Burns's *Cold Sassy Tree*, and David Payne's *Ruin Creek*.

Best Book to Read First

The Prince of Tides. With over 5 million copies in print—and a Streisand-directed movie that won Nick Nolte an Oscar nomination—this is Conroy's most popular and successful book.

When I'm writing, I have no idea where I'm going. People get married, and I didn't realize they were engaged. People die in these novels and I'm surprised. They take on this little subterranean life of their own. They reveal secrets to me even as I'm doing it. Maybe this is a dangerous way to work, but for me it becomes the pleasure of writing . . . Critics call me a popular novelist, but writing popular novels isn't what urges me on. If I could write like Faulkner or Thomas Wolfe, I surely would. I'd much rather write like them than like me. Each book has been more ambitious. I'm trying to be more courageous.

— Pat Conroy, *Chicago Tribune*, November 25, 1986

Conroy Magic in Italy

On his 1998 honeymoon, Pat Conroy discovered the exquisite Umbrian hill town of Monte Santa Maria Tiberina, and Oscari, the town's only restaurant. "Damn!" we said, for we had recently celebrated our 25th anniversary there, and now Conroy was telling the world about it in *Gourmet* (September 1999).

Our harsh feelings softened, however, as we savored his descriptions of Oscari: "The odor of truffle is as distinctive as the giveaway scent of marijuana. It enlarges the air around itself and gives you some idea of what the tree must smell like to itself." (He'd obviously ordered the sliced truffles served over pasta—as did we—and was dead-on in describing the experience.) Later, "What is prettier than a bowl of green olives or the molten green of the first pressing of extra-virgin olive oil looking, in cut-glass cruets, like watered-down jade?" Oh, yes!

Conroy is clearly far more than a "Southern writer." He is wonderful, regardless of topic. He finishes his meal with a cup of coffee that, like his writing, is *perfetto*. "The taste of Italy in a cup. My honeymoon in a cup, at Oscari in a hill town in the rain."

Patricia Cornwell

Born
June 9, 1956, in
Miami, Florida, to Sam
Daniels, an attorney,
and Marilyn Zenner
Daniels, a secretary.
Cornwell is a descen-
dent of Harriet Beecher
Stowe (*Uncle Tom's
Cabin*).

Nicknames
"Patsy" to friends and
family, "P.C." to former
colleagues at the
Virginia medical
examiner's office

Education
Attended King College
in Tennessee but had
to withdraw because of
anorexia nervosa and
bulimia. Once recov-
ered, she enrolled in
Davidson College
(North Carolina) and
earned a B.A. in
English, 1979.

Family
Married Charles
Cornwell, a Davidson
College professor 17
years her senior, in
1980. Divorced in
1990.

Home
A gated community in
Richmond, Virginia.
Also maintains resi-
dences in New York,
London, and the
Caribbean—destina-
tions she has been
known to visit (some-
times only for the day)
via private jet.

Publisher
Putnam

Patricia Cornwell wrote three conventional mystery novels, all of
them rejected, before an editor
told her to "write about what you
know." After jobs that included
crime reporting for the *Charlotte
Observer*, serving as a volunteer
uniformed policewoman, and six years in the
Virginia medical examiner's office, what she
knew led her to create Dr. Kay Scarpetta, a
forensic pathologist whose mind is as sharp
as the Stryker saws used to cut through bones
in an autopsy.

Cornwell has been writing about what she
knows ever since. Whether it means going on
night patrol with the police in the subway
tunnels of New York City—the crack vials
crunching underfoot and the rats skittering
over her boots—or placing her gloved hand in
the chest cavity of a corpse and being startled
to find that the blood is cold, Cornwell tries to
experience first hand what she later has her
characters experience. "I have said goodbye
in the morgue to a homicide detective who
was my friend, and stared stunned at the
small hole in his chest. In these ways I have
come to understand Pete Marino, the homicide detective in my books. I know he would
not speak to me had I not lived in his world
and done my best to learn its language," Cornwell wrote in the *Washington Post* (July 31,
1994).

Authenticity, fascinating details of forensic techniques, believable characters, and a
tough, smart, yet vulnerable female heroine
make for a winning combination, novel after
novel. Patricia Cornwell clearly ranks with
Sue Grafton as one of the reigning queens of
crime fiction.

Good to Know

❖ Seven publishers rejected *Postmortem* before Scribners bought it for $6,000. The book
won all five major mystery awards for 1990
and led to contracts for five more Scribner titles. In 1996, Putnam paid her $24 million for
her next three novels.

❖ Nervous about security—she knew one of
the female serial murder victims in the real-
life case that inspired *Postmortem*—Cornwell often travels with bodyguards. She
carries one or more pistols at all times: a .357
Colt Python, a .380 Walther semiautomatic,
and a .38 Smith & Wesson. (Dr. Scarpetta, in
contrast, carries a Glock 9 millimeter, a favorite of law-enforcement officials.)

❖ Cornwell has a suite of offices in Richmond
and an eight-person staff. When writing, she
typically works 14 hours a day, subsisting primarily on cottage cheese right from the carton.

❖ Her parents separated when she was five,
and mother and kids moved to North Carolina. Four years later, her mother had a nervous breakdown and tried to give her children
to neighbors Reverend Billy Graham and his
wife Ruth. Instead, the children were placed
with missionaries just back from the Congo
until their mother recovered. But the Gra-
hams have been a surrogate family for Cornwell ever since. (She has written two
biographies of Ruth Bell Graham.)

❖ A chance meeting on the Stairmasters at a
hotel gym led to a friendship with Senator Orrin Hatch, whom Cornwell later persuaded to
increase the funding for the FBI's training fa-
cility at Quantico, Virginia. *The Body Farm* is
dedicated to "Senator Orrin Hatch of Utah for
his tireless fight against crime."

❖ Cornwell learned to fly a helicopter while researching *Point of Origin* and now counts helicoptering among her hobbies.

Treatises and Treats

COMPANIONS

Scarpetta's Winter Table by Patricia Cornwell (Putnam, 1998). Described in the *Washington Post* as "a wisp of a book that visits the high-powered forensic pathologist and her small 'adopted' family as they cook their way through the holiday week [Christmas and New Year's]. No autopsy saws. No mangled bodies. Just a way for die-hard Cornwell fans to watch Scarpetta and her friends celebrate the season at home."

Cornwell readers will be also be happy to know that her first children's book, ***Life's Little Fable,*** was published in 1999. Inspired by a visit to a second-grade classroom in Los Angeles, Cornwell began writing the book on her laptop on the flight home.

BEST OF THE NET

Patricia Cornwell Web Experience

www.patricia-cornwell.com
The author's official Web site, where you'll find biographical information, book descriptions and excerpts, interviews that you can listen to through your computer's speakers, and scores of photographs. You can also follow the progress of Cornwell's current book project.

Cornwell's Crimes

FEATURING KAY SCARPETTA

Postmortem, 1990
    (winner of Edgar, Macavity, and three other awards for best first crime novel)
Body of Evidence, 1991
All That Remains, 1992
Cruel and Unusual, 1993
    (Gold Dagger award)
The Body Farm, 1994
From Potter's Field, 1995
Cause of Death, 1996
Unnatural Exposure, 1997
Point of Origin, 1998

Black Notice, 1999
The Last Precinct, 2000

OTHER CRIME NOVELS

Hornet's Nest, 1997
Southern Cross, 1999
    (sequel to *Hornet's Nest*)

If You Like Patricia Cornwell . . .

Try D. J. Donaldson or Susan Dunlap, both of whom write books featuring a medical examiner. Other possibilities: Sue Grafton, J. A. Jance, T. J. MacGregor, and Sara Paretsky.

Best Book to Read First

Postmortem introduces Dr. Kay Scarpetta, Chief Medical Examiner of Virginia, and her friends and associates, most of whom you'll meet in succeeding novels. Each book stands on its own, but why not get in at the beginning and watch the relationships grow?

The mystery genre doesn't apply to what I do, and if you expect that, you're going to be shocked or disappointed. My books are crime novels and about the people who work crime—not mysteries, which I've never read in my life anyway.

—Patricia Cornwell, *New York Times Magazine*, July 14, 1996

Courtship with Controversy

Patricia Cornwell doesn't court controversy. It comes to her. Like the Virginia couple who sued her for "breach of privacy," claiming Cornwell had used the confidential details of their daughter's autopsy in *All That Remains*. The judge dismissed the case.

There have been other minor controversies, but none tops the one revealed in an April 1997 *Vanity Fair* interview. Here, after long denying it, Cornwell admits to having had a lesbian affair with FBI agent Margo Bennett, whose husband Eugene Bennett (also an FBI agent), accused Cornwell of breaking up his marriage. In July 1996, Eugene Bennett took a minister hostage and lured his wife to a church. At least one shot was fired. (Margo came armed.) Eugene Bennett was arrested the next day and is now serving a 23-year prison term for attempted murder.

The incident generated the predictable buzz. But, as yet, no one has raised the possibility that, as she has done so often, Patricia Cornwell may simply have been doing field research to make her portrayal of Kay Scarpetta's gay niece Lucy more authentic.

Michael Crichton

Born
October 23, 1942, in
Chicago, Illinois, to
John Henderson
Crichton, executive
editor of *Advertising
Age,* and Zula Miller
Crichton

Full Name
John Michael Crichton
(pronounced "cry-ton")

Pseudonyms
Michael Douglas,
Jeffrey Hudson, and
John Lange

Education
Harvard University,
A.B. in anthropology
(summa cum laude),
Phi Beta Kappa, 1964;
Harvard Medical
School, 1969

Family
Married four times,
most recently (1987)
to actress/screen-
writer Anne-Marie
Martin (a.k.a. Eddie
Benton), with whom he
has a daughter.

Home
Northern Westchester
County, New York

Fan Mail
Michael Crichton
c/o Creative Artists
  Agency
9830 Wilshire Blvd.
Beverly Hills, CA
  90212
info@crichton-
  official.com

Publisher
Knopf

Michael Crichton is one of the most successful storytellers of all time. He doesn't create memorable characters or lyrical descriptions. His prose, while more than adequate, never soars. And while it's true that once you pick up a Michael Crichton novel you'll find it hard to put down, when you do let it slip from your fingers you're likely to discover that the story is a little difficult to remember. In contrast, the images presented in the *movies* based on his books are often quite memorable, which may explain why Crichton has spent so much of his time writing, directing, and producing films of his novels.

Crichton's novels are about ideas and information. His stories will have you turning the pages long after you should have turned off the light and gone to sleep. And unlike other successful writers of page-turning fiction, Crichton's intelligence is so far ranging that it refuses to be confined to a single field, like horror, advanced military hardware, or the law. Not that Stephen King, Tom Clancy, and John Grisham aren't intelligent (and equally entertaining). But Crichton has the ability to tell a good story whether he's dealing with the world of Victorian England (*The Great Train Robbery*), international politics (*Rising Sun*), sexual harassment (*Disclosure*), or a high-tech amusement park where nothing can go wrong (*Westworld*).

He has also written novels about scientific topics—DNA, primates, biology, drugs, and other subjects one would expect a medical doctor to know something about. And he's the author of a well-received exploration and appreciation of modern artist Jasper Johns, published by Harry N. Abrams. In short, Crichton is a phenomenon. But to fully enjoy him, don't miss the films based on his fiction.

Good to Know

❖ Working on weekends and vacations, Crichton put himself through medical school writing thrillers under the pen name John Lange. During the same period, under his own name, he wrote *The Andromeda Strain* and sold it to Hollywood, which made him something of a celebrity on campus.

❖ Big man, big income: Crichton stands six feet nine inches tall. According to *Forbes*, his 1998 earnings of $65 million made him the eighth highest-paid celebrity, behind Michael Jordan ($69 million) but ahead of Harrison Ford ($58 million) and the Rolling Stones ($57 million). Jerry Seinfeld topped the list at $267 million.

❖ He's the creator and coproducer of *ER*, the hit TV show that has won some 14 Emmys. He and wife Anne-Marie Martin cowrote the original screenplays for *Twister* (1996) and *Jurassic Park 3* (scheduled for release in 2000).

❖ In 1999, Crichton founded Timeline Studios in Cary, North Carolina, to develop and distribute "the next generation" of 3-D computer-gaming software. Cofounder Michael Backes is a leading figure in bringing the digital revolution to the movie business. For more on this new venture, visit the company's Web site (www.timelinestudios.com).

Treatises and Treats

COMPANIONS

Michael Crichton: A Critical Companion by Elizabeth A. Trembley (Greenwood Press, 1996). Includes biographical information and individual chapters devoted to Crichton's novels, from *The Andromeda Strain* to *Disclosure*.

Travels by Michael Crichton (Knopf/Random House, 1988). An autobiography of sorts that offers valuable insights into the mind and personality of this extraordinary artist.

BEST OF THE NET
Official Michael Crichton Site
www.crichton-official.com
Start here for biographical information, book descriptions, movies, frequently asked questions, and news. Also transcripts of online chat sessions, speeches, and interviews.

Michael Crichton Newsgroup
alt.books.crichton
One of the more active author-related newsgroups, this is a good place to check for readers' opinions on specific Crichton novels and to post questions about the author.

Before You See the Movie

NOVELS
The Andromeda Strain, 1969
The Terminal Man, 1972
Westworld, 1974
The Great Train Robbery, 1975
Eaters of the Dead, 1976
   (filmed as *The 13th Warrior* starring Antonio Banderas, 1999)
Congo, 1980
Sphere, 1987
Jurassic Park, 1990
Rising Sun, 1992
Disclosure, 1994
The Lost World, 1995
Airframe, 1996
Timeline, 1999

NONFICTION
Five Patients: The Hospital Explained, 1970
Jasper Johns, 1977 (revised and expanded, 1994)
Electronic Life: How to Think about Computers, 1983

If You Like Michael Crichton...

Look for these early novels he wrote under the pseudonyms John Lange, Jeffrey Hudson, and Michael Douglas:

WRITING AS JOHN LANGE
Odds On, 1966
Scratch One, 1967
Easy Go, 1968
Zero Cool, 1969
The Venom Business, 1969
Drug of Choice, 1970
Grave Descend, 1970
Binary, 1971 (filmed as *Pursuit*, 1972)

WRITING AS JEFFREY HUDSON
A Case of Need, 1968 (winner of an Edgar Award and filmed as *The Carey Treatment* in 1972)

WRITING AS MICHAEL DOUGLAS
Dealing: Or, The Berkeley-to-Boston Forty-Brick Lost-Bag Blues, 1971 (written with his brother Douglas)

Best Book to Read First

The Andromeda Strain is his most popular (30 weeks on the *New York Times* bestseller list back in the early 1970s and still highly recommended by Crichton fans). But you can't go too far wrong by simply picking up whatever his current bestseller happens to be.

One doesn't read Crichton's books for intimate peeks at inner worlds, but for heaping helpings of plot, suspense, and cosmological maunderings from popular literature's most noted polymath.

—Neal Karlen, *Los Angeles Times Book Review*

How to Write Like Crichton

In a 1995 review of *The Lost World*, *New York Times* book critic Michiko Kakutani aptly described how to write a Crichton-esque bestseller in five easy steps, as summarized here:

1. Pick a hot-button topic (like genetic engineering) to give "a glossy veneer of topicality."

2. Create clearly bad villains and clearly good heroes so the reader knows who to root for.

3. Be sure to end each chapter with "a scary, cliff-hanging note" to keep readers engaged, "regardless of the characters' vapidity."

4. Pack the book with frantic chase scenes (essential for the movie version).

5. Make sure your dialogue has ample "technical, pseudo-specialist talk" so that readers are fooled into thinking they're learning something.

Don DeLillo

Born
November 20, 1936, in New York City, the son of Italian immigrants. Grew up in the Bronx in a two-family house shared by his parents, sister, grandparents, and cousins.

Pseudonym
Cleo Birdwell

Education
Fordham University, 1958. Studied history, philosophy, and theology.

Family
Married Barbara Bennett in 1975. She was a banker at the time but now works as a landscape designer.

Home
Westchester County, New York

Fan Mail
Don DeLillo
c/o Wallace & Sheil
177 East 70th Street
New York, NY 10021

Publisher
Scribner

Don DeLillo has said that jazz, be-bop, and abstract expressionism have influenced his work more than any particular writer has. Given that, he is best approached with the same set of expectations you might bring to a top-flight *New Yorker* story: Forget about plot and character and simply savor the words—their selection, their rhythms, their cumulative effect. This is the essence of DeLillo's novels, and when he is on top of his game, no contemporary author can touch him.

An enormously talented writer, DeLillo tends to write lengthy books that almost always seem to fly out of control. This may be because he attempts too much. It may be due to the fact that his main goal often appears to be to offer a critique of one or more aspects of modern life—especially modern *American* life—that he finds affecting, while incorporating the symbolism and artistry that make for great literature. He once told an interviewer, "What writing means to me is trying to make interesting, clear, beautiful language. Working at sentences and rhythms is probably the most satisfying thing I do as a writer. I think after a while a writer can begin to know himself through his language. He sees someone or something reflected back at him from these constructions. Over the years it's possible for a writer to shape himself as a human being through the language he uses. I think written language, fiction, goes that deep."

As an introduction to DeLillo, go to your local library and read the first chapter of *Underworld*, with New York Giant Bobby Thomson's 1951 World Series–winning "shot heard 'round the world" as its unifying event. Or go to the "Don DeLillo Life & Times" Web page created by the *New York Times* to hear the author read excerpts from two of his novels. Both options offer excellent introductions to the work of this most skillful writer.

Good to Know

❖ DeLillo was raised a Roman Catholic and educated in Catholic primary and secondary schools, followed by studies at Fordham ("New York City's Jesuit University"). He attributes the "sense of last things" found in many of his novels to Catholicism's focus on death and eternity.

❖ He worked as an advertising copywriter for Ogilvy & Mather, where his clients included Sears and Zippo lighters. An ad for Sears tires took him to west Texas, a locale he later used in *End Zone*.

❖ At age 28 he left the ad agency and set about completing *Americana*, his first novel. Some years later he told an interviewer, "I quit my job just to quit. I didn't quit my job to write fiction. I just didn't want to work anymore."

❖ After years as a "critic's writer" with a small readership, DeLillo's ninth novel, *White Noise*, sold 300,000 copies. He wanted to call the novel *Panasonic*, meaning "sound everywhere," but attorneys from the famous Japanese electronics firm of the same name objected.

❖ His 1997 novel *Underworld* was bought by Scribner's for a purported $1.3 million. The next day, DeLillo's agent sold the screen rights to Paramount for close to $1 million.

❖ DeLillo uses a manual typewriter. "The physical sensation of hitting keys and watching hammers strike the page is such an integral part of the way I think and even the way I see words on the page that I'd be reluctant to give it up. There's a sculptural quality to me, of letter-by-letter, word-by-word, linear progress across a piece of paper as I type.... It's actually sensuous."

Treatises and Treats

DON DELILLO SOCIETY

For just $10.00 a year ($5.00 for students), you can join this organization for DeLillo readers and scholars throughout the world. The society meets in conjunction with the American Literature Association Conference (held each year in either Baltimore, Maryland, or San Diego, California) and publishes an annual newsletter and DeLillo bibliography. Contact:
Don DeLillo Society
Joseph Conte, Treasurer
Department of English
306 Clemens Hall
SUNY at Buffalo
Buffalo, NY 14260-4610
716-645-2575, x1009
Email: jconte@acsu.buffalo.edu
www.acsu.buffalo.edu/~jconte

COMPANIONS

Introducing Don DeLillo, edited by Frank Lentricchia (Duke University Press, 1991). "A first-rate collection of essays on DeLillo from a variety of critical viewpoints," according to the Don DeLillo Society. Covers most of the novels through *Libra.*

In the Loop: Don DeLillo and the Systems Novel by Tom LeClair (University of Illinois Press, 1988). Considered an indispensable resource for DeLillo scholars.

Don DeLillo by Douglas Keesey (Twayne, 1993). Provides a solid overview of DeLillo's career, with especially good coverage of *Americana, Ratner's Star,* and *Mao II.*

BEST OF THE NET

Don DeLillo Life & Times
www.nytimes.com/books/97/03/16/
    lifetimes/delillo.html
A great starting point, this site presents information about DeLillo drawn from the archives of the *New York Times*—book reviews, articles by and about the author, RealAudio recordings of DeLillo reading from *Mao II* and *Libra* at the 92nd Street Y in New York, and his 1997 interview with Terry Gross of NPR's *Fresh Air* about the writing of *Underworld.* The recordings provide a truly wonderful way to sample the author's work.

DeLillo's America
www.perival.com/delillo
For another good introduction to DeLillo, visit this well-organized and regularly updated fan page. You'll find biographical information, an outstanding annotated bibliography, quotations, and reviews. And don't miss the collection of tidbits called "Odds and Ends," where you'll learn, for example, that the famously reclusive DeLillo was recently rated a 7 on *Entertainment Weekly*'s "reclusiveness scale" of 1 to 10—compared with Thomas Pynchon at 8 and J. D. Salinger at 10.

DeLillo's Dozen

Americana, 1971
End Zone, 1972
Great Jones Street, 1973
Ratner's Star, 1976
Players, 1977
Running Dog, 1978
Amazons, 1980
    (writing as Cleo Birdwell)
The Names, 1982
White Noise, 1985
    (American Book Award)
Libra, 1988
    (Irish Times/Aer Lingus International
    Fiction Prize)
Mao II, 1991
    (PEN/Faulkner Award)
Underworld, 1997

If You Like Don DeLillo . . .

You might also like Paul Auster, whose novel *Leviathan* is dedicated to DeLillo. Or try T. Coraghessan Boyle, E. L. Doctorow, Mark Helprin, and Thomas Pynchon.

Best Book to Read First

Libra, built around the events leading up to the assassination of John F. Kennedy, is DeLillo's most successful novel to date. *White Noise*, an American Book Award winner, is another excellent place to start.

Because he is so deadly serious, it is not said often enough that DeLillo is tremendously funny.

—Jay McInerney,
The New Republic

DeLillo's wit is so surgical you don't even know an artery has been severed. You don't laugh until you see you're bleeding.

—Nelson Algren, in a 1972 quote posted at the "DeLillo's America" Web site

Charles Dickens

Born
February 7, 1812, in
Portsmouth, England,
to John Dickens, a
clerk in the Navy Pay
Office, and Elizabeth
Barrow Dickens

Full Name
Charles John Huffam
Dickens

Education
Primarily home-
schooled by his mother
and self-educated.
Attended Dame School
at Chatham for a short
time and Wellington
Academy.

Family
Married Catherine
Hogarth in 1836. They
had ten children before
separating in 1858.

Home
Kent, England

Died
June 18, 1870, in
Gad's Hill, Kent,
England, of a paralytic
stroke

Publisher
(one of many)
Oxford University Press

Charles Dickens is probably the greatest novelist England ever produced. His innate comic genius and shrewd depictions of Victorian life made him immensely popular, beginning in 1836 with his serial publication of *Pickwick Papers*. Serialized versions of *Oliver Twist*, *Barnaby Rudge*, and *The Old Curiosity Shop* appeared in the following years, the latter two being published in Dickens's own weekly periodical, *Master Humphrey's Clock*. It was in *Oliver Twist* that Dickens first assumed the role of social critic, which would carry over into his later works.

Dickens is a master creator of incredibly memorable characters. In his books live some of the most repugnant villains in literature, as well as some of the most likeable (and unlikely) heroes. But it is his minor figures that imbue his stories with an unexpected richness. Names like Uriah Heep, Miss Havisham, the Artful Dodger, and Mr. Pumblechook all bring to mind living characters with distinctive speech patterns and identifiable physiognomies beloved by Dickens readers the world over.

Good to Know

❖ In 1823, Dickens's family moved to London where his father was arrested for debt and incarcerated for three months in Marshalsea Debtors' Prison. Only 11 years old, Dickens was sent to work making shoe polish at Warren's Blacking Factory, where he met the boy on whom he would later base the Artful Dodger in *Oliver Twist*.

❖ Dickens's favorite of his novels was *David Copperfield*. It also happens to be the most autobiographical. (The title character's initials are the reverse of Charles Dickens's.)

❖ In one of his residences, Tavistock House, Dickens installed a hidden door in the study, made to look like part of an unbroken wall of books, complete with dummy shelves and fictitious titles. Some of the more creative titles displayed included *Five Minutes in China* (three volumes), *Noah's Arkitecture*, and *The Virtues of Our Ancestors* (so narrow that the title had to be printed sideways!).

❖ New Yorkers were so eager to read the final installment of *The Old Curiosity Shop* that they couldn't wait for the ship carrying the magazine to dock. Six thousand people crowded the wharf, yelling to the sailors as the ship approached, "Does Little Nell die?"

❖ Dickens often used nicknames, including "Wennerables," which he insisted his grandchildren call him. Another was "The Sparkler of Albion"—a reference to his firm belief that he was the brightest spark in English literature since Shakespeare. (Albion is an ancient name for Great Britain.) "Boz," one of his pen names, came about from the mispronunciation of a younger brother, whom Dickens had dubbed "Moses," the name of one of the sons in Goldsmith's *Vicar of Wakefield*. The child pronounced it "Bozes," which got shortened to "Boz."

Treatises and Treats

COMPANIONS

The Friendly Dickens: Being a Good-natured Guide to the Art and Adventures of the Man Who Invented Scrooge by Norrie Epstein (Viking, 1998). Epstein, sometime university lecturer and author of *The*

Friendly Shakespeare, has penned a lively, erudite account of the life and work of Dickens, sprinkled throughout with fascinating bits of information.

Charles Dickens A to Z: The Essential Reference to His Life and Work by Paul B. Davis (Facts on File, 1998). A veritable Dickensian encyclopedia, culled from letters, criticism, correspondence, reviews, and texts.

What Jane Austen Ate and Charles Dickens Knew: From Fox Hunting to Whist—the Facts of Daily Life in 19th Century England by Daniel Pool (Simon & Schuster, 1993). A delightful handbook for Anglophiles interested in Victorian life. Pool explains 19th-century customs that have been lost and examines various other aspects of British life such as clothing, etiquette, and marriage.

BIOGRAPHIES

Charles Dickens: His Tragedy and Triumph by Edgar Johnson (Penguin, 1986). The revised and abridged version of Johnson's comprehensive 1952 two-volume biography.

Dickens: A Biography by Fred Kaplan (Johns Hopkins University Press, 1998). This is the first full-scale account of Dickens's life since the publication of Johnson's biography. Kaplan's is a compelling and finely crafted addition to the canon of Dickens biographies, incorporating research done in the intervening years.

BEST OF THE NET

Dickens Project Web Site
humwww.ucsc.edu/dickens/index.html
Located at the University of California, the Dickens Project is recognized throughout the world as the premier center for Dickens studies. Conferences, publications, teaching resources, electronic texts, and links to other key sites—they're all at this Web site. You'll also find membership information on the many "Dickens Fellowships"—reading and discussion groups—around the world.

David Perdue's Charles Dickens Page
www.fidnet.com/~dap1955/dickens
A great resource with numerous links to information on Dickens, including selected fellowships, societies, and scholarly sites. This is a truly remarkable site.

The Best of Books

(Note: Most of these novels are available in more recent paperback editions from a variety of publishers. Oxford offers a complete set of Dickens's novels in hardcover.)

Pickwick Papers, 1837
Oliver Twist, 1838
Nicholas Nickleby, 1839
The Old Curiosity Shop, 1841
Barnaby Rudge, 1841
Martin Chuzzlewit, 1843
A Christmas Carol, 1843
Dombey and Son, 1848
David Copperfield, 1850
Bleak House, 1853
Hard Times, 1854
Little Dorrit, 1857
A Tale of Two Cities, 1859
Great Expectations, 1861
Our Mutual Friend, 1865
The Mystery of Edwin Drood, 1870

Best Book to Read First

Great Expectations, which author and scholar Angus Wilson called "[perhaps] the most completely unified work of art that Dickens ever produced."

I like Mr. Dickens's books much better than your books, Papa.

—William Makepeace Thackeray, quoting his ten-year-old daughter in his lecture, "Charity and Humour"

Take Two

The original final scene of *Great Expectations* has Pip chancing to meet Estella in London. Estella is remarried to a Shropshire doctor and very unhappy. They speak briefly and then go their separate ways, with Pip reflecting later upon Estella's change of heart and his belief that she now understood the suffering his heart had endured.

It has been suggested that this scene was inspired by Dickens's own obsession with the young Ellen Ternan and her rejection of his advances. However, he was prevailed upon to change this ending to the one with which all readers are now familiar: Pip meets Estella in the ruins of Miss Havisham's house and his final thoughts are, "I took her hand in mine, and we went out of that ruined place. . . . I saw no shadow of another parting with her."

E. L. Doctorow

Born
January 6, 1931, in
New York City, to David
Doctorow, a music
store proprietor, and
Rose Levine Doctorow,
a pianist

Full Name
Edgar Lawrence
Doctorow (named for
Edgar Allan Poe)

Education
Kenyon College, A.B.
(with honors), 1952;
Columbia University,
graduate study,
1952–53

Family
Married Helen Esther
Setzer, a writer, in
1954. Three children.

Home
Sag Harbor, New York,
and a Manhattan
apartment. He recently
sold his house in New
Rochelle, New York (a
main location in his
bestselling novel
Ragtime).

Fan Mail
E. L. Doctorow
Dept. of English
New York University
New York, NY 10003

Publisher
Random House

E. L. Doctorow is one of those rare writers who have earned both critical acclaim and popular success. His first two novels combined serious themes and popular literary genres. In *Welcome to Hard Times* (1960), he uses the format of the Western, and in *Big as Life* (1966), he employs devices of science fiction. But the books that he's best known for are the later ones—most notably *Ragtime*, *World's Fair*, *Billy Bathgate*, and *The Waterworks*—that experiment with our commonly held notions about the historical novel.

Unlike most other historical novelists, Doctorow takes liberties with the facts, juxtaposing real-life figures and historical events with pure fabrication. His writing style is always confident and declarative, conveying an impression of historical accuracy—a technique that some consider audacious but others find liberating. Asked by readers if his novels are true, Doctorow replies, "I have always been a writer who invents, and I think books are something you make. I make books for people to live in, as architects make houses."

Good to Know

❖ In the early 1960s, Doctorow was offered a writing job in California. Reluctant, he and his wife consulted the *I Ching*. It told them they would cross a great water. "That's the Mississippi," said his wife, "Let's go!" So they packed everything into the car and left for California. While there, Doctorow finished *The Book of Daniel* and received a contract for his next book, which turned out to be *Ragtime*.

❖ In *Ragtime*, his most popular book, Doctorow re-imagines the United States of America between 1902 and 1917 by means of a plot that conjoins fictional characters with Henry Ford, J. P. Morgan, Harry Houdini, Sigmund Freud, and Emma Goldman. The book sold more than 200,000 copies in hardcover in its first year, and the paperback reprint rights were purchased by Bantam Books for $1.85 million, a then-record figure.

❖ Welcome to Hollywood! In 1967, MGM produced a movie version of Doctorow's *Welcome to Hard Times* starring Henry Fonda. Doctorow has referred to it as "the second worst movie ever made." For a time he was involved with the film version of *Ragtime* (1981). Dino De Laurentiis hired Robert Altman to direct, and Altman persuaded Doctorow to write the screenplay. De Laurentiis eventually fired Altman, and then rejected Doctorow's script for being too long. Milos Forman took over the directing, and playwright Michael Weller wrote the screenplay. The movie starred James Cagney in his last big-screen performance.

❖ Doctorow says he "gets up for work in the morning like anybody else" and writes for about six hours until mid-afternoon, with a goal of producing 500 to 1,000 words (one to two single-spaced typewritten pages). He follows certain rules: the Hemingway dictum of always stopping when he knows what's coming next, and never rereading a working draft when he's tired. His drafts are always single-spaced, "because then more of the landscape is visible at one time."

❖ He has resisted purchasing a word processor because he likes the physical aspect of writing. "I like to tear up a piece of paper and throw it down and put a new piece of paper in the typewriter. When I've decided to change something, I like to retype the whole page."

❖ Doctorow admits that his research is spotty. He studies paintings and photographs to familiarize himself with the era he's writing about. But he does not want to get bogged down by facts. He describes his research as "idiosyncratic and accidental, to find something to confirm your hunch, and not to look for it until you need it."

❖ When asked by the *New York Times* to name one book that he wished he had written, Doctorow replied that it would have to be *Don Quixote*. "I think the whole world is in that book."

Treatises and Treats

COMPANIONS

Conversations with E. L. Doctorow, edited by Christopher D. Morris (University Press of Mississippi, 1999).

The Political Fiction of E. L. Doctorow by Michelle M. Tokarczyk (Peter Lang Publishing, 1999).

Understanding E. L. Doctorow by Douglas Fowler (University of South Carolina Press, 1991).

BEST OF THE NET

E. L. Doctorow Page
www.albany.edu/writers-inst/doctorow.html
Created and maintained by the New York State Writers Institute at the State University of New York, this is a good starting point for information about Doctorow and his books.

New York Times Featured Authors
www.nytimes.com/specials/ragtime/
    doctorow.html
Check here for dozens of articles and reviews from the archives of the *New York Times*.

All the Fiction

Welcome to Hard Times, 1960
Big as Life, 1966
The Book of Daniel, 1971
Ragtime, 1975
    (National Book Critics Circle Award)
Loon Lake, 1980
Lives of the Poets: Six Stories and a Novella, 1984
World's Fair, 1985
    (American Book Award)
Billy Bathgate, 1989
    (PEN/Faulkner Award)
The Waterworks, 1994
City of God, 2000

If You Like
E. L. Doctorow . . .

You might also like T. Coraghessan Boyle, Don DeLillo, Mark Helprin, William Kennedy, Joyce Carol Oates, Phillip Roth, and Jane Smiley.

Best Book to Read First

Ragtime, winner of a National Book Critics Circle Award and one of the most critically acclaimed novels of the 1970s.

Writing is an exploration. You start from nothing and learn as you go. If you do it right, you're coming up out of yourself in a way that's not entirely governable by your intellect. That's why the most important lesson I've learned is that planning to write is not writing. Outlining a book is not writing. Researching is not writing. Talking to people about what you're doing, none of that is writing. Writing is writing.

—E. L. Doctorow

Doctorow on Broadway

Doctorow has never cared much for musicals—"[They're] just a repository for easy sentiment"—but he had to reconsider when he was approached about the possibility of turning *Ragtime* into a Broadway show. Remembering occasions when he had read passages from the book to musical accompaniment, he realized that the addition of music might very well contribute to the impact of the words. After seeing the show for the first time, he changed his mind for good: "I can see now . . . that [the musical] is a very powerful medium. It creates very strong feelings and illumination."

Although Livent, Inc., the company that produced *Ragtime*, has had its financial difficulties, there is every indication that the show will continue indefinitely at the Ford Center for the Performing Arts in New York City, an architectural marvel that artfully combined two older theaters (the Lyric and the Apollo) into a single, new entertainment space.

Arthur Conan Doyle

Born
May 22, 1859, in Edinburgh, Scotland, to Charles Altamont Doyle (a civil servant and artist who was institutionalized as a result of epilepsy and alcoholism) and Mary Foley Doyle

Education
Edinburgh University, B.M., 1881; M.D., 1885

Family
Married in 1885 to Louise Hawkins, with whom he had two children. Following her death in 1906 from tuberculosis, he married Jean Leckie in 1907. They had three children.

Died
July 7, 1930, of a heart attack, in Crowborough, Sussex, England

Publisher
Bantam Doubleday Dell

Although he was never considered a great writer, Sir Arthur Conan Doyle created one of the most famous and enduring characters in the history of fiction—Sherlock Holmes. The four novels and 56 stories in which Holmes appears have been translated into more than 50 languages, and the characters of Holmes and Dr. John Watson have frequently been depicted in plays, films, radio and television programs, cartoons, comic strips, and advertising.

The incredible popularity of Sherlock Holmes was troubling to Doyle, whose dream was to be known for his painstakingly researched historical novels in the tradition of Sir Walter Scott. So in 1893, Sherlock Holmes met his end at the Reichenbach Falls in "The Final Problem." When this story appeared in *Strand* magazine, however, 20,000 readers canceled their subscriptions, businessmen dressed in mourning, and Doyle received letters addressing him as "You Brute."

In 1903 Doyle was offered $5,000 per story if he would bring Holmes back to life. Thus Holmes returned in "The Empty House." The story created a sensation, and the detective was as famous as ever. In fact, by the 1920s—years after he had given up his medical practice (as an eye specialist, he never attracted a single patient)—Doyle was the most highly paid writer in the world, commanding huge sums of money for his serialized Sherlock Holmes tales.

Good to Know

❖ A large man, Doyle stood over six feet two inches tall and weighed 210 pounds in his prime. He was an excellent all-around athlete, proficient in rugby, boxing, and cricket.

❖ He wrote almost constantly: on trains, in cabs, while posing for photographs, even while carrying on a conversation at a party. He wrote his first Sherlock Holmes novel, *A Study in Scarlet* (1887), in three weeks!

❖ Doyle served during the Boer War as chief surgeon of a field hospital in South Africa. He was knighted in 1902, not because of his mysteries, but because he wrote a pamphlet defending British actions during the Boer War.

❖ Sherlock Holmes was based on Dr. Joseph Bell, a surgeon Doyle met while attending Edinburgh University. Dr. Bell was able to deduce his patients' occupations and other information simply by observing them.

❖ American actor William Gillette made a career of portraying Sherlock Holmes. It was Gillette who introduced Holmes's "signature" curved calabash pipe (the actor needed a pipe he could hold in his teeth as he spoke his lines) and deerstalker hat. Holmes never smoked the former and wore the latter only in the country.

❖ The phrase "Elementary, my dear Watson" is never uttered by Sherlock Holmes in any of Doyle's writings. Like the pipe, it was a creation of the film adaptations.

❖ Mail is still regularly sent to Sherlock Holmes's fictional address in London—221B Baker Street.

❖ A first edition of *The Hound of the Baskervilles* was sold at auction in 1998 by Sotheby's in London for $131,541. The book commanded such a high price because it is one of only two known copies with the original dust jacket. (Dust jackets were introduced in the 1870s simply as wrappings for books, and most buyers threw them away as soon as they left the store.)

Treatises and Treats

ARTHUR CONAN DOYLE SOCIETY

This group publishes a journal and maintains a Web site that's chock full of information about Doyle, Sherlock Holmes, and Calabash Press, a small publishing company that specializes in "books by Sherlockians for Sherlockians." Annual membership is $27. For more information, contact:

Christopher and Barbara Roden
P.O. Box 1360
Ashcroft, British Columbia
Canada V0K 1A0
www.ash-tree.bc.ca/acdsocy.html

COMPANIONS

Teller of Tales: The Life of Arthur Conan Doyle by Daniel Stashower (Henry Holt, 1999). A thorough investigation of Doyle's life, particularly his historical novels and his interest in spiritualism.

BEST OF THE NET

221B Baker Street Web Site
www.members.tripod.com/~msherman/
    holmes.html

One of the most comprehensive sites available on Sherlock Holmes and his creator. Includes the full text of all four novels and 48 of the 56 Holmes stories (the other 12 are still protected by copyright). Other highlights include a Sherlock Holmes canon word search, pictures from the stories, and links to other Holmes resources.

Elementary Reads

NOVELS

A Study in Scarlet, 1887
The Sign of Four, 1890
The Hound of the Baskervilles, 1902
The Valley of Fear, 1915

STORY COLLECTIONS

The Adventures of Sherlock Holmes, 1892
The Memoirs of Sherlock Holmes, 1894
The Return of Sherlock Holmes, 1905
His Last Bow: Some Reminiscences of Sherlock Holmes, 1917
The Case-Book of Sherlock Holmes, 1927
Note: *The Complete Sherlock Holmes* (Bantam Doubleday Dell, 1998) includes all four Sherlock Holmes novels and the 56 stories.)

Best Book to Read First

Most Doyle fans consider *The Hound of the Baskervilles* (1902) to be the most chilling of the Sherlock Holmes novels. According to acclaimed mystery writer John Dickson Carr, author of *The Life of Sir Arthur Conan Doyle*, this novel is "the only tale, long or short, in which the story dominates Holmes rather than Holmes dominating the story."

I fear that Mr. Sherlock Holmes may become like one of those popular tenors who, having outlived their time, are still tempted to make repeated farewell bows to their indulgent audiences. This must cease and he must go the way of all flesh, material or imaginary.

—Sir Arthur Conan Doyle, in his preface to *The Case-Book of Sherlock Holmes*, his last story collection, published in 1927

Unanswered Mysteries

From a very young age, Doyle was obsessed with the supernatural. He attended his first séance at the age of 20. And he dedicated the final decade of his life to spiritualism, putting most of his energy into these writings. He even opened a psychic bookshop in London, which further caused his reputation to suffer.

In 1920 he sought out Harry Houdini, who he saw as another form of spiritualist, and they began a friendship. But when Houdini tried to explain to Doyle how certain "magic tricks" were done, Doyle wouldn't listen.

Other disagreements followed, the most notable involving Lady Conan Doyle, who claimed a talent for "automatic writing." At a séance in Atlantic City, Lady Doyle suggested they try to contact Houdini's deceased mother. She wrote down a 15-page message she claimed had come directly from the dead woman. But Houdini declared the event unsuccessful, since the message was written in English—a language his Hungarian mother did not speak. Doyle felt that Houdini's objections were unfounded, and the event led to the end of the friendship between the two men.

Daphne du Maurier

Born
May 13, 1907, in
London, England. The
second of three daugh-
ters of actor/manager
Gerald du Maurier and
actress Muriel
Beaumont du Maurier.

Full Name
Daphne du Maurier
Browning

Education
Governesses, then
finishing school near
Paris, France

Family
Married Frederick
Browning, 1932. Three
children: Tessa, Flavia,
and Christian.

Home
Cornwall, England

Died
April 19, 1989

Publishers
Doubleday
University of
  Pennsylvania Press

Born into a literary and theatrical family, Daphne du Maurier achieved success as a writer of popular fiction and dramas. Some like to downplay her achievement, but her works of romantic yet cynical suspense have lasted well beyond those of contemporaries who received more acceptance by literary critics of the time. She is a novelist for "us"—ordinary readers who demand a good story told well.

Suspense and plot twists are hallmarks of du Maurier's fiction. Her characters are fallible, compulsive, and driven. "I am passionately interested in human cruelty, human lust, and human avarice," she notes, adding almost as an afterthought, "and, of course, their counterparts in the scale of virtue."

The resulting works form a rogues' gallery of fascinating men and women made flesh and blood by du Maurier's skill. She captures the physical atmosphere of a particular place, adds an intuitive sense of the underlying spirit of the vanished people who lived there across centuries, and tosses in psychological insights into relations between the sexes. What more could you ask for a thoroughly engrossing read?

Good to Know

❖ Daphne du Maurier enjoyed reading the work of Sir Walter Scott, William Thackeray, Oscar Wilde, Katherine Mansfield, Robert Louis Stevenson, and Mary Webb. Literary friends of her family included thriller-writer Edgar Wallace, novelist/critic Arthur Quiller-Couch, and James M. Barrie, author of the play *Peter Pan*.

❖ Her grandfather, George du Maurier, illustrated works by Thackeray, James, and Hardy, and did caricatures for the satiric magazine *Punch*. He also created the ominously evil character Svengali in his novel *Trilby*.

❖ The British setting of du Maurier's short story "The Birds" was replaced by northern California in Alfred Hitchcock's 1963 film version. The script by Evan Hunter considerably embellished du Maurier's taut tale. Closer to the originals, but not always pleasing to the author, were the film versions of *Jamaica Inn* (1939), *Rebecca* (1940), *Frenchman's Creek* (1944), *My Cousin Rachel* (1952), *The Scapegoat* (1959), and *Don't Look Now* (1973).

❖ Fowey was the part of Cornwall that du Maurier loved best. Across an estuary, in the town of Bodinnick, her family bought a small holiday retreat called Ferryside that was part cottage and part boathouse. Walks in this area brought her to Menabilly, the house that inspired Manderley in *Rebecca* and in which she later lived.

❖ Real-life romance: *The Loving Spirit*, du Maurier's first book, was a bestseller that received critical praise and made her reputation. One impressed reader was Frederick Browning, a tall, confident, 34-year-old major in the Grenadier Guards who haunted Ferryside in his boat, trying to meet the author. He succeeded and they soon married and set off by boat on their honeymoon.

❖ In 1969 du Maurier was made a Dame of the British Empire (DBE); thereafter, she was entitled to be referred to as Dame Daphne. One friend teased that now she would have to stop wearing pants.

Treatises and Treats

DAPHNE DU MAURIER FESTIVAL

Held annually in May at the Fowey Estuary to celebrate the life and works of Daphne du Maurier, with literary events, art exhibitions, music, workshops, guided walks, films, cruises. For information, contact:
Daphne du Maurier Festival Office
Restormel Borough Council
39 Penwinnick Road
St. Austell, Cornwall PL25 5DR
United Kingdom

COMPANIONS

The du Maurier Companion, compiled by Stanley Vickers, foreword by Christian du Maurier Browning (Fowey Rare Books, 1997). Biographical information about the literary du Mauriers: Daphne, her sister Angela, and grandfather George, with a family tree and illustrations.

Daphne du Maurier, Haunted Heiress by Nina Auerbach (University of Pennsylvania Press, 1999). Praised for its engaging prose style and for rescuing du Maurier from her "*Rebecca* fate," this biography is written by a professor of literature and history at Penn.

Daphne du Maurier: The Secret Life of the Renowned Storyteller by Margaret Forster (Doubleday, 1993). A comprehensive biography that draws on unpublished letters to reveal du Maurier's complex inner life.

The Private World of Daphne du Maurier by Martyn Shallcross (Transaction Publishers, 1992). An intimate biography of du Maurier by a longtime friend.

Daphne du Maurier: Writing, Identity, and the Gothic Imagination by Avril Horner and Sue Zlosnik (St. Martin's Press, 1998). Critical evaluation of du Maurier's fiction and themes such as gender roles, identity, transgression, and desire.

Daphne du Maurier: Letters from Menabilly, Portrait of a Friendship by Oriel Malet (M. Evans, 1994). Letters by du Maurier to the younger writer, Malet.

BEST OF THE NET
Daphne du Maurier Web Site
www.westwind.co.uk/westwind/cornwall/ daphne/maurier.html
A good starting point for information about du Maurier, her work, Menabilly, and the annual festival in her honor.

Best Reads

NOVELS

The Loving Spirit, 1931
Jamaica Inn, 1936
Rebecca, 1938
Frenchman's Creek, 1941
My Cousin Rachel, 1951
The Scapegoat, 1957
The House on the Strand, 1969

SHORT-STORY COLLECTIONS

The Treasury of du Maurier Short Stories, 1960
Don't Look Now, 1971

If You Like Daphne du Maurier . . .

Unfortunately, du Maurier fans have been less than enthusiastic about Susan Hill's *Mrs. de Winter* (1994), the long-awaited sequel to *Rebecca*. Instead, try books by Patricia Highsmith, Ruth Rendell, and Minette Walters. You might also like the Brontës (Charlotte and Emily).

Best Book to Read First
Rebecca, first published in 1938 and immortalized in the 1940 Alfred Hitchcock film. The book still sells at a rate of 4,000 paperback copies a month, drawing readers in with its famous opening line, "Last night I dreamt I went to Manderley again."

There was no moon. The sky above our heads was inky black. But the sky on the horizon was not dark at all. It was shot with crimson, like a splash of blood. And the ashes blew towards us with the salt wind from the sea.

—The closing lines of Daphne du Maurier's *Rebecca*

A King Who Bows to a Dame

Stephen King calls *Rebecca* "a pretty good novel and an excellent piece of entertainment," especially praising du Maurier's "bravura pacing and narrative control." Writing in the *New York Times*, King twits what he calls the outmoded "social lessons" of the novel—for example, that older men should marry very young women. Still, he notes, feminists will enjoy *Rebecca* because du Maurier "created a scale by which modern women can measure their feelings about mating and marriage, and judge the progress our society has made toward sexual equality."

Ralph Ellison

Born
March 1, 1914 in Oklahoma City, Oklahoma, to Lewis Alfred Ellison, a construction worker, and Ida Millsap Ellison

Full Name
Ralph Waldo Ellison

Education
Attended Tuskegee Institute, 1933–36.

Family
Married Fanny McConnell, 1946.

Died
April 16, 1994, in New York City, of pancreatic cancer

Publisher
Random House

I am an invisible man." These words open Ralph Ellison's 1952 novel *Invisible Man,* the author's celebrated masterpiece on race and the struggle to be human. "I am a man of substance, of flesh and bone, fiber and liquids—and I might even be said to possess a mind. I am invisible, understand, simply because people refuse to see me…. When they approach me they see only my surroundings, themselves, or figments of their imagination—indeed everything and anything except me."

The book's nameless black protagonist is literally invisible to the white world. He is just another black face. But he uses his "invisibility" as a mask that lets him observe and comment on the world that ignores him and in so doing delivers a powerful statement about not only the black experience in America but the experience of men and women everywhere.

Although Ellison wrote numerous short stories, essays, and reviews, *Invisible Man* is the only novel he completed in his lifetime. But the book received great critical acclaim, garnering the National Book Award in 1953, the fourth year in which that award was presented. And in 1965, it was voted the most distinguished American novel published since the end of World War II by *Book Week* readers. It went on to sell millions of copies worldwide.

Ellison has been hailed by critics as "a moral historian" and "the profoundest cultural critic we have." In his view, the duty of the novelist is both moral and political. The grandson of slaves, he felt an obligation to fully explore the singular experience of being black in America, but equally important, to place this experience in the context of a universal human experience. *Invisible Man,* therefore, is in the tradition of the Bildungsroman. It is a novel in which the young black protagonist moves toward a disillusioned enlightenment as the story progresses. The book is noted for its experimental narrative techniques and complex symbolism. Ellison's use of the blues and folklore refocused attention on the importance of these elements in literature and culture in general.

Juneteenth, the much anticipated novel that Ellison would never finish, tells the story of the adopted son of a black minister whose light skin allows him to "pass" in white society. The young man eventually becomes a United States senator who espouses white supremacy. An edited version of the novel was finally published in 1999, making Ellison's absence even more strongly felt.

Good to Know

❖ A trumpet player beginning at age eight, Ellison enrolled in the Tuskegee Institute to study music but dropped out due to lack of funds. He settled in New York City where he met Langston Hughes and Richard Wright. Wright, acting as a mentor, encouraged Ellison to write, though ultimately their divergent worldviews caused them to drift apart. In New York, Ellison worked on the Federal Writers' Project from 1938 to 1942.

❖ He was named by his father after Ralph Waldo Emerson. Ellison felt pressure all his life to live up to his namesake.

❖ Ellison began work on his second novel (which was to become *Juneteenth*) sometime in the late fifties. During the course of his career, he published several excerpts, but evidence suggests that a fire in his Plainsfield, Massachusetts, home in 1967 destroyed a large portion of the manuscript. Devastated by the loss, he did not resume work on the book for several years.

Treatises and Treats

COMPANIONS

Conversations with Ralph Ellison, edited by Amritjit Singh and Maryemma Graham (University Press of Mississippi, 1995). A collection of interviews that show many sides of Ellison as he addresses the topics of race, writing, art, and culture. His humor, intellect, and independent nature shine through in these personal conversations, giving readers rare insight into the mind and heart of one of America's most esteemed writers.

The Collected Essays of Ralph Ellison, edited by John F. Callahan (Random House, 1995), who also edited the posthumously published *Juneteenth*. A collection of essays and interviews highlighting Ellison's contribution to American letters in his writings about the black experience in America, literature, folklore, jazz, and black culture. The book also includes the critically acclaimed works *Shadow and Act* (1964) and *Going to the Territory* (1986).

Ralph Ellison: Modern Critical Views Series, edited by Harold Bloom (Chelsea House Publishers, 1992). Criticism and interpretation of Ellison's major works.

BEST OF THE NET

Ralph Ellison Webliography

centerx.gseis.ucla.edu/weblio
Originally intended as a comprehensive resource for scholars of Ralph Ellison, this site has morphed into an electronic bibliography that will be especially useful to readers looking for an introduction to Ralph Ellison.

New York Times Featured Authors

www.nytimes.com/books/specials/author.html
Check here for reviews of Ellison's two novels, *Invisible Man* and *Juneteenth*, as well as his published collections of essays and short stories from the *New York Times* archives. The site also provides links to several articles, including a 1982 interview with Ellison in which he speaks about *Invisible Man* and his then unfinished second novel.

Powerful Works

Invisible Man, 1952
(National Book Award)
Flying Home and Other Stories, 1996
(edited by John F. Callahan)
Juneteenth, 1999
(posthumous publication edited by John F. Callahan)

Best Book to Read First

Invisible Man is the obvious choice because it is the product of Ellison's artistic vision and it is his alone. *Juneteenth*, though it consists of Ellison's words and is definitely recommended reading, is not the truest representation of his work.

If I'm going to be remembered as a novelist, I'd better produce a few more books.

—Ralph Ellison, in a 1981 interview

Ralph Ellison is the Charlie Parker of writers. . . . Once he finished playing, the stage was in cinders, there was nothing else to say about being black in America. . . . I mean it's done, man, just everybody finish your Long Island Iced tea and go the f**k home.

—James McBride, author of *The Color of Water: A Black Man's Tribute to His White*

The Unkindest Cut of All?

When Ralph Ellison died in 1994, he left 1,500 pages of a novel that he had started in the 1950s. He alluded to the work in progress in interviews over the years and published eight extracts in various literary magazines, but he steadfastly refused to speculate on when his long-awaited second novel would be finished. Upon his death, he left no instructions regarding the work, and one wonders what he would think about the 1999 publication of *Juneteenth*.

His widow entrusted John F. Callahan, Odell Professor of Humanities at Lewis and Clark College and Ellison's literary executor, with the Herculean task of turning the sprawling narrative into a publishable book. Callahan spent three years shaping, cutting, and rearranging the multiple plot lines and narrative voices of a novel that spans 50 years. In final form, Callahan's version is a 354-page linear narrative that bears no resemblance to the book Ellison described in a 1977 interview: "It's a crazy book, and I won't pretend to understand what it's about."

Commenting on the book in a *New York Times* magazine piece shortly after its publication, Gregory Feeley admits that it is still a "powerful and affecting read," but concedes that Ellison enthusiasts will probably be disappointed.

Louise Erdrich

Born
June 7, 1954, in Little
Falls, Minnesota, the
first of seven children.
Parents were both
teachers at the Bureau
of Indian Affairs.
Father Ralph was
German-American;
mother Rita Joanne
Gourneau was of
Ojibwa (Chippewa)
Indian descent.

Full Name
Louise Karen Erdrich
(pronounced "air-drik")

Education
Dartmouth College,
B.A., 1976; Johns
Hopkins University,
M.A., 1979

Family
Married in 1981 to
Michael Dorris, an
award-winning writer
and Dartmouth
professor of Native
American studies and
the father of three
adopted children, one
of whom died in 1991.
The couple had three
children together
before Dorris, who was
of Modoc Indian
ancestry, committed
suicide in 1997.

Home
Minneapolis,
Minnesota

Publisher
HarperCollins

Many critics have compared Louise Erdrich to William Faulkner. Her fictional town of Argus, North Dakota, like Faulkner's Yoknapatawpha County, is populated with interesting characters. And many of them show up again and again in the "Argus" novels as the stories of three interrelated families living in and around an Indian reservation are revealed and explored. Like Faulkner, Erdrich often tells her stories nonchronologically, using more than one narrator. And there is the ever-present sense of the past, of family, of the sins and glories of the fathers and mothers that came before, and the rough interface of different American cultures.

But Erdrich is more fun to read than Faulkner. Hers is a lighter touch applied by a modern Ivy League-educated female with a genetic foot in both white and Native American cultures. Though small in scope, like all the best tales, her stories are universal. And like the most enjoyable novels, hers take you somewhere you've never been and do so with a lyricism and grace that make them a pleasure to read.

Good to Know

❖ Erdrich has been a visiting poet, writing instructor, magazine editor, and textbook writer. But she has also worked as a waitress, a psychiatric hospital aide, a lifeguard, a construction flag signaler, a prison poetry teacher, and as a sugar-beet weeder and hoer. "[These jobs] turned out to have been very useful experiences, although I never would have believed it at the time," says Erdrich.

❖ She was raised in Wahpeton, North Dakota, where her Chippewa grandfather had been tribal chair of the Turtle Mountain Reservation. She told *Contemporary Authors* "My father used to give me a nickel for every story I wrote, and my mother wove strips of construction paper together and stapled them into book covers. So at an early age I felt myself to be a published author earning substantial royalties."

❖ Until enrolling in the Native American Studies Program at Dartmouth, Louise Erdrich had never explored the heritage that would serve as the inspiration for her novels. The department head was anthropologist Michael Dorris, who later became her husband and occasional collaborator. But it wasn't until she returned to Dartmouth as a visiting fellow in 1980 that the romance really caught fire.

❖ Erdrich and Dorris had a unique collaborative relationship. Whoever had the original idea for a book would be its official author and write the first draft. The other person would edit it, and another draft would be created. After five or six drafts, they would read the work aloud until they could agree on each word.

❖ At the time of Dorris's suicide, the couple had been secretly separated for more than a year. (Erdrich had moved six blocks down the street to be able to share joint custody of their children.) She is understandably reluctant to talk about the suicide, but it was something she had feared for some time. Dorris's father had committed suicide, and Dorris himself was devastated by the death of his adopted son, Abel, whose struggle with fetal alcohol syndrome was the subject of Dorris's highly acclaimed book, *The Broken Cord*.

❖ Several Errdrich short stories have been selected for O. Henry awards, and several have been included in the annual *Best American Short Story* anthologies. *The Blue Jay's Dance*, her first nonfiction book, offers her observations on motherhood. Published in 1996, *Grandmother's Pigeon*, with illustrations by Jim LaMarche, is her first children's book.

Treatises and Treats

COMPANIONS

A Reader's Guide to the Novels of Louise Erdrich by Peter G. Beidler and Gay Barton (University of Missouri Press, 1999). The geography, genealogy, chronology, and characters of the first six "Argus, North Dakota" novels, including a dictionary of characters. Essential for the true fan.

Louise Erdrich: A Critical Companion by Lorena L. Stookey (Greenwood Press, 1999). Insightful analysis that uncovers the layers of wisdom and humor and the recurring themes embedded in Erdrich's work.

The Chippewa Landscape of Louise Erdrich edited by Allan Chavkin (University of Alabama Press, 1999). Nine critical essays on various themes found in Erdrich's fiction.

Louise Erdrich's Love Medicine: A Casebook edited by Hertha D. Sweet Wong (Oxford University Press, 1999). Critical essays covering the history and culture of Native

American storytelling, with specific emphasis on the novels of Erdrich and Dorris.

BEST OF THE NET
Reader's Guides to Louise Erdrich Novels
www.harpercollins.com/readers/index.htm
HarperCollins has prepared reader's guides with plot summaries and suggested discussion topics for most of Erdrich's novels. You can view them online and print copies at this Web site. Or you can call 800-242-7737 to order them in packs of 20 for your book club or reading group.

Argus and Beyond

Love Medicine, 1984, expanded edition, 1993 (National Book Critics Circle Award)
The Beet Queen, 1986
Tracks, 1988
The Crown of Columbus (with husband Michael Dorris), 1991
The Bingo Palace, 1994
Tales of Burning Love, 1996
The Antelope Wife, 1998

If You Like Louise Erdrich . . .

You might also like books credited to her late husband, Michael Dorris, since she collaborated with him on many of them. Or try Sherman Alexie, Linda Hogan, Susan Power, and Jim Welch, Erdrich's personal favorites of the current generation of Native American writers according to a 1996 interview in the online magazine *Salon* (www.salon.com).

Erdrich is also a fan of Kay Boyle and Grace Paley, both of whom write about being writers and mothers.

Just Say "Yes!"

Thomas Disch, reviewing *Tracks* in the *Chicago Tribune*, had this to say about Erdrich's storytelling ability: "Louise Erdrich can do it in spades, for not only are each of her novels cannily and precisely plotted, but, as their several strands interconnect, there are further 'Oh-hos' and 'Eurekas' for the attentive reader...Erdrich is like one of those rumored drugs that are instantly and forever addictive. Fortunately, in her case, you can just say yes."

Best Book to Read First
Since Erdrich's characters appear and reappear in the five "Argus, North Dakota" books, read them in story order instead of in order of publication. Start with *Tracks*. Then read: *Love Medicine, The Beet Queen, The Bingo Palace,* and *Tales of Burning Love.*

People in [Native American] families make everything into a story. . . . People just sit and the stories start coming, one after another. I suppose that when you grow up constantly hearing the stories rise, break, and fall, it gets into you somehow.

—Louise Erdrich, interview in *Writer's Digest*, June 1991

William Faulkner

Born
September 25, 1897, in New Albany, Mississippi

Real Name
William Cuthbert Falkner. The *u* in the name had been dropped by his great-grandfather. Faulkner used both spellings until about 1921. The name change was *not* a publisher's misprint as has often been reported.

Education
Did not graduate from high school. Attended the University of Mississippi, 1919–20.

Family
Lost his fiancée, Estelle Oldham, to another man in 1918 but married her in 1929 after her divorce. Two daughters, one of whom died as an infant.

Home
"Rowan Oak," Oxford, Mississippi. Also a home in Charlottesville, Virginia.

Died
July 6, 1962, in Byhalia, Mississippi, of a heart attack while recuperating from a fall from his horse

Publisher
Random House

Winner of the 1949 Nobel Prize in Literature, two Pulitzers, and numerous other awards, William Faulkner is ranked among the greatest novelists of the 20th century. His stylistic innovations have influenced nearly every serious novelist in the latter half of the century worldwide. "To the young people of France," Jean-Paul Sartre said in 1945, "Faulkner is a god."

Faulkner's characters, his eye for detail, and the sheer scope of his interconnected novels as they follow the fate of several black and white Mississippi families over a century and a half, starting in 1820, are simply remarkable. The vast majority of his stories take place in a fictional, highly agricultural county in the Deep South, yet they explore human issues that are equally fundamental to people living in the urbanized North (or anywhere else). The violence, death, race relations, family ties, love, hate, integrity and dishonesty in his stories are universal themes confronted by all humanity.

It should be noted that Faulkner is not always the easiest author to read. To those who have yet to study James Joyce or T. S. Eliot, Faulkner's use of stream of consciousness, his sentence structure, and his way of presenting characters and scenes will come as a surprise. Rest assured, however, that as he manipulates your responses, Faulkner is always in complete control. Like a poet, he doesn't flatly state what he means, relying instead on implication and, most importantly, on what the reader brings to the process, to achieve the full resonance of his art.

Good to Know

❖ Faulkner's Nobel Prize was awarded a year late—in 1950—because the committee couldn't make its selection in time. In addition to Faulkner, the initial list included Hemingway, Steinbeck, Pasternak, Sholokhov, Mauriac, Camus, Winston Churchill, and Pär Lagerkvist.

❖ Too short to be a pilot for the U.S. Army during World War I, Faulkner adopted a British persona (including a fake English accent) and, with phony letters of recommendation, applied to the Royal Air Force in Canada. He was accepted, but the war ended before he graduated from flight school.

❖ Faulkner wore his RAF uniform home—sporting pilot's wings he had picked up in New York City. He also affected a limp and claimed on at least one occasion that he had a silver plate in his head, the result of injuries suffered, presumably, in a dogfight over France.

❖ Though closely modeled on Mississippi's Lafayette County, Yoknapatawpha (pronounced "YOK-nuh-puh-TAW-fuh") County, the setting for most of Faulkner's novels and short stories, is his own creation. And, just as J. R. R. Tolkien did with Middle-Earth, Faulkner prepared a hand-drawn map of the place. Published in 1936 in *Absalom, Absalom!*, the map is signed "William Faulkner, Sole Owner & Proprietor."

❖ Both Anthony Trollope and Faulkner set their stories in fictional counties, ("Barsetshire," in Trollope's case), and both had jobs they hated, working in a post office. "I reckon I'll be at the beck and call of folks with money all my life," Faulkner said after being fired as postmaster at the University of Mississippi, "but thank God I won't ever again have to be at the beck and call of every son of a bitch who's got two cents to buy a stamp." Faulkner held the post for nearly three years, during which he routinely ignored patrons (they interrupted his writing) and kept people's magazines until he had read them first.

❖ Beginning in 1949, many of Faulkner's works were made into movies with major stars: *The Tarnished Angels* (based on *Pylon*), with Rock Hudson and Robert Stack; *The Long Hot Summer* (based on *The Hamlet*), with Paul Newman, Joanne Woodward, Lee Remick, Orson Wells, and Angela Lansbury; *The Sound and the Fury*, with Yul Brynner, Joanne Woodward, Ethel Waters, and Jack Warden as Benjy; and *Sanctuary* with Lee Remick and Yves Montand. The most recent screen adaptation of his work is *Old Man* (derived from *If I Forget Thee, Jerusalem*) in 1997, starring Jeanne Tripplehorn and Arliss Howard.

Treatises and Treats

THE FAULKNER SOCIETY

Dedicated to fostering the study of Faulkner. Membership is $5 a year. For a subscription to *The Faulkner Journal*, include an additional $12. Contact:
Dr. Theresa M. Towner
3410 University Blvd.
Dallas, TX 75205

COMPANIONS

The Portable Faulkner, edited by Malcolm Cowley (Viking, 1977). Originally published in 1946 when all of Faulkner's novels except *Sanctuary* were out of print, this collection of short stories and excerpts from the novels brought Faulkner back to the attention of the literary establishment. Cowley organizes the works by story chronology and offers commentary to help readers better understand what Faulkner was up to. The book's introduction is considered the finest short analysis of Faulkner yet written.

BEST OF THE NET
Faulkner Resources on the Web
www.unf.edu/~alderman/faulkner.html
Assembled by Jim Alderman, Reference Librarian at the University of North Florida, the information and links on this site offer the ideal way to tap into Faulkner resources. Be sure to click on "William Faulkner on the Web" and "William Faulkner Society" for connections to truly superb information sites.

The Yoknapatawpha Masterpieces

Of Faulkner's 20 novels, 15 are set in Yoknapatawpha County. Here are the six that are generally rated among Faulkner's very best:

The Sound and the Fury, 1929
As I Lay Dying, 1930
Light in August, 1932
Absalom, Absalom!, 1936
The Hamlet, 1940
Go Down, Moses, 1942

Best Book to Read First

The Sound and the Fury, Faulkner's fourth novel, is his first true masterpiece. (It was reportedly his own personal favorite.) Published in 1929, it uses the then-revolutionary stream-of-consciousness narrative technique pioneered by James Joyce. This can make the narrative difficult to follow at times. For a less demanding book, try Faulkner's last novel, *The Reivers*. This comic tale won him his second Pulitzer (his first was awarded for *A Fable* in 1955), and served as the basis for the 1969 Steve McQueen movie of the same name.

Clark Who?

Faulkner spent some 20 years working in Hollywood. (He needed the money.) His most famous films include *The Big Sleep* and *To Have and Have Not*, as well as many films for which he was not credited (including *God Is My Co-pilot*). One day in 1932, Faulkner, director Howard Hawks, and Clark Gable were out dove hunting when Hawks began talking with Faulkner about books. Gable remained silent but eventually asked Faulkner his opinion of the best five writers of the day. Faulkner paused and then said, "Ernest Hemingway, Willa Cather, Thomas Mann, John Dos Passos, and myself."

"Oh," said Gable, "do you write for a living?"

"Why, yes," Faulkner replied. "And what do *you* do, Mr. Gable?"

I'm a failed poet. Maybe every novelist wants to write poetry first, finds he can't and then tries the short story, which is the most demanding form after poetry. And failing at that, only then does he take up novel writing.

—William Faulkner

F. Scott Fitzgerald

Born
September 24, 1896, in St. Paul, Minnesota

Real Name
Francis Scott Key Fitzgerald, after the author of "The Star-Spangled Banner," a paternal ancestor

Education
Attended Princeton University, 1913–17, but did not receive a degree.

Family
Married Zelda Sayre, whom he had met when stationed near Montgomery, Alabama, while in the army. On discovering his $90 per month salary as an advertising copywriter, she broke their engagement. One week after *This Side of Paradise* was published, they were married. One daughter, Frances, known as "Scottie" (1921–86).

Died
December 21, 1940, at age 44, of a second heart attack three weeks after experiencing the first. He is buried near his parents in St. Mary's Cemetery, Rockville, Maryland.

Publisher
Scribner

Highly autobiographical and offering only preliminary indications of the artistry to come, Fitzgerald's first novel, *This Side of Paradise*, was published in 1920 when he was only 23. To his great misfortune, the novel became a spectacular success and he was hailed as the voice of the Jazz Age, the 1920s era of flappers, speakeasies, bobbed hair, and short skirts that followed the pain of World War I.

Swept up by fame and fortune, Fitzgerald, who would become a heavy drinker, and his wife Zelda, who would become prone to nervous breakdowns, began to live far beyond their means. It was a lifestyle difficult to sustain, particularly since his next two novels failed to achieve the success of the first. To pay for all the flowers and champagne, Fitzgerald borrowed from his publisher and his agent and wrote short stories—which surely distracted him from developing as a novelist.

Clearly, money was always on his mind. In 1938, he wrote to Anne Ober, the wife of his literary agent, "That was always my experience—a poor boy in a rich town; a poor boy in a rich boy's school; a poor boy in a rich man's club at Princeton.... I have never been able to forgive the rich for being rich, and it has colored my entire life and works." Of course, Fitzgerald wasn't at all poor by American standards. Growing up in St. Paul, he and his family lived quite comfortably on his mother's inheritance. But he encountered *real* wealth at Princeton, which didn't place the same emphasis on academic achievement that it does today and had a reputation for being a school for the very rich.

All of which is undoubtedly to the good, for no one rich enough to actually *own* piles of London-made shirts "with stripes and scrolls and plaids in coral and apple-green and laven-der and faint orange, with monograms of Indian blue" could ever have written such a line, as Fitzgerald did in *The Great Gatsby*. A truly wealthy person would never have noticed.

When Fitzgerald is at his best, his prose is simply lambent. It flows effortlessly, leading you along, offering gentle surprises and highlighting or adding details that would never have occurred to most writers, rich or poor. Had he lived longer, there is every indication that Fitzgerald would eventually have fulfilled his dream of becoming, as he wrote to his friend and fellow Princetonian, Edmund Wilson, "one of the greatest writers who have ever lived."

Good to Know

❖ The eating clubs in *This Side of Paradise* still exist in Princeton today, including the stately University Cottage Club, which counts not only Fitzgerald himself and his character "Amory Blaine" among its members but also former U.S. Senator Bill Bradley '65 and 1999 Pulitzer Prize–winners John McPhee '53 (*Annals of the Former World*) and A. Scott Berg '71 (*Lindbergh*).

❖ Zelda Fitzgerald's final mental breakdown in 1934 left her a permanent invalid. Scott Fitzgerald visited her often at the sanitarium, but when it became clear she was not going to improve, he became a scriptwriter in Hollywood (contributing to *Gone With the Wind*, among other films). There he met and fell in love with gossip columnist Sheilah Graham. The two lived together for the rest of his life.

❖ In August 1940, Fitzgerald received what was to be his last royalty statement. It reported total sales of all of his titles of only 40 copies. "Amount due author: $13.13." Fitzgerald's works have since been translated into 35 languages and now routinely sell some 500,000 copies a year.

❖ *Living Well Is the Best Revenge* by Calvin Tomkins (Modern Library, 1998) is the real-life story of Gerald and Sara Murphy, the models for Dick and Nicole Diver in Fitzgerald's *Tender Is the Night*. Written in 1924 but not published until 1934 because he was pre-occupied writing short stories, Fitzgerald's novel of the high life in Paris during the Roaring '20s understandably failed to resonate with a world in the midst of the Great Depression.

Treatises and Treats

COMPANIONS

Some Sort of Epic Grandeur by Matthew J. Bruccoli (Carroll & Graf, 1993). Available from out-of-print sources, this is the leading modern Fitzgerald biography.

F. Scott Fitzgerald A to Z: The Essential Reference to His Life and Work by Mary Jo Tate and Matthew J. Bruccoli (Facts on File, 1998). Highly recommended, this book draws on Fitzgerald's writings and correspondence and on interviews with those who knew him for its biographical sections. Also includes synopses of all his works, critical essays, chronologies, and an extensive bibliography.

Trimalchio: An Early Version of The Great Gatsby, prepared by James L. W. West, III (Cambridge University Press, 2000). The manuscript, "hidden in plain sight" for decades, presents a Nick Carraway who is less likable and a Jay Gatsby who is more mysterious than in the published novel.

BEST OF THE NET

F. Scott Fitzgerald Centenary
www.sc.edu/fitzgerald
This superb site exists because Matthew J. Bruccoli, one of the foremost Fitzgerald scholars and collectors of the day, is also the Emily Brown Jeffries Professor of English at the University of South Carolina. Bibliographies, a Fitzgerald life chronology, essays and articles, voice and film clips, downloadable copies of his major stories as well as *This Side*

of Paradise, and links to other outstanding sites—this is the place to begin.

Gatsby and Co.

ALL THE NOVELS

This Side of Paradise, 1920
The Beautiful and the Damned, 1922
Tender Is the Night, 1924 (not published until 1934)
The Great Gatsby, 1925
The Last Tycoon, 1941 (unfinished)

SHORT-STORY COLLECTIONS

Of Fitzgerald's more than 160 stories, critics consider "The Ice Palace," "Bernice Bobs Her Hair," "A Diamond as Big as the Ritz," "May Day," "Winter Dreams," "Absolution," "Babylon Revisited," and "The Rich Boy" to be among the best. Many of them are available free of charge at www.sc.edu/fitzgerald. Here are the main collections, some of which were prepared posthumously:

Flappers and Philosophers, 1920
Tales of the Jazz Age, 1922
All the Sad Young Men, 1926
Taps at Reveille, 1935
The Crack-up and Other Pieces and Tales, 1945
The Pat Hobby Stories, 1967
Bernice Bobs Her Hair and Other Stories, 1968
Bits of Paradise, 1973
The Price Was High: Fifty Uncollected Stories, 1979

Best Book to Read First

The Great Gatsby, Fitzgerald's best-loved work and a 20th-century American classic. For a real treat, look for the unabridged audio edition read by Alexander Scourby (Audio Partners Publishing, 1989).

[Fitzgerald] had one of the rarest qualities in all literature, and it's a great shame that the word for it has been thoroughly debased by the cosmetic racketeers, so that one is almost ashamed to use it to describe a real distinction. Nevertheless, the word is "charm"—charm as Keats would have used it. Who has it today? It's not a matter of pretty writing or clear style. It's a kind of subdued magic, controlled and exquisite, the sort of thing you get from good string quartettes.

—Raymond Chandler, in a 1950 letter to his publisher

The Rich Are Different

At the peak of his fame in 1929, the *Saturday Evening Post* paid Fitzgerald $4,000 for a story—the equivalent of about $40,000 in 1990s money. But he was not among the highest paid writers of the day. In 1920 and 1921, close to 50,000 copies of *This Side of Paradise* were sold, but in his entire lifetime, *The Great Gatsby* sold under 30,000 copies and *Tender Is the Night* fewer than 15,000. Indeed, during the 1920s Fitzgerald's income from all sources rarely topped $25,000 a year, a nice living, but certainly not a fortune. In 1937, his star had fallen so far that the *Post* paid him $2,000 for "Trouble" and ran it at the back of the magazine.

Penelope Fitzgerald

Born
December 17, 1916, in Lincoln, England, to Edmund Valpy Knox (a journalist and later the editor of *Punch*) and Christina Hicks Knox

Education
Somerville College, Oxford University, 1939 (degree in English literature, first-class honors)

Family
Married Desmond Fitzgerald (an Irish soldier she met at a party; he worked in the travel business) in 1953. He died of cancer in 1976. Two children, a son and a daughter. Nine grandchildren.

Home
The North London district of Highgate, in a small flat connected to the Victorian home of her daughter and son-in-law

Publisher
Houghton Mifflin

Penelope Fitzgerald, who didn't begin her first novel until she was 59 years old, has established a reputation as an ironic and richly comic novelist with a strong sense of detail and insightful observations of human nature. *Los Angeles Times Book Review* contributor Richard Eder notes that Fitzgerald's prose is "so precise and lilting that it can make you shiver." John Bayley, writing in the *New York Review of Books*, adds: "Penelope Fitzgerald is not only an artist of a high order but one of immense originality." Three of her novels—*The Bookshop*, *The Beginning of Spring*, and *The Gate of Angels*—have been short-listed for the Booker Prize, and one novel, *Offshore*, won the award in 1979.

Fitzgerald's early novels are loosely based on her own experiences. *The Bookshop* (1978) tells the story of a courageous bookstore owner named Florence Green who defies the stuffy prejudices of her town by stocking Vladimir Nabokov's novel *Lolita*. *Offshore* (1979) presents a community of eccentric characters living on barges on the Thames River. A review in *Books and Bookmen* describes this novel as "a delicate water-colour of a novel…a small, charming Whistler etching."

With the publication of *Innocence* in 1986, Fitzgerald began to look beyond England for her stories. *Innocence* follows the decline of a patrician family in postwar Florence. *The Beginning of Spring* is a comedy of manners set in the household of a British expatriate in prerevolutionary Moscow. With this novel, according to *New York Times Book Review* contributor Robert Plunket, Fitzgerald has become "that refreshing rarity, a writer who is very modern but not the least bit hip. [She] looks into the past, both human and literary, and finds all sorts of things that are surprisingly up to date." *The Blue Flower* (1995)—based on the early years of the German romantic poet Friedrich Leopold von Hardenberg—won the National Book Critics Circle Award in 1998.

Good to Know

❖ While on scholarship at Oxford, Fitzgerald studied literature with J. R. R. Tolkien.

❖ She worked for the BBC during World War II and, after her marriage in 1953, served as a clerk in a bookstore. These experiences led to the novels *Human Voices* and *The Bookshop*.

❖ During the 1960s, her family lived on a barge anchored on the Thames, the only accommodation they could afford. The barge sank under them twice. Working at the time as a teacher, Fitzgerald recalls, "We were only allowed to use the lavatory on a falling tide…. It was terribly difficult to get respectable enough to go into work." After two years on the barge, the family rented a flat. "It seemed rather odd to come back to dry land," she said. Her experiences living on the Thames led to the Booker Prize–winning novel *Offshore*.

❖ Her husband inspired her first attempt at fiction—*The Golden Child*, a mystery written to entertain him during his final illness. She went about getting the book published in a slightly unorthodox manner, sending it to a publisher who didn't typically consider crime fiction, figuring the house would not have seen many manuscripts like it. Her plan worked—the novel was accepted. But the publisher felt it wasn't "thrilling" enough to be called a thriller, so they cut the last eight chapters and called it a mystery. Her first attempt at a mystery novel proved to be her last. "The publisher told me I'd have to write six, with the same detective—so they could make a row on the bookshelf," Fitzgerald said. "I was appalled."

❖ Fitzgerald claims to hate writing and welcomes interruptions that take her from it. As for a writing routine, she says she has none: "I don't think women ever do—they call us kitchen-table writers. Women always have to let the cat in, or something." But she does have some rituals: she always writes her books in longhand, and she won't actually begin a novel until she has her title, her first paragraph, and her *last* paragraph.

Treatises and Treats

BEST OF THE NET

Penelope Fitzgerald Reader's Guides
www.hmco.com/trade/features/
     penelope_fitzgerald.html
For book group discussions or to enhance your own personal enjoyment of Fitzgerald's novels, check here for reading guides developed by her publisher, Houghton Mifflin.

New York Times Featured Authors
www.nytimes.com/books/specials/author.html
Click on "Penelope Fitzgerald" for a collection of book reviews as they appeared in the *New York Times*.

Reading List

ALL THE NOVELS
The Golden Child, 1977
The Bookshop, 1978
Offshore, 1979
     (Booker Prize)
Human Voices, 1980
At Freddie's, 1982
Innocence, 1986
The Beginning of Spring, 1988
The Gate of Angels, 1990
The Blue Flower, 1995
     (National Book Critics Circle Award)

BIOGRAPHIES
Edward Burne-Jones, 1975 (about the Pre-Raphaelite painter)
The Knox Brothers, 1977 (recounting the lives and accomplishments of Fitzgerald's father and his brothers)
Charlotte Mew and Her Friends: With a Selection of Her Poems, 1988 (about the tragic life of an extraordinary but long-forgotten English poet)

If You Like Penelope Fitzgerald . . .

You may also enjoy Anita Brookner or George Eliot (a.k.a. Mary Ann Evans, 1819-80, author of *Silas Marner*, *Adam Bede*, and *The Mill on the Floss*).

Best Book to Read First

Readers new to Penelope Fitzgerald may want to start with her most recent novel, *The Blue Flower* (1995), which the *New York Times* calls her "most recondite and challenging book . . . Her greatest triumph." It won the National Book Critics Circle Award in 1998 (over such heavy favorites as Don DeLillo, Philip Roth, and Charles Frazier), making Fitzgerald the first non-American author to receive the award.

A Remarkable Family

Both of Fitzgerald's grandfathers were Anglican bishops. Her uncle, Dillwyn Knox, was a cryptographer and Oxford classics professor who helped crack German codes in both world wars. Another uncle, Wilfred, was an Anglican priest and a writer, and her only brother, Rawle, became a distinguished war correspondent. "It was a very brilliant family," Fitzgerald told *Publishers Weekly*, "and they were given to understatement, which is where I got it from."

Fitzgerald's aunt wrote all her life and eventually had a nervous breakdown. Even in a nursing home, her aunt continued writing. "She couldn't be stopped, and she wrote all of her life," says Fitzgerald. "I would rather have liked to have done that myself—write all my life—but that just wasn't possible in my case. I had a family to raise."

[Penelope Fitzgerald is] one of the mildest and most English of writers. . . . Mild, yes, but there is authority behind those neat, discursive, and unresolved stories of hers. . . . She is so unostentatious a writer that she needs to be read several times. What is impressive is the calm confidence behind the apparent simplicity of utterance.

—Anita Brookner, writing in *Spectator*

Richard Ford

Born
February 16, 1944, in Jackson, Mississippi, to Parker Ford, a laundry starch salesman, and Edna Akin Ford

Education
Michigan State University, B.A., 1966; University of California, Irvine, M.F.A., 1970

Family
Married Kristina Hensley, a research professor, in 1968.

Home
A house on Bourbon Street in New Orleans, Louisiana, and another in Chinook, Montana

Fan Mail
Richard Ford
c/o International Creative Management
40 West 57th Street
New York, NY 10019

Publisher
Knopf

R ichard Ford emerged on the American scene in the late 1970s as one of the "Coca-Cola Realists" or "New Minimalists," with the likes of Tobias Wolff, Raymond Carver, and Mary Robison. He heatedly rejected both labels, and time has shown that he is neither a flavor of the day nor just a regional writer.

In his five novels and two story collections, Ford traverses America—and dips into Mexico—telling tales of ordinary doubt and pain in a highly original way. And though his characters often dwell in that woozy void of arrested and unfulfilled yearnings typical of modern fiction's psychic territory, Ford usually grants them some redemption, a refuge in acceptance or insight. Critics consider his protagonist Frank Bascombe to be on a par with Willy Loman and Harry Angstrom.

If Richard Ford's work is about any one thing, it is a rumination on the contemporary American character. His people have an obsessive need to explain things—rather than confessing or justifying them—and he grants even his marginal creations a "speculative intelligence" through which the writer himself speaks, wrote John Wideman in a review for the *New York Times*. In this way, Wideman asserts, Ford is always "expanding the fashionable conventions of contemporary fiction."

Good to Know

❖ Richard Ford is "a writer's writer." He has taught creative writing at Princeton, Williams, and the University of Michigan. He writes about writing. And he talks about it insightfully. ("A lot of people could be novelists," he once said, "if they were willing to devote their lives to their own responses to things.")

❖ His father died in his arms when he was 16. After college, as the Vietnam War was expanding, he volunteered for the Marines but was discharged when he contracted hepatitis. He went to work briefly for the CIA, attended law school, and served a stint as an editor for the short-lived magazine *Inside Sports*, an experience that inspired his breakthrough novel about a man who abandons his literary ambitions to write about sports.

❖ Thanks to the encouragement and financial support of his wife (they met when we was 19), Ford has been able to devote himself exclusively to writing for most of his career. Now Executive Director of the New Orleans City Planning Commission, Kristina Ford spent a number of years as an economic researcher, a job that required a great deal of travel. Ford accompanied her around the country, living in 14 different states and 20 houses in as many years.

❖ After studying with E. L. Doctorow and Oakley Hall at the University of California, Ford began to write in earnest. He labored over two novels that no one wanted, and when he showed an editor at Knopf the manuscript for his third, *The Sportswriter*, the editor advised him to put the book in a drawer and forget about it. Vintage Contemporaries publishing the book as a paperback original in 1986. It was named one of the five best books of the year by *Time* magazine and became a PEN/Faulkner finalist.

❖ Mildly dyslexic as a boy, Ford spent extra effort on reading. But it was the way of talking in the South, the "mouthing and punning, a lot of play on words, disrespectful jiving about our elders," that steeped him in the pleasures of language. He read his award-winning novel *Independence Day* aloud twice—all 700 pages of the manuscript—to detect any rough spots.

Then, just as the book was to go to press, an editor commented that there seemed to be quite a few –*ly* adverbs. Ford agreed and spent the next two weeks striking out every one he could and strengthening the accompanying verbs. "It seemed there were about four thousand of them," he later commented.

❖ His wife is always his first reader, even though he feels she's not perfect for this role. "She's much too smart; she's much too sympathetic to me and my various efforts; and she has a great sense of humor and loves jokes. My ideal reader is somebody I have to work hard to win over…somebody like me, for instance."

❖ "I do all my own typing," Ford says, "since that's a way of staying close to the book. My biggest challenge is to stay *in* the book as long as I can, since I believe that I can make things better if I just concentrate and stay close. Young writers—and I was one—are often bothered by the worry of being able to finish a book….I'm challenged nowadays, though, by a wish to stay in without finishing."

Treatises and Treats

COMPANIONS

Ford biographies are yet to be written. But you can hear the author himself read his 1997 collection of stories, *Women with Men*. Available on audiotape from Random House, it provides a fine opportunity to indulge in Ford's mannerly, pleasurable speaking voice.

Random House also offers a reading-group guide for the novel *Independence Day*. You'll find it on the Random House Web site at www.randomhouse.com/resources.

BEST OF THE NET

The Mississippi Writers page
www.olemiss.edu/depts/english/ms-writers
A good starting point, with a heavy emphasis on bibliography. But you'll also find goodies like a 1996 interview of Ford, conducted by NPR's Elizabeth Farnsworth and available for listening via RealAudio.

New York Times Featured Authors
www.nytimes.com/books/specials/
    author.html
Ford's listing in the *New York Times* archives leads to reviews and profiles, plus some articles he wrote for the paper.

Book List

NOVELS
A Piece of My Heart, 1976
The Ultimate Good Luck, 1981
The Sportswriter, 1986
Wildlife, 1990
Independence Day, 1995
    (Pulitzer Prize, PEN/Faulkner Award)

SHORT-STORY COLLECTIONS
Rock Springs, 1987
Women with Men: Three Long Stories, 1997

If You Like Richard Ford…

Try Tobias Wolff, who is in all ways Ford's peer—they have even traveled the lecture circuit together, sometimes interviewing each other. Wolff's intensely novelistic memoir, *This Boy's Life*, is one of his best books.

Best Book to Read First

The Sportswriter (1986) was Ford's first novel to garner widespread critical praise. It sold five times as many copies as his previous two books combined. The narrator, Frank Bascombe, reappears in *Independence Day* (1995). Though *Independence Day* won the Pulitzer Prize and the PEN/Faulkner Award, *The Sportswriter* is the logical place to dig into the work of Ford's most fertile period to date.

Literary Defense

After years of perceived misreadings, gratuitous categorizations, and outright vicious pans—one critic said that *The Ultimate Good Luck* "calls to mind a cheap action picture in which hastily collaborating hacks didn't quite manage to put a story together"—Ford has a notorious dislike for reviews. When asked about the rumor that he had shot a critic's novel with a gun, he denied it. It was actually his wife Kristina who carried the book into their backyard for target practice. They sent the bullet-riddled tome to the critic's editor.

All the voices are male. All white. All approximately 25 to 40 years old. Predictably, they speak about gaining, losing or holding on to manhood … Women are lovers, mothers, daughters. And though female characters may be strong, aggressive, even in charge, their appearance signals not so much the existence of a feminine world and the author's curiosity about it, but an opportunity to observe how women affect men, how they fit into a man's world.

—John Wideman, reviewing Ford's 1987 short-story collection, *Rock Springs*

C. S. Forester

Born
August 27, 1899, in Cairo, Egypt, the son of an English schoolteacher

Real Name
Cecil Louis Troughton Smith

Education
Studied at Alleyn's, a private school near his home in London. Went on to Guy's Medical School of the University of London, where (according to a biography written by his son) he "lazed away his time" rather than attending classes.

Family
Married twice, with two sons by his first wife, to whom he was married for 18 years.

Home
Berkeley, California (from the start of World War II until his death)

Died
April 2, 1966

Publisher
Little, Brown

C. S. Forester is best known for his Horatio Hornblower stories, set during England's battles with Napoleon in the age of the tall ships. Ernest Hemingway, a fan of his work, said, "I recommend Forester to everyone literate I know."

But while Hornblower was his mainstay, so to speak, Forester wrote scores of other novels, histories, and biographies. He's the author of *The African Queen*, the book on which the famous 1951 movie was based, and *The Last Nine Days of the Bismarck*, which was made into the movie *Sink the Bismarck!* Regardless of historical setting, C. S. Forester was clearly a born storyteller.

Good to Know

❖ Born in Cairo, Forester returned to England with his mother and four older brothers and sisters when he was three, after his parents separated. The children used the top floor of their house as a gigantic playroom. A favorite game: re-enacting the Napoleonic Wars, using a cardboard model of a Nelsonian ship-of-the-line, received as a gift, and other models they built themselves.

❖ His first novel, *A Pawn Among Kings* (1924), revolves around a fictional woman who causes Napoleon to make mistakes by upsetting his judgment at crucial times. Forester also published *Napoleon and His Court* and *Josephine: Napoleon's Empress* in the same year.

❖ Supported by his parents until age 27, CSF, as he was known, had his first big hit with *Payment Deferred*, a novel about a man hanged for a murder he didn't commit be-

cause exonerating himself would prove the murder that he *had* committed. It was made into a 1932 movie starring Charles Laughton.

❖ Forester was lured to Hollywood to write a pirate movie with Arthur Hornblow and Niven Busch. But *Captain Blood* (1935) appeared first, making Errol Flynn and Olivia de Havilland stars. Since it used the same historical incidents that Forester, Hornblow, and Busch had planned to use, *their* film was cancelled.

❖ Discouraged by this (and possibly also concerned about a threatened paternity suit involving a fading opera singer), CSF caught a freighter bound for England. During the crossing he plotted *The Happy Return* with its characters Hornblower, Bush, and Lady Barbara. It was published in the United States as *Beat to Quarters*, the first of 11 Hornblower titles.

❖ During World War II, Forester was sent to Berkeley, California, with an assignment from the British government to write propaganda designed to keep the U.S. on Britain's side.

Treatises and Treats

THE C. S. FORESTER SOCIETY

Open to anyone interested in C. S. Forester's writings, especially the Hornblower series. Annual membership fee is $15, including a subscription to the quarterly publication, *The Naval Gazette* (see the Society's Web site for a sample).

The C. S. Forester Society
William A. Carpenter, Secretary
390 Hansen Ave. South
Salem, OR 97302
503-581-2179
www.teleport.com/~vamberry
vamberry@teleport.com

COMPANIONS AND BIOGRAPHIES

The Hornblower Companion by C. S. Forester (Naval Institute Press, 1999). Contains maps and personal commentary on each of the novels.

Hornblower—One More Time by C. S. Forester, et al. Published in a limited and numbered edition by the Richard Bolitho Society, Tacoma Washington. Contains an introduction by Alexander Kent (Douglas Reeman), creator of the Bolitho series, plus two autobiographical pieces by CSF ("Hornblower and I" and "Hornblower's London"), a chronology, a bibliography, and three previously uncollected short stories.

The Life and Times of Horatio Hornblower by C. Northcote Parkinson (Sutton Alan, 1998). This "biography" is so authentic it has been known to fool some people. Written by the inventor of "Parkinson's Law," the book covers Hornblower's life from his birth on July 4, 1776, to his death on January 12, 1857.

C. S. Forester by Sanford V. Sternlicht (Twayne, 1981). The standard biography.

BEST OF THE NET

The C. S. Forester Society Web Site
www.teleport.com/~vamberry
Start here. The site is a treasure trove of Forester and Hornblower information and links to other Web sites.

Sea Room Web Site
www.sea-room.com
Site creator John Berg publishes a newsletter and books related to the age of sail. He also runs Searoom-L and Seabooks-L, Internet mailing lists devoted to discussions of books and lore of wooden sailing ships, with special emphasis on the novels of C. S. Forester and Patrick O'Brian. To subscribe, visit the Sea Room site and click on "Sea Room's Internet Services."

Best Reads

THE HORNBLOWER SAGA

Listed here in "saga" order, with original publication dates.
Mr. Midshipman Hornblower, 1950
Lieutenant Hornblower, 1954
Hornblower and the Hotspur, 1962
Hornblower During the Crisis, 1967
    (unfinished at the time of CSF's death)
Hornblower and the Atropos, 1953
    (published in England as *Captain Hornblower, R.N.*)
Beat to Quarters, 1937
Ship of the Line, 1938
Flying Colors, 1939
Commodore Hornblower, 1945
Lord Hornblower, 1948
Admiral Hornblower in the West Indies, 1958

If You Like C. S. Forester...

Try Dudley Pope, Alexander Kent, C. Northcote Parkinson, Kenneth Maynard, and Richard Woodman, each of whom has written a Hornblower-like series. For a hugely deeper experience, read Patrick O'Brian's Aubrey/Maturin series, starting with *Master and Commander*. Also consider Bernard Cornwell's Richard Sharpe saga about a team of riflemen fighting Napoleon's army in Spain.

Best Book to Read First

Mr. Midshipman Hornblower, the first book in the Hornblower saga.

Radio Days

C. S. Forester was so popular in the 1950s that the BBC produced a radio series called *Captain Horatio Hornblower* starring Michael Redgrave. All 24 episodes are available on audiotape from Crabapple Sound (518-842-5962, www.crabapplesound.com).

For the first time for many months I could read a book for pleasure. Oliver Lyttelton, Minister of State in Cairo, had given me **Captain Hornblower, R.N.,** *which I found vastly entertaining. When a chance came, I sent him the message,* **"I find Hornblower admirable."** *This caused perturbation in the Middle East Headquarters, where it was imagined that "Hornblower" was the code-word for some special operation of which they had not been told.*

—Winston Churchill, *The Grand Alliance*

E. M. Forster

Born
January 1, 1879, in London, the only child of an architect father who died within two years

Full Name
Edward Morgan Forster

Education
King's College, Cambridge, B. A. in classics, 1900; B. A. in history, 1901; M.A., 1910

Family
Forster's bond with his widowed mother was so great that he lived with her until her death, when he was 66. They also traveled the world together.

Home
Lived in Greece, Italy, India, and Egypt. Returned to England in 1927, living with his mother at Abinger Hammer in Surrey. After her death, he divided his time between Cambridge and Coventry.

Died
June 7, 1970, in Coventry

Publishers
Bantam
Harcourt Brace
Vintage

E. M. Forster's novels have been turned into sumptuous films more successfully than those of any other important writer of the 20th century. Which isn't too surprising when you consider his strongest features as a writer: the creation of unique and interesting characters, the mixing of different cultures with their disparate mores and codes of conduct, and the employment of a vast array of experiences in foreign lands to create memorable backdrops for his tales.

Born into the English middle class, Forster was educated with the upper classes, and it is these two groups that he examines with his graceful style and gentle irony. He knew his people well, and his characters are exact renderings. Apart from Jane Austen, one critic noted, he is the only novelist whose characters speak in such distinct ways that no reader could ever confuse them. "And this without any of the obvious tricks and slogans which…[the characters of lesser authors] fly like identifying flags."

Forster felt the middle and upper classes lacked spontaneity and were too repressed to fathom the passion that resided within them. He explored this idea in his novels by contrasting the archetypal stiff-upper-lip Englishmen (and English women) with peoples from other cultures. Yet what makes his books such a pleasure to read is that he offers no easy solutions to this or any of life's problems. He was dedicated to conveying the complexity of life, and this, combined with his "mystical sense of landscape," helps explain why his novels are so easily adapted into films, and why his fiction remains relevant today.

Good to Know

❖ At Cambridge, E. M. Forster was elected to the Apostles, an elite secret society, and became associated with the Bloomsbury Group. As a result of these connections, he formed close ties with Virginia Woolf, Lytton Strachey, and the economist John Maynard Keynes.

❖ Forster is one of just a handful of authors to have three books (*A Passage to India*, *Howards End*, and *A Room with a View*) on the Modern Library's list of the 100 Best Novels of the 20th century.

❖ He stopped writing fiction in 1924 when he was just 45. (He lived to be 91.) Critic John Carey has suggested that he gave up novels because "as a homosexual, he was tired of pairing off boys with girls." In a letter, Forster himself said "I shall never write another novel after it (*Passage to India*). My patience with ordinary people has given out."

❖ Forster completed a novel with homosexual themes (*Maurice*) in 1914, but felt that "it could not be published until my death… and England's." It turns out he was half right. Based on an actual 30-year relationship between British social reformer Edward Carpenter and his working-class partner, the book was published in 1971, the year after Forster died.

❖ Merchant-Ivory has adapted three Forster novels for the big screen: *A Room with a View* (1986), *Maurice* (1987), and *Howards End* (1992). Helena Bonham Carter appears in all three productions, along with Simon Callow and Denholm Elliot in the first two. Hugh Grant and Rupert Graves played Clive Durham and Alec Scudder in *Maurice*. David

Lean directed *A Passage to India* (1984), which film critic Roger Ebert called "the greatest screen adaptation I have ever seen."

Treatises and Treats

BIOGRAPHIES

E. M. Forster by Lionel Trilling (New Directions, 1943; reissued by W.W. Norton, 1971). Considered by some to be the best study of Forster.

E. M. Forster: A Life by P. N. Furbank (Harcourt Brace, 1978). The authorized biography.

E. M. Forster: A Biography by Nicola Beauman (Alfred A. Knopf, 1994). An admiring treatment of Forster's life that concentrates on his novel-writing years. One reviewer compared the author of this biography to Miss Lavish in *A Room with a View*: "She shares with her reader not only the results of her research but also the process. We see her eating her sandwiches at Figsbury Rings (*The Longest Journey*) and sitting pinkly in the Taj Hotel in Bombay (*A Passage to India*), and we know her interest in many odd subjects: in graphology, for example, and the etymology of the names of Forster's characters."

COMPANIONS

Aspects of the Novel by E. M. Forster (Harcourt Brace, 1972). Originally published in 1927, this is a collection of Forster's lectures on English-language novels at his alma mater in Cambridge. "My absolute favorite Forster book," says Tracy Kidder in *For the Love of Books* (Grossett/Putnam, 1999). "It has a wonderful clarity and economy, articulating a lot of complicated thoughts about the craft of fiction, in lovely plain English."

Abinger Harvest by E. M. Forster (Harcourt Brace, 1986). Thirty years of articles, essays, reviews, and poems. "Anyone who misses this book will be missing one of the most exquisite pleasures that the contemporary market can afford." (*Saturday Review*)

Two Cheers for Democracy by E. M. Forster (Harcourt Brace, 1990). Insightful essays on politics, aesthetics, anti-Semitism, liberty, censorship, and his faith in the arts.

BEST OF THE NET

Forster Text Collection

www.hti.umich.edu/english/pd-modeng/bibl.html Forster is one of many authors whose public domain works are available here as part of the University of Michigan's Humanities Text Initiative. You can download the full text of *A Room with a View*, as well as *Howards End*, *The Longest Journey*, and *Where Angels Fear to Tread*. Better still, you can *search* the texts for words, phrases, and characters.

All the Novels

Where Angels Fear to Tread, 1905
The Longest Journey, 1907
A Room with a View, 1908
Howards End, 1910
A Passage to India, 1924
Maurice, 1971

Best Book to Read First

A Passage to India is considered Forster's greatest accomplishment, but if you are looking for a slice of English life circa 1910, try *Howards End*.

If you asked a selection of educated English readers of fiction to pick out our most distinguished living novelist, nine out of ten, I should say, would answer E. M. Forster.

—Dame Rose Macaulay, *The Writings of E. M. Forster* (1938, reissued 1970)

Only Connect!

In 1915, Forster wrote, "My defense at the Last Judgement would be: 'I was trying to connect up and use all the fragments I was born with.'" Indeed, E. M. Forster is famous for the phrase "Only connect!" which appears in chapter 22 of *Howards End*:

[S]he might yet be able to help him to the building of the rainbow bridge that should connect the prose in us with the passion. Without it we are meaningless fragments. . . . It did not seem so difficult. . . . She would only point out the salvation that was latent in his own soul, and in the soul of every man. Only connect! That was the whole of her sermon. Only connect the prose and the passion, and both will be exalted, and human love will be seen at its height. Live in fragments no longer. . . . By quiet indications the bridge would be built and span their lives with beauty.

Dick Francis

Born
October 31, 1920, in Tenby, Pembrokeshire, southwest Wales

Full Name
Sir Richard Stanley Francis (named an Officer of the most noble Order of the British Empire in 1984)

Education
Dropped out of Maidenhead County School at age 15.

Family
Married for more than 50 years to Mary Margaret Brenchley, a former teacher and assistant stage manager; two sons: Merrick and Felix.

Home
Cayman Islands, British West Indies

Fan Mail
Dick Francis
c/o Sterling Lord Literstic
1 Madison Avenue
New York, NY 10010

Publisher
Putnam

O nce famous as the steeplechase jockey for England's Queen Mother, Dick Francis is today known worldwide for his annual forays into the realm of good versus evil, bringing the thrill of horse racing (and bestseller status) to each new tale of intrigue.

"It is fascinating to see how many completely fresh and unexpected plots he can concoct about horses," wrote Anthony Boucher in the *New York Times Book Review*. With what has been described as a Dickensian attention to detail, Francis draws on extensive research and his own experiences to craft the completely believable world his protagonists inhabit.

Though some critics have complained that Francis's plots are formulaic, many commend him for consistently bringing depth to the characters he creates. And while his works tend toward violence, "Somehow," he says, "the readers like to read about it."

Good to Know

❖ The son of a professional rider, Dick Francis got his first job at age 13, riding ponies for a circus owner. Two years later, he left school to make his debut as an amateur jockey.

❖ His first serious riding accident as a boy left him with chipped teeth and a fractured palate, jaw, and nose. Over the years, he also suffered a cracked skull and broken collarbone. "I don't subject [my characters] to anything I wouldn't put up with myself," he told the *New York Times Book Review*.

❖ Francis served as a pilot in the Royal Air Force during World War II, then returned full time to the equestrian career that would

make (and break) him.

❖ When top jockey Lord Mildmay mysteriously disappeared in 1950, Francis stepped into his stirrups. Soon, trainer Peter Cazalet had him riding for the royal family, most notably for Queen Elizabeth, the Queen Mother. He was riding her horse, Devon Loch, when it inexplicably fell at the 1956 Grand National.

❖ After another serious fall in 1957, Francis retired from race riding and began a second career writing about his experiences, starting with his autobiography, *The Sport of Queens*, and six feature stories for the *London Sunday Express*, where he served as racing correspondent until 1973.

Treatises and Treats

COMPANIONS AND BIOGRAPHIES

Twelve Englishmen of Mystery, edited by Earl F. Bargainnier (Bowling Green University Popular Press, 1984). An interesting context in which to consider this icon of suspense.

Dick Francis by Melvyn Barnes (Ungar, 1986) and *Dick Francis* by J. Madison Davis (Twayne Publishers, 1989). Both books provide detailed literary analyses of the author's works, considering such topics as horse racing in literature, the crime genre, and Francis's place in British history.

AUTOBIOGRAPHY

Of course, every Francis enthusiast worth his or her oats will want to read his debut work, *The Sport of Queens: The Autobiography of Dick Francis*. First published in 1957, it has been updated and reissued several times, most recently in 1995 (Macmillan).

Dick Francis Reading Group

members.aol.com/dfbooks

Fans call this the definitive Dick Francis site. "If you want to get into discussions and book readings and all things Dick Francis," reports one such enthusiast, "this is the site for you."

Dick Francis Book Summaries

www.primenet.com/~llsmith/francis.htm

Check here for summaries of all the novels—useful for jogging the memory of seasoned Francis fans as well as inspiring new ones.

Off to the Races

NOVELS FEATURING SID HALLEY

Odds Against, 1965

Whip Hand, 1979 (Golden Dagger and Edgar Allan Poe Awards)

Come to Grief, 1995 (Mystery Writers of America Best Novel)

NOVELS FEATURING KIT FIELDING

Break In, 1985

Bolt, 1986

OTHER NOVELS

Dead Cert, 1962

Nerve, 1964

For Kicks, 1965 (Silver Dagger Award)

Flying Finish, 1966

Blood Sport, 1967

Forfeit, 1968 (Edgar Allan Poe Award)

Enquiry, 1969

Rat Race, 1970

Bonecrack, 1971

Smokescreen, 1972

Slay-ride, 1973

Knockdown, 1974

High Stakes, 1975

In the Frame, 1976

Risk, 1977

Trial Run, 1978

Reflex, 1980

Twice Shy, 1981

Banker, 1982

The Danger, 1983

Proof, 1984

Hot Money, 1987

The Edge, 1988

Straight, 1989

Longshot, 1990

Comeback, 1991

Driving Force, 1992

Wild Horses, 1994

To the Hilt, 1996

10 Lb. Penalty, 1997

Second Wind, 1999

SHORT STIRRUPS

Short fiction is an occasional indulgence for Francis, as his 1998 story collection *Field of Thirteen* attests. His short work is also anthologized in *Winter's Crimes 5* (1973), *Stories of Crime and Detection* (1974), *Ellery Queen's Crime Wave* (1976), and *Ellery Queen's Searches and Seizures* (1977).

If You Like Dick Francis . . .

Try John Francome's *Stone Cold*, Peter Lovesey's *Bertie and the Tinman*, and J. J. Maric's *Gideon's Sport*, all of which involve horse racing and are recommended by the Mystery Guide (www.mysteryguide.com). For other sports-related mysteries, go to the Mystery Guide Web site and under "Genres," click on "Special Subjects" and then on "Sports."

You might also like the Western-style thrillers of Tony Hillerman. Like Dick Francis, Hillerman immerses his readers in a particular subculture via richly detailed prose, recounting elaborate tales through recurring characters.

Best Book to Read First

Start with *Odds Against*, the first of the novels featuring Sid Halley, a jockey whose hand is crippled in a fall, forcing him to find a new career. Or try *Dead Cert*, considered one of the classics of crime fiction.

Not to read Dick Francis because you don't like horses is like not reading Dostoyevsky because you don't like God. . . . Race tracks and God are subcultures. A writer has to have a subculture to stand upon.

—John Leonard,
New York Times

Another Year, Another Ride

Did someone say retire? Not Dick Francis. This Occidental octogenarian writes roughly a book a year. "I still find the writing grindingly hard, and I approach chapter 1 each year with deeper foreboding." Still, Francis reports a rhythm to the writing process that seems to work for each new story. With a plot sketched out by mid-July or so, he begins the six months of research that are typically required to become an expert in areas like aviation, gold mining, or photography. Wife Mary pitches in, and by January, he is ready to write. But that's hardly the home stretch. "Writing the words so as to make it easy to read is very hard work," he says. "Much harder than riding a horse."

Gabriel García Márquez

Born
March 6, 1928, in
Aracataca, Colombia,
to Gabriel Eligio García
and Luisa Santiaga
Márquez Iguaran

Education
Attended Universidad
Nacional de Colombia,
1947–48, and Univer-
sidad de Cartagena,
1948–49.

Family
Married to Mercedes
Barcha; two sons.

Home
Mexico City, Mexico

Fan Mail
Gabriel García Márquez
P.O. Box 20736
Mexico City, Mexico

Publisher
Knopf

Colombian-born writer Gabriel García Márquez has been hailed as "the poet of plebian and street life." Winner of the 1982 Nobel Prize in Literature and a seasoned journalist, García Márquez is largely responsible for opening the eyes of the world to the beauty and power of the literature of Latin America. He is best known for *One Hundred Years of Solitude*, a mythical epic of seven generations of the Buendia family living in the fictitious village of Macondo. The novel has sold more than 20 million copies and has been translated into over 30 languages. William Kennedy, writing for the *National Observer*, enthusiastically proclaimed that "*One Hundred Years of Solitude* is the first piece of literature since the Book of Genesis that should be required reading for the entire human race."

García Márquez's work, with that of other Latin American authors like Jorge Luis Borges and Alejo Carpentier, has been categorized by critics as "magical realism." In this tradition, the fantastic and supernatural exist in a world grounded in fact. It is García Márquez's journalistic background that allows him to artfully meld these elements of history and fiction into stories that cause the most timeworn skeptic to suspend disbelief. He has been compared to both Ernest Hemingway and William Faulkner, two authors whom he acknowledges as profound influences.

Like Hemingway, García Márquez began his career as a journalist. He has always been active in Latin American politics, and this is reflected in his writing—engendering controversy over the years. That García Márquez can write a political novel such as *The General in His Labyrinth* and also write the heartbreaking romantic fable, *Love in the Time of Cholera*, is a testament to his virtuosity and versatility as an artist.

Good to Know

❖ After the Cuban revolution (1956–59), García Márquez, always a committed leftist, helped found the Bogotá office of Prensa Latina, Fidel Castro's official press agency.

❖ *One Hundred Years of Solitude* came to García Márquez during a creative drought. His mind finally cleared during a drive from Mexico City to Acapulco in 1965, when inspiration came to him in great detail. Over the next year and a half he worked for eight to ten hours a day, isolating himself from his family. When he was finally finished, his wife asked him, "Did you really finish it? We owe $12,000."

❖ In October 1982, García Márquez acted as an intermediary between François Mitterand and Fidel Castro to obtain the release of the jailed Cuban poet Armando Valladares.

❖ Until Congress forced an end to the practice in 1991, the U.S. State Department maintained an immigration "blacklist" barring certain people from entering the country because of their political views. García Márquez appeared on the list along with Nobel Laureate Pablo Neruda, author Graham Greene, and actor Yves Montand.

❖ "Gabo," as he is known to his friends, purchased a failing Colombian newsmagazine in 1999. Regarding his early journalism and fiction, he once said that his news editors "complained that my style was too literary," while literary critics "complained that my style was too journalistic."

Treatises and Treats

COMPANIONS

García Márquez: The Man and His Work by Gene H. Bell-Villada (University of North Carolina Press, 1990). With its extensive notes and thorough bibliography, this book is considered a must for serious García Márquez readers. It's especially strong in probing the author's literary foundations, from Sophocles, Rabelais, and Camus to Faulkner, Kafka, and Woolf.

Gabriel García Márquez: Life, Work, and Criticism by G. R. McMurray (York Press, 1987). Another book-length treatment recommended by García Márquez scholars and general readers.

Gabriel García Márquez: Modern Critical Views, edited by Harold Bloom (Chelsea House, 1992). A collection of 18 critical essays, arranged in order of their original publication.

Gabriel García Márquez: Solitude and Solidarity by Michael Bell (St. Martin's Press, 1993). Concentrates on the later novels, including *One Hundred Years of Solitude* and *The General in His Labyrinth*. Includes a brief biography and commentary on García Márquez's fiction, which is "peculiarly elusive of interpretation."

A Study Guide to Gabriel García Márquez's **One Hundred Years of Solitude** (Time Warner Audio Books, 1994). Actor F. Murray Abraham narrates the story of the Buendia family, and the audiotape is packaged with a study guide to help you get the most out of García Márquez's most popular novel.

BEST OF THE NET
Macondo Web Site
www.rpg.net/quail/libyrinth/gabo
Criticism, photos, biography, filmography, and links to papers and essays on García Márquez and his work.

Book List

(Note: Publication dates are for the English translations.)
In Evil Hour, 1979
One Hundred Years of Solitude, 1970
The Autumn of the Patriarch, 1976
Chronicle of a Death Foretold, 1982
Love in the Time of Cholera, 1988
The General in His Labyrinth, 1990
Of Love and Other Demons, 1995
News of a Kidnapping, 1997

If You Like Gabriel García Márquez...

You might like Angela Carter's *Nights at the Circus*, Peter Carey's *Oscar and Lucinda*, and Isak Dinesen's *Out of Africa*. If you're particularly interested in Latin American writers, try Laura Esquivel's *Like Water for Chocolate*, a funny and enchanting novel, or books by Isabel Allende, Carlos Fuentes, and Mario Vargas Llosa.

Best Book to Read First

One Hundred Years of Solitude. The Great Latin American Novel. Part fantasy, part family chronicle, set in the mythical village of Macondo—a place *Time* called "a kind of tropical Yoknapatawpha County"—the novel offers a microcosm of Latin America. This is the book for which García Márquez is best known.

The Novelist and the Dictator

What do a Nobel laureate and a Cuban dictator have in common? Ernest Hemingway, for one thing. García Márquez recalls getting into Castro's car some years ago and noticing a small book bound in red leather. "It's my master, Hemingway," Castro told the writer.

This revelation probably did not surprise García Márquez, who knows Castro as a "very cultured, well-read man." In fact, García Márquez actually showed Castro the manuscript for *Chronicle of a Death Foretold*, even before he submitted it to his publisher. Castro has "a keen eye for spotting contradiction in a crime story like this," he later explained.

I'm fascinated by the relationship between literature and journalism. I began my career as a journalist in Colombia, and a reporter is something I've never stopped being. When I'm not working on fiction, I'm running around the world, practicing my craft as a reporter.

—Gabriel García Márquez, in a 1983 *Playboy* interview with Claudia Dreifus

William Gibson

Born
March 17, 1948, in
Conway, South
Carolina, to contractor
William Ford Gibson
and Otey Williams
Gibson, a homemaker

Education
University of British
Columbia, B.A., 1977

Family
Married Deborah
Thompson, a language
instructor, in 1972.
Two children: Graeme
and Claire.

Home
Vancouver, British
Columbia, Canada

Fan Mail
William Gibson
c/o Martha Millard
    Literary Agency
204 Park Avenue
Madison, NJ 07940

Publisher
Viking

William Gibson is not merely a gifted writer and the originator of a controversial science fiction sub-genre briefly called "cyberpunk." He is also a one-man cultural cottage industry—screenwriter, essayist, literary mouthpiece for a generation of technologically minded desperadoes—following a trajectory more typical of celebrity rock-and-rollers than writers.

Like rock and roll, his writing was condemned by mainstream critics as raucous and incomprehensible when it first appeared, and was passionately embraced by rebellious, cyber-age youth for the same reasons. But in other ways, Gibson's themes are quite traditional. His characters may live in the grip of dangerous, unpredictable cybernetic forces, in a world despoiled by the excesses of technological capitalism, but his narratives turn on the classic—and romantic—notion of the alienated individual fighting to prevail in a mass society.

Surprisingly, Gibson is anything but a computer geek. Yet his descriptions of what it's like to be in "cyberspace" (a term he's credited with coining), moving from one database to another in search of some piece of information, are the most intellectually and emotionally accurate that you're ever likely to encounter.

Good to Know

❖ *Neuromancer* was the first noticed and most celebrated of a wave of hard-edged anti-utopian novels that appeared in the mid-1980s, and Gibson found himself chief among the demigods of the genre. Through similarly cranky dispositions and a crafty sense of self-promotion, he and other figures embarked on collaborations over the next several years, busily constructing nests of literary conspiracies. By far the most astonishing of these is *Agrippa*, a poem by Gibson accompanied by the etchings of Dennis Ashbaugh. Until the text of the poem was posted on the Internet, it existed only as a limited edition of computer disks which, on being accessed for the first time, would erase themselves once the text was read.

❖ *The Difference Engine*, a collaboration with Bruce Sterling, shows Gibson at his most contrarian. The authors recast the 19th century as if mechanical computers had shaped Victorian England and had given it devices like airplanes and steam-powered televisions. This quaint technology ends up being no less corrupting than the scourges of Gibson's modern-era works, but he participated in *The Difference Engine* for a change of pace, and to keep his readers off-balance.

❖ Gibson is now praised for a writing style that critics once thought strange and obtuse. He told a reviewer that, far from being futuristic, the language for his first two novels came from the slang of dope-dealers and bikers in the streets of Toronto, where he was hanging out in 1969. Commentators have taken to comparing the incomprehension that readers experience in Gibson's toughest narratives to the ordinary difficulties of living in a technologically complex society.

❖ As a screenwriter Gibson has had mixed success and little notoriety. He's credited with the screenplay for *Johnny Mnemonic*, a 1995 film starring Keanu Reeves that's probably best forgotten. (It's based on the Gibson short story of the same name.) The most famous screenplay that does *not* bear his name is *Alien 3*, for which he wrote a version that the producers rejected.

❖ Gibson counts musician Lou Reed among the most influential figures in his literary life, along with William S. Burroughs and Thomas Pynchon. Of Ridley Scott's film, *Blade Runner* (the cinematic equivalent of the corrosive future that Gibson and his peers have put in books), Gibson once said that the film "looked so much like the inside of my head that I fled the theater after about 30 minutes and have never seen the rest of it."

Treatises and Treats

COMPANIONS
William Gibson by Lance Olsen (Borgo Press, 1992). Although he may be a prolific public figure, Gibson is still a cub as literary lions go. This is one of the few critically-interpretive books about his writing.

To get Gibson's friendly take on some of his peers, read his forewords to *Dhalgren* by Samuel R. Delany (University Press of New England, 1996), and, if you can find copies, *The Artificial Kid* by Bruce Sterling (Cortext, 1997) and *City Come A-Walking* by John Shirley (Eyeball Press, 1996), both recent reprints that have already gone out of print.

BEST OF THE NET
William Gibson Information Page
www.ee.oulu.fi/~thefinn/gibson
The array of Gibson and cyberpunk Web sites is dizzying, but this is the place to start. You'll find handsome reproductions of the covers of Gibson's novels and a good set of links to other Internet resources. Be sure to take a look at the one for the "alt.cyberpunk FAQ," a minutely detailed document in question-and-answer format about this thing they once called "cyberpunk."

William Gibson Bibliography/Mediagraphy
www.slip.net/~spage/gibson/biblio.htm
As thorough a listing of Gibsoniana as you could want, and much more. Useful both as a resource and a demonstration of how far things can go.

Cyberstories

THE CYBERSPACE TRILOGY
Neuromancer, 1984
Count Zero, 1986
Mona Lisa Overdrive, 1988

OTHER NOVELS
The Difference Engine (with Bruce Sterling), 1990
Virtual Light, 1993
Idoru, 1996
All Tomorrow's Parties, 1999

SHORT-STORY COLLECTION
Burning Chrome (with Bruce Sterling, John Shirley, and Michael Swanwick), 1986

If You Like William Gibson . . .

Gibson got the ball rolling with *Neuromancer*, but several other novels and short-story collections have achieved legendary status with the cyber-cognoscenti. Notable among them:

Snow Crash (Bantam Spectra, 1992) and *Cryptonomicon* (Avon, 1999), both by Neal Stephenson.

Vurt, by Jeff Noon (Crown, 1993), which treads the addiction-as-a-metaphor-for-life ground that Gibson covered in *Mona Lisa Overdrive.*

Mirrorshades, the widely praised short-story collection, edited by Bruce Sterling (Arbor House, 1986).

Best Book to Read First

Neuromancer, Gibson's debut novel, won an unprecedented number of top-tier science-fiction awards when it was published in 1984—including the Hugo, the Nebula, and the Philip K. Dick Award—and it emphatically set the tone for the profanely super-charged, techno-fright Gibson narratives to come.

The future has arrived; it's just not evenly distributed.

—William Gibson

Strange Encounters

People turn out in droves for Gibson's readings, and some are dismayed by his soft-spoken voice and decidedly bland wardrobe. His encounters with fans—who he refers to as M & Ms, short for "modems and mohawks"—have sometimes been unnerving. But nothing in his experience has been as unsettling as his time in Hollywood. "Sitting in the Polo Lounge talking to 20-year-old movie producers with money coming out of their ears–that's science fiction, boy," he once said.

William Goldman

Born
August 12, 1931, in Chicago, Illinois, to businessman Maurice Goldman and home-maker Marion Weil Goldman

Pseudonyms
Harry Longbaugh (*No Way to Treat a Lady*) and S. Morgenstern (*The Princess Bride* and *The Silent Gondoliers*)

Education
Oberlin College, B.A., 1952; Columbia University, M.A., 1956

Family
Married Ilene Jones in 1961; divorced in 1988. Two daughters: Jenny Rebecca and Susanna.

Home
An apartment on East 77th Street in New York City

Fan Mail
William Goldman c/o Morton Janklow Associates 598 Madison Avenue New York, NY 10022

Publishers
Ballantine
Pantheon

William Goldman is every aspiring fiction writer's idol. He paid his dues as a serious novelist and wrote some truly memorable books, including *Soldier in the Rain* and *The Temple of Gold*. But he realized early on that if you hope to make a living writing fiction, it's a lot easier to do so writing movies than novels. And in truth, Goldman is "one of only a handful of earthlings who can write screenplays and novels—and excel at both." (*Chicago Tribune Book World*).

Unfortunately, it is also fair to say that writing for Hollywood effectively cut off and cauterized any impulse to write serious fiction ever again. Indeed, starting in the mid-1970s, many of Goldman's books appear to have been conceived as screenplays and then fleshed out into novels. Whatever the reason, with the exception of *The Silent Gondoliers* (1983), a fable written under the pseudonym S. Morgenstern, none of the novels written after *Marathon Man* (1975) are as memorable as his earlier work.

Not that he doesn't keep you turning the pages in *all* of his books (fiction and nonfiction alike). Goldman is a masterful storyteller. Bedtime story or barroom story, it doesn't matter. He shoots from the hip and onto the page, crafting deceptively casual sentences and crackling dialogue that draw you in and make you want to hear more. Yes, *hear* more. Goldman's real secret may be his narrative voice. In all of his books, the attitude, the humor, and the reassuring confidence of his storytellers make you want to hear more of what this writer has to say.

Good to Know

❖ Goldman's older brother James, who died in 1998, was an acclaimed novelist and playwright. Remembered primarily for his Oscar-winning adaptation of his play, *The Lion in Winter*, James Goldman also wrote *Robin and Marian*, the wonderful 1976 film starring Audrey Hepburn as Maid Marian and Sean Connery as an aging Robin Hood who returns from the Crusades to find that life has passed him by. The Goldman brothers collaborated on a play, *Blood, Sweat, and Stanley Poole* (1961), and the book for a musical aptly titled *A Family Affair* (1962).

❖ The screenwriter for *Butch Cassidy and the Sundance Kid*, Goldman was paid $400,000 for the script in 1968—the highest amount ever paid up until then. The film grossed $100 million, became the namesake for Robert Redford's annual independent film festival in Utah, and led to two sequels that Goldman had nothing to do with.

❖ In addition to *Butch Cassidy*, Goldman wrote the screenplays for more than a dozen other movies, including *Harper* (1966), *The Stepford Wives* (1974), *The Great Waldo Pepper* (1975), *All the President's Men* (1976), *Marathon Man* (1976), *The Princess Bride* (1987), *Misery* (1990), and *The General's Daughter* (1999).

❖ Goldman has also doctored numerous scripts, rewriting them without receiving official credit. Among these are Arnold Schwarzenegger's ill-fated *The Last Action Hero*, John Cleese's madcap zoo comedy *Fierce Creatures*, and a draft of *Mission Impossible II*.

❖ He leaves his Manhattan apartment in the morning and writes in a nearby office. At around 5:00 P.M., he's more than happy to stop writing, leave the office, and enjoy the rest of the day. "The sooner I'm done, the sooner I can go to the movies," he admits.

❖ After the breakup of his 27-year marriage, Goldman landed two gigs most middle-aged men would kill for. He became the only man ever to judge both the Cannes Film Festival and the Miss America Pageant in the same year, spending three weeks surrounded by beautiful women on the exotic beaches of the French Riviera and on the not-so-exotic beaches of Atlantic City. He documented his experiences in *Hype and Glory*.

❖ Dig out those first editions! Prices vary with condition, but a first edition of *Marathon Man* can fetch as much as $75, while *The Princess Bride* may sell for well over $500. Two good places to check for Goldman titles and prices: Alibris (www.alibris.com) and Bibliofind (www.bibliofind.com).

Treatises and Treats

COMPANIONS

William Goldman by Richard Andersen (Twayne, 1979). Criticism, interpretation, and a bibliography covering Goldman's early works. Now out of print, but available from used booksellers and libraries.

BEST OF THE NET

The Princess Bride, 25th Anniversary Page
www.randomhouse.com/delrey/promo/
    princessbride

While there are countless Web sites dedicated to Goldman's novels and films, there are few that feature any substantial information about the author himself. Random House's page commemorating the 25th anniversary of *The Princess Bride* is among the better offerings. It includes a biography, Goldman's new introduction to the book, and information about the sequel, *Buttercup's Baby*.

Best Reads

NOVELS

The Temple of Gold, 1957
Soldier in the Rain, 1960
Boys and Girls Together, 1964
The Thing of It Is…, 1967
The Princess Bride, 1973
Marathon Man, 1975
The Silent Gondoliers, 1983

NONFICTION

The Season: A Candid Look at Broadway, 1969
Adventures in the Screen Trade: A Personal View of Hollywood and Screenwriting, 1983
Hype and Glory, 1990
Which Lie Did I Tell: More Adventures in the Screen Trade, 2000

Best Book to Read First

Boys and Girls Together, an incredibly rich, funny, sad novel with indelible characters, is Goldman at his best as a novelist. From its opening sentence, "Aaron would not come out," to its final sentence, "Aaron entered into agony," it is a stunning performance.

No one has ever heard me use the word "good" about any of my screenplays. I would never attribute that kind of quality—good, bad, or beautiful—to a screenplay. A screenplay is a piece of carpentry, and except in the case of Ingmar Bergman, it's not an art, it's a craft. And you want to be as good as you can at your craft, and you want to give them what they need within the limits of your talents—and the only reason I am "hot" now has nothing to do with the quality of the films that I have been involved with. It has to do with two things: some of the films have been successful, but more important, they have been made.

—William Goldman, Esquire (October 1981)

Dad's Copy

*T*he Princess Bride was almost *not* a movie. After the book's publication in 1973, the film rights bounced from studio to studio, frustrating Goldman so much that he bought them back with his own money. Little did he know what wheels had been set in motion years earlier.

While working on his 1969 book about Broadway, *The Season*, Goldman came to admire the play *Something Different* and its author, Carl Reiner. He sent a complimentary copy of *The Season* to Reiner, and continued to send copies of his books to the Reiner home for years. One of those books was *The Princess Bride*, which became a favorite of Reiner's son, Rob. And it was Rob Reiner who in 1986 put the project on its feet and ended up directing *The Princess Bride*, starring Cary Elwes, Robin Wright Penn, Mandy Patinkin, Chris Sarandon, Christopher Guest, Wallace Shawn, and the late André the Giant as Fezzik, Goldman's favorite character.

Born
April 24, 1940, in
Louisville, Kentucky

Education
University of Louisville,
1961, B.A. in English
Literature

Family
Married third husband,
Steven F. Humphrey, in
1978. Three children
from her first two
marriages and two
grandchildren,
including one named
Kinsey.

Homes
A four-and-a-half-acre
estate in Montecito,
California, with pool,
croquet court, putting
green, and elaborate
gardens. Also main-
tains a home in
Louisville, Kentucky.

Fan Mail
suegrafton@fsb.
superlink.net

Publishers
Putnam
Henry Holt

Sue Grafton

Sue Grafton is the author of the well-known "alphabet" mystery series that begins with *"A" Is for Alibi*. Her heroine is California-based private investigator Kinsey Millhone, a character that *Newsweek* (June 7, 1982) described as a "thoroughly up-to-date, feminine version of Philip Marlowe, Raymond Chandler's hard-boiled hero." That she is. But plunking Marlowe down in today's Santa Barbara and forcing him to deal with the complexities of modern life wouldn't capture the essence of Kinsey Millhone.

That essence is a female sensibility that women will identify with and men will find fascinating. Kinsey notices things that an equally hard-boiled male detective would completely miss. Whether you're a mystery fan or not, if you have yet to discover Sue Grafton, you're in for a real treat.

Good to Know

❖ Grafton novels have sold over 2 million copies in hardback and over 16 million in paperback in the U.S. alone. Her books are published in 28 other countries and have been translated into 26 languages.

❖ She wrote her first novel at 22, but it never saw the light of day—with good reason, according to Grafton. Writing at night after the kids were asleep, working days as a medical secretary, she wrote and sold *Keziah Dane* (1967) and *The Lolly-Madonna War* (1969). But *"A" Is for Alibi* (1982) really launched her career.

❖ Grafton spent 15 years writing TV and movie screenplays, sometimes in collaboration with husband Steven F. Humphrey. Joint credits include Agatha Christie adaptations:

A Caribbean Mystery and *Sparkling Cyanide*.

❖ Grafton is the granddaughter of Presbyterian missionaries and the daughter of the late C. W. Grafton, a Kentucky municipal-bond attorney who wrote mysteries in his spare time.

❖ Where did the idea for the alphabet series come from? In an interview posted at her Web site, Grafton says, "I was always fascinated by mysteries that had linking or related titles. I knew about John D. MacDonald, whose titles were connected through color, and Harry Kemelman, who joined his titles by the days of the week. One day I was reading *The Gashly-crumb Tinies*, a book of cartoons by Edward Gorey [in which] little Victorian children [are] 'done in' by various means...'A is for Amy who fell down the stairs...B is for Basil assaulted by Bears...C is for Clara who wasted away,' etc.

"A cartoon lightbulb formed above my head and I thought to myself, 'Gee, why couldn't you do a series of novels based on the alphabet?' At that point, I sat down and made an alphabetical list of all the crime-related words I could think of. So here I am now, nearly half-way through, probably tied up until the year 2015 or so."

❖ Grafton hasn't yet settled on titles for *P* through *Y* in the alphabet series, but she told *Publishers Weekly* in a 1998 interview that the last book will be called *"Z" Is for Zero*.

Treatises and Treats

COMPANIONS
"G" Is for Grafton: The World of Kinsey Millhone by Natalie Hevener Kaufman and Carol Kay (Henry Holt, 1997). Sue Grafton's biography has yet to be written. But this guide

to the fictional universe of Kinsey Millhone—complete with maps, floor plans, photos, time lines, and case logs—presents a wealth of biographical information about Kinsey's creator. Written with Grafton's cooperation, the book includes an essay on the role she has played in the development of the detective novel. One caveat: If you plan to read the complete alphabet series but haven't done so yet, you may want to hold off reading this book in order to avoid spoilers.

Kinsey and Me: A Collection of Short Stories by Sue Grafton (Bench Press, 1992). Limited-edition collection of eight stories, selected by husband Steven Humphrey and published in hardcover as a gift for his wife. Includes "The Parker Shotgun" (Anthony Award) and "A Poison That Leaves No Trace" (American Mystery Award). For a signed copy from the first printing of 350, send $250 (plus $3.95 for shipping and 7.75% California sales tax) to Bench Press, P.O. Box 50505, Santa Barbara, CA 93150.

BEST OF THE NET
Sue Grafton Web Site
www.suegrafton.com
A truly superb Web site—interviews, sample chapters, Kinsey Millhone's favorite foods, recipes, bios, photos, author tour schedule, and more. Click on "Press Room" for information on signing up for the Sue Grafton Mailing List.

Grafton A–O

The Kinsey Millhone alphabet series:

"A" Is for Alibi, 1982
   (Mysterious Stranger Award)
"B" Is for Burglar, 1985
   (Shamus and Anthony Awards)
"C" Is for Corpse, 1986
   (Anthony Award)
"D" Is for Deadbeat, 1987
"E" Is for Evidence, 1988
"F" Is for Fugitive, 1989
"G" Is for Gumshoe, 1990
"H" Is for Homicide, 1991
"I" Is for Innocent, 1992
"J" Is for Judgement, 1993
"K" Is for Killer, 1994
"L" Is for Lawless, 1995.

"M" Is for Malice, 1996.
"N" Is for Noose, 1998.
"O" Is for Outlaw, 1999

If You Like Sue Grafton . . .

Try Sara Paretsky's *Burn Marks*, one of several books in the V. I. Warshawski series. Like Kinsey Millhone, Paretsky's freelance P. I. is extremely popular—so much so that Kathleen Turner agreed to play the part in the 1991 movie *V. I. Warshawski.*

For a British twist, try Liza Cody's novels featuring the no-nonsense P. I., Anna Lee. And don't miss *An Unsuitable Job for a Woman* by P. D. James, the grandmother of the genre.

Other authors recommended by Grafton fans include Linda Barnes, Linda Grant, Karen Kijewski, Margaret Maron, Lia Matera, Marcia Muller, Gilliam Slovo, Julie Smith, and Susan Steiner.

Or try some of Grafton's favorite books. Her top reads, according to the 1996 edition of *The Book Lover's Calendar* (Workman), include:
Cat Chaser by Elmore Leonard
High Window by Raymond Chandler
Drowning Pool by Ross Macdonald
Double Indemnity by James M. Cain
Beyond a Reasonable Doubt by her father,
   C. W. Grafton

Best Book to Read First

Each book in the alphabet series stands on its own, but you'll have an even richer experience if you read them in order. So start with *A Is for Alibi.*

Why Kinsey Won't Go Hollywood

I'm adamant about not surrendering control of Kinsey's character or the books. I used to picture Debra Winger in the role, but . . . the truth is, I don't want an actress's face superimposed on Kinsey's . . . Books are like movies of the mind and it's better to leave Kinsey where she is. Hollywood can't believe writers aren't panting for the money and the recognition—the glamour of film—but I wrote in Hollywood for 15 years and believe me, I'm cured. I know how the game is played and it's not one I admire. Because of Kinsey, I can afford to have integrity.

[Source: Sue Grafton Web site]

John Grisham

Born
February 8, 1955, in
Jonesboro, Arkansas,
the son of a construc-
tion worker and a
homemaker

Education
Mississippi State, B.S.
in accounting, 1977;
law degree from
University of Missis-
sippi, 1981

Family
Married Renee Jones
in 1981. They have
two children, a boy and
a girl.

Homes
Oxford, Mississippi,
and Albemarle County,
Virginia

Fan Mail
John Grisham
P.O. Box 1780
Oxford, MS 38655

Publisher
Doubleday

A former criminal attorney, John Grisham is the king of legal-thriller novels. From the time he wrote his first novel, inspired by a heart-breaking courtroom scene he had witnessed in which a 12-year-old girl testified against her rapist, Grisham has drawn on his legal background to write one successful page turner after another. More than 60 million Grisham books are in print worldwide.

Grisham's novels are masterpieces of conspiracy, duplicity, and high-level corruption. Yet, while loved by his fans for his compelling, complex, and thrilling narratives, critics regularly lament his formulaic writing style and one-dimensional characters. Grisham admits that his early novels were based on a singular premise: entangling an innocent person in a conspiracy and then extracting them from it. However, he doesn't apologize for sticking to a formula that works. "I've succeeded in spite of [my critics]," Grisham once told Mel Gussow of the *New York Times*.

Formulaic or not, Grisham's novels sell like nobody's business. *The Firm*, his blockbuster second novel, gave Grisham the financial freedom to quit his law practice and work full-time as a novelist. His fans have responded by making him a millionaire several times over in the years since.

Good to Know

❖ Grisham practiced criminal and civil law in Southaven, Mississippi. He won a seat in the Mississippi legislature in 1983, just two years out of law school, and was re-elected in 1987. But he resigned in 1990 out of frustration with the slow pace of government, particularly regarding educational reform.

❖ Finding an agent and publisher for his first novel, *A Time to Kill,* wasn't easy. It eventually sold for $15,000 to Wynwood Press, which printed 5,000 copies. (Grisham himself bought 1,000 of them to sell at garden club meetings and to give to friends.) After the success of *The Firm*, Wynwood reissued *A Time to Kill*, which went on to spend 80 weeks on the bestseller lists. There are now 8.6 million copies in print and first editions are worth upwards of $3,900.

❖ In writing his second novel, *The Firm*, Grisham followed *Writer's Digest* guidelines for plotting a suspense novel. The strategy worked: two weeks before selling the manuscript to Doubleday (which had previously rejected *A Time to Kill*), a bootlegged copy prompted Paramount to offer Grisham $600,000 for the film rights.

❖ Although he stopped practicing law in 1991, Grisham returned to the courtroom in 1996 to honor a previous commitment. He won his largest verdict ever ($683,500) for the family of a railroad brakeman who had been killed on the job. Clearly the man is more than a "paper" lawyer.

❖ Grisham produces a new novel every spring, and he writes each in a remarkably short period of time. (*The Pelican Brief*, for example, took only 100 days to complete.) His earnings are a closely guarded secret, but in 1998, *Publishers Weekly* estimated the worldwide gross of his novels and their spinoffs, including move rights, at more than $1 billion.

❖ Other writings include screenplays, like *The Gingerbread Man*, which has been made into a Robert Altman film featuring Kenneth Branagh (doing a convincing Southern accent) and an all-star cast.

❖ Grisham devotes considerable time to charitable causes, church activities, and to one of his greatest passions—baseball. He serves as a local Little League coach and commissioner, regularly playing on one of six ball fields he had built on his property in Albemarle County, Virginia.

Treatises and Treats

COMPANIONS

John Grisham: A Critical Companion by Mary Beth Pringle (Greenwood, 1997). Biographical information, a discussion of the legal thriller and Grisham's contributions to the genre, and individual chapters on the novels themselves.

GRISHAM ON TAPE

The Testament, unabridged and read by actor Frank Muller (BDD Audio, 1999). Muller, whose television credits include *Law and Order*, *Harry and the Hendersons*, and *All My Children*, narrates Grisham's tenth novel about a disillusioned litigator, an oddball billionaire, and a heroic female. Considered the leading narrator in the industry, Muller is also the reader for *The Street Lawyer*, *The Partner*, *The Runaway Jury*, and *The Rainmaker*.

BEST OF THE NET

John Grisham Web Site
www.jgrisham.com
The official site, created and maintained by Doubleday. (Says Grisham, "Stephen King has one, so I thought I'd better keep up with the competition.") Fans can check here for descriptions of all the novels, cover art, and excerpts. There's also a trivia quiz to test your knowledge of Grisham characters and plot lines, and a survey that you can submit in exchange for a chance to win a signed, leatherbound edition of Grisham's latest novel.

The Mississippi Writers Page
www.olemiss.edu/depts/english/ms-writers
Another good source of Grisham information, this site offers an especially good bibliography and links to other Internet resources.

Grisham's Docket

A Time to Kill, 1989
The Firm, 1991
The Pelican Brief, 1992
The Client, 1993
The Chamber, 1994
The Rainmaker, 1995
The Runaway Jury, 1996
The Partner, 1997
The Street Lawyer, 1998
The Testament, 1999
The Brethren, 2000

If You Like John Grisham . . .

Try the 1998 short-story anthology, *Legal Briefs: Stories by Today's Best Thriller Writers*, edited by William Bernhardt. You might also like the novels of David Baldacci, Patricia D. Benke, Joseph T. Klempner, Phillip M. Margolin, Steven Martini, Brad Meltzer, Richard North Patterson, Scott Turow, and Judith Van Gieson.

Also consider *Mistaken Identity* and other books by Lisa Scottoline (rhymes with *linguine*). An expert tale-teller, Scottoline has been described as "the distaff Grisham," only funnier.

Best Book to Read First

Fans will tell you that *any* Grisham book is a good first book to read, but you might want to start with his second novel, *The Firm,* since it was the one that began the Grisham phenomenon.

I'm not going to write about sex because my mother is still alive, and my wife says I don't know anything about it.

—John Grisham's response to Bryant Gumbel on the *Today Show,* when asked how *The Firm* and *The Pelican Brief* could have sold 46 million copies without including sex scenes

The Grisham Influence

Doubleday's yearly spring publication of the newest John Grisham novel has a tremendous influence on the selling strategies of other top publishers, many of whom shape their seasons around the Grisham release to avoid head-to-head competition. If Doubleday's schedule slips, watch out!

One year, a late Grisham release entered the bookstores just before Mother's Day—the traditional selling season for mystery author Mary Higgins Clark. When asked by her publisher if she wanted to postpone her release, Clark declined, knowing that her fans expected to see her book on the shelves at that time of year. The decision cost her the top spot on most of that season's bestseller lists.

Dashiell Hammett

Born
May 27, 1894, in St.
Mary, Maryland, to
Richard Thomas
Hammett and Annie
Bond Hammett

Full Name
Samuel Dashiell
Hammett

Education
Attended Baltimore
Polytechnic Institute.

Family
Married in 1921 to
Josephine Dolan, with
whom he had two
daughters. Divorced in
1937.

Home
Katonah, New York,
and New York City

Died
January 10, 1961, in
New York of lung
cancer, after a lifetime
of heavy smoking and
hard drinking

Publishers
Knopf
Library of America
Vintage

Erle Stanley Gardner once said of Dashiell Hammett, "I think of all the early pulp writers who contributed to the new format of the detective story, the word 'genius' was more nearly applicable to Hammett than to any of the rest." Hammett was the first major writer of crime fiction to tell his stories in the first person, through the eyes of his detectives. By incorporating criminal argot and using his superb skill at characterization, Hammett brought a new level of realism to the genre. His detectives rely on street smarts and attitude to get them out of tough situations, rather than the muscle and firepower used by their opponents. Characters, such as the unnamed Continental Op, Sam Spade, and Nick Charles, live according to a strict code of behavior, lone detectives trying to make things right in a corrupt world.

Thirty-two of Hammett's short stories were published in *Black Mask* magazine between 1923 and 1927. The stories were so good that the editors encouraged him to write longer fiction, and in November 1927, the magazine published the first installment of the four-part *Red Harvest*, Hammett's first novel. After the publication of *The Thin Man* in 1934, he stopped writing novels and turned to Hollywood. This essentially marked the end of his creative output. The last sentence he wrote reads: "If you are tired you ought to rest, I think, and not try to fool yourself or your customers with colored bubbles."

Good to Know

❖ Hammett worked as an operative for the Pinkerton detective agency between 1915 and 1922. During his career, he was employed by the defense during the Fatty Arbuckle rape-and-murder trial. He also foiled a heist of $125,000 in gold when he discovered the booty stuffed down the smokestack of a ship about to embark for Australia.

❖ Looking lean and stylish, Hammett's full-length photo on the cover of his novel, *The Thin Man*, caused confusion about who "the thin man" really was. In the story, it is the thin man's disappearance that is at the heart of the mystery, but the cover photo and the films starring William Powell and Myrna Loy encouraged people to identify the thin man with the boozed up, sophisticated detective Nick Charles, and ultimately with Hammett himself.

❖ In 1951, after refusing to testify regarding bail violation by 11 members of the Communist Party, Hammett was sentenced to six months in jail. During that time, the IRS filed a $100,000 tax-lien against him. A $140,000 lien followed in 1957. Whether he owed the money or not, given what is now known about the period, there can be little doubt that much of this was politically motivated.

❖ In 1930, while still a married man, Hammett fell in love with playwright Lillian Hellman. It was a tempestuous relationship that lasted until his death in 1961. Hellman was the inspiration for the character of Nora Charles. But she clearly abandoned him when he was jailed. Fearing that her own career would be ruined by an association with a known Communist, she decamped to London.

Treatises and Treats

COMPANIONS

Shadow Man: The Life of Dashiell Hammett by Richard Layman (Harcourt, 1981). A highly informative and entertaining biography, with a complete bibliography of Hammett's writings.

Hellman and Hammett by Joan Mellen (HarperCollins, 1996). With unprecedented access to Hellman's personal papers and closest friends, the author of this book provides a fascinating account of the passionate and volatile relationship of two of this century's most eccentric writers. The book also includes 32 pages of photos.

The Critical Response to Dashiell Hammett, edited by Christopher Metress (Greenwood Press, 1994). Includes reviews and commentary of Hammett's novels of the 1920s and 1930s, as well as recent scholarly essays. For a better understanding of the contributions of Hammett's writing to twentieth-century literature, start with this book.

BEST OF THE NET

The Hammett List

www.cigarsmokers.com/hammett
This is the best place to begin your online search for information on Dashiell Hammett. You'll find scores of links to Hammett resources on the Web—plot summaries, bibliographies, movie adaptations, and so forth. You can also sign up for a Hammett mailing list.

Book List

NOVELS

Red Harvest, 1929
The Dain Curse, 1929
The Maltese Falcon, 1930
The Glass Key, 1931
The Thin Man, 1934

SHORT-STORY COLLECTIONS

The Big Knockover: Selected Stories and Short Novels, edited by Lillian Hellman (1966)
The Continental Op, edited by Steven Marcus (1974)

Nightmare Town, edited by Kirby McCauley, Martin Harry Greenberg, and Edward Gorman (Knopf, 1999). Twenty stories and other items that have been kept out of print for the last 50 years due to copyright complications.

If You Like Dashiell Hammett . . .

Try Ross Macdonald. When he died in 1983, Macdonald was the most widely known and respected crime-fiction writer in America. His private investigator, Lew Archer, is an updated version of the hard-boiled detective of the original school: a little more introspective, but the same cynical dreamer trying to make right out of wrong.

Raymond Chandler (creator of Philip Marlowe) is also a must-read for any fan of the genre. Another good choice is James M. Cain (*Double Indemnity*, *Mildred Pierce*, *The Postman Always Rings Twice*). And, of course, Mickey Spillane.

Best Book to Read First

The Maltese Falcon, which introduces Sam Spade, the tough-talking, hard-bitten detective who has served as the paradigm for hard-boiled characters (with a soft spot, of course) ever since. In 1930, W. R. Brooks said that the *Maltese Falcon* "is not only probably the best detective story we have ever read, it is an exceedingly well written book." The classic screen version is John Huston's 1941 film starring Humphrey Bogart.

The slang in use among criminals is for the most part a conscious, artificial growth, designed more to confuse outsiders than for any other purpose, but sometimes it is singularly expressive...

—Dashiell Hammett, "From the Memoirs of a Private Detective," 1923

What's in a Name?

Poisonville, The Seventeenth Murder, Murder Plus, The Wilson Matter, The City of Death, The Cleansing of Poisonville, The Black City—these were all proposed titles for Dashiell Hammett's first novel, all of them rejected by publisher Alfred Knopf, who finally approved calling the book *Red Harvest*.

Knopf also groused about the title Hammett came up with for his third novel, saying, "Whenever people can't pronounce a title or an author's name, they are, more than you would think, too shy to go into a bookstore and try." But Hammett won out in the end, and the book was published as *The Maltese Falcon*.

Thomas Harris

Born
Circa 1940 in Jackson, Mississippi, to William Thomas Harris, an electrical engineer and farmer, and Polly Harris, a high school chemistry and biology teacher

Education
Baylor University, B.A., 1964

Family
Married a fellow Baylor student with whom he has a daughter, Anne, who works for his publisher. Divorced in the 1960s. Has lived with Pace Barnes for the last 20 years. She used to work in publishing and is reportedly as outgoing as he is shy.

Home
Sag Harbor, New York, and Miami Beach, Florida

Fan Mail
Thomas Harris
c/o Morton L. Janklow
598 Madison Avenue
New York, NY 10022

Publisher
Delacorte

Thomas Harris's first novel, *Black Sunday* (1975), placed him firmly on the bestseller list, and he has kept readers up late at night ever since. A former crime reporter, Harris's countless hours of research allow him to imbue his tales of madmen and murder with a spine-tingling authenticity. Critics have praised his intelligent and tasteful treatment of gruesome subjects as well as his skilled plotting and characterization.

Red Dragon (1981) tells the story of the FBI's search for a deformed murderer and introduces Harris's best-known character, Dr. Hannibal "The Cannibal" Lecter. (The movie version was called *Manhunter*, a 1986 film directed by Michael Mann.) A brilliant but deranged psychopathic killer with a taste for human flesh, Lecter turns up again in what many consider a masterpiece of suspense, *The Silence of the Lambs*. Selling over 5 million copies in paperback, the book enabled Harris to negotiate a $5.2 million deal for his next two books. *Hannibal*, the long-awaited follow-up to *Silence of the Lambs*, was published in 1999.

Whereas *Silence* was an intense, realistic thriller—a true exploration of evil—some feel that the tone of *Hannibal* is almost campy. There are probably just as many, however, who love the book, including Stephen King, who calls it "the third and most satisfying part of one very long and scary ride through the haunted palace of abnormal psychiatry."

Good to Know

❖ Harris's intimate knowledge of the criminal mind comes from his six years as a general-assignment reporter for the Associated Press in New York, where he covered the crime beat daily. He has also spent time at the FBI's Behavioral Science Unit in Quantico and has interviewed serial killer Ted Bundy in the course of researching his novels.

❖ *The Silence of the Lambs* became the third movie in history to claim the top five Academy Awards: Best Actor (Anthony Hopkins), Best Actress (Jodie Foster), Best Screenplay (Ted Tally), Best Director (Jonathan Demme), and Best Picture. Harris never actually saw the movie in a theater.

❖ *Hannibal* was the first book in a two-book deal that stipulates there's to be no editing of Harris's manuscripts. Short-circuiting the editorial process speeds up the production cycle, so the manuscript Harris delivered to the publisher in March 1999 appeared in bookstores only four months later. The first printing was 1.3 million copies.

❖ Harris hasn't granted an interview in 20 years, though he will pose for a photograph or two. *Hannibal* was launched with no publicity tour or book signings, but that didn't keep it from being the hottest book on Amazon.com the week before its publication date. Some publishers even rescheduled their 1999 summer books so that they wouldn't be lost in the excitement over *Hannibal*.

❖ For a highly successful author, Harris lives a fairly quiet life. His only apparent luxuries are his summer and winter homes in Sag Harbor and Miami. He also he owns a Jaguar and a Porsche.

❖ One of his passions is gourmet food. But Harris doesn't have to go to a four-star restaurant when he wants a sumptuous meal: he has taken cooking lessons at the renowned Le Cordon Bleu culinary school in Paris.

❖ Harris was burned out of the writing studio above Marty's barbershop in Sag Harbor where he wrote *Silence of the Lambs*. But maybe he needed a change of scenery, anyway. The fire occurred a few years after he had signed his million-dollar book deal, and he still hadn't presented his publisher with anything. In 1998 he sequestered himself somewhere in Paris and finally completed the manuscript for *Hannibal*.

Treatises and Treats

BEST OF THE NET

Official Thomas Harris Web Site
www.thomasharris.com
Includes excerpts from all four of Harris's books, and, as a bonus, you can listen to the author read a chapter from his latest, *Hannibal*. It is the only Web site with Harris's seal of approval.

Mississippi Writers Page
www.olemiss.edu/depts/english/
   ms-writers/dir/harris_thomas
Offers what biographical information is known about Thomas Harris, lists selected book reviews and critical commentary on his work, and provides links to other Internet resources, like the Dr. Hannibal Lecter Fan Club.

Page Turners

Black Sunday, 1975
Red Dragon, 1981
The Silence of the Lambs, 1988
Hannibal, 1999

If You Like Thomas Harris...

You might also like books by John Sandford (*Certain Prey* and others featuring Minneapolis detective Lucas Davenport). Other possibilities include Caleb Carr, Jonathan Kellerman, and Andrew Vachss.

Best Book to Read First

The Silence of the Lambs, Harris's most popular book, brings together Dr. Hannibal Lecter—the brilliant madman, serial killer, and partaker of human flesh—and FBI trainee Clarice Starling. Lecter agrees to help Clarice track down a serial murderer named Buffalo Bill (who is killing young women in order to use their skin to make a coat) in exchange for information about herself. According to the *Arizona Republic*, Hannibal Lecter, with Dracula and the shark from *Jaws*, is among the ten scariest literary monsters of all time.

Naked Came the Goodyear Blimp

Thomas Harris's first book, *Black Sunday*, was actually a collaborative effort. In the early 1970s, *Naked Came the Stranger*, a sexy novel by one "Penelope Ashe," appeared on the scene. As insiders knew, however, Ms. Ashe was actually a group of some 25 *Newsday* reporters, who wrote the novel in a kind of literary relay race, each person adding chapters and handing off the script to the next writer.

The book became a mini-sensation, and Harris and fellow reporters Sam Maull and Dick Riley, who were working the four-to-midnight shift at AP at the time, said, "Hell, we can do that." So they came up with the idea of using the Goodyear Blimp as the vehicle for an attempted terrorist bombing of the Super Bowl, wiping out 100,000 spectators—including the president of the United States. (Directed by John Frankenheimer, the 1977 movie stars Robert Shaw and Bruce Dern.)

In the beginning, all three did the research and the writing together, but eventually Harris took over the project. When the book was sold to Putnam, Harris, always the Southern gentleman, split the advance three ways. Then Harris split for bestsellerdom. After publication of *Black Sunday*, he was able to devote himself to writing full-time.

Harris is not for all people of course—I don't think many of the Danielle Steel crowd will be rushing out to buy the book in which one character is eaten from the inside out by a ravenous moray eel—but for those who like what Harris can do so brilliantly, no book report is required.

—Stephen King on *Hannibal*

Robert A. Heinlein

Born
July 7, 1907, in Butler, Missouri, one of seven children of Rex Ivar Heinlein, an accountant, and Bam Lyle Heinlein

Full Name
Robert Anson Heinlein (rhymes with "fine line")

Education
Graduate of U.S. Naval Academy, 1929; attended University of California, Los Angeles, 1934, for graduate study in physics and mathematics.

Family
First marriage to Leslyn MacDonald ended in divorce in 1947. Married Virginia ("Ginny") Doris Gerstenfeld, 1948.

Died
May 8, 1988, in Carmel, California, of emphysema and related disabilities. His ashes were scattered from the stern of a Navy warship near "Bonny Doon," his Santa Cruz home of 20 years.

Publisher
Putnam

Heinlein began writing science fiction stories at precisely the moment that John W. Campbell Jr. (editor of *Astounding Science Fiction* magazine) had begun a program to lift the genre out of the morass of space opera and turn it into genuine, thought-provoking literature. The result was the Golden Age of Science Fiction. Heinlein so completely fit the bill that Campbell would run two or more of his stories in each issue, assigning pseudonyms to conceal the fact that so many stories were written by the author who became known as "the dean of science fiction."

In retrospect, Heinlein's voice is so distinctive that it's hard to imagine anyone reading a story credited to "Anson MacDonald" and not seeing the similarity between it and a Heinlein-signed story. (The identity of Anson MacDonald was actually one of the SF world's most open secrets.) After all, Heinlein was not a literary stylist. Most of his work features the same three characters: the wise old man; the smart, uninhibited young woman; and the big lunk who excels when physical courage is called for. Often, the lunk and the woman end up signing a marriage contract, renewable after five years, and set out to use their respective skills and talents to carve out a life for themselves.

A marriage with an expiration date and renewable if both parties agree? That's pure Heinlein. Or consider: What would society be like if every adult were required to carry a sidearm and take training in how to use it? What if everything we've always thought of as "magic" turned out to be solid science? What if slavery reappeared as the planets are colonized? Heinlein uses his stock characters—and their snappy dialogue—to present ideas like these. The science is always strong, and the logic, once you grant the premise, is rigorously consistent.

Just about everything Heinlein wrote from 1940 through 1970 is worth reading, even the "juveniles" he produced for Scribner's during the 1940s and '50s. After about 1970, however, many of his books became self-indulgent, preachy, and poorly organized. This was partially due to failing health. But the power of the Heinlein name—*Stranger in a Strange Land* had sold over 3 million copies—unquestionably permitted the publication of even unedited material, and in hardback books, no less.

Good to Know

❖ Heinlein had planned a naval career. "I write stories for money," he told an interviewer. "What I *wanted* to be was an admiral." After serving on the *Lexington*, he was transferred to a destroyer (U.S.S. *Roper*), where he contracted tuberculosis in 1934. Eventually cured, he was mustered out as "totally and permanently disabled" and given a small pension.

❖ A variety of civilian activities followed, including operating a silver mine and running unsuccessfully for the California State Assembly (as a Democrat). Broke, married, and struggling with a mortgage, he saw an announcement of a "short-story contest" (actually an on-going talent search) in *Thrilling Wonder Stories*. He produced "Life-Line" in four days in April 1939 and submitted it, not to *TWS*, which he assumed would be swamped, but to John Campbell at *Astounding Science Fiction*. Campbell paid him

$70—$20 more than the Grand Prize for the *TWS* contest. "And there was never a chance that I would ever again look for honest work," he later wrote.

❖ Heinlein has added at least three terms to the English language: Grok, waldo, and puppet masters. *Grok*, a Martian word from *Stranger in a Strange Land*, means to completely and thoroughly understand something or someone as if you were one with it or them. Today's remote control devices used to manipulate radioactive material and other objects safely are called *waldoes* because of "Waldo and Magic, Inc.," the 1950 Heinlein story in which they were first conceived. *Puppet masters* comes from the 1951 novel, later made into a movie of the same name starring Donald Sutherland (1994).

❖ With the possible exception of Isaac Asimov and his "Foundation" series, no other SF writer has created anything comparable to Heinlein's "Future History"—the author's informal projection of the progress of the people of Earth and their civilizations as they reached outward to the stars over the next millennium. Heinlein reportedly created a gigantic chart that occupied an entire wall of his study to make it easier for him to slot in his novels and short stories.

Treatises and Treats

COMPANIONS

Robert A. Heinlein: A Reader's Companion by James Gifford, (Nitrosyncretic Press, 2000). A comprehensive guide to Heinlein's life work by a devoted fan, who is also the creator of the Internet's best Heinlein resource.

The Robert Heinlein Interview and Other Heinleiniana by J. Neil Schulman and Brad Linaweaver (Pulpless.com, 1999). The transcript of what is purported to be the writer's longest interview, conducted in 1973, covering his beliefs about UFOs, life after death, and libertarianism, among other things. Endorsed by Ginny Heinlein herself.

Grumbles from the Grave, edited by Virginia Heinlein (Del Ray, 1990). A collection of letters written by Heinlein, mostly to his agent,

Lurton Blasingame, detailing his writerly life. Some say the book portrays a determined artist, others say it shows a censorious rager.

BEST OF THE NET
The RAH Home Page
www.nitrosyncretic.com/rah
Home of the Heinlein FAQ, a thorough, opinionated, and deeply affectionate compendium of Heinlein lore by James Gifford, along with an abbreviated biography, bibliography, and advice on various topics.

Vintage Heinlein

HUGO AWARD WINNERS

Double Star, 1956
Starship Troopers, 1960
Stranger in a Strange Land, 1961
The Moon Is a Harsh Mistress, 1966

OTHER NOVELS AND STORY COLLECTIONS

Beyond this Horizon, 1948
The Puppet Masters, 1951
The Door into Summer, 1956
Methuselah's Children, 1958
Glory Road, 1963
Farnham's Freehold, 1964
The Past Through Tomorrow, 1967
  (all the Heinlein "Future History" stories in a single volume)

If You Like Robert A. Heinlein...

Try Frank Herbert's *Dune* series, remarkable for its logical extrapolations of survival and culture on a desert planet. You might also like *Foundation* by Isaac Asimov, and *The Space Merchants*, a classic, futuristic tale about advertising by Frederik Pohl and C. M. Kornbluth.

Best Book to Read First

Stranger in a Strange Land is his best-known work, but it's not typical Heinlein. Instead, start with *Starship Troopers*, featuring a world where the right to vote must be earned by voluntary service to society, or *The Moon Is a Harsh Mistress*, with its fascinating hands-on description of how to organize a successful revolution. Both of these books are much closer to the essence of this most influential of all science fiction writers.

Citizenship is an attitude, a state of mind, an emotional conviction that the whole is greater than the part...and that the part should be humbly proud to sacrifice itself that the whole may live.

—Colonel Dubois in *Starship Troopers*

Joseph Heller

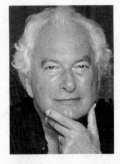

Born
May 1, 1923, in Brooklyn, New York, to Lena and Isaac Heller. Isaac, who drove a bakery truck, died just five years later of complications from a bleeding ulcer. Heller later wrote that he recalled nothing about his father or the funeral. "I simply lost interest in him after he was gone."

Education
Attended the University of Southern California; New York University, B.A. in English, Phi Beta Kappa, 1948; Columbia University, M.A., 1949; graduate study at Oxford University, 1949–50, as a Fulbright Scholar.

Family
Married in 1945 to Shirley Held, with whom he had two children. They were divorced in 1982. In 1987, he married Valerie Humphries, a nurse he met while he was ill.

Home
East Hampton, Long Island, New York

Died
December 12, 1999, at home, of a heart attack

Publishers
Knopf
Simon & Schuster

Joseph Heller's *Catch-22* is considered one of the best novels of the 20th century. With its strangely believable absurdities and dark humor, it is certainly one of the funniest. Yet when it was published in 1961, it received lukewarm reviews and had only modest sales. *Catch-22* challenged the comfortably held, Hollywood-enhanced, post–World War II conviction that U. S. soldiers willingly and routinely faced death with a coolness and courage born of the knowledge that they were fighting for a higher cause. The book's protagonist, bombardier John Yossarian, in contrast, would (and does) do anything to be excused from combat. He is frantic and furious that thousands of people he hasn't even met are trying to kill him, including, in his view, the officers who keep sending him out on flak-filled bombing missions.

The book's greatest power, wrote former Navy Secretary James Webb in a *Wall Street Journal* commentary following Heller's death, "was that it took the ultimately justifiable war and stripped away cant and hypocrisy from the telling of how difficult it is to serve." What kept it alive and selling year after year was word of mouth: people who had read it would strongly recommend it or pass along copies to friends.

By the mid-1960s, with the Vietnam War heating up, the book found a large and enthusiastic audience among the nation's college students, many of whom would be drafted into the military if they were to lose their college deferments. Heller spent much of the 1960s speaking out against the war on college campuses, and his book eventually sold over 10 million copies.

Joseph Heller wrote plays, short stories, memoirs, and six other novels over the last three decades of his life. *Closing Time* (1994) has been described as a sequel to *Catch-22*—though it's really a separate novel that happens to involve some of the characters from his first and most enduring work. In response to those who complained over the years that he had never written another book like *Catch-22*, he typically replied, "Neither has anyone else."

Good to Know

❖ Definition: According to the rules, anyone who is declared insane must be excused from flying combat missions. But you have to *ask* to be excused. That's *Catch-22*, since anyone who shows "rational fear in the face of clear and present danger" is obviously sane and therefore must continue to fly. Similar situations occur so frequently in life that it is no wonder the term has entered the language.

❖ Heller was a lieutenant in the Army Air Corps during World War II, serving as a bombardier on a B-25. After flying 60 missions, he was discharged in June 1945. Until his 37th mission, "it was all play, all games, it was being in a Hollywood movie." Then he saw planes flown by his friends blown out of the sky and his own plane was hit by flak, wounding the top-turret gunner. From then on, "I was scared even on the milk runs."

❖ *Catch-22* was filmed in 1970 by Mike Nichols. Adapted by Buck Henry, it starred Alan Arkin as Yossarian and featured in other roles Art Garfunkel, Orson Welles, Bob Newhart, Anthony Perkins, Richard Benjamin, Paula Prentiss, Jack Gilford, and Jon Voight.

❖ In 1986, Heller noticed that he was having trouble swallowing and couldn't pull a sweater over his head. He was diagnosed with Guillain-Barré syndrome, a neurological disorder that could have killed him. He fought back and won, but only after racking up $300,000 in medical expenses—and he had let his health insurance lapse! Friend Mario Puzo helped him out with a loan. The story is recounted in *No Laughing Matter* (1986) by Heller and Speed Vogel.

❖ Mario Puzo once said of Heller, "I never knew anyone so determined to be unhappy, so suspicious of happiness." Barbara Gelb, a friend of over 20 years, wrote that she overlooked "his frequent sulkiness, his gluttonous table manners, and his tendency to growl 'No'" before even knowing what the question was because she so relished his "aberrant sense of humor and his skewed way of looking at life."

Treatises and Treats

COMPANIONS

Now and Then: From Coney Island to Here by Joseph Heller (Knopf, 1998). A memoir covering the author's boyhood in the 1920s and 1930s.

Conversations with Joseph Heller, edited by Adam J. Sorkin (University Press of Mississippi, 1993). A selection of the most significant interviews with Heller. Topics discussed include the themes of his work, major influences, writing methods, and political opinions.

Understanding Joseph Heller by Sanford Pinsker (Greenwood Publishing Group, 1991). This book of critical commentary is currently out of print, but it's available from used book dealers on the Web and elsewhere.

BEST OF THE NET

New York Times Featured Authors
www.nytimes.com/books/specials/author.html
An excellent source of articles about Heller, reviews of his books, and lectures he has given. You can also listen to the author reading excerpts from *Catch-22*.

All the Novels

Catch-22, 1961
Something Happened, 1974
Good As Gold, 1979
God Knows, 1984
Picture This, 1988
Closing Time, 1994
A Portrait of an Artist as an Old Man, 2000

If You Like Joseph Heller . . .

Try *Slaughterhouse Five* by Kurt Vonnegut, *Corelli's Mandolin* by Louis De Bernieres, and *The Jukebox Queen of Malta* by Nicholas Rinaldi, which Heller calls "a beguiling, romantic story in an illuminating and surprising setting." You might also like *Face of a Hero* by Louis Falstein, a novel/memoir that predates *Catch-22*. It has some remarkable similarities to Heller's masterpiece, but Heller denied ever reading it. There are also a number of Vietnam-war novels that owe a great debt to *Catch-22*. Try Tim O'Brien's classic *Going After Cacciato* as a short but powerful example.

Best Book to Read First

Catch-22. One of the first books to portray the absurdity of war—comic and horrific at the same time—through one man's struggle to survive. You will laugh so hard, you'll cry. It's number seven on the Modern Library's list of the 100 Best Novels of the 20th century.

What's in a Number?

Believe it or not, *Catch-22* was to have been published as *Catch-18*, and Simon & Schuster would have released it as such had not rival publisher Doubleday stepped into the picture. Doubleday was getting ready to launch bestselling author Leon Uris's *Mila 18*, and when they heard that Simon & Schuster was coming out at about the same time with an unknown writer's first novel with a "similar title," they raised a ruckus.

In the end, Simon & Schuster backed off, and Heller changed the title to avoid trouble. Heller's editor also recalled that *Catch-22* had been years in the writing and had originally been called *Catch-14*.

I get an opening line, and a concept of the book as a full, literary entity. It's all in my head before I even begin to write. Many of my ideas for dialogue and plot twists come to me while I'm jogging. And when I'm close to finishing a book, nothing is more important to me. I might stop to save a life, but nothing less.

—Joseph Heller

Mark Helprin

Born
June 28, 1947, in New York City to Morris Helprin, a *New York Times* film critic and later a motion-picture executive, and Eleanor Lynn Helprin, a leading lady on Broadway in the 1930s. He grew up in New York City, the Hudson River Valley, and the British West Indies.

Education
Harvard University, A.B., 1969; A.M., 1972. Postgraduate study at Magdalen College, University of Oxford, 1976–77.

Family
Married Lisa Kennedy, a tax attorney and banker, in 1980; two daughters.

Home
A farmhouse in upstate New York

Publisher
Harcourt

Once upon a time there were two mayoral candidates. One made a promise a minute, none of which he ever intended to keep. The other never talked about garbage, electricity, or police. He spoke instead "almost hypnotically about love, loyalty, and esthetics.... He promised them love affairs and sleigh races, cross-country skiing on the main thoroughfares, and the transfixing blizzards that howled outside and made the heart dance."

Wow!

Mark Helprin's *Winter's Tale*, like the rest of his fiction, is filled with passages and images that are just as transfixing and pleasing to the heart as this one. His work has been described as "magical realism," a genre in which fantastical things happen in settings derived from ordinary locations. In the New York City of *Winter's Tale*, for example, Helprin places a burglar's lair above the zodiac in Grand Central Station's vaulted ceiling. The trick is to somehow make it all believable and meaningful, and Helprin is able to do just that.

His 1995 novel, *Memoir from Antproof Case*, features a narrator who has been a World War II fighter ace, an investment banker and confidante of popes and presidents, the thief of the century, a murderer, and a vigorous opponent of the world's most insidious enslaver: coffee. In lesser hands, such a character would be a cartoon, but not with Helprin. Indeed, a lesser writer could not have conceived of such a character, much less made him seem real.

But imagination is only part of what Mark Helprin has to offer. He is also a born story-teller who is highly skilled at getting you intensely interested in knowing what happens next. And he is a master of language. Dante, the Bible, and Shakespeare are his models, but he is said to consult old dictionaries to find just the right wonderful, historically appropriate words. As some critics have noted, Helprin's plots may not always be as tight as they could be, but his language, images, and imagination never fail.

Good to Know

❖ A contributor to the *Wall Street Journal*'s opinion page for more than a decade, Helprin is a political conservative (a "Theodore Roosevelt Republican") and an expert on the Middle East. He wrote Bob Dole's Senate resignation speech, which all agreed was uncharacteristically lyrical for the former majority leader.

❖ As a Harvard undergrad, he submitted a dozen short stories to the *New Yorker*, which finally accepted two at the same time: "Because of the Waters of the Flood" and "Leaving the Church," a story Helprin says he wrote while sitting on the grave of Henry James.

❖ His military experience includes service in the British Merchant Navy and in the Israeli Infantry and Air Force. He became an Israeli citizen and served in a combat unit that went on dozens of patrols at the Lebanese border.

❖ Helprin doesn't smoke, drink, or consume caffeine. An accomplished mountain climber, he reached the top of the 14,410-foot Mount Rainier in 1987. He has also climbed Mount Etna and nearly made it to the summit of the Matterhorn. Khaki pants and hiking boots are a mainstay of his wardrobe.

❖ Working in a rosewood-paneled office overlooking an alfalfa field, Helprin writes rough drafts on loose-leaf notebook paper in black ink and second drafts in red ink. Only then does he type a third version into his computer. His office houses over 4,000 books, but no wastebasket. (To have a single crumpled paper in a trash bin would throw off his extreme sense of order.)

❖ Helprin refuses to review fiction, endorse books for other authors, or seek blurbs for his own books. He usually acts as his own literary agent, successfully snaring six-figure advances for his fiction.

Treatises and Treats

BEST OF THE NET

Mark Helprin Fan Page

www.rigroup.com/~candi/helprin

Filled with goodies for the Helprin enthusiast—including favorite excerpts and a wide-ranging bibliography listing his fiction as well as newspaper and journal commentaries. And for ravenous readers (Helprin just doesn't write fast enough!), there are recommendations of other books and authors that may satisfy until the next Helprin release.

Book List

ALL THE NOVELS

Refiner's Fire, 1977
Winter's Tale, 1983
A Soldier of the Great War, 1991
Memoir from Antproof Case, 1995

SHORT-STORY COLLECTIONS

A Dove of the East and Other Stories, 1975
Ellis Island and Other Stories, 1981
 (PEN/Faulkner Award)

BOOKS FOR CHILDREN

All three include enchanting illustrations by Chris Van Allsburg.
Swan Lake, 1989
A City in Winter: The Queen's Tale, 1996
The Veil of Snows, 1997

If You Like Mark Helprin . . .

You might also like books by these authors, all of whom combine the fantastical, the historical, and the allegorical with a powerful emphasis on language: A. S. Byatt (*Possession*), Caleb Carr (*The Alienist*), Jack Finney (*Time and Again*), Gabriel García Márquez (*One Hundred Years of Solitude*), Richard Powers (*The Gold Bug Variations*), and Terri Windling (*The Wood Wife*).

Best Book to Read First

Winter's Tale. A big, broad, sweeping fantastical work of such shimmering beauty, clarity, and exhilarating use of language that the "inner eye is stunned" (*Publishers Weekly*). It remained on the *New York Times* bestseller list for 16 weeks in 1983.

Too Natural a Storyteller?

Helprin is infamous for telling journalists tall tales about his life. In a 1981 interview for *Publishers Weekly*, he claimed that when he was a child his father required him to make up a story before he would be allowed to eat dinner (prepared by the family's French chef who was once employed by the Hotel Pierre). If his story wasn't interesting enough, little Mark would go hungry. At his infuriated father's urging, Helprin later admitted that he'd made it all up. In another instance, he told a radio interviewer that he had once been a mercenary in Africa and that, following a coup, he left with a sack of diamonds.

Helprin insists that these are the only two stories he has fabricated. So the one in which a 13-year-old Mark was almost killed in Jamaica by a Pakistani immigrant and had to have 60 stitches in the head and legs—administered by a Canadian psychiatrist without the aid of anesthesia and with only a rag to bite on—is true?

All my life I've allowed what I dream to influence me. My dreams are usually very intense and extremely detailed and always in the most beautiful colors.... Frequently I will dream, and simply retrace that dream the day after when I write. It's just like planning ahead, only I do it when I'm unconscious.

—Mark Helprin, in a 1984 interview in *Openers* magazine

Ernest Hemingway

Born
July 21, 1899, in Oak Park, Illinois, to Clarence Edmunds, a physician, and Grace Hall Hemingway, a music teacher

Full Name
Ernest Miller Hemingway

Family
Married four times, to Hadley Richardson in 1921 (divorced 1927); Pauline Pfeiffer, a writer, in 1927 (divorced 1940); Martha Gellhorn, also a writer, in 1940 (divorced 1945); and to a third writer, Mary Welsh, in 1946. Three children: John Hadley Nicanor by his first marriage, and Patrick and Gregory by his second.

Homes
Oak Park, Illinois; Key West, Florida; Ketchum, Idaho; and Havana, Cuba

Died
Committed suicide with a shotgun on July 2, 1961, three weeks shy of his 62nd birthday, in Ketchum, Idaho.

Publisher
Scribner

This 1954 Nobel Prize–winning author is one of the true giants of modern American literature. Hemingway's punchy, pared-down style and ability to zero in on the perfect characterizing detail of a person or scene has influenced every serious novelist of the second half of the 20th century. Everyone reads him at one time or another.

Rising to prominence as he did after the cataclysm of the First World War, he was the right man in the right place—with the right skills—at the right time. With Fitzgerald, Dos Passos, e.e. cummings, Archibald MacLeish, and many others, Hemingway was part of "the Lost Generation," a term coined by Gertrude Stein to refer to a group of writers who came of age during the Great War and made their literary reputations in the 1920s. Hemingway's terse, economic style, with its superb dialogue and unflinching portrayal of violence, perfectly suited the disillusionment of those who survived the War. People had the sense that everything was different, everything had changed, and Hemingway was in the vanguard of the charge of the literary wing.

Unfortunately, he seems to have gotten stuck in that period, for he published nothing of significance between his 1940 novel about the Spanish Civil War, *For Whom the Bell Tolls*, and his 1952 Pulitzer Prize–winning novella *The Old Man and the Sea*. Instead, he became famous as the midcentury embodiment of machismo. His tempestuous marriages, his headlong pursuit of danger as a big-game hunter, in the bullring, and in the boxing ring always made headlines.

Ernest Hemingway was one of the first public figures to be celebrated as much for who he was and how he lived as for what he created. Unwittingly, perhaps, he turned "Hemingway" into a recognizable brand name. People who had never read him knew that he was a great writer who led an adventurous life. And the media and public of the time made him a personage with an image he may have felt he had to live up to.

Some have suggested that the pressures this entailed led to his suicide. We will never know. What we do know is that a lot of inferior work—unfinished sketches, early drafts of novels, and other writings that the author probably should have burned—has been published under the "Hemingway" brand since his death. Do not let this distract you from the greatness of his earlier work. Read *A Farewell to Arms* (1929) and some of his short stories before forming an opinion.

Good to Know

❖ Hemingway's pals included Ezra Pound and Gertrude Stein—members of a group that has attained near mythic status and was both honored and brilliantly skewered in Alan Rudolph's hilarious 1988 film, *The Moderns*.

❖ The most prominent annual celebrations bearing the author's name are a festival in Key West featuring a "Papa Hemingway" look-alike contest, an expensive bill-fishing tournament in Havana, and the International Imitation Hemingway Competition sponsored by PEN Center USA and Harry's Bar & American Grill (also known as the "Bad Hemingway Contest"). It's all in great good fun.

❖ Mary Hemingway chose the title for her husband's posthumous memoir, *A Moveable*

Feast, which characterized the bohemian life of the Parisian Latin Quarter in the 1920s. Her inspiration came from some lines her husband had once written to a friend: "If you are lucky enough to have lived in Paris as a young man, then wherever you go for the rest of your life, it stays with you, for Paris is a moveable feast."

Treatises and Treats

SOCIETIES

The Hemingway Society. An international organization of academics and enthusiasts. Publishes *The Hemingway Review* and organizes an annual conference in a place with special relevance to Hemingway. Membership is $25. Contact: The Hemingway Society, c/o Department of English and Foreign Languages, University of West Florida, Pensacola, FL 32514.

Michigan Hemingway Society. Fly-fishers as well as educators, writers, and journalists make up this group, which holds a Hemingway weekend in Petoskey, Michigan, each October. Dues are $10. Contact: Michigan Hemingway Society, P.O. Box 953, Petoskey, MI 49770 (www.upnorth.net/hemingway).

COMPANIONS

Ernest Hemingway: A Life Story by Carlos Baker (Collier Books, 1988). First published in 1969, this is the standard biography. In addition to the primary sources, Princeton Professor Baker relies on testimony of Hemingway's peers, including John Dos Passos, F. Scott Fitzgerald, Ezra Pound, and Gertrude Stein. The book is also available on audiocassette from Blackstone Audio (800-729-2665, www.blackstoneaudio.com).

Ernest Hemingway A to Z: The Essential Reference to the Life and Work by Charles M. Oliver (Facts on File, 1999). An encyclopedic resource, with detailed synopses of all of the author's fiction and nonfiction writings.

BEST OF THE NET

Ernest Hemingway Oak Park Foundation
www.hemingway.org
A thorough, intelligent, and reverential place,

offering a useful chronology and a long list of interesting links. Don't miss "The *Kansas City Star* Stories" with its audio files of Hemingway readings, the "Deux Magots Café" page (Web site of the Paris café where Hemingway and his cohorts gathered in the 1920s), and "The Sharks in Literature."

New York Times Featured Authors
www.nytimes.com/books/specials/
   author.html
Click on "Ernest Hemingway" for book reviews and articles from the *New York Times* archives, a slide show from the Hemingway Collection of Boston's JFK Library, and an audio file of the author's Nobel Prize acceptance speech. Also his obituary and related articles that appeared soon after his death.

The Memorable Feast

ALL THE NOVELS

Many of these books are available in more recent editions, sometimes with new introductions.

The Torrents of Spring, 1926
The Sun Also Rises, 1926
A Farewell to Arms, 1929
To Have and Have Not, 1937
For Whom the Bell Tolls, 1940
Across the River and into the Trees, 1950
The Old Man and the Sea, 1952
   (Pulitzer Prize)
Islands in the Stream, 1970
The Garden of Eden, 1986

SHORT-STORY COLLECTION

The Complete Short Stories of Ernest Hemingway: The Finca Vigia Edition, 1998

NOTABLE NONFICTION

A Moveable Feast, 1964
True at First Light, 1999

Best Book to Read First

A Farewell to Arms, one of Hemingway's earliest novels, is generally regarded as his best. But many readers and critics feel that his short fiction displays the terse power of his language to greater effect. *The Complete Short Stories of Ernest Hemingway: The Finca Vigia Edition* (Scribner, 1998) is thus an excellent place to start reading Hemingway.

Reconciling literature and action, [Hemingway] fulfilled for all writers the sickroom dream of leaving the desk for the arena, and then returning to the desk. He wrote good and lived good, and both activities were the same. The pen handled with the accuracy of the rifle; sweat and dignity; bags of cojones.

—Anthony Burgess, *Contemporary Authors*

Tony Hillerman

Born
May 27, 1925, in Sacred Heart, Oklahoma, to August Alfred Hillerman and Lucy Grove Hillerman. He is the youngest of three children.

Education
University of Oklahoma, B.A., 1946; M.A., University of New Mexico, 1966

Family
Married Mary Unzner in 1948; six children.

Home
Albuquerque, New Mexico

Fan Mail
Tony Hillerman
c/o Curtis Brown, Ltd.
10 Astor Place
New York, NY 10003

Publisher
HarperCollins

Tony Hillerman is far more than a successful mystery writer. For one thing, the Southwest setting of his stories and his understanding of the modern and the traditional American West make him a writer of Westerns. Then there is his focus on the Navajo, or Dineh, which makes him something of an anthropologist, naturalist, lobbyist, ambassador, journalist, and bard. His awards—including the Edgar and Grand Master Awards from Mystery Writers of America, the Golden Spur from Western Writers of America, and the Special Friend of Dineh from the Navajo Tribal Council—reflect some of these facets of his work.

Critics praise Hillerman's clever plots and authenticity, as well as his descriptive powers and sense of place. His two leading characters, Joe Leaphorn and Jim Chee, members of the Navajo Tribal Police, are worthy additions to the pantheon of crime-fiction detectives. In books like *Talking God*, *Skinwalkers*, *Coyote Waits*, and *The Blessing Way*, Navajo customs are as important as forensics in finding out "who done it," and they can be even more helpful in figuring out why. The older Leaphorn is a comfortable presence, while the younger Chee has more of an edge. But neither is a simple or symbolic icon. Each provides a realistic depiction of what it takes to reconcile traditional beliefs and modern ways.

In a *Publishers Weekly* interview, Hillerman expressed his strong interest in the cultures of the Southwest. "For me, studying them has been absolutely fascinating," he says, "and I think it's important to show [my readers that] aspects of ancient Indian ways are still very much alive and are highly germane." He has done just that in his mystery novels as well as in works of nonfiction (*Hillerman Country* and *New Mexico, Rio Grande and Other Essays*, for example) that open up the geography and history of the Southwest for a wide audience.

Good to Know

❖ Hillerman grew up on a farm in Oklahoma during the Depression. From 1930 to 1938, he and other farm children attended St. Mary's Academy, a boarding school for Native American girls, where many of his friends and playmates were Potawatomi and Seminole.

❖ He joined the army in 1943 and saw combat during World War II, receiving the Silver Star, Bronze Star, and Purple Heart. On a convalescent furlough in 1945, he first encountered Navajos and witnessed an Enemy Way ceremony intended to restore the health and harmony of Navajo marines who had served in the Pacific. The experience created lasting impressions of a generous, deeply religious, and hospitable people whose approach to life he valued.

❖ Before becoming a mystery writer, Hillerman was a journalist with the *Borger* (Texas) *News Herald*. He later covered politics and crime for newspapers in Oklahoma and New Mexico, rising to the position of executive editor with the *New Mexican* in Santa Fe. Joining the faculty of the University of New Mexico in Albuquerque in the 1960s, he soon became chair of the journalism department. He's now an emeritus professor of journalism.

❖ Hillerman researches his stories by reading books and articles, but he then relies on his friends on the Navajo reservation for authoritative details of ceremony, taboo, and other cultural elements. He knows, for example, that instead of knocking on a door, a

Navajo police officer will wait in the car until the Navajo homeowner comes outside.

❖ He typically writes without an outline. "I begin knowing a kernel of the plot," he says. "I daydream my way into each scene." Because he revises extensively as he creates each chapter, he tends to produce only one draft.

❖ Most of Hillerman's novels feature Joe Leaphorn and Jim Chee. But in *Finding Moon* (1996), he introduces Moon Mathias and sends him on a risky mission near the end of the Vietnam War. (It was a novel he tried to write decades earlier about the Belgian pull-out from Congo, but he couldn't make it work.) In 1980, he decided to use the U.S. pullout from Vietnam as his backdrop. Unable to get permission to enter Vietnam or Cambodia, Hillerman (like Francis Ford Coppola filming *Apocalypse Now*) turned to the Philippines to research the settings for the book.

Treatises and Treats

COMPANIONS

Talking Mysteries: A Conversation with Tony Hillerman, with Ernie Bulow (University of New Mexico Press, 1991). Essays and an interview explore Hillerman's writing methods, sources, and philosophy. Bulow is Hillerman's friend and an adviser on Navajo cultural details.

Tony Hillerman: A Critical Companion by John M. Reilly (Greenwood Publishing Group, 1996). Biographical information, bibliography, and critical discussions of the novels.

The Tony Hillerman Companion: A Comprehensive Guide to His Life and Work, edited by Martin Greenberg (HarperCollins, 1994). Essays on the author, Navajo culture, and the clans and characters in his fiction, as well as an interview, photos, and a chronology of Hillerman's life.

Tony Hillerman's Indian Country Map and Guide (Time Traveler Maps, 1998). A nifty, highly detailed, hardcover map of "Hillerman country."

BEST OF THE NET

Unofficial Tony Hillerman Home Page
www.umsl.edu/~smueller/index.htm
A very thorough site offering biography, criticism, interviews, photos, map, and links to other resources on the Net.

Hillerman Country

The Blessing Way, 1970
The Fly on the Wall, 1971
Dance Hall of the Dead, 1973
    (Edgar Award)
Listening Woman, 1977
The People of Darkness, 1978
The Dark Wind, 1981
Ghostway, 1984
A Thief of Time, 1985
Skinwalkers, 1986
Talking God, 1989
Coyote Waits, 1990
Sacred Clowns, 1993
The Fallen Man, 1996
Finding Moon, 1996
The First Eagle, 1999
Hunting Badger, 1999

If You Like Tony Hillerman . . .

Try the novels of Nevada Barr, Jean Hager, J. A. Jance, Sharyn McCrumb, and Aimee and David Thurlo.

Best Book to Read First

Skinwalkers. "A good introduction to Hillerman's work," according to Charles Petersen in *Chicago Tribune Books*. "If you start the book, you won't stop reading until the end."

I admire Tony Hillerman for his plots, the ease of his style, the quiet tension he draws between traditional and modern Navajo... but I admire even more the fact that he gets his Zuni rituals just right, that he knows Navajo land like the back of his hand, and that he can make the vast, sunny open spaces of the American Southwest as fully threatening...as the dark canyons of our corroding cities.

—Yale history professor Robin W. Winks, *Washington Post Book World*

Landscape into Art

Whenever Tony Hillerman gets writer's block, he drives out to the Navajo reservation to "take a fresh look at the landscape." Details of the physical world are important to his creative process. For each scene, he wants to know the time of day and the "way the wind is blowing." He often refers to maps while working on a story, and tries to be accurate. But in one book, he confesses, "I moved Burnt Water about 200 miles north of its actual locale because I love that name."

Alice Hoffman

Born
March 16, 1952, in
New York City. She and
her brother were raised
by her mother, a
teacher and social
worker, in the Long
Island community of
Levittown, New York.

Education
Adelphi University,
B.A., 1973; Stanford
University, M.A., 1975.
Her thesis project in
the Stanford writing
program became her
first novel, *Property Of*.

Family
Married to Tom Martin,
a writer; two children,
Jake and Zack.

Home
A Victorian house in
Brookline, Massachu-
setts

Fan Mail
Alice Hoffman
c/o Elaine Markson
   Literary Agency
44 Greenwich Avenue
New York, NY 10011

Publisher
Putnam

Alice Hoffman's books—described in the *Boston Review* as displaying "a shimmering prose style, the fusing of fantasy and reality"—are often classified as "magic realism." She writes about rebels, eccentrics, and distracted women, all of whom, despite their typical domestic settings, gain some mystical wisdom. Hoffman explains that she writes about such people "because they're outsiders and to some extent, we all think of ourselves as outsiders."

The author's early novels, *Property Of*, *The Drowning Season*, *Angel Landing*, and *White Horses*, were praised for their fusion of gritty modern-day reality and the symbolic, mythic qualities of legend. Then came *Fortune's Daughter*, hailed in the *Chicago Tribune Book World* as "modern-day female mythology." Though a bit sentimental, the book earned high marks for its offbeat humor and beautiful prose style. *Illumination Night* has been called Hoffman's most subtle work, described as "a powerful if often disturbing look at the interior lives, domestic and emotional, of a young family and a teenage girl set on destroying them all" (*Boston Review*).

In her 1988 novel, *At Risk*, Hoffman deals with the subject of AIDS and the slow death of an eight-year-old girl who suffers from the disease. But she returns to the interweaving of the real and the supernatural with *Seventh Heaven*, deemed by critics her best novel, and continues this device in *Turtle Moon*, *Second Nature*, and *Practical Magic*, also highly praised.

Good to Know

❖ Growing up on Long Island, Hoffman never imagined that she would eventually be the author of more than a dozen books, most of them bestsellers: "Unhappiness was trapped in the house like a bubble. My mother was a teacher and social worker, and my father wasn't there. My brother was the smart one, the scientist. I wanted to be a veterinarian, but I didn't think a girl could be that. I never thought somebody like me could grow up to be a writer."

❖ Her early novels didn't earn very much, so she and her husband Tom Martin worked together on screenplays. One of their most notable efforts: *Independence Day* (1983), a critically praised film starring Kathleen Quinlan and Dianne Wiest. Though the couple still work together on screenwriting projects, Hoffman remains happily detached from the adaptations of her own novels to film. "I don't want to take my own book apart and put it back together again," she once told a reporter. "That's a difficult process."

❖ Hoffman has also collaborated on two children's books (*Fireflies* and *Horsefly*) with another author—her nine-year-old son, Zack. She describes the experience of being edited by a nine-year-old as "humbling."

❖ On weekdays, she begins writing at 5:30 A.M. "I think it's before the senses are turned on and before I have to deal with the real world and get phone calls. And since I have kids, it's always been a time when I don't have to get somebody a drink or something. For me it's my best time of day."

❖ Hoffman never asks about how her books are selling. "I write a book, I give it to my editor, then I go back and write another one. That's what I do."

❖ She characterizes her most recent novel, *Here on Earth* (based on Emily Brontë's *Wuthering Heights*) as the most deep and intense book she has ever written. She even set it aside for a time in order to work on the more lighthearted *Practical Magic* (the book that served as the basis for a 1998 movie starring Sandra Bullock, Nicole Kidman, Stockard Channing, and Dianne Wiest).

❖ Grace Paley is one of Hoffman's favorite authors. She once met the acclaimed short-story writer. "I wanted to tell her how important she was to me, but I couldn't. I was too embarrassed."

Treatises and Treats

BEST OF THE NET

New York Times Featured Authors
www.nytimes.com/books/specials/
    author.html
Includes reviews of Hoffman's work as well as a collection of articles by and about her.

Oprah's Book Club
www.oprah.com
Check here for an author bio and reading guide to the novel *Here on Earth*, which was featured on Oprah's Book Club in March 1998.

Reading List

ALL THE NOVELS
Property Of, 1977
The Drowning Season, 1979
Angel Landing, 1980
White Horses, 1982
Fortune's Daughter, 1985
Illumination Night, 1987
At Risk, 1988
Seventh Heaven, 1990
Turtle Moon, 1993
Second Nature, 1994
Practical Magic, 1995
Here on Earth, 1997
    (Oprah's Book Club selection)

SHORT-STORY COLLECTION
Local Girls, 1999

If You Like Alice Hoffman . . .

You might also like the writings of Amy Bloom, Ellen Gilchrist, Shirley Jackson, and Barbara Kingsolver.

Best Book to Read First

Illumination Night, a novel of magic and mystery set in Martha's Vineyard and considered by many to be Hoffman's finest book to date. The title refers to a Fourth of July tradition of illuminating the island's Victorian houses with old-fashioned lanterns.

Magical Thinking

Alice Hoffman does not distinguish between "magic realism" and "realism" in fiction. In fact, she believes that magic is around us all the time. "I have magical thinking," she says, "Like a kid. When I'm with my little kid in a store, he'll say, 'The ceiling is talking to me,' and I'll realize that it's the loudspeaker. It's like the world is very magical and the things that happen happen for magical reasons." Hoffman discovered the enchantment of the world when she was a child: "The fireflies on the lawn, the voices of the adults inside the house. It felt like magic..."

Perhaps the real sorcery occurs between Hoffman and her characters. She says they feel like real people to her when she's writing. "Sometimes it's as if they're sitting on the couch and I'm writing their story and I'm sitting on the couch with them." Sadly though, when she finishes writing a book, her relationship with the characters also comes to an end. Says Hoffman: "I'm done, they're done." They disappear—like magic.

I think it's important to feel affected and moved by things internally, and that's how I hope people feel about my books, affected and moved. That's what literature is supposed to do.

—Alice Hoffman

Zora Neale Hurston

Born
January 7, 1903, in
Eatonville, Florida, to
preacher/carpenter
John Hurston and
teacher/seamstress
Lucy Potts Hurston;
fifth of eight children

Education
Barnard College, B.A.,
1928 (the school's
first black graduate).
Went on to study
anthropology at
Columbia University.

Family
Two short-lived
marriages, both of
which ended in divorce:
Herbert Sheen,
1927–31, Albert Price
III, 1939–43

Home
Various locations in
Florida, and for a time
Baltimore, New York,
and Washington, D.C.

Died
January 28, 1960, in
Fort Pierce, Florida

Publishers
HarperCollins
Library of America

During that richly expressive artistic period in the 1920s known as the Harlem Renaissance, Zora Neale Hurston was the leading black female writer in the country. The first black graduate of Barnard, she collaborated with Langston Hughes on *Mule Bone*, wrote stories for major magazines, and produced four novels, many essays, an autobiography, and two volumes on black mythology and folklore. She also studied anthropology at Columbia.

Yet by the late 1950s, she was working as a hotel maid in her native Florida. She died in 1960 at a county welfare home and was buried in an unmarked grave, completely forgotten—until Alice Walker, author of *The Color Purple* and other novels, discovered her, arranged to have a gravestone placed at the site, and almost singlehandedly revived interest in this most remarkable lady with a 1975 article for *Ms.* magazine called "In Search of Zora Neale Hurston."

In *Their Eyes Were Watching God*, her best-known book, Hurston tells the story of Janie Crawford, a black woman living in a black town in Florida who has been married to three men and tried for the murder of one of them. The town talks. Indeed, everyone talks. And they do so in the Deep South black language of the 1930s. Some, notably Richard Wright, were furious at Hurston for reinforcing the stereotype whites liked to hold regarding blacks at the time. And, in truth, it is difficult not to wince today when encountering dialogue like "Dat's just de same as me 'cause mah tongue is in mah friend's mouf."

But Hurston wasn't writing about black people and their confrontations with the white world. She was writing about a human community and capturing the way its members talked. Had she been writing about Eskimos or Italians in America, she would have used the same approach. Remember, Hurston had done advanced work in anthropology at Columbia. Surely getting it right, as opposed to getting it politically correct, would always have been her goal.

In retrospect, the country probably had to experience the civil rights movement and the turmoil of the 1960s and 1970s before Zora Neale Hurston could come into her own. Today, writers, scholars, and readers of every race can appreciate what Hurston captured and passed on to us all. Forget about labels. Zora Neale Hurston was an extraordinary human being with exceptional gifts of observation and communication. And she is a treat to read.

Good to Know

❖ Eatonville, Florida, Hurston's hometown, is the setting for many of her stories. Located a few miles northeast of Orlando, Eatonville was America's first incorporated all-black town. Her father once served as Eatonville's mayor.

❖ In 1927, Charlotte Mason, a wealthy white New Yorker, provided Hurston with a car, a movie camera, and $200 a month to travel the Deep South collecting black folklore, stories, and songs. As a black women traveling alone, Hurston's cover story was that she was simply killing time until her bootlegger husband got out of jail. Her 300-page account was only recently discovered in the Smithsonian and has yet to be published in full.

❖ A Guggenheim Fellowship in 1936 funded Hurston's study of the West Indian practice of Obeah, a belief system characterized by the use of sorcery and magic ritual. During that time, in a seven-week period, she also wrote *Their Eyes Were Watching God*, her second novel.

Treatises and Treats

ZORA NEALE HURSTON FESTIVAL

Hurston fans celebrate the author's life and work each January in Eatonville, Florida, with a program of literary events, music, dance, drama, juried art exhibit, folk arts, and ethnic cuisine. For more information, contact:

Zora Neale Hurston Festival
227 East Kennedy Blvd.
Eatonville, FL 32751
407-647-3307
longwood.cs.ucf.edu/~zora

ZORA'S WORKS ON AUDIO TAPE

Listen to Ruby Dee read an abridged two-cassette version of *Their Eyes Were Watching God* from HarperAudio's Caedmon imprint, available from Amazon.com or BarnesandNoble.com for about $15. Or revel in the full-length, five-cassette version narrated by Michele-Denise Woods, rented from Recorded Books for $14 (www.recordedbooks.com). Either way, hearing the patois spoken by Hurston's characters reproduced by such talented actresses is an even richer experience than reading the dialogue on the page.

COMPANIONS

Zora Neale Hurston: A Literary Biography by Robert E. Hemenway (University of Illinois Press, 1977). The definitive biography, with extensive notes and bibliography.

Zora Neale Hurston: Critical Perspectives Past and Present, edited by Henry Louis Gates and K. A. Appiah (Amistad Press, 1993). Essays, reviews, chronology, bibliography.

Zora Neale Hurston: An Annotated Bibliography and Reference Guide by Rose Parkman Davis (Greenwood Publishing Group, 1997). A guide to books, articles, manuscripts, and Internet resources about Hurston and her work. Also catalogs where her manuscripts, letters, and memorabilia can be found.

BEST OF THE NET
Zora Home Page
i.am/zora

An especially good fan page, with a nicely organized collection of stories, photographs, and essays, and links to other "Zora Resources" on the Net. You can also post messages to the site's Zora Bulletin Board and search an archive of previous postings.

Folk's Tales

NOVELS

Jonah's Gourd Vine, 1934
Their Eyes Were Watching God, 1937
Moses, Man of the Mountain, 1939
Seraph on the Suwanee, 1948

AUTOBIOGRAPHY

Dust Tracks on a Road, 1942

COLLECTED WORKS

A two-volume set of Hurston's major work has been published by the Library of America:
Novels and Stories, 1995
Folklore, Memoirs, and Other Writings, 1995

If You Like
Zora Neale Hurston . . .

Try *The Bluest Eye* by Toni Morrison, *The Color Purple* by Alice Walker, *Dessa Rose* by Sherley Anne Williams, and *The Wedding* by Dorothy West.

Best Book to Read First

Their Eyes Were Watching God. Considered a classic in feminist literature and the author's finest novel, it tells the story of one woman's life journey for fulfillment and freedom, emphasizing the strengths of African-American culture.

I am not tragically colored. There is no great sorrow dammed up in my soul, nor lurking behind my eyes. I do not mind at all. I do not belong to that sobbing school of Negrohood who hold that nature somehow has given them a lowdown dirty deal and whose feelings are all hurt about it. . . . No, I do not weep at the world— I am too busy sharpening my oyster knife.

—Zora Neale Hurston, 1928

Day's End, Eatonville, Florida,

I t was the time for sitting on porches beside the road. It was the time to hear things and talk. These sitters had been tongueless, earless, eyeless conveniences all day long. Mules and other brutes had occupied their skins. But now, the sun and the boss-man were gone, so the skins felt powerful and human. They became lords of sounds and lesser things. They passed nations through their mouths. They sat in judgment."

—Zora Neale Hurston, *Their Eyes Were Watching God*

John Irving

Born
March 2, 1942, in
Exeter, New Hampshire. His adoptive
father was a teacher of
Russian history and
his mother was a
social worker.

Real Name
John Wallace Blunt Jr.
at birth. Changed to
John Winslow Irving
when adopted by his
stepfather at age six.

Education
B.A. (cum laude) from
the University of New
Hampshire, 1965.
(While attending UNH,
Irving studied at the
University of Vienna;
Austria is prominently
featured in some of his
work.) Earned M.F.A. in
1967 from the Iowa
Writers' Workshop,
where he studied with
Kurt Vonnegut Jr.

Family
Married his literary
agent, Janet Turnbull,
in 1987. They have
one son. Irving also
has two sons from his
17-year marriage to
Shyla Leary, which
ended in divorce in
1981.

Home
A luxurious mountain
hideaway in Vermont,
with spectacular views
of the Green Mountains

Publisher
Random House

John Irving is that rare hybrid of contemporary author who has achieved both bestseller status and literary acclaim. His novels are dark, hilarious, life journeys populated with bizarre characters. Despite their eccentricity, Irving protagonists summon incredible sympathy. Irving delves into topics that many authors wouldn't touch with a ten-foot pencil: prostitution, rape, abortion, transsexuality, dwarfism, speech impediments, castration, and other disfigurements. And he manages to make you laugh all the while. He has described his stories as "artfully disguised soap opera." To Irving, literature and entertainment are *not* mutually exclusive.

Long before Quentin Tarantino's *Pulp Fiction*, Irving revealed the fine line between violence and love, cruelty and civility, tragedy and happily-ever-after. He leaves you shocked and open-mouthed at plot twists, and chuckling at the macabre turn the tale has taken. Irving told the *New York Times Book Review*, "In just the same way that I don't see comedy and tragedy as contradictions…I don't see that unhappy endings undermine rich and energetic lives."

Good to Know

❖ A dyslexic child, John Irving did not excel in school. It took him five years to get through Exeter Academy, where his adoptive father taught Russian history.

❖ When starting a novel, Irving typically writes the last line first. He works at his desk, doing the first draft in longhand and the second on an electric typewriter.

❖ *The World According to Garp* made Irving a literary star. Winner of the American Book Award in 1980, *Garp* spent six months on the bestseller lists. Irving was so pleased he treated himself to a "GARP" license plate but eventually had to get rid of it because it made him too conspicuous.

❖ Irving's fiction is often cited for its sensitivity to feminist issues, but he told the *Los Angeles Times* that his "interest in women as a novelist is really very simple….I see every evidence that women are more often victims than men. As a novelist I'm more interested in victims than winners."

❖ Cinema Irving: Academy Award–winner Robin Williams brought Garp to life on the silver screen in 1982, costarring with Glenn Close and John Lithgow. Watch closely—Irving has a cameo as a wrestling-match referee. *The Hotel New Hampshire*, starring Jodie Foster and Rob Lowe, made its film debut in 1984. *Simon Birch*, a 1998 movie featuring Jim Carrey, was inspired by *A Prayer for Owen Meany*. Michael Caine stars in the 1999 Miramax production of *The Cider House Rules*.

Treatises and Treats

COMPANIONS

John Irving: A Critical Companion by Josie P. Campbell (Greenwood Publishing Group). Analyzes all the novels, from *Setting Free the Bears* (1969) to *A Widow for One Year* (1998). Includes a biographical chapter, insightful reviews and criticism, and text that offers readers a unique approach to Irving's work.

IRVING FOR THE EARS

Pension Grillparzer Audiobook (Audio Partners Publishing Corporation, 1989). Irving himself reads this little gem, first published in *The*

World According to Garp as a story written *by* the character Garp, who is also a writer. *Pension* earned acclaim on its own merit and was honored in *The Pushcart Prize II: Best of the Small Presses* (1977) before its "host" novel was ever published. It later became the outline for *The Hotel New Hampshire*. Order on the Web at www.audiopartners.com or call 800-231-4261.

BEST OF THE NET

New York Times Featured Authors

www.nytimes.com/books/specials/
   author.html

Click on "John Irving" for a collection of book reviews, articles, and interviews from the *New York Times* archives. Other goodies include a set of zinging letters to the editor—a moral and intellectual Ping Pong match—between Irving and feminist Andrea Dworkin on the relation-ship between pornography and sexual violence against women.

John Irving Fan Page

hometown.aol.com/forestben/irving.htm
Billed by its creator as "A Very Unofficial John Irving Page," this site is well worth a visit. Highlights include a reliable biographical sketch, an extensive bibliography, reader-favorite poll results, and links to other even *less* official sites, including one that features color photographs of the author's alleged maple-leaf-shaped tattoo that strategically camouflages a shoulder scar.

The World According to Irving

ALL THE NOVELS

Setting Free the Bears, 1969
The Water-Method Man, 1972
The 158-Pound Marriage, 1974
The World According to Garp, 1978
   (American Book Award)
The Hotel New Hampshire, 1981
The Cider House Rules, 1985
A Prayer for Owen Meany, 1989
Son of the Circus, 1994
A Widow for One Year, 1998

IRVING SOUP

Trying to Save Piggy Sneed, 1996. A hodge-podge collection of Irving's short stories, memoirs, and homage pieces written over three decades. Though it received lukewarm reviews, the collection is a good bet for the die-hard Irvingonian. Readers just discovering his work, however, should stick to the bigger fiction.

My Movie Business: A Memoir, 1999. In this slim little volume, Irving explains what motivated him to join the ranks of Hollywood film producers in putting *The Cider House Rules* on the big screen. The book includes 32 pages of black-and-white photographs.

Wrestling His Muse

John Irving may well be America's only novelist-wrestler. His deep passion for the sport began during his prep-school days at Exeter. He continued as an amateur wrestler throughout college and later graduated to coaching. Today, his fully-equipped home health club features a regulation-size wrestling mat. And when neither of his two adult sons (also skilled matsmen) is available to provide some healthy competition during his daily two-hour workout, Irving goes head-to-head with a life-like dummy. Although he has never won a tournament, he's been named one of the National Wrestling Hall of Fame's "Outstanding Americans" for his literary contribution to the sport.

Has wrestling inspired Irving's writing? Definitely. T. S. Garp, his best-known creation, spends time as a wrestling coach. For insight into Irving's love affair with the sport, see *The Imaginary Girlfriend* (1977), a memoir detailing his wrestling adventures.

Best Book to Read First

Start with *The World According to Garp*, considered by readers and critics alike to be Irving's finest book.

The World According to Garp . . . contains almost intolerable pain. It is a bloody package, and if [Irving] had flung this in front of us, we would have backed away in horror. As it is, we read on, at first entertained, then puzzled, then trapped, wanting to look away, but by this time unable to avert our eyes.

—Margaret Drabble, *Harper's*

Irving's philosophy is basic stuff: One must live willfully, purposefully, and watchfully. Accidents, bad luck . . . and open windows lurk everywhere—and the dog really bites. It is only a matter of time. Nobody gets out alive, yet few want to leave early. Irving's popularity is not hard to understand. His world is really the world according to nearly everyone.

—R. Z. Sheppard, *Time*

Henry James

Born
April 15, 1843, in New York City, to Henry James Sr., a noted theologian, philosopher, and son of one of the first American millionaires; and Mary Walsh James

Education
Attended school in France and Switzerland; Harvard Law School, 1862–63.

Family
Older brother William James, the famous philosopher and psychologist (with whom Henry had an intense and competitive relationship all his life), sister Alice (an important diarist), and two younger brothers; never married

Home
Settled in London in 1876, when he was 33; became a British citizen in 1915 in a show of solidarity with British and French soldiers fighting World War I.

Died
February 28, 1916, in London, of edema following a series of strokes. His ashes are buried in Cambridge, Massachusetts.

Publishers
Library of America
Penguin

Were he alive today, Henry James would probably be a revered film director. His sense of place, his insightful, minute observations, and the great psychological depth of his characters would guarantee him critical acclaim and, with a bit of Miramax-style marketing, a level of popular success. But Henry James died in 1916 at the age of 72, and thus had to tell his stories in print. At the time of his death, his novels were all but unread. Only after the observance of his 100th birthday in 1943—when World War II had focused America's attention on Europe—did critics realize that James was one of the greatest novelists of the 19th century.

Henry James believed that every line should count and that there should be none of "the baseness of the arbitrary stroke"—a wonderful concept for poetry or for a short story, but not so much for a long, intricately wrought novel. One must pay attention to every word, something many readers are not willing to do, regardless of the manifest rewards. Thus the suggestion that film, where an image or nuance really is worth a thousand words, would have been the perfect medium for Henry James.

There were later financial reversals, but during his formative years, James's family had lots of money. His father, a friend of Thoreau, Emerson, and Hawthorne, could afford to move the family to London in 1844 in order to be close to Thomas Carlyle and other thinkers, and he entertained writers and artists wherever they lived (Geneva, Paris, Bonn, and elsewhere). By the time James was 21, he had spent almost one-third of his life in foreign countries and most of his time learning foreign languages.

In 1869, at age 26, he arrived in London and soon had introductions to Darwin, George Eliot, Ruskin, Rossetti, William Morris, and others. To put James and his worldview in perspective, one should note that Mark Twain's *The Innocents Abroad* was published that same year. For Twain, James's beloved Venice was an impoverished, faded lady and a gondola was a "rusty old canoe with a sable hearse body clapped onto the middle of it," while the Uffizi museum and Pitti Palace in Florence were "weary miles of picture galleries."

To James, "citizen of the world," Twain and the Americans who read him had to be an embarrassment, at best. At worst, they were uncultured louts concerned only with making money in the "here and now," totally lacking any sense of or appreciation for the past. Henry James was undoubtedly correct. But then, unlike Twain, Melville, and other great 19th-century American novelists, Henry James could afford such lofty views.

Good to Know

❖ Three Henry James novels made the Modern Library's list of the 100 Best Novels of the 20th century: *The Wings of the Dove* (26), *The Ambassadors* (27), and *The Golden Bowl* (32).

❖ Although a master of virtually every form of writing, James felt that criticism was intellectually superior to creative writing and saw himself primarily as a critic. A person of genuinely refined tastes, he was ideally suited to showing his fellow Americans the path to true culture and sophistication.

❖ James's fiction was often inspired by stories and conversations heard at the many dinner parties he attended in London. (During 1878 and 1879, he dined out 140 times.) At one such event, an actress related an anecdote that became the plot of *Washington*

Square. At another, a dining companion advised James to "live all you can...it's a mistake not to," which became the central theme of *The Ambassadors*, rendered as an impassioned plea from Lambert Strether to Little Bilham, "Live all you can, live, live!"

❖ Henry James's stories and novels present only the experience or perception of his characters. This approach to the problem of "point of view" in the novel was first identified and labeled "stream of consciousness" by elder brother William. It's a Jamesian invention that may represent the biggest effect he had on the novelists who followed.

❖ "The James family was the most creative in 19th-century America, and perhaps the most remarkable family America has ever known." So says *A Reader's Guide to Twentieth Century Writers* (Oxford University Press). Descendents of the Adamses, Kennedys, Rockefellers, and Roosevelts may beg to differ. Yet in their time, both Henry and William James certainly made important, indelible marks on their respective occupations. What mother could wish for more?

Treatises and Treats

The Henry James Society
Open to scholars and general readers. Membership is $31 a year and includes a subscription to *The Henry James Review*. For more information, contact Leland S. Person, University of Alabama at Birmingham (205-934-5293, lsperson@uab.edu).

COMPANIONS
Henry James: A Life by Leon Edel (Harper, 1985). Published as both a five-volume work and a single-volume abridged edition, this biography was written by the world's leading James authority and is considered one of the great biographies of our time. Both versions are currently out of print but widely available from used book sources.

The Cambridge Companion to Henry James, edited by Jonathan Freedman (Cambridge University Press, 1998). A collection of essays and critical commentary to introduce new readers to Henry James and his work.

A Henry James Encyclopedia by Robert L. Gale (Greenwood Publishing, 1989). Assembled by a respected Henry James scholar, this 800-page reference work presents more than 3,000 entries, organized alphabetically, describing each of James's works, fictional characters, friends, relatives, and correspondents.

BEST OF THE NET
Henry James Scholar's Guide
www.newpaltz.edu/~hathaway
An extensive, well-organized archive and directory, this is *the* place to begin looking for information about Henry James, including the complete text of many of his novels, discussion groups, conferences, and teaching materials.

Best Novels

Washington Square, 1880
The Portrait of a Lady, 1881
The Bostonians, 1886
The Wings of the Dove, 1902
The Ambassadors, 1903
The Golden Bowl, 1904

If You Like Henry James . . .

You might also like the novels and short stories of his friend Edith Wharton.

Best Book to Read First

The Portrait of a Lady is his masterpiece and perhaps the best expression of his fundamental theme: the contrast between New World "innocence" and Old World "sophistication," and the comedy and tragedy generated when someone from one of these worlds (typically a well-to-do but naive American) is immersed in the other.

James Goes to Hollywood

Since his rediscovery in 1943, many of Henry James's works have been turned into movies. The newest is the Merchant-Ivory film of *The Golden Bowl*, but *Washington Square*, *The Portrait of a Lady*, and *The Wings of the Dove* have also appeared on the big screen in recent years with all-star casts. For the best classic versions of James on film, try *The Heiress* (1949), based on *Washington Square* and starring Olivia de Havilland in an Oscar-winning performance, and *The Turn of the Screw* (1959), a made-for-TV version of James's famous ghost story, with Ingrid Bergman, who won an Emmy for her portrayal of the governess.

P. D. James

Born
August 3, 1920, in
Oxford, England, to
Sidney Victor James, a
tax official, and
Dorothy Hone James.
She was the eldest of
their three children.

Full Name
Phyllis Dorothy James
White

Education
Attended the
Cambridge High School
for Girls from 1931 to
1937 and later took
evening classes in
hospital administra-
tion.

Family
Married Ernest White
in 1941. (He died in
1964.) Two daughters
and five grandchildren.

Home
A large house in
London's Holland Park
area and a cottage in
Southwold

Fan Mail
P. D. James
c/o Greene & Heaton
Ltd.
37 Goldhawk Road
London W12 8QQ
England

Publisher
Knopf

P. D. James occupies a rank in the pantheon of mystery writers equivalent to Agatha Christie, Dorothy L. Sayers, Ngaio Marsh, and Margery Allingham. All five created interesting, urbane, male detectives whose characters and neuroses in some way offset their brilliance and dandyism. James's Scotland Yard detective Adam Dalgliesh (named for one of her teachers) writes poetry, mournfully misses his deceased wife and child, and seems never to fully connect with romantic partners or colleagues. He holds back emotionally, just as one of his suspects might hold back the complete truth.

James is known for her intricate plots and complex characters. In fact, in a P. D. James mystery, the minor figures are as interesting as the major suspects. And when she probes the psychological and sometimes warped depths of her characters, even the innocent reveal dark interior terrains of the heart and mind. Besides extolling her prose style, critics praise her attention to character, motive, plot, and descriptive detail, and the realistic nature of the world she creates in each story. Dalgliesh's cases have allowed her to write not only convincing police procedurals, but also "country house cozies."

"There is a closed circle of suspects," James says of her mysteries, noting that the reader finds the clues along with the detective and has the same opportunity to solve the crime. "And at the end of the story there is a credible and satisfactory resolution." A mystery novel is the modern version of the morality play, James asserts: "The values are basic and unambiguous. Murder is wrong." Her novels provide an antidote to what she calls "an age in which gratuitous violence and arbitrary death have become common."

Good to Know

❖ James's early years were spent in Southwold, on the eastern coast of England in the East Anglia region, the setting for several of her mysteries. "Almost always," James notes, "the idea for a book comes to me as a reaction to a particular place and setting." This could be "an empty stretch of beach or a community of people."

❖ During World War II, while working as a Red Cross nurse, James met and married Ernest White, a doctor. After the war, with her husband suffering from mental illness, James supported the family through her work as a hospital administrator.

❖ She wrote her first novel, *Cover Her Face* (1962), while working as an administrative assistant for a London hospital board. Penned in longhand during two-hour stints before going to work each morning, the book took her three years to complete.

❖ Insider knowledge of police operations came from James's decade of work (1968 to 1979) as principal administrative assistant in London's police and criminal policy departments. She became a full-time writer after retiring in 1979. By that time, she had produced seven successful novels.

❖ From 1979 to 1984, P. D. James served as a justice of the peace in London. The Order of the British Empire was awarded her in 1983, and she was made a peer—Baroness James of Holland Park—in 1991, which entitles her to sit in the House of Lords.

❖ James claims "a murderous instinct," pointing out that by writing a murder mystery, she can "get it out of my system." But friends describe her as an extrovert—friendly, unassuming, hospitable, and good-natured.

❖ She enjoys reading George Eliot, Anthony Trollope, Henry James, and Evelyn Waugh. But her favorite author—one she reads and rereads—is Jane Austen. Favorite mystery writers include Dashiell Hammett, Raymond Chandler, Dorothy L. Sayers, Ross Mac-Donald, Ruth Rendell, Dick Francis, Amanda Cross, and Sue Grafton.

Treatises and Treats

COMPANIONS

P. D. James by Richard G. Gidez (Twayne, 1986) and *P. D. James* by Norma Siebenheller (Ungar, 1981) offer critical commentary and a bibliography. Both books are currently out of print, but you can probably find them through used book sources or at your local library.

P. D. JAMES ON VIDEO

Although several "Dalgliesh" and "Cordelia Gray" novels have been filmed for the PBS series *Mystery*, they're not easy to find on videotape. One excellent source for these videos (as well as many other well-loved PBS/BBC dramas and mysteries) is Brits, a store in Lawrence, Kansas, that specializes in all things British (including food, pub equipment, and London transport posters). Call 888-382-7487 or visit their Web site at www.britsusa.com.

BEST OF THE NET

P. D. James Page

pantheon.yale.edu/~yoder/mystery/
    james.html
A fan page with a short biography and list of works.

New York Times Featured Authors

www.nytimes.com/books/specials/
    author.html
Check here for an interesting collection of reviews and articles, including a 1986 profile of "The Queen of Crime" that appeared in the *New York Times Magazine*.

All the Novels

ADAM DALGLIESH NOVELS

Cover Her Face, 1962
A Mind to Murder, 1963
Unnatural Causes, 1967
Shroud for a Nightingale, 1971
The Black Tower, 1975
Death of an Expert Witness, 1977
A Taste for Death, 1985
Devices and Desires, 1989
Original Sin, 1995
A Certain Justice, 1997

OTHER NOVELS

An Unsuitable Job for a Woman, 1972
Innocent Blood, 1980
The Skull Beneath the Skin, 1982
The Children of Men, 1992 (science fiction)

If You Like
P. D. James . . .

You might also like books by Elizabeth George, Reginald Hill, B. M. Gill, Ruth Rendell, and Minette Walters.

Best Book to Read First

The Adam Dalgliesh mystery *A Taste for Death,* or *An Unsuitable Job for a Woman,* featuring Cordelia Gray.

When some of us heard P. D. James at the Pump Room a few years ago, she said she must have had the mind of a crime writer even as a child, because when she first heard the nursery rhyme about Humpty Dumpty, her thought was "Did he fall, or was he pushed?"

—A character in Peter Lovesey's 1996 mystery novel *Bloodhounds*

The Other Detective

Cordelia Gray is the detective in charge of P. D. James's *An Unsuitable Job for a Woman* and *The Skull Beneath the Skin*. Created in 1972, Gray is an early entry in the ranks of the now numerous fictional women who earn a living as professional detectives. Once a denizen of various foster homes as a child, she seems the opposite of James's primary crime solver, Adam Dalgliesh, in her acceptance of life's chaotic or grim flourishes. Instead of brooding, Gray gets on with it. While Dalgliesh solves murders as a member of the police, Gray is a private eye with her own London agency. Dalgliesh is middle aged; Gray is in her 20s.

Not surprisingly, Cordelia Gray shares some elements of P. D. James's own past. Both left school when they were 16 and had difficult relationships with their fathers. Gray's first solo case takes her to Cambridge, where the teenage James was an assistant stage manager at the Festival Theater. What Gray, Dalgliesh, and P. D. James all share is a meticulously observant eye for detail.

Robert Jordan

Born
October 17, 1948, in Charleston, South Carolina, to James Rigney and Eva May Grooms Rigney

Real Name
James Oliver Rigney Jr.

Pseudonyms
In addition to Robert Jordan, Rigney has written under the names Reagan O'Neal, Jackson O'Reilly, and Chang Lung.

Education
The Citadel (The Military College of South Carolina), B.S. in physics, 1974

Family
Married Harriet McDougal in 1981. One son, William Popham McDougal.

Home
Charleston, South Carolina, in a house built in 1797

Publisher
Tor Books

Robert Jordan has dominated the fantasy/sword-and-sorcery genre for almost a decade. As soon as the latest installment in his "Wheel of Time" series is published, it immediately jumps to the top of the *New York Times* bestseller list.

Jordan has been compared to J. R. R. Tolkien, whose "Lord of the Rings" series captivated an earlier generation of readers. Both authors create "an entirely convincing and compelling alternative world, complete with social systems, cultural differences, and competing motivations" (Jo-Ann Goodwin, *New Statesmen and Society*). Yet Tolkien's work, as one would expect of an Oxford don, has many historical, cultural, and linguistic antecedents. And he sets forth his epic in three volumes (four, if you count *The Hobbit*).

Jordan's books offer echoes of Christian and biblical iconography, allusions to Arthurian legend, and other substantive references. But *The Path of Daggers*, the current installment at this writing, is merely the eighth (and certainly not the last) book in the "Wheel of Time" saga. Perhaps Jordan is more similar to Terry Brooks and the "Shannara" fantasy series than to Tolkien.

More than seven million copies of the books in the "Wheel of Time" series have been sold in North America, and over 100,000 copies of *each* volume are sold in paperback every year—reason enough for any author to keep on writing. Although some critics have noted that the saga's enormous length and huge cast of characters may overwhelm new readers, others have said that "Jordan's talent for sustaining the difficult combination of suspense and resolution, so necessary in a multi-volume series such as this one…is nothing short of remarkable" (*Publishers Weekly*).

Good to Know

❖ Jordan served two tours of duty in Vietnam with the U.S. Army, winning the Distinguished Flying Cross, the Bronze Star with "V," and two Vietnamese Crosses of Gallantry. From 1974 to 1978, he worked for the U.S. Civil Service as a nuclear engineer.

❖ A man of many names: Robert Jordan is not the only pseudonym used by James Rigney. He has also written historical novels as Reagan O'Neal (*The Fallon Blood*, 1980; *The Fallon Pride*, 1981; *The Fallon Legacy*, 1982), Westerns as Jackson O'Reilly (*Cheyenne Riders*, 1982), and articles for periodicals such as *Library Journal*, *Fantasy Review*, and *Science Fiction Review* as Chang Lung.

❖ During the 1980s, Jordan wrote seven novels for the popular "Conan the Barbarian" series created by Robert E. Howard in the 1930s: *Conan the Invincible*, *Conan the Unconquered*, *Conan the Magnificent*, *Conan the Victorious*, *Conan the Triumphant*, *Conan the Destroyer*, and *Conan the Defender*.

❖ When he's not writing, Jordan's favorite pastimes include hunting, fishing, sailing; playing poker, chess, and pool; and adding to his pipe collection.

❖ Wife Harriet McDougal is executive editor and vice president at Tor Books, Jordan's publisher. She edits all the books in his "The Wheel of Time" series, the last several of which have been dedicated to her. Jordan—or rather James Rigney—has also worked as an editor for Tor Books.

Treatises and Treats

COMPANIONS

The World of Robert Jordan's The Wheel of Time by Robert Jordan (Tor Books, 1997). This illustrated guide to "The Wheel of Time" series features portraits of the central characters, landscapes, objects of power, new world maps, and national flags. It also includes the first seven book-jacket paintings by renowned fantasy artist Darrell K. Sweet.

BEST OF THE NET

Robert Jordan's Wheel of Time
www.tor.com/sites/wheel_of_time
The official "Wheel of Time" Web site, with samples of Jordan's work and descriptions of every book in the series.

Wheel of Time Index
student-www.uchicago.edu/users/kor2/ WOT/WOTindex
A fan page offering an exhaustive set of links to the Net's "Wheel of Time" resources—author bios and interviews, discussion groups and fan clubs, plot summaries and character references, literary sources, and more. (Note: The Web address is case-sensitive, so be sure to enter it exactly as shown above.)

Wheel of Time FAQ
linuxmafia.com/jordan
Answers to the most common fan questions, including "What should I do if I become obsessed?" (A humorous five-step program is suggested.) The FAQ also covers what can only be classified as "extreme trivia," such as the age and height of individual characters.

The Complete Wheel

The Eye of the World, 1990
The Great Hunt, 1990
The Dragon Reborn, 1992
The Shadow Rising, 1992
The Fires of Heaven, 1993
Lord of Chaos, 1994
A Crown of Swords, 1996
The Path of Daggers, 1998

If You Like Robert Jordan . . .

You might also like J. R. R. Tolkien's "Lord of the Rings" series, the "Shannara" books by Terry Brooks, and Isaac Asimov's "Foundation Trilogy." Or try Marion Zimmer Bradley, Orson Scott Card, and Terry Goodkind.

How Did It Start, How Will It End?

Jordan started thinking about what would eventually become the "Wheel of Time" series in the mid-1980s, beginning with the last scene of the last book. "I could have written that 15 years ago, and if I had, it would differ from what I would write today only in the words. . . . So, I've known where I'm going from the start."

When asked during a Barnes & Noble online chat if he ever takes fan speculation into consideration when plotting new books, he replied: "I very seldom see any of the speculation. Occasionally someone will send me printouts of things that have been posted on the Web sites. . . . About a third of the speculation there is right, about a third is almost right—it's sort of in the right direction, but they're not quite going in the direction I am—and the remaining third is totally blue sky. But I won't tell anybody which third is which."

Best Book to Read First

The Eye of the World (1990), the initial volume in "The Wheel of Time" series. "No one should expect to start a work of this size except at the beginning." (Roland Green, *Booklist*)

[In fantasy] you can talk about good and evil, right and wrong, and nobody tells you that you're being judgmental. And . . . there's always the belief that you can overcome whatever obstacles there are, that you can make tomorrow better. And not only that you can, but that you will, if you work at it.

—Robert Jordan

James Joyce

Born
Born February 2,
1882, in Dublin,
Ireland, to John Stanis-
laus Joyce, an election
agent who was
appointed tax collector
for Dublin as a reward
for his success in
electing "Irish Home
Rule" candidates, and
Mary Jane Murray
Joyce. He was the
eldest of ten children.

Full Name
James Augustine
Aloysius Joyce

Education
University College,
Dublin, B.A., 1902

Family
Married in 1931 to
Nora Barnacle, a cham-
bermaid he had met
and fallen in love with
in 1904. They lived
together for many
years without marrying
because of his anti-
religious principles.
Two children, a son
and a daughter.

Home
Trieste, Italy, and
Zurich, Switzerland

Died
January 13, 1941, in
Zurich following
surgery for a perfo-
rated ulcer

Publishers
Penguin
Vintage

In 1998, James Joyce's *Ulysses* was declared to be the greatest novel of the 20th century by the Modern Library, confirming an opinion long held by many critics. The same book has also been called the greatest *unread* novel of the century. And it's easy to see why. Over 800 pages long, *Ulysses* details the events of a single day in the life of Leopold Bloom. The book turns a critical eye on Irish culture and society, but these themes have little to do with its literary impact, which was undoubtedly of the same magnitude as Picasso's on the art world. Nothing quite like it had ever been seen before, and everything after follows in its wake.

Joyce's experimentation with language and with the conventional methods of storytelling did nothing less than reconstitute the form of the novel. Employing stream-of-consciousness narration, alternating points of view, interior monologue, puns, literary references, word play, and multiple layers of meaning, Joyce altered the traditional relationship between reader and author. Rather than seeing the reader as a passive party, he invites active interpretation. Thus, the reader who truly engages will discover (among countless other delights) that each episode in *Ulysses* deals with a particular art or science and includes a particular symbol, organ of the human body, and color; and that the three main characters form a trinity of sorts with Stephen as "intellect," Molly as "flesh," and Leopold as the central "everybody" in which can be found both extremes.

Like all great works of art, *Ulysses* can be visited again and again, providing additional and deeper rewards with each encounter. Yet this was not his only book. "James Joyce," a critic once wrote, "was and remains almost unique among novelists in that he published nothing but masterpieces." Joyce's final novel, *Finnegans Wake*, is even more challenging than *Ulysses*. Fortunately, his masterpieces also include the short-story collection *Dubliners* and the novel *A Portrait of the Artist as a Young Man*, both of which offer a much more accessible introduction to this dazzling light of 20th-century fiction.

Good to Know

❖ According to David Lodge in *The Practice of Writing*, Joyce once explained why *Ulysses* was taking so long to write this way: "I have the right words already. What I'm seeking is the perfect order of the words in the sentences I have." *Ulysses* took seven years. *Finnegans Wake*, known until publication as "Work in Progress," required 17.

❖ Joyce's poor eyesight deteriorated until he was almost as blind as Homer. Much like John Milton, he had to rely heavily on his memory and on the secretarial help of friends.

❖ Rejection slips: The story collection *Dubliners* was turned down 22 times before being accepted for publication. *Ulysses* was rejected by two governments before it was finally published in France in 1922. The book was banned in the United States until 1933, when a judge declared that it was not obscene.

❖ The first chapter of *Ulysses* opens in a tower containing a gun platform in its living room and offering a panoramic view of the countryside. The actual tower Joyce describes—one of several built to withstand an invasion by Napoleon—has been turned into the James Joyce Museum, located in Sandycove, just nine miles south of Dublin.

Treatises and Treats

INTERNATIONAL JAMES JOYCE FOUNDATION

Sponsor of an international James Joyce symposium held every other year, this group also serves as a central clearinghouse for information about Joyce—publications, societies and clubs, discussion groups and mailing lists, special events, and Internet resources. The $20 annual membership fee includes a subscription to the group's newsletter. For more information, contact:

International James Joyce Foundation
Department of English
Ohio State University
164 West 17th Avenue
Columbus, OH 43210
614-292-2061
E-mail: ijjf@magnus.acs.ohio-state.edu
Web site: english.ohio-state.edu/
    organizations/ijjf

COMPANIONS

Of the many excellent references and guides to James Joyce's life and work, here are several that new readers will find especially helpful:

A Reader's Guide to James Joyce by William York Tindall (Syracuse University Press, 1995). First published in 1959 and still considered by many to be the best introduction to Joyce's work.

Re Joyce by Anthony Burgess (W.W. Norton & Company, 1968). Burgess makes Joyce accessible for newcomers, but also offers brilliant and insightful analysis sure to fascinate readers already familiar with Joyce's canon.

James Joyce by Richard Ellmann (Oxford University Press, 1983). Considered the definitive account of Joyce's life. A brilliantly styled, witty tour de force that succeeds in showing the genius and the humanity of a most daunting subject.

James Joyce by Edna O'Brien (Viking, 1999). Part of the "Penguin Lives" series of short biographies written by leading novelists, O'Brien's 176-page book offers "Joyce without the footnotes and other academic impedimenta," according to *Booklist*.

BEST OF THE NET

In Bloom: A James Joyce Page

www.joycean.com

A "master site" featuring electronic versions of Joyce's major works, biographical information, essays and reading guides, and an extensive set of links to scores of other Joyce-related resources on the Net. Also includes a discussion board where you can ask questions and exchange views with other readers.

Stately, Plump Volumes

Dubliners, 1914 (collection of short stories)
A Portrait of the Artist as a Young Man, 1916
Ulysses, 1922
Finnegans Wake, 1939

If You Like James Joyce . . .

You might also like *The Sound and the Fury* by William Faulkner and *Jacob's Room* by Virginia Woolf. Both Faulkner and Woolf use a stream-of-consciousness narrative technique to tell their stories.

Best Book to Read First

A Portrait of the Artist as a Young Man, a semi-autobiographical novel remarkable for the intimacy it offers the reader and for its astonishingly vivid passages. The book introduces Stephen Dedalus (who is Joyce) and Joyce's Dublin—both of which are central to *Ulysses*.

Bloomsday Worldwide

For the last seven decades, "Bloomsday" has been celebrated in locations throughout the world on June 16, the day Leopold Bloom in *Ulysses* walked the streets of Dublin and fulfilled the experiences of a lifetime. In many cities, the celebration includes marathon readings of *Ulysses* that typically last 24 hours or more. But nowhere is Bloomsday marked so enthusiastically or imaginatively as in Dublin. Here the events of Leopold Bloom's day are reenacted by anyone who cares to join. Fans retrace his itinerary across Dublin, stopping off for a glass of burgundy and a Gorgonzola sandwich at Davy Byrne's Pub on Duke Street (just as Bloom did), or having an afternoon pint in the Ormond Hotel where Bloom was tempted by the barmaids in the "Sirens" episode.

For information on readings and other Bloomsday events in your area, contact the English department of your nearest college or university. Or use a Web search engine like Yahoo or AltaVista and type this in the search box:
+"James Joyce" +Bloomsday

Jan Karon

Born
1937 in Lenoir, North Carolina, a small town in the western part of the state near the foothills of the Blue Ridge Mountains. Raised by her grandparents with at least one sister.

Real Name
She was named Janice Meredith Wilson after *Janice Meredith: A Story of the American Revolution*, a popular novel by Paul Leicester Ford, published in 1899.

Education
Dropped out of school after eight years.

Family
Married, gave birth, and divorced someone surnamed Karon (pronounced like the name "Karen") by the time she was 18. She prefers not to talk about this part of her life and offers few details. Daughter Candace Freeland is a professional photographer.

Home
Blowing Rock, North Carolina

Publisher
Viking

Sharing a café table with an American couple in Florence, we describe the book we're working on about popular fiction authors. "Oh, you *must* include Jan Karon," they say. Fortunately, we had the good sense not to reply, "Jan who?" Instead, with only the vaguest hope that the IRS would let us write off the meal as a working lunch, we dug for more detail. Our new friends were passionate about Karon and her "Mitford" novels, with their Christian themes and stories of small-town life. And as we have since learned, so are millions of other readers. But why?

The lives of Jan Karon's characters revolve around the church because of her strong belief that people are hungry for novels that show the spiritual as an integral part of everyday life: choir, youth group, summer camp, outreach, spiritual healing, and weekly services. That brought us up short because, although we have lived most of our adult lives on the East Coast, our roots are in the Midwest, and we know (and are related to) people who live like that. They aren't all that "God-fearing"—some have appalling social views—but they are solid citizens who are definitely not part of any lunatic fringe. And the church plays a major role in their lives.

Jan Karon's novels speak to these people by reflecting their reality. Some critics have called her writing treacly and overly sentimental. But in her books, bad things do happen to good people. What sets Karon apart is how her characters confront their misfortunes. They don't whine. They don't give up on life. Instead, they rely on their community and their church to help them through. For they know that this life is but a passing shadow on their greater journey.

Combine this message of hope that resonates so fully in so many lives with an idealized town like Mitford, populated as it is with so many likable, interesting characters, and you may have the answer to the Jan Karon phenomenon. No town is as perfect as Mitford—her novels contain no sex, profanity, or violence—but there are tens of thousands of towns across the country that match Mitford so closely that residents can justifiably feel that Jan Karon is writing about *them*. And so she is.

Good to Know

❖ Jan Karon took it on faith—literally. In 1987, she left a successful advertising career with a Charlotte, North Carolina, ad agency, traded her Mercedes for a rusty Toyota, and moved to a tiny town just 30 miles from where she was raised. Her goal was to become a writer—at age 50, with no track record of published works. The path was never easy, but 12 years later, she was not only a published writer but a bestselling author with millions of devoted fans.

❖ The inspiration for her original book and the resulting series came to her as she lay in bed one night shortly after she had made her move: the image of an Episcopal priest walking down the street. That priest became Father Tim Kavanaugh. And the streets he walked became part of a charming little town named Mitford.

❖ Livermush is one of Jan Karon's favorite foods. A concoction of pork liver, cornmeal, and spices, Mitford fans know that it's a standard menu item at the Main Street Grill. But for the recipe, you'll have to wait until the planned Mitford cookbook is published.

❖ Karon says that there's a little of her in each of her characters, but she has a special affinity for Cynthia Coppersmith, an outspoken woman who has had to rely on her God-given talents to succeed in life. The wedding of Cynthia and Father Tim is the subject of the sixth book in the Mitford series, *A Common Life: A Wedding Story*, due in 2001.

❖ She writes every day, but not on a set schedule—30 minutes one day, three or four hours the next. To be a writer, you must simply write, Karon believes, even when you don't feel like it.

❖ There isn't a town called Mitford anywhere in the United States, though there are at least five "Milfords." Karon says that two of her readers confessed to having bought her first book because they thought the title was *At Home in Milford*.

Treatises and Treats

MORE FROM MITFORD NEWSLETTER
With the help of her publisher, Jan Karon produces a twice-yearly newsletter called *More from Mitford*. Regular features include the author's book-signing schedule, answers to readers' questions, and news concerning Mitford and the series. The newsletter is free, so you can either print it directly from the publisher's Web site (www.penguinputnam.com/mitford), or add your name to the mailing list by calling the Penguin Marketing Department (800-778-6425).

BEST OF THE NET
Mitford Web Site
www.penguinputnam.com/mitford
Created and maintained by Jan Karon's publisher, this site offers book descriptions and excerpts, the complete first chapter of the most recent book in the Mitford series, reading group guides, and an archive of current and past editions of the *More from Mitford* newsletter.

Sweetacre's Jan Karon Links Page
www.geocites.com/Heartland/Hills/3272/
   Jkaron.html
This fan-created Web site features a collection of links to Jan Karon resources on the Web, including articles and interviews, transcripts of online chats, discussion groups, and reviews of the novels.

The Mitford Series

At Home in Mitford, 1994
A Light in the Wind, 1995
These High, Green Hills, 1996
Out to Canaan, 1997
A New Song, 1999

If You Like Jan Karon . . .

Other inspirational writers you might enjoy are Anne Lamott and Iyanla Vanzant. Or try some of these book recommended by Jan Karon herself: the "village novels" of British writer Miss Read (a.k.a. Dora Saint); *A Green Journey* and *Dear John* by Jon Hassler; and the works of Conrad Richter and A. B. Guthrie Jr.

Best Book to Read First
At Home in Mitford, the first book in the Mitford series. You'll meet Episcopal priest Father Tim Kavanaugh and the rest of the residents of Mitford, including the big dog who has moved into the priest's home uninvited. You will also discover why Mitford is known as "the little town with the big heart."

My own world has to be kept very gentle or I can't write these books. My work comes out of a place that's very deep and very tender, and if I allow it to be assaulted, there will be no more Mitford.

—Jan Karon, *BookPage* (1997)

Little Pink House on the Mountain

If you were to walk into Jan Karon's cottage, you might suspect you had stumbled into the home of a romance writer, or perhaps a "love doctor." The color scheme consists of varying shades of pink, accented by floral fabrics, old-fashioned hatboxes, and antique white dressers.

The décor may scream "romance," but the overall effect is one of warmth and welcome. And although readers can't visit Karon in her home, they can visit the mountain village of Blowing Rock, North Carolina, and get the same feeling. Blowing Rock is most certainly the model for Karon's fictional Mitford, a town where Christian folks respect and look after one another, and the church and the local diner serve as gathering places. Karon's "little pink house" is a place of inspiration and comfort for her, as Mitford is for her readers. But she's in the process of buying a farm and moving into a house even farther away from the distractions of the world. Says Karon, "I grow with each book . . . and I think it will help to be around cows being born and seeds being planted and things that aren't just writing."

Garrison Keillor

Born
August 7, 1942, the third of six children, in Anoka, Minnesota, to John Philip Keillor, a railway mail clerk, and Grace Denham Keillor, a homemaker

Real Name
Gary Edward Keillor, but he has used the pen name Garrison since he was 13.

Education
University of Minnesota, B.A., 1966. He paid his tuition by working at the campus radio station and remains a fan of college radio to this day.

Family
Married to his third wife, violinist Jenny Lind Nilsson. One son by his first marriage and a daughter by his third.

Home
A log cabin in Wisconsin, built by Swedish immigrants a century ago. His studio, a tiny frame house on stilts, is within walking distance up a dirt road.

Fan Mail
Garrison Keillor
Minnesota Public
   Radio
45 East Seventh Street
Saint Paul, MN 55101
phc@mpr.org

Publisher
Viking

An unabashed political liberal, humorist Garrison Keillor has created a multi-million dollar empire out of a tiny, imaginary town. Lake Wobegon was born on public radio and later grew into literature.

In 1974, an essay Keillor wrote for the *New Yorker* about the Grand Ole Opry planted the seeds for his own live radio program, *A Prairie Home Companion*. Built around Keillor's monologue about the lives and loves of the residents of mythic Lake Wobegon, this folksy radio program entertains with a wide variety of music, other featured humorists, recurring characters, and humorous bits like "Guy Noir, Private Eye" and "The Lives of the Cowboys." The show is "sponsored" by fake products like Powder Milk Biscuits ("they help shy people get up and do what needs to be done").

Although stories from *Prairie Home* had been collected and published earlier, it wasn't until 1985 that Keillor made his debut as a novelist with *Lake Wobegon Days*, which roosted for over 20 weeks on the *New York Times* bestseller list. Distinctly American in tone and topic, Keillor is a master at coaxing readers into the barbershop, the feed store, the one-room post office, and filling their lazy afternoons with juicy local gossip or a welcome jaunt down memory lane.

And it is often the story within the story—when the storyteller props his boots onto the porch railing and begins, "That reminds me of the time . . ."—that we most savor. Somehow, these small tales are large in impact. Readers take pleasure and comfort in believing that somewhere, in a place called Lake Wobegon, there's still an America populated by folks you can count on, people who are content simply being who they are. The twist is that it's all a midwestern mirage—we feel better about our own Everytown because of Keillor's.

Good to Know

❖ The six-foot-four-inch Keillor performs *A Prairie Home Companion* wearing a white suit with red socks and red suspenders. He has often claimed that the program's signature "News from Lake Wobegon" monologue is performed extemporaneously. But he has also frequently extolled the joys of being a writer and being paid to lie for a living.

❖ Fickle about fiction: Keillor admires John Updike, his "old hero," and enjoys Carl Hiaasen. But he doesn't read much fiction, claiming "it either bores me or it makes me faint with envy."

❖ Keillor's marriage to second wife Ulla Skaerved was highly publicized because of how they came together—and how they fell apart. He rediscovered his "true love" at his 25th high school reunion—she had been an exchange student from Denmark his senior year. He broke off a live-in relationship with the producer of his radio program and married Skaerved in Copenhagen in 1985, only to divorce six years later. Skaerved licked her wounds in a letter to a Minneapolis newspaper, claiming Keillor had left her for another woman.

❖ "Pink Boas, Spangly Tights, Dangly Earrings, and now Governor of Minnesota—WHAT A GUY!," reads the book jacket for Keillor's satire, *Me by Jimmy (Big Boy) Valente*. Pro-wrestler-turned-politician Jesse Ventura was reportedly not pleased, prompting Keillor to respond, "I'm sorry the Governor is steamed about it. A Minnesota humorist would be crazy to ignore Mr. Ventura. . . . He is the best show in town." (*Publishers Weekly*)

Treatises and Treats

COMPANIONS

A Prairie Home Commonplace Book: 25 Years on the Air by Garrison Keillor (Penguin, 1999). The perfect gift book for *Prairie Home Companion* fans, with amusing facts, recollections, scripts, behind-the-scenes photos, recipes, and commercials—everything from "Autoharp" to "Zenith."

Garrison Keillor by Peter A. Scholl (University of Iowa Press, 1994). Takes a look at how Keillor's radio oeuvre has influenced his written storytelling, and how the author's public persona as a performer puts him at odds with his solitary life as a writer.

Garrison Keillor: A Voice of America by Judith Yaross Lee (University of Mississippi Press, 1991). The first-ever full-length analysis of Minnesota's most loved humorist, with discussions of the themes and comic techniques in his songs, poems, commercials, and audience-participation events.

The Man from Lake Wobegon: An Unauthorized Biography of Garrison Keillor by Michael Fedo (St. Martin's Press, 1987). This book is no longer in print, and it leaves off more than a dozen years ago. But it's the only biography that's been done to date, so it might be worth tracking down at the library or through used book sources.

RECORDINGS

Minnesota Public Radio, the official home of *Prairie Home*, offers more cassettes and compact disks than you can shake a stick at. Favorites include *A Prairie Home Companion 20th Anniversary Collection*, *Garrison Keillor's Comedy Theater*, and *A Prairie Home Christmas*. To order, call 800-755-0387.

BEST OF THE NET

Prairie Home Companion Web Site
phc.mpr.org
A must for Keillor fans. One of the really neat features is the searchable archive of *Prairie Home* scripts and audio files.

New York Times Featured Authors
www.nytimes.com/books/specials/author.html
Click on "Garrison Keillor" for a collection of book reviews and articles from the archives of the *New York Times*.

A Keillor Companion

NOVELS AND STORIES

Happy to Be Here, 1982 (stories)
Lake Wobegon Days, 1985
Leaving Home, 1987 (stories)
We Are Still Married, 1989 (stories)
WLT: A Radio Romance, 1991
The Book of Guys, 1993
Wobegon Boy, 1997
Me by Jimmy (Big Boy) Valente, 1999

CHILDREN'S BOOKS

Cat, You Better Come Home, 1995
The Old Man Who Loved Cheese, 1996
The Sandy Bottom Orchestra, 1996

If You Like Garrison Keillor . . .

You might also like that masterful yarn-spinner Mark Twain, with whom he is often compared, and humorists Ring Lardner and James Thurber.

> **Best Book to Read First**
>
> *Lake Wobegon Days*, a proper introduction to Keillor's beloved American Everytown.

> *And that's the news from Lake Wobegon, where all the women are strong, all the men are good looking, and all the children are above average.*
>
> —Garrison Keillor, every Saturday night on *A Prairie Home Companion*

When Keillor Speaks, America Listens

The first broadcast of *A Prairie Home Companion* entertained a live theater audience of 20 people. The program is now heard weekly (broadcast live each Saturday, 6:00 to 8:00 P.M.) on over 400 public radio stations by some 2.2 million listeners. Keillor also hosts a daily five-minute program, *The Writer's Almanac*.

As a child, Keillor lay sprawled for hours in front of his family's big console radio, soaking up the sounds wafting over the airwaves. Some of his favorites: Fred Allen, Fibber McGee and Molly, and Jack Benny. On launching his on-air career in the early 1960s, Keillor says he "walked in, asked for a job, made an audition tape using my biggest, boomiest voice, and got the gig. They were semi-desperate." He went on to win a Grammy Award for his recording of *Lake Wobegon Days* and has been inducted into the Radio Hall of Fame.

Stephen King

Born
September 21, 1947, in Portland, Maine, to Donald Edwin King, a merchant sailor, and Nellie Ruth Pillsbury King

Full Name
Stephen Edwin King

Pseudonym
Richard Bachman

Education
University of Maine at Orono, B.Sc. in English, 1970

Family
Raised by his mother after his father (whose surname was originally Spansky before he legally changed it to King) went out for cigarettes one night and never returned. Married Tabitha Jane Spruce (a novelist who publishes as Tabitha King) in 1971; three children.

Home
Bangor, Maine

Fan Mail
Stephen King
49 Florida Avenue
Bangor, Maine 04401

Publisher
Scribner

Stephen King may be "the world's bestselling novelist." Since 1974, his books have sold 300 million copies in 33 languages. Thanks to his multivolume *The Green Mile*, he is the first writer to have had three, four, and finally five titles appear *simultaneously* on the *New York Times* bestseller list. Most people have either read a Stephen King novel or at least seen a movie based on one of them. Simply stated, he has single-handedly changed the place of horror fiction in the publishing industry and in popular culture. He is famous for terrifying tales replete with vampires, ghosts, and normal people struggling against the supernatural.

Throughout his career, Stephen King has been criticized for writing novels lacking in "literary" merit, but perhaps such comments come from writers who anticipate that King may be remembered long after they are forgotten. Or from those unaware of the fact that the films *Stand by Me* and *The Shawshank Redemption* are based on King novellas, and that several years ago he won first prize in the prestigious O. Henry awards, presented for the best "literary" fiction written each year.

Good to Know

❖ Stephen King says that the people who taught him the most about being a novelist were Max Brand, John D. MacDonald, Richard Matheson, and James M. Cain (*The Postman Always Rings Twice*).

❖ In 1984, King published the novel *Thinner* under the pseudonym Richard Bachman. A Literary Guild reader described the novel as "what Stephen King would write like if Stephen King could really write."

❖ King plays rhythm guitar, sometimes with a rock-and-roll band called the Rock Bottom Remainders. Other members include Dave Barry, Roy Blount Jr., Barbara Kingsolver, Amy Tan, and more than a dozen writers and music critics, plus a few professional musicians. In 1993 the band did a six-city tour, with the proceeds benefiting charities that fight illiteracy and homelessness.

❖ Watch the credits closely and you'll find that Stephen King sometimes appears in the movies based on his fiction. His roles have included: a band leader in *The Shining* (1980), a hoagie man in *Knightriders* (1981), a truck driver in *Creepshow* (1982) and *Creepshow II* (1989), a priest in *Pet Sematary* (1989), a bus driver in *Golden Years* (1991), and a cemetery caretaker in *Sleepwalkers* (1992).

❖ Although he is busy writing a minimum of six pages every day—except Christmas, the Fourth of July, and his birthday—King will autograph a book for anyone willing to send one to his office address (49 Florida Avenue, Bangor, Maine 04401). You must enclose a prepaid, self-addressed book mailer and be prepared to wait up to a year. King signs about 100 books a month and typically has a backlog of 1,200 or more. He will only sign two books per person. That means two books in your entire lifetime. (His assistants maintain strict records.)

❖ King has rarely said "no" to film and television versions of his books, though some have pleased him more than others. His top-ten favorites: *The Green Mile, Stand by Me, Storm of the Century, The Shawshank Redemption, Cujo, Misery, The Stand, Dolores Claiborne, Christine,* and *Pet Sematary*.

Treatises and Treats

COMPANIONS

The Stephen King Companion, edited by George Beahm (Andrews & McMeel, 1989). Contains a wealth of information on King, including almost 70 articles, profiles, and interviews, as well as trivia and rare photographs.

The Complete Stephen King Encyclopedia: The Definitive Guide to the Work of America's Master of Horror by Stephen J. Spignesi (NTC/Contemporary Publishing, 1993). Covers the people, places, and things mentioned in King's novels, as well as helpful reference guides, sidebars, photographs, and drawings.

BEST OF THE NET

Official Stephen King Web Site
www.stephenking.com
The only official, sanctioned Stephen King site on the Web. All information on this site is provided and monitored by King and/or his assistants.

Unofficial Stephen King Web Site
www.utopianweb.com/king
An information-packed fan page, with the latest news on King, as well as interviews, reviews of his books, an extensive bibliography, and more.

New York Times Featured Authors
www.nytimes.com/books/specials/author.html
Click on "Stephen King" for a collection of interviews, book reviews, and a RealAudio recording of the author reading from his work. Also a roundtable debate/discussion about which book is King's best.

King's Crown Jewels

Carrie, 1974
Salem's Lot, 1975
The Shining, 1977
The Stand, 1978
   (uncut edition, 1990)
The Dead Zone, 1979
Firestarter, 1980
Cujo, 1981
Pet Sematary, 1983
Christine, 1983
It, 1986
Misery, 1987
The Tommyknockers, 1987
The Dark Half, 1989
Needful Things, 1991
Gerald's Game, 1992
Dolores Claiborne, 1993
Insomnia, 1994
Rose Madder, 1995
Bag of Bones, 1998

Best Book to Read First

Carrie is the book that launched King's career, though *Firestarter*, *It* and *The Stand* are his most popular hardcover titles to date, each having spent 35 weeks on the *New York Times* best-seller list. Many of King's fans have predicted that *The Stand*, a post-apocalyptic novel, will be his most enduring.

Working His Way Up

Before he became famous, King pumped gas for $1.25 an hour and worked in a commercial laundry for $1.60 an hour. He was paid $35 for his first short story ("The Glass Floor"). In 1971, he earned an annual salary of $6,400 teaching high school English.

During this time, King began working on a novel that would eventually be published as *Carrie*. He wrote several pages, but after deciding that the story had no potential, he crumpled them up and threw them into the trash. Fortunately for King and his fans, his wife retrieved the pages, read them, and convinced King to go ahead with his plans to write the novel. In 1973 he submitted *Carrie* to Doubleday, which bought the book and subsequently sold the paperback rights to New American Library for $400,000.

Jump ahead a couple of decades, and the 1997 *Forbes* magazine survey of the world's 40 most ridiculously overpaid entertainers listed King at the number-eight position, with estimated annual earnings of $50 million. One year later, *Forbes* reported that King had slipped to an estimated income of $40 million, more than John Grisham or Tom Clancy but $25 million less than Michael Crichton.

Muse is a ghost. In a real sense, writing comes as it comes. It really is like ghost-writing. It's like it comes from some-place else. Maxwell Perkins, I think, said that Thomas Wolfe wasn't a writer, he was a divine wind chime. The wind blew through him and he just rattled. And I think that's true of a lot of writers. It's true of me.

—Stephen King, in a 1998 *New Yorker* profile by Mark Singer

Barbara Kingsolver

Born
April 8, 1955, in
Annapolis, Maryland,
to physician Wendell
Kingsolver and Virginia
Henry Kingsolver. Grew
up in eastern
Kentucky.

Education
DePauw University,
B.A., magna cum
laude, 1977. (Her
piano-playing skills won
her a music scholar-
ship, but she studied
biology.) Went on to
study biology and
ecology at University of
Arizona, M.S., 1981.

Family
Married chemist
Joseph Hoffman in
1985. They had one
child, Camille, before
the marriage ended in
divorce. Married
second husband
Steven Hopp, an
ornithologist and guitar
player, in 1996. They
have a daughter, Lily.

Home
Lives outside Tucson,
Arizona, with her
husband and two
daughters.

Fan Mail
Barbara Kingsolver
c/o Frances Goldin
305 East 11th Street
New York, NY 10003

Publisher
HarperCollins

On hearing that Barbara King-solver's novels discuss topics like the Sanctuary movement to shel-ter Central American refugees, laws regulating the adoption of In-dian children, Americans who worked with the Sandinista gov-ernment, and the CIA's installation of the dic-tator Mobutu in the Congo, you might say, "Uh-oh. Political correctness alert. Prepare to be bored silly." But that would be a huge mis-take, for it would mean missing some of the most finely drawn, likable characters—many of them strong-willed women—in modern fiction. To say nothing of good-natured humor that will make you laugh out loud, language woven with great beauty, and an emotional wallop that can leave you short of breath.

Barbara Kingsolver has never denied wanting to make a difference in the world by drawing attention to social and political is-sues in her novels. But she realizes that if she were to write nonfiction books about such topics, "probably all 85 people who are inter-ested in the subject" would read them. Com-menting on *The Poisonwood Bible*, she notes, "Instead I can write a novel that's ostensibly about family and culture and an exotic lo-cale....I really believe that complex ideas can be put across in simple language. And a good plot never hurt anybody. It doesn't cost you in literary terms to give your readers a reason to turn a page."

Combining political advocacy with fiction is nothing new. But doing it *successfully* re-quires extraordinary talent—and Barbara Kingsolver has it. As Karen Karbo noted in the *New York Times Book Review*, Kingsolver is "possessed of an extravagantly gifted narra-tive voice, she blends a fierce and abiding moral vision with benevolent, concise humor.

Her medicine is meant for the head, the heart, and the soul—and it goes down dan-gerously, blissfully, easily." Or, as the *Wash-ington Post* puts it, "There is no one quite like Barbara Kingsolver in contemporary litera-ture." Read one of her novels, and you're sure to agree.

Good to Know

❖ As a child, Kingsolver wrote constantly—anything from stories to essays—and at eight, she began to keep a journal. She says, "I used to beg my mother to let me tell *her* a bedtime story."

❖ In 1963, the Kingsolver family moved to what was then the Belgian Congo. Two years later, the late Mobutu Sese Seko seized power, renaming the country Zaire. It is against that backdrop, instead of the small-town America of her previous novels, that Kingsolver's best-seller *The Poisonwood Bible* is set.

❖ During her college years and two years in Greece and France, Kingsolver worked as an archaeologist, copyeditor, X-ray technician, housecleaner, biological researcher, transla-tor of medical documents, and science writer. She also spent a couple of years (1985–87) as a freelance journalist, doing articles and fea-tures for the *Nation, Smithsonian*, and the *New York Times* and writing fiction at night.

❖ Suffering from insomnia after becoming pregnant with her first child, she ignored her doctor's suggestion that she try to overcome it by scrubbing her bathroom tiles with a tooth-brush. Instead, she sat in a closet and began to write *The Bean Trees*.

❖ Part of the nearly one million dollars Kingsolver received for *The Poisonwood Bible* will go toward the Bellwether, a literary prize she's established for writers of unpublished novels addressing issues of "social injustice." The award, to be announced every two years on May Day, includes a $25,000 cash prize and a publishing contract.

Treatises and Treats

COMPANIONS

Barbara Kingsolver: A Critical Companion by Mary Jean Demarr (Greenwood Publishing, 1999). An extensive analysis of Kingsolver's first four novels, plus discussion of her background as a feminist, journalist, and humanist.

Reader's Guides are available from Harper-Collins for *Animal Dreams*, *The Bean Trees*, *Homeland and Other Stories*, *Pigs in Heaven*, and *The Poisonwood Bible*. Packaged in sets of 20 for book clubs and reading groups, the guides can be ordered from bookstores or by calling 800-242-7737. Or visit www.harpercollins.com/readers and print as many copies as you need.

Barbara Kingsolver: A PBS Documentary. Ideal for book groups or classroom use, this video features Kingsolver speaking in great detail about her writing, background, and published works. Available for $39.95 from the Annenberg/CPB Multimedia Collection (800-532-7637).

BEST OF THE NET

Official Barbara Kingsolver Web Site
www.kingsolver.com
The official site. A great source of book descriptions and excerpts, bibliography, questions and answers, and biography.

New York Times Featured Authors
www.nytimes.com/books/specials/author.html
Click on "Barbara Kingsolver" for book reviews, articles by and about the author, and links to other Internet resources.

Book List

ALL THE NOVELS
The Bean Trees, 1988
Animal Dreams, 1990
Pigs in Heaven, 1993
The Poisonwood Bible, 1999

SHORT-STORY COLLECTION
Homeland and Other Stories, 1989

NONFICTION
Holding the Line: Women in the Great Arizona Mine Strike of 1983, 1989
High Tide in Tucson: Essays from Now or Never, 1995 (Thoughtful, charming, and witty. On a par, some would say, with the essays of Forster, Updike, and just a few other novelists.)

If You Like Barbara Kingsolver . . .

Try Andrea Barrett, Harry Crews, Louise Erdrich, Jane Hamilton, Doris Lessing, Thomas McGuane, John Nichols, and Anne Tyler.

Best Book to Read First

The Bean Trees, winner of the 1988 American Library Association Award, showcases the storytelling, sensitivity, humor, and vibrant characters that are Kingsolver's hallmark.

And on That Note . . .

The soundtrack of the PBS documentary about Barbara Kingsolver, as well as the musical interludes between poems on the audiocassette version of her poetry collection *Another America*, all come from the CD *Fingers Crossed*, an instrumental album by Kingsolver's guitarist husband, Steven Hopp. The CD is available from:

Vireo Music
P.O. Box 31870
Tucson, AZ 85751
members.xoom.com/vireomusic

I don't ever write about real people. That would be stealing, first of all. And second of all, art is supposed to be better than that. If you want a slice of life, look out the window. An artist has to look out that window, isolate one or two suggestive things, and embroider them together with poetry and fabrication, to create a revelation. If we can't, as artists, improve on real life, we should put down our pencils and go bake bread.

—Barbara Kingsolver, in reply to a frequently asked question about whether her work is autobiographical

Dean Koontz

Born
July 9, 1945, in Everett, Pennsylvania, to Ray and Florence Koontz

Pseudonyms
David Axton (adventure)
Brian Coffey (crime/suspense)
K. R. Dwyer (suspense)
Deanna Dwyer (horror)
John Hill (science fiction)
Leigh Nichols (romantic suspense)
Anthony North (thrillers)
Richard Paige (romantic suspense)
Owen West (horror)
Aaron Wolfe (science fiction)

Education
Shippensburg University, B.A., 1966; Litt. D. (honorary degree), 1989

Family
Married Gerda Ann Cerra, his high school sweetheart, in 1966. She serves as his business manager.

Home
Three houses, including a palatial estate overlooking the ocean in Newport Beach, California

Fan Mail
Dean Koontz
P.O. Box 9529
Newport Beach, CA 92658

Publisher
Bantam

According to his publisher, Dean Koontz is one of the five or six most popular writers in the world. The author of more than 60 novels, he has had 7 books reach the number-one spot on the *New York Times* hardcover bestseller list and 11 on the paperback list. His books have sold more than 200 million copies worldwide (a figure that is currently growing by about 17 million copies a year) and have been translated into 33 languages.

Although he has written in most popular genres under many different names, Koontz currently writes "suspense fiction"—page-turning stories with tightly constructed, good-versus-evil plots that combine the styles of horror, science fiction, and romance. His novels often depict violence and the macabre, but Koontz shuns the label of "horror writer," explaining that "too many current horror novels are misanthropic and senselessly bleak. . . . We live in a time of marvels, not a time of disaster." Because of this optimistic view of life, his heroes and heroines most often emerge battered but victorious over the evil forces that try to spell their doom.

Koontz freely admits that much of his early work was not of the highest quality. Inexperience combined with low book advances forced him to churn out title after title to remain afloat. *Whispers*, published in 1980, marked a turning point and signaled his breakout from genre fiction into mainstream success. The story revolves around Bruno Frye's obsession with Hollywood screenwriter Hilary Thomas, who must somehow find the strength to fend off his psychopathic intentions. According to one reviewer, "Frye ranks as one of the most original psychological aberrations in horror fiction."

Known in the industry as a consummate professional and a genuinely nice guy, Koontz clearly cares about his craft. He normally allows only complete and unabridged audio versions of his books, for example, but when abridged versions are produced, he insists on personally making any cuts that are needed. And he is known to have revised several of his early books, including a science fiction novel that he rewrote to more than double the original length, without using a single sentence from the original.

Good to Know

❖ Koontz wrote his first stories at age eight. "I'd write them, draw little covers and staple the edge, and I'd put tape over the staples so nobody hurt their fingers, and sell them for a nickel to relatives. Of course, they were bought under duress."

❖ After teaching English in a Harrisburg, Pennsylvania, high school for a couple of years in the late sixties, Koontz was offered a deal by wife Gerda. "I'll support you for five years," she told him, "and if you can't make it as a writer in that time, you'll never make it." By the end of five years, Koontz was doing well enough to allow Gerda to quit her job and begin working full time as his business manager. He now reportedly commands nearly $6 million per book.

❖ Married for more than 30 years, Koontz and his wife typically work between 60 and 70 hours a week. For years, they have been eating dinner at the same restaurant five nights a week. They employ two assistants, but often answer their own phones. Their personal library includes over 50,000 books, arranged alphabetically by author.

❖ Koontz has never appeared on *Today*, *Good Morning America*, or any of the other East Coast programs normally frequented by authors, partially because he doesn't fly and partially due to an aversion to publicity. He spends no time online and granted his first extensive magazine interview relatively recently—to *Rolling Stone* in 1998.

❖ Thousands of fans write to Koontz each year asking where they can get a copy of *The Book of Counted Sorrows*, frequently mentioned in his books as the source of verse used in his stories. Turns out the book doesn't exist. The verse is made up by Koontz to underline certain themes, and he made up the "source" as well.

Treatises and Treats

COMPANIONS

Dean Koontz: A Writer's Biography by Katherine Ramsland (Harper Prism, 1998). A 528-page biography based on interviews with Koontz and his family, friends, and colleagues. Fans call the book "must reading" but warn potential readers that Ramsland gives away the endings to some of Koontz's novels.

The Dean Koontz Companion by Ed Gorman and others (Berkley, 1994). Interviews, summaries of film and TV adaptations, short writings by Koontz, and an annotated bibliography of his 60-odd novels. Called "pure, uncritical publicity" by *Booklist*, but generally recommended by fans.

Dean Koontz: A Critical Companion by Joan G. Kotker (Greenwood Publishing Group, 1996). Critical commentary on Koontz's "mature" fiction, intended "to provide both conventional and alternative readings" of 16 of the author's later novels.

BEST OF THE NET

Random House Web Site
www.randomhouse.com/features/koontz
A great resource for biographical information, excerpts from recent books, reviews, and interviews—many of which display Dean Koontz's quirky sense of humor.

Dean Koontz Fan Page
www.call-us.demon.co.uk
Highlights of this popular fan page include answers to frequently asked questions about Dean Koontz and his books, a collection of trivia, author quotes, and a picture gallery.

Best of the Bestsellers

Seven Dean Koontz novels have appeared in the number-one spot on the *New York Times* hardcover bestseller list:

Lightning, 1988
Midnight, 1989
Cold Fire, 1991
Hideaway, 1992
Dragon Tears, 1992
Intensity, 1995
Sole Survivor, 1997

If You Like Dean Koontz . . .

Try Thomas Harris, Jonathan Kellerman, and Stephen King. You might also want to look for books written under one of his many pseudonyms. Or try Koontz's own favorite suspense writer, John D. MacDonald.

Best Book to Read First

Intensity. One of the author's favorites, this book is a "pulse-pounder" that lives up to its name.

Looking for the kind of suspense that will raise goosebumps on your goosebumps? Cozy up to the latest pulse-quickener from Dean Koontz.

—*People* magazine

Real-Life Terror

As a suspense writer who deals in fear and how his characters react to it, Koontz has powerful childhood memories that allow him to understand his characters' plight. "I was always frightened when [my father] was there," Koontz told *Entertainment Weekly* in a 1996 interview. "I always thought, 'This is the night he's going to kill me and my mother.'"

His father, Ray Koontz, was a paranoid schizophrenic and an alcoholic who would often fly into a rage with little warning, hitting his wife and breaking furniture. "He'd usually come home drunk, and the drunker he was the angrier he got," remembers Koontz. "If he came up the driveway really fast with gravel flying, and you'd hear bonk, bonk, bonk on the horn, that's when my mother would usher me into my room, close the door, and say, 'Don't come out.'"

Wally Lamb

Born
October 17, 1950, in
Norwich, Connecticut,
to Walter Lamb, a
superintendent for the
gas company at the
local power utility, and
Anna Pedace Lamb, a
homemaker. He was
the third of their three
children and the only
boy.

Full Name
Walter Lamb

Education
University of
Connecticut, B.A. in
Education, Phi Beta
Kappa, 1972, and
M.A. in education,
1977. Also earned an
M.F.A. in creative
writing from Vermont
College, 1984.

Family
Married elementary
school teacher Chris-
tine Grabarek in 1978.
They have three sons,
two cats, and a golden
retriever.

Home
The suburban commu-
nity of Willimantic,
Connecticut

Fan Mail
Wally Lamb
c/o Linda Chester
   Literary Agency
1035 Fifth Avenue
New York, NY 10028

Publisher
HarperCollins

Wally Lamb has captivated millions of readers by creating endearing heroes and heroines—survivors stuck at the crossroads of self-discovery. Described by one reviewer as a "modern-day Dostoyevsky with a pop sensibility," Lamb creates humor from his protagonist's endurance of pain and perpetual sense of hope. His lively narratives are ripe with cultural references and filled with the struggles of the Baby Boom generation.

Touched by Lamb's balance of tragedy and comedy in his first novel, *She's Come Undone*, Oprah Winfrey declared, "It's not just a book, it's a life experience." Winfrey's selection of the book for her monthly book club changed Lamb's own life experience. Propelled by the "Oprah Effect" five years after it was first published, the book catapulted to the top of bestseller lists and transformed him from a simple high school English teacher into one of the most popular writers in America.

Good to Know

❖ Wally Lamb began writing fiction on Memorial Day 1981, the morning his first son was born. Exhausted and energized by an all-nighter in the delivery room, he returned home and started his first short story, "Mister Softee," about a teenage ice cream vendor. It was published three years later in *Northeast* magazine.

❖ From Rags to Power Windows: In 1991, high-school-teacher Lamb was on his hands and knees scraping a wad of chewing gum from the classroom floor when publisher Judith Regan called. She'd just finished reading the manuscript for *She's Come Undone* and offered to buy it for an advance of $150,000— a phenomenal sum for a first novel. Lamb used part of the money to purchase a new Honda, his family's first air-conditioned car.

❖ His female characters are so convincing that readers are often stunned to learn that Wally Lamb is a man. How does he do it? Lamb says that a good deal of the credit goes to his wife Chris ("the most honestly critical fan a writer could have") and to the women in his 15-year-old writer's group who have served as advisors over the years. And then there are his two older sisters. "I was cast in the role of the observer very early on," Lamb told *Book* magazine. "I would watch their odd behavior. They dressed as harem girls, they ironed each other's hair on the ironing board trying to look like Cher, and I was the dopey little brother annoying them."

❖ Though he hasn't yet earned a Pulitzer or a Nobel, Lamb has won a number of literary awards in his short career. *She's Come Undone* was a finalist for the *Los Angeles Times* Book Awards first-fiction prize and was named a Notable Book of the Year by the *New York Times* and *People* magazine.

❖ Hooray for Hollywood! Twentieth Century Fox paid upwards of seven figures for the movie rights to *I Know This Much Is True*, to be directed by Oscar-winning director/producer Jonathan Demme (*The Silence of the Lambs*, *Philadelphia*, *Beloved*). And Lamb has agreed to write the screenplay for *She's Come Undone* before starting his third novel, *Sire of Sorrow*.

❖ Despite his commercial and critical success, Lamb still loves the classroom. He taught creative writing at Norwich Free Academy until 1998, when he joined the English Department of his alma mater, the University of Connecticut. Already the popular professor, he launched the *Long River Review*, an annual literary journal featuring the work of creative-writing students.

❖ Family rather than career is Lamb's first priority. His three sons keep their famous father humble. ("There's no danger in my house of success going to my head," says Lamb. His nickname around the house is "the Geezer.") He's also actively involved in his community, serving on the board of directors of the local public library and volunteering at a day care center for children of high school students.

Treatises and Treats

BEST OF THE NET

Oprah's Book Club

www.oprah.com

Wally Lamb has appeared twice on Oprah Winfrey's Book Club, so this Web site offers lots of information about him and his books,

including a set of 20 discussion questions for *She's Come Undone* and for *I Know This Much Is True*.

University of Connecticut Web Site

www.uconn.edu

Curious to know what courses Wally Lamb is teaching this semester? Visit the home page of his employer and alma mater and key in a search for "Wally Lamb." You'll find information about his classes and other activities on campus, as well as a collection of articles from the archives of the campus newspaper.

Reading List

NOVELS

She's Come Undone, 1992
I Know This Much Is True, 1997
Sire of Sorrow (scheduled for 2001)

ANTHOLOGIES FEATURING LAMB'S SHORT STORIES

Streetsongs: New Voices in Fiction, 1990
Pushcart Prize XV: Best of the Small Presses 1990–1991, 1990
Best of the Missouri Review 1978–1990, 1991

If You Like Wally Lamb . . .

You might like some of these contemporary authors who Lamb says have inspired him and helped him to better understand the themes in his own writing: Margaret Atwood, Gabriel García Márquez, Harper Lee, Toni Morrison, Flannery O'Connor, Anne Tyler, John Updike, and Alice Walker.

Best Book to Read First

She's Come Undone, praised on Oprah's Book Club as "a deeply affecting, often hilarious novel that centers around one of the most extraordinary characters in recent American fiction: wisecracking, ever-vulnerable Dolores Price."

The Early Bird Gets the Bestseller

It took Wally Lamb more than eight years to write *She's Come Undone*. During that time, he would typically leave his house at 4 A.M., pick up gallons of coffee, and write with pen and pad in the University of Connecticut's library. At around 7 A.M., he would pack up and head for his teaching job.

These days, still busy teaching and even busier giving interviews and lectures, he's found himself a new place that offers the peace and quiet he needs to write. It's an almost bare apartment in Willimantic, furnished with just a desk and chair and decorated with bulletin boards that he uses for outlining his plots. The biggest advantage of the apartment? No phone.

John Updike once observed that J. D. Salinger loves some of his characters "more than God loves them," which might be said about Wally Lamb. Excess is tolerable, however, when those characters are equally endearing to the reader, as Dolores Price is, even in her most self-deprecatory moments: this reader kept rooting for her to overcome all adversity and find peace and happiness.

—Hilma Wolitzer, in a review of *She's Come Undone* for the *New York Times Book Review*

Louis L'Amour

Born
March 22, 1908, in
Jamestown, North
Dakota, to Louis
LaMoore, a veterinarian
and farm-machinery
salesman, and Emily
Dearborn LaMoore; the
youngest of seven
children

Real Name
Louis Dearborn
LaMoore (he used the
French pronunciation
"Louie" and changed
his last name back to
the original French
spelling)

Pseudonyms
Tex Burns and Jim
Mayo

Education
Self-educated (left
school when he was
15)

Family
Married in 1956 to
Kathy Adams, an
actress who had
appeared on *Gunsmoke*
and *Death Valley Days*.
Two children.

Home
Los Angeles, Cali-
fornia, and an
1,800-acre ranch in
Durango, Colorado

Died
June 10, 1988, of lung
cancer, although he
never smoked

Publisher
Bantam

Louis L'Amour was one of America's most prolific bestselling authors. He wrote over 115 novels, most of them published as paperback originals, and when he died, over 200 million copies of his books were in print. Indeed, L'Amour is said to have written more million-copy bestsellers than any other American fiction writer. "Probably the biggest reason for L'Amour's success," according to Ben Yagoda in *Esquire*, was "his attention to authenticity and detail. . . . His books are full of geographical and historical information."

Initially ignored by critics, who found his characters simplistic and his plots predictable, L'Amour found a vast audience that was hungry for characters who believed in honor, duty, and loyalty. His Western heroes respected the environment, admired the Indian way of life, overcame villains and the chaos they represented, and enjoyed the company of beautiful women. "I think of myself in the oral tradition," L'Amour once said, "as a troubadour, a village tale-teller, the man in the shadows of the campfire. That's the way I'd like to be remembered—as a storyteller. A good storyteller."

Good to Know

❖ L'Amour didn't publish his first novel until he was past 40. By then, his work history included jobs as a longshoreman, lumberjack, miner, circus-elephant handler, hay shocker, bare-fisted boxer, flume builder, fruit picker, and seaman on an African schooner. But he always knew he wanted to be a writer, "almost from the time I could walk," he once said. (Since 1816, over 30 members of his family had been writers.)

❖ Before turning to Westerns, L'Amour tried his hand at poetry. In fact, his first book was a privately published collection of poems called *Smoke from This Altar* (1939). Reprinted by Bantam years later, the book is his least popular title, with a "mere" 107,000 copies in print.

❖ He met his future wife Kathy on a double date in 1952. But the woman L'Amour had been paired up with was actress Julie Newmar, who later played Catwoman on the 1966 TV series *Batman*. The two went to New York together but eventually broke up. "And one day," Kathy L'Amour remembers, "I was driving down the street, and he was buying a newspaper on Sunset Boulevard. . . . I stopped and said, 'I don't know if you'll remember me,' and he said, 'I've been looking everywhere for you!'"

❖ More than 45 L'Amour novels and short stories have been filmed, beginning with *Hondo*, starring John Wayne, in 1953. The novel is based on the author's short story, "The Gift of Cochise," which first appeared in *Colliers*. Wayne bought the screen rights for $4,000 in 1952 for his newly formed production company.

❖ Louis L'Amour wrote three novels a year for over 30 years. Yet he wasn't even close to exhausting the material he had gathered. At the time of his death in 1988, he had developed outlines for 50 more novels and had his own book-of-the-month club.

❖ He once considered switching from an electric typewriter to a computer. But when son Beau told him that it would take about six weeks to become a proficient PC user, he decided against making the switch, concluding that it would cost him an entire book.

Treatises and Treats

COMPANIONS

The Louis L'Amour Companion by Robert Weinberg and Louis L'Amour (Bantam, 1994). From his first published story to a complete chronicle of L'Amour's novels and short stories, the *Companion* is an excellent resource for fans and newcomers alike.

The Sackett Companion: A Personal Guide to the Sackett Novels by Louis L'Amour (Bantam, 1992). L'Amour himself walks the reader through the creation of his 17-book saga of the Sackett family, beginning with *The Daybreakers* in 1960. Covers plots, characters, settings, a glossary, and the Sackett family tree.

Education of a Wandering Man by Louis L'Amour, with an introduction by Daniel J. Boorstin (Bantam, 1990). Though a bit rambling, according to a review in *Library Journal*, L'Amour demonstrates in this book of memoirs "a raw enthusiasm for life and for books that is too rarely encountered today." Dedicated fans will treasure the book, despite its flaws. Others may want to wait for Beau L'Amour's biography of his dad, which is in the works.

A Trail of Memories: The Quotations of Louis L'Amour by Angelique L'Amour (Bantam Books, 1988). Compiled by his daughter, *Quotations* offers selections drawn from L'Amour's best-loved works.

BEST OF THE NET

Official Louis L'Amour Web Site
www.louislamourbooks.com
An excellent starting point for information about L'Amour and his books. You'll find a brief biography, descriptions of each book, a bulletin board and mailing list, trivia contest, and suggestions for further reading.

Louis L'Amour Fan Page
www.veinotte.com/lamour
Another well-organized and informative site, with biographical information, bibliography, movie adaptations, and a very active discussion forum where you can ask questions and share thoughts with other L'Amour fans.

On the Range

THE "SACKETT FAMILY" NOVELS

The Daybreakers, 1960
Sackett, 1961
Lando, 1962
Mojave Crossing, 1964
The Sackett Brand, 1965
Mustang Man, 1966
The Sky-Liners, 1967
The Lonely Men, 1969
Galloway, 1970
Ride the Dark Trail, 1972
Treasure Mountain, 1972
Sackett's Land, 1974
To the Far Blue Mountains, 1976
Sackett's Gold, 1977
The Warrior's Path, 1980
Ride the River, 1983
Jubal Sackett, 1985

OTHER RECOMMENDED NOVELS

Hondo, 1953
Flint, 1960
Down the Long Hills, 1968
    (Spur Award)
Bendigo Shafter, 1978
    (American Book Award)
The Lonesome Gods, 1983
The Walking Drum, 1984
Last of the Breed, 1986
The Haunted Mesa, 1987

If You Like Louis L'Amour . . .

You might also like books by Max Brand, Zane Grey, Larry McMurtry, and Luke Short.

Best Book to Read First

Either *Hondo* or *Flint*, both of which were voted among the 25 best Western novels ever written by the Western Writers of America.

There's no difference in the Western novel and any other novel. . . . A Western starts with a beginning and it goes to an end. It's a story about people, and that's the important thing to always remember. Every story is about people— people against the canvas of their times.

—Louis L'Amour, in a 1987 interview for *Contemporary Authors*

Friends in High Places

Both Jimmy Carter and Ronald Reagan are Louis L'Amour fans. In fact, President Reagan awarded him the Presidential Medal of Freedom in 1984. L'Amour also received the Congressional Gold Medal, the first writer to have been so honored.

D. H. Lawrence

Born
September 11, 1885, in Eastwood, Notting-hamshire, England, the fourth of five children of John Arthur Lawrence, a coal miner, and Lydia Beardsall Lawrence, a school teacher

Full Name
David Herbert Richard Lawrence. Called "Bert" by his family.

Pseudonyms
Jessie Chambers and Lawrence H. Davison

Education
Nottingham University College, teacher train-ing certificate, 1908

Family
Eloped in 1911 with German aristocrat Frieda von Richthofen Weekley, sister of the celebrated World War I ace known as "The Red Baron." The couple married in 1914.

Home
Lived in England, but also at various times in Italy, Ceylon, Australia, Mexico, and the U.S.

Died
March 2, 1930, in Vence, France, of tuber-culosis

Publishers
Bantam
Modern Library
Penguin

You're an adolescent boy who chances upon *Lady Chatterley's Lover* tucked away behind the re-spectable books in your grandpar-ents' library. On reading the blurb, your first thought is "Can I get it out of here without being noticed?" Somehow you do and, with skills honed paging through a copy of Harold Robbins's *The Carpet-baggers* that was passed around your school cafeteria, you quickly zero in on the sexy parts. Said parts are stunning in their sensuality, at least by 1960s standards.

But with eyes now nearly as old as those of that set of grandparents, one can look back on *Lady Chatterley* and realize, first, that it is among the author's lesser works, and second, that D. H. Lawrence was anything but a pornog-rapher. Sex and sensuality were important to him and his worldview, but not for salacious reasons. To a greater degree than most novel-ists, Lawrence had a philosophical message to convey. The message was constantly evolving, but fundamentally, it was one of naturalism, of what he called "blood consciousness" that ex-ists independently of "mental consciousness." It was his answer to the question, "How should we human beings live in this world?"

Consider this passage from *The Rainbow*:

> They felt the rush of the sap in spring, they knew the wave which cannot halt, but every year throws forward the seed to begetting, and, falling back, leaves the young-born on the earth. They knew the intercourse between heaven and earth, sunshine drawn into the breast and bowels, the rain sucked up in the daytime, nakedness that comes under the wind in autumn, showing the birds' nests no longer worth hiding.

You need to catch your breath and read the passage again. This is William Blake. This is Walt Whitman. Mystical. Sensual. Connected to the earth, to life, and to one part of the greater Being. Today, D. H. Lawrence's ideas, literary style, and explicit sensuality would not raise a ripple. But appearing as they did at the end of one era and the beginning of another, his works were challenged under obscenity statutes. (Scotland Yard even confiscated some of the paintings he had done.)

Lawrence believed in the transformative power of literature, and, as Anthony Burgess wrote, his exertions disturbed both readers and writing itself. "Lawrence's world is the di-vine unconscious," said Burgess, "and it sits strangely with the chairs, newspapers, and ashtrays of the modern realistic novel."

Good to Know

❖ Lawrence's writing left many readers baf-fled. But some of his peers "got it," including E. M. Forster, who called him "the greatest imag-inative genius of our generation." Ezra Pound said, "I think Lawrence learned the proper treatment of modern subjects before I did."

❖ Five years after his death and burial in France, Frieda Lawrence arranged to have her husband's body exhumed, cremated, and brought to Taos, New Mexico, where Lawrence had once dreamed of establishing a utopian community. Angelo Ravagli, Frieda's lover at the time, was to accompany the ashes to Taos. Some years later, Ravagli confessed that he had dumped the author's ashes in France to avoid the expense and trouble of transporting them, and the ones he delivered to Frieda had been picked up in New York.

❖ Lawrence wrote over 5,500 letters—a body of work viewed by critics as one of his major achievements—placing him next to Byron as one of the greatest correspondents in the language. The letters are available as *Reflections on the Death of a Porcupine and Other Essays* from Cambridge University Press.

Treatises and Treats

COMPANIONS

D. H. Lawrence: A Reference Companion by Paul Poplawski (Greenwood, 1996). A comprehensive but easy-to-use guide to Lawrence's life and work, designed so that readers can quickly find information on a specific aspect of his career—even a specific novel or story.

A Flame into Being: The Life and Work of D. H. Lawrence by Anthony Burgess (Arbor House, 1985). This book is currently out of print, but it's worth looking for at your local library or favorite used book source. For a lengthy excerpt, visit the *New York Times* Web site (search.nytimes.com/books/search) and type the phrase "The Literature of Natural Man" (including quote marks) in the box labeled "Entire Books Archive."

D. H. Lawrence, The Early Years, 1885–1912 by John Worthen (1991); *D. H. Lawrence, Triumph to Exile, 1912–1922* by Mark Kinkead-Weekes (1996); and *D. H. Lawrence: Dying Game, 1922–1930* by David Ellis (1998). This three-part biography from Cambridge University Press aims to be the definitive record.

BEST OF THE NET

Rananim Society Web Site
www.ukonline.co.uk/rananim/lawrence
With biographical information, reviews, critical commentary, online texts, and photographs, this site also serves as a virtual community of Lawrence enthusiasts. ("Rananim" is the name Lawrence used to refer to the utopian society he hoped to create.)

D. H. Lawrence Collection
www.library.nottingham.ac.uk
This is a no-nonsense repository of news, writings, and links of particular interest to Lawrence scholars and students. The site also provides contact information for D. H. Lawrence Societies throughout the world.

Best Reads

The White Peacock, 1911
The Trespasser, 1912
Sons and Lovers, 1913
The Rainbow, 1915
Women in Love, 1920
The Lost Girl, 1920
The Plumed Serpent, 1926
Lady Chatterley's Lover, 1928
The Virgin and the Gypsy, 1930

If You Like D. H. Lawrence . . .

Part of the excitement of reading Lawrence is the sense that he is trying something new. He and his compatriots were part of the great artistic upheaval of modernism in its most vital years. Reading other writers of his day conveys both an impression of the times and literary history in the making.

Try *Antic Hay* or *After Many a Summer Dies the Swan* by Lawrence's friend, Aldous Huxley. Or Henry Miller, who was also popularly known as a rollicking sexualist and who was also banned—though his writing was adored by the avant-garde everywhere. Miller's *Tropic of Cancer*, *Black Spring*, and *Tropic of Capricorn* are autobiographies fictionalized in the Laurentian manner, but supercharged with a furious bohemianism that Lawrence could never have mustered.

Best Book to Read First

Sons and Lovers, his most widely read book. Or *Women in Love*, a masterpiece that was made into a 1969 film starring Alan Bates, Oliver Reed, and Glenda Jackson.

Such Beautiful People . . .

Lawrence died intestate. But Frieda Lawrence managed to land his entire literary estate—one of the most valuable in the world—after a legal battle with his family. She ended up with over 100 manuscripts, some handwritten, including all three versions of *Lady Chatterley's Lover*.

Frieda did quite well over the years, dribbling the works out through a dealer in Los Angeles. But even before Lawrence's death she had taken up with Angelo Ravagli, a former sharpshooter in the Italian army. They lived together in Taos, New Mexico. On occasion they would dole out a parcel of their literary wealth, just to impress visitors. They sold the three *Lady Chatterley* manuscripts for a mere $10,000 to "a beautiful international couple" they barely knew.

John le Carré

Born
October 19, 1931, in Poole, Dorsetshire, England, to Ronald and Olive Cornwell. A shady businessman, Ronnie Cornwell was eventually jailed for fraud.

Real Name
David John Moore Cornwell

Education
Attended Bern University, Switzerland, 1948–49; Oxford, B.A. in German literature (with honors), 1956.

Family
Married Alison Sharp in 1954. They had three sons before divorcing in 1971. Married Valerie Jane Eustace in 1972, with whom he has one son. Ten grandchildren.

Home
Cornwall and Hampstead, England

Fan Mail
John le Carré
c/o David Higham, Ltd.
5-8 Lower John Street
Golden Square
London W1R 4HA
England

Publisher
Knopf

Like many other novelists who specialized in Cold War themes and backgrounds, John le Carré has had to move on. Still, his suspenseful tales of espionage are considered the finest in the genre, and they never were about the Cold War per se. His lean prose, ear for dialogue, and suspenseful plotting draw readers into a world of betrayal and fear, where moral ambiguity rules and decent men are enticed into treachery. In an article for the *New Yorker* (March 15, 1999), Timothy Garton Ash writes that le Carré's true subject matter is not really espionage, but "the endlessly deceptive maze of human relations: the betrayal that is a kind of love, the lie that is sort of truth, good men serving bad causes and bad men serving good."

In his first novels, *Call for the Dead* and *A Murder of Quality*, le Carré introduces George Smiley, an intelligence agent featured in many of his later novels. However, it was the 1963 publication of *The Spy Who Came in from the Cold* that distinguished le Carré as both a critical and commercial success. Many critics believe that with this book, he transcended the genre, raising the spy novel to the level of serious literature. His success continued with subsequent books, and in 1974 he published *Tinker, Tailor, Soldier, Spy*, the first book in a loosely connected trilogy in which George Smiley is pitted against the Russian master spy "Karla," who artfully planted a "sleeper" in Smiley's operation years ago. The sleeper has been activated and Smiley must deduce who he or she is.

A number of le Carré's books have been made into movies, including *Tinker, Tailor*, which was filmed for television by the BBC in 1980 with an all-star cast: Alec Guinness, Joss Ackland, Warren Clarke (of *Dalziel and Pascoe* on PBS), Ian Richardson (of the three-part *House of Cards* PBS drama), and many other leading actors and actresses. More recently, his 1989 book *The Russia House* was adapted for the big screen in a 1990 film starring Sean Connery and Michelle Pfeiffer.

Good to Know

❖ Ronnie Cornwell admonished his son against reading in his presence. But young David Cornwell read books secretly and was influenced by the works of authors such as Charles Dickens and Joseph Conrad. In fact, several critics have noted similarities between le Carré's *The Honourable Schoolboy* and Conrad's *Lord Jim*.

❖ Le Carré's first two novels were written while he worked for the British Foreign Office in London. Prior to that, he had worked for an undisclosed length of time with the British Secret Service. It was the success of *The Spy Who Came in from the Cold* that enabled him to quit his job and write full-time.

❖ His most famous character is George Smiley, a short, fat, quiet man who wears "really bad clothes, which hung about his squat frame like skin on a shrunken toad." But, of course, Smiley is a brilliant espionage agent who is strangely at home in the moral ambiguities of the profession. His finest hours are spent battling the Soviet superspy "Karla" through three sequential novels. "[Smiley] grew out of two people," le Carré told the London *Sunday Times*. "One was a spook I was working with who wrote novels under the name of John Bingham and was otherwise the Lord Clanmorris." About the other, le Carré would say only that he was an Oxford lecturer "who became effectively my confessor and godfather." The newspaper speculated that he was the Reverend Vivian Green, the author's tutor at Oxford.

❖ Because of his diplomatic position, Cornwell was required to publish his writing under a pseudonym. He settled on John le Carré (*le carré* is French for "the square").

❖ Never having learned to type, le Carré writes all of his novels the old-fashioned way: by hand. He's the inventor of a spy lexicon that is widely used today. Terms like *babysitters* (bodyguards), *honey-traps* (sexual entrapment), and *mole* (deep-penetration agent) all first appeared on the pages of his novels.

Treatises and Treats

COMPANIONS

Understanding John le Carré by John L. Cobbs (University of South Carolina Press, 1997). Analyzing each of le Carré's novels, Cobbs builds a convincing case that le Carré is first and foremost a social critic who writes novels of manners that transcend the espionage genre. Cobbs also presents a biographical sketch, including the author's often overlooked academic success as well as his career with British Intelligence.

John le Carré by Lynndianne Beene (Macmillan, 1992.) A comprehensive study that examines the significance of le Carré's work as a thriller writer and a serious literary novelist.

BEST OF THE NET

John le Carré Resources on the Web
www.robotwisdom.com/jorn/lecarre.html
A nicely organized collection of links to interviews, book reviews, fan pages, and biographical information about John le Carré. A great place for any fan or just the curious reader.

Book List

INTRODUCING GEORGE SMILEY . . .

Call for the Dead, 1961 (published in the
  U.S. as *The Deadly Affair*, 1966)
A Murder of Quality, 1963
The Spy Who Came in from the Cold, 1963
The Looking Glass War, 1965

THE SMILEY/"KARLA" TRILOGY

Tinker, Tailor, Soldier, Spy, 1974
The Honourable Schoolboy, 1977
Smiley's People, 1980

THE REST OF THE STORIES

A Small Town in Germany, 1968
The Little Drummer Girl, 1983
A Perfect Spy, 1986
The Russia House, 1989
The Secret Pilgrim, 1991
The Night Manager, 1993
Our Game, 1995
The Tailor of Panama, 1996
Single & Single, 1999

If You Like John le Carré . . .

You might also like books by Eric Ambler, William F. Buckley, John Creasey, Len Deighton, John Gardner, Bill Granger, and Graham Greene.

A Boy's Life

Graham Greene once remarked that childhood is a novelist's bank balance. In that regard, John le Carré is a wealthy man. Growing up without a mother (she defected from the family when he was five) and being raised by a father who was a womanizer and a con man gave le Carré a great deal of material from which to draw.

In a 1999 interview for the *New York Times*, le Carré alludes to these childhood influences: "Why did I, as a chap of 29 years old, invent a hero of Smiley's age, and somebody of such flawed perfection as Smiley? Perhaps he was the dad I wished I had had."

Traces of Ronnie Cornwell appear in many of le Carré's characters, most recognizably in *A Perfect Spy* and *Single & Single*. When his father died in 1975, le Carré paid for the memorial service but did not attend.

Best Book to Read First

The Spy Who Came in from the Cold, the story of Alec Leamas, a 50-year-old British intelligence agent who wants to retire but is persuaded to take on one last assignment. (Richard Burton played the role in the 1965 movie.) Le Carré's literary role model, Graham Greene, describes it as "the best spy novel I have ever read." A close second: *Smiley's People*.

Artists, in my experience, have very little center. They fake. They are not the real thing. They are spies. I am no exception.

—John le Carré, in remarks made to the Knopf sales force, 1996

Elmore Leonard

Born
October 11, 1925, in
New Orleans,
Louisiana, the son of
Elmore John Leonard,
an executive for
General Motors, and
Flora Rive Leonard, a
homemaker

Full Name
Elmore John Leonard Jr.
Nicknamed "Dutch" in
high school, after a
famous Washington
Senators' knuckleballer

Education
University of Detroit,
Ph.B. (Bachelor of
Philosophy), 1950

Family
Married three times.
First to Beverly Cline,
1949, with whom he
had five children;
divorced in 1977.
Second marriage to
Joan Shepard, 1979;
she died in 1993.
Third wife is Christine
Kent, whom he
married in 1993.

Home
Bloomfield Village,
Michigan, a suburb of
Detroit

Fan Mail
Elmore Leonard
2192 Yarmouth Road
Bloomfield Village, MI
48301

Publisher
Delacorte

The fact that Elmore Leonard has achieved the all-but-impossible state of getting glowing reviews from the literary critics while simultaneously achieving popular acclaim as a bestselling novelist is puzzling—until you read him. Characters, plot, compression, dialogue, wryness, and wit combine to provide a reading experience unlike any other. He considers his precursors to be Ernest Hemingway and John Steinbeck instead of the more obvious Chandler-Hammett-MacDonald line, and his own reading habits favor an edgier strain of storytellers like Jayne Anne Phillips.

Washington Post reviewer Michael Kernan describes the typical Leonard novel as offering readers "guns, a killing or two or three, fights and chases and sex. Tight, clean prose, ear-perfect, whip-smart dialogue. And, just beneath the surface, an acute sense of the ridiculous." Leonard's style is almost entirely devoid of narration and description, and he moves his stories along, Hemingway-like, by what his characters say.

"Leonard's viewpoint is not exactly cynical," said the *Washington Post*'s Jonathan Yardley, "inasmuch as he admits the possibility of something approximating redemption, but it certainly is worldly and unsentimental." As a result, Yardley wrote, "his world bears a striking resemblance to the real one."

Good to Know

❖ Leonard twice had to give up book writing for "real" work—the first time as an ad copy writer and the second writing scripts for educational and industrial movies—until the sale of his Western novel *Hombre* to Hollywood in 1967 gave him enough money to support his family while he struggled to start writing books again.

❖ To assemble background material for his low-life adventures, Leonard relies in part on a research assistant. But he also spends considerable time dealing personally with both law enforcement and criminal types. One convict wrote Leonard of his efforts to get his fellow inmates to read Leonard's books instead of Sidney Sheldon's. He had convinced some former heroin dealers, the convict said, but had not yet converted the crack-and-cocaine crowd.

❖ Leonard has said that he puts his characters through a sort of audition in the opening scenes, before he decides whether they will stay or go, to see if they can "talk." This technique has earned him a reputation as one of the best dialogue writers in contemporary fiction. He says, however, "It isn't the words that are authentic but rather the rhythm of the way people talk."

❖ He is an innovator not only in his minimalist writing style but also in his approach to the morality of the crime-fiction genre. The good-versus-evil simplicity of Raymond Chandler and Dashiell Hammett is nowhere to be found in Leonard's books, replaced by a wary, fatalistic ambiguity.

❖ Master of two genres: The Western Writers of America have named Elmore Leonard's novel *Hombre* one of the 25 best Westerns of all time. And the Mystery Writers of America have honored him with their Grand Master Award, in recognition of his overall contributions to the field of mystery writing.

Treatises and Treats

COMPANIONS

Elmore Leonard by David Geherin (Continuum, 1989). The only book-length treatment of Elmore Leonard and his work, now out of print but worth tracking down at the library or through used book sources. The first chapter takes a broad look at the first six decades of the author's life. After that, Geherin devotes individual chapters to each period in his writing career, starting with the 1950s westerns and finishing with his 1988 masterpiece, *Freaky Deaky*.

Elmore Leonard's Criminal Records: Profile of a Writer. Highly recommended by "Dutch" fans, this 1991 video (available from Amazon.com and elsewhere), includes interviews with Leonard, who talks about his life and work, with particular emphasis on his crime novels.

BEST OF THE NET

Official Elmore Leonard Web Site
www.elmoreleonard.com
Not nearly as much fun as the books themselves, but since it's the "official" site, created and maintained by Random House, it's a good place to check for information about Leonard's latest bestseller. You'll also find book descriptions and, in some cases, excerpts.

New York Times Featured Authors
www.nytimes.com/books/specials/
    author.html
Reviews and articles from the *New York Times* archives, plus an audio reading by Leonard.

Get Leonard

SELECTED CRIME NOVELS

The Big Bounce, 1969
Fifty-Two Pickup, 1974
Swag, 1976
Stick, 1983
LaBrava, 1983
    (Edgar Award)
Glitz, 1985
Freaky Deaky, 1988
Get Shorty, 1990
Rum Punch, 1992
Cuba Libre, 1998
Be Cool, 1999

SELECTED WESTERN NOVELS

The Bounty Hunters, 1953
Last Stand at Saber River, 1957
Hombre, 1961
Valdez Is Coming, 1970
Forty Lashes, Less One, 1972
Gunsights, 1979

If You Like Elmore Leonard…

You might also like books by Thomas Berger, Carl Hiaasen, and Donald E. Westlake.

Best Book to Read First

Leonard is the author of at least eight Westerns, including *Hombre*, the book from which the 1967 Paul Newman film was made. But he's best known for his nearly 30 crime novels. Try his early-career bestseller *The Big Bounce* (1969), mid-career *Swag* (1976), or late-career *Get Shorty* (1990)—made into a movie of the same name starring John Travolta, Gene Hackman, Rene Russo, and Danny DeVito in 1995.

A Fine Idea

In the early 1970s, Donald I. Fine, the head of a small publishing firm called Arbor House, decided to create an Elmore Leonard buzz more or less out of whole cloth. He bombarded key reviewers with Leonard in manuscript, galley, and bound-edition form, accompanying each packet with a personal letter. Following the hallowed publishing tradition of "blurbing," he also solicited comments from other writers of the genre. John D. MacDonald responded with the simple question, "Who is Elmore Leonard?" Fine turned the innocent query into the centerpiece for a media blitz. Thus began Leonard's climb from being intensely admired by a knowing few to being "discovered."

Criminals are so much more interesting than people up at the country club talking about their golf game or their stocks. All those bad guys have a mother, too. . . . They worry about what they are going to wear when they commit a crime, I'm sure they do.

—Elmore Leonard,
    in an interview
    for the London
    Sunday Telegraph
    (March 7, 1999)

C. S. Lewis

Born
November 29, 1898, in Belfast, Ireland, to Albert James Lewis, a solicitor, and Flora Hamilton Lewis

Full Name
Clive Staples Lewis ("Jack" to his friends, from a beloved childhood dog, Jacksie, who was struck and killed by a car)

Pseudonyms
N. W. Clerk, Clive Hamilton, and Nat Whilk

Education
University College, Oxford, A.B., classics, 1920; philosophy, 1922; English, 1923 (first-class honors for all three degrees)

Family
Married American poet and novelist Joy Davidman Gresham in 1956 when he was 58. She died four years later of cancer.

Home
The Kilns, near Oxford University

Died
November 22, 1963 (the same day that John F. Kennedy and Aldous Huxley died), of heart failure following a long illness

Publishers
Harcourt Brace
HarperCollins
Scribner

C. S. Lewis's honesty and intellect were such that he would be long remembered even if he had never written a word of fiction. In 1936 he published *The Allegory of Love: A Study in Medieval Tradition*, a work of great scholarship and originality focusing on courtly love in medieval romances. This book laid the foundation for his academic reputation. But in 1938, he published a science fiction book, *Out of the Silent Planet*, that launched his career as a novelist. He also made contributions in the areas of philosophy, mythology, theology, literary criticism, poetry, and memoirs. In all, he published some 52 books, 153 essays, and a great many prefaces, letters, and book reviews. To this day, he remains one of the world's most popular authors, with more than 1.5 million copies of his works sold each year.

As a young man, Lewis was an atheist, and he defended and argued for this philosophy with all the considerable energy, intellect, and wit at his disposal. But, as he later wrote, he would often feel "the steady, unrelenting approach of Him whom I so earnestly desired not to meet." In 1929, he "gave in, and admitted that God was God, and knelt and prayed: perhaps, that night, the most dejected and reluctant convert in all England." From then on, Lewis focused his powers in active support of the Christian view of the universe and the world.

It is important to emphasize, however, that Lewis's Christianity couldn't be further from the preaching of the Moral Majority or the Religious Right. Nor does it have much in common with the soft and comfortably reassuring sermons and homilies delivered in suburban churches. He may slip under your guard with a "children's" tale like *The Lion, the Witch, and the Wardrobe* (part of the Narnia Chronicles), or he may delight you with the wit of *The Screwtape Letters*, in which Satan advises his nephew on the best way to tempt mankind. But his work ultimately confronts your intellect. He says, in effect, "Look around you. How could anyone *not* accept the existence of a Supreme Creator? As for Christ, well, let me tell you a story..."

Good to Know

❖ An expert on allegory, Lewis did not consider the Narnia Chronicles to be allegorical: "I did not say to myself, 'Let us represent Jesus as He really is in our world by a Lion in Narnia.' I said, 'Let us suppose that there were a land like Narnia and that the Son of God, as he became a Man in our world, became a Lion there, and then imagine what would happen.'"

❖ Lewis once said of J. R. R. Tolkien's latest contribution to his monumental *Lord of the Rings*, "Not another f***ing dwarf!" He could be so frank because the two men were great friends who, with Charles Williams and other Oxford writers, were known as the Inklings. The group met at pubs, especially the Eagle and Child (they called it "the Bird and Baby"), to smoke pipes, drink beer, and read aloud from their works in progress.

❖ Wheaton College in Wheaton, Illinois, offers an extensive C. S. Lewis collection, including the elaborately decorated wardrobe said to have served as his imagination's gateway to Narnia. For more information, call 630-752-5908 or visit www.wheaton.edu/learnres/wade on the Web.

❖ *Shadowlands*—a play, BBC TV drama, and then a movie starring Anthony Hopkins and Deborah Winger—depicts C. S. Lewis's relationship with Joy Davidman Gresham, an American-born poet and novelist whom he met and married in his late 50s. Says stepson Douglas Gresham: "In terms of hard facts it is deliberately and by necessity very inaccurate, but emotionally it is spot on."

Treatises and Treats

COMPANIONS

C. S. Lewis: A Companion and Guide, edited by Walter Hooper (HarperSanFrancisco, 1998). Considered by many to be the definitive book on C. S. Lewis's life and work, this award-winning 960-page volume was edited by an eminent Lewis scholar and close personal friend.

The C. S. Lewis Readers' Encyclopedia, edited by Jeffrey D. Schultz and John G. West (Zondervan, 1998). Another comprehensive treatment by students of C. S. Lewis's work.

Companion to Narnia by Paul F. Ford (HarperSanFrancisco, 1994). A beautifully illustrated and well-researched reference book designed to give readers a deeper appreciation of the Narnia Chronicles. Includes a foreword by Madeleine L'Engle.

BEST OF THE NET

Into the Wardrobe
cslewis.drzeus.net
An excellent entrée to all things Narnia and beyond: biography, critical commentary, FAQs (frequently asked questions), message forums, and more. Click on "Useful Contacts" to find out about the various branches of the C. S. Lewis Society around the world. To access the popular C. S. Lewis newsgroup (alt.books.cs-lewis) and searchable archives of the group's past discussions, click on "Other Lewis Links."

C. S. Lewis and the Inklings
ernie.bgsu.edu/~edwards/lewis.html
Another good starting point, where you'll learn about Tolkien, Charles Williams, and Lewis's other literary drinking buddies. Also, advice for young Lewis researchers, photo gallery, and annotated guide to audio and video adaptations of Lewis's work.

Narnia and Beyond

THE NARNIA CHRONICLES

(Note: Often packaged as a boxed set, the books are listed here in story order, along with original publication date. For an introduction to the series, *The Lion, the Witch, and the Wardrobe* is a good first choice.)

The Magician's Nephew, 1955
The Lion, the Witch, and the Wardrobe, 1950
The Horse and His Boy, 1954
Prince Caspian, 1951
The Voyage of the Dawn Treader, 1952
The Silver Chair, 1953
The Last Battle, 1956

THE SPACE TRILOGY

Out of the Silent Planet, 1938
Perelandra, 1943
That Hideous Strength, 1945

OTHER NOVELS

The Screwtape Letters, 1941
The Great Divorce: A Dream, 1945
Till We Have Faces: A Myth Retold, 1956

AUTOBIOGRAPHY

Surprised by Joy: The Shape of My Early Life, 1955
A Grief Observed, 1961
All My Road Before Me: The Diary of C. S. Lewis, 1991

Best Book to Read First

Till We Have Faces: A Myth Retold. An extraordinarily powerful, potentially life-changing retelling of the Cupid and Psyche myth, said to be Lewis's own favorite. Begin by reading his synopsis of the myth itself, found at the back of the book.

Have You a First-Class Ticket?

Jack Lewis's main hobby was walking, something he shared with the main character in his space trilogy. Once when he'd been on a vigorous tramp through the countryside, he boarded a train for the journey back to Oxford. His unkempt appearance startled an elderly lady as he sat down in the first-class compartment. "Excuse me, sir, have you a first-class ticket," she said. "Yes, madam, I do," replied Lewis, "but I'm afraid I'll be needing it for myself."

Robert Ludlum

Born
May 25, 1927, in New York City; to businessman George Ludlum and Margaret Wadsworth Ludlum

Pseudonyms
Jonathan Ryder and Michael Shepherd

Education
Wesleyan University, B.A., 1951

Family
Married actress Mary Ryducha in 1951. Three children: Michael, Jonathan, and Glynis.

Home
Naples, Florida

Fan Mail
Robert Ludlum
c/o Henry Morrison
Box 235
Bedford Hills, NY
    10507

Publisher
St. Martin's Press

Robert Ludlum writes slam-bang thrillers designed to keep you turning the pages long after you know you should have gone to bed. With 21 bestselling books to his credit and legions of devoted fans, he's one of the most widely read and wealthiest authors in the world.

Ludlum has conjured up plots involving a conspiracy among five military figures to take over the world, the kidnapping of the pope, the theory that FBI Director J. Edgar Hoover was really assassinated, and a neo-Nazi secret brotherhood dedicated to restoring the glories of the Third Reich. (Your kids may say, "The Third what?" but never mind.) Few writers can take such fanciful plots and spin them into such engrossing tales. Corruption at the highest levels, Byzantine secret plans, and unsuspecting ordinary people drawn into a web of deceit are key elements of his novels—and are what keep fans desperate for more.

As Newgate Callendar, writing in the *New York Times Book Review*, said of *The Matlock Papers*, "The basic situation is unreal—indeed, it's unbelievable—but a good writer can make the reader suspend his disbelief, and Ludlum is a good writer." Well, yes and no. You will definitely suspend your disbelief, but Robert Ludlum will never win any prizes for creating fully developed characters or evoking an enchanting sense of place. And as with many thriller and spy novelists whose popularity soared during the Cold War—when the threat of nuclear annihilation was anything but fanciful—some of Ludlum's plots can seem a bit dated.

On the other hand, "Robert Ludlum" is a powerful brand name. In 1998, after more than 20 years with Bantam, Ludlum signed a three-book deal with St. Martin's Press for a reported $4 million per book, the first of which is scheduled to appear in 2000. He will also "create" a four-book mass market paperback series that will be written by other authors. But consider his publisher's description of his 1997 novel, *The Matarese Countdown*:

> Twenty years ago, top agents from the CIA and KGB banded together to bring down the Matarese Circle, an international cabal of powerbrokers and assassins whose sole objective was to achieve worldwide economic domination. Now the bloody Matarese dynasty is back—and the only man with the power to stop it may have already run out of time.

You say, "Well of course it's absurd." And then, "Isn't it? But what if something like this *could* happen. I wonder what happens next." And you're hooked. He's got you. Now in his seventies, the master clearly has not lost his touch.

Good to Know

❖ Ludlum began acting professionally at 16 in the 1943 Broadway production of *Junior Miss*. He enlisted in the Marines at 18, earned a college degree, got married, and resumed his acting career with roles in summer stock, Broadway shows, and television. He appeared in over 200 TV dramas for such early live programs as *Studio One* and *Kraft Television Theater*.

❖ To have greater creative control, Ludlum became a producer. He brought *The Owl and the Pussycat* to Broadway in 1956. Four years later he took the play to a new venue of his creation: the country's first shopping-center theater, Playhouse-on-the-Mall in Paramus, New Jersey. (A then-unknown Alan Alda played the lead.)

❖ *The Scarlatti Inheritance*, Ludlum's first novel, came out in 1971 when he was 44. This tale of espionage and corruption, about a group of financiers who help to fund Hitler's Third Reich, set the pattern for Ludlum's career. The novel quickly became a bestseller, as did the 20 books that followed.

❖ Carlos, the Jackal, the villain in *The Bourne Identity*, is a real person. After 30 years of murder and terrorism in support of an independent Palestine, the Argentine Ilich Ramirez Sanchez ("Carlos") was captured in Sudan in 1994 and smuggled into France in a sack.

❖ All of Ludlum's books—which have sold more than 210 million copies and have been translated into over 30 languages—are still in print. But sales per book, which used to average 5.5 million copies, have leveled off in recent years to about 450,000 copies, prompting Ludlum to leave Bantam Books to seek a fresh approach at St. Martin's Press.

Treatises and Treats

COMPANIONS

Robert Ludlum: *A Critical Companion* by Gina MacDonald (Greenwood Press, 1997). A personal interview granted by Ludlum sheds light on his approach to his craft. MacDonald offers an in-depth analysis of 17 of the novels and uncovers "the serious themes running through" the novelist's work, including the temptations of power, the importance of personal loyalties, and the nature of evil.

The Robert Ludlum Companion, edited by Martin H. Greenberg (Bantam Books, 1993). Currently out of print, this companion offers criticism and interpretations of Ludlum's work.

BEST OF THE NET

The Ludlum Mosaic

nedhosting.com/users/ludlum

This fan page offers a nice collection of Ludlum news, book information, and advice on what to read first. But the real gem is the Ludlum discussion board, where fans exchange views, reviews, and information.

Random House Online Catalog

www.randomhouse.com/catalog

Until recently, most of Ludlum's novels have been published by Bantam, a division of Random House, so this is a good place to check for book descriptions, excerpts, and audio editions.

All the Novels

The Scarlatti Inheritance, 1971
The Osterman Weekend, 1972
The Matlock Paper, 1973
Trevayne, 1973
The Rhinemann Exchange, 1974
The Road to Gandolfo, 1975
The Gemini Contenders, 1976
The Chancellor Manuscript, 1977
The Holcroft Covenant, 1978
The Matarese Circle, 1979
The Bourne Identity, 1980
The Parsifal Mosaic, 1982
The Aquitaine Progression, 1984
The Bourne Supremacy, 1986
The Icarus Agenda, 1988
The Bourne Ultimatum, 1990
The Road to Omaha, 1992
The Scorpio Illusion, 1993
The Apocalypse Watch, 1995
The Cry of the Halidon, 1996
The Matarese Countdown, 1997

If You Like Robert Ludlum . . .

You'll probably also like Len Deighton, Ken Follett, Frederick Forsyth, and John le Carré. But for fresher plots, consider William F. Buckley's "Blackford Oakes" novels and thrillers by Tom Clancy, John Gilstrap, Jonathan Rabb, Chris Stewart, and the writing team of Douglas Preston and Lincoln Child.

> **Best Book to Read First**
>
> *The Chancellor Manuscript*, *The Matarese Circle*, or *The Bourne Identity*. If you don't like these books, Robert Ludlum is not for you.

> *I start with a concept that outrages me, something that bothers the hell out of me. I think arresting fiction is written out of a sense of outrage. I try to find something with an underpinning of reality. I generally go back over recent history looking for a situation where the events have a conceivable official explanation but where the solution might be other than it is purported to be.*
>
> —Robert Ludlum,
> *Writer's Digest*
> (September 1977)

Alison Lurie

Born
September 3, 1926, in
Chicago, Illinois, to
Harry Lurie, a Latvian-
born teacher, scholar,
and socialist who
founded the Council of
Jewish Federations and
Welfare Funds, and
Bernice Stewart Lurie

Education
Radcliffe College, A.B.,
1947

Family
Married to Edward
Hower, a novelist and
professor. (An earlier
37-year marriage to
Jonathan Bishop
ended in divorce in
1985.) Three sons
from her first marriage:
John, Jeremy, and
Joshua.

Home
Lives most of the year
in Ithaca, New York,
but also owns a flat in
London and a winter
getaway in Key West,
Florida.

Fan Mail
Alison Lurie
Department of English
Cornell University
Ithaca, NY 14853

Publisher
Henry Holt

Alison Lurie is best known for her witty, insightful novels dealing with crises in the everyday lives of well-educated, upper-middle-class people who are often in some way connected to academe. As Sara Sanborn writes in the *New York Times*, "Lurie's protagonists are always academics or writers; well read and well controlled, thoughtful and successful, people of good taste—and hence people especially susceptible to the Call of the Wild and the perfectly rational processes of self-deception."

Lurie has been compared to Jane Austen for her ironic, detached humor and to Henry James for her precision of expression. Most critics agree that *The War Between the Tates* (1974) and *Foreign Affairs* (1984) represent the author at her best. *The War Between the Tates* examines the collapse of the apparently perfect marriage of a professor and his wife, a story juxtaposed with campus unrest caused by the Vietnam War. Critic John Leonard praised the book for its "faultless prose, like an English lawn. One could play polo on such prose, swatting ideas with a mallet up and down the pastoral field. There are brilliant scenes, dozens of them...[and] a detachment so profound that we might be looking at tropical fish in a tank instead of people in extremis." *Foreign Affairs*, the story of two academics on sabbatical in England who learn more about love than scholarship, is the book that helped propel Lurie into the forefront of American novelists.

Some critics have declared that Lurie's writing is too intelligent for popular tastes. Others have argued that her novels are too programmatic, too reliant on contrivances to heighten irony or to make a larger point. But most agree with Joyce Carol Oates that Lurie's work "is triumphantly in the comic mode, and she knows its contours and idio-syncrasies and its meticulous pacing exceptionally well." She is a lively, funny writer with the wry wit to produce a modern comedy of manners.

Good to Know

❖ Lurie began writing at an early age: "I was encouraged to be creative . . . because I didn't have much else going for me. I was a skinny, plain, odd-looking little girl, deaf in one badly damaged ear from a birth injury, and with resultant atrophy of the facial muscles that pulled my mouth sideways whenever I opened it to speak and turned my smile into a sort of sneer."

❖ After college, she worked as an editorial assistant for Oxford University Press in New York, with the hope of eventually making a living as a writer. Years of rejection slips, however, caused her to abandon that goal and devote herself to raising her three sons. Her first novel, *Love and Friendship*, wasn't published until 1962. The book's central characters were modeled rather closely on friends and colleagues, leading to many hurt feelings when the book came out. "Now I try my best not to reproduce anyone I know," says Lurie.

❖ In addition to her novels, Lurie has written *The Language of Clothes*, a study of the conscious and unconscious use of clothes as a means of self-expression, and *Don't Tell the Grown-Ups*, a study of children's literature. She has also edited volumes of children's literature.

❖ She has taught at Cornell University since 1968 and became a full professor in 1976, specializing in folklore and children's literature. Her short-take on academia: "The one thing you see in academia is that people have much younger second wives. There's an endless supply of female students who are impressed by professors. There they are all starry-eyed and spread out in front of you."

❖ The truth about Alison Lurie: "When you meet a writer, you're bound to be disappointed. Because what you're meeting is a sort of unedited first draft. My books have been through at least four or five drafts and then they've been through an editor so everything's spelled right and nothing goes wrong. But when you meet a writer they've been to the dentist so their face is all puffed up and the cream curdles and not everything they say is clever—in fact most of the things they say are not clever at all. . . ." (Alison Lurie, in a 1994 interview for the *Independent*.)

Treatises and Treats

COMPANIONS
Alison Lurie by Richard Hauer Costa (Twayne, 1992). The first and only book-length study of Lurie's major works of adult fiction and nonfiction.

BEST OF THE NET
New York Times Featured Authors
www.nytimes.com/books/specials/author.html
Click on "Alison Lurie" for a collection of some two dozen book reviews and articles by and about the author, all from the *New York Times* archives.

All Her Novels

Love and Friendship, 1962
The Nowhere City, 1965
Imaginary Friends, 1967
Real People, 1969
The War Between the Tates, 1974
Only Children, 1979
Foreign Affairs, 1984
    (Pulitzer Prize)
The Truth About Lorin Jones, 1988
The Last Resort, 1998

If You Like Alison Lurie . . .

You might like Jane Austen and Henry James. Also try Anthony Powell, whose 12-novel series known as *A Dance to the Music of Time* is an influence Lurie readily admits.

For another take on university life, read Jane Smiley's academic comedy *Moo*. Or try David Lodge's *Changing Places* and *Small World*, and *The Salterton Trilogy* by Robertson Davies.

American or British?

Lurie's most recent novel, *The Last Resort* (1998) was published in Great Britain first, where she is more popular than she is in America—though her novels sell well in American college and university towns. "My manner is somewhat British, even if my style is American," she has said.

Her attachment to Great Britain started when she was much younger. As soon as she learned to read, she discovered *Winnie the Pooh*, *Peter Pan*, *The Wind in the Willows*, and the books of E. Nesbitt in the school library. Britain, she says, was "the country I read about from the age of six, the country of all my children's books and then of all the books I read when I was growing up."

Best Book to Read First
Foreign Affairs, her most successful novel and winner of the Pulitzer Prize.

Making up stories . . . was what I did for fun. With a pencil and paper I could revise the world. I could move mountains; I could fly over Westchester at night in a winged clothes basket; I could call up a brown-and-white-spotted milk-giving dragon to eat the neighbor who had told me and my sister not to walk through her field and bother her cows.

—Alison Lurie
(*New York Times*,
June 6, 1982)

Norman Mailer

Born
January 31, 1923, in Long Branch, New Jersey, to Isaac Barnett Mailer, an accountant, and Fanny Schneider Mailer, owner of a small business

Real Name
Nachem Malech Mailer

Education
Harvard University, B.S. (cum laude) in aeronautical engineering, 1943; Sorbonne, Paris, 1947–48

Family
Married six times, most recently in 1980 to Norris Church, with whom he has a son, John Buffalo. He has seven other children from his earlier marriages.

Home
Provincetown, Massachusetts, and an apartment in Brooklyn Heights, New York

Fan Mail
Norman Mailer
c/o Rembar
19 West 44th Street
New York, NY 10022

Publisher
Random House

Norman Mailer, cofounder of New York's *Village Voice* and brilliant, two-time Pulitzer Prize winner, is among the 20th century's most notorious American writers—not for his prose but for what *Contemporary Authors* calls his "special talents as antic public gadfly." That said, he is also among the elder statesmen of American letters, with some 30 books to his credit and countless nonfiction articles and short stories.

Bursting onto the literary scene in 1948 with *The Naked and the Dead,* Mailer built a reputation as a compelling craftsman who tempered his obsessions—sex, greed, and violence—with a thoughtful, if intense, sensibility. He won his first Pulitzer Prize in 1969 for *The Armies of the Night,* an account of a massive anti–Vietnam War march on the Pentagon that blended fact and fiction to present a "firsthand" account using the techniques of the New Journalism. (In the book, Mailer refers to himself in the third person.) His second Pulitzer came a decade later with *The Executioner's Song,* his exhaustive "true-life novel" about the sad, strange life of death-row inmate Gary Gilmore.

An outspoken critic of politics and popular culture, Mailer has injected himself into countless national controversies—feminist polemics, boxing, space exploration, the peace movement. But his personal exploits have been at least as controversial. Barroom brawls, forays into acting and activism, accusations of madness, and macho grandstanding attest to the fact that he has lived life fully, having long ago "bade farewell to an average man's experience."

Good to Know

❖ Mailer grew up in Brooklyn and still keeps a top-floor apartment in Brooklyn Heights. But he writes at his home in Provincetown, Massachusetts. There, during the Cape Cod winters, "it's wonderful to wake up and you don't feel sorry for yourself that you're missing anything, because nothing is happening."

❖ Drafted in 1944, the 21-year-old Mailer spent two years in the Philippines as an artillery surveyor before requesting a transfer to a front-line Intelligence and Reconnaissance infantry unit. His World War II experiences provided him with the material for *The Naked and the Dead*, a startlingly candid portrayal of life under fire.

❖ Mailer ran for mayor of New York City in 1960, advocating that the city secede from New York State. With fellow New Journalist Jimmy Breslin as his running mate, he made another unsuccessful bid for mayor in 1969, this time proposing to bring back the death penalty in the form of gladiator-style public battles.

❖ The pugnacious Mailer's legendary ego has ignited feuds with Gore Vidal, William Styron, Tom Wolfe, and others. Some have been acerbic. Others were more good-natured: *National Review* founder and author William F. Buckley once sent Mailer a copy of his latest book. Disappointed that Buckley had failed to inscribe it, Mailer quickly flipped to its index in search of his name. There, he discovered Buckley's handwritten salutation: "Hi!"

❖ Mailer's wife of two decades is Norris Church, a statuesque former artist, model, and actress who once dated President Clinton. Church recently set aside her paintbrush to work on her first book, a thriller about three

1960s-era Arkansas women titled *Windchill Summer*. Like her husband, she draws on her own experience in crafting the novel. Her days as an onion-peeler in a pickle factory are said to have inspired the book's opening scene.

Treatises and Treats

COMPANIONS

Mailer: A Biography by Mary V. Dearborn (Houghton Mifflin, 1999). This 450-page, well-researched unauthorized biography offers a "solid, intelligent portrait of Norman Mailer that views him with a critical yet sympathetic eye" (*Kirkus Reviews*).

Conversations with Norman Mailer, edited by J. M. Lennon (University Press of Mississippi, 1988). Mailer the literary lion reflects on both his demons and his muse.

BEST OF THE NET

New York Times Featured Authors
www.nytimes.com/books/specials/author.html
Cull the *New York Times* archives for timely reviews of Mailer's many notable books, along with profiles and coverage of his notorious assault on his second wife, Adele.

Best Reads

FICTION

The Naked and the Dead, 1948
An American Dream, 1965
Ancient Evenings, 1983

Tough Guys Don't Dance, 1984
Harlot's Ghost, 1991
The Gospel According to the Son, 1997

NONFICTION

The Armies of the Night, 1968
 (Pulitzer Prize, National Book Award)
Miami and the Siege of Chicago, 1968
 (National Book Award)
The Prisoner of Sex, 1971
Marilyn: A Biography, 1973
The Executioner's Song, 1979
 (Pulitzer Prize)
Portrait of Picasso as a Young Man, 1995
Oswald's Tale: An American Mystery, 1995

COLLECTIONS

Advertisements for Myself, 1959
The Time of Our Time, 1998

If You Like Norman Mailer . . .

Try Ernest Hemingway, perhaps the grandfather of Mailer's genre of manly yet sensitive prose. Like Mailer, Hemingway examines machismo's costs and payoffs, drawing on a journalist's eye for detail to place his characters in time and circumstance. Hemingway, not surprisingly, is Mailer's personal literary hero.

Best Book to Read First

The Naked and the Dead, the 1948 *New York Times* bestseller about World War II that catapulted the 25-year-old Mailer to a literary stardom.

I'd say the most surprising thing for me that emerged from working on [The Time of Our Time] was how little difference there is between my fiction and my nonfiction. The piece on Marilyn Monroe and Arthur Miller could be a chapter in a novel. When you have good nonfiction, you have fiction. Really, you do. And when you have bad nonfiction, you have bad journalism.

—Norman Mailer, 1998

Disorderly Conduct

In 1960, during a boisterous all-night party at their West 94th Street apartment, Mailer stabbed his second wife Adele with a "dirty three-inch penknife" for calling him a "faggot." From her bed in the Intensive Care Unit at University Hospital, the soon-to-be-ex-Mrs. Mailer declined to press charges. But police arrested Mailer for felonious assault. (The week before, he had been arrested for disorderly conduct after he was refused credit for a $7.60 liquor bill at Birdland, a jazz nightclub.)

Given a suspended sentence, Mailer was committed to Bellevue Hospital for observation. "It's important for me not be sent to a mental hospital," Mailer protested, "because my work will be considered that of a disordered mind. My pride is that I can explore areas of experience that other men are afraid of. I insist I am sane."

Divorced in 1962, Adele Mailer would eventually go on to write a tell-all memoir, *The Last Party: Scenes from My Life with Norman Mailer* (Barricade Books, 1997), about her heavily drugged and drinking days on Mailer's arm, hobnobbing with the likes of Marlon Brando, Montgomery Clift, and Lillian Hellman.

Bernard Malamud

Born
April 28, 1914, in
Brooklyn, New York, to
Max Malamud, a
grocery store owner,
and Bertha Fidelman
Malamud

Education
Erasmus Hall High
School in Brooklyn;
City College of New
York (now City College
of the City University of
New York), B.A., 1936;
Columbia University,
M.A., 1942

Family
Married Ann de Chiara
in 1945; two children:
Paul and Janna.

Died
March 18, 1986, in
New York City

Publisher
Farrar, Straus & Giroux

Because his work is so good and because so much of it features characters deeply involved in the culture and customs of non-assimilated American Jews, Bernard Malamud has long been considered one of the most important "Jewish writers" of this century. But for Malamud, Jewishness was more a spiritual than a cultural or religious quality. "I was concerned with what Jews stood for," he once said, "with their getting down to the bare bones of things. I was concerned with their ethicality—how Jews felt they had to live in order to go on living." Malamud never considered himself only a "Jewish writer" but rather a writer "writing for all men." And anyone who reads his work will agree.

Malamud twice won the National Book Award for Fiction, for *The Magic Barrel*, a collection of stories, and for *The Fixer*, a novel that also won the Pulitzer Prize. His fiction is populated with rabbis, confidence men, schlemiels, and fathers and sons in strained relationships. Early in his career, he was able to perfect the Jewish-American dialect that characterized much of his work. "Where Malamud excels is in his subtle and nearly always comical juxtaposition of a neurotic character against a deeper and wider moral and historic context," writes Barbara Lefcowitz in *Literature and Psychology*. His characters are often found struggling to change and renew their lives in the face of human loneliness, and his fiction achieves a rare balance of humor, sadness, and compassion.

Good to Know

❖ Malamud began creating stories at an early age. In elementary school, after going to the movies, he would recount the plots for his friends, sometimes substituting a plot of his own invention. "The pleasure, in the beginning," Malamud said, "was in retelling the impossible tale."

❖ After college, he supported himself in a variety of jobs, including a stint as a clerk at the Census Bureau: "No one seemed to care what I was doing so long as the record showed I had finished a full day's work. Therefore after lunchtime I kept my head bent low while I was writing short stories at my desk."

❖ In the 1940s he began teaching in various New York City night schools, which allowed him time during the day for writing. He went on to spend 11 years teaching at Oregon State College, 25 years at Bennington College, and 2 years as a visiting lecturer at Harvard.

❖ Malamud would typically write each of his novels and stories at least three times—"once to understand it, the second time to improve the prose, and a third to compel it to say what it still must say." He used the technique of "swift transition"—changing a scene in one sentence between paragraphs—that he learned from Charlie Chaplin. "I was influenced very much by Charlie Chaplin movies," he said, "by the rhythm and snap of his comedy and his wonderful, wonderful mixture of comedy and sadness."

❖ An intensely private man, he rarely gave interviews. Some have speculated that he was the inspiration for the character E. I. Lonoff in Philip Roth's 1979 novel *The Ghost Writer*.

Lonoff is a novelist who is skeptical of the world and therefore lives a life of solitude.

❖ Media adaptations of Malamud's novels and stories include: *The Fixer*, filmed by John Frankenheimer for MGM (1969); *Angel Levine*, a movie starring Zero Mostel and Harry Belafonte (1970), and an off-Broadway musical (1995); and *The Natural*, filmed by Barry Levinson and starring Robert Redford, Robert Duvall, Glenn Close, and Kim Basinger (1984).

❖ Malamud's fans included fellow writer Flannery O'Connor, who wrote to a friend in 1958: "I have discovered a short-story writer who is better than any of them, including myself." That writer was Bernard Malamud.

Treatises and Treats

COMPANIONS

Talking Horse: Bernard Malamud on Life and Work, edited by Alan Cheuse and Nicholas Delbanco (Columbia University Press, 1996). A collection of Malamud's essays, interviews, lectures, and notes that provide insights into the way he thought about and practiced his craft.

Conversations with Bernard Malamud, edited by Lawrence M. Lasher (University Press of Mississippi, 1991). Thirty interviews transcribed from various sources—an especially valuable resource since Malamud rarely granted interviews.

READINGS

Jewish Stories from the Old World to the New, an 18-hour radio series created by NPR radio station KCRW, includes two unforgettable stories by Bernard Malamud: "The Silver Crown," read by Alan Arkin, and "The Magic Barrel," read by Elliott Gould. You can buy the complete series from KCRW for $100 (800-292-3855, www.kcrw.org/jewish). Audio clips are available at the KCRW Web site.

Symphony Space's Selected Shorts, another multivolume series, also includes "The Magic Barrel" (on volume X), and another delightful Malamud story, "The Jewbird" (on volume VI), both read by Joseph Wiseman. Each volume contains five or six stories by major authors,

read by leading actors, and costs about $18 plus shipping. For a complete listing of stories or to order tapes, contact Symphony Space (212-864-1414, www.symphonyspace.org).

BEST OF THE NET

New York Times Featured Authors

www.nytimes.com/books/specials/
    author.html

Check here for book reviews, interviews, and articles about Bernard Malamud, including his 1986 obituary from the *New York Times* archives.

Reading List

ALL THE NOVELS

The Natural, 1952
The Assistant, 1957
A New Life, 1961
The Fixer, 1966
    (National Book Award, Pulitzer Prize)
The Tenants, 1971
Dubin's Lives, 1979
God's Grace, 1982

SHORT-STORY COLLECTIONS

The Magic Barrel, 1958
    (National Book Award)
The Complete Stories, 1997 (edited and introduced by Malamud's longtime editor, Robert Giroux)

If You Like Bernard Malamud...

Try Isaac Bashevis Singer, particularly *The Family Moskat*. Another book you might enjoy is Henry Roth's *Call It Sleep*. Originally published in 1934 and rediscovered in the early 1960s, it is now considered a classic of Jewish-American literature. Other possibilities include Saul Bellow, Cynthia Ozick, Philip Roth, and John Updike.

Best Book to Read First

The Assistant is considered by many to be Malamud's finest novel—a classic of American as well as Jewish literature. Malamud's father, who worked in a grocery store 16 hours a day, served as the basis for the Jewish grocer who takes on a gentile hold-up man as his assistant.

With me, it's story, story, story. Writers who can't invent stories often pursue other strategies, even substituting style for narrative. I feel that the story is the basic element of fiction though that ideal is not popular with disciples of the "new novel." They remind me of a painter who couldn't paint people, so he painted chairs. The story will be with us as long as man is.

—Bernard Malamud

Carson McCullers

Born
February 19, 1917, in
Columbus, Georgia, to
Lamar Smith, a
jeweler, and Marguerite
Waters Smith

Full Name
Lula Carson Smith
McCullers (she
dropped the name
"Lula" when she was
13 and dreaming of a
career as a concert
pianist)

Education
Attended Columbia
University and New
York University,
1935–36.

Family
Married Reeves
McCullers twice, first
in 1937 (divorced in
1940) and again in
1945. (Reeves
committed suicide in
1953.)

Home
Nyack, New York

Died
September 29, 1967,
in Nyack, New York, at
age 50, following a
stroke and subsequent
brain hemorrhage

Publishers
Bantam
Houghton Mifflin
Modern Library

Carson McCullers made her literary debut at age 23 with the publication of *The Heart Is a Lonely Hunter* (1940). The story concerns the relationships among five people living in a small town in Georgia. All are damaged spirits, struggling to find meaning in their own lives, yet paralyzed by an inability to connect on a meaningful level with other human beings or with a power greater than themselves. One critic called the book "the most pessimistic novel ever written," but also "one of the ten greatest American novels." It went on to become a highly acclaimed bestseller and brought McCullers to the attention of the international literary community.

The theme of spiritual isolation combined with images of violence and the grotesque permeate McCullers's writing, consistent with the Southern gothic school. But she often tempers shock with mercy, striving to evoke sympathy rather than revulsion in her readers. Much of her work is autobiographical, and it is perhaps this personal identification with her characters that enables her to treat the outcast with such compassion.

Her second novel, *Reflections in a Golden Eye*, did not meet the critical expectations raised by her first, but with *The Ballad of the Sad Café* and *The Member of the Wedding*, McCullers confirmed her reputation as an extraordinary literary talent. Her style, one critic said, allowed her to "transcend the bizarre and violent nature" of her stories. Author Gore Vidal praised her in 1961, saying that her "genius for prose remains one of the few satisfying achievements of our second-rate culture."

Good to Know

❖ "Wunderkind," her first published work, was an autobiographical piece for *Story* magazine. It tells of a 15-year-old girl's realization that she is not, after all, a musical prodigy. When she drops her music lessons, she loses her circle of musical friends and the special treatment her parents used to give her. (McCullers herself had to give up a musical career due to repeated bouts of rheumatic fever.)

❖ *Reflections in a Golden Eye* was written at a time when her marriage to Reeves McCullers was falling apart, and the novel reflects her desperation over the situation. (Reeves had taken a male lover, and Carson's response was to take a female lover.) Shortly after finishing the book in 1940, she separated from her husband and went to live in a brownstone rented by the editor of *Harper's Bazaar*. According to Rex Reed, the brownstone became "the only important literary salon in America," home to such celebrities as W. H. Auden, Christopher Isherwood, and Richard Wright.

❖ With the guidance of Tennessee Williams, McCullers reshaped *The Member of the Wedding* into a play, which won the New York Drama Critics Circle Award in 1950. But her professional triumphs were offset by marital problems and ailments that included pneumonia, breast cancer, and a series of strokes that left her partially paralyzed.

❖ Reeves McCullers became increasingly depressed and suicidal after they remarried in 1945 and began talking of a double suicide. While they were living in Europe in 1953, Carson became so frightened by her husband's insistence on suicide that she fled to the United States alone. A few weeks later, Reeves overdosed on sleeping pills in a Paris hotel room.

❖ In her last decade, Carson McCullers began dressing like Emily Dickinson, all in white. Biographer Virginia Spencer Carr notes that the author was obsessed with "the image of whiteness and its ambivalent connotations [of everything and nothingness]. Soon she was granting interviews dressed in a white nightgown and tennis shoes."

Treatises and Treats

CARSON MCCULLERS SOCIETY

This group meets annually and holds special sessions on Carson McCullers at the Modern Language Association and American Library Association conferences. For a $10 annual membership fee, you can join the society and get on the mailing list for the group's annual newsletter, with articles, reviews, bibliography, and information on events relating to the author. For more information contact:
Carson McCullers Society
c/o Carlos L. Dews, President
Department of English
University of West Florida
Pensacola, FL 32514
904-474-2923
www.uwf.edu/~english/McCullers

COMPANIONS

The Lonely Hunter: A Biography of Carson McCullers by Virginia Spencer Carr (Carroll & Graf, 1985). A compelling portrait of the eccentric genius who captivated the literary world at the age of 23.

Illumination and Night Glare: The Unfinished Autobiography of Carson McCullers (University of Wisconsin Press, 1999). Finally released by the author's very protective estate, this 280-page autobiography will, according to *Booklist*, "whet the appetite of literary groupies... [but leave them] pining for a full-scale biography."

Carson McCullers (Chelsea House, 1992) and *Critical Essays on Carson McCullers* by Melvin J. Friedman and Beverly Lyon Clark (Macmillan, 1996) both offer collections of reviews and commentary.

BEST OF THE NET
The Carson McCullers Project
www.carson-mccullers.com
Fans of Carson McCullers couldn't ask for a nicer site—comprehensive, well organized, and regularly updated with new information, like the recently published autobiography.

Reading List

ALL THE NOVELS

The Heart Is a Lonely Hunter, 1940
Reflections in a Golden Eye, 1941
The Ballad of the Sad Café, 1943
The Member of the Wedding, 1946
Clock Without Hands, 1961

COLLECTIONS

The Mortgaged Heart: The Previously Uncollected Writings of Carson McCullers, 1971
Collected Stories of Carson McCullers, 1987

If You Like Carson McCullers...

Other writers in the Southern gothic tradition include William Faulkner, Harper Lee, Flannery O'Connor, and Eudora Welty.

Best Book to Read First

The Member of the Wedding, a novel about adolescent loneliness and isolation, is generally considered her masterpiece.

The Road Not Taken

Carson McCullers might have become a famous concert pianist had she not lost all of her money upon arriving in New York City to attend the Julliard School of Music. Just 17 and away from home for the first time, she accidentally left her pocketbook on the subway.

Her financially strapped family had made enormous sacrifices to send their daughter to the famous school—even selling an heirloom diamond-and-emerald ring to raise money for the tuition. So young Carson could not bring herself to tell them of her predicament. Instead, she took odd jobs and enrolled in writing classes at Columbia and at New York University. This turn of events, combined with health problems, caused her to give up a career in music. But she never abandoned her love for it, and music often appears as a theme or metaphor in her fiction.

Colleen McCullough

Born
1938 in Wellington,
New South Wales,
Australia

Education
Attended University of
Sydney.

Family
Married Ric Robinson,
a housepainter/land-
scaper 13 years her
junior, in 1984.

Home
Norfolk Island, 1,000
miles off the Australian
coast

Fan Mail
Colleen McCullough
c/o Janklow & Nesbit
598 Madison Avenue
New York, NY 10022

Publisher
William Morrow

From a love story to a multi-genera-tional epic to the politics of an-cient Rome, Colleen McCullough's novels are versatile enough to please a wide range of readers. McCullough believes "a lot of writ-ers keep feeding people the same book." She told Edwin McDowell in a *New York Times Book Review* interview that she had "de-cided long ago…to have a bash at different kinds of books."

McCullough expresses her extraordinary insight into ordinary people through sympa-thetic, engaging characters of depth, com-plexity, and intelligence. She has been described as a consummate storyteller, so good that readers often have difficulty putting her novels down. One of her favorite themes pairs characters who don't "logically" belong together romantically. She stirs up sexual tension amid lush settings, and often her romantic heroes and heroines do not wind up happily ever after. In *Tim*, a middle-aged businesswoman becomes romantically entangled with a 25-year-old mentally re-tarded man. *The Thorn Birds* pairs a young woman with a Roman Catholic priest. And in *An Indecent Obsession*, a war nurse is en-gaged to one patient although she is sexually attracted to another.

Comparing themes of *Tim*, *The Thorn Birds*, and *An Indecent Obsession*, *Chicago Tribune Book World* reviewer Julia M. Ehres-mann observes that "in these times when per-sonal gratification is valued so highly, Colleen McCullough is writing about old-time moral dilemmas and largely discarded qualities: self-denial, self-control, and notions of duty, honor, and love as self-displacing virtues."

Virtue is something the characters of her Roman novels understood well, even if they did not always practice it. Anyone who has ever emerged from a high school Latin course with an interest in Roman history will find these books irresistible. The rivalries, the in-fighting, the ever-present factor of one's lin-eage, the sex, the money, and what people talked about are so realistically presented that one concludes, "Why, yes, these people were human beings, not marble statues. This is how it *must* have been."

Good to Know

❖ Doctor or writer? In 1963 McCullough left Australia to pursue a career in medicine. But that notion was ended by an allergy to soap and a shortage of money. After studying neu-rophysiology in London, she worked as a re-search assistant in Yale's College of Medicine. The pay was so terrible, however, that she de-cided to try writing. "I belonged to that group of women who were grossly underpaid for what they did. I told myself, 'Coll, ol' gal, you better try writing or you're going to be a very poor old spinster.'"

❖ She earned $50,000 from her first novel, *Tim*. Next came *The Thorn Birds*, which she wrote at night while working days at the Yale research-assistant job. She produced the first two drafts in three months, often turning out nearly 50 double-spaced pages each night. The final 1,000-page draft was completed af-ter working at that pace for a year.

❖ Her publisher backed the release of *The Thorn Birds* with an extensive publicity cam-paign, and the buzz helped to sell the paper-back rights for $1.9 million—a record amount at the time. The novel went on to sell over half a million copies in hardcover and more than seven million in paperback.

❖ In 1993, *The Thorn Birds* was made into a ten-hour television miniseries starring Richard Chamberlain and Rachel Ward. It became the second-most-watched miniseries ever, after *Roots*. Based on that success, CBS followed up three years later with *The Thorn Birds: The Missing Years*, covering the period of time that the blockbuster 1993 miniseries left out (1943 to about 1946). McCullough had this to say about the television versions of her novel: "The first TV series was terrible, and I figure [the second] one will be ghastly. I didn't write any of it. What on earth could they find to write about, since I covered all that I did and killed everybody off anyway?"

❖ McCullough is passionate about the last years of the Roman Republic and the rise of Julius Caesar. Her Roman books are meticulously researched and include maps of the city and portraits of the leading characters (drawn by McCullough), as well as helpful glossaries that even provide illustrated instructions on the correct way to drape a toga. She makes ancient Rome come alive!

Treatises and Treats

COMPANIONS

Colleen McCullough, A Critical Companion by Mary Jean DeMarr (Greenwood Press, 1996). Discussion, analysis, and evaluation of each of McCullough's novels, along with biographical information and commentary on the variety of genres in which she has written.

BEST OF THE NET

Fictional Rome Home Page

www.stockton.edu/~roman/fiction
Colleen McCullough is one of several authors featured at this Web site, hosted by Richard Stockton College of New Jersey. For readers of her "Masters of Rome" series, the site offers a rich and well-organized collection of information: historical figures, reference works, glossary, timeline, discussion groups, and descriptions and reviews of books by McCullough and other authors of historical novels set in Ancient Rome.

Book List

"MASTERS OF ROME" SERIES

The First Man in Rome, 1990
The Grass Crown, 1991
Fortune's Favorites, 1993
Caesar's Women, 1996
Caesar, 1997
The October Horse (not yet published)

OTHER NOVELS

Tim, 1974
The Thorn Birds, 1977
An Indecent Obsession, 1981
A Creed for the Third Millennium, 1985
The Ladies of Missalonghi, 1987

If You Like Colleen McCullough . . .

You're sure to like Robert Graves's *I, Claudius* and its successors. Graves starts with Augustus, who won the civil war that followed the murder of Julius Caesar.

You might also want to try Margaret George, starting with *Mary, Queen of Scotland and the Isles*, one of the most compelling historical novels ever written. Like McCullough, George does her homework and tells a great story.

Best Book to Read First

The Thorn Birds or *The First Man in Rome*, both of which offer page-turning stories with wonderfully developed characters and a fine sense of place.

I always wrote to please myself. I was a little snobby about it—that way I could write entirely as I wished. To write for publication, I thought, was to prostitute myself.

—Colleen McCullough, commenting on her early years as a writer in an interview for *Publishers Weekly*

When in Rome . . .

A sprawling replica of ancient Rome (at three-quarters the size of the original)—Colosseum, Forum, fake River Tiber and all—is being built near the town of Orvieto in Umbria, Italy, at an estimated cost of $39 million. Tourists are expected in droves to visit "Roma Vetus" (ancient Rome), where they'll feast on authentic ancient Roman meals, stroll through the Forum's markets and temples, and watch gladiator fights and chariot races. A television series based on *The First Man in Rome*, the beginning of McCullough's Roman series, is expected to be the first—but hopefully not the last—movie filmed there.

Alice McDermott

Born
June 27, 1953, in Brooklyn, New York, to William J. McDermott, a power company business representative, and Mildred Lynch McDermott. Grew up in suburban Long Island in an Irish Catholic family with two older brothers.

Education
State University of New York (Oswego), B.A., 1975; University of New Hampshire, M.A., 1978

Family
Married David M. Armstrong, a research neuroscientist, in 1979; three children.

Home
A large, red-brick colonial in the Washington, D.C., suburb of Bethesda, Maryland

Fan Mail
Alice McDermott
c/o Harriet Wasserman Literary Agency
137 East 36th Street
New York, NY 10016

Publisher
Farar, Straus & Giroux

At about 250 pages each, Alice McDermott's novels may be comparatively short, but they are filled to the brim with descriptive detail and imagery, complex and memorable characters, emotion, lyrical writing, and inventiveness. Set on and around her native Long Island, McDermott's novels chronicle the many nuances of the Irish-American family, aspects of love, and of friendship. Family is central to her work, she once said, because she wants "to reconstruct the inner life. Family is the first source of that."

Yet McDermott does not in any way consider her work to be "Irish American." She merely takes advantage "of the material at hand.... I know their homes, what they eat, how they turn a phrase." Hers are the stories of families everywhere projected against a background that happens to be Irish American. "I said after *At Weddings and Wakes* that I'm finished with the Irish, I'm not gong to write another thing about an Irish American. Then there was this one character [Billy Lynch], and I couldn't leave until I had taken a look at him."

The resulting novel, *Charming Billy*, won the National Book Award in 1998, a year when Tom Wolfe's *A Man in Full* was considered the odds-on favorite. "Billy is in every extended Irish-American family," McDermott said. "He's the loveable drunk. It's not a party or a family gathering unless he's there." You don't have to be Irish—all families embrace people like Billy. And that, of course, is McDermott's appeal. She and her characters speak to everyone, everywhere.

McDermott does not like to write linear narratives. She told *USA Today*, "I want to re-create life more as we store it, rather than how we lived through it.... What we have to say about what happens is more important than what actually happens.... [Memory is] where the drama is. The memory is what endures, what we retell, what is carried on into the lives of others who retell it."

Good to Know

❖ Alice McDermott told *Newsday* in a 1998 interview, "My mother told me from a very early age, 'If anything was bothering you, don't tell anybody about it because you might say something that you wish you hadn't. But write it down ... and then tear it up so no one ever reads it.' I think she's regretting I didn't take the second part of her advice."

❖ Her family discouraged her from becoming a professional writer, suggesting instead that she opt for a career as a lawyer, as her two brothers had done.

❖ While she was in college, one of her teachers told her, "I got bad news for you kid, you're a writer." But it wasn't until she won a scholarship to the writing program at the University of New Hampshire and came under the influence of her writing mentor, Mark Smith, that she got serious about writing and sold a story to a magazine. She then began a novel about a girl working at a vanity press. Smith contacted his agent, who, after reviewing some pages, agreed to represent her. A week later, McDermott was offered a contract.

❖ Before selling her first novel, McDermott read manuscripts for *Redbook*, earning 40 cents for every story while her husband attended graduate school. They decided they could stay afloat financially for six months—her deadline to make it as a writer. When the deal for *A Bigamist's Daughter* came through, her husband bought a case of Guinness to celebrate. "We were going to take a ride on the Staten Island ferry," says McDermott, "but we fell asleep."

❖ She combats her terror of writing by working on two novels at the same time. If one is giving her trouble, she puts it aside and focuses on the other. A mother of three, she does most of her writing between 9 A.M. and 3 P.M. when her children are at school. But she also teaches writing at Johns Hopkins University.

❖ She composes her first drafts in longhand and then modifies them on a computer. "I don't worry about the thoughts coming too quickly for my pencil to move across the page. I worry about what could get lost forever. You can crumple up a piece of paper or cross out lines, but the words are still there."

❖ In addition to winning the National Book Award for *Charming Billy*, McDermott has twice been a finalist for the Pulitzer Prize—for *That Night* and for *At Weddings and Wakes*.

❖ In her acceptance speech for the National Book Award, she told the assembled audience, "I wouldn't be true to my Irish heritage if I thought this were entirely a good thing. I will clutch onto my Irish humility with great

vigor." So how did she celebrate her victory? She and her husband went to the bar at New York's Parker Meridian Hotel and had a glass of wine. Then they went home.

Treatises and Treats

BEST OF THE NET

New York Times Featured Authors
www.nytimes.com/books/specials/author.html
The *New York Times* archives is your best bet for information about Alice McDermott online. You'll find at least two interviews with the author, along with reviews of her books by fellow writers Anne Tyler and David Leavitt, among others.

News Hour Interview with Alice McDermott
www.pbs.org/newshour
Shortly after winning the National Book Award, Alice McDermott was interviewed by Elizabeth Farnsworth on *The NewsHour with Jim Lehrer*. You can read the transcript and listen to the complete interview by visiting the PBS Web site and clicking on "News Hour Index" and then "Arts & Entertainment."

All the Novels

A Bigamist's Daughter, 1982
That Night, 1987
At Weddings and Wakes, 1991
Charming Billy, 1998
   (National Book Award)

If You Like Alice McDermott...

You might also like the novels and short stories of William Trevor and Alice Munro. Or try James Joyce's story, "The Dead," to which *Charming Billy* has been compared.

Best Book to Read First

Charming Billy, winner of the 1998 National Book Award. Thomas Mallon, chairman of the judging panel, describes the book as having "a voice like nothing we could recall...It found us. It was what we kept hearing."

A novel is not just what it's about. I don't think we talk about that enough. In this country in particular, in describing books we're so plot-obsessed and anxious to categorize by subject—black kids in the ghetto, the Civil War, the Holocaust. The question of memoirs competing with the novel is silly. Fiction is not a series of events copied down or a long personality profile. It's the language, the rhythm, the use of metaphor, that capture moments in time and the way people think.

—Alice McDermott, in an interview for the *Minneapolis Star Tribune*

A Wake for Billy Lynch

Somewhere in the Bronx, only twenty minutes or so from the cemetery, Maeve found a small bar-and-grill in a wooded alcove set well off the street that was willing to serve the funeral party of forty-seven medium-rare roast beef and boiled potatoes and green beans amandine, with fruit salad to begin and vanilla ice cream to go with the coffee. Pitchers of beer and of iced tea would be placed along the table at intervals and the bar left open—it being a regular business day—for anyone who wanted a drink.
   —from *Charming Billy*, chapter 1

Terry McMillan

Born
October 18, 1951, in
Port Huron, Michigan
(about 60 miles north-
east of Detroit), to a
black working-class
family in a predomi-
nantly white city. She
was the first of the
family's five children.
Her parents divorced
when she was 13 and
her father died three
years later, leaving her
mother to support the
family.

Education
Los Angeles City
College; University of
California, Berkeley,
B.S. in journalism,
1979. Studied film at
Columbia University,
where she received an
M.F.A., 1980.

Family
One son, Solomon
Welch, with her former
lover, Leonard Welch.

Home
Danville, California,
across the bay from
San Francisco

Publisher
Viking

Terry McMillan is leading the charge toward a surge of interest in African-American women writers and literature, challenging the mistaken assumption that blacks don't buy books. But make no mistake, her readership extends far beyond professional, middle-class black women.

It's been said that her heartbreaking and humorous novels have created a new literary genre, somewhere between popular fiction and more literary work by other black authors such as Toni Morrison and Alice Walker. Her dialogue-driven plots address the lives of contemporary middle-class black women, with observations and discussions on everything from genuinely serious issues to the best way to do nails and hair. She also explores relationships—female friendships, mothers and children, and, above all, romances between professional black women and blue-collar black men and the resulting tension of class differences. A good man really is hard to find in her novels.

McMillan's female characters are in touch with their strength and sexuality (or trying hard to get there). They are bawdy, earthy, complex, imperfect, smart, attractive—and typically alone. Looking for love in all the wrong places, they have a strong sense of heritage and use it to advantage with other African Americans in professional settings. Like her characters, the author is brassy, forthright, and unapologetic for offending the sensibilities of others. Her books are an autobiographical tour of her life, which helps explain why devoted fans say reading a Terry McMillan novel is like "having a conversation with your girlfriends."

Good to Know

❖ After college, McMillan supported herself working as a word processor technician. She published her first short story, "The End," when she was 25. But it wasn't until she was 36 that she came out with her first novel, *Mama* (1987), the story of the struggling Mildred Peacock and her five children.

❖ *Mama* started out as a short story that McMillan couldn't sell. After joining the Harlem Writer's Guild, she was advised that Mildred's story would really work better (and possibly be more saleable) as a novel. Taking the group's advice, in just six weeks McMillan expanded *Mama* into a 400-page book and sent some sample pages to Houghton Mifflin. Four days later she received word back that they wanted to buy it.

❖ In 1990, McMillan's former lover Leonard Welch tried to cash in on her success by filing a $4.75 million defamation suit against her. The suit claimed that McMillan had used Welch as the model for Franklin Swift, the sometimes violent leading male character in her second novel, *Disappearing Acts*. The following year, the New York Supreme Court ruled in favor of McMillan.

❖ The paperback rights to McMillan's third novel, *Waiting to Exhale*, garnered a massive $2.64 million, making the deal the second largest of its kind in publishing history. The book hit the *New York Times* bestseller list within one week of publication and remained there for several months. It has sold nearly four million copies. As a result of the book-turned-movie's box-office success (the film version directed by Forest Whitaker was one of the most highly praised movies of 1996), McMillan was offered $6 million for her fourth novel, *How Stella Got Her Groove Back*.

❖ *Stella*, written in less than a month, is the closest thing to an autobiography Terry McMillan has ever written. The first printing of 800,000 copies in hardcover was a record for an African-American novelist, and the film rights were sold before publication.

❖ McMillan has done wonders for the tourist business in Jamaica. The country's tourist board screened *How Stella Got Her Groove Back* for U.S. travel agents and aired TV spots promoting the island as a lovers' getaway. One month after the movie came out, travel to Jamaica jumped 10 percent over the same month the year before.

❖ Terry McMillan's mother died in 1993 of an asthma attack. At the time, McMillan was working on a novel called *A Day Late and a Dollar Short* that featured a loving mother very similar to her own. Too distraught to continue working on the book, McMillan put it aside and has not yet returned to it.

All the Novels

Mama, 1987
Disappearing Acts, 1989
Waiting to Exhale, 1992
How Stella Got Her Groove Back, 1996

If You Like Terry McMillan...

You might also like books by Alice Adams, Bebe Moore Campbell, Zora Neale Hurston, John Irving, Sheneska Jackson, Barbara Neely, Alice Walker, and Dorothy West.

Best Book to Read First

Waiting to Exhale, a bawdy, vibrant, deliciously readable story of four "thirty-something" middle-class black women and their frequently disastrous encounters with black men. (McMillan gives a powerful performance reading the abridged audiotape version, available from Penguin Audiobooks.)

Treatises and Treats

COMPANIONS

Terry McMillan: A Critical Companion by Paulette Richards (Greenwood Press, 1999). Richards offers the first book-length treatment of Terry McMillan's fictional characters, themes, and narrative technique. The book includes discussions of all four novels as well as earlier writings.

Terry McMillan: An Unauthorized Biography by Diane Patrick (St. Martin's Press, 1999). Though reviewers and fans give the author of this book credit for trying, the general consensus is that she wasn't terribly successful in telling Terry McMillan's life story. (McMillan, after all, had decided she wasn't ready to have her biography written and refused to grant interviews or provide material for the book.) Still, until another biography comes along, dedicated McMillan fans may want to take a look at this one.

Taking Charge and Telling It Like It Is

When her debut novel *Mama* was released, McMillan's publisher would only agree to the standard publicity campaign for first-time-authors—sending out press releases and review copies. So McMillan decided to promote the book herself. She wrote over 3,000 letters—to chain bookstores, independent booksellers, colleges and universities, and African-American groups—urging them to stock and promote her book and offering to come and do readings. She got such a good response that she planned her own book publicity tour, with some 39 stops. Her efforts paid off. *Mama* was reviewed in numerous publications, most of which gave the book high marks. And the publisher, caught off guard by the demand, went back to press twice in six weeks to print additional copies.

Aspiring blockbuster authors take note: For more details on Terry McMillan's do-it-yourself book promotion campaign, look for her article "Publicizing Your Commercially Published Novel," which first appeared in the January/February 1988 issue of *Poets & Writers Magazine* and was later reprinted in *Quarterly Black Review of Books* (May 31, 1994).

Larry McMurtry

Born
June 3, 1936, in
Wichita Falls, Texas.
Father and grandfather
were cattle ranchers.

Education
North Texas State
University, B.A., 1958;
Rice University, M.A.,
1960. Also studied at
Stanford University.

Family
Married Josephine
Ballard in 1959;
divorced in 1966. One
son, folksinger James
McMurtry. Close
companion and collab-
orator of many years,
Diana Ossana.

Home
The Taylor Mansion in
Archer City, Texas (two
hours northwest of
Dallas; population:
1,800). He has filled
the house with his
personal library of over
16,000 volumes.

Fan Mail
Larry McMurtry
Booked Up, Inc.
216 S. Center
Archer City, TX 76351
bookedup@wf.net

Publisher
Simon & Schuster

McMurtry writes novels that are usually about the Southwest, particularly Texas, past and present. He is best known for *Lonesome Dove*. Yet of some 25 books written in the last 40 years, only seven are really about the frontier. And even when he's writing about cowboys and cattle drives, there is always much more to a McMurtry novel than you'll find in the typical Western.

McMurtry always comes up with interesting, three-dimensional characters who talk the way people really talk. Think of Aurora Greenway in *Terms of Endearment* (the part played by Shirley MacLaine in the movie version). His evocation of place is legendary, even when he's writing about Las Vegas or Hollywood instead of the Southwest. The plots are generally good as well, propelling you from page to page to find out what happens next to the characters. The result is usually a novel that resonates—a book that stays with you long after you read the final page.

Good to Know

❖ McMurtry worked as a cowhand on his father's Texas cattle ranch until he was 22, but never aspired to be a rancher. "I never really liked it," explains McMurtry. "I knew, and my father knew, that it wasn't going to last another generation."

❖ He published his first novel, *Horseman, Pass By*, when he was just 25. The book was turned into the Academy Award–winning movie *Hud* (starring Paul Newman) in 1962.

❖ The title for McMurtry's first novel, *Horseman, Pass By*, comes from the poem "Under Ben Bulben" by William Butler Yeats, whose tombstone also bears these lines:

> Cast a cold eye
> On life, on death.
> Horseman, pass by!

❖ He wrote *The Last Picture Show* in 1966. Then, with Peter Bogdanovich, he created the screenplay for the 1971 movie, which was nominated for eight Oscars (including best screenplay adaptation) and made Cybill Shepherd a star.

❖ *Terms of Endearment* (1975)—though well liked—got very little attention until 1983, when the movie version won five Oscars, including Best Picture. Ten years later, *Lonesome Dove* (1985) earned McMurtry a Pulitzer Prize and spawned two enormously popular TV miniseries.

❖ Following a heart attack in 1991, McMurtry had quadruple-bypass surgery, then suffered severe depression for over a year. "I faded out of my life. Suddenly I found myself becoming an outline, and then what was within that outline vanished," McMurtry recalls. During this period he wrote *Streets of Laredo*, a dark sequel to *Lonesome Dove*.

❖ McMurtry's companion Diana Ossana helped pull him out of his depression by pushing him to continue writing. He agreed to do so only if she would collaborate. The result was *Pretty Boy Floyd* (1994) and *Zeke and Ned* (1997), both of which got mixed reviews.

Treatises and Treats

COMPANIONS

McMurtry and his novels are the subject of more than a dozen books. Some of the more recent titles include **Larry McMurtry and the Victorian Novel** by Roger Walton Jones (Texas A&M University Press, 1994), **Larry McMurtry and the West: An Ambivalent Relationship** by Mark Busby (University of North Texas Press, 1995), **Larry McMurtry's Texas: Evolution of the Myth** by Lera Patrick Tyler Lich (Eakin Press, 1987), and **Taking Stock: A Larry McMurtry Casebook** edited by Clay Reynolds (Southern Methodist University Press, 1989).

For general background information about the language and culture of the West, try **Western Words: A Dictionary of the Old West** by Ramon F. Adams (Hippocrene Books, 1997) and **Cowboys of the Old West** (Time-Life Books, 1997), praised for both the quality of the writing and the lavish illustrations—drawings, maps, and photographs.

BEST OF THE NET

New York Times Featured Authors
www.nytimes.com/books/specials/author.html
Click on "Larry McMurtry" for profiles, book excerpts, first chapters, book reviews, and reviews of films based on his work.

Archer City Web Page
www.archercity.org
Check here for the latest on the restoration of the Royal Theater (immortalized in *The Last Picture Show* book and movie and now a burned-out shell) and other goings on in McMurtry's hometown.

McMurtry's World

LONESOME DOVE SERIES
(in story order)
Dead Man's Walk, 1995
Lonesome Dove, 1985
   (Pulitzer Prize and Spur Award)
Streets of Laredo, 1993
Comanche Moon, 1997

LAST PICTURE SHOW TRILOGY
The Last Picture Show, 1966
Texasville, 1987
Duane's Depressed, 1999

URBAN TRILOGY AND SEQUELS

Moving On, 1970
All My Friends Are Going to Be Strangers, 1972
Some Can Whistle, 1989 (sequel to *All My Friends...*)
Terms of Endearment, 1975
The Evening Star, 1992 (sequel to *Terms of Endearment*)

OTHER POPULAR BOOKS
Horseman, Pass By, 1961 (also published as *Hud*)
Leaving Cheyenne, 1963
Somebody's Darling, 1978
Anything for Billy, 1988
Buffalo Girls, 1990
The Late Child, 1995
Crazy Horse, 1999

If You Like Larry McMurtry...

You might also like *Whatever Happened to Jacy Farrow?* by Ceil Cleveland, a high school classmate of McMurtry's. The title refers to the smart-mouthed teenage beauty in *The Last Picture Show*. Also consider James Carlos Blake, Ivan Doig, Cormac McCarthy, and Thomas McGuane.

Best Book to Read First

Lonesome Dove. Quintessential McMurtry. In his memoir, *Walter Benjamin at the Dairy Queen* (1999), the author himself discounts the other books in the saga.

I'm a critic of the myth of the cowboy. I don't feel that it's a myth that pertains, and since it's a part of my heritage, I feel it's a legitimate task to criticize it.... Sometimes the resistance is total. [People] are clinging to an idealization, to the pastoral way of life as being essentially less corrupt than the urban way.

—Larry McMurtry, in a *New York Times* interview

A Reader's Roundup

Larry McMurtry is one of the country's leading antiquarian book dealers. His dream is to create, in Archer City, Texas, an American version of Hay-on-Wye, the legendary British town that attracts antiquarian book dealers and book lovers from around the world. He's well on his way—with over 300,000 volumes in four huge buildings. "The tradition I was born into was essentially nomadic, a herdsman tradition, following animals across the earth," McMurtry told the *New York Times Magazine* (11/30/97). "The bookshops are a form of ranching. Instead of herding cattle, I herd books."

Herman Melville

Born
August 1, 1819, in New York City, one of eight children. Father Allan Melvill (the final *e* was added in 1834), was a merchant from a prominent Boston family. Mother Maria Gansevoort Melvill was the daughter of General Peter Gansevoort of Albany, New York—a hero during the Revolutionary War.

Education
Attended the Albany Academy in Albany, New York, until age 15.

Family
Married Elizabeth Shaw, daughter of a wealthy chief justice of Massachusetts, in 1847. Four children: two boys who died before reaching adulthood, and two girls.

Home
Arrowhead, his beloved 160-acre farm in the Berkshire Mountains near Pittsfield, Massachusetts (1850–62), which he was forced to leave because he couldn't support his family as a writer. Spent his last 29 years in New York City.

Died
September 28, 1891, of a heart attack

Publishers
Library of America
Modern Library

"To read *Moby-Dick* and absorb it," wrote poet and critic Violet Meynell, "is the crown of one's reading life." It may well be the greatest American novel of all time. The problem is that Ahab, with his peg leg and mad obsession, and the Great White Whale itself have been so parodied and so freighted with symbolism and "significance" that most prospective readers either think they already know what the book is about or have zero interest in finding out.

In reality, *Moby-Dick* is a heck of a good story from start to finish. Its characters are fascinating, its descriptions are firsthand accurate, and its narrator is quite human and likeable. The book is studded with gems of humor and insight and filled with images that will forever linger in your mind. At its very least, the novel makes real many details of early 19th-century life—such as a traveler's concern about the fireplace in his room, or the necessity of sharing a bed (and body warmth) with another guest, or the food one could expect to be served.

Read it simply as a story, and you'll find *Moby-Dick* as powerful as your favorite Shakespeare play. By the time you get to the end of the book—"then all collapsed, and the great shroud of the sea rolled on as it rolled five thousand years ago"—you will be drained of dull care and quite possibly dazed.

The tragedy is that, with the notable exception of his friend Nathaniel Hawthorne, few of Melville's contemporaries "got it" when it came to *Moby-Dick*. Most preferred his earlier travel/adventure-based books like *Typee*, *Omoo*, and *Redburn*. After the publication of *Moby-Dick* and its poor reception, Melville, who had poured everything he had into the book, essentially gave up. As was common at the time, he sought a political appointment and ended up spending 20 years at the Port of New York as a customs inspector, writing very little and even less of merit. His death in 1891 passed unnoticed. Only 30 years later—and 70 years after the publication of *Moby-Dick* (1851)—was Herman Melville "rediscovered" by literary scholars.

Good to Know

❖ Melville's grandfather, Major Thomas Melvill, participated in the Boston Tea Party and is the subject of Oliver Wendell Holmes's "The Last Leaf." His father prospered as an importer of French fabrics, hose, and perfumes but went bankrupt in 1830 and died two years later, leaving 13-year-old Herman and the rest of the family in dire financial straits.

❖ At odds with his mother (who he later declared hated him), Melville quit school at 15 and left home a short while later. He worked at various jobs—clerking at a New York bank, working in his brother's fur and cap store, farming, and teaching. He studied to be a surveyor on the Erie Canal project, but the job fell through, so he went to sea.

❖ During an early South Sea voyage, he deserted the *Acushnet* and was reportedly held captive for four months among the cannibalistic Typees. He escaped, signed on with another ship, and became involved in a mutiny. He worked on several Pacific islands, eventually making his way home as an able seaman aboard an American ship of war. These experiences were the basis for several popular novels.

❖ On another voyage, a Gansevoort cousin was forced by his ship's captain to court-martial and condemn to death three young sailors. This event inspired Melville to write *Billy Budd*, his last work, which remained unpublished until 1924.

❖ Melville's lifetime earnings from his writing have been estimated at about $5,900 from the United States and $4,500 from Great Britain. Gifts from his wealthy father-in-law were frequently all that kept the family afloat.

Treatises and Treats

THE MELVILLE SOCIETY

A long-established organization of almost 700 members, this group publishes a newsletter, *Melville Society Extracts*, and sponsors an online discussion group called Ishmail (short for "Ishmael Mailing List"). For more information, contact:
The Melville Society
c/o Christopher Sten
George Washington University
Washington, D.C. 20052
www.melville.org/ishmail.htm

COMPANIONS

The Cambridge Companion to Herman Melville, edited by Robert S. Levine (Cambridge University Press, 1998). A collection of specially commissioned essays covering all of Melville's novels as well as most of his poetry and short fiction.

Melville: A Biography by Laurie Robertson-Lorant (University of Massachusetts Press, 1998). Working with 500 family letters found in 1983, Robertson-Lorant "brings to life the Melville who wrote like an angel one day and a madman the next." (*New York Times Book Review*)

Herman Melville: A Biography: 1819–1851 by Hershel Parker (Johns Hopkins University Press, 1996). This 900-page first volume of Melville's biography uses letters, diaries, and newspaper accounts to tell the story of the author's early life and career (through the writing of *Moby-Dick*).

AUDIOTAPES

Moby-Dick and **Billy Budd** unabridged audiobooks, read by the critically acclaimed Frank Muller, "the first true superstar of spoken audio" (*Library Journal*). Accept no substitutes! Both books are available from Recorded Books (800-638-1304, www.recordedbooks.com).

BEST OF THE NET

Life and Works of Herman Melville

www.melville.org/melville.htm
This truly remarkable Web site is organized into four major sections: Breaking News (a guide to special Melville events and exhibits), Biography (featuring both Melville and Hawthorne), The Works (excerpts, e-texts, and criticism), and Other Net Resources (with links to Arrowhead, the Melville in Film page, and more).

All the Novels

Typee, 1846
Omoo, 1847
Mardi, 1849
Redburn, 1849
White-Jacket, 1850
Moby-Dick, 1851
Pierre, 1852
Israel Potter, 1855
The Confidence Man, 1857
Billy Budd, 1924

Best Book to Read First

Moby-Dick, without question. Skip the introductory stuff. Go directly to the famous opening line, "Call me Ishmael," and plunge right in.

> **What I feel most moved to write, that is banned—it will not pay. Yet, altogether, write the other way I cannot.**
>
> —Herman Melville, in a letter to Nathaniel Hawthorne, 1851

The Great Failure

The original title for *Moby-Dick* was *The Whale*. But after a newspaper account of a real-life sea chase involving a white whale called "Mocha Dick," Melville's publisher suggested he take advantage of the publicity with a very subtle change of name. Even the name *Moby-Dick* couldn't help, however: The book was one of the greatest publishing failures of its time. Two years after publication, the printing plant burned down, destroying the plates and most of the unsold copies. Melville's publisher, which had advanced him $700 for *Moby-Dick*, refused to give him any more money, and they certainly weren't going to reset the book. In the end, only 3,715 copies of *Moby-Dick* were sold during Melville's life.

James A. Michener

Born
February 3, 1907, according to *Who's Who in America*, though the date is uncertain because he was adopted and never had a birth certificate

Education
Won a basketball scholarship to Swarthmore College; B.A. in English and history, Summa Cum Laude, Phi Beta Kappa, 1929. University of Northern Colorado, A.M., 1937. Began a doctorate in education at Harvard in 1939.

Family
First two marriages ended in divorce. In 1955, married third wife Mari Yoriko Sabusawa, the daughter of Japanese immigrants. "Cookie" was their pet name for each other. Mari died of cancer in 1994. No children.

Home
Grew up in Doylestown, Pennsylvania. Spent his last decade in Austin, Texas.

Died
October 16, 1997, of kidney failure, ten days after terminating his dialysis machine treatment

Publisher
Random House

James A. Michener began writing in his teens, as an editor on the high school yearbook and as a sports reporter for a local newspaper. But he spent years as a teacher and was on track to become a university professor studying the teaching of social studies when Macmillan offered him a job as social studies editor with its textbook division. That's the job he held in 1943 when he was activated from the Naval Reserve and sent to the South Pacific.

His assignment as a "super-secretary" to an aviation maintenance unit in the Solomon Islands left him plenty of time to write, and the results were published by Macmillan in 1947 as *Tales of the South Pacific*. The book won the Pulitzer Prize in 1948, but sales were a modest 25,000 copies. Then Rodgers and Hammerstein used the book as the basis for their hit musical and film, *South Pacific*. Reissued in paperback, the collection of stories sold more than two million copies, and Michener, 42 when the musical opened, had been handed a new career.

In the books that immediately followed, Michener mined his familiarity with the South Pacific and Asia and the experiences of his youth. With the publication of *Hawaii* in 1959, however, he hit upon "the formula." As critic Webster Schott says, the "formula calls for experts, vast research, travel to faraway places and fraternizing with locals. And it calls for good guys and bad guys (both real and imagined) to hold the whole works together. It's a formula millions love. Mr. Michener gratifies their curiosity and is a pleasure to read."

When he died in 1997, James A. Michener was one of only eight authors to have written six or more number-one bestsellers in the half-century history of the weekly *New York Times* bestseller list. "I am not a stylist like Updike or Bellow, and don't aspire to be," the author once told an interviewer. "I'm not interested in plot or pyrotechnics, but I sure work to get a steady flow. If I describe a chair, I can describe it so that a person will read it to the end." Voting with their book-buying dollars, literally tens of millions of readers would agree.

Good to Know

❖ When *Tales of the South Pacific* won the Pulitzer Prize for fiction in 1948, the award was controversial because many considered it a collection of stories rather than a novel. "There were editorials that declared it was the least-deserving book in recent years to win the Pulitzer," Michener said. "I had no time to develop a swelled head."

❖ A lifelong Democrat, Michener campaigned for John F. Kennedy and served as chairman for the President's Food for Peace Program in 1961. His own candidacy for Congress from Pennsylvania's Eighth District wasn't a success. But he drew on his political experiences for several books and articles.

❖ After suffering a serious heart attack in 1964, Michener eased his workload by employing a team of researchers. While he would listen attentively to staff critiques and suggestions, it was always Michener who did the actual writing, rewriting, and revisions.

❖ In 1981, he was invited by Texas Governor William Clements to write about Texas for the state's 1986 Sesquicentennial Celebration. Supplied with a research staff and an office at the University of Texas, Michener nevertheless invested two years and $100,000 of his own money traversing the state to do research and interview experts.

❖ Michener and his wife gave over $100 million to museums, universities, writing programs, libraries, and other charities. A quiet philanthropist, he never wanted anything to be named after him but gave in when his hometown of Doylestown opened its new art museum in 1988. Housed in a renovated late-19th-century prison, the James A. Michener Art Museum features American art, with an emphasis on Pennsylvania impressionists (215-340-9800, www.michenerartmuseum.org).

Treatises and Treats

COMPANIONS

The World Is My Home: A Memoir by James A. Michener (Fawcett Books, 1998). Helps the Michener reader understand the roots of some of his most appealing "novels of place."

James A. Michener: A Biography by John Phillip Haynes (Bobbs-Merill Co. 1987). Written by one of his researchers, this biography explores the drive behind Michener's success, as well as his public and personal relationships.

Michener and Me: A Memoir by Herman Silverman (Running Press, 1999). About as close as you'll get to knowing the real Mich-

ener. Written by a close friend of 50 years, it includes personal photos and previously unpublished letters.

BEST OF THE NET

James A. Michener: Tales of the Storyteller
www.jamesmichener.com
Highlights of this site include photos and video clips, an interactive map showing the areas Michener wrote about, as well as a chronological timeline of his life and an excellent annotated bibliography.

Michener's World Tour

Tales of the South Pacific, 1947
    (Pulitzer Prize)
Hawaii, 1959
The Source, 1965 (Israel)
Centennial, 1974 (Colorado)
Chesapeake, 1978 (Chesapeake Bay region)
The Covenant, 1980 (South Africa)
Space, 1982 (American space program)
Poland, 1983
Texas, 1985
Mexico, 1992

If You Like James Michener . . .

Try some of these other authors who weave history and interesting geographical locations into their fiction: John Jakes, Colleen McCullough, Irving Stone, Leon Uris, Gore Vidal, and Herman Wouk.

A Pair of Wonderful Guys

The royalties from Rodgers and Hammerstein's *South Pacific*—which produced such memorable songs as "Some Enchanted Evening," "Bali Ha'i," and "A Wonderful Guy"—freed Michener to write full time, prompting him some years later to quip, "I have only one bit of advice to the beginning writer: Be sure your first novel is read by Rodgers and Hammerstein."

Best Book to Read First

Michener's novels are differentiated by subject, not by style, character, or story. So your best bet is to pick one covering a topic or geographical area you want to know about—make that "want to know a *lot* about"—and plunge right in.

I knew exactly what I was hoping for. I was hoping I could write a series of stories that would tell men who were drafted into the military in those difficult years what life was like. I gambled that when they returned home and demobilized, they would remember their experiences as the most vital of their lives, and they would want to read about it, and my book would be there.

—James A. Michener, talking about *Tales of the South Pacific*, a collection of stories he hammered out on a typewriter using the backs of letters from home and official navy correspondence for stationery

Born
November 29, 1943.
She grew up in
Chicago, Illinois, where
her father was a
minister.

Education
Radcliffe College, B.A.,
1964

Family
Married second
husband Doug Bauer,
a writer, in the mid-
1980s. One child, from
her first marriage.

Home
A townhouse in
Boston's South End
and a country home in
Vermont

Fan Mail
Sue Miller
c/o Maxine Groffsky
  Literary Agency
2 Fifth Avenue
New York, NY 10011

Publisher
Knopf

Sue Miller

Sue Miller is a writer recognized for her skillful renderings of domestic life. Her books and stories provide readers with windows into the worlds of nontraditional families and include such recurring themes as the tension between parents and children, the demands of family and career, and the impact of sexual liberation. Though she often writes about female characters, Miller does not like to be called a "women's writer" because of the label's inherent implication that the work would not appeal to a male audience. Says Miller: "I don't want to let men off the hook. They need to learn how to read women's metaphors just the way women have learned to read men's metaphors."

Miller's first novel, *The Good Mother* (1986), about a divorced woman embroiled in a fierce custody battle, was highly praised by critics and stayed on bestseller lists for six months. Her next novel, *Family Pictures* (1990), also a bestseller, tells the story of a Chicago-based family that Miller portrays as a character in itself. *Newsweek*'s Laura Shapiro called *Family Pictures* "a big, wonderful, deeply absorbing novel that retains the vivid domestic focus of *The Good Mother* while spiraling far beyond it."

Miller continued her exploration of the struggles of domestic life in her next two novels, *For Love* (1993) and *The Distinguished Guest* (1995). But she also attempted in *The Distinguished Guest* to broaden her range to include racial issues. When that book proved less popular than her three earlier novels, she left long-time publisher HarperCollins for Alfred A. Knopf. Her latest novel, *While I Was Gone* (1999), finds her back in familiar territory, examining "the artificially tamed wilderness inhabited by husbands and wives...[in a book that] swoops gracefully between the past and the present, between a woman's complex feelings about her husband and her equally complex fantasies—and fears—about another man," writes Jay Parini in the *New York Times*.

While some critics fault Sue Miller for not always providing the answers to the domestic problems that arise in her novels, she is nevertheless credited with bringing the issues to light and exploring the possibilities for change.

Good to Know

❖ Miller was a high school teacher, a cocktail waitress, and a model before becoming a full-time mother. Shortly after the birth of their child, she divorced her first husband and found herself struggling to make ends meet. During that time, she helped found the Harvard Day Care Centers, where she worked as a preschool teacher.

❖ She didn't begin writing until she was 35 and joined a writing workshop. She sold her first story, but when she tried her hand at a first novel, she couldn't find an agent who was interested. What was the novel about? Well, nothing really happened in the book, admits Miller, but "nothing happened rather elegantly." Nevertheless, she has since destroyed the manuscript.

❖ Experimental writer Robert Coover was a boarder in Miller's parents' basement while he attended the University of Chicago. Years later, seeing a review of his first novel in a newspaper inspired Miller to try to get a book published. "It suddenly occurred to me that publishing a book was not such a remote thing. It was something to which I could actually aspire."

❖ Miller believes that, like her fictional characters, we all have a desire to reinvent our lives. When she was in college, she would create new personas, accents, and stories for herself on the bus from Chicago to Boston.

❖ When people tell Sue Miller that they "read her book," she knows they mean *The Good Mother*. "I'm very grateful," says Miller, "but sometimes I want to say, 'You know, there have been four more.'"

❖ The *New York Times* has called Miller a "doyenne of domesticity." Miller says, "I don't understand it. Yes, there is usually a family in the middle of my books, but most of us live in families, that's how we came into the world."

❖ Movie adaptations include: *The Good Mother* (1988), directed by Leonard Nimoy and starring Diane Keaton and Liam Neeson; *Family Pictures* (1993), starring Anjelica Huston and Sam Neill; and *Inventing the Abbotts* (1997), starring Liv Tyler. Miller refuses to see any of the films that were made from her fictional creations.

❖ As a child, Sue Miller liked stories that made her cry. She would read and reread them until she could no longer cry over them. "You owe your readers an engaging experience," she says, "Your book should not make itself difficult. I know there are writers who feel very differently, who say to hell with the reader who won't do an enormous amount of work to read their stuff. But not me. It's a lot to ask of people, at this time in our culture, to stop and read a book. And it's a great privilege to be read, so your work should justify itself, as Conrad said, word by word."

Treatises and Treats

BEST OF THE NET
Books@Random Reading Group Guide
www.randomhouse.com/resources/rgg.html
Check here for a book description, questions, and discussion topics for *While I Was Gone*.

Reading List

ALL THE NOVELS
The Good Mother, 1986
Family Pictures, 1990
For Love, 1993
The Distinguished Guest, 1995
While I Was Gone, 1999

SHORT-STORY COLLECTION
Inventing the Abbotts and Other Stories, 1987

If You Like Sue Miller...

Try Anita Brookner, John Irving, Alison Lurie, Jane Smiley, John Updike, Alice Munro, Anne Tyler, and Amy Tan.

Best Book to Read First

The Good Mother, a suspenseful story of a divorced woman caught in the confusion of a bitter custody battle that "mesmerizes the reader until the last page is turned" (*Chicago Tribune*).

Inspired by O. J.

It's been noted that *While I Was Gone*, a novel dealing largely with themes of infidelity, family dynamics, and forgiveness, was released around the time of the Lewinsky Affair in Washington, D.C. Miller, however, states that she was by no means planning to cash in on the scandal. Nor was she influenced by it. (In fact, the novel was written well before word of the scandal hit the newsstands.)

According to Miller, it was actually the O. J. Simpson trial, not President Clinton's impeachment trial, that inspired her book. Says Miller: "I was struck by how heartfelt O. J.'s claims of innocence were, though I didn't believe them. It was almost as if he were saying, 'I'm not the kind of person who would have done this.' We all do that, don't we?"

Though inspired by O. J., Miller says she considered sending President Clinton a copy of her book, because she felt that "he could really use it."

I knew a woman who compared writing a novel to knitting an argyle sock the size of a football field. I think that is very apt. It's just such a struggle to shape it all up. And then it's published and I worry about it making its way in the world. And then I worry about getting another idea. It's always something.

—Sue Miller, in a 1999 interview for *Arizona Republic*

Margaret Mitchell

Born
November 8, 1900, in Atlanta, Georgia, to Eugene Muse Mitchell, a prominent attorney, and Maybelle Stephens Mitchell, a suffragette

Education
Attended Smith College (1918–19) with hopes of studying psychiatry, but returned to Atlanta after her mother's death during the great flu epidemic of 1918.

Family
Married Red Upshaw in 1922, but he left her three months later and the marriage was eventually annulled. (Red was the inspiration for Rhett Butler in *Gone with the Wind*.) Married John Marsh (the best man at her first nuptials) in 1925. He died in 1952.

Home
Atlanta, Georgia

Died
August 16, 1949, of injuries suffered after being struck by an intoxicated cabdriver as she crossed Peachtree Street in Atlanta. So many friends and fans mourned her death that tickets had to be distributed for the funeral.

Publisher
Simon & Schuster

Margaret Mitchell's *Gone with the Wind*, the bestselling novel of all time, was an indisputable blockbuster from its debut. Over a million copies of the 1,037-page Pulitzer Prize winner were sold within the first six months of its publication, even at the exorbitant price of $3—an unheard of sum for a book in 1936. It's never been out of print since and has sold more than 21 million copies in the United States alone. Sixty-plus years after its original publication, *GWTW* continues to sell some 25,000 hardcover and 250,000 paperback copies a year.

The book received mixed reviews, but few critics would dispute its power. The *New York Times Book Review* (July 5, 1936) recognized the story's mass appeal early on: "This is beyond a doubt one of the most remarkable first novels produced by an American writer. It is also one of the best."

Mitchell's unforgettable characters have become American icons. No one who has spent time with Scarlett O'Hara will ever forget her. She's a Southern belle with a spine. When the Civil War breaks out, she sets aside her fan and flowing gowns and uses her wits, charm, and steely determination to battle for survival. Perhaps this is what accounts most for the book's runaway popularity. *GWTW* offered the nation a sweeping, entertaining story of overcoming hardship that mirrored the average American's struggle during the Great Depression.

Good to Know

❖ The makings of a writer: With the encouragement of her English teacher at Washington Seminary, a private girls' school, Mitchell wrote her first book, *The Big Four*, about the adventures of four schoolgirls and their valiant leader, Margaret. Displeased with her 400-page handwritten story, she inscribed on the inside back cover of her copybook: "There are authors and authors, but a true writer is born and not made. Born writers make their characters real, living people, while 'made writers' have merely stuffed figures who dance when the strings are pulled—that's how I know I'm a 'made' writer."

❖ Mitchell's first fiancé, Lieutenant Clifford Henry, was killed in France during World War I. Critics have identified the idealistic, attractive, and serious-minded Henry as the model for Ashley Wilkes. Mitchell later declared her former intended as the one great love of her life.

❖ Act like a lady? Fiddle-dee-dee! At her father's insistence, Margaret joined the prestigious Debutante Club. But her style was more the free-spirited flapper. Public drinking, smoking, and finally, her shocking performance of an Apache dance, complete with a sensually-slitted costume, ended her career as a debutante. The Atlanta Junior League refused her membership.

❖ Mitchell began her writing career as a feature writer for the *Atlanta Journal*. She also authored a freelance column for the paper called "Elizabeth Bennett's Gossip."

❖ *GWTW* was bought by Macmillan editor Harold S. Latham, who had heard of Mitchell's magnum opus while on a scouting trip in Atlanta. She flatly refused him twice, but finally agreed to a meeting on the eve of his departure. "I went to the lobby," Latham recounted, "and there, sitting on a divan, was Margaret Mitchell, and beside her was the biggest manuscript I had ever seen. The pile of sheets reached to her shoulders. She rose and said: 'Here, take the thing before I change my mind.'" Latham bought a suitcase to haul the book with him on the next leg of his trip. Mitchell, having second thoughts, wired him in New Orleans, asking for return of the manuscript. But Latham ignored her plea and sent the oversized parcel to New York.

❖ Selznick International Pictures paid $50,000 for motion picture rights to the novel. The 1939 film was a smash hit and won ten Academy Awards.

❖ Would Scarlett by any other name smell as sweet? Mitchell's infamous heroine was originally named Pansy, the book's working title. But editors insisted on a new name to avoid any connection with the word sometimes used in the North to refer to a homosexual. Other early titles for the book: *Tote the Weary Load* and *Tomorrow Is Another Day*.

Treatises and Treats

COMPANIONS

Gone with the Wind: The Definitive Illustrated History of the Book, the Movie, and the Legend by Herb Bridges and Terryl C. Boodman (Fireside, 1989). The ultimate behind-the-scenes history of the book and its offspring, with some 300 photographs.

Southern Daughter: The Life of Margaret Mitchell by Darden Asbury Pyron (Oxford University Press, 1991). The most respected of Mitchell's life stories. It's out of print but available from the Margaret Mitchell House (404-249-7012, www.gwtw.org).

Margaret Mitchell & John Marsh: The Love Story behind Gone with the Wind by Marianne Walker (Peachtree Publishers, 1993). The private story of the couple's 24-year marriage, drawn from hundreds of previously unpublished letters and extensive interviews with relatives, coworkers, and friends.

BEST OF THE NET

Margaret Mitchell House Web Site
www.gwtw.org
A good starting point for *GWTW* information, created and maintained by the Margaret

Mitchell House and Museum in Atlanta. You'll find all sorts of interesting facts about the author and the ground-floor apartment she lovingly called "the Dump," now restored to look just as it did in Mitchell's day.

Reading List

Gone with the Wind, 1936
Lost Laysen, 1996
    (a novella written in 1915 by 15-year old Mitchell as a gift for her boyfriend)

If You Like Margaret Mitchell . . .

You'll probably want to stay far, far away from the highly publicized sequel to *GWTW* by Alexandra Ripley, *Scarlett* (Warner Books, 1991). It was widely criticized for its failure to even remotely live up to the original. Instead, try Colleen McCullough's blockbuster romance *The Thorn Birds*.

Best Book to Read First

Alas, *Gone with the Wind* is the only novel Mitchell ever published. She spent her post-*GWTW* years answering fan letters and volunteering in the World War II effort. Her posthumously published novella *Lost Laysen* is of interest more for its letters and vintage photographs than for its fictional fare.

Gone With the Wind is going to be the biggest flop in Hollywood history. I'm just glad it'll be Clark Gable who's falling flat on his face and not Gary Cooper.

—Gary Cooper in 1938, commenting on Gable's acceptance of the Rhett Butler role after he had turned it down

---

Image and Truth

At the time of its re-release in 1998, no other movie in history had sold more tickets at the box office than *Gone With the Wind*. Yet, as historian Arthur Schlesinger Jr. once noted in an *Atlantic Monthly* piece, "How badly written it is!" Schlesinger also acknowledged the movie's "idealization of slavery," but expressed the view that *GWTW* should not be condemned for this, as it was simply reflecting the stereotypes of the day.

Schlesinger is probably right. But in an age dominated by the visual image, *GWTW's* portrayal of slavery and Reconstruction, though completely flawed, becomes the "truth" for millions of people. The 1977 TV miniseries *Roots* may be the best visual antidote. But for verbal truth, the narratives of ex-slaves themselves have no equal, starting with *Puttin' on Ole Massa*, edited by Gilbert Osofsky (Harper, 1969) and *I Was Born a Slave*, edited by Yuval Taylor (Lawrence Hill Books, 1999). Also consider Jennifer Fleischner's *Mastering Slavery: Memory, Family, and Identity in Women's Slave Narratives* (New York University Press, 1996), James McPherson's *The Negro's Civil War* (Ballantine, 1991), and the Pulitzer Prize–winning *Mary Chesnut's Civil War* (Yale University Press, 1983).

Toni Morrison

Born
February 18, 1931, in Lorain, Ohio, the second of George and Ramah Wofford's four children

Full Name
Chloe Anthony Wofford. She changed her name to Toni (short for her middle name) when she went to college because people didn't know how to pronounce Chloe.

Education
Graduated with honors from high school. Howard University, B.A. in English, 1953; Cornell, M.A., 1955.

Family
Married Harold Morrison, a Jamaican architecture student, in 1958. Divorced in 1964. Two sons.

Homes
Princeton, New Jersey, where she teaches a course at Princeton University. Also has an apartment in New York City's SoHo district.

Fan Mail
Toni Morrison
c/o International
  Creative Management
40 West 57th Street
New York, NY 10019

Publisher
Knopf

Toni Morrison has been hailed as "black America's best novelist and one of America's best." In 1993, she became the first African-American woman to win the Nobel Prize in Literature and the first American woman to be so honored since Pearl Buck in 1938. In 1977, her *Song of Solomon* won the National Book Critics' Circle Award, and *Beloved* earned her the Pulitzer Prize for Fiction in 1988.

But don't let all these awards, or the fact that Morrison now teaches at Princeton, put you off. She doesn't write the kind of academic novels that are often so prized by critics and awards committees but avoided by passionate readers. In her own words, she writes "village" or "peasant" literature about the American black experience and culture. But she does so with language of such lyrical power and such vivid dialogue that, regardless of her subject, reading her words is a genuine pleasure.

Good to Know

❖ Morrison grew up in a gritty steel-town suburb of Cleveland, Ohio, a community she first fictionalized nearly 40 years later in *The Bluest Eye*.

❖ She read voraciously as a girl, devouring Flaubert, Jane Austen, and the great Russian novelists, among others. Her parents sacrificed greatly to send her to college.

❖ At Cornell University, Morrison wrote her masters thesis on William Faulkner and Virginia Woolf. She returned to Howard as an instructor in 1957. Her students there included Andrew Young, Stokely Carmichael, Leroi Jones (later Amiri Baraka), and others who became leaders in the civil rights movement.

❖ She published *The Bluest Eye* to respectable reviews in 1970. Shortly thereafter she become an editor with Random House. Over some 18 years, Morrison acquired and edited books by Angela Davis, Toni Cade Bambara, Gayl Jones, and other black women authors. She also edited Muhammad Ali.

❖ *Song of Solomon* was the first novel written by an African American to be chosen as a Book-of-the-Month-Club selection since Richard Wright's *Native Son* in 1940.

❖ Morrison resigned from Random House in 1983 to write full-time. That career move paid off just five years later in 1988, when she was awarded the Pulitzer Prize for *Beloved*.

❖ In 1993, the Swedish Academy honored Morrison with the Nobel Prize in Literature, lauding her for the "visionary force and poetic import" of her novels. As for the prize money ($817,771), she made a few small purchases—some fine china and silverplate—but invested most of it for her retirement.

❖ On Christmas morning in 1993, Morrison's home, a converted boathouse overlooking the Hudson River in Nyack, New York, was destroyed by fire. Notes, memorabilia, revised manuscripts, and much else of scholarly value were lost.

❖ Some 12 years in the making, the movie version of Morrison's *Beloved*, directed by Jonathan Demme and starring Oprah Winfrey and Danny Glover, opened in 1998 to mixed reviews. *New Yorker* critic David Denby asked "whether some novels shouldn't be left in peace as mere books, unredeemed by the movies."

Treatises and Treats

COMPANIONS

Toni Morrison: A Critical Companion by Missy Dehn Kubitschek (Greenwood Publishing, 1998). Written for college students, teachers, and reading groups rather than the literary community. Includes chapters on each of Morrison's novels, including her most recent book, *Paradise*. "Toni Morrison wants people to talk about [her books], especially in groups" says Kubitschek, a professor of English and Afro-American Studies at Purdue University, "because she thinks that the books aren't really finished until readers emerge with an interpretation."

Conversations with Toni Morrison, edited by Danille Taylor-Guthrie (University Press of Mississippi, 1994). A collection of interviews in which Morrison discusses her life and her novels.

BEST OF THE NET

Nobel Prize Internet Archive
www.nobelprizes.com
An excellent starting point for information about Toni Morrison and her novels. Click on "Literature" and then scroll down the page to find her name. The site's creators have collected news stories and links to other Web sites that present interviews, quotes, biographical information, and critical commentary.

Toni Morrison Page
www.cwrl.utexas.edu/~mmaynard/
    Morrison/home.html
Created and maintained by students in the University of Texas English department, this site is especially strong on information about *Beloved*. Includes a reading guide for the novel, with discussions about the major themes and the historical events that affect the characters. (The Web address is case-sensitive, so type it exactly as shown.)

Oprah's Book Club
www.oprah.com
Two of Morrison's novels, *Song of Solomon* and *Paradise*, have been featured on Oprah, so there's lots of good information here—an interesting author bio, reviews of both books, and reading guides that you can print out and use for group discussions of the novels. You'll find both books in the section called "Previous Book Club Selections."

Every Last Novel

The Bluest Eye, 1969
Sula, 1973
Song of Solomon, 1977
    (National Book Critics Circle Award)
Tar Baby, 1981
Beloved, 1987
    (Pulitzer Prize for Fiction, 1988)
Jazz, 1992
Paradise, 1998

If You Like Toni Morrison . . .

Try some of these authors who have also written powerfully and effectively about the black experience in America: Maya Angelou (*I Know Why the Caged Bird Sings*), James Baldwin (*Go Tell It on the Mountain*), Ralph Ellison (*Invisible Man*), Zora Neale Hurston (*Their Eyes Were Watching God*), Alice Walker (*The Color Purple*), and Richard Wright (*Native Son*).

In Her Own Voice

Most of Toni Morrison's novels are offered on tape from Random House Audiobooks in both abridged and unabridged format. No surprise there. The neat part is that Morrison herself does the reading. And known as she is for her wonderful voice and for conveying "the music of black talk," as one reviewer put it, there is no better way to enjoy Morrison's books than by hearing them read in the author's own voice. The tapes are available in bookstores, or you can order them directly from Random House (800-793-2665, www.randomhouse.com).

Best Book to Read First

Song of Solomon or *Jazz*, both of which are considered more approachable than the prize-winning *Beloved*.

I am from the Midwest so I have a special affection for it. My beginnings are always there. . . . No matter what I write, I begin there. . . . It's the matrix for me. . . . Ohio also offers an escape from stereotyped black settings. It is neither plantation nor ghetto.

—Toni Morrison, in an essay for *Black Women Writers at Work* (Continuum, 1986)

Vladimir Nabokov

Born
April 23, 1899, in St. Petersburg, Russia, the eldest son of one of Russia's noble families

Education
Trinity College, Cambridge, with honors, 1922. Studied Romance and Slavic languages.

Pseudonym
Vladimir Sirin

Family
Married Vera Slonim in 1925; one son, Dmitri.

Home
Emigrated to the U.S. in 1940. Lived in Ithaca, New York, while employed as a professor of Russian literature at Cornell University until 1958, when the commercial success of *Lolita* allowed him to give up teaching and move to Switzerland.

Died
July 2, 1977, at his home at the Palace Hotel in Montreux, Switzerland, of a viral infection

Publishers
Vintage
Library of America

Vladimir Nabokov (pronounced "na-BOAK-off") has been called "the most original, the most tantalizing, the most unpredictable author" of his time. He was known for his "brilliant poetic imagination, pervasive sense of paradox, vivid wit, obscure literary allusions, and erudite word games." But he probably never would have rocketed to fame and fortune had he not written a dirty book.

First published in Paris in 1955 by the Olympia Press, and then in the United States in 1958, *Lolita* was Nabokov's ninth novel. It deals with an aging professor's sexual preoccupation with a 12-year-old girl. Of course it wasn't a dirty book. But people thought it was. In the words of the *New York Times*, the "serious novel succeeded for salacious reasons."

There is so much going on *Lolita*, and in any Nabokov novel, and at so many different levels (anagrams, trilingual puns, parody, and Joycean depths of cultural and literary references and echoes) that it isn't surprising that even some major critics didn't appreciate the author's work at first. Nabokov's supreme accomplishment, however, is that the fictional integrity of his work is never sacrificed to his trickery. You can read Nabokov, as most do, savoring the ecstatic enjoyment of the words, the colorful characters, the rampant humor, and feel wholly satisfied. The trickery and multiple levels of meaning, should one happen to be aware of them, only enrich the experience.

You won't want to miss Nabokov's nonfiction either. His *Lectures on Literature* (Harcourt Brace, 1982), delivered while he was a professor at Cornell University, and his autobiography *Speak, Memory* (Knopf, 1999), are both well regarded for their insights and as works of art.

Good to Know

❖ "Without my wife, I wouldn't have written a single novel," Nabokov once said. According to *Vera: Mrs. Vladimir Nabokov* by Stacy Schiff, Vera Slonim, a Jewish Russian émigré, handled nearly every aspect of their lives, from placating landlords to typing manuscripts to negotiating book contracts and chasing royalty payments. In their correspondence with others, they were known to swap authorship in mid-sentence, depending on the topic. Nabokov even imitated Vera's handwriting at such times, a bit of whimsy that fans of his fiction will find particularly appealing.

❖ Nabokov, who grew up speaking and reading English before he could read Russian, inherited a $2 million estate near St. Petersburg. But his family fled to Berlin to escape the Bolshevik Revolution and lost everything. There, his father was killed trying to shield his political rival from an assassin's bullet.

❖ Graduating from Cambridge with first-class honors in French and Russian literature, Nabokov wrote, usually in Russian, in nearly every genre. He even created the first Russian crossword puzzle.

❖ A distinguished lepidopterologist (butterfly expert), he discovered several species and subspecies and served six years as a research fellow in entomology at Harvard's Museum of Comparative Zoology when he and Vera first arrived in the U.S.

❖ Nabokov did not write in a linear fashion. Instead, he composed his novels on index cards, often while standing at a lectern, which allowed him to shuffle his story into its final form.

Treatises and Treats

INTERNATIONAL VLADIMIR NABOKOV SOCIETY

With a leadership rooted in academia, this organization is not for the dim of wit. But any lover of Nabokov can join the society simply by subscribing to *The Nabokovian*, a twice-yearly journal, for an annual $15 contribution:
Stephen Jan Parker
Slavic Languages & Literature
University of Kansas
Lawrence, Kansas 66045
www.libraries.psu.edu/iasweb/nabokov

COMPANIONS

The Annotated Lolita, edited by Alfred Appel, Jr. (Vintage Books, 1991). An excellent way to crack the code. Includes, in addition to the novel itself, over 900 line-by-line notes explaining the book's countless references, word games, anagrams, and other bits of mind candy strewn throughout the novel. A great guide to the art and artifice of Nabokov at his best.

Lolita, read by Jeremy Irons (Random House Audio, 1997). "Irons captures Humbert's voice perfectly," and reads "with a sensitivity to the language that conveys all of Nabokov's humor, passion, and lyricism." (Caryn James, *New York Times*)

The Garland Companion to Vladimir Nabokov, edited by Vladimir E. Alexandrov (Garland, 1995). Focuses on all aspects of Nabokov's legacy—novels, poems, lectures, lepidoptera studies, even chess problems. At 848 pages and a price of $50, this collection is for serious Nabokophiles.

Vladimir Nabokov: The Russian Years and *The American Years* by Brian Boyd (Princeton University Press, 1990 and 1991). Drawing upon the recollections of Nabokov's friends and his private files, this two-volume biography presents a full-bodied picture of the author and his life.

BEST OF THE NET

New York Times Featured Authors

www.nytimes.com/books/specials/author.html
For a plethora of goodies from the *New York Times* archives, click on "Vladimir Nabokov" on the author list. Highlights include audio readings and lectures, and articles such as "Why Nabokov Detests Freud" and "Is *Lolita* a Love Story?"

Best Reads

The Real Life of Sebastian Knight, 1941
Bend Sinister, 1947
Lolita, 1958
Pnin, 1957
Pale Fire, 1962
Ada or Ardor: A Family Chronicle, 1969
Transparent Things, 1972
Look at the Harlequins!, 1974

Best Book to Read First

Lolita. A sophisticated examination of obsessive love and the eternal quest for innocence. "My knowledge of nymphets," Nabokov said, using the term he had coined, "is purely scholarly." Read the book, and then treat yourself to the film versions by Stanley Kubrick (1962) and Adrian Lyne (1998).

Lolita, the Movie

Vladimir Nabokov wrote thoughtful, multilayered, hugely rich novels seemingly focused on chess (*The Defense*), murder (*Despair*), politics (*Invitation to a Beheading*), and other topics, all of which made statements about art. *Lolita* was no exception. The difference is that it was popular and supposedly salacious. So naturally it's the one that gets made into a movie. Twice. The money from the first one, which was directed by Stanley Kubrick in 1962, enabled Nabokov to move to Switzerland to concentrate on writing.

The second, a 50-million-dollar film directed by Adrian Lyne (*Flashdance*, *Fatal Attraction*, and *9½ Weeks*), appeared in 1998 and starred Jeremy Irons, Melanie Griffith, Frank Langella, and Dominique Swain. But although it had a successful European run, no U.S. studio would distribute it. Eventually, U.S. rights to the film were bought by Viacom's Showtime Network.

V. S. Naipaul

Born
August 17, 1932, in
Chaguanas, Trinidad,
the son of Seepersad
Naipaul, a journalist
and writer, and
Dropatie Capildeo
Naipaul

Full Name
Vidiadhar Surajprasad
Naipaul

Education
Attended Queen's
Royal College in
Trinidad, 1943–48.
Earned a B.A. from
University College,
Oxford, in 1953.

Family
Married Patricia Ann
Hale in 1953.
Following her death in
1996, he married
Nadira Khannum Alvi, a
newspaper columnist.

Home
A comfortable house in
Wiltshire, England, with
a well-stocked wine
cellar and room
enough for his collec-
tion of classical Indian
paintings; Also a
duplex in London

Fan Mail
V. S. Naipaul
c/o Aitken & Stone
29 Fernshaw Road
London SW10
England

Publisher
Knopf

To Americans, the term "postcolonial" has little personal meaning. But for V. S. Naipaul, born and raised in a Hindu family in Trinidad, an extraordinarily multicultural island nation off the coast of Venezuela, it means living with a past that stops at your grandparents, with nothing but a blank beyond. It means being forced to forge a national identity out of the remnants of native and colonial cultures from which many citizens feel estranged. And it means trying to find your own identity in the face of such rootlessness.

Naipaul explores these themes in many locales, including his native Caribbean as well as East Africa and England. But he does so in unique ways, blurring the distinctions among many genres. His travel writing is filled with dramatic tension, while his novels are characterized by detailed evocations of place and culture. Colorful, vivid characters populate almost all his work, and as they confront their circumstances with joy, bitterness, humor, and sorrow, you realize anew that human beings are the same everywhere.

He has, as Irving Howe put it in the *New York Times*, "an almost Conradian gift for tensing a story, a serious involvement with human issues, a supple English prose, a hardedged wit, a personal vision of things." Some critics say his vision, though thoughtful, may be too gloomy. On the other hand, Naipaul has seen much in his journeys to support a pessimistic viewpoint.

Raised in Trinidad's Indian community, he won a scholarship to Oxford University at 18 and left the Caribbean for good. Though he settled in London after college, much of his life has been taken up with world travel. In a sense, his writings can be seen as autobiographical journeys in search of an identity— he has said as much himself—and the restlessness of the exile permeates even his most comedic work.

Good to Know

❖ *A House for Mr. Biswas*, based loosely on the life of Naipaul's father, details the misfortunes of a sign painter with chronically modest expectations who is suddenly and somewhat ruthlessly absorbed into a vast, grasping Indian-Trinidadian family. Exuberant critics outdid themselves with superlatives for the book.

❖ Naipaul has a refined taste for food, wine, and art, but also prides himself on a life that is hermetic and austere. He dislikes music, reads no contemporary literature (preferring Balzac, Flaubert, and Proust to "pretentious" writers like William Golding), and once delighted in telling director George Lucas that he had never seen the *Star Wars* movies or Spielberg's *Indiana Jones*.

❖ Naipaul describes his early years in London, writing endless book reviews while struggling with his first novels, as "hard and mean." But it wasn't just the poverty and lack of recognition. He also experienced what he later described as "the spiritual meanness of not knowing how to move, of not being able to look at experiences and make books out of them."

❖ Though knighted in 1990, he refuses to use his title. His second wife, Nadira, however, likes to refer to herself as Lady Naipaul.

Treatises and Treats

COMPANIONS

Between Father and Son: Family Letters
(Knopf, 2000). A collection of letters between
the author and his father, as well as other
family members, written in the early 1950s
before Naipaul was a published novelist. Prepared with Naipaul's consent, but without his
participation.

V. S. Naipaul by Bruce Alvin King (St. Martin's Press, 1993). An accessible guide to the
writer, with an excellent introductory essay
and good plot synopses.

Conversations with V. S. Naipaul, edited by
Feroza Jussawalla (University Press of Mississippi, 1997). Covering the full span of
Naipaul's 40-year career, *Conversations* reveals a protean individual who has become
less enigmatic and less severe with time. The
book also sheds light on how fear and hysteria
motivated the author.

BEST OF THE NET

New York Times Featured Authors
www.nytimes.com/books/specials/author.html
The dependable *New York Times* archive offers trenchant views on Naipaul's books, plus
the usual articles by and about the author.

All the Novels

The Mystic Masseur, 1957
The Suffrage of Elvira, 1958
Miguel Street, 1959
A House for Mr. Biswas, 1961
Mr. Stone and the Knights Companion, 1963
The Mimic Men, 1967
In a Free State, 1971
   (Booker Prize)
Guerrillas, 1975
A Bend in the River, 1979
The Enigma of Arrival, 1987
A Way in the World: A Sequence, 1994

If You Like V. S. Naipaul . . .

For dense, sensual language equal to
Naipaul's—but a somewhat different view of
the personal price of colonialism in a time of
critical change—try Nadine Gordimer's
Burger's Daughter. You might also enjoy Milan
Kundera's *The Unbearable Lightness of Being*
and books by Joseph Conrad. Naipaul's *A Bend
in the River* has been called a modern-day
Heart of Darkness, with a disturbing Kurtz-like
character said to be modeled on the late dictator Mobutu (Zaire/Congo).

Best Book to Read First

A House for Mr. Biswas. Published in 1961, this is an antic and deeply humane novel. Anyone taking up Naipaul in his dark maturity might be surprised to learn that, as he wrote in a new introduction to this comic epic in 1983, he has "no higher literary ambition than to write a piece of comedy that might complement or match this early book."

One always writes comedy at the moment of deepest hysteria.

—V. S. Naipaul, in a 1994 interview

And Then He Said . . .

It was the literary brouhaha of the late 1990s, and it involved V. S. Naipaul and his protégé and friend of
over 30 years, Paul Theroux. The episode amounts to little more than a literary footnote, but at the time it
caused much hooting and jeering around the world. The occasion was a 1998 book by Theroux called *Sir
Vidia's Shadow: A Friendship Across Five Continents*, in which Theroux claimed that a slight by the older
man—really by Naipaul's second wife, Nadira—gave him reason to reveal some awful truths.

Theroux credits Naipaul as the person most responsible for his literary success. But his book launches a
litany of indictments that portray the notoriously private Naipaul as a racist, sadistic, philandering, tight-
fisted, opinionated monster, so self-centered that he once made a scene over being served a vegetarian
meal without taking notice of the fact that his fellow dinner guests had all been presented with similar fare.
One reviewer called the book the spleen of "a vindictive younger writer who evolved from worshipful appren-
tice to resentful colleague."

New York Times book reviewer Michiko Kakutani faulted Theroux for his refusal to acknowledge Naipaul's
sensitive writing about racial issues. And Zoe Heller, in the online magazine *Salon*, said that a recounting of
Naipaul's words out of context completely missed the complexity and irony of his thinking. "There is an element of vituperation in this outpouring...that is not explained by Theroux's disapproval of racism, or even
his compassion for slighted book-tour escorts. In part, it suggests the fury of scorned love," says Heller.

Joyce Carol Oates

Born
June 16, 1938, in
Lockport, New York, to
Frederic James Oates,
a tool-and-die designer,
and Caroline Bush
Oates

Pseudonym
Rosamond Smith

Education
Syracuse University,
B.A. (Phi Beta Kappa),
1960; University of
Wisconsin, M.A., 1961

Family
Married in 1961 to
Raymond Smith,
formerly a professor of
English; now concen-
trates on the *Ontario
Review Press*, which
the couple founded in
1961 to publish books
and a literary journal
(www.ontarioreview
press.com).

Home
Princeton, New Jersey

Fan Mail
Joyce Carol Oates
Dept. of Creative
  Writing
Princeton University
Princeton, NJ 08544

Publisher
Dutton

Joyce Carol Oates published her first book, a collection of short stories called *By the North Gate*, when she was 25. She has averaged two books a year ever since. Her enormous body of work includes novels, short stories, poetry, drama, essays, and literary criticism. Her astounding output has moved some to suggest that she emphasizes quantity over quality. But as feminist critic Elaine Showalter (a Princeton colleague and good friend of Oates) pointed out in *Ms.* magazine, "Some criticism is plainly envious; Oates herself has noted that 'perhaps critics (mainly male) who charged me with writing too much are secretly afraid that someone will accuse them of having done too little with their lives.'"

And consider the record: National Book Award for *Them* in 1970; Bobst Award for Lifetime Achievement in Fiction, 1990; Pulitzer Prize finalist in 1993 for *Black Water* and in 1995 for *What I Lived For*; 14 O. Henry Awards; 16 stories selected for the annual Best American Short Stories anthologies; 6 Pushcart Prizes.

Despite its wide variety, critics have noted two characteristics that appear throughout Joyce Carol Oates's work: a rootedness in "American naturalism and American reality" and a preoccupation with violence that sometimes borders on the obsessional. Some readers and critics find her work almost too dark and violent. Yet she's "not concerned with the gory details....That explicit sort of violence is kept at an amazing minimum, given her novels' various dark subjects" according to the *Chicago Tribune Book World*. She is able to "find just where it hurts—then press," wrote Henry Louis Gates Jr. in the *Nation*.

Good to Know

❖ Joyce Carol Oates submitted her first novel to a publisher when she was 15. But the manuscript—about an addict who is rehabilitated by caring for a black stallion—was rejected as too depressing for the young adult market.

❖ Oates, who refers to her *public* persona as "JCO," does very little rewriting and often produces an entire story in a single evening. She's been known to write ten hours a day or more, and, according to her authorized biography, views eating as little more than one of life's necessary complications. She has reportedly had bouts of anorexia.

❖ Hobbies include bicycling and jogging with her husband, watching boxing matches, and "being owned by two cats," one of whom (Christobel), lets JCO know when she thinks the writing sessions have been going on for too long.

❖ Oates is one of several well-known writers who call Princeton, New Jersey, home: Russell Banks, Peter Benchley, Daniel Halpern, John McPhee, and Toni Morrison, to name a few. She has used Princeton as the setting for several novels, prompting one writer to note, "Everybody's both extremely hopeful and extremely scared that Joyce is going to put them in her next novel."

❖ Several JCO stories formed the basis for the 1999 movie *Getting to Know You*, featuring Bebe Neuwirth. Other movie adaptations of her work include *Foxfire* (1996), *Lives of the Twins* (1991), and *Smooth Talk* (1981), based on the story "Where Are You Going, Where Have You Been?"

Treatises and Treats

COMPANIONS

Invisible Writer: A Biography of Joyce Carol Oates by Greg Johnson (E. P. Dutton, 1998). The authorized biography. Fiction-writer Johnson was granted full access to Joyce Carol Oates's letters and journals in order to create this 560-page account, which focuses more on *why* she writes so much rather than *how*. Includes over 40 photographs.

Lavish Self-Divisions: The Novels of Joyce Carol Oates by Brenda O. Daly (University Press of Mississippi, 1995). Analyzing three decades of JCO's work, Daly looks at the novels by period and type and attempts to defend the author from her male critics and feminist detractors.

Joyce Carol Oates, edited by Harold Bloom (Chelsea House, 1992). A collection of critical essays on Oates and her work.

Conversations with Joyce Carol Oates, edited by Lee Milazzo (University Press of Mississippi, 1990). A collection of interviews that Oates has given over the years.

BEST OF THE NET

Celestial Timepiece
storm.usfca.edu/~southerr/jco.html
Created by a JCO fan, this attractive site offers regularly updated news about the author (including interviews and public appearances), book excerpts, critical commentary, a discussion group, and photographs.

New York Times Featured Authors
www.nytimes.com/books/specials/
    author.html
Check here for dozens of book reviews and articles by and about Joyce Carol Oates, all from the *New York Times* archives.

Best Reads

Them, 1969
    (National Book Award)
Do With Me What You Will, 1973
Bellefleur, 1980
You Must Remember This, 1987
Because It Is Bitter, and Because It Is My Heart, 1990
Black Water, 1992
Where Are You Going, Where Have You Been?: Selected Early Stories, 1993
What I Lived For, 1994
We Were the Mulvaneys, 1996

If You Like Joyce Carol Oates...

You might also like Margaret Atwood, Anita Brookner, Alice Hoffman, Cormac McCarthy, and Susan Sontag.

Best Book to Read First
Them, winner of the 1970 National Book Award. The *New York Times* called it "a vehement, voluminous, kaleidoscopic novel, more deeply rooted in social observation than current fiction usually tends to be."

Over a period of three decades I seem to have published somewhere beyond four hundred short stories—a number as daunting, or more daunting, to me, as to any other. The motives have nearly always to do with memorializing people, or a landscape, or an event, or a profound and riddlesome experience that can only be contemplated in the solitude of art. There is the hope too of 'bearing witness' for those who can't speak for themselves; the hope of recording mysteries whose very contours I can scarcely define, except through transforming them into structures that lay claim to some sort of communal permanence.

—Joyce Carol Oates, in the afterword to *Where Are You Going, Where Have You Been?: Selected Early Stories* (1993)

The Name Game

In 1987, Joyce Carol Oates wrote the mystery novel *Lives of the Twins*, using the pen name Rosamond Smith (a variation on the name of her husband, Raymond Smith). But instead of submitting it to her longtime literary agent or her editor at Dutton, she gave it to Rosalie Siegel, a literary agent and neighbor in Princeton, and took the first offer—a $10,000 advance from Simon & Schuster.

Oates said later, "I wanted a fresh reading; I wanted to escape from my own identity." But in the end her literary cover was blown. Her agent was shocked, and her editor at Dutton was none too pleased, since they were scheduled to publish a new Oates novel, *You Must Remember This*, during the same year as *Lives of the Twins*. Oates declared that she would never again try to hide behind a pseudonym. She published her sixth "Rosamond Smith" novel, *Double Delight*, in 1997. But each book cover identifies the author as "Joyce Carol Oates writing as Rosamond Smith."

Patrick O'Brian

Born
December 12, 1914, in Chalfont St. Peter, Buckinghamshire, to Dr. Charles Russ and Jessie Naylor Goddard; the eighth of nine children

Real Name
Richard Patrick Russ (legally changed to Patrick O'Brian in 1945)

Education
Shebbear College, near Torrington, Devon. Fluent in French, Italian, Spanish, and Catalan; read Latin with ease.

Family
First marriage in 1936 ended in divorce. One son and a daughter who died at three. Second marriage in 1945 to Frieda Mary Wicksteed, ex-wife of Demitry, Count Tolstoy Miloslavsky, son of one of Tsar Nicholas's principal advisors. One stepson. Mary died in 1998.

Home
A cottage in Collioure, France, on the Mediterranean Sea near the Spanish border

Died
January 2, 2000, in Dublin, Ireland, fittingly enough

Publisher
W. W. Norton

Patrick O'Brian, far from being a Catholic Irishman, as he claimed, was in reality the grandson of an evangelical Lutheran who had come to London from a town near Dresden in the 1860s and built a prosperous Bond Street business supplying furs to royalty. These and other secret details of O'Brian's life were reported late in 1998, but few paid attention until his obituary appeared in January 2000.

All novelists are liars. But few can lay claim to *living* a completely false identity. Far from detracting from his work, however, this makes it all the more intriguing. O'Brian is most famous for his 20-book series chronicling the exploits of Captain Jack Aubrey and ship's surgeon Dr. Stephen Maturin as they fight Napoleon during the golden age of the square-rigged men o' war whose cannon made the world safe for the British Empire. Sounds like C. S. Forester's much-loved Hornblower series.

But it is so much more. O'Brian does nothing less than *re-create* the age. His characters speak as they would have spoken at the time, using the words of their professions. Aubrey, a strapping man of natural good looks, is completely at home on a ship and often completely "at sea" on land. Maturin, a short, unattractive Irish-Catalan physician, is most at home in a book-filled study. He knows little of seamanship but is an expert medical man and a passionate naturalist. He is also a consummate spy for the Admiralty. The two share a passion for music.

The battles they fight are historically accurate, with some alterations for plot that are always acknowledged at the beginning of each book. But as good as the action scenes may be, the books are really about the late 18th and early 19th centuries, English culture at the time, and wonderful characters—all laced with O'Brian's huge intelligence and very dry sense of humor.

Good to Know

❖ O'Brian's favorite author was Jane Austen, a novelist to whom he is often compared, owing to his wry humor and detailed portrayal of characters' lives. *Post Captain*, much of which takes place in English drawing rooms and country houses, is O'Brian's homage to Austen.

❖ The Aubrey/Maturin series wasn't available in the U.S. until the late 1980s. Former Navy Secretary John Lehman once recounted how, for many years, he would ask anyone traveling to England to bring back the latest O'Brian, almost like smuggled goods. Fortunately, someone at W. W. Norton twigged to the O'Brian phenomenon and began publishing him to great success.

❖ As Patrick Russ, O'Brian published *Caesar* (1930), about a "panda-leopard," and *Hussein* (1938), about an Indian boy growing up under the British Raj. He also wrote much praised biographies of Picasso and Joseph Banks, the naturalist who accompanied Captain James Cook to Australia. But much of his life he spent in genteel poverty, relying for income on his translations of the works of Simone de Beauvoir, André Maurois, and others.

Treatises and Treats

COMPANIONS

A Sea of Words: A Lexicon and Companion for Patrick O'Brian's Seafaring Tales, edited by Dean King (Henry Holt, 1997). This handy guide illuminates what the old salts are saying.

Harbors and High Seas: An Atlas and Geographical Guide to the Aubrey-Maturin Novels of Patrick O'Brian by Dean King, et al. (Owl Books, 1999). A detailed guide to the routes of our heroes' wanderings, with maps and commentary.

Lobscouse and Spotted Dog by Anne Chotzinoff Grossman and Lisa Grossman Thomas (W. W. Norton, 1997). A cookbook that faithfully reconstructs such 18th-century dishes as haggis, a savory recipe for rat, and Jack Aubrey's favorite pudding, spotted dog (a suet-based bread pudding with currants).

Patrick O'Brian: A Life Revealed by Dean King (Henry Holt, 2000). The untold story of a novelist whose greatest fictional creation was his own identity.

AUDIOTAPES AND CDS

Aubrey/Maturin on Tape. The unabridged recordings of O'Brian's novels from Recorded Books (800-638-1304, www.recordedbooks.com) are an unsurpassed listening experience. Patrick Tull perfectly renders the accents of the characters and unfolds the stories with a dimension not available to Americans reading a period British novel.

Musical Evenings with the Captain. Join Jack Aubrey and Stephen Maturin in the music room to hear works by Handel, Haydn, Mozart, and other 18th-century composers they enjoy and talk about in the novels. Available on CD in stores, or order directly from Essay Recordings (800-973-7729, www.essaycd.com).

BEST OF THE NET
The Patrick O'Brian Page
www.wwnorton.com/pob
An omnibus collection of all things O'Brian. Highlights include a lively frequently-asked-questions list, reading-group guides, book excerpts, back issues of the *Patrick O'Brian Newsletter*, and a link to the "Gunroom Guide to O'Brian Web Resources."

Aubrey/Maturin Novels

Master and Commander, 1969
Post Captain, 1972
H.M.S. Surprise, 1973
The Mauritius Command, 1977
Desolation Island, 1978
The Fortune of War, 1979
The Surgeon's Mate, 1980
The Ionian Mission, 1981
Treason's Harbour, 1983
The Far Side of the World, 1984
The Reverse of the Medal, 1986
The Letter of Marque, 1988
The Thirteen-Gun Salute, 1989
The Nutmeg of Consolation, 1991
The Truelove, 1992
The Wine-Dark Sea, 1993
The Commodore, 1995
The Yellow Admiral, 1996
The Hundred Days, 1998
Blue at the Mizzen, 1999

Best Book to Read First

Start with the first book in the Aubrey/Maturin series, *Master and Commander*, and prepare to be amazed.

Not only in literary craftsmanship, but in the mastery of complex relationships, deep philosophical conflict, and intensity of passion, he is unmatched. The subtlety of his personalities and the gaudy parade of characters are used to explore war, anthropology, engineering, botany, medicine, and metaphysics and yet weave all this complexity into a grand and continuing flow of life.

—Former Navy Secretary John Lehman, in a *Wall Street Journal* review of *The Wine-Dark Sea*

A Key to "Patrick O'Brian"

Shortly before his death, Patrick O'Brian was interviewed by Walter Cronkite on C-SPAN2. Though charming throughout, the author was evasive whenever the conversation even lightly touched on his life. Audience questions were accepted under the strict proviso that no personal questions would be entertained.

Today the world knows why. O'Brian's son, Richard Russ, now in his 60s, told a London newspaper that he had not spoken to his father in 36 years. "When a man walks out on everybody, leaving a two-year-old daughter severely disabled [by spina bifida], a small boy, and his mother with no financial support, what sort of respect can you have for him?"

It makes you want to cry. Particularly when you learn that Stephen Maturin, O'Brian's alter ego, rescues his fictional daughter Bridget from the near oblivion of autism and twice rescues two children from certain death in faraway countries. The pain for O'Brian—prim, proper, and able to wield his wit and perfect manners like a weapon—must have been unimaginable. *Requiem in pacem.*

Rosamunde Pilcher

Born
September 22, 1924, in Lelant, Cornwall, England, to Charles Scott, a Royal Navy commander, and Helen Harvey Scott

Pseudonym
Jane Fraser

Education
St. Clare's Polwithen and Howell's School Llandaff, then Miss Kerr-Sanders' Secretarial College. Served with the Women's Royal Naval Service, 1943–46.

Family
Married in 1946 to Graham Pilcher, a company director; two daughters and two sons.

Home
Invergowrie by Dundee, Scotland

Fan Mail
Rosamunde Pilcher
c/o Curtis Brown Ltd.
10 Astor Place
New York, NY 10003

Publisher
St. Martin's Press

Few romance writers have been as successful at crossing over into mainstream commercial fiction as Rosamunde Pilcher. She began her career at age 18 writing stories for a women's magazine in London. By the time she was 25, she had expanded her repertoire to include romance novels under the pseudonym Jane Fraser. She honed her craft writing these light romances ("frightfully wet little novels—romantic stuff with red roses on the cover") and then moved on to more complex historical romances and family sagas, many of them written under her own name. In 1987, almost four decades after the publication of her first book, she came out with her first serious novel, *The Shell Seekers*, and both British and American readers bought out the store shelves. The book has sold over 3.5 million copies around the world.

Pilcher writes of the extraordinariness in the ordinary lives of everyday people, effortlessly transporting readers to another time and place with her picturesque prose. Reviewers can seem to find no fault with her writing or her deceptively simple plots, describing her novels as pleasurable, satisfying reads and welcoming her unpretentious style. A reviewer for *Publishers Weekly* called Pilcher "one of the best current practitioners of literate commercial fiction." Her skillful use of flashbacks, attention to detail, and ability to make fictional characters seem like old friends in bestsellers such as *September* and *Coming Home* have won her a loyal readership.

Good to Know

❖ Pilcher is Scotland's highest-earning resident, according to *Scotland on Sunday*, with an estimated income of about $7.1 million.

❖ She began writing at age 7 and was sending out stories at age 16: "I wrote a little short story and sent it to Winnifred Johnson, an elderly lady who edited three women's magazines in London. She wrote back and said, 'It's not right yet, but you'll get it.' She was a tremendous help to me . . . like a very nice headmistress, a great lucky break in my life."

❖ The "lucky break" actually occurred two years later when Ms. Johnson finally bought one of Pilcher's stories. She has since earned the distinction of selling more stories to *Good Housekeeping* than any other writer.

❖ "I don't ever write about a place or a person or an experience that I don't know a lot about," says Pilcher. And her stories, she says, are "not so much love stories, but more about human relations. . . . If the stories do not have a happy ending, then they always have a hopeful ending."

❖ Many thought that her 1995 novel *Coming Home* (with sales of over one million copies) would be her last. But in the summer of 1999, Pilcher signed a contract for a substantial advance for *The Winter Solstice*, a novel set in modern times.

❖ Pilcher fans were generally disappointed with the made-for-TV movies of *The Shell Seekers* (1989) and *Coming Home* (1998). Both had great casts, but neither succeeded in capturing the essence of the novels.

Treatises and Treats

COMPANIONS

The World of Rosamunde Pilcher by Rosamunde Pilcher (St. Martin's Press, 1996). A richly illustrated gift book that Pilcher fans will treasure. Includes an introduction by the author, who recounts her life growing up in Cornwall and her later years in Scotland and London. Also family snapshots, recipes, and extracts from Pilcher's best-loved novels and short stories.

Christmas with Rosamunde Pilcher by Rosamunde Pilcher (St. Martin's Press, 1998). Another gift book that invites fans to celebrate the holidays with the Pilcher family. Includes Christmas recipes, descriptions of some of the family's holiday traditions, and lovely photographs of scenic Scotland.

AUDIOTAPES

Many of Rosamunde Pilcher's novels are available in abridged audiotape editions. One of the best is ***Coming Home***, narrated by actress Lynn Redgrave (Bantam Audio, 1995). Redgrave gets high marks for the warmth and clarity of her delivery, and her ability to bring Pilcher's characters to life.

For the largest selection of *unabridged* versions of Pilcher's novels and story collections, contact Books-on-Tape (800-88-BOOKS, www.booksontape.com).

BEST OF THE NET

Scottish Writers Page

www.users.globalnet.co.uk/~crumey/
    scot.html

Check here for an informative Pilcher biography, book list, discussion area, and suggestions for further reading.

Reading List

ALL THE NOVELS

A Secret to Tell, 1955
April, 1957
On My Own, 1965
Sleeping Tiger, 1967
Another View, 1969
The End of Summer, 1975

Snow in April, 1972
The Empty House, 1973
The Day of the Storm, 1975
Under Gemini, 1976
Wild Mountain Thyme, 1979
The Carousel, 1982
Voices in Summer, 1982
The Shell Seekers, 1988
September, 1990
Coming Home, 1995
The Winter Solstice, 2000

SHORT-STORY COLLECTIONS

The Blue Bedroom and Other Stories, 1985
Flowers in the Rain and Other Stories, 1991

If You Like Rosamunde Pilcher...

You might also enjoy books by Maeve Binchy. Or try some of these leading Scottish writers of romance and family sagas: Emma Blair, Margaret Thomson Davis, Alexandra Raife, Eileen Ramsay, Mary Stewart, and Jan Webster.

You might also want to check used book sources like Alibris (www.alibris.com) or Bibliofind (www.bibliofind.com) for these early genre romances, which Rosamunde Pilcher published under the pseudonym Jane Fraser:

Halfway to the Moon, 1949
The Brown Fields, 1951
Dangerous Intruder, 1951
Young Bar, 1952
A Day Like Spring, 1953
Dear Tom, 1954
Bridge of Corvie, 1956
A Family Affair, 1958
A Long Way from Home, 1963
The Keeper's House, 1963

Best Book to Read First

The Shell Seekers is the novel that made Rosamunde Pilcher's reputation. History and suspense, offbeat characters, tragedy and triumph— *Publishers Weekly* called it "A satisfying and savory family novel."

All my life I've had people coming up and saying, "Sat under the hair dryer and read one of your little stories, dear. So clever of you. Wish I had the time to do it myself." I just say, "Yeah, fine, pity you don't." I've been beavering away. And now I'm hoping that nobody will ever, ever say that again.

—Rosamunde Pilcher in *Publishers Weekly*, on publication of *The Shell Seekers*

E. Annie Proulx

Born
August 22, 1935, in
Norwich, Connecticut,
to George N. Proulx, a
textile executive, and
Lois Gill, an artist

Full Name
Edna Annie Proulx
(rhymes with "true")

Education
Attended Colby College
in the 1950s.
Completed undergrad-
uate studies much
later at the University
of Vermont, with a
B.A., cum laude, 1969.
Earned her M.A. from
Sir George Williams
University (now
Concordia University)
in 1973. Passed her
doctoral orals in 1975,
but abandoned her
dissertation to become
a freelance writer.

Family
Married and divorced
three times; four
children.

Home
LaBarge, Wyoming

Fan Mail
E. Annie Proulx
c/o Darhansoff &
Verrill Literary Agency
179 Franklin Street
New York, NY 10013

Publisher
Scribner

E. Annie Proulx began writing novels relatively late in life—just past 50—but she has achieved the kind of success that most novelists can only dream of. With a mere three novels and two collections of short stories since 1988, she has won the PEN/Faulkner Award, the National Book Award, and a Pulitzer Prize for Fiction, among other honors. John Updike included one of her stories in *The Best American Short Stories of the Century*, which he edited for Houghton Mifflin, and Proulx herself was selected to edit the 1997 edition of the venerable *Best American Short Stories* series. Her books are not just critics' choices, either; they are hugely popular with the reading public.

Proulx is a purveyor of a kind of contemporary gothic fiction. Her settings tend to be forbidding landscapes—which play as important a role in the narratives as any character—and she composes intricate dramas of people trying to adapt to tragic circumstances. *Postcard* protagonist Loyal Blood, for example, flees his ancestral home after the mysterious death of his girlfriend, and the novel chronicles his aimless 30-year odyssey and the simultaneous ruin of the family farm he left behind.

What distinguishes Proulx's novels, besides a voice that has been praised for both its lyricism and its extraordinary authenticity, is an historian's rigor for details. Proulx has said that research is the best part of writing, and her stories have an immediacy that is rare in fiction. Every book also has its quirky motif: Each chapter in *Postcards* begins with a correspondence between Blood and his family; in *The Shipping News*, chapters are introduced with a drawing of a knot and a bit of philosophy from *The Ashley Book of Knots*; and in *Accordion Crimes*, the motif is the movement of a musical instrument through the hands of several generations of American immigrants.

Good to Know

❖ An habitual driver of the country's back roads, Proulx is known for capturing the minutiae of out-of-the-way American life. Her willingness to examine and haul away small-town rubbish is so eager and indiscriminate that her bookshelves are stuffed with such threadbare oddments as a pamphlet of Spam recipes, a history of corncob pipes, and a guide to gate crashing. It is in these rural outbacks that she also finds the snippets of conversation and the place names like Joe Batt's Arm and Seldom Come By that lend her books their eccentric ring of truth.

❖ Nostalgic for the public libraries of days gone by, Proulx says she misses the old wooden card-catalog trays because they offered chance, "browse-by" encounters with information you might not have known existed. Furthermore—and this is a bit surprising from a writer with highly developed literary sympathies for suffering humankind—she dislikes the fact that "in bad weather homeless folk exuding pungent odors doze at the reading tables."

❖ Proulx rarely grants interviews and is known to be rather prickly on occasion. Despite the fact that fame has relieved her forever from waitressing, postal clerking, and the tedium of writing magazine articles—which sustained her for 19 years before her success—like many literary writers she resents the system that tries so hard to foster celebrity. Especially since the process of her art requires quiet and privacy. "In a sense

[fame] is like someone continually ransacking your personal life," she says.

❖ In addition to her many honors, Proulx also holds the distinction of being the first woman to receive the prestigious PEN/Faulkner Award, for *Postcards*.

Treatises and Treats

AUDIO PROULX

Simon & Schuster offers abridged audiotape versions of Proulx's novels and story collections, which are fine for sampling the author and her work. Even better, contact Recorded Books (800-638-1304, www.recordedbooks.com) for the 13-hour, full-length version of *The Shipping News*, narrated by actor Paul Hecht.

BEST OF THE NET

New York Times Featured Authors
www.nytimes.com/books/specials/author.html
Leave it to the *New York Times* archive to rescue those few contemporary writers who have almost no other presence on the World Wide Web. Reviews, articles about Proulx, and those she penned herself, along with some intriguing links, can all be found here.

Book List

ALL THE NOVELS
Postcards, 1992
    (PEN/Faulkner Award)
The Shipping News, 1993
    (Pulitzer Prize, National Book Award,
    Irish Times/Aer Lingus International
    Fiction Prize)
Accordion Crimes, 1996

SHORT-STORY COLLECTIONS
Heart Songs and Other Stories, 1988
Close Range: Wyoming Stories, 1999

If You Like
E. Annie Proulx . . .

You might also like *Snow Falling on Cedars* by David Guterson, *The Stone Diaries* by Carol Shields, *A Thousand Acres* by Jane Smiley, and *Breathing Lessons* by Anne Tyler.

Best Book to Read First

The Shipping News. Lavishly praised by critics, it won several coveted prizes and became an enduring bestseller. The book displays all of the author's gifts: descriptive gusto, an unflinching eye for wounded humanity, and a taste for harsh landscapes and peculiar place names. Inspired by a canoeing trip to Newfoundland, Proulx centers her story around anti-hero Quoyle, who returns to the island with two disturbed daughters and an eccentric aunt to make a new life for himself.

Why Don't I Write About Women, You Ask?

A nnie Proulx's best-known protagonists have been men—Loyal Blood in *Post-cards* and Quoyle in *The Shipping News*—and more than once she has had to answer to her fans on this issue.

"Readers often ask me why don't you write about women, implying that if you are a woman, that's all you can write about," she once told a reporter. "Writers can write about anything they want, any sex they want, any place they want."

Given the exhaustive way she prepares for her novels—not to mention her generally contrarian outlook—it's not surprising that her thinking about writing goes against conventional wisdom. In another interview, Proulx said that she found the idea of writing about one's personal experience an unpleasant trend. "If only people would write about what intrigues them, what they *don't* know, would do a little research, would become questioning as well as observant. That's the pleasure in writing."

The digging involves more than books. I need to know which mushrooms smell like maraschino cherries and which like dead rats.

—E. Annie Proulx, on the myriad pleasures of her favorite pastime, research

Mario Puzo

Born
October 15, 1920, in New York City, to Antonio Puzo, a railroad trackman, and Maria Le Conti Puzo, a homemaker

Education
Attended New York City's New School for Social Research and Columbia University.

Family
Married Erika Lina Broske in 1946. They had five children. Following his wife's death from breast cancer in 1978, her nurse, Carol Gino, became his companion.

Home
Bay Shore, Long Island, in a modest house that he bought in 1968 and added onto over the years. (According to friend and fellow author Joseph Heller, "It was a model house in a development, and he asked them to leave the furniture.")

Died
July 2, 1999, at his home in Bay Shore, of heart failure

Publisher
Random House

Even though Mario Puzo did not consider it his best novel, *The Godfather* is his legacy. It has sold over 21 million copies, set the standard for books about the Mafia, and spawned three award-winning movies (two of which are generally considered among the best films of all time). The fame and money became very important to Puzo. His first two novels, *The Dark Arena* and *The Fortunate Pilgrim*, were well received critically but were unsuccessful commercially. They made him a total of $6,500.

The Godfather was written to make money. It became the bestselling novel of the 1970s, outselling the decade's other blockbusters—*The Exorcist, Love Story,* and *Jaws*—by millions. In addition to its commercial success, *The Godfather* was also praised critically. Robert Lasson of the *Washington Post Book World* wrote that "Puzo sat down and produced . . . a novel which still had enormous force and kept you turning the pages." *Newsweek*'s Pete Axthelm called Puzo "an extremely talented storyteller . . . [whose narrative] moves at breakneck speed without ever losing its balance."

The book's enormous popularity produced high expectations for Puzo's long-awaited fourth novel, *Fools Die*. New American Library paid an unprecedented $2.2 million for the paperback rights, plus $350,000 for the reprint rights to *The Godfather*. In spite of the publicity, or perhaps as a result of it, critical reception to this novel was mixed at best. James Wolcott of the *Village Voice* wrote: "In all this commotion, a fundamental question has gone unasked. . . . Has anyone at [the publisher] actually read this book?" Puzo spent the rest of his career trying to top *The Godfather*—and failing.

Good to Know

❖ Inspired by Dostoyevsky, Puzo began writing stories in high school and dreamed of making writing his career. At 15, he was told by two different teachers that his compositions were good enough to be published.

❖ He served in the United States Army Air Forces during World War II. Assigned to the military government of French towns, he never fired a shot but won five battlefield stars for coming under enemy fire. "As a soldier, I was so inept," he said, "that it's a good thing I never had to handle a rifle!"

❖ In 1960, Bruce Jay Friedman hired him as an assistant editor of a group of men's magazines (*Male, Gent,* and others). Puzo wrote action stories for these magazines, many based on versions of World War II battles.

❖ Finally, an offer he couldn't refuse: In 1965, a Putnam editor happened to stop by the magazine offices where Puzo was working and overheard him telling Mafia stories. The editor offered him a $5,000 advance for a book about the Italian underworld. The result was *The Godfather*.

❖ Mama Mia! Puzo has said that his mother was the model for the character of Don Vito Corleone. It was *her* voice that Puzo heard whenever the Godfather spoke. "My mother was a wonderful, handsome woman," said Puzo, "but a fairly ruthless person."

❖ Puzo won Academy Awards for best screenplay adaptation for both *The Godfather* and *The Godfather: Part II*, and Golden Globe Awards for best screenplay for *The Godfather* and *The Godfather: Part III*. He also cowrote the screenplays for other popular Hollywood films such as *Earthquake* (1974), *Superman* (1978), and *Superman II* (1981).

❖ A self-described book addict, Puzo would sometimes read 16 hours a day. He once told Camille Paglia that he liked to have 20 books available at all times, and that he had a "weakness of rereading." His favorite authors: John le Carré and Larry McMurtry, whose *Lonesome Dove* he considered "a perfect novel." He also enjoyed "English lady novelists" like Fay Weldon and Muriel Spark, and the nonfiction of Norman Mailer and Gay Talese.

❖ Before he died, Puzo completed *Omerta* (Sicilian for "code of silence"). He considered this book the third in his Mafia trilogy.

Treatises and Treats

COMPANIONS

The Godfather Papers and Other Confessions by Mario Puzo (Putnam, 1972). Out of print but worth tracking down for insights like this one into the creation of Puzo's book (rather than the three movies): "I'm ashamed to admit that I wrote *The Godfather* entirely from research. I never met a real honest-to-god gangster."

The Godfather Legacy by Harlan Lebo (Fireside, 1997). A fully illustrated, behind-the-scenes look at how Francis Ford Coppola turned *The Godfather* into one of the most stunning films of all time.

The Godfather Companion: Everything You Ever Wanted to Know About All Three Godfather Films by Peter Biskind (Harper-Perennial, 1990). A meticulously detailed treatment of the production and events surrounding the making of the three *Godfather* movies. It's currently out of print, but you can probably find it at your local library or favorite used book source.

BEST OF THE NET

Official Mario Puzo Library

www.jgeoff.com/puzo
A good starting point for biographical information, bibliography, filmography, and interviews.

Reading List

THE MAFIA TRILOGY

The Godfather, 1969
The Last Don, 1996
Omerta, 2000

OTHER NOVELS

The Dark Arena, 1955
The Fortunate Pilgrim, 1964
Fools Die, 1978
The Sicilian, 1984
The Fourth K, 1991

If You Like Mario Puzo ...

You will probably also like *The Wise Guy* by Nicholas Pileggi and *Unto the Sons* by Gay Talese. But also consider *The Leopard* by Giuseppe di Lampedusa, a classic novel about an aristocratic family and a Sicilian prince, who sees the old ways falling to the onslaught of the new during Garibaldi's campaign to forge a unified Italy in the 1850s and 1860s.

Best Book to Read First

The one for which Puzo will be remembered is *The Godfather* (67 weeks on the *New York Times* bestseller list). Alternatively, go with *The Fortunate Pilgrim*, the book that Puzo and many others consider his best and most literary work. The *New York Times Book Review* called it "a small classic."

It was Christmas Eve and I had a severe gallbladder attack. I had to take a cab to the [hospital], got out, and fell into the gutter. There I was, lying there, thinking, "Here I am a published writer, and I am dying like a dog." That's when I decided I would be rich and famous.

—Mario Puzo in *Time*, March 13, 1971

Speculation: Was Puzo "Connected"?

Many readers of *The Godfather* have suspected that Puzo's knowledge of the Mafia had to have been first-hand. In fact, after the book's release, real-life underworld figures began approaching Puzo, convinced he was linked to organized crime. "I was introduced to a few gentlemen related to the material," Puzo told *Time*. They were flattering. They refused to believe that I had never had the confidence of a don."

Puzo also had an unpleasant encounter with Frank Sinatra (on whom many readers assume Puzo based the character Johnny Fontane—a singer past his prime who comes to the Godfather for help with his career). "The worst thing he called me was a pimp," writes Puzo, "which rather flattered me. But what hurt was that there he was, a northern Italian, threatening me, a southern Italian, with physical violence."

Thomas Pynchon

Born
May 8, 1937, in Glen Cove, Long Island, New York, to Thomas Ruggles Pynchon, an industrial surveyor, and Katherine Bennett Pynchon

Full Name
Thomas Ruggles Pynchon Jr.

Education
Cornell University, B.A., 1958

Home
He's rumored to be living in New York City with his literary agent, whom he married in 1990.

Publisher
Henry Holt

No American writer of the 20th century—not even J. D. Salinger—has been shrouded in more mystery than Thomas Pynchon. Not that it really matters, but no one is even quite sure what he looks like. He communicates with his publisher only with elaborate precautions designed to conceal his whereabouts and identity.

It's a great gimmick. Make a fetish of avoiding publicity in order to *get* publicity. That might work even if you have no talent. But as Richard Schickel writes in the *World*, "I don't see how anyone who cares the least bit seriously about modern fiction can deny Pynchon's richness of imagination, his mastery of craft, or his power of vision. Attention must be paid to him as an artist of the very first—and most dangerous—quality."

There is simply no question: The guy's good; very, very good. And he knows it. So he doesn't have to play by anyone else's rules. For whatever reason, he does not seem to care about money. So he's either an ascetic or the beneficiary of a trust fund. For all you know, he could be the middle-aged fellow behind the deli counter slicing the oh-so-thin pieces of corned beef for your lunchtime sandwich.

Still, the Pulitzer Prize editorial board refused to grant him the fiction award in 1974 for *Gravity's Rainbow*. The nominating jurors were unanimous in their choice, but the board declared the book "obscene" and "unreadable." As a result, no one received the Pulitzer for fiction that year. The novel went on to win the National Book Award, and Edward Mendelson, writing in the *Yale Review*, ranked *Gravity's Rainbow* with Joyce's *Ulysses* and Mann's *The Magic Mountain*.

In all likelihood Pynchon is having us on with his publicity phobia. But the apparent depth and complexity of his work, combined with his unavailability for comment, amount to a kilo of catnip for academics. In Pynchon they have a new, fully equipped intellectual gymnasium to use for verbal workouts leading to learned articles, studies, grant-funded summer projects, and possibly even tenure-track books. Pynchon himself could probably not care less.

Forget the commentary and the reclusiveness of the author. Borrow any Pynchon book from the library and start reading anywhere. Approach it not as a novel but as a book of prose images. Read five or ten pages. If nothing strikes an internal chord, strike the fellow off your list. Pynchon writes on the outer edge. Society may "require" you to like certain aspects of Dickens or Joyce, but Pynchon has not yet achieved that status.

Good to Know

❖ Pynchon went to Cornell to study engineering and physics but left to serve in the navy from 1955 to 1957. When he returned, he enrolled in the College of Arts and Sciences and took a course given by Vladimir Nabokov, who later said that he did not remember Pynchon (though Nabokov's wife remembered Pynchon's unusual handwriting: half printing, half cursive).

❖ Lewis Nichols in *In and Out of Books* writes that Pynchon, during his last years at Cornell, was "a constant reader—the type who read books on mathematics for fun... [and] who started the day at 1 P.M. with spaghetti and a soft drink...and read and worked until 3 A.M. the next morning."

❖ When *Gravity's Rainbow* won the National Book Award in 1974 (shared with Isaac Bashevis Singer's *A Crown of Feathers*), Pynchon sent a stand-up comic, Irwin Corey, to accept for him. (Yet another put-on.) When the same novel won the William Dean Howell's Medal in 1975, Pynchon declined the award through a letter, suggesting that another author be chosen. (Had Pynchon simply accepted the medal, even in absentia, no one would comment. But doing what he did…well, if he didn't want the publicity, why didn't he simply refuse to respond in any way? Think about it.)

Treatises and Treats

COMPANIONS

A Gravity's Rainbow Companion: Sources and Contexts for Pynchon's Novel by Steven C. Weisenburger (University of Georgia Press, 1990). Provides a page-by-page, often line-by-line, guide to the historical references, scientific data, cultural fragments, jokes, and puns found in *Gravity's Rainbow*.

Thomas Pynchon: A Bibliography of Primary and Secondary Materials by Clifford Mead (Dalkey Archive Press, 1989). A thorough bibliography that lists Pynchon's own writings and magazine contributions, as well as translations and criticism of his work. Also includes contributions to his high school newspaper and rare photographs from his high school yearbook.

JOURNALS

Pynchon Notes. *American Literary Scholarship* calls this journal "The most trustworthy repository for the finest Pynchon scholarship." Subscriptions are $10.Contact:
Bernard Duyfhuizen
College of Arts and Sciences
University of Wisconsin—Eau Claire
Eau Claire, WI 54702-4004

BEST OF THE NET

Pomona Pynchon Page
www.pomona.edu/pynchon
Provides a good starting point for information about Thomas Pynchon's life and work, including the five-page Pynchon FAQ with answers to frequently asked questions about the author. Also includes information on subscribing to the Pynchon-L mailing list.

Spermatikos Logos
www.rpg.net/quail/libyrinth/pynchon
Another comprehensive, well organized source, offering a Pynchon bibliography, a collection of his essays and papers, a look at his fictional characters, criticism, quotations, and information on musical artists who have been influenced by Pynchon.

All the Novels

V., 1963
The Crying of Lot 49, 1966
Gravity's Rainbow, 1973
   (National Book Award)
Vineland, 1990
Mason & Dixon, 1997

If You Like Thomas Pynchon…

You might also like Jorge Luis Borges, Italo Calvino, Don DeLillo, William Gaddis, James Joyce, Joseph McElroy, and Gertrude Stein. Also consider Oakley Hall's *Warlock*, a college favorite of Pynchon's.

Best Book to Read First

The Crying of Lot 49 introduces many of the themes found in Pynchon's work but is shorter and more clearly plotted than his other novels.

Getting a Sense of Pynchon

Mason & Dixon tells the story of the astronomer and the surveyor who laid out the Mason-Dixon line. It begins more or less in 1761 and is written in the vernacular of the 18th-century, hence the strange capitalizations. Just listen to the language!

Snow-Balls have flown their Arcs, starr'd the Sides of Outbuildings, as of Cousins, carried Hats away into the brisk Wind off Delaware, —the Sleds are brought in and their Runners carefully dried and greased, shoes deposited in the back Hall, a stocking'd-foot Descent made upon the great Kitchen, in a purposeful Dither since Morning, punctuated by the ringing Lids of Boilers and Stewing-Pots, fragrant with Pie-Spices, peel'd Fruits, Suet, heated Sugar, —the Children, having all upon the Fly, among rhythmic slaps of Batter and Spoon, coax'd and stolen what they might, proceed, as upon each afternoon all this snowy Advent, to a comfortable Room at the rear of the House, years since given over to their carefree Assaults.

Ayn Rand

Born
February 2, 1905, St. Petersburg, Russia. Came to the U.S. in 1926, arriving in New York City with only $50.

Real Name
Alice Rosenbaum. She changed it to Ayn Rand when she came to the U.S., borrowing a Finnish writer's first name (Ayn rhymes with "pine") and adopting a surname in honor of her trusty Remington Rand typewriter.

Education
Graduated with highest honors in history from the University of Petrograd, 1924.

Family
Married actor Charles "Frank" O'Connor in 1929. They were together for 50 years. No children.

Home
Lived mostly in California until 1951; then moved back to New York City, where she lived until her death.

Died
March 6, 1982, in her New York City apartment

Publishers
Dutton
Penguin

More than a novelist, Ayn Rand was a philosopher. This is not to say that her fiction even remotely resembles some bone-dry philosophical text. On the contrary, her stories are compelling in plot and keep the reader swiftly turning pages—a fortunate effect, considering the heft of her anvil-sized books.

Rand was a product of the Bolshevik Revolution, and the suffering she witnessed in the name of promoting communism caused her to cling to the pure principles of capitalism and many things "American." In a 1979 interview with Phil Donahue, over 50 years after her emigration, she described her feelings for Russia as "complete loathing." Russia, she said, is "the ugliest, and incidentally, most mystical country on earth." Rand was that brand of American, strict and serious in her patriotism, who can only be born elsewhere.

An atheist, her personal religion was a staunch belief in the sanctity of individualism and laissez-faire government. According to Rand, humans are inherently selfish creatures who act only out of personal interest. A selfish act, therefore, is a rational one. It is under this philosophical umbrella that her fictional characters play out their lives. Her heroes are larger-than-life individuals who struggle for unfettered freedom and rate self-worth not by anything as foolishly "collective" as altruism, but on material gain. Sure, they may *sound* like id-driven jerks, but they come off as grand beacons of truth, pillars of authenticity, and models for the person each of us should strive to be.

Good to Know

❖ Ayn Rand dreamed of becoming a screenwriter and quickly found her way to Hollywood after immigrating to the U.S. On her second day in town, Cecil B. DeMille spotted her standing at the gate of his studio and gave her a job as an extra in *King of Kings*. She also worked as a script reader and wardrobe girl before selling *Red Pawn* to Universal Studios in 1932.

❖ After moving back to New York City in the 1950s, Rand hosted Saturday-night "salons" in her apartment to share ideas with like-thinkers, a group she called "the collective." Among the frequent attendees: Federal Reserve Chairman Alan Greenspan, whom Rand often referred to specifically as a "disciple."

❖ *The Fountainhead*, one of the most influential and widely read philosophical novels of the 20th century, was rejected by 12 publishers before it was bought by Bobbs-Merrill. Published in 1943, it soon rose to bestseller status, not because of advertising or author recognition but through favorable word-of-mouth.

❖ In 1998, following publication of its controversial list of the 100 Best Novels of the 20th century, the Modern Library asked readers to cast *their* votes for the best novels written in English since 1900. All four of Rand's novels made the top ten: *Atlas Shrugged*, #1; *The Fountainhead*, #2; *Anthem*, #7; and *We the Living*, #8. In another survey conducted by *Reader's Digest* and the Library of Congress, readers named *Atlas Shrugged* as the book that, second only to the Bible, had most influenced them.

❖ Of all other writers, Victor Hugo and Feodor Dostoyevsky received Rand's greatest admiration. But she also enjoyed poetry, and her favorite verse, Rudyard Kipling's "If," was read at her funeral. She was, by the way, buried beside a six-foot floral dollar sign.

Treatises and Treats

AYN RAND SOCIETY

Membership in this group is limited to those who belong to the American Philosophical Association. But anyone can become affiliated with the society as a "contributor" by making an annual donation of $30. Contributors receive society mailings and invitations, just like regular members. For more information, contact:

Professor Allan Gotthelf
Ayn Rand Society
Department of Philosophy
The College of New Jersey
Ewing, NJ 08628-0718
www.aynrandsociety.org

COMPANIONS

The Ayn Rand Reader by Ayn Rand, edited by Gary Hull (Plume, 1999). A "Rand sampler platter" of sorts, with excerpts from all of her novels. Provides a good introduction to those who have never read Ayn Rand and who might feel intimidated by the sheer size of *The Fountainhead* and *Atlas Shrugged*.

The New Ayn Rand Companion by Mimi Reisel Gladstein (Greenwood Publishing, 1999). Written by an independent scholar who has no part in either the Rand "establishment" or her detractors, this book offers the most comprehensive bibliography published to date, commentary on Rand's posthumous publications, and summaries of books and articles about Rand that have appeared since her death.

VIDEO DOCUMENTARY

Ayn Rand: A Sense of Life, directed by Michael Paxton (1998). This Academy Award–nominated documentary is a sweeping portrait of the drama of Rand's life and fiction. Narrated by actress Sharon Gless, it includes rare photos and an original film-noir scene from Rand's 1934 play, *Ideal*. Also available, **Ayn Rand: A Sense of Life—The**

Companion Book by Michael Paxton (Gibbs Smith, 1998). Compiled by the documentary's director, this hardcover delight provides the script from the film, rare photos, transcripts, and original sheet music.

BEST OF THE NET
Ayn Rand Institute Web Site
www.aynrand.org

Sponsored by the institute that bears her name, this site proposes Objectivism as a vital philosophy to live by and acts as guardian of Rand's reputation. Aimed especially at high school and college students, the site also provides commentary on current events and seeks to offer opinions on the world in a "what-Rand-would-have-said" style.

All the Novels

We the Living, 1936
Anthem, 1938
The Fountainhead, 1943
Atlas Shrugged, 1957

Best Book to Read First

Head straight for the novel that is considered her greatest achievement: *Atlas Shrugged*.

Ayn Rand is a writer of great power. She has a subtle and ingenious mind and the capacity for writing brilliantly, beautifully, bitterly.... Her characters are romanticized, larger than life as representations of good and evil. But nothing she has to say is said in a second-rate fashion.

—*New York Times Book Review*, May 16, 1943

Randy Rand

In 1950, Ayn Rand received a fan letter from a young man named Nathaniel Branden. She was so impressed by the thoughts expressed in the letter that, quite uncharacteristically, she wrote back to him. The correspondence eventually developed into an affair that lasted for more than a decade. In fact, Rand told others that she needed to have sex with Branden (who was married and 25 years her junior) at least twice a week in order to combat writer's block.

But Branden became much more than Rand's boy toy. She made him her "intellectual heir" and chief spokesperson. He codified the principles of her novels into a strict philosophical system (Objectivism) and founded an institute bearing his own name. The affair ended in 1968 when Branden took up with another Rand disciple. (He's now a Beverly Hills psychotherapist.)

For more details, read Branden's tell-all memoir, *My Years with Ayn Rand* (Jossey-Bass, 1999). Or look for the confessional by his wife Barbara, *The Passion of Ayn Rand* (Anchor, 1986). But skip the video of the same name, as it is muddled at best.

Anne Rice

Born
October 4, 1941, in New Orleans to Howard O'Brien, a postal worker, novelist, and sculptor, and Katherine Allen O'Brien

Real Name
Howard Allen O'Brien, a name she hated. She began calling herself Anne in 1947.

Pseudonyms
A. N. Roquelaure and Anne Rampling, names she used for several explicit bondage and dominance-and-submission novels.

Education
San Francisco State University, B.A., 1964; M.A., 1971

Family
Married her high school sweetheart, Stan Rice, a poet and painter, in 1961. Two children, writer Christopher Rice and a daughter who died of leukemia at age five.

Home
Several antebellum mansions in New Orleans, Louisiana

Fan Mail/Messages
Anne Rice
1239 First Street
New Orleans, LA 70130
504-522-8634

Publisher
Random House

One of the most unusual writers of our time, Anne Rice has mastered the balancing of fact and figment, morals and sin, fiction and autobiography. Grabbing readers' attention with her Vampire Chronicles by turning "the undead" lore on its head, Rice breathes life into ancient legends while weaving her own myths and history. Susan Ferraro in the *New York Times Magazine* describes Rice's writing as "florid, both lurid and lyrical, full of sensuous detail. She supports her fantasies with superb narrative, unabashed eroticism, and a queasy but ultimately cathartic indulgence in the forbidden."

Anne clearly enjoys tackling the controversial, titillating, and taboo. Her vast body of work delves into religion, homosexuality, the joys of sin, voodoo, sadomasochism, and witchcraft, among other subjects. Not surprisingly, New Orleans offers a perfect backdrop for dark, carnal indulgences. "The passionate energy that infuses Rice's prose is personal," Ferraro observes. Anne Rice confirmed this in a *People* interview: "When I'm writing, the darkness is always there. I go where the pain is."

Good to Know

❖ Anne Rice wrote her first book—about two kids from Mars who commit suicide—when she was in the fifth grade.

❖ Before her daughter Michele was diagnosed with leukemia, Rice had a dream that showed the little girl dying as a result of something wrong with her blood—a prophecy that unfortunately came true. She wrote *Interview with the Vampire* in five weeks—in a grief-ridden haze after five-year-old Michele's death. In the book, she created Claudia, a six-year-old vampire child who is granted immortality.

❖ Anne Rice does all her own editing and has been quoted as saying that any errors that readers discover in her books are her responsibility—not that of her publisher.

❖ You can tour one of Anne Rice's New Orleans homes, the Violin house at 2524 St. Charles Avenue, between 3:00 P.M. and 6:00 P.M. on Mondays. The tour is free, but don't expect to see the author. (She is *not* part of the tour!)

❖ Autographed and special edition Anne Rice books can be purchased at the Garden District Book Shop, 2727 Prytania Street, New Orleans, Louisiana (504-895-2266, betbooks@aol.com).

Treatises and Treats

ANNE RICE VAMPIRE LESTAT FAN CLUB

The only Anne Rice club sanctioned by the author, ARVLFC was founded in 1988 by fans who met in a book-signing line for *Queen of the Damned*. Membership includes a photo postcard of Anne, a subscription to the fan club newsletter, invitations to "The Annual Gathering of the Coven" party, and occasional members-only merchandise offers. For more information, contact:
ARVLFC
P.O. Box 58277
New Orleans, LA 70158-8277
www.arvlfc.org

COMPANIONS

Prism of the Night: A Biography of Anne Rice by Katherine Ramsland (Plume, 1994). The "official" biography of Anne Rice, with an exploration of her personal life as well as an analysis of her work.

The Vampire Companion: The Official Guide to Anne Rice's The Vampire Chronicles by Katherine Ramsland and Anne Rice (Ballantine Books, 1995). An in-depth guide to the world, history, and characters of Rice's vampires.

The Witches' Companion: The Official Guide to Anne Rice's Lives of the Mayfair Witches by Katherine Ramsland and Anne Rice (Ballantine Books, 1996). The ultimate diviner of the history and mystery of these extraordinary witches.

The Anne Rice Reader, edited by Katherine Ramsland (Ballantine Books, 1997). Provocative interviews, essays, articles, and explanations of Anne Rice's work by journalists, scholars, and authors.

In the Shadow of the Vampire: Voices from the World of Anne Rice, by Jana Marcus (Thunder's Mouth Press, 1997). A book of photo interviews about Anne Rice, created by award-winning documentary photographer Jana Marcus.

The Anne Rice Trivia Book by Katherine Ramsland (Del Ray, 1994). A collection of trivia questions based on twelve of Rice's novels.

BEST OF THE NET

Official Anne Rice Web Site
www.annerice.com
The author's personal home page, packed with information that's sure to delight her readers: book descriptions, answers to questions from fans, photos, news on her latest projects, catalog of Rice paraphernalia offered for sale, and more.

Random House's Anne Rice Page
www.randomhouse.com/features/annerice
Check here for information about audiobooks, trivia, and house tours.

Vampires and More

THE VAMPIRE CHRONICLES
Interview with the Vampire, 1976
The Vampire Lestat, 1985
The Queen of the Damned, 1988
The Tale of the Body Thief, 1992

Memnoch the Devil, 1995

NEW TALES OF THE VAMPIRES
Pandora, 1998
The Vampire Armand, 1998
Vittorio the Vampire, 1999

LIVES OF THE MAYFAIR WITCHES
The Witching Hour, 1990
Lasher, 1993
Taltos, 1994

OTHER ANNE RICE NOVELS
The Feast of All Saints, 1979 (historical)
Cry to Heaven, 1982 (historical)
The Mummy, 1989
Servant of the Bones, 1996
Violin, 1997

EROTICA BY "ANNE RAMPLING"
Exit to Eden, 1985
Belinda, 1986

EROTICA BY "A. N. ROQUELAURE"
The Claiming of Sleeping Beauty, 1983
Beauty's Punishment, 1984
Beauty's Release, 1985

If You Like Anne Rice...

Her most ardent fans will tell you that there's simply no one else quite like her. But you might try books by Sara Adamson, Stephen King, Pauline Réage, and Chelsea Quinn Yarbro. Or look for son Christopher Rice's *Density of Souls*.

Best Book to Read First

Her first novel, *Interview with the Vampire*, which has sold more than four million copies and was subsequently made into a movie of the same name starring Tom Cruise and Brad Pitt.

Anne Rice brings a fresh and powerful imagination to the staples of vampire lore; she makes well-worn coffins and crucifixes tell new tales that compose a chillingly original myth.

—*New York Times Book Review*

Long Live the Queen of Vampires!

Much like the immortality of her vampires, Rice seeks to live on through her work. "I want people to carry dog-eared copies of *Interview with the Vampire* in their backpacks," she says. "I want my books to live, to be read after I'm dead. That will be justification enough for all the pain and work and struggling and doubt."

Philip Roth

Born
March 19, 1933, in
Newark, New Jersey, to
Herman Roth, an insur-
ance salesman, and
Bess Finkel Roth

Full Name
Philip Milton Roth

Education
Bucknell University,
B.A. in English, 1954;
University of Chicago,
M.A. in English, 1955.
Has also taught at
various universities
and served as writer-in-
residence at Princeton
(1962–64) and the
University of Pennsyl-
vania (1965–80).

Family
First marriage to
Margaret Martinson in
1959 ended with her
death in 1968. Second
marriage to actress
Claire Bloom in 1990
ended in an acrimo-
nious divorce in 1994.

Home
An 18th-century farm-
house in Connecticut.
Notoriously reclusive,
he changes his phone
number frequently to
avoid unwanted
contact.

Fan Mail
c/o Andrew Wylie
The Wylie Agency
250 West 57th Street
New York, NY 10107

Publisher
Houghton Mifflin

Hailed as one of the best contemporary fiction writers in America, Philip Roth has focused his
considerable gifts on recording
the modern Jewish experience.
A satirist with a keen sense of
humor and biting sarcasm,
Roth has been both acerbically denounced by
the Jewish religious establishment for anti-
Semitism and honored by the literary elite
for these explorations.

Roth attained celebrity at the age of 26
with the publication of his first book, *Goodbye Columbus*, a National Book Award winner that was later turned into a popular film
starring Richard Benjamin and Ali MacGraw.
But it was with his fourth novel, *Portnoy's
Complaint*, that both his fame and infamy
were established. Called a "desperately dirty
novel," *Portnoy's Complaint* depicts sexually
explicit acts. The prepublication buzz about
the book was so fierce that Roth earned close
to a million dollars from magazine excerpts,
long before the book itself hit the shelves.

Roth's work is sometimes drawn so directly from his own life that the line between
fiction and reality is fuzzy—a theme that he
toys with in many of his novels. Of this, author
Tobias Wolff says, "Roth's purpose in all this is
not merely playful or cantankerous; what he
means to do, and does, is make the strongest
possible case for fiction's autonomy by suggesting and then repudiating its connection
with 'the facts.' It's a nervy, sometimes hilarious, now and then exasperating performance;
his road of excess doesn't always lead to the
palace of wisdom. But often it does."

Good to Know

❖ When Jacqueline Susann's novel *The Love
Machine* was competing with Roth's *Portnoy's Complaint* (and its graphic depictions
of masturbation) for top ranking on bestseller lists, Susann was asked her opinion of
Roth. "He's a fine writer," she replied, "but I
wouldn't want to shake hands with him."

❖ Critics tended to be less impressed by the
post-*Portnoy* novels until Roth introduced
his fictional alter ego, Nathan Zuckerman, in
The Ghost Writer (1979). Many critics consider this and the Zuckerman books that followed to be Roth's best work.

❖ In 1976, Roth became general editor of
Writers from the Other Europe, a Penguin series that published works by authors living
behind the Iron Curtain. He was motivated to
take the job out of an intellectual debt to
Franz Kafka.

❖ And speaking of Kafka...just as that
Czech master turned his famous character
Gregor Samsa into a beetle in *The Metamorphosis*, Roth transformed comp. lit. professor
David Kepesh into a six-foot-long mammary
gland in his novella, *The Breast*. John Gardner called the 78-page curiosity "inventive
and sane and very funny, though filthy.... It's
incredible, in fact, how smart [Roth] is for a
man so hung up with his you-know-what."

❖ Writing as therapy: Following knee surgery
in 1987, Roth suffered from severe depression. But he was able to "write myself out of it"
with his widely praised memoir *The Facts: A
Novelist's Autobiography*.

❖ Roth received America's four major literary prizes with the successive publication of four books in the 1990s: *Patrimony*, National Book Critics Circle Award (1991); *Operation Shylock*, PEN/Faulkner Award (1993), *Sabbath's Theater*, National Book Award (1995); *American Pastoral*, Pulitzer Prize (1998).

Treatises and Treats

AUTOBIOGRAPHIES

The Facts: A Novelist's Autobiography (Farrar, Straus & Giroux, 1988). Roth gives a candid portrait of his life in this unconventional autobiography, concentrating on five emotional episodes.

Patrimony: A True Story (1991, repr. Vintage Books, 1996). Chronicling his 86-year-old dad's struggle with a terminal brain tumor, Roth takes readers on a touching father-son journey in this witty, beautifully written memoir.

BEST OF THE NET

New York Times Featured Authors
www.nytimes.com/books/specials/author.html
Click on "Philip Roth" for reviews of his books, personal interviews, articles by and about him, and interesting side notes, such as a piece by author William Styron recalling an unforgettable day he spent with Roth in Ireland called "Dear Dirty Dublin: My Joycean Trek With Philip Roth."

Reading List

NATHAN ZUCKERMAN NOVELS

The Ghost Writer, 1979
Zuckerman Unbound, 1981
The Anatomy Lesson, 1983
Zuckerman Bound, 1985
　　(a trilogy including the three works listed above and an epilogue, *The Prague Orgy*)
The Counterlife, 1986
　　(National Book Critics Circle Award)
I Married a Communist, 1998

ALL THE OTHER NOVELS

Goodbye Columbus and Five Short Stories, 1959
　　(National Book Award)
Letting Go, 1962
When She Was Good, 1967
Portnoy's Complaint, 1969
Our Gang, 1971
The Breast, 1972
The Great American Novel, 1973
My Life as a Man, 1974
The Professor of Desire, 1977
Deception, 1990
Operation Shylock: A Confession, 1993
　　(PEN/Faulkner Award)
Sabbath's Theater, 1995
　　(National Book Award)
American Pastoral, 1997
　　(Pulitzer Prize)

If You Like Philip Roth . . .

Try Bernard Malamud, another contemporary legend who captured Jewish culture with grace and humor. You might also like books by Saul Bellow and Bruce Jay Friedman.

Best Book to Read First

To sample Roth's most scandalous book, try the "masturbation novel" *Portnoy's Complaint*. But if you're not up for all that "self love," *Goodbye, Columbus* is a sure bet—for both supreme entertainment and literary mastery.

Philip Roth is our Kafka: a Jewish comic genius able to spin a metaphysical joke to a far point of ingenuity—the point at which artistic paradox becomes moral or religious parable.

　　　　—David Lehman,
Washington Post Book World

Claire Bloom's Complaint

It seems no celebrity's life is now complete unless an ex-spouse or lover writes about it in a kiss-and-tell memoir. So as if to affirm Philip Roth's fame, his ex-wife, actress Claire Bloom, composed the memoir *Leaving a Doll's House* (Little, Brown & Company, 1996). She devotes the first part of the book to describing her early years in London and bragging about the big-name stars she slept with as a young actress (Richard Burton, Yul Brynner, and Laurence Olivier). But then she shines her blinding spotlight at Roth, taking exception to the ironclad prenuptial agreement he insisted that she sign before their marriage and accusing him of harboring "a deep and irrepressible rage" toward women.

Well, it's not as though she hadn't been warned. "Do not involve yourself with Portnoy," Gore Vidal recalls telling Bloom when she first began her romance with Roth.

J. K. Rowling

Born
In 1966 at Chipping Sodbury General Hospital near Bristol, England, to Peter Rowling, an aircraft factory manager, and Ann Rowling, a lab technician

Full Name
Joanne Kathleen Rowling (pronounced "rolling"). "Jo" to her friends. The initials were a marketer's ploy to disguise her gender so that her books would appeal to boys as well as girls.

Education
Studied French at Exeter University.

Family
Married in 1990 to a Portuguese journalist she declines to name. Daughter Jessica, born 1993; couple divorced soon afterward.

Home
Grew up in England's Forest of Dean near the Welsh border. Now lives in Edinburgh, Scotland, with daughter Jessica. Sister Di lives nearby.

Fan Mail
J. K. Rowling
c/o Christopher Little
   Literary Agency
48 Walham Grove
London SW6 IQR
England

Publisher
Scholastic Press

"No other author in living memory," according to the *New York Times*, has had three books simultaneously occupy the top slots on that publication's bestseller list. But that's exactly where J. K. Rowling's first three "Harry Potter" children's books were as 1999 drew to a close. Yet children aren't the only fans of this orphaned British ten-year-old who discovers he has a magical heritage and enters Hogwarts School to learn how to be a wizard. In the *New York Review of Books*, Alison Lurie reports that a plain-cover edition of the first book—aimed at adults embarrassed to be seen reading a children's book—sold out its first printing of 20,000 in the U.K., even though it cost two pounds more than the original.

Rowling's novels have sold over seven million copies in the U.S. and Britain alone, with millions more to come in other languages. In September 1999, Harry Potter even made the cover of *Time* magazine, which called the phenomenon "one of the most bizarre and surreal in the annals of publishing." Equally unfathomable is the power these books have over young boys, luring them away from their video games and getting them to actually sit down and read. So what's up?

As Richard Bernstein said in the *New York Times*, the Harry Potter stories are fairly conventional, and "not nearly as brilliant or literary as, say, *The Hobbit* or the *Alice in Wonderland* books." The explanation for their popularity, he suggests, can be found in Bruno Bettelheim's classic study of children's literature, *The Uses of Enchantment*. The essence of Bettelheim's theory is that children live with greater terrors than most adults can understand, and that the classic fairy tales help express that terror while showing a way to a better future. In effect, J. K. Rowling's novels

fill a basic need for children everywhere and for the child in every adult.

That seems quite sound. But there is also the fact that Rowling has a degree of whimsicality not to be found in Tolkien, C. S. Lewis, or her other antecedents. She is much closer to L. Frank Baum's "Wizard of Oz" series in that regard. And she has a sense of humor tuned to her era. Thus, Harry's school supplies include "one plain pointed hat (black) for day wear." Mail at the school is delivered by owls of different sizes, including "tiny scops owls ('Local Deliveries Only')." And exams at Hogwarts include practical tests, like making a pineapple tap-dance across a desk and turning a mouse into a snuffbox, "with points given for how pretty the snuffbox was, but taken away if it had whiskers."

Warner Bros. has already bought the movie rights to the first book. One can only hope that, in the *Star Wars*–like onslaught to come, the sly wit, the charm, and the childlike wonder of Rowling's books won't get lost to the evils of commercialism. Indeed, here's a spell we can all conjure with: "Aroint thee, witch!" (*Macbeth*, I, iii, 4) Begone! No Harry Potter McDonald's Happy Meals, backpacks, or action figures. Begone! No sugar-cereal-sponsored Saturday morning cartoons. Begone!

Good to Know

❖ At age six Rowling wrote her first story, "Rabbit," the tale of a rabbit with measles who was visited by his friends, including a giant bee named, appropriately enough, Miss Bee.

❖ She attended a small, old-fashioned grammar school where a failing grade on a quiz landed her in the "stupid row." The teacher "positioned everyone in the class according to how clever she thought they were; the brightest sat on her left, and everyone she thought dim sat on the right. I was as far right as you could get without sitting in the playground."

❖ Rowling spent five years inventing Harry Potter's world, writing her first novel, and making notes on the other six books in the series. She has already written the last chapter of the final book "to remind myself where I'm going."

❖ Because she couldn't afford to have her first manuscript photocopied, she typed it out twice before sending it off. She sold it to U.K. publisher Bloomsbury for about $4,000. Then Scholastic Press in the U.S. paid over $100,000 for the rights—the largest advance ever paid for a first-time author of a children's book.

❖ The village Little Whinging, where Harry's evil aunt, uncle, and cousin live, would be called "Little Whining" in American English. As for some of the other unique names: Hedwig was a saint, Dumbledore is an old English word for bumblebee, and Snape is an actual place in England.

❖ The dominance of Rowling's books on the *New York Times* bestseller list has been a point of discussion in the publishing community. Some feel it's appropriate to include children's books on the list, while others are grousing. In a millennium spoof, the newspaper's Sunday book review ran its projections for the January list in 2020. Included were *Harry Potter and the Initial Public Offering*

and *Harry Potter and the Receding Hairline*, with *Chicken Soup for Harry Potter's Soul* listed under "Advice and How-to."

Treatises and Treats

LISTEN UP, POTTER FANS!

Harry Potter and the Sorcerer's Stone unabridged audiocassettes (Listening Library, 1999). Let Stephen Fry (*Jeeves, Black Adder II,* etc.) take you on a magical journey into Harry Potter's world of wizardry (800-243-4504, www.listening.lib.com).

BEST OF THE NET

Official Harry Potter Web Site
www.scholastic.com/harrypotter.com
A must-browse site for Harry Potter fans. Includes sample chapters, discussion guides, a reading circle, author interview, and more.

Harry Potter, So Far

Harry Potter and the Sorcerer's Stone, 1998
Harry Potter and the Chamber of Secrets, 1999
Harry Potter and the Prisoner of Azkaban, 1999

If You Like
J. K. Rowling . . .

Try some of these authors recommended for Harry Potter fans by *Book* magazine (January/February 2000): Lloyd Alexander, Paul Jennings, Robin McKinley, Tamora Pierce, Philip Pullman, Patricia Wrede, and Diana Wynne Jones.

Best Book to Read First

Harry Potter and the Sorcerer's Stone, the first book in a planned seven-book series—one book for each year of Harry's education as a wizard.

A Wizard's World

Muggles: Nonmagical people who can't see wizards.

Floo powder: A pinch will transport you around the country in seconds.

Drago Dormiens Nunquam Titillandus: The Hogwarts School motto: "Never Tickle a Sleeping Dragon."

Every Flavor Beans: A candy that can taste like everything from chocolate to earwax. Says so right on the package.

J. K. Rowling is determined that once Harry Potter leaves wizard school, that will be the end. "There will be no Harry Potter's midlife crisis or Harry Potter as an old wizard." Rowling might even turn her hand to "adult" novels, but she is adamant that this is not a pinnacle of achievement. "I think it's wrong to think of adult books as 'real literature.' Real literature can be for people of nine and that's what I'm trying to write."
—Sunday Telegraph (July 19, 1998)

J. D. Salinger

Born
January 1, 1919, in New York City, to Sol Salinger, a cheese importer, and Miriam Jillich Salinger

Full Name
Jerome David Salinger

Education
Graduated from Valley Forge Military Academy, 1936; attended New York University, Ursinus College, and Columbia University.

Family
First marriage to a French physician lasted only two years (1945–47). Second marriage in 1955 to Claire Douglas (with whom he has two children, Margaret Ann and Matthew) ended in divorce in 1967.

Home
Cornish, New Hampshire

Fan Mail
J. D. Salinger
c/o Harold Ober
 Associates
425 Madison Avenue
New York, NY 10017

Publisher
Little, Brown

Perhaps no author has garnered more attention for so few published books than J. D. Salinger. His first novel, *The Catcher in the Rye* (1951), quickly became a classic, particularly with younger readers, and it is one of the most popular "serious" novels to be published after World War II. Salinger won high praise for his deft handling of teenage slang and speech patterns. The narrator of the novel, Holden Caulfield, who declares war on all that is "phony," is one of the most enduring characters in the history of literature.

After the publication of *Catcher*, however, Salinger chose to live the life of a recluse, continuing to write but publishing his work sparingly. His later work raised questions as to whether he had matured enough as a writer to warrant all the attention he was receiving. Several of his stories appeared in the *New Yorker* and were subsequently published in book form: *Franny and Zooey* (1961) and *Raise High the Roof Beam, Carpenters, and Seymour: An Introduction* (1963). A novella-length story written in the form of a letter, *Hapworth 16, 1924*, was first published in the *New Yorker* in 1965 and issued as a book in 2000.

Many of these stories focus on the fictional Glass family, leading some critics to declare that all of these stories, when put together, comprise a short-story cycle. But Salinger has refused to participate in the debate over his work. He gives no lectures or readings, and rarely does he grant interviews.

Good to Know

❖ Salinger used Valley Forge Military Academy as the model for Pencey Prep in *The Catcher in the Rye*. It was at Valley Forge that he began to write fiction, often by flashlight under his blankets after "lights out."

❖ While at Columbia in 1939, Salinger attended a class on short-story writing. A year later he published his first story, "The Young Folks," in *Story* magazine, founded and edited by his Columbia professor, Whit Burnett. In an unpublished letter to a friend who had congratulated him on this first publication, Salinger replied: "I have of course an ardent admirer in myself, but mostly when I'm at work. When I'm finished with a piece, I'm embarrassed to look at it again, as though I were afraid I hadn't wiped its nose clean."

❖ Salinger served in the army in Europe during World War II. He eventually became staff sergeant and received five battle stars. But he also continued to write, using a portable typewriter. He witnessed heavy combat and was once hospitalized for combat-related stress, an experience that inspired his story "For Esme—with Love and Squalor."

❖ When *The Catcher in the Rye* was chosen as the main selection of the Book-of-the-Month Club in 1951, the club's president expressed anxiety over the book's somewhat ambiguous title. When asked if he would consider a change, Salinger simply replied, "Holden Caulfield wouldn't like that." (The name "Holden Caulfield" most likely came from joining the first name of a boyhood friend with the last name of movie actress Joan Caulfield, on whom Salinger once had a crush.)

❖ In 1974 Salinger tried everything—including the use of lawyers and the FBI—to prevent the publication of his earliest stories in book form. Despite his efforts, some 25,000 copies found their way into public hands. The books were peddled to bookstores at $1.50

each by different men who always introduced themselves as "John Greenberg" and claimed to come from Berkeley, California.

❖ People close to Salinger say that he does his writing in a tiny concrete bunker on his New Hampshire property and has at least two complete manuscripts stored in a vault there. He gets up most days at the crack of dawn, walks down the hill to the bunker, and spends 15 or 16 hours at his typewriter. Later, he may watch a movie from his vast collection of 1940s videos.

Treatises and Treats

COMPANIONS

Salinger: A Biography by Paul Alexander (Renaissance Books, 1999). The first full-length popular account of the famously private Salinger's entire life and career, based on published sources and interviews with some 40 literary figures (George Plimpton, Gay Talese, and Tom Wolfe, among others).

In Search of J. D. Salinger by Ian Hamilton (Random House, 1989). This biography confines itself to the author's life from 1919 to 1965, the year that he published his last *New Yorker* story. The book's planned release led to a court battle between Hamilton and Salinger, who declared that his letters could not be quoted without his permission.

At Home in the World by Joyce Maynard (Picador, 1998). The centerpiece of this memoir is Maynard's account of her highly publicized yearlong relationship with Salinger.

The Dream Catcher by Margaret Salinger (Pocket Books, 2000). Another memoir, written by Salinger's daughter, about her childhood and relationship with her father.

BEST OF THE NET
Bananafish Web Site
slf.gweep.net/~sfoskett/jds/index.html
A good fan-created Web site, with information on Salinger's fictional characters, bibliography, critical commentary, anecdotes, articles, and news.

New York Times Featured Authors
www.nytimes.com/books/specials/author.html
Click on "J. D. Salinger" for a collection of book reviews and articles from the *New York Times* archives.

All the Books

The Catcher in the Rye, 1951
Nine Stories, 1953
Franny and Zooey, 1961
Raise High the Roof Beam, Carpenters, and Seymour: An Introduction, 1963
The Complete Uncollected Stories of J. D. Salinger, 1974 (unauthorized edition)
Hapworth 16, 1924, 2000

If You Like J. D. Salinger . . .

Try these classic "growing-up" stories: Angela Carter's *The Magic Toyshop*, Roddy Doyle's *The Commitments*, John Knowles's *A Separate Peace*, C. D. Payne's *Youth in Revolt*, Philip Roth's *Portnoy's Complaint*, and Anne Tyler's *Dinner at the Homesick Restaurant*.

Best Book to Read First
The Catcher in the Rye is the book that made Salinger famous and continues to sell a quarter of a million copies every year.

There is a marvelous peace in not publishing. . . . Publishing is a terrible invasion of my privacy. I like to write. I love to write. But I just write for myself and my own pleasure.

—J. D. Salinger

The Joyce Maynard Letters

In 1972, Joyce Maynard was featured on the cover of the *New York Times Magazine*, along with her article, "An 18-Year-Old Looks Back on Life." It was all part of the publicity campaign for the young woman's forthcoming memoirs, *Looking Back: A Chronicle of Growing Up Old in the Sixties* (Doubleday, 1973). Salinger, then 53, was impressed, and a correspondence developed. Maynard dropped out of Yale and moved in with the author. But she seemed more concerned with *TV Guide* and her own blossoming fame than with serious writing. After nine months, Salinger kicked her out.

In 1999, amid much controversy, Maynard auctioned 14 of their letters at Sotheby's. (She said she needed the money in order to send her children to college.) Fortunately for Salinger, the successful bidder was Peter Norton (the wealthy, retired creator of the Norton Utilities software package and an excellent writer himself), who paid $156,500 for the letters and then immediately announced that he would return them to Salinger.

Dorothy L. Sayers

Born
June 13, 1893, in
Oxford, England, the
only child of Anglican
clergyman and school-
master Henry Sayers
and Helen Leigh
Sayers

Education
Somerville College,
Oxford University, B.A.
(with honors) in
medieval literature,
1915; M.A., and B.C.L.
(Bachelor of Civil Law),
1920

Family
Married in 1926 to
Captain Oswald
Atherton Fleming, a
former war hero turned
wastrel, whom she
essentially supported
until he died in 1950.
One child, John
Anthony, from a casual
affair two years prior to
her marriage.

Home
A flat in London's
Bloomsbury district,
and a house in
Witham, Essex,
England. Fellow
mystery writer Margery
Allingham was a
neighbor at both loca-
tions.

Died
December 17, 1957,
of coronary thrombosis

Publishers
Harcourt
HarperCollins
St. Martin's Press

It is impossible to read about Dorothy L. Sayers without wishing one could have met her. For openers, she was among the first women to be allowed to graduate from Oxford. And while there (beginning in 1911), she sported unconventional attire, liked walking down High Street smoking a cigar, and was generally considered a "free thinker." Later in life she listed motorcycling as her hobby and was known to like a gin and tonic (or two).

In 1924, unmarried, she concealed giving birth to a son—no small matter at that time. Although she supported him financially and was part of his life, he knew her as "Cousin Dorothy" and the two were estranged as adults. Sayers died at the age of 64 of a coronary thrombosis brought on by drinking and chain-smoking.

And to top it all off, this fascinating lady is one of the most important figures in the development of modern detective fiction. In Lord Peter Wimsey she invented a complete subset of the British detective novel—one featuring a foppish, witty, aristocratic detective who, while seeming a bit of a twit, has a razor-sharp mind and impressive powers of deduction.

She wrote 11 novels and 21 short stories featuring Lord Peter. But in her fifth novel *Strong Poison* (1930), she introduced Harriet Vane, a mystery writer whose fiancé dies in a manner described in one of her stories. Harriet is in the dock because she has an extensive knowledge of poisons. Lord Peter is determined to prove her innocence, and to make her his wife.

The two sleuths appear as a husband-and-wife team in three subsequent novels. One of them, *Gaudy Night* (1935), finds Harriet Vane caught in a tug-of-war between her love for Lord Peter and her growing satisfaction with her work, and struggling to balance womanhood and personhood. Sayers may have been inspired by Christie's *Partners in Crime* stories, each featuring Tuppence and Tommy,

and each parodying some other mystery writer. But Dashiell Hammett was surely influenced by Sayers when creating his "Nick and Nora Thin-Man" series several years later.

Sayers started as an advertising copywriter and began writing mysteries because it was the easiest way to break free and become a professional writer. But she eventually became bored with detective fiction and turned her talents to religious plays, poems, and essays. Detective stories, she said, falsely persuade us that problems like poverty and hatred can be "solved in the same manner as the death in the library." Although the murderer is caught, "nothing at all has been said about the healing of his murderous soul."

Good to Know

❖ The first Lord Peter Wimsey mystery, *Whose Body?*, appeared in 1923, and the series continued into the 1930s. Sayers never completed the last novel, *Thrones, Dominations*. She produced 170 pages in the late 1930s, then set the manuscript aside. The book was later completed by Jill Paton Walsh and published in 1998.

❖ In the 1920s, Sayers worked as a copywriter for the advertising agency S. H. Benson Ltd. (Benson's, for short), where she absorbed details that she would later put to use in *Murder Must Advertise*. In the book, Lord Peter goes undercover at an ad agency called Pym's.

❖ Both Ian Carmichael and Edward Petherbridge have appeared as Lord Peter Wimsey in BBC productions of Sayers's books. Each played the role quite differently: Carmichael opted for the hale and hearty Englishman, while Petherbridge offered a more cerebral character. Both actors have also recorded audio versions of Sayers's works. Sadly, however, only *Clouds of Witness* is currently available on videotape.

❖ As a cofounder of the Detection Club, Sayers got together with other mystery writers, including Agatha Christie, Freeman Wills Crofts, G. K. Chesterton, and Anthony Berkeley. In collaboration, members of the club wrote *The Floating Admiral* (1931), *Ask a Policeman* (1933), and *Six Against the Yard* (1936).

Treatises and Treats

DOROTHY L. SAYERS SOCIETY

Led by Barbara Reynolds, who knew Sayers personally and has written several books about her, this group holds annual conventions and publishes a newsletter six times a year. Dues are $24, $15 for students. Contact:
Dorothy L. Sayers Society
Attn: Membership Secretary
6 Constantius Court
Brandon Rd., Church Crookham
Hampshire GU13 0YF
England
www.sayers.org.uk

COMPANIONS

Dorothy L. Sayers: Her Life and Soul by Barbara Reynolds (St. Martin's Press, 1997). Written by a close personal friend of Sayers, this 400-page biography draws on excerpts from Sayers's own letters to tell the story of the author's life and loves.

The Letters of Dorothy L. Sayers, 1899–1936: The Making of a Detective Novelist (St. Martin's Press, 1996) and *The Letters of Dorothy L. Sayers, 1937–1943: From Novelist to Playwright* (St. Martin's Press, 1998). Volumes I and II of the author's entertaining letters, from literate child to literary sensation, both edited by Barbara Reynolds. The first volume includes a preface by mystery writer P. D. James.

BEST OF THE NET

Dorothy L. Sayers Society Web Site
www.sayers.org.uk
Here you'll find information about the society, of course, but also a brief biography, frequently asked questions, and links to other Net resources such as online texts, a guide to TV adaptations, and the popular DorothyL mailing list.

The Wimsey Pages
members.xoom.com/jentalley/wimsey.htm
Billed as the "unofficial home of Lord Peter Wimsey on the Web," this site offers a good introduction to Sayers's most popular creation, along with biographical information, a bibliography, and a discussion group.

Best Reads

LORD PETER WIMSEY MYSTERIES
Whose Body?, 1923
Clouds of Witness, 1925
Unnatural Death, 1927
The Unpleasantness at the Bellona Club, 1928
The Five Red Herrings, 1931
Murder Must Advertise, 1933
The Nine Tailors, 1934

LORD PETER/HARRIET VANE MYSTERIES
Strong Poison, 1930
Have His Carcase, 1932
Gaudy Night, 1935
Busman's Honeymoon, 1937

If You Like Dorothy L. Sayers...

You *must* try Margery Allingham. Then consider P. D. James, Martha Grimes, Amanda Cross, Elizabeth Peters, Carole Nelson Douglas, and Laurie R. King.

Best Book to Read First

The Nine Tailors, featuring Lord Peter Wimsey, her master sleuth, at his best.

In the end, what we admire about Dorothy L. Sayers is that she tells a good—and enduring—mystery story....One reads [her novels] again and again, even though one knows their plots by heart...and honors her because her indelible detective hero played fair, sharing with the reader every clue he had in his possession, keeping nothing up his sleeve.

—*New York Times*

American Sayers

Over 200 of Dorothy L. Sayers's manuscripts—including the majority of her published works—are housed at the Marion E. Wade Center of Wheaton College in Wheaton, Illinois. Also in the collection are unpublished manuscripts, over 30,000 pages of letters, books that Sayers owned, and photographs. For tour information: 630-752-5908, www.sayers.org.uk/wade.html.

Sidney Sheldon

Born
February 11, 1917, in
Chicago, Illinois, to
salesman Otto
Sheldon and Natalie
Marcus Sheldon

Education
Attended Northwestern
University, 1935–36.

Family
First wife Jorja
Curtright, to whom he
was married in 1951,
was an actress and
later a prominent
interior decorator. She
died in 1985. Married
Alexandra Kostoff, a
former child actress
and more recently an
advertising executive,
in 1989. One daughter
from his first marriage.

Home
Divides his time
between London, Palm
Springs, and a hilltop
mansion on Sunset
Boulevard in Beverly
Hills.

Publisher
William Morrow

Sidney Sheldon created the TV series *Hart to Hart* (starring Robert Wagner and Stefanie Powers) and was executive producer of *I Dream of Jeannie* (starring Larry Hagman and Barbara Eden). But at age 50 he had never considered writing a novel until one day he got an idea "so introspective [he] could see no way to do it as a television series, movie, or Broadway play, because you had to get inside the character's mind." The result was *The Naked Face* (1970), which won several prestigious awards for mystery writing but sold only 17,000 copies. "I was horrified," said Sheldon, "because 20 million people watched *Jeannie*."

Sheldon's book-writing career took off with his next novel, however. *The Other Side of Midnight* (1974) sold three million copies in paperback, and he has since published seven additional novels that have sold in the millions—making him one of the bestselling authors in the world.

The typical Sheldon story involves a beautiful woman exacting revenge on her enemies. As Sarah Booth Conroy explains in the *Washington Post*: "The beautiful but often poor and pure heroines are raped...and defrauded, and go on to avenge themselves by questionable, often illegal, but ingenious methods." As might be expected, literary critics describe Sheldon's prose as lackluster and his plots as unbelievable. But then, as Carol E. Rinzler notes in the *Washington Post*, "There aren't a whole lot of writers around who can be depended on to produce good junk reading time after time; Sheldon is one of the few."

Good to Know

❖ Both of Sheldon's parents were third-grade dropouts. His father had never read a book in his life, and Sidney was the first one in his family to finish high school. He sold his first poem to a children's magazine when he was ten years old.

❖ Sheldon served as a script reader for Universal and Twentieth Century Fox studios (initially earning $17 a week)—no doubt good training for his later roles as creator, producer, and writer of hit television shows, including *The Patty Duke Show*, *I Dream of Jeannie*, and *Hart to Hart*. At one point during the 1965–66 season when *The Patty Duke Show* and *I Dream of Jeannie* overlapped, he was writing two half-hour scripts a day.

❖ He won an Academy Award for best original screenplay in 1948 for *The Bachelor and the Bobby-Soxer* (Cary Grant and Myrna Loy); a Screen Writers' Guild Award for best musical of the year in 1948 for *Easter Parade* (Judy Garland and Fred Astaire) and in 1950 for *Annie Get Your Gun*; a Tony Award in 1959 for *Redhead*; and multiple Emmy Awards for *I Dream of Jeannie*.

❖ Sheldon's novels have sold over 280 million copies. According to *The Guinness Book of World Records*, "The world's most translated author is Sidney Sheldon, whose books have been distributed in more than 180 countries in 51 languages."

❖ Sheldon on preferred medium: "When you write a movie, you have a hundred collaborators. But when you write a novel, it's yours. There's this sense of excitement because you invent and control the characters. You decide whether they live or die. I find this type of creative process tremendously stimulating."

❖ Sheldon on research: "Accuracy and authenticity are very important to me in my novels, because a reader can always tell if an author is 'faking' it. If you read about one of my characters eating a meal in a restaurant in some exotic part of the world, you can bet that I've had that very meal in that same restaurant. Caring about details makes the difference between a fair book and a really good one."

❖ When Sheldon begins a novel he has no plot in mind, only a central character. He dictates his first draft to his secretary six days a week, from early morning to late dinnertime. " As I begin to talk, the novel comes to life," states Sheldon. "I feel that the story is given to me—I don't know where it comes from, but when it starts to roll, the characters take over. They tell the story, and I just get swept along." A first draft takes several months and may total 1,000 to 2,000 pages. Then the manuscript may go through more than a dozen rewrites.

❖ Of his many novels, Sheldon says his personal favorites are *The Best Laid Plans* and *The Other Side of Midnight*.

Treatises and Treats

COMPANIONS

The Other Side of Me by Sidney Sheldon (not yet published). The author tells his own story in this autobiography, due out soon from William Morrow.

BEST OF THE NET
Official Sidney Sheldon Web Site
www.sidneysheldon.com
Everything you'd expect from an "official" author Web site—biographical information, book descriptions, author interviews, awards and publications, media appearances and book signings, even a trivia contest. Whether you're a Sidney Sheldon fan or simply want to try to get a handle on his phenomenal popularity, this is a good place to start.

All the Novels

The Naked Face, 1970
  (Edgar Award)
The Other Side of Midnight, 1974
A Stranger in the Mirror, 1976
Bloodline, 1977
Rage of Angels, 1980
Master of the Game, 1982
If Tomorrow Never Comes, 1985
Windmills of the Gods, 1987
The Sands of Time, 1988
Memories of Midnight, 1990
The Doomsday Conspiracy, 1991
The Stars Shine Down, 1992
Nothing Lasts Forever: The New Novel, 1994
Morning, Noon, and Night, 1995
The Best Laid Plans, 1997
Tell Me Your Dreams, 1998

If You Like Sidney Sheldon . . .

You might also like books by Barbara Taylor Bradford, Jackie Collins, Harold Robbins, and Danielle Steel.

Best Book to Read First

The Naked Face (1970) won the Edgar Award for best first mystery novel, but Sheldon's second book, *The Other Side of Midnight* (1974) is the one that launched his career.

Anticipation . . .

Sidney Sheldon's fans have proven several times that they cannot wait for his next novel—literally! In 1980, *Rage of Angels* reached number one on the bestseller lists the week *before* its official publication date. It stayed in the top spot for an additional 17 weeks and on the lists for 42 weeks.

Advance orders for his eighth novel, *Windmills of the Gods* (1987), were the heaviest in publisher William Morrow's history. The novel debuted at number one two days before its official release date. The same happened with *The Sands of Time* (1988), with advance orders exceeding one million copies.

I have this goal. And it's for a reader to not be able to go to sleep at night. I want him to keep reading another four pages, then one more page. The following morning, or night, he's anxious to get back to the book.

—Sidney Sheldon,
Los Angeles Times

Anne Rivers Siddons

Born
January 9, 1936, in Atlanta, Georgia, to Marvin Rivers, an attorney, and Katherine Kitchens Rivers, a secretary. Her family has lived in the same small Georgia railroad town (Fairburn, population 2,000) for six generations.

Full Name
Sybil Anne Rivers Siddons

Education
Auburn University, B.A. (studied illustration), 1958; also attended Atlanta School of Art, 1958.

Family
Married in 1966 to Heyward L. Siddons, now a retired printing executive; four stepsons.

Home
Charleston, South Carolina (after many years in Atlanta), and a summer home in Maine overlooking Penobscot Bay

Fan Mail
Anne Rivers Siddons c/o Virginia Barber Literary Agency 101 Fifth Avenue New York, NY 10003

Publisher
HarperCollins

Described in the *Atlanta Journal–Constitution* as "the Jane Austen of modern Atlanta," Anne Rivers Siddons, although she is certainly a Southern writer, has become much more than just a regional writer. "Anne is simply one of the best writers writing about the South today," says friend Pat Conroy. "*Gone with the Wind* comparisons drive Anne crazy, but the truth is, she is covering the territory Margaret Mitchell would have covered if she'd lived. The difference is that Anne is a much better writer."

Siddons has described her obsession as a writer—the subject she continually returns to—as the issue of a woman becoming strong enough to stand alone. Her first novel, *Heartbreak Hotel* (1976), provides a marvelously detailed look at the South during the 1950s. Later novels such as *Homeplace* (1987) and *Peachtree Road* (1988) won even greater praise from critics and became bestsellers. Bob Summers wrote in *Publishers Weekly* that *Homeplace* "struck a national chord" with its account of a Southern-born woman returning home after 20 years.

Though Siddons has occasionally moved her novels out of the South, she has continued to write about Southern women and the culture they carry with them wherever they go. "I have found I can move anywhere in my fiction," she said in a 1994 interview. "If I take it from the point of view of a Southerner traveling there, it's still an honest point of view."

Good to Know

❖ Working as a senior editor at *Atlanta* magazine, Siddons thought it was a prank when a Doubleday editor sent her a letter suggesting that she write a book. She ignored the letter. But Doubleday followed up, offering a two-book contract. Siddons took the deal and produced *John Chancellor Makes Me Cry* (1975), a collection of essays chronicling a year of her life in Atlanta, and *Heartbreak Hotel* (1976), her first novel (later made into the 1989 movie *Heart of Dixie* starring Ally Sheedy).

❖ Erma Bombeck loved the book of essays, praising Siddons for her ability to "combine humor, intimacy, and insight into a marriage." Bombeck's favorite essay: the one in which Siddons describes a single month in her life during which her husband lost his job, her grandmother died, a Siamese cat she was tending for a friend was hit by a car, her own cat contracted an expensive disease, and her house was burglarized.

❖ Siddons did a brief stint as a horror writer. Her second novel, *The House Next Door* (1978), was "something of a lark. It's different from anything I've ever written, or probably ever will. But I like to read occult, supernatural stories. Some of the world's great writers have written them, and I guess I wanted to see what I could do with the genre." Stephen King dedicated an entire chapter of his *Danse Macabre* (a critique of the horror genre) to *The House Next Door*, comparing it to Shirley Jackson's classic, *The Haunting of Hill House*.

❖ There have been times when Siddons has been stuck on a novel and the problem has worked itself out in her dreams: "I literally dreamed a scene from start to finish and woke up thinking, 'Of course, it has to be that way. Why didn't I think of that?'...I don't know how it would be possible to use that side of yourself, to write or create, without recognizing your dreams or drawing from them."

❖ When Siddons's mother read her 1990 novel *King's Oak*, which contains several sex scenes, she told her daughter, "You know, dear, it's not too late to get your teaching certificate."

❖ Husband Heyward Siddons (Princeton '48, and inspiration for her famous essay, "Reunions Make Me Cry"), manages her business affairs. He says that when Anne is preparing to start a new book, she makes "a nest of papers, like a mouse getting ready for the winter," and then she starts walking into walls. (She once put her kitten in the refrigerator and the orange juice carton out the back door.) When ready to begin writing, she makes a big breakfast, cleans up the house, and disappears to her backyard cottage for two or three days. Heyward helps her edit each day's work by reading it aloud over evening cocktails.

Treatises and Treats

COMPANIONS

True Grits: Tall Tales and Recipes from the New South by the Junior League of Atlanta (Cookbook Marketplace, 1997). A collection of 318 regional recipes, as well as stories from some of the South's most renowned authors, including Anne Rivers Siddons and the late Lewis Grizzard.

A Southern Belle Primer: Or Why Princess Margaret Will Never Be a Kappa Kappa Gamma by Maryln Schwartz (Doubleday, 1991). A very funny and irreverent guide to the mores and manners of the South. Anne Rivers Siddons, Tri-Delt member and good little Southern girl, would (and almost certainly does) chuckle over every page. Her novel *Outer Banks* is based on her 1988 pledge-class reunion.

BEST OF THE NET

Anne Rivers Siddons Fan Page

www.geocities.com/athens/delphi/8435
Includes reviews of all the books, both fiction and nonfiction; a biography; and a recent interview.

All the Novels

Heartbreak Hotel, 1976
The House Next Door, 1978
Fox's Earth, 1980
Homeplace, 1987
Peachtree Road, 1988
King's Oak, 1990
Outer Banks, 1991
Colony, 1992
Hill Towns, 1993
Downtown, 1994
Fault Lines, 1995
Up Island, 1997
Low Country, 1998

If You Like Anne Rivers Siddons...

You might also like books by Maeve Binchy, Pat Conroy, Carson McCullers, Flannery O'Connor, Rosamunde Pilcher, Belva Plain, and Lee Smith. And, on the lighter side, try Rebecca Wells.

Best Book to Read First

Hill Towns, in which a Southern woman and her husband travel to Tuscany and encounter the corrupting influences not of Europeans but of fellow Americans living abroad. The book earned high praise for its stunning character portrayals.

[Anne Rivers Siddons] breaks your heart, knocks your socks off, and writes with such lyrical beauty that you want to read her aloud to anyone you ever loved.

—Pat Conroy

Southern Belle

Siddons had the upbringing of a Southern belle: "I was all those things that Southern girls long to be," she told *People Weekly*. "Homecoming queen in the white formal, then Centennial Queen of Fairburn, Georgia, riding on a float in an organdy dress. . . . And of course I was a cheerleader; I was captain of the cheerleaders. I was best all-around in high school, 'Loveliest of the Plains' at Auburn University."

Despite all this attention, she felt that something was missing. "No matter what I did, I always ended up with this hollow feeling. It finally hit me that that's why I write: I am writing about the journey we all take to find out what lives in that hole."

Isaac Bashevis Singer

Born
July 14, 1904, in Radzymin, Poland, to Pinchos Menachem Singer, a rabbi and author, and Bathsheba Zylberman Singer. Came to the United States in 1935 and was granted citizenship in 1943.

Pseudonym
Isaac Warshofsky

Education
Attended Tachkemoni Rabbinical Seminary in Warsaw, Poland, 1920–27.

Family
Married in 1940 to Alma Haimann, a refugee from Nazi Germany who worked for many years in a New York department store. One child, Israel Zamir, from an earlier marriage that ended in divorce.

Home
Lived most of his adult life on the Upper West Side of Manhattan in New York City.

Died
July 24, 1991, after several strokes, in Surfside, Florida

Publisher
Farrar, Straus & Giroux

Years ago, a famous advertising slogan for a baker of rye bread appeared on the buses and subways of New York City. It read, "You don't have to be Jewish to love Levy's." The phrase could be applied with equal accuracy to Isaac Bashevis (pronounced "buh-SHEV-us") Singer. He is considered one of the greatest writers of Yiddish literature, but he is also arguably one of the greatest writers of all time.

Though fluent in English, Singer always wrote in Yiddish, that wonderfully expressive combination of German, Hebrew, and other languages that offers handy, useful words for which there is no equivalent in American speech. His output was remarkable: novels, memoirs, short-story collections, children's books, and plays flowed from his pen. Most of his fiction is set in the *shtetls* (small Jewish settlements or villages) of eastern Europe that were destroyed by Hitler and the Nazis, a setting so far removed from modern life as to appear exotic. Yet the stories he tells are those of men and women and children and families *everywhere*. And his insights are as sharp as a freshly honed scythe.

"I never thought that my fiction…had any other purpose than to be read and enjoyed by the reader," Singer once said. "I never sit down to write a novel to make a better world." According to the *New York Times*, his first story collection, *Gimpel the Fool and Other Stories* (1957) earned him a place among "the epic storytellers, transcending geographical and chronological boundaries." He went on to win the National Book Award in 1974 for *A Crown of Feathers and Other Stories*. And in 1978, he was presented with the only Nobel Prize ever awarded a writer of Yiddish literature. "Yiddish is the wise and humble language of us all, the idiom of the frightened and hopeful humanity," he said in his acceptance speech.

Good to Know

❖ Singer was expected to become a Hasidic rabbi. But his older brother, novelist I. J. Singer, broke the family's orthodox tradition by moving to New York and writing secular stories. A year later, Singer joined him, working for the *Jewish Daily Forward* newspaper.

❖ He lived most of his life on Manhattan's Upper West Side, where he described his recreation as "walking in the bad air" of the place. He preferred local dairy restaurants and cafeterias to writers' hangouts and was a vegetarian, he said, "not for my health, but for the health of the chicken." He once remarked that in his next life, he would come back as a pig. "And the other animals will ask me what I was in the previous life. I will tell them I was a writer, and they will say, 'That's what all the pigs claim.'"

❖ Singer once said he began writing children's stories because "Children are the best readers of genuine literature. Grownups are hypnotized by big names, exaggerated quotes, and high-pressure advertising…. The child is still the independent reader who relies on nothing but his own taste." *Schlemiel Went to Warsaw and Other Stories* (1968) is one of his most popular children's books.

❖ The movies *The Magician of Lublin* (1978) starring Alan Arkin and *Enemies: A Love Story* (1989) with Ron Silver and Anjelica Huston are based on Singer's novels. His short story "Yentl, the Yeshiva Boy" became the award-winning *Yentl* (1983) starring Barbra Streisand. Singer later wrote: "I did not find artistic merit, neither in the adaptation, nor in the directing. There was too much singing, much too much."

Treatises and Treats

COMPANIONS

Isaac Bashevis Singer: Conversations by Grace Farrell (University Press of Mississippi, 1992). A collection of interviews conducted by authors Irving Howe, Richard Burgin, and others, in which Singer discusses the nature of his writing, its ethnic roots, the importance of free will, and the place of storytelling in human life.

Isaac Bashevis Singer: A Life by Janet Hadda (Oxford University Press, 1997). Yiddish scholar and psychoanalyst Hadda draws on extensive interviews with Singer's wife, translators, and fellow writers, as well as Yiddish sources, to trace the author's rise to literary fame and his uneasy relations with his family. The book is generally considered an unsympathetic, but thorough and interesting, portrait.

Journey to My Father, Isaac Bashevis Singer by Israel Zamir and Barbara Harshav (Arcade, 1996). Singer's only son describes their reunion 20 years after Singer left for the United States, abandoning his wife and child, and the relationship that followed.

READINGS

Jewish Stories from the Old World to the New is an 18-hour series produced by NPR station KCRW at Santa Monica College. Hosted by Leonard Nimoy, it features readings of Singer's stories, along with those of other writers (Saul Bellow, Bernard Malumud, Cynthia Ozick, and Philip Roth, etc.) by Edward Asner, Adam Arkin, Richard Dreyfuss, Joanna Gleason, Charlton Heston, Carl Reiner, and others. Hearing Jewish stories read with the proper tone and appropriate accent offers a resonance not available from the printed page. The entire series is available on tape or CD from KCRW (800-292-3855, www.kcrw.org/jewish).

BEST OF THE NET

New York Times Featured Authors
www.nytimes.com/books/specials/
  author.html

Check here for reviews of Singer's books, a collection of interviews and speeches (including his 1978 Nobel Prize acceptance speech), and his 1991 obituary, all from the *New York Times* archives.

Best Reads

NOVELS

Satan in Goray, 1935
The Family Moskat, 1950
The Magician of Lublin, 1960
The Slave, 1962
Enemies: A Love Story, 1972
Shosha, 1978
The Penitent, 1983
Scum, 1991

SHORT-STORY COLLECTIONS

*Schlemiel Went to Warsaw, and Other
  Stories*, 1968
A Crown of Feathers and Other Stories, 1973
  (National Book Award)
*The Collected Stories of Isaac Bashevis
  Singer*, 1982

If You Like Isaac Bashevis Singer . . .

You might also like Saul Bellow and Bernard Malamud. But don't forget Sholem Aleichem, whose stories formed the basis for *A Fiddler on the Roof*. Or the lesser known but equally good Russian writer Sholem Yankev Abramovitsch, who wrote about the exploits of Benjamin the Third, a Jewish Don Quixote, and Fishe the Lame, a long-suffering beggar, in *Tales of Mendele the Book Peddler. Booklist* called Abramovitsch (1835–1917) the architect of modern fiction in Yiddish and Hebrew.

Best Book to Read First

The Collected Stories of Isaac Bashevis Singer. Although Singer was an acclaimed novelist, he is best known for his short stories, and this book includes some of his gems.

It's true that since I know the Jewish people best and since I know the Yiddish language best, so my heroes, the people of my stories, are always Jewish and speak Yiddish. I am at home with these people. But just the same, I'm not just writing about them because they speak Yiddish and are Jewish. I'm interested in the same things you are interested in and the Japanese are interested in—in love, and in treachery, and in hopes and in disappointments.

—Isaac Bashevis
Singer

Jane Smiley

Born
September 26, 1949, in Los Angeles, California, to James Laverne Smiley, a career soldier in the U.S. Army, and Frances Graves Smiley, a writer/editor. Following her parents divorce when she was four, she moved with her mother to St. Louis, Missouri.

Education
Vassar College, B.A. in English, 1971. University of Iowa, M.A., 1975; M.F.A, 1976; and Ph.D., 1978

Family
Married and divorced three times. She has three children: two daughters from her second marriage and a son from her third.

Home
A three-acre spread christened the "Do-Re-Mi ranchette" in northern California, where she raises thoroughbred horses

Fan Mail
Jane Smiley
c/o Aaron Priest
  Agency
122 East 42nd Street
New York, NY 10168

Publisher
Knopf

Jane Smiley is every English professor's secret dream. She's smart, she has the educational background and personal and political skills to thrive in the academic world, and she has the special gifts and talents needed to write bestselling novels that give her the freedom to leave academe forever, if she wants, and concentrate on her writing.

She has two secret weapons. The first is a battery of impeccable research skills. From Old Norse folklore to campus-set satirical comedy, from a mystery to a romance adventure set in the Old West, you can count on Smiley to get the historical details right. (If she has a fault in this regard, it may be that she tells readers a bit more than they really need to know about topics like modern hog farming or Norse mythology. Others revel in the perceptive detail.) The second, and the one that makes Jane Smiley truly special and beloved by readers, is her accurate, insightful, and loving portrayals of families, individual family members, and the interactions among them.

As Joanne Kaufman said in *People*, Smiley "has an unerring, unsettling ability to capture the rhythms of family life gone askew." Her award-winning *A Thousand Acres*, for example, begins with aging farmer Larry Cook announcing his intention to turn over one of the largest farms in Zebulon County, Iowa, to his three daughters—Caroline, Ginny, and Rose. It's *King Lear* on the prairie, with the story told by Ginny, Jane Smiley's modern version of Goneril. The concept is simply irresistible.

Or consider *Moo*, an "uproariously funny and at the same time hauntingly melancholy portrait of a college community," according to the *New York Times*. Anyone who has spent even one semester at an institution of higher learning will recognize the characters Smiley develops and presents and will chuckle at their interactions and their relations with family members.

Indeed family relations and relationships among family members are consistent Smiley themes. You read her books and exclaim, "Yes! I know that person," or "I've been in just that situation."

Good to Know

❖ For her senior thesis at Vassar, Smiley wrote a novel. Years later, she said the experience led her to become a fiction writer.

❖ She has made it a personal goal to write each one of the four major narrative forms—epic (*The Greenlanders*), tragedy (*A Thousand Acres*), comedy (*Moo*), and romance (*The All-True Travels and Adventures of Lidie Newton*). "She's constantly looking for a new challenge, some new project that makes her have to do something differently," says Neil Nakadate, author of *Understanding Jane Smiley*.

❖ *The Greenlanders* was conceived during a Fulbright Scholarship year in Iceland, where she studied Old Norse literature (the subject of her doctoral dissertation). The novel took five years to research and write.

❖ Smiley contends that she does not mine her own life for material. "I rarely write in any autobiographical way," she told *Redbook* in 1998. But her 15 years as a college professor (teaching English at Iowa State University and serving as visiting professor at the University of Iowa) no doubt provided inspiration for the settings and characters in *Moo*, a comic novel about professors and academe.

Now breeding horses on a California ranch, her current project is a novel called *Horse Heaven*, about the turbulent world of thoroughbred horse racing.

❖ It was the success of her Pulitzer Prize–winning *A Thousand Acres* and the subsequent movie deal that allowed Smiley to give up teaching. But she won't give up writing any time soon. "No, my writing just goes on," she said in a 1998 online interview for *Atlantic Unbound*. "It wasn't affected by children, it wasn't affected by marriage, it wasn't affected by teaching, it wasn't affected by quitting teaching. It's never been affected by anything."

❖ Standing six-foot-two in her stocking feet, Smiley may well be "the tallest woman in American fiction," according to her third ex-husband.

Treatises and Treats

COMPANIONS

Understanding Jane Smiley by Neil Nakadate (University of South Carolina Press, 1999). Nakadate knows Jane Smiley as a neighbor and fellow professor for 15 years at Iowa State University and brings that knowledge to bear in this comprehensive book. Through a close reading of Smiley's novels and stories, he shows the connections between her life and her work, examining her interests, social and political concerns, and ability to delve into new creative challenges with each book.

BEST OF THE NET

New York Times Featured Authors
www.nytimes.com/books/specials/author.htm
Click on "Jane Smiley" for a collection of interviews, articles, and reviews of her work from the archives of the *New York Times*.

Reading List

NOVELS

Barn Blind, 1980
At Paradise Gate, 1981
Duplicate Keys, 1984

The Greenlanders, 1988
A Thousand Acres, 1991
  (Pulitzer Prize, National Book Critics Circle Award)
Moo, 1995
The All-True Travels and Adventures of Lidie Newton, 1998
  (Spur Award)

OTHER

The Age of Grief, 1987 (story collection)
Catskill Crafts: Artisans of the Catskill Mountains, 1987 (nonfiction)
Ordinary Love and Good Will, 1989 (novellas)
The True Subject: Writers on Life and Craft, 1993 (coauthor; nonfiction)

If You Like Jane Smiley...

Try Mary McCarthy's *The Groves of Academe* and John L'Heureux's *The Handmade of Desire*, two send-ups of university life. Or try Jane Hamilton's *A Map of the World*, the story of two parents trying to raise their daughters in the pastoral safety of a Wisconsin dairy farm who find that safety is an illusion. You might also like the novels of E. L. Doctorow, John Irving, and Anne Tyler.

Best Book to Read First

A Thousand Acres, a retelling of the tragedy of King Lear set on an Iowa farm. Winner of the 1992 Pulitzer Prize, it was turned into a 1997 movie starring Michelle Pfeiffer, Jessica Lange, and Jennifer Jason Leigh.

Most of my books are in some sense historical novels, because they all draw on an analysis of what happened at a particular historical moment. I tend to get into things, kind of obsessed with them. I've stuck with my interests in my children, in my writing, and in horses, but other than that I get involved in new things, and I want to write about them. I'm more of an outward-looking writer than an inward-looking writer, and I'm drawn to lots of different kinds of subjects.

—Jane Smiley, *Atlantic Unbound* (1998)

The Book I Would Most Like to Have Written...

Asked by the *New York Times* what book she would most like to have written (other than her own), Smiley named *Our Mutual Friend*, Charles Dickens's last completed novel. What appealed to her most is that Dickens "perfected his writing style so that every word is right in half a dozen or more ways so that the book becomes, as you are reading, a huge network of meanings that the more you read the more meanings you apprehend, and it just builds and builds and builds. It's just perfect from beginning to end."

Not surprisingly, Smiley has been asked to write the Dickens volume in the "Penguin Lives" series of short biographies, published by Viking.

Danielle Steel

Born
August 14, 1947, in
New York City to John
and Norma Steel

Full Name
Fernande Danielle
Steel

Education
Educated in France.
Also attended Parsons
School of Design,
1963, and New York
University, 1963–67.

Family
Married five times.
Most recently in 1998
to venture capitalist
Thomas J. Perkins (of
the San Francisco-
based venture-capital
firm Kliener Perkins
Caulfield & Byers), who
helped found the high-
tech firms Genentech,
Compaq, and Tandem.
Seven children of her
own and two stepsons
from earlier marriages.

Home
The Pacific Heights
section of San Fran-
cisco, California

Fan Mail
Danielle Steel
c/o Morton L. Janklow
598 Madison Avenue
New York, NY 10022

Publisher
Delacorte

I f you're in the mood for a little romance, one of Danielle Steel's novels
may be just what you need. With some
60 books to her credit, including a
moving nonfiction account of her son
Nick's death from a heroin overdose
(*His Bright Light*), Steel's forte is
telling romantic tales of glamorous and powerful women confronted with tough decisions
about life and love—tales that have made her
one of the most popular novelists of the day.

Critics, of course, typically dismiss romance novels as pure escapism. However, reviewers like Peggy Hill (*Toronto Globe &
Mail*) have recognized in Danielle Steel the
ability to give the genre enough strength so
that it does not "collapse into an exhausted
state of cliché." Steel's fun, readable style
combined with her talent for creating intricate, compelling plots driven by engaging
characters have earned her a permanent
place on the *New York Times* bestseller list
and distinguished her as a publishing phenomenon with total sales topping 380 million
copies.

Danielle Steel also writes novels centering on serious, thought-provoking issues such
as infertility, child abuse, and child abduc-
tion. These are the issues faced by the characters in *Mixed Blessings*, *Malice*, and
Vanished. As these topics suggest, familial relationships are quite often at the core of a
Danielle Steel novel. She explores how families cope when they are confronted with
tragedy: in *Accident*, a couple must deal with
their teenaged daughter's brain injury; and
The Gift follows one family as its members
move through the grieving process after the
death of their youngest member.

In the end, Danielle Steel's goal is to inform
as well as entertain. And given her enormous
worldwide readership, she has certainly
achieved that goal.

Good to Know

❖ Danielle Steel earned a place in the *Guinness Book of World Records* for having at least
one book on the *New York Times* bestseller
list every week for 381 consecutive weeks
(more than seven years!). In addition, she's
had a novel on *Publishers Weekly*'s annual
bestseller list every year since 1982.

❖ She often has multiple projects in different
stages of development at any given time.
When she finally sits down at her 1946
Olympia manual typewriter, she has typically
done two to three years of research for that
one project. And once she starts writing, she
may spend 18 to 20 hours a day pounding the
keys.

❖ Don't hold your breath waiting for the sequel to your favorite Danielle Steel novel. She
has never written a sequel to any of her books,
feeling that it would be "an invitation to unfa-
vorable comparison." Besides, she has too
many original story ideas to spend more than
one book on a particular character or story-
line.

❖ Even though their mother is a bestselling
author, selling books that are read by both
men and women in 47 countries and 28 languages, Steel's children do not come to her for
creative-writing advice. According to Steel,
"they all write wonderful poetry, but they do it
all on their own."

❖ Between her children and her pets,
Danielle Steel's home is a literal and figura-
tive zoo! When she is not chauffering her children between school and extra-curricular
activities, helping with homework, or just
spending time with them, she tends to the
needs of her five miniature Brussels Griffon

dogs, Bugs the rabbit, Rosie the yellow parakeet, and Coco, the Vietnamese potbellied pig.

❖ She also serves as national chairman for the American Library Association and as a spokesman for two organizations dealing with child abuse, the National Committee for the Prevention of Child Abuse and the American Humane Association.

❖ Steel reportedly paid upwards of $6 million for her palatial Pacific Heights mansion overlooking San Francisco Bay. (See the "Scrapbook" section of her Web site for pictures.) She married her latest husband there, under an arch of lavender roses and violets. Mayor Willie Brown, actor Don Johnson, and media mogul Rupert Murdoch attended the celebratory dance that followed.

Treatises and Treats

COMPANIONS

The Lives of Danielle Steel: The Unauthorized Biography of America's #1 Best-Selling Author by Lorenzo Benet and Vickie L. Bane (St. Martin's Press, 1994). An in-depth portrait that reveals how closely Steel's own life tracks with her fiction. Fans are sure to relish this book, described by *Entertainment Weekly* as "steamy."

Danielle Steel by Nicole Hoyt (Kensington Publishing Group 1994). For all her beauty, talent, and wealth, Steel has had her share of struggles and heartbreak, all revealed here. Includes a 12-page photo insert.

BEST OF THE NET

Official Danielle Steel Web Site

www:daniellesteel.com
Created by her publisher, this site is sure to delight Danielle Steel fans with its author interviews and photos of her pets and lavish home. You can also sign up for the Danielle Steel Reading Group.

Best of the Bestsellers

Here's a baker's dozen of the Danielle Steel novels that have enjoyed the longest runs on the bestseller lists:

Mixed Blessings, 1992
Vanished, 1993
The Gift, 1994
Accident, 1994
Wings, 1994
Five Days in Paris, 1995
Lightning, 1995
Malice, 1996
Silent Honor, 1996
The Ranch, 1997
Special Delivery, 1997
The Ghost, 1997
The Long Road Home, 1998

If You Like Danielle Steel . . .

Try the novels of Catherine Cookson, Steel's British counterpart. Before she died in 1998, Cookson was confirmed as Britain's best-selling author of the decade, with more than 100 million copies of her books sold worldwide.

You might also like books by Barbara Taylor Bradford, Janet Dailey, Judith Krantz, Judith Michael, Nora Roberts, and Sidney Sheldon.

Best Book to Read First

Mixed Blessings. Deals with the often devastating effects of infertility as it affects three California couples. Though not typical Steel subject matter, it is considered one of her all-time best books.

Steel, our American Cookson, is a marvel among writers of hairdryer-and-beachchair hefty romantic performances.

—*Kirkus Reviews*

Rated G

If you think Danielle Steel only writes steamy romance novels, think again. Children have always been an important part of her life, and in recent years, she has written two series of books for the preschool set.

"Max and Martha" is an illustrated series intended to comfort young children and help them get through their growing pains. Potentially problematic situations such as a new baby in the family (*Max's New Baby*), a new stepparent (*Martha's New Daddy*), or the loss of a grandparent (*Max and Grandma and Grandpa Winky)* are addressed. The "Freddie Books" deal with topics like a child's first visit to the doctor (*Freddie and Doctor*) and spending the night away from home (*Freddie's First Night Away*).

Wallace Stegner

Born
February 18, 1909, in Lake Mills, Iowa, to George Stegner and Hilda Paulson Stegner

Full Name
Wallace Earle Stegner

Education
University of Utah, B.A. (Phi Beta Kappa), 1930; courses at University of California, 1932–33; State University of Iowa, Ph.D., 1935

Family
Married Mary Stuart Page in 1934. One child: Stuart Page.

Home
Los Altos Hills, California

Died
April 13, 1993, from injuries resulting from a car accident

Publisher
Penguin

Growing up, Wallace Stegner lived successively in Iowa, Utah, North Dakota, Washington, Montana, Wyoming, and Saskatchewan—experiences mirrored in his acclaimed novel *The Big Rock Candy Mountain* (1942). If these were his formative years, what they "formed" was a writer of the West. Yet Stegner is much more than a regional writer. His themes are universal: finding one's identity, the need for love and understanding, and sense of home.

Stegner's early professional years were also nomadic. He taught at Augusta College in Rock Island, Illinois; the University of Utah in Salt Lake City; the University of Wisconsin in Madison; Harvard University in Cambridge, Massachusetts; and finally Stanford University in Palo Alto, California, where he settled in for a run of several decades. He had found *his* home.

The West of the 19th and early 20th centuries was Stegner's literary terrain, and he evoked in his novels the lingering wildness and mythical contours of the frontier—what he called "that place of impossible loveliness that pulled the whole nation westward." He also wrote of the struggle of humans to live among each other while living with themselves. There is, Stegner believed, "a kind of hunger for order in the world that I think afflicts westerners more than easterners."

A recurring theme in Stegner's work is the person who looks into the past to make peace with the present. His nonfiction also dips into history. In *Beyond the Hundredth Meridian: John Wesley Powell and the Second Opening of the West* (1954), Stegner looks at a Western explorer whose life, he says, represents "an ideal of public service that seems peculiarly a product of the American experience." Many of Stegner's essays reflect on the geography and history of the West and of his place in the mix. His life, art, and thought coalesced in one of his last works, *Where the Bluebird Sings to the Lemonade Springs: Living and Writing in the West* (1992), a collection of anecdotes and essays.

Good to Know

❖ Stegner wrote his first book, *Remembering Laughter,* in response to a contest sponsored by the publisher Little, Brown and Company. First prize was $2,500. Stegner won, and the book was published in 1937.

❖ He founded Stanford University's creative writing program in 1946, and ran the program for 25 years. Highly regarded nationally, the Stanford program now offers a writing fellowship in Stegner's honor.

❖ From his years in Utah, Stegner became interested in Mormon history, producing two books on the subject. *Mormon Country* (1941), his first nonfiction book, presents the geography of Utah and a brief history of the Mormons. *The Gathering of Zion: The Story of the Mormon Trail* (1964) is based on journal accounts of Mormons who traveled from Illinois to Utah in the mid-19th century.

❖ Stegner the "Western" writer set his 1987 novel *Crossing to Safety* in Vermont. It's the story of the lifelong friendship between two very different couples, one from the East and one from the West, who first met when the husbands were colleagues at the University of Wisconsin in 1937. Stegner once said that the novel is the closest he has come to writing his autobiography.

❖ In addition to the Pulitzer Prize for *Angle of Repose*, his literary honors include the National Book Award for *The Spectator Bird* and three O. Henry Awards for short stories.

Treatises and Treats

COMPANIONS

Wallace Stegner: His Life and Work by Jackson J. Benson (Viking Books, 1996). A friend's admiring account of Stegner and his place in literature.

Stealing Glances: Three Interviews with Wallace Stegner, edited by James R. Hepworth (University of New Mexico Press, 1998). Stegner discusses his work, how he learned his craft, the teaching of writing, and his views on environmental issues, history, and Western writers.

Conversations with Wallace Stegner on Western History and Literature, with Richard W. Etulain (University of Nevada Press, 1996). A collection of interviews in which Stegner talks about his life, his early works and major novels, and his views on Western history and the changing American West.

BEST OF THE NET

Wallace Stegner Page
water.montana.edu/stegner
Created by Montana State University, which honored Stegner in 1993 by establishing the Wallace Stegner Chair in Western American Studies, this site offers biographical information, bibliography, quotes, and photographs.

Wallace Stegner Environmental Center
sfpl.lib.ca.us/stegner
Another good source of information on Stegner's life and work, compliments of the San Francisco Public Library.

Book List

ALL THE NOVELS
Remembering Laughter, 1937
The Potter's House, 1938
On a Darkling Plain, 1940

Fire and Ice, 1971
The Big Rock Candy Mountain, 1943
Second Growth, 1947
The Preacher and the Slave, 1950
    (reissued as *Joe Hill*, 1969)
A Shooting Star, 1961
All the Little Live Things, 1967
Angle of Repose, 1971
    (Pulitzer Prize)
The Spectator Bird, 1976
    (National Book Award)
Recapitulation, 1979
Crossing to Safety, 1987

SHORT-STORY COLLECTIONS
The Women on the Wall, 1948
The City of the Living and Other Stories, 1956
Where the Bluebird Sings to the Lemonade Springs, 1992
Collected Stories of Wallace Stegner, 1994

If You Like Wallace Stegner . . .

You might also like Edward Abbey, Wendell Berry, Annie Dillard, Larry McMurtry, Jean Stafford, and Tobias Wolff.

Best Book to Read First

Angle of Repose, winner of the Pulitzer Prize. (The title refers to the geological term for the slope at which a rock ceases to roll.) "Reading it is an experience to be treasured." (*Boston Globe*)

If there is such a thing as being conditioned by climate and geography, and I think there is, it is the West that has conditioned me. It has the forms and light and colors that I respond to in nature and in art. If there is a western speech, I speak it; if there is a western character or personality, I am some variant of it; if there is a western culture in the small-c, anthropological sense, I have not escaped it.

—Wallace Stegner,
Where the Bluebird Sings to the Lemonade Springs

Stegner, the Environmentalist

In the 1950s, Stegner fought construction of a dam on the Green River in order to preserve the Dinosaur National Monument, an area straddling northeast Utah and northwest Colorado where fossils bear witness to America's prehistoric animals. In the 1960s, he served on the National Parks Advisory Board and worked briefly as an assistant to Secretary of the Interior Stuart Udall during the Kennedy administration.

Perhaps his most famous piece of environmental writing is the *Wilderness Letter*, in which he states: "Something will have gone out of us as a people if we ever let the remaining wilderness be destroyed." The letter has been called a manifesto of the environmental movement, and it provided the introduction to the 1964 bill establishing the National Wilderness Preservation System.

John Steinbeck

Born
February 27, 1902, in
Salinas, California, to
John Ernst Steinbeck,
a county treasurer, and
Olivia Hamilton Stein-
beck, a teacher

Education
Studied marine biology
at Stanford University,
1919–25.

Family
First two marriages
ended in divorce: Carol
Henning (1930–43),
Gwyn Conger
(1943–48). Married
third wife Elaine Scott
in 1950. Two sons
from his second
marriage.

Died
December 20, 1968,
in New York City, of
heart disease. Buried
in Salinas, California.

Publishers
Library of America
Penguin

The quick handle on John Steinbeck is that he wrote powerful
protest novels of the 1930s and
early 1940s that, because they
were seen to lean to the political
left, were as controversial in
their time as Harriet Beecher
Stowe's *Uncle Tom's Cabin* (1852) was in the
mid-19th century. Both novelists laid bare
the plight of the least fortunate Americans,
be they black African slaves or white migrant
farm workers.

But no thoughtful reader of Steinbeck
would conclude that he was a hard-bitten ide-
ologue. He used his enormous talents to
awaken the country's social conscience at a
time when the power of mass media was not
as great as it is now. As a result, as was the
case with Harriet Beecher Stowe, his books
were banned and burned.

Steinbeck won the Nobel Prize in 1962 for
his "realistic as well as imaginative writings"
and his "keen social perception." He also won
the Pulitzer and National Book Award. But the
controversies surrounding his works—including his use of four-letter words as he reproduced the way people actually speak—
overshadowed his writing talent. Today he is
considered passé and is largely ignored by
academia. Yet the fact is that, while no one ever
read *Uncle Tom's Cabin* for its literary merits,
decades from now people will be reading Steinbeck's novels because the writing and the characters and the emotions they evoke are so very,
very powerful.

Should you doubt it, you need only consider this: Steinbeck wrote 17 novels, several
of which have been adapted for film, stage,
and television. Today, more than three
decades after his death, *all* of John Steinbeck's novels are in print, and they sell a combined total of more than 700,000 copies each
year!

Good to Know

❖ Researching *The Grapes of Wrath*, Steinbeck spent two years traveling with a group of
migrant farmers from Oklahoma to California. He completed the actual writing of the
book in five months, writing 2,000 words—
about eight double-spaced pages—a day.

❖ Two Steinbeck novels are among the 50
most frequently banned books in the United
States: *Of Mice and Men* (#2) and *The Grapes
of Wrath* (#34). For details, see Herbert Foerstel's *Banned in the U.S.A.* (Greenwood
Press, 1994).

❖ Concerned that bookstores might not accept *The Grapes of Wrath* because of its "obscene language," the publisher sent an editor
out to work with the author on changing the
four-letter words. When transmitting the
changes to New York, the editor had an unexpected problem. The Western Union operator
was horrified at the words she was asked to
key in and chastised the editor, "You are obviously not a Christian, madam!"

❖ In 1960, when he was almost 60 years old,
Steinbeck set out on a road trip across
America with his "old French gentleman
poodle," Charley. His book *Travels with
Charley* recounts the many fascinating
events and people he encountered on his
journey to rediscover America.

Treatises and Treats

NATIONAL STEINBECK CENTER

Steinbeck once said of his birthplace, Salinas,
California, "They want no part of me, except in
a pine box." But in 1998 the town opened the

National Steinbeck Center, with a $10 million museum and extensive archives devoted to the author's life and work. Among the exhibits: *Rocinante*, the pickup that Steinbeck drove around the United States gathering stories for *Travels with Charley*. The Center also hosts the annual Steinbeck Festival and sponsors a short-story competition. Contact: 831-796-3833, www.steinbeck.org.

FRIENDS OF STEINBECK

This fan club of sorts is sponsored by the Center for Steinbeck Studies at San Jose State University—home to a collection of rare editions, manuscripts, and other memorabilia. The $25 annual fee includes a subscription to *The Steinbeck Newsletter*. Contact:
Center for Steinbeck Studies
San Jose State University
One Washington Square
San Jose, CA 95192-0202
www.sjsu.edu/depts/steinbec/srcnewsl.html

COMPANIONS

John Steinbeck: A Biography by Jay Parini (Henry Holt, 1996). Written by an admiring Steinbeck scholar, this account attempts to demythologize the man and present an honest representation of his literary contributions. *Booklist* called it a "finely wrought portrait."

John Steinbeck: Comprehensive Research and Study Guide, edited by Harold Bloom (Chelsea House, 1999). A great resource for anyone wanting to better understand and appreciate Steinbeck's work. Bloom has compiled a selection of critical responses to Steinbeck's fiction, presented in order of publication.

BEST OF THE NET

Center for Steinbeck Studies

www.sjsu.edu/depts/steinbec/srchome.html
A nicely organized collection of information. Highlights include "Steinbeck and His Times," "Steinbeck's Homes," and the "Nobel Prize."

John Steinbeck Page

tlc.ai.org/steinbec.htm
A treasure trove of information, with guides to all the novels and links to organizations such as the National Steinbeck Center, the Cannery Row Foundation, and Steinbeck House.

Best Reads

FICTION

Tortilla Flat, 1935
Of Mice and Men, 1937
The Red Pony, 1937
The Grapes of Wrath, 1939
    (Pulitzer Prize)
Cannery Row, 1945
The Wayward Bus, 1947
The Pearl, 1947
East of Eden, 1952
Sweet Thursday , 1954
The Winter of Our Discontent, 1961

NONFICTION

Travels with Charley, 1962

If You Like John Steinbeck . . .

You might also like Theodore Dreiser, Jack London, and Emil Zola. Dreiser's *An American Tragedy* examines American society in the early days of capitalism, exposing the harsh realities and the dark side of the American dream.

Best Book to Read First

The Grapes of Wrath is Steinbeck's masterpiece. But the best book to start with is the novella *Of Mice and Men*. If it doesn't knock you off your feet, then nothing else Steinbeck wrote will affect you, and you should move on. If the novella reaches you, however, then by all means turn to *Grapes*, taking full advantage of the Web and other resources listed here as you progress.

A Raisin Scorned!

Steinbeck's first wife Carol found the title for his best-known work in Julia Ward Howe's "The Battle Hymn of the Republic": *Mine eyes have seen the glory of the coming of the Lord, He is trampling out the vintage where the grapes of wrath are stored.* (The author insisted that the first edition of the book include all the verses of this Union anthem.) His third wife Elaine found the title for *East of Eden* in the 16th verse of *Genesis*: "Then Cain went away from the presence of the Lord, and settled in the land of Nod, east of Eden."

But titles don't always translate well into other languages. When Elaine Steinbeck visited a Yokohama bookstore, she asked if they had her husband's most famous novel. The clerk checked and reported that they did indeed carry *The Angry Raisins*.

William Styron

Born
June 11, 1925, in
Newport News,
Virginia. Only child of
William Clark Styron, a
marine engineer, and
Pauline Abraham
Styron, who died when
he was 13. Descended
from the Stioring family
that arrived in Virginia
in 1650.

Full Name
William Clark Styron

Education
Early studies at
Christchurch School,
Virginia. Then Davidson
College and Duke
University, both in
North Carolina.
Courses at the New
School for Social
Research in New York
City set him on his
writing career.

Family
Married Rose
Burgunder in 1953.
They have four
children.

Home
Roxbury, Connecticut,
and Vineyard Haven,
Massachusetts

Fan Mail
William Styron
12 Rucum Road
Roxbury, CT 06783

Publisher
Random House

William Styron is one of the genuine heavyweights among American writers. His work receives the accolades of critics for its substance, style, and power. Unafraid of tackling the difficult or controversial, Styron adopted the narrative voice of the real-life black leader of an 1831 slave uprising in Virginia in *The Confessions of Nat Turner*. It was a bold step for a white Southern writer in the 1960s.

But the jewel in Styron's career is *Sophie's Choice*, a searing novel about the Holocaust and its shadow-filled legacy. Meryl Streep's award-winning portrayal of Sophie in the 1982 movie version was not only a jewel in her own career, but one of the deepest, fullest, richest performances by any actor. (You have two healthy children, a boy and a girl. Only one can live, the other will die, and you must choose. Now.)

Styron mixes compelling characters into tragic love stories, and at the same time manages to comment on great issues that confront us all: the abuse of authority, the existence and nature of evil, the effects of domination and rebellion, and the possibility of redemption.

Styron grew up listening to his grandmother's stories of her struggles during the Civil War, and he experienced firsthand the Sunday picnics, saltwater baptisms, and polarized world of the Tidewater South. Themes of social injustice and the abuse of power give shape to his fiction. From childhood on, he has considered himself a rebel against authority, believing that "this impulse toward freedom is probably at the heart of all human action."

Good to Know

❖ Able to read at age five, the precocious author was publishing short stories in his high school newspaper by the time he hit adolescence. In college, he wrote poems for the literary magazine. Literary influences include William Faulkner, Joseph Conrad, Thomas Wolfe, Hannah Arendt, and classic Greek tragedies.

❖ Styron was a Marine lieutenant during World War II and was recalled from the reserves during the Korean War, but faulty eyesight disqualified him for active service. Soon after, he was in Paris helping George Plimpton start a magazine called the *Paris Review*, for which he remains an advisory editor.

❖ *Lie Down in Darkness*, his first novel, earned him an advance of $100 from Crown Publishers. At the time, he considered that amount "enormous."

❖ In the 1950s, Styron lived and traveled in France and Italy. He and Rose were married in Rome on May 4, 1953. For a look at how American expatriates got along in Italy during this time period, read Styron's fictional account in *Set This House on Fire*.

❖ Surfacing from severe depression in the 1980s, Styron wrote about the experience in *Darkness Visible*, a nonfiction work that takes its title from Milton's *Paradise Lost*. When the angel Lucifer fell from Heaven, he arrived in Hell and found no light there, only "darkness visible."

❖ The movie *Shadrach*, starring Harvey Keitel and Andie MacDowell, is based on a short story in *A Tidewater Morning*. Styron wrote the screenplay with his daughter Susanna

Styron, who directed the film. It's the tale of an elderly former slave who travels on foot back to Virginia, seeking burial where he grew up.

Treatises and Treats

COMPANIONS

William Styron: A Life by James L. W. West (Random House). The authorized biography, and a key to the author's life, fiction, and creative process.

The Critical Response to William Styron, edited by Daniel William Ross (Greenwood Publishing Group). Essays, reviews, and articles that chronicle Styron's controversial body of work while providing valuable insights.

Conversations with William Styron, edited by James L. W. West (University Press of Mississippi). A collection of 25 conversations across 30 years, covering the writer's mentors, ideas, experiences, and work. Includes a foreword by Styron.

BEST OF THE NET

William Styron Fan Page
www.sirius.com/~fillius/styron.htm
A nicely organized fan page, with quotes, photos, and full-text articles by and about William Styron.

That Summer in New York

Styron used autobiographical elements for *Sophie's Choice,* basing the character Stingo on himself. Like Stingo, who also wanted to be a writer, Styron embarked on an unfruitful job at a New York publishing firm. It was the summer of 1947, and living in a rooming house in Brooklyn, he met the woman who inspired Sophie. Most of the novel, however, is straight out of the author's imagination.

William Styron Cybercast
www.broadcast.com/news/events/loc/
 styron/locsite
Styron and his biographer, James L. W. West, discuss the author's life and work in a video presentation made available through the Library of Congress. Styron's daughter, Susanna, also joins the conversation.

Book List

FICTION

Lie Down in Darkness, 1951
The Long March, 1955
Set This House on Fire, 1960
The Confessions of Nat Turner, 1967
 (Pulitzer Prize)
Sophie's Choice, 1979
 (American Book Award)
A Tidewater Morning, 1993

NONFICTION

This Quiet Dust and Other Writings, 1982
Darkness Visible: A Memoir of Madness, 1990

If You Like William Styron . . .

Try some of these books:

Go Tell It on the Mountain by James Baldwin
Humboldt's Gift by Saul Bellow
The Living by Annie Dillard
As I Lay Dying by William Faulkner
The Tin Drum by Günther Grass
Wise Blood by Flannery O'Connor

Best Book to Read First

Sophie's Choice. "A great book should leave you . . . slightly exhausted at the end," Styron has said, and this one certainly does. But it's well worth it.

When, in the autumn of 1947, I was fired from the first and only job I have ever held, I wanted one thing out of life: to become a writer. . . . I burned to write a novel and I could not have cared less that my bank account was close to zero, with no replenishment in sight. At the age of twenty-two I had such pure hopes in my ability to write not just a respectable first novel, but a novel that would be completely out of the ordinary, that when I left the McGraw-Hill Building for the last time I felt the exultancy of a man just released from slavery and ready to set the universe on fire.

—William Styron,
This Quiet Dust and Other Writings (1982)

Amy Tan

Born
February 19, 1952, in
Oakland, California, to
immigrants John Yueh-
han Tan, a minister and
electrical engineer, and
Daisy Tu Ching Tan, a
vocational nurse

Real Name
En-Mai (which means
"Blessing of America")
Tan

Education
Graduate of San Jose
State University, where
she earned a B.A.,
English and linguistics,
1973; and M.A., 1974.
Postgraduate study at
University of California,
Berkeley, and Univer-
sity of California, Santa
Cruz.

Family
Married Louis M.
DeMattei, a tax
attorney, in 1974. No
children, Tan told the
New York Times,
because "I remember
being such an unhappy
child, and I can't guar-
antee that I won't do
the same things my
mother did."

Homes
San Francisco's presti-
gious Presidio district
and Manhattan

Fan Mail
Amy Tan
c/o Sandra Dijkstra
1155 Camino del Mar
Del Mar, CA 92014

Publisher
Putnam

Amy Tan's novels explore familial relationships against a background of cultural and generational differences and conflicts. Tan once remarked that although she was originally ambivalent about her ethnicity and tried to distance herself from it, writing *The Joy Luck Club* helped her discover "how very Chinese I was. And how much had stayed with me that I had tried to deny."

The book uses the traditional Chinese "talk story" to explore the lives of four Chinese immigrant mothers, their four American-born daughters, and the impact past generations have had on their relationships. A mother-daughter relationship is also the theme of her second book, *The Kitchen God's Wife*. It begins with an American-born daughter's reluctant visit to her mother's home in Chinatown and ends with revelations that surprise them both. In her third novel, *The Hundred Secret Senses*, Tan explores sisterhood and what it means to be a family.

As the late Michael Dorris said in the *Chicago Tribune*, "Tan's characters, regardless of their cultural orientation or age, speak with authority and authenticity. The details of their lives, unfamiliar to most American readers, are rendered with such conviction that almost immediately their rules seem to become the adages and admonitions with which we ourselves grew up."

Good to Know

❖ When she was 14, Amy Tan's father and older brother both died of brain tumors. Shortly afterward, doctors discovered that her mother also had a tumor, though it was benign. Anxious to escape what she viewed as the evil influence of the family's "diseased house," Tan's mother took her and her younger brother to live in Europe.

❖ Tan completed high school at an exclusive school in Montreux, Switzerland, where her classmates included the children of ambassadors, princes, and tycoons—people with whom she had little in common. Feeling alienated and realizing that "being good" had not saved her father or brother, she went through a period of rebellion and fell in with a drug dealer who claimed to be a German Army deserter but who was in fact an escapee from a mental hospital. They nearly eloped to Australia.

❖ Great Expectations: Amy Tan's mother expected her to be a neurosurgeon by day and a concert pianist on the side. When she defied those wishes by switching college majors from premed to English, her mother refused to speak to her for six months. As part of their later reconciliation, Tan videotaped her mother for hours as she spoke of her past. The information played a key role in her subsequent writing.

❖ Tan has worked as a language consultant to programs for disabled children. She was also a reporter, managing editor, and associate publisher for *Emergency Room Reports* (now *Emergency Medicine Reports*) and a freelance technical writer for companies such as IBM, AT&T, and Apple Computer.

❖ She began writing fiction (and taking jazz piano lessons) as an antidote to her workaholic lifestyle as a freelance technical writer. Her first efforts were short stories, one of which won her a spot in the Squaw Valley Community of Writers, a fiction writers' workshop. The story, "Rules of the Game," later became part of *The Joy Luck Club*.

❖ Amy Tan's books are assigned reading in many high schools and colleges. *The Joy Luck Club* was selected for the literature portion of the 1992–93 Academic Decathlon, a national scholastic competition for high school students.

❖ Her own all-time favorite books: *Jane Eyre* by Charlotte Brontë, *Love Medicine* by Louise Erdrich, *Annie John* by Jamaica Kincaid, *Lolita* by Vladimir Nabokov, and the dictionary (she says she reads lists of words as though they were stories).

Treatises and Treats

COMPANIONS

Amy Tan: A Critical Companion by E. D. Huntley (Greenwood Publishing, 1998). Explores Tan's first three novels—their characters, language, plot, setting, major themes, and literary devices.

TAN ON TAPE

Amy Tan does the reading for the audiobook versions of her novels and children's books, earning praise from *AudioFile* magazine for her "contrasting American and Chinese accents" that bring the characters vividly to life. The tapes are available from Dove Audio (800-368-3007, www.doveaudio.com) and other audiobook sources.

BEST OF THE NET

www.luminarium.org/contemporary/amytan
A fan page offering biographical information, book excerpts, reviews, interviews, and schedule of upcoming appearances by the author.

Reading List

ALL THE NOVELS

The Joy Luck Club, 1989
    (National Book Award)
The Kitchen God's Wife, 1991
The Hundred Secret Senses, 1995

BOOKS FOR CHILDREN

The Moon Lady, 1992
The Chinese Siamese Cat, 1994

If You Like Amy Tan …

Try Edwidge Danticat, Cristina Garcia, Barbara Kingsolver, Penelope Lively, Toni Morrison, and Gloria Naylor.

Stranger Than Fiction . . .

When she isn't writing, Amy Tan can be found dressed in thigh-high patent-leather boots performing with a band called the Rock Bottom Remainders. Other members of the mostly author group include Dave Barry, Roy Blount Jr., Robert Fulghum, Matt Groening, Stephen King, Barbara Kingsolver, Al Kooper, and Dave Marsh. "The band plays music as well as Metallica writes novels," says Dave Barry.

You can order the group's *Stranger Than Fiction* double CD, tour video, and T-shirts from Don't Quit Your Day Job Records (415-284-6363, www.dqydj.com). The T-shirts feature caricatures by Gretchen Shields, the illustrator for Amy Tan's children's books.

Best Book to Read First

The Joy Luck Club, her first novel and winner of the 1989 National Book Award.

The Joy Luck Club is so powerful, so full of magic, that by the end of the second paragraph, your heart catches; by the end of the first page, tears blur your vision; and one-third of the way down on page 26, you know you won't be doing anything of importance until you have finished this novel.

—Carolyn See,
Los Angeles Times

J. R. R. Tolkien

Born
January 3, 1892, in
Bloemfontein, South
Africa, where his
father, Arthur Reuel
Tolkien, was working
temporarily as a bank
manager. Shortly
before his father's
death in 1896, he
moved with his mother,
Mabel Suffield Tolkien,
to Birmingham,
England, where both
parents' families had
lived for generations.

Full Name
John Ronald Reuel
Tolkien (pronounced
TOLE-keen)

Education
Exeter College, Oxford,
B.A., 1915; M.A.,
1919

Family
Married Edith Mary
Bratt, a pianist, in
1916. Four children:
John, Michael, Christo-
pher, and Priscilla.

Died
September 2, 1973

Publisher
Houghton Mifflin

I n a hole in the ground there lived a hobbit. Not a nasty, dirty, wet hole, filled with the ends of worms and oozy smell, nor yet a dry, bare, sandy hole with nothing in it to sit down on or eat: it was a hobbit hole, and that means comfort." In 1937, J. R. R. Tolkien published *The Hobbit*, introducing the richly imagined world of Middle-Earth, inhabited not just by hobbits, but by elves, dwarves, trolls, and other strange and wonderful creatures, including human beings.

In the years that followed, Tolkien wrote *The Lord of the Rings*, a trilogy that revealed more of this extraordinary place and its inhabitants' struggle against implacable evil. "Wait a minute," you say, "we've all been there and done that." True, but only because Tolkien is the model that the writers of all modern fantasy epics and games strive to emulate. This bookish Oxford don, who was highly respected for his scholarly works, never imagined that his fiction would establish a new genre and make him the central figure in a literary cult. But in the 1960s and 1970s, that's exactly what happened as Baby Boomers went to college. To this day, millions of copies of Tolkien books are bought worldwide every year.

What makes Tolkien so special is that all actions in Middle-Earth take place within clearly defined rules against a fully developed background and history. Magical powers exist, for example, but they are limited. No one can simply wave a wand and make everything right. The details of the past are presented as necessary, but there is never any doubt that these are but the barest tip of a huge iceberg of lore about the world, its peoples, their customs, and the languages they speak. This is why it is so easy to suspend disbelief.

It is also why one readily accepts the idea that some weapons have proper names and histories, like Gandalf's sword Glamdring ("foe-hammer"), which was forged for a king of Gondolin. In a "Conan" or "Xena" book or video, you'd laugh your head off because the idea sounds so lame. But Tolkien makes it real. And he does so with a purpose. *The Hobbit* is a delightful children's tale. But the trilogy is far deeper and far richer.

Good to Know

❖ Orphaned at 14, Tolkien spent several impressionable years in the care of Father Francis Xavier Morgan, a Roman Catholic priest to whom his widowed mother had entrusted his upbringing before her own death. He remained a devout Catholic all his life.

❖ Tolkien served in World War I (1915–18) and later became a professor at Oxford University, teaching Anglo-Saxon (1925–45) and English language and literature (1945–49). His scholarly works include *A Middle English Vocabulary* (1922), an edition of *Sir Gawain and the Green Knight* (1925), and *Beowulf: The Monster and the Critics* (1937).

❖ His fiction grew out of a linguistic exercise when he was a philology major at Oxford. "Elvish," a language of Tolkien's invention, had its own rules, root words, and inflections. Eventually, he created a mythology that matched this tongue, and thus Middle-Earth was born.

❖ Tolkien and close friends C. S. Lewis and Charles Williams were the core of a group that called itself "The Inklings." The group met on Tuesdays at an Oxford pub and on Thursdays at Lewis's home to read aloud from their works in progress, offer critiques, and discuss literature. Other regular members of the group included Owen Barfield, Hugo

Dyson, W. H. Lewis, Nevill Coghill, Christopher Tolkien, and Dorothy L. Sayers. W. H. Auden also stopped by on occasion.

❖ Milwaukee's Marquette University holds most of the manuscripts of *The Hobbit*, *The Lord of the Rings*, *Farmer Giles of Ham*, and *Mr. Bliss*. The University of Texas at Austin and Wheaton College in suburban Chicago both have portions of his correspondence.

Treatises and Treats

THE TOLKIEN SOCIETY

The premier organization for Tolkien readers and scholars, this group publishes a newsletter and journal, hosts annual festivals and special events, and answers Tolkien-related questions from members. Annual fee: £26 (about $42). For more information, contact:
Trevor Reynolds, Membership Secretary
65 Wentworth Crescent
Ash Vale
Surrey GU12 5LF
England
www.tolkiensociety.org

COMPANIONS

Tolkien: A Biography, by Humphrey Carpenter (Ballantine, 1985). Though out of print, this authorized biography is widely available from used bookstores.

J. R. R. Tolkien: Architect of Middle-Earth by Daniel Grotta (Courage Books, 1996). Fans treasure this critical biography, which candidly explores Tolkien's unconventional life, from his traumatic childhood through combat service in World War I, and later as an Oxford professor.

The Atlas of Middle-Earth by Karen Wynn Fonstad (Houghton Mifflin, 1991). A geographer/cartographer uses Tolkien's posthumously published drafts, alternative versions, and notes to compile this exhaustively thorough reference. Mapped by theme, war, timescale, climate, people, and languages.

BEST OF THE NET

J. R. R. Tolkien Information Page
www.csclub.uwaterloo.ca/u/relipper/tolkien/rootpage.html
The mother lode of information for Tolkien readers, this clearinghouse offering links to articles, chat rooms, fan clubs and societies, and more (even "elvish" fonts and graphics).

Best Reads

The Hobbit, 1937

THE LORD OF THE RINGS TRILOGY
The Fellowship of the Ring, 1954
The Two Towers, 1955
The Return of the King, 1956

POSTHUMOUS HIGHLIGHTS
The Father Christmas Letters, edited by Baillie Tolkien, 1976
Pictures, with foreword and notes by Christopher Tolkien, 1979
Unfinished Tales of Numenor and Middle-Earth, edited by Christopher Tolkien, 1980
The Letters of J. R. R. Tolkien, 1981

If You Like Tolkien . . .

Try C. S. Lewis's *Chronicles of Narnia*, Stephen R. Donaldson's *The Chronicles of Thomas Covenant, the Unbeliever*, Marion Zimmer Bradley's "Darkover" series, Terry Brooks's "Shannara" series, and Gene Wolfe's "Book of the New Sun" series.

Best Book to Read First

The Hobbit, featuring Bilbo Baggins, a wizard named Gandalf, a troupe of dwarves, and a dragon named Smaug. Plus a ring that makes its wearer invisible. But that is the least of its (unsuspected) powers. If you don't like *The Hobbit*, you won't like Tolkien.

I think that a fairy story has its own mode of reflecting 'truth...' But first of all it must succeed just as a tale, excite, please, and even on occasion move, and within its own imagined world be accorded literary belief. To succeed in that was my primary object.

—J. R. R. Tolkien

Tolkien on Tape

Many companies offer audiobook versions of Tolkien's works but none can compare with the readings done by Rob Inglis for Recorded Books. Inglis presents *The Hobbit* and *The Lord of the Rings* trilogy with the kind of verbal drama and panache simply not available to readers of the printed page. He not only infuses each character with a unique voice but also adds an entirely new dimension by singing the many songs beautifully. For rentals, contact Recorded Books (800-638-1304, www.recordedbooks.com).

Leo Tolstoy

Born
September 9, 1828, in
Tula Province, Russia,
to Count Nikolay Ilyich
Tolstoy, a retired army
officer and landowner,
and Maria Bolkonskaya
Tolstaya, who died
when he was just two
years old

Full Name
Leo Nikolayevich
Tolstoy

Education
Privately educated by
French and German
tutors; attended the
University of Kazan,
1844–47.

Family
Married in 1862 to
Sofya Andreyevna
Bers, with whom he
had 13 children. His
wife was just 18 at the
time of their marriage;
he was 34.

Died
November 20, 1910,
of pneumonia, at the
railway station in
Astapovo, Russia

Publishers
Dutton
HarperCollins
Modern Library

Leo Tolstoy is one of the most important figures in Russian literary and cultural history. For many years he was famous not only for his writings—novels, short stories, plays, nonfiction—but also for his spirituality. The influence of his moral thought was felt beyond Russia's borders by such figures as George Bernard Shaw, Mohandas "Mohatma" Gandhi, and William Dean Howells. But today, Tolstoy is known for his writing more than his moral authority, particularly his two sprawling masterpieces, *War and Peace* and *Anna Karenina*, and his shorter novel, *The Death of Ivan Ilych*.

Much of Tolstoy's writing is preoccupied with the gap between a life lived in harmony with nature and a life lived according to the false norms of society. His fiction is characterized by its precision of both physical and psychological detail. He often used an "inner monologue" to convey his microscopic observations—a technique some critics have likened to "psychological eavesdropping." Another technique employed brilliantly in *War and Peace* is "decentralization," the use of multiple perspectives in order to provide a sense of objectivity. This was necessary in *War and Peace*, given the novel's more than 600 characters.

While *War and Peace* deals with Napoleon Bonaparte's military campaigns at the beginning of the 19th century, *Anna Karenina* explores questions of love, sex, and marriage. The title character is caught in a loveless marriage to an older man, but when she leaves him for a younger man she discovers that her efforts to find happiness are doomed to failure. *The Death of Ivan Ilych* is the culmination of Tolstoy's lifelong obsession with death. It tells the story of a man faced with the certainty of his own death and is considered a classic of existential literature.

Good to Know

❖ Tolstoy studied Oriental languages and law, but he abandoned his academic pursuits in 1847 before getting a degree and returned home to the family estate, where he spent much of the next four years gambling and carousing.

❖ He served in the Russian army from 1851 to 1856. During that time, he produced his first published work of fiction, the novel *Childhood* (1852).

❖ *War and Peace*, which he started in 1860, took nearly ten years to write and went through many drafts, copied and recopied by his young wife, Sofya. It was originally published in six volumes.

❖ Soon after finishing *War and Peace*, Tolstoy began work on what was to become his second great novel, *Anna Karenina*, another multiyear/multivolume endeavor. Following the success of that book, he became caught up in what his wife called a "disease," an experiment in living according to the rules laid down by Christ. He set out to prove that the Church did not exist in accord with the Gospels, an exercise that eventually led to his excommunication.

❖ In 1891–92, Tolstoy organized a relief effort to aid the starving population of middle Russia. And in 1896, he renounced all rights to his books, personal property, and money (including whatever he might have inherited from his wealthy family).

❖ During Tolstoy's last years, he was surrounded by admirers and disciples, worsening his relationship with his wife. She resisted his efforts to give away his property and literary income and was constantly at odds with his followers. Tolstoy blamed her for his inability to live a simple, spiritual life.

Treatises and Treats

TOLSTOY STUDIES JOURNAL

An annual publication of the Tolstoy Society of North America, featuring scholarly articles, roundtable discussions, news and events, and book reviews. Subscription fee: $10 (individuals), $35 (institutions). For more information and an order form, visit the Society's Web site (www.utoronto.ca/tolstoy) or contact Professor Edwina Cruise, Department of Russian, Mount Holyoke College, South Hadley, MA 01075.

COMPANIONS

Tolstoy: A Biography by A. N. Wilson (Ballantine, 1989). A study of how Tolstoy's art grew out of the three unresolved relationships in his life—with God, with women, and with Russia. *Publishers Weekly* called this biography "a magnificent achievement, a work of seamless scholarship."

The Last Station: A Novel of Tolstoy's Last Year by Jay Parini (Henry Holt, 1998). Set during the last few years of Tolstoy's life, this novel chronicles the conflict between Tolstoy's professed doctrine of poverty and his enormous wealth. Gore Vidal called it "one of the best historical novels written in the last 20 years."

BEST OF THE NET

Tolstoy Library

www.tolstoy.org

An expansive and useful site on Tolstoy, with a biography, discussion board, "Who's Who" list for *War and Peace*, literary criticism and analysis, information on Tolstoy gifts and featured videos, and links to the Tolstoy Foundation and *Tolstoy Studies Journal*.

Best Reads

Family Happiness, 1859
The Cossacks: A Tale of the Caucasus in 1852, 1863
War and Peace, 1864–69
Anna Karenina, 1873–77
Childhood, Boyhood, and Youth, 1876
The Death of Ivan Ilych, 1886
The Kreutzer Sonata, 1891
Master and Man, 1895
Resurrection, 1899
The Devil, 1899

If You Like Leo Tolstoy . . .

You might also enjoy reading Isaac Babel, Feodor Dostoyevsky, Nikolai Gogol, and Boris Pasternak. Also try Flaubert's *Madame Bovary* and Ibsen's *A Doll's House*. And, perhaps, the Robert Fagles translation of *The Iliad* for its portrayal of men at war.

Best Book to Read First

War and Peace, Tolstoy's masterpiece, is considered one of the greatest novels ever written. But if you can't quite bring yourself to crack the spine of such a hefty book, start instead with *The Great Short Works of Leo Tolstoy* (HarperCollins, 1972), which includes an excellent introduction by world-class Tolstoy authority John Bayley.

The truth . . . I care a great deal . . . how they . . .

—Tolstoy's last words

An Obsession with Death

Tolstoy was obsessed with death, frequently filling up notebooks with his observations on battlefield slaughters, executions, and even the deaths of some of his children. When his son Petya died, Tolstoy panicked and fled from his house to Moscow because he thought he might "catch death," as one catches an infection. During the years 1873–75, he lost three children and two aunts, prompting him to write: "It is time to die. That is not true. What *is* true is there is nothing else to do in life but die. I feel it every instant."

Tolstoy's fear of death was so great that often he would begin to tremble and sweat, and he would feel a presence behind his back. But his reaction to his brother Dmitry's death was quite different. He deserted Dmitry in his sickroom, not wanting to look at him. "I honestly believe that what bothered me most about his death," Tolstoy later wrote, "was that it prevented me from attending a performance at Court to which I had been invited." Perhaps this reaction was due to the fact that Dmitry had rejected a spiritual life for one of debauchery.

Born
April 12, 1949, in
Chicago, Illinois, to
David D. Turow, an
obstetrician, and Rita
Pastron Turow, a writer.
Last name is
pronounced "tur-OH."

Education
Amherst College, B.A.
in English, 1970;
Stanford University,
M.A., 1974; Harvard
University, J.D., 1978

Family
Married Annette
Weisberg, an artist, in
1971; three children.

Home
A suburban community
near Chicago, Illinois

Fan Mail
Scott Turow
Sonnenschein, Carlin,
  Nath, and Rosenthal
Sears Tower
Suite 8000
Chicago, IL 60606
scott@scottturow.com

Publisher
Farrar, Straus & Giroux

Scott Turow

Scott Turow started the legal-thriller revolution in 1987 with his bestseller, *Presumed Innocent*, the story of a married, politically connected prosecutor who begins investigating the murder of a woman who was his former lover and ends up being accused of the crime. He was four years ahead of John Grisham, the undisputed current king of the genre, who didn't publish *The Firm* until 1991. But Grisham, a graduate of Mississippi State University (in accounting) and the University of Mississippi Law School, stopped practicing law that same year and began writing full time, producing novels that have sold over 60 million copies.

Why hasn't Turow done equally well? Two reasons (at least). First, Turow is much the better writer, and good writing takes time. (Grisham is a lot of fun, and hats off, he really has grasped and molded the legal-thriller formula. But few would be motivated to read any of his novels a second time.) Second, despite his literary success, Turow has remained a full partner at his law firm, where he often works 60-hour weeks.

This dedication to maintaining a "real job" apparently has deep roots. His parents wanted him to become a doctor. He wanted to be a writer. Amherst and Stanford followed, as did 25 rejection slips for his first (and still unpublished) novel, *The Way Things Are*. Which made him realize "I wasn't one-tenth the writer I hoped to be.... I could not sustain the vision of myself as a writer only." He became convinced that he could not make a living in the U.S. writing serious fiction. "I was never bitter about that. I didn't see why the world had an obligation to support novelists."

On the other hand, producing a first novel that threw off gross proceeds of over $4.2 million, and a second whose paperback rights alone sold for $3.2 million, might make one think seriously about quitting the day job—or at least clocking back. But quitting the law might cut a novelist off from new material, just as it has done with John Grisham. So Scott Turow, lawyer and storyteller, labors on.

Good to Know

❖ Turow's publisher, Farrar, Straus & Giroux, offered $200,000 in 1986 for the rights to his first novel, *Presumed Innocent*. The investment paid off, of course. Turow is currently FSG's bestselling author, no mean accomplishment considering that this is also the house that publishes Tom Wolfe, Philip Roth, and John McPhee.

❖ Instead of writing his novels straight through from beginning to end, Turow typically records interesting anecdotes and vignettes from his daily life and uses these independent stories to form and shape his novels. The cut-and-paste function of his computer's word processor has proven invaluable: "I think that my career as a writer owes a lot to the fact that the computer can organize all of it. You just move those blocks of text around."

❖ The Internet also figures into his writing process. He uses several Web sites, most notably Findlaw (www.findlaw.com), to track down court decisions. He also frequents the *USA Today* site (www.usatoday.com)—not for doing research but to check out their bestseller list!

❖ Turow's very first book was a personal, nonfiction exposé of life at law school. Taking notes throughout his busy class schedule and writing during summer break, he produced

One L: An Inside Account of Life in the First Year at Harvard Law School (Putnam, 1977). Now considered "required reading for anyone contemplating a career in law," the book examines the curriculum, the ideologies promoted by professors, and the competitiveness that develops among fellow law students. It also offers an inside look at what graduates are really qualified to do.

❖ In 1990, Turow became the 92nd writer to grace the cover of *Time* magazine, joining the ranks of literary icons such as Ernest Hemingway, Alex Haley, J. D. Salinger, and John Updike. *Time* dubbed him the "Bard of the Litigious Age." The cover kicked off the media blitz surrounding the release of Turow's second legal thriller, *The Burden of Proof*, and the film version of *Presumed Innocent*, starring Harrison Ford.

❖ Turow says that knowing that his novels are likely to become films does not affect his writing process. "I can't psych out Hollywood. I never can understand the way those people think, and I'm really not devoted to trying."

Treatises and Treats

COMPANIONS

Scott Turow: Meeting the Enemy by Derek Lundy (ECW Press, 1995). Biographical information and analysis of Turow's first three hit novels, *Presumed Innocent*, *The Burden of Proof*, and *Pleading Guilty*.

BEST OF THE NET

Scott Turow Web Site

www.scottturow.com
The official Turow Web site, with a brief biography, book descriptions and excerpts, quotes from the author about how he works and the writers who have influenced him, and book-tour information. The site also includes a link to wife Annette Turow's Web site (www.annetteturow.com), where you can see some of her paintings and learn about her philosophy of art.

Reading List

ALL THE NOVELS

Presumed Innocent, 1987
  (Silver Dagger Award)
The Burden of Proof, 1990
Pleading Guilty, 1993
The Laws of Our Fathers, 1996
Personal Injuries, 1999

NONFICTION

One L: An Inside Account of Life in the First Year at Harvard Law School, 1977

If You Like Scott Turow...

There's always John Grisham, of course. Or try books by some of these legal-thriller authors: David Baldacci, Patricia D. Benke, Joseph T. Klempner, Phillip M. Margolin, Steven Martini, Brad Meltzer, Richard North Patterson, Lisa Scottoline, or Judith Van Gieson.

Best Book to Read First

Presumed Innocent, a tightly plotted, gripping murder and courtroom drama that is also justly considered a work of serious fiction. (The movie was great, too, but read the novel first.)

We talk about literary truths as implausible, fictitious, and yet there's a way in which the mystery novel delivers a truth that real life can't deliver. Often you get that in a trial: the jury says not guilty, and you don't know who did it.

—Scott Turow

Turow on Writing

With degrees from Amherst, Stanford, and Harvard, Scott Turow is an intellect to be reckoned with. Yet he doesn't sound like an academic when he talks about writing. "I don't have a lot of fixed rules," he says. "But I definitely do not have an outline until the later stages. Usually the outline is for the second or third draft."

"I didn't know what the theme of *Presumed Innocent* was until I was finished. I was interested in the resonance of the character, the story . . . the whole gritty courthouse world, that incredibly dense community with its extraordinary network of relationships."

As for why he sets his novels in the fictional Kindle County, he explains, "I didn't want to get stuck with having a geography I couldn't alter. I find novels set in real places, involving fictionalized historical events, to be hokey. I'd rather make the fictional cut at the first level and just say this is a nonexistent place, these are nonexistent people. Now, we're all gonna sit around and agree it's real."

Mark Twain

Born
Born November 30, 1835, in Florida, Missouri, the sixth child of John Marshall Clemens, a lawyer, shopkeeper, and politician, and Jane Lampton Clemens

Real Name
Samuel Langhorne Clemens

Education
Formal schooling till age 12 when he was forced to quit school to help support his family after his father died.

Family
Married in 1870 to Olivia Langdon (died 1904). Of their four children, one died of meningitis, another was epileptic and drowned in the bathtub, and a third suffered a nervous collapse and was forbidden by doctors to communicate with her father.

Home
Childhood in Hannibal, Missouri. Later years with his wife and children in Hartford, Connecticut, where he lived for 20 years.

Died
April 21, 1910, in Redding, Connecticut, of heart disease

Publishers
Library of America
Oxford University Press

The first thing any modern reader needs to know about "Mark Twain" is that he was a construct created by a person named Samuel Clemens. It is a construct that will forever be embodied by Hal Holbrook's wonderful 1967 one-man-show, *Mark Twain Tonight*. The white suit, the nimbus of white hair, the cigar, the rocking chair, and the casually delivered but precisely worded zinger. But Samuel Clemens was much more than Mark Twain, the persona and American icon.

He was undoubtedly happiest as a riverboat pilot, but the Civil War ended traffic on the Mississippi, forcing him to return to being a newspaperman and journalist. He didn't set out to become a great writer, and you never read of him studying past masters. Yet he evolved from being a Western humorist and travel writer to become one of the giants of American literature, producing what many consider *the* Great American Novel, *The Adventures of Huckleberry Finn*.

In this book, as in *The Adventures of Tom Sawyer* that preceded it, Twain defied literary conventions and rules of grammar and allowed his characters to speak in the vernacular. This was unheard of at the time, and it ranks as one of his major influences on American letters. In addition, like all good humorists, Twain was a keen observer of society, and *Huckleberry Finn* has been praised for its insights into racism and slavery. As a result, it was banned in several states in Twain's time. (On hearing that the Concord, Massachusetts library had banned the book, Twain exclaimed, "That will sell 25,000 books for sure!")

Mark Twain was also a superb creator of memorable characters. Characters like Tom Sawyer, Huckleberry Finn, and the escaped slave, Jim, are familiar even to those who haven't read the novels in which they appear. And some scenes, like Tom Sawyer whitewashing the fence and Jim and Huck on the raft, are permanent parts of our culture. Few other authors have had that kind of influence or lasting impact.

Good to Know

❖ It's well known that "Mark Twain" was what a riverboat's leadsman called out when his soundings showed water "two fathoms deep." Most people don't know, however that the 12 feet of water it refers to is a depth just barely safe for navigation. Clemens first used the pseudonym at age 27.

❖ Fleeing Virginia City, Nevada, in 1864 after being challenged to a duel, Twain arrived in San Francisco, where he met Bret Harte and Charles Farrar Browne, who as "Artemus Ward" was one of the most popular humorists and platform lecturers of the day.

❖ A libel suit by the San Francisco police department forced Twain to leave town for the Angels Camp gold mine. There he heard the tale that became "The Celebrated Jumping Frog of Calaveras County," the story that brought him national fame and acclaim in November 1865.

❖ Many of his books were published by subscription houses. Interested readers paid in advance, and only after there were enough subscribers would the book actually be published. Twain himself profitably published Ulysses S. Grant's memoirs this way, a work written by the former president to recover from a devastating financial loss.

❖ Funding the development of an alternative typesetting machine that proved worthless, along with other bad financial decisions, forced Twain into bankruptcy in 1894. He paid every creditor in full by writing *The Tragedy of Pudd'nhead Wilson*, *The Personal Recollections of Joan of Arc*, and *Following the Equator*, and going on a world lecture tour.

Treatises and Treats

SOCIETIES AND SPECIAL EVENTS

Mark Twain Circle of America

A $15 annual membership fee includes a subscription to the quarterly *Mark Twain Circular*, providing news of Twain events and scholarships, commentary, and more. Contact:
Prof. John Bird, Executive Coordinator
Mark Twain Circle
English Department
Winthrop University
Rock Hill, SC 29733
www.citadel.edu/faculty/leonard/
    mtcircular.htm

Mark Twain Days Festival

Sponsored by the Mark Twain House in Hartford, Connecticut, this annual three-day event in August celebrates Mark Twain and Victorian-era Hartford. For more information about the festival and regular tours of the house, call 860-493-6411 or visit www.hartnet.org/~twain/tour.htm.

COMPANIONS

Mark Twain A to Z: The Essential Reference to His Life and Writing by R. Kent Rasmussen (Facts on File, 1995). Over 1,300 entries on Twain, including his major and minor works, characters, friends and family, and even residences.

The Mark Twain Encyclopedia by J. R. Lemaster (Garland, 1993). Over 740 entries covering the private and personal life, including little-known facts about Twain's darker side. "An excellent guide to Twain's life and works for students, scholars, and devotees." (*Booklist*)

Mark Twain: A Biography by Albert Bigelow Paine (Chelsea House, 1997). First published in 1912, this is still considered the "official" Mark Twain biography.

AUDIO/VIDEO

Mark Twain Tonight (Kultur Video, 1999), a 90-minute video of Hal Holbrook's dazzling 1967 television performance. You'll swear you're seeing and hearing the great man himself. A two-cassette audio recording (Audio Partners, 1988) is also available.

BEST OF THE NET

Mark Twain Guide

marktwain.about.com
An impressive collection of links to Twain-related materials—traditional biographical and critical information, bulletin board, chat room, plus other items of interest such as collectibles, Twain impersonators, and used and rare books. Use the site's search feature to access the "Mark Twain FAQ."

Best-Loved Novels

The Adventures of Tom Sawyer, 1876
The Prince and the Pauper, 1881
The Adventures of Huckleberry Finn, 1884
*A Connecticut Yankee in King Arthur's
    Court*, 1889
The Tragedy of Pudd'nhead Wilson, 1894

Best Book to Read First

The Adventures of Huckleberry Finn. Considered by many to be the greatest of all American novels. According to Ernest Hemingway in *The Green Hills of Africa*, "All modern literature comes from [this] one book by Mark Twain."

The Curmudgeon's Guide

A few words of wisdom from Mark Twain for your amusement and/or use:

1. It takes your enemy and your friend, working together, to hurt you to the heart; the one to slander you and the other to get the news to you. (*Following the Equator*)
2. Truth is the most valuable thing we have. Let us economize it. (*ibid.*)
3. Always do right. This will gratify some people and astonish the rest. (Card sent to the Young People's Society, Greenpoint Presbyterian Church, Brooklyn.)
4. Nothing so needs reforming as other people's habits. (*The Tragedy of Pudd'nhead Wilson*)
5. Put all your eggs in one basket and—WATCH THAT BASKET. (*ibid.*)

Anne Tyler

Born
October 25, 1941, in Minneapolis, Minnesota, to Lloyd Parry Tyler, an industrial chemist, and Phyllis Mahon Tyler, a social worker. Much of her childhood was spent among various Quaker communities in the Midwest and South.

Education
At 16, entered Duke University, where she majored in Russian, was elected to Phi Beta Kappa, and graduated in 1961. Graduate study at Columbia University, 1961–62.

Family
Married Taghi Modarressi, an Iranian psychiatrist and writer, in 1963. (He died in 1999.) Two daughters: Tezh and Mitra.

Home
Baltimore, Maryland

Fan Mail
Anne Tyler
c/o Russell & Volkening
50 West 29th Street
New York, NY 10001

Publisher
Knopf

In one of her rare interviews, Anne Tyler told the *New York Times*, "I think of my work as a whole. And really what it seems to me I'm doing is populating a town. Pretty soon it's going to be just full of lots of people I've made up. None of the people I write about are people I know. That would be no fun.... I want to live other lives."

Apparently so do Anne Tyler's readers, many of whom see her as a modern-day Jane Austen and who (like Austen's fans) read and reread her novels again and again. They are addicted to her writing style and marvelous sense of humor. But most of all, they fall in love with the genuinely quirky characters she so skillfully evokes, and her ability to make you care about them as they face the small triumphs and tragedies of everyday life. Focusing on "the minute detail of quotidian existence," Tyler gives us access to the lives of ordinary people: the outsiders, the visionaries, and the lost souls.

Anne Tyler has been compared to Flannery O'Connor, Carson McCullers, and Eudora Welty. But her novels, at once unusual and traditional, are difficult to characterize. Although she was born in Minnesota, most of her fiction takes place in Baltimore, and her novels are "Southern in their sure sense of family and place but lack the taste for violence and the Gothic that often characterizes self-consciously Southern literature." (*New York Times Book Review*)

Although her earlier work was well-received, *Dinner at the Homesick Restaurant*, published in 1982, was Tyler's breakthrough book. It begins with an 85-year-old woman on her deathbed recalling her past and her children. But then the focus widens to include her children as *they* knew their mother and home growing up. As Benjamin De Mott wrote in his *New York Times* review, Anne Tyler "has cre-ated, in her books, a half-dozen individual, idiosyncratically charming, completely believable young women; nobody I know of now writing matches this accomplishment."

The book that brought Anne Tyler fame and commercial success was soon followed by the critically acclaimed *The Accidental Tourist* and Pulitzer Prize–winning *Breathing Lessons*. Succeeding titles were also well received. The *New Yorker*, for example, called *A Patchwork Planet*, "a wonder of construction: everything fits, it's seamless."

Good to Know

❖ Reynolds Price, the prolific North Carolina writer, poet, and critic, encouraged Tyler to pursue her writing career while she was studying at Duke. But, although she wrote and published novels in her 20s, she didn't take writing seriously until 1967 when she began to write full-time.

❖ Tyler dislikes her first two novels, *If Morning Ever Comes* and *The Tin Can Tree*, both of which received some harsh criticism. When asked about these books, she essentially disowns them. (*Dinner at the Homesick Restaurant* is Tyler's favorite.)

❖ Eudora Welty was one of her main literary influences. "She taught me there were stories to be written about the mundane life around me." But Tyler confesses to never thinking about the process of writing, claiming a superstition about examining it too closely.

❖ Time and old age are Tyler obsessions. Her bestselling 1995 novel *Ladder of Years* takes place at a retirement home where residents are moved to increasingly higher floors as they grow older and more infirm.

❖ Several of Anne Tyler's novels have been adapted for television and film, including *The Accidental Tourist*, an award-winning 1988 movie directed by Lawrence Kasdan and starring Kathleen Turner and William Hurt.

Treatises and Treats

COMPANIONS

An Anne Tyler Companion by Robert W. Croft (Greenwood Publishing Group, 1998). Includes an overview of her life and career; alphabetically arranged entries for her works, characters, and prominent themes; and bibliographies, reviews, and critical commentary.

Anne Tyler: A Critical Companion by Paul Bail (Greenwood Publishing Group, 1999). Biographical information, literary influences, and critical discussion of each novel.

Anne Tyler as Novelist, edited by Dale Salwak (University of Iowa Press, 1994). A collection of critical essays on Tyler's writings.

BEST OF THE NET

New York Times Featured Authors

www.nytimes.com/books/specials/author.html Click on "Anne Tyler" for book reviews, articles, and a rare interview with the author, all from the *New York Times* archives. You'll also find a delightful essay by Tyler about her 1980 visit with literary kindred spirit Eudora Welty in Jackson, Mississippi.

Books@Random Reading Group Guides

www.randomhouse.com/resources/rgg.html Tyler's publisher has produced reading guides for two of her novels, *Patchwork Planet* and *Ladder of Years*. Each one includes a plot summary, discussion topics, and a brief author bio.

All the Novels

If Morning Ever Comes, 1964
The Tin Can Tree, 1965
A Slipping-Down Life, 1970
The Clock Winder, 1972
Celestial Navigation, 1974
Searching for Caleb, 1976
Earthly Possessions, 1977
Morgan's Passing, 1980
Dinner at the Homesick Restaurant, 1982
    (PEN/Faulkner Award)
The Accidental Tourist, 1985
    (National Book Critics Circle Award)
Breathing Lessons, 1988
    (Pulitzer Prize)
Saint Maybe, 1991
Ladder of Years, 1995
Tumble Tower, 1993 (illustrated by daughter Mitra Modarressi)
A Patchwork Planet, 1998

If You Like Anne Tyler . . .

You might also like books and stories by these authors: John Cheever, Pat Conroy, Gail Godwin, Nadine Gordimer, Alice Hoffman, Carson McCullers, Sue Miller, Flannery O'Connor, Alice Walker, and Eudora Welty.

Best Book to Read First

The Accidental Tourist (winner of the 1986 National Book Critics Circle Award). Masterfully combining the tragedy and comedy that appear in previous books, it recounts the story of a man whose attempts to keep the world from changing fall short when he's confronted with his own tragedy at home.

Tyler is especially gifted at the art of freeing her characters and then keeping track of them as they move in their unique and often solitary orbits. Her fiction is filled with displaced persons who persist stubbornly in their own destinies.

—Gail Godwin,
New York Times

Index Cards: White and Unlined

When she was raising her children, Anne Tyler would write from precisely 8:05 A.M. until 3:30 P.M., when school let out. At other times, she would jot down her thoughts on white, unlined index cards. "There are cards scattered in almost every room of the house," wrote a reporter for the *New York Times* following a 1977 interview. "And ballpoint pens. The pen in the bedroom has a light on it. The cards—with their random thoughts trapped—are eventually filed in one of two small metal boxes. . . . Her novels are written in longhand with a Parker ballpoint pen on white paper attached to a clipboard. 'I used to use Bics,' says Tyler, 'but after a few hours the ridges became painful.'"

John Updike

Born
March 18, 1932, in Reading, Pennsylvania. Father was a junior high school math teacher; mother, Linda Grace Hoyer, an aspiring author (one novel, *Enchantment*, 1971).

Education
Harvard University, A.B. in English (summa cum laude), 1954. Also studied at the Ruskin School of Drawing and Fine Art in Oxford, England.

Family
Married second wife Martha Bernhard in 1977. Four children from his 24-year first marriage to Mary Pennington (divorced, 1977), and three stepchildren.

Home
A seaside house in Beverly, Massachusetts, just north of Boston, where he writes for about three hours each day (10 A.M. to 1 P.M.). Prefers to write with a pencil instead of his word processor because "you can sneak into your imagination a little easier."

Publisher
Knopf

John Updike's essays, short stories, novels, and poetry have earned him nearly every major American literary award. He is one of only three Americans to win two Pulitzer Prizes. (The other two are Booth Tarkington and William Faulkner.) All that's left is the Nobel Prize in Literature.

Although he has written on many topics, by his own admission, "My subject is the American Protestant small town middle class." Probably the best quick handle on Updike is that he is a poet who writes bestselling novels. Some critics complain about thin plot lines or, as one put it, that "Updike's fiction is not overburdened by action." But virtually no one denies his exceptional powers of observation and his absolute mastery of language. As another critic said, "His work is worth reading if for no reason other than to enjoy the piquant phrase, the lyric vision, the fluent rhetoric."

Good to Know

❖ Updike grew up in Shillington, Pennsylvania, a small town near Reading, and on an 80-acre farm in nearby Plowville. Encouraged to write by his mother, he fictionalized Shillington as the town of Olinger and used Reading as the model for Brewer in his novels and stories.

❖ Co-valedictorian of his high school class, he was awarded a scholarship to Harvard, where he wrote and drew cartoons for the *Harvard Lampoon*. He did his senior essay on Cavalier poet Robert Herrick.

❖ Soon after graduating from Harvard, Updike sold his first piece to the *New Yorker* (a short story called "Friends from Philadelphia"). He went on to the Ruskin School of Drawing and Fine Art at Oxford. While in England, he met E. B. White, who hired him as a staff writer for the *New Yorker's* "The Talk of the Town" column.

❖ Updike left the magazine in 1957 and moved to Ipswich, Massachusetts (fictionalized as Tarbox in *Couples*), to write full-time. His first novel, *The Poorhouse Fair*, was scheduled to be published by Harper in 1958. But rather than change the ending as the publisher requested, Updike took the book to Knopf, where he has remained ever since.

❖ Updike has twice made the cover of *Time* magazine. The first was April 26, 1968, for a cover story called "The Adulterous Society," pegged to his book *Couples*, which had been published earlier that year. The second was October 18, 1982, for a cover story entitled "Going Great at 50."

Treatises and Treats

COMPANIONS

John Updike Revisited by James A. Schiff (Twayne, 1998). Considered one of the best overall surveys of Updike's work, especially for new readers.

The John Updike Encyclopedia by Jack De Bellis, soon to be published by Greenwood Press. Professor De Bellis, who teaches English at Lehigh University in Bethlehem, Pennsylvania, has been called "one of the most knowledgeable and obsessed of Mr. Updike's devoted readers." His 800-page encyclopedia will include descriptions of each of Updike's books, along with discussions of major characters, themes, and images. There will also be entries devoted to Updike's family, friends, associates, fellow writers, and critics.

AUTOBIOGRAPHY AND BIBLIOGRAPHIES

Self-Consciousness: Memoirs by John Updike (Knopf, 1989). Six essays in which the author talks with candor and humor about growing up in Shillington, his struggles with psoriasis and a sporadic stammer, the consequences of fame and recognition, and other aspects of his life and work.

John Updike: A Bibliography by C. Clarke Taylor (Kent State University Press, 1968). Covering the period from 1949 to 1967, this is the definitive source for publishing details on Updike's early writings, including contributions to his high school paper *The Chatterbox* and to the *Harvard Lampoon.*

John Updike: A Bibliography, 1967–1993 by Jack De Bellis (Greenwood Press, 1994). Picks up where the Taylor bibliography leaves off, providing details on published works by and about John Updike, including his many unsigned pieces that have appeared in the *New Yorker* and elsewhere.

BEST OF THE NET

The Centaurian

www.users.fast.net/~joyerkes

A rich and well-organized collection of "Updikiana," created and maintained by Professor James Yerkes of Moravian College. Illustrated chronology of Updike's life and literary achievements, information about upcoming public appearances, selected reviews and essays. Also a discussion area for sharing thoughts with other readers.

John Updike Life & Times Page

www.nytimes.com/books/97/04/06/
lifetimes/updike.html

A *New York Times* feature with some 40 reviews of Updike's books dating back to 1959, along with two entertaining voice interviews conducted by Terry Gross, host of *Fresh Air* on National Public Radio.

Best Reads

HARRY ANGSTROM SERIES

Rabbit, Run, 1960
Rabbit Redux, 1971

Rabbit Is Rich, 1981
    (Pulitzer Prize, American Book Award, National Book Critics Circle Award)
Rabbit at Rest, 1990
    (Pulitzer Prize, National Book Critics Circle Award)

HENRY BECH SERIES

Bech: A Book, 1970
Bech Is Back, 1982
Bech at Bay: A Quasi-Novel, 1998

OTHER NOVELS

The Poorhouse Fair, 1959
The Centaur, 1963
    (National Book Award)
Couples, 1968
Marry Me: A Romance, 1976
The Coup, 1978
The Witches of Eastwick, 1984

If You Like John Updike...

You might like the novels of British writer Henry Green (*Blindness*, *Party Going*, *Loving*), whose work Updike has said "made more of a stylistic impact upon me than those of any other writer in English, living or dead." Also try Nicholson Baker's *U and I: A True Story*, a comically self-obsessed book about its author's fixation on Updike from age 15 on.

Best Book to Read First

Rabbit, Run. Like all great books, it offers images and characters that will remain with you the rest of your life. It's an excellent introduction to two 20th-century icons—Harry "Rabbit" Angstrom and John Updike.

I read all through my adolescence for escape. From the age of 12 I had my own library card to the Reading Public Library, a beautiful, palatial haven; for . . . I loved books, their bindings, their order, their fragrance. I read all the books the library had by Erle Stanley Gardner, Ellery Queen, Agatha Christie, and John Dickson Carr, in that order. Also humorists: Benchley, Thurber, Leacock, Perelman. Fifty books by P. G. Wodehouse I consumed . . .

—John Updike,
in "Nineteen Forties"
(1965)

Unmistakable Style

I deally, I'd only write poems," Updike once said, "but they're a luxury that must be maintained by other means." Here's a good example of his unmistakable poetic prose from *Rabbit at Rest*:

In this cumbersome sandstone church with its mismatched new wing . . . he was baptized and confirmed, in a shirt that chafed his neck like it had been starched in lye, and here, further along Central . . . he first felt himself in love, with Margaret Schoelkopf . . . His heart had felt numb and swollen above the sidewalk squares like one of those zeppelins you used to see in the sky, the squares of cement like city blocks far beneath his floating childish heart.

Gore Vidal

Born
October 3, 1925, at
the U.S. Military
Academy, West Point,
New York, to Eugene
Luther Vidal, director of
civil aviation under
President Franklin
Roosevelt, and Nina
Gore Vidal

Full Name
Eugene Luther Gore
Vidal

Pseudonym
Edgar Box (mysteries)

Education
Attended St. Albans.
Graduated from Phillips
Exeter Academy, 1943.
No college.

Family
Howard Austen, his
partner of close to five
decades

Home
La Rondinaia, a villa in
Ravello, Italy; and Los
Angeles, California

Fan Mail
Gore Vidal
c/o Owen Laster
William Morris Agency
1350 Avenue of the
    Americas
New York, NY 10019

Publisher
Random House

Gore Vidal has been one of the most unabashed, outrageous, politically aggressive, outspoken novelists of this century, gaining many fans and also many detractors along the way. Called "the Gentleman Bitch of American Letters" by the *New Republic*'s Stefan Kanfer, Vidal is known for his eloquence, intelligence, and biting satire, as well as his attacks on the cultural and political establishment. He was instantly recognized as a talented writer with the publication of his first novel *Williwaw* (1946) at age 21. His third novel, *The City and the Pillar* (1948), immediately appeared on bestseller lists, and its subject matter—the naturalness of homosexual relations—stirred controversy in the New York publishing world.

In 1964 Vidal wrote his first historical novel, *Julian*, introducing the style that has become his trademark—a style characterized by "cutting remarks, catty asides, ribald jokes...[and the] humorous interjection of the trivial and the personal into an impeccably researched historical novel," in the words of one critic. "[Vidal] can make old facts look like contemporary gossip. And he takes wicked pleasure in turning accepted notions about the past upside down," said another.

The many historical novels that followed focus on subjects ranging from the fourth-century Roman Empire to Persian courts to American political history. Several were bestsellers, and when *Lincoln* appeared in 1984, it was considered must reading for politicians.

Vidal has also written satires about American culture, the most popular of which is *Myra Breckinridge* (1968), which takes on almost everything, especially our culture's views of sexuality. John Weightman's praise of this novel in *Observer Review* may also be a perfect way to sum up Vidal's life and career:

"It is a queer, queer book, a virtuoso exercise in kinkiness, a draught of fizzy hemlock, a strikingly intelligent attempt to go as far as possible in outrageousness."

Good to Know

❖ After a scathing *New York Times* review of his controversial 1948 novel about the homosexual demimonde, *The City and the Pillar*, and after the *Times* refused to advertise the novel and gave negative reviews to the books that followed, Vidal resorted to publishing several mystery novels under the pseudonym Edgar Box.

❖ Vidal moved to Hollywood in the mid-1950s after his next five novels failed. He planned to work for five years to make enough money to last him the rest of his life. (It took him closer to ten years.) He wrote lots of Golden Age of Television teleplays, plus films, including *I Accuse, Suddenly Last Summer* (with Tennessee Williams), *Is Paris Burning?* (with Francis Ford Coppola), and *Ben-Hur*.

❖ He's famous for his verbal brawling with such literary heavyweights as William F. Buckley, Norman Mailer, and Truman Capote. He once sued Capote for libel and won. "Truman could not tell you the truth about anything," says Vidal. "He was a psychopath, and the lies would get crazier and crazier."

❖ Vidal says that the secret to his decades-long companionship with Howard Austen is that they never have sex with each other. "If you're not in the business of baby making," he says, "the anonymous or paid encounter is far more satisfactory. It takes so much time the other way." He claims to have had legions of sexual partners, most of whom he did not know. One he *did* know: Jack Kerouac, who agreed with Vidal that they "owed it to literary history to couple."

❖ A bit of gossip: Vidal's maternal grandfather was Oklahoma Senator Thomas Gore. The author is a distant cousin of Vice President Al Gore. His mother was beautiful, alcoholic, and promiscuous. She left to marry Hugh Auchincloss, later stepfather to Jacqueline Kennedy Onassis. Vidal had romantic (though sexless) attachments to actress Claire Bloom (to whom he dedicated his novel *1876*) and *Delta of Venus* author Anaïs Nin.

Treatises and Treats

COMPANIONS

Gore Vidal: A Critical Companion, edited by Susan Baker and Curtis S. Gibson (Greenwood Press, 1997). The first full-length study of Vidal's work to cover his most recent novels. Includes a biographical sketch of Vidal, and groups his novels into two categories: historical fiction and social satire.

The Essential Gore Vidal, edited by Fred Kaplan (Random House, 1999). Selected Vidal writings, as well as critical essays and reviews.

Gore Vidal: A Biography by Fred Kaplan (Doubleday, 1999). Kaplan, who has written biographies of Dickens, Carlyle, and Henry James, was invited by Vidal to write this book and given complete access to the author and his papers. "The facts are all there," according to a *New York Times* review. "Making the facts freely available, though, Mr. Vidal keeps successful control of the insights. His openness is pre-emptive: a tour of a shrewdly arranged Potemkin village."

BEST OF THE NET

New York Times Featured Authors
www.nytimes.com/books/specials/author.html
Includes articles by and about Vidal, reviews of most of his books, excerpts from his work, and links to other sites.

Best Book to Read First

Lincoln, published in 1984 with an extraordinary 200,000-copy first printing. Described by one reviewer as "a momentous fictional biography," the book's intelligence, wit, humor, and outrageousness are quintessential Vidal.

A Political Life

A s the Democratic candidate for Congress in New York in 1960 (encouraged to run by President Kennedy), Gore Vidal received more votes than any other upstate Democrat in 50 years. He ran for nomination as Democratic senatorial candidate in California in 1982 and finished second. He also originated the idea of the Peace Corps. "The only thing I've ever really wanted in my life was to be President," he once told *Time* magazine.

Vidal had a role in the satirical movie *Bob Roberts*, playing an incumbent politician. Says Vidal: "I realized I was playing my grandfather [Oklahoma Senator Thomas Gore]." But despite his interest in all things political, he has not participated in a presidential election since 1964, when he voted for Lyndon Johnson, "the peace candidate," and later vowed never to be so taken in again.

Best Reads

Williwaw, 1946
The City and the Pillar, 1948
Julian, 1964
Washington, D.C., 1967
Myra Breckinridge, 1968
Burr, 1973
Myron, 1974
1876, 1976
Lincoln, 1984
Empire, 1987
Hollywood, 1990

If You Like Gore Vidal ...

You might also like Margaret George, whose historical novels about the lives of Cleopatra, Henry VIII, and Mary Queen of Scots are well-researched and richly detailed page-turners. Also try Colleen McCullough's novels about ancient Rome (*The First Man in Rome*, et al.) and T. C. Boyle's wickedly funny *The Road to Wellville*.

Gore Vidal isn't what I set out to be. Early on I wanted to be Franklin Roosevelt, and then as I realized I had to make a choice I saw myself more in the great tradition, somebody like Thomas Mann, going on and on into my old age turning everything into literature like a bivalve collecting sea water. But I don't mind what I've become. My God, what a lucky life. I do exactly what I want to do and I've made a living—which you're not supposed to do if you write the way you want to. I've had really great luck.

—Gore Vidal, in an interview for *Newsweek*

Kurt Vonnegut

Born
November 11, 1922,
in Indianapolis,
Indiana, to Kurt
Vonnegut Sr., an archi-
tect, and Edith Lieber
Vonnegut

Education
Cornell University,
1940–42; Carnegie
Institute of Technology
(now Carnegie-Mellon
University) 1943; and
University of Chicago,
1945–47, M.A., 1971

Family
Married Jane Marie
Cox in 1945 (divorced,
1979). Married photog-
rapher Jill Kremetz in
1979. Three children
from his first marriage
and four adopted
children.

Home
An apartment on New
York City's East Side
and a getaway cottage
in the Hamptons

Fan Mail
Kurt Vonnegut
c/o Donald C. Farber
Hartman & Craven
460 Park Avenue
New York, NY 10022

Publisher
Putnam

Kurt Vonnegut, known as "K" to his family and friends, is among the most popular and respected authors living today. His rich satires, packed with both jokes and provocative philosophical ideas, helped raise what many call "science fiction" from the level of pulp paperbacks to bestselling hardback fiction.

Vonnegut's narrative view is almost always off-center, cockeyed, and yet accurate and perceptive on some fundamental level. Things typically begin "normally" and then spin off into unusual but seemingly plausible situations. At the end of *The Sirens of Titan*, for example, you really will believe (for at least a minute or two) that Earth was created for the sole purpose of helping some very patient interstellar visitors send a galactic telegram. That and only that, Vonnegut proposes, is the meaning of human/earthly life.

Though his books are often shelved in the science fiction section, Vonnegut is not really part of that genre. Like Ray Bradbury, Rod Serling, and possibly Gene Wolfe, he has created his own genre—with a viewpoint, voice, and imaginative reality all his own. It is a reality that grows from moral, social, and political ideas that can be summed up in his character Eliot Rosewater's statement, "Goddamn it, you've got to be kind," (from *God Bless You, Mr. Rosewater*, 1965).

Good to Know

❖ Before becoming a bestselling author, Vonnegut worked as a police reporter in Chicago, a publicist for GE's research labs, an English teacher on Cape Cod, a salesman of space-age technology, a copywriter for an advertising agency, and a Saab dealership manager.

❖ After holding teaching positions at Harvard and the University of Iowa's Writers Workshop in the late 1960s and early '70s, Vonnegut settled permanently in New York City. Like many of the socially elite mocked in his novels, he also keeps a cedar-shingle cottage in the Hamptons.

❖ With his success in writing novels and short stories, Vonnegut lived out the dream of his mother, a failed writer. (Upset by her own shortcomings, she committed suicide in 1944.) Prone to bouts of depression, Vonnegut attempted to follow in his mother's footsteps and tried to kill himself by overdosing on barbiturates 40 years after her death. Now firm in his belief that the only respectable form of suicide is smoking, he goes through several packs a day.

❖ A POW and Purple Heart recipient during World War II, Vonnegut admits that in real life he is ambivalent about the pacifism he promotes in his novels. Once asked what person in American history he would most like to be, he named Joshua Lawrence Chamberlain, a college professor from Maine and Civil War colonel whose heroic deeds in the Battle of Gettysburg were recounted in Michael Shaara's 1993 Pulitzer Prize–winning *The Killer Angels*.

❖ After years of filling pages of his books with his doodles and drawings, Vonnegut purchased a silk-screen printer. Working in a shed beside his Hamptons house, he prints out cartoons, starbursts, and self-portraits. Several galleries have held shows for his pictures, which have sold for upwards of $1,500.

Treatises and Treats

COMPANIONS

The Vonnegut Encyclopedia by Marc Leeds and Kurt Vonnegut (Greenwood Press, 1994). A comprehensive catalog of the characters, themes, phrasing, and imagery found in Vonnegut's novels, short stories, plays, and essays.

The Vonnegut Chronicles: Interviews and Essays, edited by Peter Reed and Marc Leeds (Greenwood Press, 1996). This collection of 11 essays and three interviews with the master himself is a celebration and retrospective of Vonnegut's work.

AUDIOTAPES

Kurt Vonnegut Jr. Audio Collection (HarperCollins, 1995). Vonnegut himself reads *Breakfast of Champions*, *Cat's Cradle*, *Slaughterhouse Five*, and three of his short stories on this four-cassette compilation.

BEST OF THE NET

Vonnegut Web

www.duke.edu/~crh4/vonnegut

It's Vonnegut infomania! Replete with archives of "Vonnegut writings from forgotten places," individual pages for each book, biographical information, and annotated bibliography. Start by clicking on "Frequently Asked Questions," the official FAQ of the Kurt Vonnegut discussion group (alt.books.kurt-vonnegut).

New York Times Featured Authors

www.nytimes.com/books/specials/author.html

This is another good source of Vonnegut book reviews, articles, and interviews, including a couple that are available as RealAudio files that you can play through your computer's speakers.

Reading List

ALL THE NOVELS

Player Piano, 1952
The Sirens of Titan, 1959
Mother Night, 1961
Cat's Cradle, 1963
God Bless You, Mr. Rosewater, 1965
Slaughterhouse Five, 1969
Breakfast of Champions, 1973

Slapstick, 1976
Jailbird, 1979
Deadeye Dick, 1982
Galapagos, 1985
Bluebeard, 1987
Hocus Pocus, 1990
Timequake, 1997

SHORT-STORY COLLECTIONS

Canary in a Cathouse, 1961
Welcome to the Monkey House, 1968

If You Like Kurt Vonnegut . . .

Take a look at William Gibson's *The Difference Engine*, a novel that wonders what the world would be like if Charles Babbage and Lady Augusta Ada Lovelace, the daughter of Lord Byron, had succeeded in their attempt to create a computer in 1855. You might also like books by J. G. Ballard, Donald Barthelme, William S. Burroughs, Joseph McElroy, and Tom Robbins.

Best Book to Read First

Slaughterhouse Five, his most innovative, most powerful, and most touching novel. Though much shorter, it ranks with *Catch-22* in its ability to make you see the absurdity of war. And laugh at our sorry human race. "So it goes."

To be literate is like trying to play French horn for a symphony orchestra. And people learned how to do it because there was nothing else to do in the winter. But Christ, now television does a wonderful job of just making the time pass.

—Kurt Vonnegut

Wear Sunscreen!

It was the first e-mail to be recorded as a pop song. Forwarded across the Internet and back, the 1997 MIT commencement address was classic Vonnegut, beginning with the opening line: "Ladies and gentlemen of the class of 1997: Wear sunscreen . . . be kind to your knees, you'll miss them when they're gone. Floss. Keep your old love letters; throw away your old bank statements . . ."

It wasn't until Australian director Baz Luhrmann contacted the novelist about buying the rights for use in a pseudo-rap song that the actual author became widely known. The text originated as a column by Mary Schmich of the *Chicago Tribune*. She says she wrote the whole thing "while high on coffee and M&M's." The hoax began when someone known as "Culprit Zero" put Vonnegut's name on Schmich's mock commencement address and began circulating it on the Net. Just about everyone was duped. Someone e-mailed Vonnegut's own wife a copy, and she was so impressed by her husband's cleverness that she forwarded it to all his children.

Luhrmann, director of *Romeo + Juliet* and *Strictly Ballroom*, bought the rights from the newspaper, and in the spring of 1999, "Everybody's Free (to Wear Sunscreen)" rocketed to the top of the American pop music charts.

Alice Walker

Born
February 9, 1944, in
Eatonton, Georgia, to
sharecroppers Willie
Lee Walker and Minnie
Grant Walker

Full Name
Alice Malsenior Walker

Education
Attended Spelman
College, 1961–63;
Sarah Lawrence
College, B.A., 1965.

Family
Married in 1967 to civil
rights lawyer Melvyn
Leventhal, with whom
she has a daughter.
Divorced 1976.

Home
San Francisco,
California

Fan Mail
Alice Walker
c/o Joan Mira
327 25th Avenue, #3
San Francisco, CA
    94121

Publisher
Random House

Alice Walker has earned critical and popular acclaim as a major American novelist and intellectual. Though best known for her novels, she is an equally talented poet and essayist. She writes of the struggle of the human spirit to grow and flourish in dignity, even in the most undignified situations. Her central characters are almost always black women, who she feels are among America's greatest unsung heroes. But she speaks powerfully about the universal female experience because, according to Gloria Steinem, she is "able to pursue it across boundaries of race and class."

Walker's first novel, *The Third Life of Grange Copeland* (1970), examines the effects of racism on three generations of a family of black sharecroppers in rural Georgia in the 1920s. *Meridian*, published six years later in 1976, is often cited as the best novel of the civil rights movement. But it was her 1982 Pulitzer Prize–winning third novel, *The Color Purple*, and the subsequent film adaptation, that brought Walker to the attention of mainstream America. The book also provoked a hailstorm of criticism and controversy for its sexually explicit content and negative portrayal of black men. Nevertheless, Peter S. Prescott in *Newsweek* described it as "an American novel of permanent importance, that rare sort of book which (in Norman Mailer's felicitous phrase) amounts to 'a diversion in the fields of dread.'"

Throughout her career, Walker has received her fair share of accolades from fans and censure from critics. Neither has influenced her choice of subject matter. In recent years she has tackled the controversial practice of female genital mutilation in African, Asian, and Middle Eastern countries in both fiction (*Possessing the Secret of Joy*, 1992)

and nonfiction (*Warrior Marks: Female Genital Mutilation and the Sexual Blinding of Women*, 1993). Her dedication to exposing oppression and using her writing as a vehicle for activism prompted University of Pennsylvania scholar Houston A. Baker Jr. to proclaim her a writer unlike any other in American letters today.

Good to Know

❖ While playing "cowboys and Indians" with her brothers, eight-year-old Alice was accidentally shot in her right eye with a BB-gun pellet, blinding her in that eye. Six years later, brother Bill paid for his sister to have the "cataract" removed, but her sight never returned.

❖ After graduation from Sarah Lawrence College, Walker moved to Mississippi and met and married Melvyn Leventhal, a Jewish civil rights lawyer. In 1967, they were the only legally married interracial couple living in Jackson, Mississippi.

❖ The filming of *The Color Purple* was one of the high points of Walker's life, but it was also a time fraught with difficulty. First, Spielberg rejected her screenplay of the book and chose to use a script with which Walker was not entirely happy. Then she was diagnosed with Lyme disease. She writes about the experience in her book *The Same River Twice: Honoring the Difficult* (1996).

❖ Walker remembers three gifts her mother bought for her with her meager income: a sewing machine so she could make her own clothes, a suitcase so she could travel, and a typewriter so she could write.

❖ Years later, when Walker's daughter was born, her mother presented her with another gift: cuttings from a 37-year-old petunia bush. Minnie Walker had rescued the lone petunia from the front yard of a deserted house. The bush accompanied the family through 12 moves, never failing to bloom each spring. Walker's poem "Revolutionary Petunias" was inspired in part by this true story of the petunia's adaptability and perseverance, qualities that she also associates with black people.

Treatises and Treats

COMPANIONS

Alice Walker: Critical Perspectives: Past and Present, edited by Henry Louis Gates Jr. and K. A. Appiah (Amistad, 1993). This anthology, the first of six volumes of literary criticism in the Amistad Literary Series, includes reviews, essays, and interviews that provide a highly personalized account of the author and her craft.

Banned by Alice Walker (Aunt Lute Books, 1996). Presents the full text of two of Walker's award-winning but controversial stories, "Roselily" and "Am I Blue," along with an introduction by Patricia Holt (*San Francisco Chronicle Book Review*), who traces the series of events that led to their being censored in California. Offers insight into literary censorship in general as well as the controversies surrounding Alice Walker's work.

Alice Walker by Donna Haisty Winchell (Twayne, 1992). A comprehensive study of Walker's first four novels and other writings.

BEST OF THE NET

Anniina's Alice Walker Page

www.luminarium.org/contemporary/alicew
A good starting point, this fan page includes a biography, list of works, links to Alice Walker interviews and reviews, and other Web resources.

Voices from the Gaps: Alice Walker

voices.cla.umn.edu/authors/alicewalker.html
Another good source of information about Alice Walker's life and work, created at the University of Minnesota.

New York Times Featured Authors

www.nytimes.com/books/specials/author.html
Check here for an excellent collection of book reviews, articles, and interviews with Alice Walker that you can listen to on your computer.

All the Novels

The Third Life of Grange Copeland, 1970
Meridian, 1976
The Color Purple, 1982
  (Pulitzer Prize, American Book Award)
The Temple of My Familiar, 1989
Possessing the Secret of Joy, 1992
By the Light of My Father's Smile, 1998

If You Like Alice Walker...

Try Maya Angelou's *I Know Why the Caged Bird Sings* and Toni Morrison's *Beloved*. You might also like Harlem Renaissance writers Zora Neale Hurston (*Their Eyes Were Watching God*), Nella Larsen (*Quicksand, Passing*), and Dorothy West (*The Wedding*).

Best Book to Read First

The Color Purple, Walker's most famous book, won both the Pulitzer Prize and the American Book Award. Steven Spielberg made it into a 1985 film starring Whoopi Goldberg.

I believe in listening— to a person, the sea, the wind, the trees, but especially to young black women whose rocky road I am still traveling.

—Alice Walker

Remembering Those Who Came Before

While a professor at Wellesley in the 1970s, Alice Walker began the first women's studies course in the nation. Though she included writers like Kate Chopin and Virginia Woolf, Walker made a special point of introducing her students to black women writers—Zora Neale Hurston, Nella Larsen, Ann Petry, Frances Watkins Harper, Dorothy West, and others. She holds a special admiration for Hurston, one of "the least appreciated writers of this century."

Walker wrote a 1975 article for *Ms.* magazine entitled "In Search of Zora Neale Hurston" that helped to renew interest in the Harlem Renaissance writer's work. She also saw to it that a headstone was placed on her previously unmarked grave in Florida. (She had to pass herself off as Hurston's illegitimate niece to accomplish this task.)

Evelyn Waugh

Born
October 28, 1903, in West Hampstead, London, to Arthur Waugh, an editor and publisher, and Catherine Raban Waugh

Full Name
Evelyn Arthur St. John Waugh (first name pronounced "EVE-lun," last name rhymes with "law")

Education
Hertford College, Oxford, 1921–24 (expelled for poor grades); Heatherley's Art School, 1924

Family
First marriage (1928–30) to the Honorable Evelyn Gardiner was annulled. Married second wife Laura Herbert, granddaughter of the Earl of Carnarvon, in 1937. Seven children, the first of whom, Auberon, became a writer. Several grandchildren are also writers.

Home
Combe Florey, his house in Somerset, England

Died
April 10, 1966

Publisher
Little, Brown

In these days of political correctness, perhaps no one is so refreshing a read as the scathingly satirical British writer Evelyn Waugh, whom American critic Edmund Wilson called "the only first-rate comic genius that has appeared in English since Bernard Shaw." Waugh's sneering send-ups of the travails of London's elite belie his dedication to the aristocratic traditions that were the bedrock of English society.

At 25, Waugh wrote *Decline and Fall*, which loosely parallels his own youthful false starts, including expulsion from Oxford and exposure to perceived indignity at every turn that followed. Military service and work as a war correspondent in Africa led to *Scoop* and *Black Mischief*, novels that spoof journalism and politics. And *A Handful of Dust* turns a darkly comical mirror on the adulterous end of his first marriage.

But *Brideshead Revisited*, published in 1945, is his magnum opus. Chronicling decades in the decline of the upper-crust Marchmain family, this controversial best-seller disappointed some critics with its sentimental story and its genuflections before the aristocracy and the Catholic faith. (Waugh himself had become a passionate convert to Roman Catholicism in 1930.) Nonetheless, the novel has been an enduring favorite over the years, and enjoyed renewed popularity in the 1980s as a highly acclaimed TV miniseries starring Anthony Andrews and Jeremy Irons.

Good to Know

❖ With a father in publishing and a brother who was a successful novelist, Waugh began his writing career in somewhat of a spotlight.

But he quickly distinguished himself as something more than "Alec Waugh's brother." Still, he remained defensive about charges that he felt competitive with his sibling. Later in life, he sued the *Daily Express* for claiming he was professionally jealous of Alec—and won. With the proceeds, he commissioned a Wilton rug.

❖ During his Oxford days, Waugh experimented with homosexuality and drank heavily, ignoring his studies until at last he was asked to leave. After a brief stint as an art student, he took a teaching job at Arnold House in North Wales; he was fired from this and two similar positions in the ensuing two years. "I have always been a dud," he said.

❖ When Great Britain declared war in 1939, Waugh enlisted in the Royal Marines and later became a major in the Commandos, fighting in Crete, North Africa, and Yugoslavia. There, as he hid in a cave, the proofs of *Brideshead Revisited* were air-dropped for his review.

❖ The father of seven, Waugh is known for relentless vitriole on the subject of children: "I abhor their company because I can only regard children as defective adults, hate their physical ineptitude, find their jokes flat and monotonous….I do not see them until luncheon, as I have my breakfast alone in the library, and they are in fact well trained to avoid my part of the house; but I am aware of them from the moment I wake. Luncheon is very painful."

❖ Waugh never learned to drive an automobile and disliked using the telephone. In his later years, he used an ear trumpet to correct his failing hearing. Ever the dandy, he wore well-cut tweeds; round, metal spectacles; and a bowler hat over slicked-back hair.

❖ Three of Waugh's books made the Modern Library's list of the top 100 English novels of the 20th century: *A Handful of Dust* (34), *Scoop* (75), and *Brideshead Revisited* (80).

Treatises and Treats

COMPANIONS

Evelyn Waugh: A Biography by Selena Hastings (Houghton Mifflin, 1995). Though not personally acquainted with her subject, the author sees her role as giving "as close an impression as possible of what it was like to know Evelyn Waugh."

The Brideshead Generation: Evelyn Waugh and His Friends by Humphrey Carpenter (Houghton Mifflin, 1990). Some might say Waugh's irascibility made him incapable of friendship, but he nonetheless is associated with a circle of Oxford contemporaries—Harold Acton, Cyril Connolly, Graham Greene, and others—who were like-minded in their resistance to social change. The book's title is misleading, however, since this is actually a study of Waugh's entire life and work.

Will This Do? by Auberon Waugh (Carroll & Graf, 1998). Being a child of Evelyn Waugh cannot have been easy, but Auberon Waugh recounts his upbringing (and beyond) with wit and wistfulness, and none of the *Mommy Dearest* sensationalism to which a lesser writer might have resorted.

BEST OF THE NET

Worldwide Evelyn Waugh Resources
e2.empirenet.com/~jahvah/waugh
An excellent starting point for Waugh research, with a search engine to uncover basic bibliographic information and connections, as well as special items that will delight true Waugh aficionados.

New York Times Featured Authors
www.nytimes.com/books./specials/
    author.html
With over a dozen reviews of Waugh and books about him, this is a great resource for gaining historical context.

Best Reads

NOVELS

Decline and Fall, 1928
A Handful of Dust, 1934
Scoop, 1938
Brideshead Revisited, 1945
The Loved One, 1948

SHORT-STORY COLLECTION

The Complete Stories of Evelyn Waugh, 1999

If You Like Evelyn Waugh . . .

You might also like two contemporary British writers praised for their biting satires: Tom Sharpe (*The Midden* and *Blott on the Landscape*) and David Lodge (*Therapy* and *Changing Places*). Both of these authors will have you rolling on the floor laughing!

Best Book to Read First

The Loved One, a novella that spoofs the California funeral industry. Or *Brideshead Revisited*, his most famous novel, which is less satirical and much longer, but worth the investment.

My feeling is that these novels of Waugh's are the only things written in England that are comparable to Fitzgerald and Hemingway. They are not so poetic; they are perhaps less intense; they belong to a more classical tradition. But I think that they are likely to last...

—Edmund Wilson,
Classics and Commercials

A *Brideshead* Weekend

Of all Waugh's novels, *Brideshead Revisited* is the least satirical, the most heartfelt, and the most beloved. The award-winning BBC miniseries, scripted by John Mortimer (*Rumpole, Voyage Round My Father*) is available on videotape. Fans say the 13 hours are best enjoyed over a single weekend—rather than being parceled out one episode per week as they were when the miniseries was originally aired.

The cast includes Anthony Andrews as Sebastian Flyte and Jeremy Irons as Charles Ryder, with cameo appearances by Sir Lawrence Olivier and the inimitable John Gielgud. Castle Howard is the setting for the estate of Brideshead. Available for purchase from PBS (call 800-645-4727 or use the A–Z listing at shop.pbs.org), the cost is $120 plus shipping and handling. But you may also be able to borrow it from your local library.

Rebecca Wells

Born
Probably in the mid- to late 1950s, the second of five children. She was raised on a working plantation in Rapides Parish, Louisiana (population 17,000) near Alexandria, where her family has lived since 1795.

Education
English degree from Louisiana State University in the 1970s. Also attended the Naropa Institute in Boulder, Colorado, where she studied language and consciousness with Allen Ginsberg.

Family
Married to Tom Schworer, a photographer.

Home
Bainbridge Island, across Puget Sound from Seattle, Washington

Publisher
HarperCollins

There are to date only two Rebecca Wells novels, but her Ya-Ya sisterhood has become a worldwide phenomenon. The term *ya-ya* comes from the Creole term *gumbo ya-ya*—meaning "everybody talking at the same time." But since Wells's two bestsellers, ya-ya has come to symbolize a certain kind of woman— "A person who is afraid and still drinks of life very deeply, who climbs on the back of an elephant and rides," Wells says. "A ya-ya is perfectly imperfect and her biggest secret is her sense of humor." Astoundingly, many readers claim her books have literally changed their lives.

The author has said she was "very lonely for friendship" when writing *Divine Secrets*. "I wrote it because I wanted a group like the ya-yas." Well, with Ya-Ya groups now springing up around the world, Wells certainly has more "sisters" than she can count. "The formation of Ya-Ya groups nationwide has turned [*Divine Secrets*] into a phenom," reports *Publishers Weekly*.

Wells's two novels celebrate the power of women and their relationships with friends and family. So it's fitting that the books have been propelled to bestseller status as a result of the force of women readers and their informal word-of-mouth campaign—friends passing books to friends, mothers to daughters, sisters to sisters. The books also explore child abuse and abandonment. But unlike other novels that deal with such subjects with a whiney, blaming tone, Wells focuses on humor, understanding, acceptance, healing, forgiveness and redemption. Imperfection is a given and that's okay.

Examining the life of four unconventional, strong, feisty Southern belles who think vices are wonderful and that it's more fun to be bad than good, the reader sees how friendship has kept them physically, spiritually, and emotionally alive through restrictive and difficult times. Their loyalty begins in childhood and strengthens and extends into adulthood. One of the charms of the novels is their deeply steeped Southern culture, though the love and laughter portrayed will resonate with readers everywhere, no matter where they're from.

Good to Know

❖ *Divine Secrets* was first published in hardcover in 1996 to lukewarm reviews and unimpressive sales. But in 1997, when the paperback version appeared and word-of-mouth had spread about just how divine *Divine Secrets* was, the book rose to the top of the *New York Times* paperback bestseller list, with 24 printings and two million copies sold.

❖ Rebecca Wells's first novel, *Little Altars Everywhere*, was published by Broken Moon Press in 1992. It sold 20,000 copies. Reissued by HarperCollins in 1996 and benefiting from the incredible popularity of *Divine Secrets*, it has since sold some 800,000 copies.

❖ Wells has received a multitude of fellowships and awards, including the Western States Book Award for fiction in 1992 for *Little Altars* and the 1999 American Booksellers Association ABBY Award for *Divine Secrets*. (Now known as the BookSense Award, this literary prize is given each year to the book that independent booksellers most enjoyed recommending to customers during the previous year.)

❖ A performer at heart, young Rebecca staged plays with her siblings, cousins, and friends at an early age and eventually began performing at her local community theater. In college, she developed a one-woman show as well as a series of short plays. After college, she left for New York City, where she performed in off-Broadway productions and studied the Stanislavski method of acting.

❖ Wells's stage performances include *Splittin' Hairs* and *Gloria Duplex*, for which she created the lead roles. *Splittin' Hairs* was nominated for Showtime's Excellence in American Theater and toured in 50 states. She has also written teleplays for ABC and CBS and currently tours the country doing a one-woman show based on her two books.

Treatises and Treats

COMPANIONS

The Ya-Ya Audio Collection. Excerpts from *Divine Secrets of the Ya-Ya Sisterhood* and *Little Altars Everywhere*, available separately or as a special boxed set, read by Rebecca Wells herself on audiotape and CD from HarperAudio (800-242-7737, www.harperaudio.com).

A Southern Belle Primer by Marlyn Schwartz ((Doubleday, 1991). While you're waiting for Rebecca Wells to come out with her next book, run out and buy yourself a copy of this one. You'll learn about the difference between calling someone "darlin'" or "precious," the importance of the Junior League, what your choice of silver pattern says about you, and how to make a proper chicken salad—all the stuff that Vivi and the other Ya-Yas learned growing up but that you might need some help with.

BEST OF THE NET

Official Rebecca Wells Web Site

www.ya-ya.com

Anyone ga-ga for Ya-Yas will want to bookmark this site, which offers periodic letters posted by Rebecca Wells, reading group guides, dates and locations of book signings and author appearances, chat rooms and bulletin boards, and a directory of Ya-Ya chapters around the country (plus information on starting your own chapter).

Book List

Little Altars Everywhere, 1992
Divine Secrets of the Ya-Ya Sisterhood, 1996
  (ABBY/BookSense Award)

If You Like Rebecca Wells . . .

You might like *Crazy Ladies* by Michael Lee West, *Fried Green Tomatoes at the Whistle Stop Café* by Fannie Flagg, and *A Big Storm Knocked It Over* and other books by Laurie Colwin. Also try Mary McCarthy and Anne Rivers Siddons.

Yippee Ya-Ya!

Divine Secrets has touched a real chord with readers and has risen to cult status, with *Ya-Ya* clubs (currently some 35 of them) springing up around the country to celebrate the depth of female friendship. Not to be left out, there's a New Orleans chapter of men called the "Ya-Yums," a Georgia chapter called the "Ya-Yis," and a Houston chapter called "The Gay Men of the Ya-Ya Sisterhood."

Club members will be thrilled to know that Wells is already hard at work on a *Ya-Ya* follow-up. And movie rights to *Divine Secrets* have been sold to Bette Midler's All Girl Productions, which is developing the property for Warner Bros.

Best Book to Read First

Divine Secrets of the Ya-Ya Sisterhood. Even though it's the sequel to *Little Altars Everywhere*, somehow they're even better read out of order.

[I grew up] in a world that valued storytelling immensely and where your status in the community was determined not solely by your wealth or profession, but by how good you could tell a tale. . . . [Y]ou might be a thief, but if you were a good storyteller you would work well at a dinner party. . . .

—Rebecca Wells

Edith Wharton

Born
January 24, 1862, in New York City to George Jones, heir to a merchant-shipping fortune, and Lucretia Rhinelander Jones

Full Name
Edith Newbold Jones Wharton

Education
Educated privately in New York and Europe.

Family
Married Edward "Teddy" Robbins Wharton, a banker, in 1885. Divorced in 1913.

Home
The Mount, a large estate in Lenox, Massachusetts, until 1911, when she sold the property and moved to France, where she lived for the rest of her life

Died
August 11, 1937, in St. Brice-sous-Forêt, France, of cardiac arrest. Buried in Versailles, France.

Publishers
Penguin
Scribner

Edith Wharton was an accomplished poet, essayist, and writer of short stories, but she is best known as a novelist. In 1921, she became the first woman to win the Pulitzer Prize for her novel, *The Age of Innocence*. She was also the first female recipient of the Gold Medal of the National Institute of Arts and Letters, paving the way for future literary award winners such as Pearl S. Buck, Toni Morrison, and Alice Walker.

Although she did not win the Nobel Prize, for which she was nominated in 1927, the nomination validated her contribution to literature and solidified her reputation as one of the most distinguished writers of her generation. Her first novel, *The Valley of Decision*, was published when she was 36, and she went on to write some 40 books before her death in 1937.

Wharton has been praised for her attention to detail, cleverness, and skillful narrative structure and technique. While her novels display her trademark satiric wit, they also address serious issues of morality and integrity. She shines a light on the pretensions and moral failings of the New York elite and depicts the Darwinian struggle of the individual to prevail in a world where wealth, power, and conformity are the conditions for acceptance. Her privileged upbringing afforded her intimate knowledge of the lifestyles of the rich and powerful, though she herself was more an observer than a participant.

She often turned her critical eye to the oppressed role of women in society and the limited choices made available to them. Ultimately, however, her novels transcend issues of class and gender as they explore the universal human quest for identity and purpose. Though her reputation declined after her death, there has been a resurgence of interest in and critical study of her work in recent years, helped in no small measure by Hollywood's release of three major motion pictures based on three of her best-loved novels.

Good to Know

❖ *The House of Mirth* was considered scandalous when it was first published in 1905. Of course, Americans love to read about scandal—especially when it involves the rich—and the book sold 100,000 copies within ten days of publication.

❖ Wharton's marriage to Teddy Robbins was on shaky ground from the start. A ten-year age difference, his worsening mental illness, and his many infidelities eventually took their toll. Not only was Teddy a philanderer, Wharton discovered that he was stealing from her to finance his affairs. The couple divorced in 1913.

❖ A love affair with the American journalist W. Morton Fullerton inspired a creative renaissance for the author that resulted in many poems and was the passionate force behind her novel *The Reef* (1913).

❖ Wharton was well known and accepted in European social and literary circles. She spent her later years exclusively in Europe, enjoying summers at her villa in St. Brice-sous-Forêt near Paris and winters on the Riviera. Her home in France was one of the stops on President Theodore Roosevelt's world tour in 1909–10.

❖ Henry James sometimes referred to Edith Wharton as "the Angel of Desolation." Meant as a teasing term of endearment, the title belies the close relationship between the two American expatriate writers. Wharton was greatly influenced by James, and critics have often noted the similarities between the two authors' works.

❖ Wharton on the Big Screen: *The Age of Innocence* (1993), a wonderful, lush Martin Scorsese film starring Daniel Day-Lewis, Michelle Pfeiffer, and Winona Ryder. (Watch for the special-effects period shot of the Dakota apartment building, so named because at the time it was built it was so far from the center of town.) Also *Ethan Frome* (1993), starring Liam Neeson and Joan Allen, and *The House of Mirth* (2000), with Gillian Anderson of *The X-Files* as Lily Bart.

Treatises and Treats

EDITH WHARTON SOCIETY

This group publishes a twice-yearly journal, *The Edith Wharton Review*, hosts meetings and social events, and sponsors online discussions through the WHARTON-L mailing list. Annual membership fee is $20 ($15 for students). For more information, contact:
Dr. Dale FlynnCampus Writing Center
University of California
Davis, CA 95616
www.gonzaga.edu/faculty/campbell/wharton

COMPANIONS

Edith Wharton: A Biography by R. W. B. Lewis (Harper & Row, 1975). After a period of neglect following her death, this Pulitzer Prize–winning biography helped to revive discussion of Wharton's work. *Newsweek* called it "masterly" and predicted that it would inspire readers to revisit Wharton's books.

A Feast of Words: The Triumph of Edith Wharton by Cynthia Griffin Wolff (Addison-Wesley, 1995). This revised edition of Wolff's fascinating study of Wharton's life and work includes two new chapters, one on the character of Lily Bart from *The House of Mirth* and another tracing the author's sensual awakening from *Ethan Frome* to *Summer*.

The Cambridge Companion to Edith Wharton, edited by Millicent Bell (Cambridge University Press, 1995). An excellent companion for first-time Wharton readers as well as those looking for insights from Wharton scholars.

BEST OF THE NET
Edith Wharton Society Web Page
www.gonzaga.edu/faculty/campbell/wharton
The site provides a good starting point for information on Wharton's life and work, including where to find the full text of her fiction and nonfiction online.

Edith Wharton Catalog
www.edithwharton.org/catalog
Top source for books by and about Wharton. The catalog is nicely annotated.

Wharton Society Picks

THE BIG THREE
The House of Mirth, 1905
The Age of Innocence, 1920
   (Pulitzer Prize)
Ethan Frome, 1911

THE NEXT LEVEL
The Reef, 1913
Summer, 1917
The Mother's Recompense, 1925
Hudson River Bracketed, 1929
The Gods Arrive, 1932 (sequel to *Hudson River Bracketed*)

If You Like Edith Wharton . . .

You might also like books by her mentor and friend, Henry James.

Best Book to Read First

The Age of Innocence is considered by many her finest work. A satirical portrait of New York society life in the 1870s, it presents the story of a young couple who enter into a loveless marriage rather than violate the code of their aristocratic society. Alternatively, start with *The House of Mirth*, an equally skilled (and satirical) tale of missed connections and ill-advised choices. Here you will meet Lily Bart, perhaps Wharton's most memorable heroine.

Decidedly, I'm a better landscape gardener than novelist, and this place, every line of which is my own, far surpasses The House of Mirth.

—Edith Wharton, referring to her garden design at The Mount

House of Worth

Widely credited with inventing the concept of interior design, Edith Wharton first set forth her theories on the subject in *The Decoration of Houses* (1897) and later in *Italian Villas and Their Gardens* (1904). Her passion for architecture and design was fully realized in her dream home, The Mount, in Lenox, Massachusetts. The estate is undergoing an extensive restoration, but visitors can still enjoy the lovely views and appreciate Wharton's exquisite taste and style from May through October. For tour information call 888-637-1902 (toll free) or 413-637-1899.

P. G. Wodehouse

Born
October 15, 1881, in Guildford, Surrey, England, to Henry Ernest Wodehouse, a civil servant and judge, and Eleanor Deane Wodehouse

Full Name
Pelham Grenville Wodehouse (pronounced "Wood-house")

Pseudonyms
P. Brooke-Haven, Pelham Grenville, J. Plum, C. P. West, J. Walker Williams, and Basil Windham

Education
Dulwich College, 1894–1900

Family
Married Ethel Rowley in 1914; one step-daughter.

Home
Emigrated to the U. S. in 1910. Became a citizen in 1955. Moved to Remsenburg, New York, where he lived from 1955 until he died.

Died
February 14, 1975, in Southampton, New York

Publishers
HarperColllins
Viking Penguin
Vintage

More than 100 years after his birth, P. G. Wodehouse remains a master of contemporary humor. The author of some 100 books, as well as a dozen plays, more than 300 song lyrics, and countless articles and reviews, Wodehouse has won legions of fans since his first novel was published in 1902. Wrote Auberon Waugh: "Wodehouse has been more read than any other English novelist by his fellow novelists."

Born of aristocratic ancestry, Wodehouse spent his early days in Hong Kong, where his father was a judge. At age two, his parents sent him and his older brothers back to England, where they lived with a number of aunts. Little Plum, as he was called (a nickname derived from "Pelham"), began to observe the peculiarities of Edwardian English gentry.

Wodehouse achieved literary stardom in the 1920s, just after the first of the Jeeves adventures was published. His most famous character and the star of countless books and stories, Jeeves is the long-suffering gentleman's gentleman of one Bertram Wilberforce Wooster, a hapless aristocrat who requires rescue from countless scrapes and near-engagements. But other characters—Psmith (the *p* is silent, "as in phthisis, psychic, and ptarmigan"), Mr. Mulliner, Lord Emsworth of Blandings Castle—are almost as unforgettable, and have provided generations of chortles and guffaws.

Good to Know

❖ After graduating from college, Wodehouse worked as a clerk at the Hong Kong & Shanghai Bank for two years before joining the *London Globe* as an assistant on the "By the Way"

column. In 1903 he took over the column, serving as writer until 1909. Under various pseudonyms, he wrote articles for *Vanity Fair* from 1915 to 1919, and also served as its drama critic.

❖ His snappy repartee can be seen as the over-achieving grandfather of the best in television situation comedy. A seasoned playwright himself, Wodehouse inspired Edward Duke to write a play derived from his novels called *Jeeves Takes Charge*, which debuted in 1984.

❖ Jeeves is a walking encyclopedia of both academic and practical knowledge who expounds on an extraordinary range of subjects and uses his wisdom to save his young charge from certain peril. The natural-language Internet search engine "Ask Jeeves" (www.askjeeves.com) takes its name from this famously intelligent and well-read character.

❖ Wodehouse was a lyricist of the caliber of Cole Porter. He collaborated on more than 23 musical comedies and is credited as a major force in the evolution of the American musical. George and Ira Gershwin, Jerome Kern, and Guy Bolton turned to him for help on their musicals, including *Sitting Pretty* and *O, Kay!* The song "Bill," written with Kern in 1918, was used in Kern and Oscar Hammerstein's *Show Boat* in 1927.

❖ Living in France when the Nazis invaded in 1940, Wodehouse and his wife were taken to Berlin, where he made several jovial radio addresses. Though hardly sympathetic to the Third Reich, they nonetheless inspired vitriolic Parliamentary demands that Wodehouse be tried for treason. (In fact, he included numerous subtle jokes at the Germans' expense.) George Orwell weighed in with an essay entitled "In Defense of P. G. Wodehouse."

❖ Despite Wodehouse's wartime "treason," Great Britain quite rightly continued to claim him as its own. He was made Knight of the British Empire just weeks before his death on Valentine's Day at the age of 93.

Treatises and Treats

THE WODEHOUSE SOCIETY

This 800-member international club has chapters in major U.S. cities. Its newsletter, *Plum Lines,* keeps members apprised of conventions and other notable events. Dues are $20 a year. For more information, contact:
Marilyn MacGregor
3215-5 Bermuda Avenue
Davis, CA 95616

WODEHOUSE ON VIDEO

A number of Wodehouse short stories were produced by the BBC in the 1970s for the TV series *Wodehouse Playhouse.* Two collections, *Jeeves and Wooster I* and *Jeeves and Wooster II,* are available from the PBS Home Video Catalog (800-645-4727, shop.pbs.org). They star the famous and incomparable comedy team of Stephen Fry as Jeeves and Hugh Laurie as Bertie Wooster.

COMPANIONS

P. G. Wodehouse: A Centenary Celebration: 1881–1981, edited by James H. Heineman and Donald R. Bensen (Pierpont Morgan Library/Oxford University Press, 1981). Published in conjunction with the 100th anniversary exhibition at the Pierpont Morgan Library in New York City.

P. G. Wodehouse: A Portrait of a Master by David A. Jasen (Continuum, 1981). This comprehensive illustrated biography is a must for Wodehouse fans. Jasen's love of his subject brings warmth and appreciation to the master humorist.

Who's Who in Wodehouse by Daniel Garrison (International Polyglonics, 1991). A master reference that lists every character who ever tripped onto the Wodehouse page, using the author's own words to describe them.

P. G. Wodehouse: A Literary Biography by Benny Green (Pavilion, 1981). This study explores Wodehouse's literary influences and lays the groundwork for understanding the far-reaching influence he enjoys.

BEST OF THE NET
Junior Ganymede Club Book
www.serv.net/~camel/wodehouse
Who is P. G. Wodehouse and why all this bally fuss? Enter this "virtual drawing room" to find out. It's here that aficionados gather to "ponder the unexplainable temptations of cow creamers, toss a bread roll or two, and generally have a grand time together" via chat rooms, role-playing, and the use of various "Noms de Plum."

Best Reads

Leave It to Psmith, 1923
Jeeves, 1925
The Code of the Woosters, 1938
Week-end Wodehouse, 1939
French Leave, 1956
The Plot That Thickened, 1973

If You Like
P. G. Wodehouse . . .

You might also like Jerome K. Jerome's delightfully funny *Three Men in a Boat: To Say Nothing of the Dog*, originally published in 1900, and John Mortimer's "Rumpole" stories.

Best Book to Read First

Anything "Jeeves"—short story, novel, it doesn't matter. Favorites include *Jeeves* and *The Code of the Woosters*. For a delicious entrée, try *Week-end Wodehouse*, a collection of stories and excerpts.

I was writing stories when I was five. I don't remember what I did before that. Just loafed, I suppose.

—P. G. Wodehouse, in a 1975 interview for *Paris Review*

Wodehouse Funhouse

Above all, it is P. G. Wodehouse's linguistic innovations that readers remember. In *The Comic Style of P. G. Wodehouse* (Archon, 1974), author Robert A. Hall examines these stylistic twists. Imbuing the character's emotions into a nearby inanimate object is one such device—"I balanced a thoughtful lump of sugar" or "He waved a concerned cigar."

Wodehouse employs some original prefixes—as in "de-Beaned the cupboard" (when Elsie Bean is removed from same). Characters wander "pigward" as they might homeward or northward. In *Heavy Weather*, Wodehouse plays on the noun *hussy*: "I regard the entire personnel of the ensemble of our musical comedy theatres as—if you will pardon me being Victorian for a moment—painted hussies. They've got to paint. Well, they needn't huss."

Thomas Wolfe

Born
October 3, 1900, in
Asheville, North
Carolina, the youngest
of eight children of
William Oliver Wolfe, a
tombstone cutter, and
Julia Westall Wolfe, a
boardinghouse propri-
etor

Full Name
Thomas Clayton Wolfe

Education
University of North
Carolina, Chapel Hill,
B.A., 1920; Harvard
University, M.A., 1922;
graduate study, 1923

Died
September 15, 1938,
at the age of 37, in
Baltimore, Maryland,
of tuberculosis of the
brain

Publishers
HarperCollins
Scribner
Simon & Schuster

It is all but impossible to read any critical commentary on Thomas Wolfe
without encountering the word
sprawling. He was known for his ex-
uberance of spirit, over-the-top
rhetoric, and near mystical celebration of youth, sex, and America. His
were among the most completely autobiographical novels ever written.

Early in his career he told his mother "I
will go everywhere and see everything. I will
meet all the people I can. I will think all the
thoughts, feel all the emotions I am able, and
I will write, write, write." True to his word,
Wolfe would appear to have recorded everything that ever happened to him and, some
critics would aver, every thought that ever
flickered through his brain. If he hadn't had
two great editors, none of his work would ever
have been published.

The first editor was the legendary
Maxwell Perkins. As recounted in A. Scott
Berg's *Max Perkins: Editor of Genius*,
Perkins essentially invented the modern profession of book editing. His three most famous authors were Fitzgerald, Hemingway,
and Thomas Wolfe, whom he virtually
adopted as the son he'd never had. Perkins
clearly saw much of value in the huge manuscripts Wolfe presented to him, and he was
able to whip them into shape. But the editor's
celebrity led critics to suggest that the author couldn't write and that any success was
Perkins's doing.

So Wolfe jumped ship and, in December
1937, signed with Harper & Brothers, where
his editor was Edward C. Aswell. No one knew
it, but Wolfe had less than a year to live. A
case of pneumonia activated the tuberculosis
he had unknowingly contracted in his youth.
It went to his brain, and he died a few weeks
before his 38th birthday. He left Aswell with a
manuscript that was literally eight feet high,
from which the editor extracted *The Web and
the Rock*, *You Can't Go Home Again*, *The Hills
Beyond*, a collection of short stories, a play,
and a novel fragment.

More than 60 years after his death, critics
are still debating the merits of Wolfe's work.
New York Post contributor Herschel Brickell
summed up both sides of the argument when
he wrote: "You can't, if you are of ordinary
stature and vitality, believe completely in
[Wolfe's] gigantic world of shadow shapes,
where everything is magnified and intensi-
fied, but you will be fascinated just the same,
swept along on the tides of his passions, carried away with the gargantuan appetite of a
man who wishes to swallow life whole when
most of us are content to chew a tiny fragment
in our frightened and dyspeptic way."

Good to Know

❖ Wolfe's original title for his first novel, *O
Lost*, was rejected by the Scribner sales force
as "too flabby." His alternatives included: *The
Exile's Story*, *The Lost Language*, and *They
Are Strange and They Are Lost*, all of which
were also considered duds. Finally, Maxwell
Perkins saved the day with a line from Milton's "Lycidas": "Look homeward, Angel, now,
and melt with ruth…"

❖ *Look Homeward, Angel* was dedicated to
Aline Bernstein, a well-to-do set and costume designer in the New York theater.
Wolfe and Bernstein had met several years
earlier and began a turbulent love affair. She
was 20 years his senior, married, and the
mother of two grown children. Wolfe used
her as the model for the character Esther
Jack in *The Web and the Rock*.

❖ Adapted as a play, *Look Homeward, Angel* was first produced in New York in 1957. A year later, the play was published by Scribner and won the Pulitzer Prize.

Treatises and Treats

THOMAS WOLFE SOCIETY

Encourages the study of Wolfe's work through annual meetings and the *Thomas Wolfe Review*, included with the $30 annual membership fee ($10 for students). Contact:
David Strange
Thomas Wolfe Society Membership
P.O. Box 1146
Bloomington, IN 47402-1146
dstrange@ait.net

COMPANIONS

Look Homeward: A Life of Thomas Wolfe by David Herbert Donald (Little, Brown, 1987). A Pulitzer Prize–winning biography. "A six-and-a-half foot, hard-drinking monomaniac who believes himself to be the Great American Writer would appear to be fiction rather than fact, but Mr. Donald's Wolfe is very real," according to Harold Bloom (*New York Times Book Review*).

A Thomas Wolfe Companion by John L. Idol (Greenwood Publishing, 1987). In addition to a biographical sketch, bibliography, and essays on Wolfe's writings, this 205-page reference book includes a glossary of characters and places in his novels, and genealogical charts of fictional characters and real-life family members.

Memories of Thomas Wolfe: A Pictorial Companion to **Look Homeward, Angel** by John Chandler Griffin (Summerhouse Press, 1996). Photographs of Wolfe's family, friends, and acquaintances, with accompanying passages from *Look Homeward, Angel*, help readers see how Wolfe transformed his life into literature.

BEST OF THE NET

Thomas Wolfe Web Site

coast.lib.uncwil.edu/wolfe/wolfe.html
Includes a biography of Wolfe, a bibliography of his works, a photo gallery, and information about the Thomas Wolfe Memorial and the Thomas Wolfe Fiction Prize.

Best Reads

Look Homeward, Angel, 1929
Of Time and the River, 1935
From Death to Morning (short-story collection), 1935
The Web and the Rock, 1939
You Can't Go Home Again, 1940

If You Like Thomas Wolfe . . .

Try the novels and stories of William Faulkner and William Styron. But you might also enjoy *The Town and the City* by Beat Generation novelist and poet Jack Kerouac, who deliberately imitated the style and approach of Thomas Wolfe in his first published novel.

The Wolfe Memorial

The rambling Victorian boarding house in Asheville, North Carolina, where Wolfe grew up is now the Thomas Wolfe Memorial, a North Carolina Historic Site. Located at 52 North Market Street, the house remains virtually unchanged since Wolfe's boyhood. For tour information, call 828-253-8304 or send e-mail to wolfe@ncsl.dcr.state.nc.us.

Best Book to Read First

Look Homeward, Angel, the novel that began Wolfe's career. The *New York Times Book Review* called it "enormously sensuous, full of the joy and gusto of life, and shrinkingly sensitive, torn with revulsion and disgust. Mr. Wolfe's style is sprawling, fecund, subtly rhythmic, and amazingly vital."

Thomas Wolfe at his best is the only contemporary American writer who can be mentioned in the same breath with Dickens and Dostoyevsky. But the trouble is that the best passages are scattered, that they occur without logic or pattern...and they lack the cumulative effect, the slow tightening of emotions to an intolerable pitch, that one finds in great novels.

—Malcolm Cowley,
New Republic,
March 20, 1935

Tom Wolfe

Born
March 2, 1931, in Richmond, Virginia, to Thomas Kennerly Wolfe, a farmer and professor of agronomy at Virginia Polytechnic University, and also editor of the magazine *Southern Planter*, and Helen Hughes Wolfe

Full Name
Thomas Kennerly Wolfe Jr.

Education
Washington and Lee University, B.A., cum laude, 1951; Yale University, Ph.D., American Studies, 1957

Family
Married Sheila Berger, art director of *Harper's* magazine, in 1978; three children.

Home
New York City

Fan Mail
Tom Wolfe
c/o International Creative Management
40 West 57th Street
New York, NY 10019

Publisher
Farrar, Straus & Giroux

According to William F. Buckley, Tom Wolfe "is probably the most skillful writer in America. I mean by that he can do more things with words than anyone else." As one of the creators of the "New Journalism," a school of writing popular in the 1960s and '70s that employs the techniques of fiction to report on nonfiction topics, Wolfe has been doing things with words for quite a while. He has always had a substantial following, but when he turned to fiction his popularity began to soar.

"I was curious," he told the *New York Times*, "having spouted off so much about fiction and nonfiction, and having said that novelists weren't doing a good job, to see what would happen if I tried." The result was *The Bonfire of the Vanities* (1987), a witty, satirical story about a Wall Street bond salesman who, with his cell phone and fancy car, is a "master of the universe"—until he is implicated in the hit-and-run traffic death of a black man in the South Bronx and is reduced to a political pawn. Critic Jonathan Yardley called it "the first novel ever to get contemporary New York, in all its arrogance and shame and heterogeneity and insularity, exactly right."

Bonfire spent over a year on the bestseller list and raised expectations for Wolfe's next novel, which arrived more than a decade later: *A Man in Full* (1998). This book also uses a city as its main character—this time Atlanta, the unofficial capital of the New South. It tells the tale of a real estate developer and conglomerate owner with huge financial problems and all the lives they affect. It tied with Tom Clancy's *Rainbow Six* for the longest run as the number one bestseller (seven weeks), and was the ninth bestselling book in 1998.

A third novel is currently in the works. Wolfe is doing research on the campus of Stanford University for a story set in the world of academia. Booksellers are pleased, for Tom Wolfe writes the kind of novels that "will pay our bills!"

Good to Know

❖ Tom Wolfe's contributions to the language include *the right stuff*, *radical chic*, *the Me decade*, *pizza grenade ties*, *social x-rays* (extremely thin society women), and, of course, those cell-phone wielding *masters of the universe*.

❖ He is famous for the hand-tailored three-piece white suits (with functioning buttons at the cuffs) that he wears whenever appearing in public. He always carries a hat and umbrella. "I had a white suit made [in 1962], started wearing it in January, and found it annoyed people tremendously.... It's kind of a harmless form of aggression, I guess."

❖ In 1965 Wolfe began a literary feud when he published a series of articles about the *New Yorker* magazine. His original plan was to do a profile of the magazine and its then editor, William Shawn, but no one would cooperate. Wolfe wrote the articles anyway, calling the *New Yorker* "the most successful suburban women's magazine in the country." He unquestionably mocked John Updike, a longtime leading light of the magazine. The two authors have been exchanging barbs ever since.

❖ *Bonfire of the Vanities*, the 1990 Brian De-Palma movie starring Tom Hanks, Melanie Griffith, and Bruce Willis, was universally panned. Most critics agree that the movie bears little relationship to Wolfe's novel. So read the book and skip the film.

❖ Though his novels have been serialized in *Rolling Stone* as they are written, you can't judge a book by its excerpt. Critics agree that *Bonfire* in its final form "ended up being far better than the earlier excerpts…suggested it would be." (*Book*, October/November 1998)

Treatises and Treats

COMPANIONS

Tom Wolfe by William McKeen (Twayne Publishing, 1995). Traces Wolfe's innovative work from his early days as a newspaper and magazine writer to his second career as a fiction writer.

The Critical Response to Tom Wolfe, edited by Doug Shomette (Greenwood Publishing, 1992). A collection of reviews of and critical commentaries on each of Wolfe's books. Also includes a chronology of important events in Wolfe's career and a bibliography of additional readings.

Conversations with Tom Wolfe, edited by Dorothy M. Scura (University Press of Mississippi, 1990). Over 30 interviews with Wolfe conducted by William F. Buckley, Bill Moyers, and others.

Ambush at Fort Bragg by Tom Wolfe, narrated by Edward Norton (BDD Audio, 1997). Distilled from the author's early false start on *Bonfire of the Vanities* and available only on audiotape, this story of media excess and arrogance in covering the murder of a gay soldier is a "high-octane verbal cartoon on a par with his best-selling [novels]." (*Dallas Morning News*)

BEST OF THE NET

Official Tom Wolfe Web Site
www.tomwolfe.com
Created by Tom Wolfe's publisher to promote *A Man in Full*, this Web site also offers biographical information, descriptions of Wolfe's other books, and a schedule of his appearances.

New York Times Featured Authors
www.nytimes.com/books/specials/author.html
Check here for a collection of book reviews and articles from the *New York Times* archives, and some highly entertaining audio clips of Wolfe reading from his books.

Reading List

NOVELS

The Bonfire of the Vanities, 1987
A Man in Full, 1998

NONFICTION

The Kandy-Kolored Tangerine-Flake Streamline Baby, 1965
The Electric Kool-Aid Acid Test, 1968
The Pump House Gang, 1968
Radical Chic and Mau-mauing the Flak Catchers, 1970
The Painted Word, 1975
The Right Stuff, 1979
    (American Book Award and National Book Critics Circle Award)
From Bauhaus to Our House, 1981

If You Like Tom Wolfe…

You might also enjoy Caleb Carr's *The Alienist*, Truman Capote's *In Cold Blood*, and E. L. Doctorow's *Ragtime*. Or try Tom Wolfe's own favorite author, Charles Dickens.

Best Book to Read First

Either *The Bonfire of the Vanities* or *A Man in Full*. Different topics, but the same patented Wolfe style. Then, for comparison, try *The Right Stuff* (1979), Wolfe's nonfiction account of the early years of the U.S. space program.

Verdict: Excellent book by a genius who will do anything to get attention.

—Kurt Vonnegut, in a 1965 *New York Times* review of *The Kandy-Kolored Tangerine-Flake Streamline Baby*

Dear Byron…

In 1963, Tom Wolfe racked up a $750 tab at the Beverly Wilshire Hotel researching a magazine article on custom cars. But he couldn't finish. The journalistic techniques he had used as a newspaper writer could not adequately describe the bizarre people and machines he had encountered.

The night before his deadline, he called *Esquire* editor Byron Dobell, who suggested that he just type his notes. A staff writer would then finish the piece. Wolfe started typing at 8:00 P.M. He began with "Dear Byron," and simply wrote all his thoughts in a stream-of-consciousness style, including random thoughts and musings.

"I wrapped up the memorandum at about 6:15 A.M.," says Wolfe, "and by this time it was 49 pages long. I took it over to *Esquire* as soon as they opened. . . . About 4 P.M. I got a call from Byron Dobell. He told me they were striking out the 'Dear Byron' part at the top of the memorandum and running the rest of it in the magazine." Thus began the unique style of writing that would make Tom Wolfe famous.

Virginia Woolf

Born
January 25, 1882, in London, England, to Sir Leslie Stephen (noted scholar, biographer, and critic), and Julia Jackson Stephen of the Duckworth publishing family

Full Name
Adeline Virginia Stephen Woolf

Education
A sickly child, Virginia was educated at home where she had access to her father's extensive private library.

Family
Married to writer and social reformer Leonard Woolf for 29 years.

Died
March 28, 1941; suicide by drowning

Publisher
Harcourt Brace

Virginia Woolf is one of the most influential and innovative authors of the 20th century. A prolific writer of essays, letters, journals, and short fiction, she is best known for her experimental novels. With her third book, *Jacob's Room*, Woolf broke away from the conventions of traditional, linear storytelling and, paralleling James Joyce, employed stream-of-consciousness and interior monologue narrative devices to explore the idea of a subjective reality. External action and conflict were ancillary to the thoughts and feelings of her characters. Woolf's writings revolutionized the British novel in their exploration of the nature of reality and the idea of a women's aesthetic.

The characters that inhabit Woolf's fiction are derived from her own memories and experience. Most are pilgrims in one way or another, searching for meaning in a cold world. *The Voyage Out* is a tragic coming-of-age novel about a young woman traveling in South America. *Jacob's Room* chronicles the life and wartime death of Jacob Flanders and his personal struggle in an unforgiving world. *Mrs. Dalloway*, set in post–World War I England, addresses issues of sexuality, class, gender, death, and madness, while *To the Lighthouse* deals with death and rebirth and examines how the past informs the future. Woolf's novels reflected her own life struggles, and as a result, writing them was simultaneously torturous and liberating for her.

Good to Know

❖ Virginia Woolf did not sit down to write until she was 30—literally! In her teens, she noticed that her sister Vanessa always stood to paint, as many painters do. According to Woolf's nephew and biographer Quentin Bell, "This led Virginia to feel that her own pursuit might appear less arduous than that of her sister unless she stood as well."

❖ Virginia Woolf was a member of the circle of Cambridge-educated intellectuals known as the Bloomsbury group. Members included future husband Leonard Woolf; sister Vanessa and her husband, art critic Clive Bell; biographer Lytton Strachey; economist John Maynard Keynes; E. M. Forster; and artist Roger Fry. The friends gathered regularly at her house in the Bloomsbury district of London to discuss art, literature, and politics.

❖ In 1917, Virginia and Leonard Woolf founded the Hogarth Press to publish experimental works by Woolf and other writers, including W. H. Auden, E. M. Forster, Robert Graves, Katherine Mansfield, Gertrude Stein, and H. G. Wells. They published the first edition of T. S. Eliot's *The Waste Land* and the first English edition of Sigmund Freud.

❖ At an early age, Woolf suffered the loss of several loved ones in rapid succession. Her own lifelong battle with depression and a family history of mental illness informed the creation of some of her most significant characters, especially that of Septimus Smith in *Mrs. Dalloway*. This character's suicide eerily mirrors Woolf's own. In 1941, fearing further bouts of madness, she loaded her pockets with stones and drowned herself in the River Ouse.

❖ Virginia Woolf struggled with questions of her own sexuality. At 16 she had her first crush—on one of her female cousins. She later had two passionate lesbian affairs, one with an older woman when she was 20 and the other with her good friend, writer Vita Sackville-West (the inspiration for the lead character in *Orlando*).

Treatises and Treats

INTERNATIONAL VIRGINIA WOOLF SOCIETY

Open to Woolf readers and scholars throughout the world, IVWS holds two annual meetings and publishes a newsletter, *Virginia Woolf Miscellany*. Annual dues are $15.00. Contact:

Laura Davis, Secretary/Treasurer
International Virginia Woolf Society
105 Bowman Hall
Kent State University
Kent, Ohio 44242-0001

COMPANIONS

Virginia Woolf: A Biography by Quentin Bell (Harcourt Brace, 1972). A personal account of the author's life, written by her nephew.

Virginia Woolf by Hermione Lee (Knopf, 1997). A more recent and highly praised treatment of the author's life and work.

BEST OF THE NET

International Virginia Woolf Society

www.utoronto.ca/IVWS
The essential first stop for Virginia Woolf information online. (The Web address is case-sensitive, so use capital letters for *IVWS*.)

Dazzling Radiance

Some critics imply that Woolf's literary achievements are overrated. But John Lehmann vouches for the importance of her work in his piece for *English Critical Essays*: "The dazzling surface radiance of the world and a terror and despair always lurking beneath—nowhere in modern writing have these things found symbols more audacious and memorable than in the novel-poems of Virginia Woolf, so that one can truly say that she enlarged the sensibility of her time, and changed English literature."

The site offers a comprehensive and well-organized collection of resource materials—electronic texts, publishers, book and movie reviews, and links to other good Woolf-related sites.

Virginia Woolf on Woman and Fiction

www.cygneis.com/woolf/pageone.htm
A virtual "Virginia Woolf Book Club." Participate in ongoing discussions or simply use the site for background materials, bibliographic references, and discussion notes.

New York Times Featured Authors

www.nytimes.com/books/specials/
    author.html
Click on "Virginia Woolf" for reviews of her books from the *New York Times* archives, as well as the article that appeared shortly after she committed suicide ("Virginia Woolf Believed Dead," April 4, 1941).

Reading List

NOVELS

The Voyage Out, 1915
Night and Day, 1919
Jacob's Room, 1922
Mrs. Dalloway, 1925
To the Lighthouse, 1927
Orlando, 1928
The Waves, 1931
The Years, 1937
Between the Acts, 1941

If You Like Virginia Woolf...

Try Dorothy Richardson (1873–1957), the first English novelist to employ the stream-of-consciousness technique in her fiction. A one-time mistress of H. G. Wells, Richardson's major work is *Pilgrimage*, a series of 13 novels based on her life. Also consider Michael Cunningham's Pulitzer Prize–winning *The Hours*, an updated version of (and homage to) Woolf's *Mrs. Dalloway*.

Best Book to Read First

Mrs. Dalloway. Considered one of Woolf's greatest triumphs and perhaps her most accessible work, it examines themes of love and death and one of her chief preoccupations—the moral disintegration of society.

There can be little question that she was the greatest woman novelist of her time, though she herself would have objected to the separation of her sex implied in such a judgement.

—David Daiches, in his biography of the author, *Virginia Woolf* (Greenwood Press, 1979)

Richard Wright

Born
September 4, 1908, near Natchez, Mississippi, to Nathan Wright, an illiterate sharecropper, and Ellen Wright, a teacher

Full Name
Richard Nathaniel Wright

Education
Attended school in Jackson, Mississippi.

Family
Married twice. First in 1939 to Dhimah Rose Meadman, a dancer. Then in 1941 to Ellen Poplar, a member of the Communist Party. Two daughters from his second marriage.

Home
Spent his adult life in Chicago (1927–37), New York City (1937–44), and Paris (1944–60).

Died
November 28, 1960, in Paris, France, of a heart attack

Publisher
HarperCollins

Richard Wright was among the first African-American writers to achieve literary fame and fortune, and today he is generally considered one of the most influential writers of this century. Perhaps his most significant contribution was to destroy the white myth of the humorous, patient, subservient black man. He was the first black novelist to write of life in the ghettos of northern cities and of the rage felt by blacks at the white society that excluded them. Wright's concern with the social roots of racism led him to join the Communist Party in 1932, but his individualism caused other members to regard his writing with suspicion, and in 1942 he resigned.

Native Son (1940), Wright's first novel, established his reputation. It is the story of Bigger Thomas, a young black man in Chicago who murders two women and is condemned to death. Wright specifically chose as the hero of the novel a man who is not fully aware of his status as a second-class human being and is therefore completely at the mercy of the violent impulses that status has created. Much of the book is written in the tradition of the naturalist writers Wright admired, and readers are left with a sense that violence is the only means Bigger Thomas has of defining himself. James Baldwin called *Native Son* "the most powerful and celebrated statement we have yet had of what it means to be a Negro in America."

Wright's reputation waned during the 1950s as younger black writers such as James Baldwin and Ralph Ellison rejected his naturalistic approach, but in the 1960s there was a resurgence of interest in his work. *American Hunger*, the second part of his autobiography, was published in 1977, almost 20 years after his death.

Good to Know

❖ After finishing his formal schooling at the age of 15, Wright began to read widely, starting with H. L. Mencken. He was able to borrow books from the Memphis "whites only" public library by forging a note from a white patron: "Dear Madam: Will you please let this nigger boy have some books by H. L. Mencken?"

❖ In 1924 the *Southern Register*, a local black newspaper, printed his first story, "The Voodoo of Hell's Half Acre." Another story, "Superstition," appeared in *Abbot's Monthly* in 1931.

❖ While living in Greenwich Village in the 1930s, Wright's friends included Ralph Ellison (who served as best man at his wedding), Langston Hughes, Countee Cullen, Nelson Algren, John Hammond, Carson McCullers, and John Steinbeck.

❖ J. Edgar Hoover's FBI investigated Wright in 1942 to determine if he could be prosecuted for sedition. The FBI continued to investigate him, as did the CIA, for the rest of his life. His autobiography, *Black Boy*, was declared obscene by the U.S. Senate in 1945.

❖ *Black Boy* sold 195,000 copies in its Harper edition and another 315,000 copies through the Book-of-the-Month Club. (*Native Son* sold 215,000 copies in three weeks as a Book-of-the-Month-Club main selection.) For the BOMC editions, Wright had to cool down some of the sexual passages and eliminate his political experiences.

❖ He wrote a play and a screenplay based on his novel *Native Son*. The play was produced on Broadway by Orson Welles at the St. James Theatre in 1941, and the film was released in 1951, with Wright himself in the title role.

❖ In his last years, Wright was plagued by illness and financial difficulties. During this period, he wrote approximately 4,000 English haikus, some of which were published posthumously in a volume called *Haiku: This Other World* (Arcade, 1998). His attempts to move to England were thwarted by both the British and U.S. governments, which conspired to keep him in France, where he died in poverty.

Treatises and Treats

COMPANIONS

Richard Wright, Daemonic Genius: A Portrait of the Man, a Critical Look at His Work by Margaret Walker (Amistad Press, 1992). The only critical biography of Richard Wright written by another accomplished African-American writer, scholar, and close friend. This book was the subject of a legal dispute over using Wright's unpublished materials.

Exiled in Paris: Richard Wright, James Baldwin, Samuel Beckett and Others on the Left Bank by James Campbell (Scribner, 1995). An informative and entertaining literary history covering the years Wright spent in exile in Paris and his encounters with other notable figures, including Vladimir Nabokov, George Plimpton, Allen Ginsberg, Chester Himes, Eugene Ionesco, William S. Burroughs, and Gertrude Stein.

Conversations with Richard Wright, edited by Keneth Kinnamon and Michel Fabre (University Press of Mississippi, 1993). Conversations with Wright that touch on a wide range of subjects, including communism, jazz, race relations, living in Paris, and the craft of writing.

Richard Wright: Critical Perspectives Past and Present, edited by Henry Louis Gates Jr. and K. A. Appiah (Amistad Press, 1993). A collection of reviews of Wright's work by his contemporaries and colleagues, including Zora Neale Hurston, Ralph Ellison, and Alain Locke. The book covers Wright's fiction, his nonfiction, and autobiographical writings.

Richard Wright: Early Works and *Richard Wright: Later Works*, with notes by Arnold Rampersad (The Library of America, 1992).

Two significant volumes of Wright's fiction, with notes that shed light on his career and his influence on contemporaries and future generations of black writers. For the first time, the complete text of Wright's autobiography has been brought together.

BEST OF THE NET
Mississippi Writers Page
www.olemiss.edu/depts/english/ms-writers
A good starting point for learning about Richard Wright, with an overview of his personal life and career, publications list, biographical and critical sources, media adaptations, and links to other online resources. Also includes information about a 1995 PBS-TV film biography, *Richard Wright: Black Boy*.

The Wright Stuff

Native Son, 1940
Black Boy, 1945
The Outsider, 1953
Savage Holiday, 1954
The Long Dream, 1958
Lawd Today, 1963
American Hunger, 1977

If You Like Richard Wright...

Try Nelson Algren's *The Man with the Golden Arm* and James T. Farrell's Studs Lonigan trilogy. You might also like books by James Baldwin, Ralph Ellison, and Toni Morrison.

Best Book to Read First

Black Boy (1945), the first volume of Wright's autobiography. According to *American Poetry Review*, "if not Wright's biggest book, it is perhaps his best, and surely his best written." Because it uses many of the techniques of fiction, *Black Boy* is considered by many to be more novel than autobiography.

[Wright was] a man praised too soon for the wrong reasons and too soon dismissed for more wrong reasons. . . . In death as in life, Wright has been forced to win as a Negro who happened to be a writer the recognition that he desired as a writer who happened to be a Negro.

—Warren French

What Else to Read

From the days of our very first outline sketches for this book, we'd always envisioned providing two approaches for helping passionate readers find great books to read. The main body of the book would present information on specific authors and expand the focus with "If you like . . ." lists and other references. The second part of the book would take a different approach, highlighting the major literary awards and other forms of recognition for books and authors. What we didn't know was how fascinating and rewarding this approach would turn out to be.

In all honesty, had some TV game-show host asked, "For one million dollars, what's the difference between the National Book Award and the Pulitzer Prize for Fiction?" we would have said, "Uh . . ." The host would have asked, "Is that your final answer?" And we would have again responded, "Uh . . ." There would have been no point in asking for help from a friend under the rules of the game because, though we know many voracious readers, we don't know anyone who could have come up with the right answer.

There are so many important literary awards, but there is so little knowledge about them. Ever curious, we were driven to collect the details: How are books nominated? Who are the judges? What is the evaluation process? And, yes, what does the author get—cash or some dust-collecting piece of bric-a-brac? Who are the previous award winners and where can one find the latest information on this year's nominees? You'll find answers to all of these questions in "Prize Winners and Prized Books," along with an array of "best of" lists, some of them quirky, some of them not, depending on your point of view. You'll also learn everything you need to know about the leading bestseller lists, including how they're created and where to find them online.

And far from limiting things to "literature," we have devoted considerable space to genre fiction. "For one mil-

lion dollars, what's the difference between the Hugo Award and the Nebula Award for science fiction? Or the Edgar and the Agatha for mystery authors? And for extra points, what are the RITA Awards?" The answers can be found in the pages that follow, along with lists of the award-winning novels and "Grand Masters" for each genre.

In short, the "Prize Winners and Prized Books" section is a delight. But the "Readers' Resources" section bears down and offers hands-on information regarding book groups and the tools and publications available to help you establish a book group among your friends, plus contact information for wonderful audiobook presentations of your favorite fiction. Please do not buy the abridged cassette version until you have explored the unabridged possibilities. You will be cheating yourself of such pleasure. As this section points out, audiobooks are available from most local libraries, so listening costs you nothing.

Here you will also find wonderful catalogs of "unsuspected" books, and you will learn how easy it is, in the age of the Internet, to locate and purchase books that are no longer in print. Books you've been after for years may be only a mouse-click away, once you check these Web sites. (At least that has been our experience.) And if it's book reviews you're after, you'll find recommendations on the best sources.

Finally, in "Special Events and Publishers," you'll learn about book-related events large and small, and the land addresses you should use to send fan mail to authors via their publishers. But why would you want to? The answer is simple: Because you loved a particular book. Or because it infuriated you. Either way, there isn't an author alive—even those who are famous recluses—who secretly doesn't enjoy hearing from readers.

In summary, we're convinced that you'll find this part of the book to be invaluable in enhancing and expanding the scope of your reading life, regardless of your specific interests.

Prize Winners and Prized Books

A wards and prizes are an important part of every industry, but nowhere more so than in publishing, where they can serve as a pretty reliable guide for people interested in what to read next. Yet, while most people have at least a vague understanding of who votes for, say, the Academy Awards, virtually no one outside the publishing and literary community has any idea of what the major book awards are all about. Who nominates the books? Who judges them? And on what basis are the winners selected?

You'll find the answers here. The section begins with the leading awards and prizes for literature and then moves to literature of another sort—genre fiction—to consider awards for writers of horror, mysteries, romance, science fiction and fantasy, and Westerns. In each case you'll find explanations and Web addresses you can use to get more information. But to save you a bit of time, we've also included lists of the award winners, including, in the genre fiction section, the authors who have been awarded Grand Master status by their peers in recognition of their lifetime achievements. Once you know what the major awards are all about, you'll be able to make better use of them in your book purchase and what-to-read-next decisions.

MAJOR LITERARY FICTION AWARDS

Book Sense Book of the Year Award

Most literary awards are given by writers to other writers. The Book Sense Book of the Year, in contrast, is voted on by the unsung heroes of the book world—independent booksellers and book clerks who heft the cartons, stock the shelves, and sell with their hearts as well as their hands. They give two awards each year for "hidden treasures"—books that they most enjoyed recommending to their customers in the previous year—one for adult fiction or nonfiction and one for a children's book. From 1991 to 1999, it was known as the ABBY (short for "American Booksellers Book of the Year").

Five finalists are nominated in each category and voted on by the booksellers. One book is selected as the winner, and runners-up become "Honor Books." The awards are announced and presented at the annual American Booksellers Association (ABA) convention, held in conjunction with BookExpo America. Winning authors receive $500 and an engraved Tiffany glass prism. For more information and a list of all the past winners and nominees, visit www.bookweb.org/news/awards on the Web.

Here are the winners in the "Adult Trade" category (which includes both fiction and nonfiction) going back to 1993, as well as the winners for 1991 and 1992, when there was only a single category:

Divine Secrets of the Ya-Ya Sisterhood by Rebecca Wells (1999)
Cold Mountain by Charles Frazier (1998)
Angela's Ashes: A Memoir by Frank McCourt (1997)
Snow Falling on Cedars by David Guterson (1996)
Chicken Soup for the Soul by Jack Canfield and Mark Victor Hansen (1995)
Like Water for Chocolate by Laura Esquivel (1994)
The Bridges of Madison County by Robert James Waller (1993)
Brother Eagle, Sister Sky by Chief Seattle, illustrated by Susan Jeffers (1992)
The Education of Little Tree by Forrest Carter (1991)

Booker Prize

Awarded annually to the best full-length novel written in English by a British or Commonwealth author, this prize is funded by Booker Plc, owner of Booker Cash & Carry, the largest food wholesaler in the United Kingdom. Established in 1968 and administered with the help of Book Trust, an independent charity devoted to promoting books and reading, the Booker Prize is judged by a different panel of novelists, professors, and editors each year.

In September, the committee announces its short list of candidates, each of whom receives £1,000 (about $1,650) and a specially bound edition of his or her book.

The winner is announced at a dinner in October and presented with £21,000 (about $34,500). For more information, visit www.bookerprize.co.uk. Here are all the winners:

Disgrace by J. M. Coetzee (1999)
Amsterdam by Ian McEwan (1998)
The God of Small Things by Arundhati Roy (1997)
Last Orders by Graham Swift (1996)
The Ghost Road by Pat Barker (1995)
How Late It Was, How Late by James Kelman (1994)
Paddy Clark Ha Ha Ha by Roddy Doyle (1993)
The English Patient by Michael Ondaatje (1992)
Sacred Hunger by Barry Unsworth (1992)
The Famished Road by Ben Okri (1991)
Possession by A. S. Byatt (1990)
The Remains of the Day by Kazuo Ishiguro (1989)
Oscar and Lucinda by Peter Carey (1988)
Moon Tiger by Penelope Lively (1987)
The Old Devils by Kingsley Amis (1986)
The Bone People by Keri Hulme (1985)
Hotel du Lac by Anita Brookner (1984)
Life and Times of Michael K by J. M. Coetzee (1983)
Schindler's Ark by Thomas Keneally (1982)
Midnight's Children by Salman Rushdie (1981)
Rites of Passage by William Golding (1980)
Offshore by Penelope Fitzgerald (1979)
The Sea, the Sea by Iris Murdoch (1978)
Staying On by Paul Scott (1977)
Saville by David Storey (1976)
Heat and Dust by Ruth Prawer Jhabvala (1975)
The Conservationist by Nadine Gordimer (1974)
The Siege of Krishnapur by J. G. Farrell (1973)
G by John Berger (1972)
In a Free State by V. S. Naipaul (1971)
The Elected Member by Bernice Rubens (1970)
Something to Answer For by P. H. Newby (1969)

Literary Awards Quick Reference

Book Sense Book of the Year Award
www.bookweb.org/news/awards

Booker Prize
www.bookerprize.co.uk

Nobel Prize in Literature
www.nobel.se

PEN/Faulkner Award
www.folger.edu/public/pfaulk/menu.htm

Hemingway Foundation/PEN Award
ww.pen-ne.org

National Book Award
www.publishersweekly.com/nbf

National Book Critics Circle Award
www.publishersweekly.com/nbcc

Pulitzer Prize
www.pulitzer.org

Nobel Prize in Literature

This is one of several prizes established by Alfred Nobel, the Swedish engineer and industrialist who discovered that mixing nitroglycerine with silica produced a paste that could be shaped into rods and used in mining, canal-building, and other blasting operations. In 1867, he patented the product under the name "dynamite."

In his will, Nobel directed that his fortune be used for annual prizes in physics, chemistry, physiology or medicine, literature, and peace. (The prize for economics was added in 1969.) The Nobel Prize in Literature—the most prestigious and financially rich of all literary awards (winners receive about $960,000)—is announced each year in October. It's given to a writer, not for a single work of prose or poetry, but in recognition of an outstanding body of work. The nationality of the nominees is not a consideration. The awards ceremony is conducted in Stockholm on December 10, the anniversary of Alfred Nobel's death. For more information, visit www.nobel.se.

Here are the winners for each year that the Nobel Prize in Literature has been presented:

Günter Grass, Germany (1999)
José Saramago, Portugal (1998)
Dario Fo, Italy (1997)
Wislawa Szymborska, Poland (1996)
Seamus Heaney, Ireland (1995)
Kenzaburo Oe, Japan (1994)
Toni Morrison, United States (1993)
Derek Walcott, St. Lucia (1992)
Nadine Gordimer, South Africa (1991)
Octavio Paz, Mexico (1990)
Camilo José Cela, Spain (1989)
Naguib Mahfouz, Egypt (1988)
Joseph Brodsky, United States (1987)
Wole Soyinka, Nigeria (1986)
Claude Simon, France (1985)
Jaroslav Seifert, Czechoslovakia (1984)
William Golding, Great Britain (1983)
Gabriel García Márquez, Colombia (1982)
Elias Canetti, Bulgaria (1981)
Czeslaw Milosz, Poland (1980)
Odysseus Elytis, Greece (1979)
Isaac Bashevis Singer, United States (1978)
Vicente Aleixandre, Spain (1977)
Saul Bellow, United States (1976)
Eugenio Montale, Italy (1975)
Harry Martinson, Sweden (1974)
Eyvind Johnson, Sweden (1974)
Patrick White, Australia (1973)
Heinrich Böll, Germany (1972)
Pablo Neruda, Chile (1971)
Alexander Solzhenitsyn, Russia (1970)
Samuel Beckett, Ireland (1969)
Yasunari Kawabata, Japan (1968)
Miguel Asturias, Guatemala (1967)
Nelly Sachs, Germany (1966)
Shmuel Agnon, Austria (1966)
Mikhail Sholokhov, Russia (1965)
Jean-Paul Sartre, France (1964)
George Seferis, Greece (1963)
John Steinbeck, United States (1962)
Ivo Andric, Yugoslavia (1961)
Saint-John Perse, France (1960)
Salvatore Quasimodo, Italy (1959)
Boris Pasternak, Russia (1958)
Albert Camus, France (1957)
Juan Jiménez, Spain (1956)
Halldór Laxness, Iceland (1955)

Ernest Hemingway, United States (1954)
Sir Winston Churchill, Great Britain (1953)
François Mauriac, France (1952)
Pär Fabian Lagerkvist, Sweden (1951)
Bertrand Russell, Great Britain (1950)
William Faulkner, United States (1949)
T. S. Eliot, Great Britain (1948)
André Gide, France (1947)
Hermann Hesse, Germany (1946)
Gabriela Mistral, Chile (1945)
Johannes Jensen, Denmark (1944)
Frans Sillanpää, Finland (1939)
Pearl S. Buck, United States (1938)
Roger Martin du Gard, France (1937)
Eugene O'Neill, United States (1936)
Luigi Pirandello, Italy (1934)
Ivan Bunin, Russia (1933)
John Galsworthy, Great Britain (1932)
Erik Axel Karlfeldt, Sweden (1931)
Sinclair Lewis, United States (1930)
Thomas Mann, Germany (1929)
Sigrid Undset, Norway (1928)
Henri Bergson, France (1927)
Grazia Deledda, Italy (1926)
George Bernard Shaw, Ireland (1925)
Wladyslaw Reymont, Poland (1924)
William Butler Yeats, Ireland (1923)
Jacinto Benavente y Martínez, Spain (1922)
Anatole France, France (1921)
Knut Hamsun, Norway (1920)
Carl Spitteler, Switzerland (1919)
Henrik Pontoppidan, Denmark (1917)
Karl Adolph Gjellerup, Denmark (1917)
Verner von Heidenstam, Sweden (1916)
Romain Rolland, France (1915)
Sir Rabindranath Tagore, India (1913)
Gerhart Hauptmann, Germany (1912)
Maurice Maeterlinck, Belgium (1911)
Paul Ludwig von Heyse, Germany (1910)
Selma Lagerlöf, Sweden (1909)
Rudolf Eucken, Germany (1908)
Rudyard Kipling, Great Britain (1907)
Giosuè Carducci, Italy (1906)
Henryk Sienkiewicz, Poland (1905)
Frédéric Mistral, France (1904)
José Echegaray, Spain (1904)
Björnstjerne Björnson, Norway (1903)
Theodor Mommsen, Germany (1902)
René François Armand Sully-Prudhomme, France (1901)

PEN/Faulkner and Hemingway Foundation/PEN Awards

PEN stands for "Poets, Playwrights, Editors, Essayists and Novelists." The PEN American Center (in New York City) is the largest of nearly 130 PEN Centers around the world that comprise International PEN, an organization that strives to "defend freedom of expression wherever it may be threatened, and promote and encourage the recognition and reading of contemporary literature." PEN American Center offers numerous awards for translating, editing, poetry, and drama. (You can find more information about them at the organization's Web site at www.pen.org.) But the PEN/Faulkner and Hemingway Foundation/PEN Awards are administered by others.

The PEN/Faulkner Award was established in 1980 by writers to honor their peers. Though funded by an endowment, it's named for William Faulkner in recognition of the fact that he used his Nobel Prize money to create an award for young writers. The PEN/Faulkner judges, all fiction writers themselves, are charged with selecting five outstanding books from among 250 novels and short-story collections published during the calendar year. The winning prize is $15,000, but the others on the shortlist receive $5,000 each. All five authors read from their works and are honored at an award ceremony held at the Folger Library in Washington, DC, each May. For more information, visit www.folger.edu/public/pfaulk/menu.htm.

Here are all the PEN/Faulkner Award winners:

The Hours by Michael Cunningham (1999)
The Bear Comes Home by Rafi Zabor (1998)
Women in Their Beds by Gina Berriault (1997)
Independence Day by Richard Ford (1996)
Snow Falling on Cedars by David Guterson (1995)
Operation Shylock by Philip Roth (1994)
Postcards by E. Annie Proulx (1993)
Mao II by Don DeLillo (1992)
Philadelphia Fire by John Edgar Wideman (1991)
Billy Bathgate by E. L. Doctorow (1990)
Dusk by James Salter (1989)
World's End by T. Coraghessan Boyle (1988)
Soldiers in Hiding by Richard Wiley (1987)
The Old Forest by Peter Taylor (1986)
The Barracks Thief by Tobias Wolff (1985)
Sent for You Yesterday by John Edgar Wideman (1984)
Seaview by Toby Olson (1983)
The Chaneysville Incident by David Bradley (1982)
How German Is It? by Walter Abish (1981)

The Hemingway Foundation/PEN Award, established in 1976 by the late Mary Hemingway, is a $7,500 prize for a distinguished first work of fiction by an American citizen or resident. Now administered by the Hemingway Society, the award is judged by a panel of three PEN authors. Both novels and short-story collections are eligible. The award ceremony takes place under the auspices of PEN New England at Boston's John F. Kennedy Library, which holds some 95 percent of Hemingway's manuscripts and correspondence. For more information, visit www.pen-ne.org.

Here are the books and authors that have won the Hemingway Foundation/PEN Award:

A Private State by Charlotte Bacon (1998)
Ocean of Words by Ha Jin (1997)
Native Speaker by Chang-Rae Lee (1996)
The Grass Dancer by Susan Power (1995)
The Magic of Blood by Dagoberto Gilb (1994)
Lost in the City by Edward P. Jones (1993)
Wartime Lies by Louis Begley (1992)
Maps to Anywhere by Bernard Cooper (1991)
The Ice at the Bottom of the World by Mark Richard (1990)
The Book of Ruth by Jane Hamilton (1989)
Imagining Argentina by Lawrence Thornton (1988)
Tongues of Flame by Mary Ward Brown (1987)
Lady's Time by Alan V. Hewar (1986)
Dreams of Sleep by Josephine Humphreys (1985)
During the Reign of the Queen of Sheba by Joan Chase (1984)
Shiloh and Other Stories by Bobbie Ann Mason (1983)
Housekeeping by Marilynne Robinson (1982)
Household Words by Joan Silber (1981)
Mom Kills Kids and Self by Alan Saperstein (1980)
Hasen by Reuben Bercovitch (1979)
A Way of Life, Like Any Other by Darcy O'Brien (1978)
Speedboat by Renata Adler (1977)
Parthian Shot by Loyd Little (1976)

National Book Award

Established in 1950 by several American publishing trade groups to promote outstanding works by American authors, the National Book Award was originally managed by volunteers from publishers' publicity departments. (Between 1980 and 1986, it was called the American Book Award.) In 1989, sponsorship of the award was shifted to the National Book Foundation, an independent institution that also promotes reading throughout the United States.

There are currently four award categories: fiction, nonfiction, poetry, and children's literature. Nominations are made by publishers, and judging is done by panels of five writers who change every year. The panels read more than 200 books to winnow the list down to five finalists, whose names are released in early November. Winners are announced at a gala dinner later that month. The prizes are $10,000 for the winner in each category and $1,000 for each runner-up. For more information about the National Book Awards and other activities of the National Book

Foundation, visit www.publishersweekly.com/nbf.
Here are all the winners in the fiction category:

Waiting by Ha Jin (1999)

Charming Billy by Alice McDermott (1998)

Cold Mountain by Charles Frazier (1997)

Ship Fever and Other Stories by Andrea Barrett (1996)

Sabbath's Theater by Philip Roth (1995)

A Frolic of His Own by William Gaddis (1994)

The Shipping News by E. Annie Proulx (1993)

All the Pretty Horses by Cormac McCarthy (1992)

Mating by Norman Rush (1991)

Middle Passage by Charles Johnson (1990)

Spartina by John Casey (1989)

Paris Trout by Pete Dexter (1988)

Paco's Story by Larry Heinemann (1987)

World's Fair by E. L. Doctorow (1986)

White Noise by Don DeLillo (1985)

Victory over Japan: A Book of Stories by Ellen Gilchrist (1984)

Collected Stories of Eudora Welty by Eudora Welty (1983, paperback)

The Color Purple by Alice Walker (1983, hardcover)

So Long, See You Tomorrow by William Maxwell (1982, paperback)

Rabbit Is Rich by John Updike (1982, hardcover)

The Stories of John Cheever by John Cheever (1981, paperback)

Plains Song by Wright Morris (1981, hardcover)

The World According to Garp by John Irving (1980, paperback)

Sophie's Choice by William Styron (1980, hardcover)

Going After Cacciato by Tim O'Brien (1979)

Blood Ties by Mary Lee Settle (1978)

The Spectator Bird by Wallace Stegner (1977)

JR by William Gaddis (1976)

The Hair of Harold Roux by Thomas Williams (1975)

Dog Soldiers by Robert Stone (1975)

A Crown of Feathers and Other Stories by Isaac Bashevis Singer (1974)

Gravity's Rainbow by Thomas Pynchon (1974)

Augustus by John Williams (1973)

Chimera by John Barth (1973)

The Complete Stories of Flannery O'Connor by Flannery O'Connor (1972)

Mr. Sammler's Planet by Saul Bellow (1971)

Them by Joyce Carol Oates (1970)

Steps by Jerzy Kosinski (1969)

The Eighth Day by Thornton Wilder (1968)

The Fixer by Bernard Malamud (1967)

The Collected Stories of Katherine Anne Porter by Katherine Anne Porter (1966)

Herzog by Saul Bellow (1965)

The Centaur by John Updike (1964)

Morte D'Urban by J. F. Powers (1963)

The Moviegoer by Walker Percy (1962)

The Waters of Kronos by Conrad Richter (1961)

Goodbye, Columbus by Philip Roth (1960)

The Magic Barrel by Bernard Malamud (1959)

The Wapshot Chronicle by John Cheever (1958)

The Field of Vision by Wright Morris (1957)

Ten North Frederick by John O'Hara (1956)

A Fable by William Faulkner (1955)

The Adventures of Augie March by Saul Bellow (1954)

Invisible Man by Ralph Ellison (1953)

From Here to Eternity by James Jones (1952)

The Collected Stories of William Faulkner by William Faulkner (1951)

The Man with the Golden Arm by Nelson Algren (1950)

National Book Critics Circle Award

The National Book Critics Circle (NBCC) is a nonprofit organization comprising nearly 700 active book reviewers. The group's mission is to raise the quality of book criticism and to provide a mechanism for communicating with fellow professionals. But it also awards prizes each year for the best books in each of five categories: fiction, nonfiction, biography and autobiography, poetry, and criticism.

Starting in 1999, the award criteria were changed to allow nominations of books by authors outside the U.S. Winners are selected from a list of five finalists in each category and presented with a scroll and a citation. For more information, visit www.publishersweekly.com/nbcc.
Here are all the winners in the fiction category:

Motherless Brooklyn by Jonathan Lethem (1999)

The Love of a Good Woman by Alice Munro (1998)

The Blue Flower by Penelope Fitzgerald (1997)

Women in Their Beds by Gina Berriault (1996)

Mrs. Ted Bliss by Stanley Elkin (1995)

The Stone Diaries by Carol Shields (1994)

A Lesson Before Dying by Ernest J. Gaines (1993)

All the Pretty Horses by Cormac McCarthy (1992)

A Thousand Acres by Jane Smiley (1991)

Rabbit at Rest by John Updike (1990)

Billy Bathgate by E. L. Doctorow (1989)

The Middleman and Other Stories by Bharati Mukherjee (1988)

The Counterlife by Philip Roth (1987)

Kate Vaiden by Reynolds Price (1986)

The Accidental Tourist by Anne Tyler (1985)

Love Medicine by Louise Erdrich (1984)

Ironweed by William Kennedy (1983)

George Mills by Stanley Elkin (1982)

Rabbit Is Rich by John Updike (1981)

The Transit of Venus by Shirley Hazzard (1980)

The Year of the French by Thomas Flanagan (1979)

The Stories of John Cheever by John Cheever (1978)
Song of Solomon by Toni Morrison (1977)
October Light by John Gardner (1976)
Ragtime by E. L. Doctorow (1975)

Pulitzer Prize

Among the most coveted of literary prizes, the Pulitzer is named for and was endowed by Joseph Pulitzer. Born in Hungary in 1847 of a Jewish father and a German Roman Catholic mother, Pulitzer was fluent in Hungarian, German, and French. He didn't learn English until coming to America to take the place of a draftee in the Civil War.

After the war he went to St. Louis, where he first owned a German-language newspaper and then the *St. Louis Post-Dispatch*. Later, he bought the *New York World*, and used cartoons, crusades, news stunts, and illustrations to build it into the largest circulation newspaper in the country.

In his will, Pulitzer provided for establishing the nation's first school of journalism at Columbia University and set up the mechanism for awarding annual prizes for excellence in journalism, literature, music, and drama. Nominees must be Americans. Entries are judged by juries of distinguished figures in their respective fields. The awards ($5,000 each) are announced each April and presented by the president of Columbia at a luncheon held each May. For more information, visit www.pulitzer.org.

Here are all the winners for fiction:

The Hours by Michael Cunningham (1999)
American Pastoral by Philip Roth (1998)
Martin Dressler: The Tale of an American Dreamer by Steven Millhauser (1997)
Independence Day by Richard Ford (1996)
The Stone Diaries by Carol Shields (1995)
The Shipping News by E. Annie Proulx (1994)
A Good Scent from a Strange Mountain by Robert Olen Butler (1993)
A Thousand Acres by Jane Smiley (1992)
Rabbit at Rest by John Updike (1991)
The Mambo Kings Play Songs of Love by Oscar Hijuelos (1990)
Breathing Lessons by Anne Tyler (1989)
Beloved by Toni Morrison (1988)
A Summons to Memphis by Peter Taylor (1987)
Lonesome Dove by Larry McMurtry (1986)
Foreign Affairs by Alison Lurie (1985)
Ironweed by William Kennedy (1984)
The Color Purple by Alice Walker (1983)
Rabbit Is Rich by John Updike (1982)
A Confederacy of Dunces by John Kennedy Toole (1981)
The Executioner's Song by Norman Mailer (1980)
The Stories of John Cheever by John Cheever (1979)

Elbow Room by James Alan McPherson (1978)
Humboldt's Gift by Saul Bellow (1976)
The Killer Angels by Michael Shaara (1975)
The Optimist's Daughter by Eudora Welty (1973)
Angle of Repose by Wallace Stegner (1972)
Collected Stories by Jean Stafford (1970)
House Made of Dawn by N. Scott Momaday (1969)
The Confessions of Nat Turner by William Styron (1968)
The Fixer by Bernard Malamud (1967)
The Collected Stories of Katherine Anne Porter by Katherine Anne Porter (1966)
The Keepers of the House by Shirley Ann Grau (1965)
The Reivers by William Faulkner (1963)
The Edge of Sadness by Edwin O'Connor (1962)
To Kill a Mockingbird by Harper Lee (1961)
Advise and Consent by Allen Drury (1960)
The Travels of Jaimie McPheeters by Robert Lewis Taylor (1959)
A Death in the Family by James Agee (1958)
Andersonville by MacKinlay Kantor (1956)
A Fable by William Faulkner (1955)
The Old Man and the Sea by Ernest Hemingway (1953)
The Caine Mutiny by Herman Wouk (1952)
The Town by Conrad Richter (1951)
The Way West by A. B. Guthrie, Jr. (1950)
Guard of Honor by James Gould Cozzens (1949)
Tales of the South Pacific by James A. Michener (1948)
All the King's Men by Robert Penn Warren (1947)
A Bell for Adano by John Hersey (1945)
Journey in the Dark by Martin Flavin (1944)
Dragon's Teeth by Upton Sinclair (1943)
In This Our Life by Ellen Glasgow (1942)
The Grapes of Wrath by John Steinbeck (1940)
The Yearling by Marjorie Kinnan Rawlings (1939)
The Late George Apley by John P. Marquand (1938)
Gone with the Wind by Margaret Mitchell (1937)
Honey in the Horn by Harold L. Davis (1936)
Now in November by Josephine W. Johnson (1935)
Lamb in His Bosom by Caroline Miller (1934)
The Store by T. S. Stribling (1933)
The Good Earth by Pearl S. Buck (1932)
Years of Grace by Margaret Ayer Barnes (1931)
Laughing Boy by Oliver LaFarge (1930)
Scarlet Sister Mary by Julia M. Peterkin (1929)
The Bridge of San Luis Rey by Thornton Wilder (1928)
Early Autumn by Louis Bromfield (1927)
Arrowsmith by Sinclair Lewis (1926)
So Big by Edna Ferber (1925)
The Able McLaughlins by Margaret Wilson (1924)
One of Ours by Willa Cather (1923)
Alice Adams by Booth Tarkington (1922)
The Age of Innocence by Edith Wharton (1921)
The Magnificent Ambersons by Booth Tarkington (1919)
His Family by Ernest Poole (1918)

GENRE FICTION

According to the classical ideal, literature should both delight and instruct. Other theories and philosophies have been propounded over the centuries, of course, giving rise to a whole range of "isms" (naturalism, realism, formalism, etc.). Unfortunately, the typical "ism" tends more toward the "instruct" side of things, while "delight" usually gets lost in the shuffle.

Genre fiction reverses the emphasis, and in so doing probably comes closer to what the Roman poet Horace had in mind when he set forth the delight-and-instruct ideal in *Ars Poetica*. His point: If your purpose is to instruct, then you'll catch more flies with honey than with vinegar. Of the many forms of delight in literature—delight in a well-turned phrase, a complex character, scenes and descriptions that sear themselves into your memory—genre fiction offers the most basic. It is the delight we all feel when an author responds to our request, "Tell me a story." Simple, childlike, and universal, the human need for "story" is what powers everything from fantasy to horror to romance to Westerns. And over the years, it has sold billions of books.

In general, such books tend to be avoided by serious readers, no matter how passionate and broadminded they may be. After all, "Ninety percent of all science fiction is crap," as the late SF writer Theodore Sturgeon put it, "But then, 90 percent of *everything* is crap." Informally known as "Sturgeon's Law," the last part of this quote certainly applies in some degree to a great deal of genre fiction. But the 10 percent that *is* good is usually quite good indeed, and it would be a shame to miss it.

One good way to identify that magic 10 percent is to start with the genre's top authors as chosen by its writers and fans—authors who have been presented with a "Grand Master" or "Lifetime Achievement" award for their overall contributions to the genre. Another trick for ensuring a good read is to zero in on specific top-rated titles, since even the best novelists aren't always at the top of their form. If you try several of a genre's leading authors and "top titles" and don't like them, you can probably say with some authority that you don't care for a particular genre.

However, you might find that these lists open doors to delights you never suspected existed and would not otherwise have discovered. For answering the request to "Tell me a story," is only the beginning of what genre fiction has to offer.

Horror

The World Horror Convention (WHC)—an annual gathering of readers, professionals, and "anyone else interested in imaginative literature, but especially the fiction, art, or dramatization of the dark fantastic"—confers its Grand Master Award each year to a horror writer who has had "a significant influence on the members' interest in and appreciation of horror literature and art." The person must be living in order to qualify and may only receive the award once. For more information, including an updated list of winners, visit www.worldhorror.org.

GRAND MASTERS

Clive Barker
Robert Bloch
Ramsey Campbell
Stephen King
Dean Koontz
Brian Lumley
Richard Matheson
Anne Rice
Peter Straub

Genius in Genres

"For the past 30 years the greatest novelists writing in English have been genre writers: John le Carré, George Higgins and Patrick O'Brian.

"Each year, of course, found the press discovering some writer whose style, provenance and choice of theme it found endearing. These usually trig, slim tomes shared a wistful and self-commendatory confusion at the multiplicity of life and stank of Art. But the genre writers wrote without sentimentality; their prose was concise and perceptive; in it the reader sees the life of which they wrote, rather than the writer's 'technique.'

"For to hell with this putrid and despicable Graduate Degree sensitivity. Le Carré had been a spy, Higgins was a working lawyer and district attorney, and God knows what Patrick O'Brian had not been up to in his 80-plus years."

—David Mamet,
New York Times, January 17, 2000

The Top 40 Horror Books of All Time

As the Horror Writers Association (HWA) notes, "Horror often has a poor reputation. It's hard to convince people who have read one too many second-rate horror novels that there is, indeed, horror worth reading." Consequently, the group established the Bram Stoker Awards for Superior Achievement in horror writing, determined by a vote of active HWA members and presented at the group's annual meeting and awards banquet. A complete list of all the winners and nominees going back to 1988 is available at the HWA Web site (www.horror.org/stoker.htm).

The HWA has also assembled a list of what its members feel are the very best horror books of all time. It's important to emphasize that *no ranking* is implied. The list is arranged alphabetically by author.

Best Ghost Stories of Algernon Blackwood by Algernon Blackwood
The Exorcist by William Peter Blatty
Something Wicked This Way Comes by Ray Bradbury
Lost Souls by Poppy Z. Brite
The Hungry Moon by Ramsey Campbell
The Between by Tananarive Due
Darklands by Dennis Etchison
Raven by Charles L. Grant
Dead in the Water by Nancy Holder
The Haunting of Hill House by Shirley Jackson
The Lottery and Other Stories by Shirley Jackson
The Turn of the Screw by Henry James
The Ghost Stories of M. R. James by M. R. James
Dr. Adder by K.W. Jeter
The Metamorphosis and Other Stories by Franz Kafka
Pet Sematary by Stephen King
The Shining by Stephen King
The Stand by Stephen King
Skin by Kathe Koja
Dark Dance by Tanith Lee
Conjure Wife by Fritz Leiber
Rosemary's Baby by Ira Levin
Songs of a Dead Dreamer by Thomas Ligotti
Lovers Living, Lovers Dead by Richard Lortz
The Dunwich Horror and Others by H. P. Lovecraft
At the Mountains of Madness by H. P. Lovecraft
The Hill of Dreams by Arthur Machen
Tales of Horror and the Supernatural by Arthur Machen
Sineater by Elizabeth Massie
I Am Legend by Richard Matheson
Relic by Douglas Preston and Lincoln Child
Frankenstein by Mary Shelley
Book of the Dead edited by John Skipp and Craig Spector
Ghoul by Michael Slade
Vampire Junction by S. P. Somtow
The Strange Case of Dr. Jekyll and Mr. Hyde by Robert Louis Stevenson
Dracula by Bram Stoker
Some of Your Blood by Theodore Sturgeon
Phantom by Thomas Tessier
Sacrifice by Andrew Vachss

Mystery

The Mystery Writers of America (MWA) presented their first Grand Master Award in 1955 to Agatha Christie. Since then, more than three dozen authors have been recognized for their important contributions to the mystery field and for producing "a significant output of consistently high quality." For more information about the award, visit the MWA Web site at www.mysterywriters.net/awards.

GRAND MASTERS

Eric Ambler
Lawrence Block
W. R. Burnett
James M. Cain
John Dickson Carr
Agatha Christie
George Harmon Coxe
John Creasey
Dorothy Salisbury Davis
Daphne du Maurier
Mignon G. Eberhart
Stanley Ellin
Dick Francis
Erle Stanley Gardner
Michael Gilbert
Graham Greene
Tony Hillerman
Alfred Hitchcock
Dorothy B. Hughes
P. D. James
Baynard Kendrick
John le Carré
Elmore Leonard
John D. MacDonald
Ross Macdonald
Ngaio Marsh
Ed McBain
Helen McCloy
Barbara Mertz
Margaret Millar

Judson Philips
Ellery Queen
Ruth Rendell
Georges Simenon
Mickey Spillane
Vincent Starrett
Aaron Marc Stein
Rex Stout
Julian Symons
Hillary Waugh
Phyllis A. Whitney

The Top 25 Mystery Novels: The Edgars for 1975–99

For specific mystery titles, start with this list of recent Edgar Award–winning novels. The Mystery Writers of America (MWA) present the Edgars each year for distinguished mystery works in various categories, including Best Novel, Best First Novel by an American Author, Best Paperback Original, and several others. Named for the group's patron saint, Edgar Allan Poe, the awards have been given annually since 1945. For lists of all past winners and nominees, visit www.mysterywriters.net.

Mr. White's Confession by Robert Clark (1999)
Cimarron Rose by James Lee Burke (1998)
The Chatham School Affair by Thomas H. Cook (1997)
Come to Grief by Dick Francis (1996)
The Red Scream by Mary Willis Walker (1995)
The Sculptress by Minette Walters (1994)
Bootlegger's Daughter by Margaret Maron (1993)
A Dance at the Slaughterhouse by Lawrence Block (1992)
New Orleans Mourning by Julie Smith (1991)
Black Cherry Blues by James Lee Burke (1990)
A Cold Red Sunrise by Stuart M. Kaminsky (1989)
Old Bones by Aaron Elkins (1988)
A Dark-Adapted Eye by Barbara Vine (1987)
The Suspect by L. R. Wright (1986)
Briarpatch by Ross Thomas (1985)
La Brava by Elmore Leonard (1984)
Billingsgate Shoal by Rick Boyer (1983)
Peregrine by William Bayer (1982)
Whip Hand by Dick Francis (1981)
The Rheingold Route by Arthur Maling (1980)
The Eye of the Needle by Ken Follett (1979)
Catch Me: Kill Me by William H. Hallahan (1978)
Promised Land by Robert B. Parker (1977)
Hopscotch by Brian Garfield (1976)
Peter's Pence by Jon Cleary (1975)

Other Mystery Awards

In addition to the Edgar Awards, there are three other important prizes for mystery fiction that are worth knowing about:

AGATHA AWARD

Presented by Malice Domestic, a nonprofit group of over 700 authors, academics, fans, dealers, editors, and agents from all over the world, the Agathas are presented at an annual convention in Washington, D.C., each April. Eligible books must have been published in the United States and qualify as a "Malice Domestic." That means no explicit sex, gore, or violence; an amateur as the detective; a confined setting; and characters who know each other. In other words, the American equivalent of a British "cozy" of the sort that Agatha Christie (for whom the award is named) did so well.

Though suggestions for nominations are considered by the Agatha Awards Committee, the committee itself monitors the year's mysteries for those meeting the Malice Domestic criteria. Voting is done by convention attendees. The award is a teapot with the Malice skull and crossbones on its side. For more information, visit www.erols.com/malice.

GOLD AND SILVER DAGGER AWARDS

These awards are administered by the Crime Writers Association, a group founded in 1953 for British crime writers of both fiction and nonfiction. The Gold Dagger is awarded to the best crime novel of the year, the Silver Dagger to the second best. Books are nominated by publishers. The award consists of a metal-plated dagger and a check. For more information, visit www.twbooks.co.uk/cwa/cwa.html.

MACAVITY AWARD

A readers' award, this is among the newest of the many honors for mystery fiction. It's named for the "mystery cat" of the musical *Cats* and T. S. Eliot's *Old Possum's Book of Practical Cats*, on which the musical is based.

Nominations and voting are done by members of Mystery Readers International—"the largest mystery fan/reader organization in the world." Founded by respected mystery writer Janet A. Rudolph, this organization is open to readers, fans, critics, writers, and anyone else with an interest in mysteries. Annual membership is $24 and entitles members to four issues of *Mystery Readers Journal*, plus the opportunity to nominate and vote for the Macavities. For more information, visit murderonthemenu.com or send an e-mail message to whodunit@murderonthemenu.com.

Romance

The Romance Writers of America (RWA) call their annual book prizes the RITA Awards, in honor of Rita Clay Estrada, the group's first president. Winners are announced each year at the RWA conference. Literally hundreds of romance novels are nominated by authors, editors, agents, and readers. The books are read and judged by a panel of five published romance authors. Finalists are selected in several categories, and then those finalists are judged by a second panel of five authors to select the winners. The prize itself is a golden statuette of a woman writing with a quill pen.

The RWA also honors one author each year with its Lifetime Achievement Award (known as the Golden Treasure from 1983 to 1989). Winners are selected for their "significant contributions to romantic fiction and the romance genre" over at least a 15-year period, and they must be currently active in promoting the genre, either by publishing or teaching. For more information, including lists of past RITA Award winners, visit the RWA Web site at www.rwanational.com.

LIFETIME ACHIEVEMENT AWARD WINNERS

Rosalyn Alsobrook
Ethel Bangert (a.k.a. Virginia Mann)
Sandra Brown
Janet Dailey
Roberta Gellis
Elanor Burford Hibbert
Jayne Ann Krentz
Ann Maxwell (a.k.a. Elizabeth Lowell)
Patricia Maxwell (a.k.a. Jennifer Blake)
Virginia Nielson McCall
Barbara Mertz
Virginia Myers
Nora Roberts
Mary Stewart
Anne Stuart
Phyllis A. Whitney
Kathleen Woodiwiss

Genre Awards Quick Reference

HORROR

Bram Stoker Award
www.horror.org/stoker.htm

Grand Master Award
www.worldhorror.org

MYSTERY

Agatha Award
www.erols.com/malice

Edgar Award
www.mysterywriters.net

Gold and Silver Dagger Awards
www.twbooks.co.uk/cwa/cwa.html

Grand Master Award
www.mysterywriters.net/awards

Macavity Award
murderonthemenu.com

ROMANCE

Lifetime Achievement Award
www.rwanational.com

RITA Award
www.rwanational.com

SCIENCE FICTION AND FANTASY

Grand Master Award
www.sfwa.org

Hugo Award
www.worldcon.org/hugos.html

Mythopoeic Award
www.mythsoc.org

Nebula Award
www.sfwa.org

World Fantasy Convention Award
www.worldfantasy.org

WESTERN

Owen Wister Award
www.westernwriters.org

Spur Award
www.slco.lib.ut.us/spur.htm

The Top 25 Romance Novels

The "All About Romance" Web site (www.likesbooks.com) is a popular and vigorously maintained spot on the Internet for romance readers. With an eye toward the millennium, in the fall of 1999, the site polled its mailing-list subscribers, asking them for their 100 favorite romances of the century. The tabulated results, "Romance Readers' Top 100 Romances," are published on the Web at www.likesbooks.com/top100.html.

The top 25 titles are listed here, along with the applicable subgenre (classic, contemporary, historical, etc.) for each.

1. *A Knight in Shining Armor* by Jude Deveraux (time travel)
2. *The Secret* by Julie Garwood (historical)
3. *Nobody's Baby But Mine* by Susan Elizabeth Phillips (contemporary)
4. *Outlander* by Diana Gabaldon (time travel)
5. *Dream Man* by Linda Howard (romantic suspense)
6. *Heaven, Texas* by Susan Elizabeth Phillips (contemporary)
7. *Lord of Scoundrels* by Loretta Chase (historical)
8. *The Gift* by Julie Garwood (historical)
9. *Whitney, My Love* by Judith McNaught (historical)
10. *It Had to Be You* by Susan Elizabeth Phillips (contemporary)
11. *The Bride* by Julie Garwood (historical)
12. *Almost Heaven* by Judith McNaught (historical)
13. *Dream a Little Dream* by Susan Elizabeth Phillips (contemporary)
14. *Pride and Prejudice* by Jane Austen (classic)
15. *Flowers from the Storm* by Laura Kinsale (historical)
16. *Paradise* by Judith McNaught (contemporary)
17. *Perfect* by Judith McNaught (contemporary)
18. *Saving Grace* by Julie Garwood (historical)
19. *The Prize* by Julie Garwood (historical)
20. *Bewitching* by Jill Barnett (paranormal historical)
21. *Born in Fire* by Nora Roberts (contemporary)
22. *After the Night* by Linda Howard (contemporary)
23. *Born in Shame* by Nora Roberts (contemporary)
24. *Ravished* by Amanda Quick (historical)
25. *The Rake* by Mary Jo Putney (historical)

Science Fiction and Fantasy

What is science fiction? There are scores of definitions. The most trenchant is probably the one offered by John Campbell, the visionary editor who was largely responsible for bringing along the writers who created the "Golden Age of Science Fiction" in the 1940s. In 1966, he said, "The basic rule of science fiction is, 'Set up a basic proposition—then develop its consistent, logical consequences.'" The definition many fans prefer, however, was offered by author and critic Damon Knight, who said "Science fiction is what we point at when we say it."

Thanks to decades of B-movies, comic books, and low-quality pulp fiction, many readers think they know what SF is about—and want no part of it. Real SF is nothing like that at all, however. When it's good, science fiction will open your mind and make you really think. When it's great, it will also touch your soul.

Grand Masters of Science Fiction and Fantasy

The Grand Master Award for lifetime achievement in science fiction and/or fantasy is administered by the Science Fiction and Fantasy Writers of America (SFWA). Founded in 1965 by Damon Knight, the group counts among its 1,200 members most of the leading writers, editors, and artists in the field of science fiction and fantasy. The award is voted on by the SFWA officers and announced at the group's annual banquet, during which they also present their Nebula Awards. For more the latest Grand Master and Nebula Award winners, visit (www.sfwa.org).

GRAND MASTERS

Poul Anderson
Isaac Asimov
Alfred Bester
Ray Bradbury
Arthur C. Clarke
Hal Clement
L. Sprague de Camp
Lester del Rey
Robert A. Heinlein
Damon Knight
Ursula K. Le Guin
Fritz Leiber
Andre Norton
Frederik Pohl
Clifford D. Simak
A. E. Van Vogt
Jack Vance
Jack Williamson

The Top 25 Science Fiction Novels: The Hugos for 1976–99

Here are the top SF novels published in the last 24 years, as determined by science fiction fans, who honored each book with the Hugo Award in the year shown in parentheses after each title. To view the complete list dating back to 1953, visit www.wsfs.org/hugos.html.

The Hugos are named for Hugo Gernsback, who in 1926 began publishing *Amazing Stories*, the world's first science fiction magazine. (The Nebula Awards, in contrast, are voted on by SF writers.) The award is managed by the nonprofit World Science Fiction Society, which also organizes each year's World Science Fiction Convention or "WorldCon." Winners receive a chrome-plated model of a rocket ship.

To Say Nothing of the Dog by Connie Willis (1999)
Forever Peace by Joe Haldeman (1998)
Blue Mars by Kim Stanley Robinson (1997)
The Diamond Age by Neal Stephenson (1996)
Mirror Dance by Lois McMaster Bujold (1995)
Green Mars by Kim Stanley Robinson (1994)
A Fire Upon the Deep by Vernor Vinge (1993, tie)
Doomsday Book by Connie Willis (1993, tie)
Barrayar by Lois McMaster Bujold (1992)
The Vor Game by Lois McMaster Bujold (1991)
Hyperion by Dan Simmons (1990)
Cyteen by C. J. Cherryh (1989)
The Uplift War by David Brin (1988)
Speaker for the Dead by Orson Scott Card (1987)
Ender's Game by Orson Scott Card (1986)
Neuromancer by William Gibson (1985)
Startide Rising by David Brin (1984)
Foundation's Edge by Isaac Asimov (1983)
Downbelow Station by C. J. Cherryh (1982)
The Snow Queen by Joan D. Vinge (1981)
The Fountains of Paradise by Arthur C. Clarke (1980)
Dreamsnake by Vonda McIntyre (1979)
Gateway by Frederik Pohl (1978)
Where Late the Sweet Birds Sang by Kate Wilhelm (1977)
The Forever War by Joe Haldeman (1976)

The Top 25 Fantasy Novels (1977–99)

Though many have tried, in the end, it is impossible to define "fantasy" in genre fiction. It is Rod Serling's *Twilight Zone* and Ray Bradbury's *Fahrenheit 451*. It is Mark Helprin's *Winter's Tale* and Ursula K. Le Guin's *A Wizard of Earthsea*. Ultimately, whether it takes place in this world, in a world parallel to ours, in the world of myth and magic, or some place else, a tale of fantasy engenders a sense of wonder—though the best fantasy builds on this sensation to offer considerably more.

Here are the best fantasy novels from the 23-year period between 1977 and 1999, selected by a panel of judges from books nominated by the 850 author and fan members of the World Fantasy Convention (WFC). All types of fantasy are considered: supernatural horror, Tolkienesque, sword and sorcery, occult, magic realism, and beyond. For more information, and the names of the runners up, plus awards for best novella, best short fiction, best anthology, and best collection of a single author's works, visit www.worldfantasy.org.

The Antelope Wife by Louise Erdrich (1999)
The Physiognomy by Jeffrey Ford (1998)
Godmother Night by Rachel Pollack (1997)
The Prestige by Christopher Priest (1996)
Towing Jehovah by James Morrow (1995)
Glimpses by Lewis Shiner (1994)
Last Call by Tim Powers (1993)
Boy's Life by Robert R. McCammon (1992)
Only Begotten Daughter by James Morrow (1991, tie)
Thomas the Rhymer by Ellen Kushner (1991, tie)
Lyonesse: Madouc by Jack Vance (1990)
Koko by Peter Straub (1989)
Replay by Ken Grimwood (1988)
Perfume by Patrick Suskind (1987)
Song of Kali by Dan Simmons (1986)
Mythago Wood by Robert Holdstock (1985, tie)
Bridge of Birds by Barry Hughart (1985, tie)
The Dragon Waiting by John M. Ford (1984)
Nifft the Lean by Michael Shea (1983)
Little Big by John Crowley (1982)
The Shadow of the Torturer by Gene Wolfe (1981)
Watchtower by Elizabeth A. Lynn (1980)
Gloriana by Michael Moorcock (1979)
Our Lady of Darkness by Fritz Leiber (1978)
Doctor Rat by William Kotzwinkle (1977)

The Top 24 Novels of the Land of Faerie: The Mythopoeic Awards for 1971–99

Though fantasy they may be, the novels of J. R. R. Tolkien and C. S. Lewis don't really fit in that classification. They are clearly part of something else, a fact recognized by the Mythopoeic Society when it presents its annual awards—statuettes of a seated lion, evoking Aslan from Lewis's *Chronicles of Narnia*—to books "in the tradition" of Tolkien and Lewis. The setting is frequently the "land of faerie" in some form or another, at some time or another. But the stories are always deeper and more resonant than simple fairy tales or most novels of "sword and sorcery." There is wonder, but there is also much meaning, and the writing is always top-drawer.

Winners of the Mythopoeic Award are selected by committees composed of volunteers from the Mythopoeic Society and presented at the group's annual convention, Mythcon. For more information, including a complete list of award winners, visit www.mythsoc.org.

Here are the "Best Fantasy Novels" for 1971 through 1999. The gap from 1976 to 1980 is due to fact that the award wasn't presented in those years.

Stardust by Neil Gaiman and Charles Vess (1999)
The Djinn in the Nightingale's Eye by A. S. Byatt (1998)
The Wood Wife by Terri Windling (1997)
Waking the Moon by Elizabeth Hand (1996)
Something Rich and Strange by Patricia A. McKillip (1995)
The Porcelain Dove by Delia Sherman (1994)
Briar Rose by Jane Yolen (1993)
A Woman of the Iron People by Eleanor Arnason (1992)
Thomas the Rhymer by Ellen Kushner (1991)
The Stress of Her Regard by Tim Powers (1990)
Unicorn Mountain by Michael Bishop (1989)
Seventh Son by Orson Scott Card (1988)
The Folk of the Air by Peter Beagle (1987)
Bridge of Birds by Barry Hughart (1986)
Cards of Grief by Jane Yolen (1985)
When Voiha Wakes by Joy Chant (1984)
The Firelings by Carol Kendall (1983)
Little, Big by John Crowley (1982)
Unfinished Tales by J. R. R. Tolkien (1981)
A Midsummer Tempest by Poul Anderson (1975)
The Hollow Hills by Mary Stewart (1974)
The Song of Rhiannon by Evangeline Walton (1973)
Red Moon and Black Mountain by Joy Chant (1972)
The Crystal Cave by Mary Stewart (1971)

The Western

For many years, the Western Writers of America (WWA) recognized their "Grand Masters" with the Levi Strauss Golden Saddleman Award. But in 1991, they changed the name to the Owen Wister Award, in honor of the author of the 1902 bestselling novel, *The Virginian: A Horseman of the Plains*. This is the book that established the conventions for the classic Western novel and went on to be voted the "Top Western of All Time" by WWA members some 75 years later. For additional information, visit the WWA Web site at www.westernwriters.org.

OWEN WISTER/GOLDEN SADDLEMAN AWARD WINNERS

Henry W. Allen (Will Henry)
Eve Ball
S. Omar Barker
Dee Brown
Benjamin Franklin Capps
José Cisneros
Max Evans
Frederick Glidden (Luke Short)
Fred Grove
A. B. Guthrie Jr.
Dorothy Johnson
Douglas C. Jones
Alvin M. Josephy
Elmer Kelton
Louis L'Amour
David Lavender
Tom Lea
Leon C. Metz
Nelson C. Nye
Wayne Overholser
Lewis B. Patten
Mari Sandoz
Jack Schaefer
Gordon D. Shirreffs
Charles L. Sonnichsen
Glendon Swarthout
Thomas Thompson
Robert M. Utley
Glenn Vernam
Dale L. Walker
Jeanne Williams
Don Worcester
Norman Zollinger

The Top 20 Westerns: The Spur Awards for 1990–99

Established by the Western Writers of America (WWA) in 1953, the Spur Awards are given annually for distinguished writing about the American West. There are more than a dozen categories, including two for hardcover adult fiction—Best Western Novel (under 90,000 words) and Best Novel of the West (over 90,000 words). Works must be written by a living author and set in the American West or on the early frontier. For more information about award criteria, visit the WWA Web site at www.westernwriters.org.

A complete list of all winners—including Larry McMurtry's *Lonesome Dove*, Michael Blake's *Dances with Wolves*, Tony Hillerman's *Skinwalker*, and Glendon Swarthout's *The Shootist*—is maintained by the Salt Lake County Library System (www.slco.lib.ut.us/spur.htm).

BEST WESTERN NOVEL (UNDER 90,000 WORDS)

Journey of the Dead by Loren D. Estleman (1999)
The Kiowa Verdict by Cynthia Haseloff (1998)
Blood of Texas by Preston Lewis, writing as "Will Camp" (1997)
The Dark Island by Robert J. Conley (1996)
St. Agnes' Stand by Tom Edison (1995)
Friends by Charles Hackenberry (1994)
Nickajack by Robert J. Conley (1993)
Journal of the Gun Years by Richard Matheson (1992)
Sanctuary by Gary Svee (1991)
Fool's Coach by Richard Wheeler (1990)

BEST NOVEL OF THE WEST (OVER 90,000 WORDS)

The All-True Travels and Adventures of Lidie Newton by Jane Smiley (1999)
Comanche Moon by Larry McMurtry (1998)
Sierra by Richard S. Wheeler (1997)
Stone Song: A Novel of the Life of Crazy Horse by Win Blevins (1996)
The Far Canyon by Elmer Kelton (1995)
Empire of Bones by Jeff Long (1994)
Slaughter by Elmer Kelton (1993)
The Medicine by Jory Sherman (1992)
Home Mountain by Jeanne Williams (1991)
Panther in the Sky by James Alexander (1990)

BEST OF THE "BEST"

What's the answer to an era of "overchoice?" Why the "best of" list, of course! We all love lists, even when, most of the time, there is no statistical basis whatsoever for the rankings. Some lists are whipped up to fill magazine and newspaper pages. Some are designed primarily to provoke discussion and controversy. And, of course, some really are designed to alert people to the best in the field.

The quirky collection that follows includes lists of every type. All are interesting. All are informative. And, by design, their quantity is limited. After all, "best of" lists are like fine chocolates—the first few are delicious, but consumed in great numbers, they soon begin to cloy. Accordingly, we've made every attempt to make each list count.

The Modern Library's 100 Best Novels

Talk about buzz! Few lists in modern memory have stirred such controversy—or served as fodder for so many columnists and commentators—as the Modern Library's "100 Best Novels" of the 20th century written in English, which was leaked to the *New York Times* and published on July 20, 1998. Why aren't there more women and minorities on the list? Where are the South Africans? Where are the Australians? Writers and critics had a field day.

Counterlists were drawn up, of course, one of which you'll find immediately following the Modern Library list. Lists of award-winning writers *not* on the Modern Library list were soon issued (Updike, DeLillo, Barthelme, Pynchon, etc.). And Joyce's difficult, experimental, and largely unread *Ulysses* as the number-one novel of the century raised eyebrows everywhere. Others noted that if 19th-century novelists had been included, Melville, Dickens, Twain, and the like would have knocked many names off the current list, "which says a great deal about 20th-century fiction."

In other words, a good time was had by all.

As more details were made public, it became clear that the ten distinguished (but all white and relatively senior) men from the Modern Library's editorial advisory board who were consulted for the list had no idea of the methodology behind the compilation or how seriously their selections would be taken. The panel members didn't "wrinkle their brows" over the selections, as one judge later put it.

Christopher Cerf, chairman of the board of the Modern Library, told the *Washington Post* (August 5,

1998), "I think the process is to some degree a scam, but it's a good scam. I mean that in the best sense of the word. The statistics weren't valid, but if you had a list that was really diverse and incredibly thought out, it would cause less controversy. And then people wouldn't be talking about books."

So in the end, it was a harmless controversy that got people talking. Which is probably exactly what former Random House chief Harold Evans had in mind when he set the idea in motion. Not incidentally, Amazon.com reported sharp sales spikes in many of the titles on the Modern Library list. *Ulysses* shot to number two on the Amazon.com paperback list. *Brave New World* rose to number seven, *Lolita* to number eight, and *The Great Gatsby* to number ten.

Here is that much storied Modern Library Best Novels list. Discuss amongst yourselves:

1. *Ulysses* by James Joyce
2. *The Great Gatsby* by F. Scott Fitzgerald
3. *A Portrait of the Artist as a Young Man* by James Joyce
4. *Lolita* by Vladimir Nabokov
5. *Brave New World* by Aldous Huxley
6. *The Sound and the Fury* by William Faulkner
7. *Catch-22* by Joseph Heller
8. *Darkness at Noon* by Arthur Koestler
9. *Sons and Lovers* by D. H. Lawrence
10. *The Grapes of Wrath* by John Steinbeck
11. *Under the Volcano* by Malcolm Lowry
12. *The Way of All Flesh* by Samuel Butler
13. *1984* by George Orwell
14. *I, Claudius* by Robert Graves
15. *To the Lighthouse* by Virginia Woolf
16. *An American Tragedy* by Theodore Dreiser
17. *The Heart Is a Lonely Hunter* by Carson McCullers
18. *Slaughterhouse-Five* by Kurt Vonnegut
19. *Invisible Man* by Ralph Ellison
20. *Native Son* by Richard Wright
21. *Henderson the Rain King* by Saul Bellow
22. *Appointment in Samarra* by John O'Hara
23. *U.S.A.* (trilogy) by John Dos Passos
24. *Winesburg, Ohio* by Sherwood Anderson
25. *A Passage to India* by E. M. Forster
26. *The Wings of the Dove* by Henry James
27. *The Ambassadors* by Henry James
28. *Tender Is the Night* by F. Scott Fitzgerald
29. The Studs Lonigan trilogy by James T. Farrell
30. *The Good Soldier* by Ford Madox Ford
31. *Animal Farm* by George Orwell
32. *The Golden Bowl* by Henry James
33. *Sister Carrie* by Theodore Dreiser
34. *A Handful of Dust* by Evelyn Waugh
35. *As I Lay Dying* by William Faulkner
36. *All the King's Men* by Robert Penn Warren
37. *The Bridge of San Luis Rey* by Thornton Wilder
38. *Howards End* by E. M. Forster
39. *Go Tell It on the Mountain* by James Baldwin
40. *The Heart of the Matter* by Graham Greene
41. *Lord of the Flies* by William Golding
42. *Deliverance* by James Dickey
43. *A Dance to the Music of Time* (series) by Anthony Powell
44. *Point Counter Point* by Aldous Huxley
45. *The Sun Also Rises* by Ernest Hemingway
46. *The Secret Agent* by Joseph Conrad
47. *Nostromo* by Joseph Conrad
48. *The Rainbow* by D. H. Lawrence
49. *Women in Love* by D. H. Lawrence
50. *Tropic of Cancer* by Henry Miller
51. *The Naked and the Dead* by Norman Mailer
52. *Portnoy's Complaint* by Philip Roth
53. *Pale Fire* by Vladimir Nabokov
54. *Light in August* by William Faulkner
55. *On the Road* by Jack Kerouac
56. *The Maltese Falcon* by Dashiell Hammett
57. *Parade's End* by Ford Madox Ford
58. *The Age of Innocence* by Edith Wharton
59. *Zuleika Dobson* by Max Beerbohm
60. *The Moviegoer* by Walker Percy
61. *Death Comes for the Archbishop* by Willa Cather
62. *From Here to Eternity* by James Jones
63. *The Wapshot Chronicles* by John Cheever

Behind the Scenes at the Modern Library

The Modern Library was founded in 1917 by Boni and Liveright, an important early 20th-century publisher. The concept was to bring American readers inexpensive reprints of modern European novels, plus a few contemporary American works. It was a profitable enterprise, but financial difficulties at its parent publisher resulted in the sale of Modern Library to one of its employees: a 27-year-old vice president named Bennett Cerf.

Cerf and partner Donald Klopfer expanded the list, and by 1927 they had made the Modern Library an even greater success. With time on their hands, they established a subsidiary that would allow them to publish books that interested them more or less at random. That, of course, was Random House, the entity that eventually made Modern Library its imprint.

64. *The Catcher in the Rye* by J. D. Salinger
65. *A Clockwork Orange* by Anthony Burgess
66. *Of Human Bondage* by W. Somerset Maugham
67. *Heart of Darkness* by Joseph Conrad
68. *Main Street* by Sinclair Lewis
69. *The House of Mirth* by Edith Wharton
70. *The Alexandria Quartet* by Lawrence Durrell
71. *A High Wind in Jamaica* by Richard Hughes
72. *A House for Mr. Biswas* by V. S. Naipaul
73. *The Day of the Locust* by Nathanael West
74. *A Farewell to Arms* by Ernest Hemingway
75. *Scoop* by Evelyn Waugh
76. *The Prime of Miss Jean Brodie* by Muriel Spark
77. *Finnegans Wake* by James Joyce
78. *Kim* by Rudyard Kipling
79. *A Room with a View* by E. M. Forster
80. *Brideshead Revisited* by Evelyn Waugh
81. *The Adventures of Augie March* by Saul Bellow
82. *Angle of Repose* by Wallace Stegner
83. *A Bend in the River* by V. S. Naipaul
84. *The Death of the Heart* by Elizabeth Bowen
85. *Lord Jim* by Joseph Conrad
86. *Ragtime* by E. L. Doctorow
87. *The Old Wives' Tale* by Arnold Bennett
88. *The Call of the Wild* by Jack London
89. *Loving* by Henry Green
90. *Midnight's Children* by Salman Rushdie
91. *Tobacco Road* by Erskine Caldwell
92. *Ironweed* by William Kennedy
93. *The Magus* by John Fowles
94. *Wide Sargasso Sea* by Jean Rhys
95. *Under the Net* by Iris Murdoch
96. *Sophie's Choice* by William Styron
97. *The Sheltering Sky* by Paul Bowles
98. *The Postman Always Rings Twice* by James M. Cain
99. *The Ginger Man* by J. P. Donleavy
100. *The Magnificent Ambersons* by Booth Tarkington

The Radcliffe Publishing Course 100

On July 21, 1998, students at the Radcliffe Publishing Course, a highly regarded six-week program for college graduates interesting in pursuing a publishing career, released their own list of the 20th century's top 100 novels written in English. The list was prepared at the request of the Modern Library and formally presented to its board chairman, Christopher Cerf.

As with the Modern Library list, students selected from a list of some 400 possible titles. Course instructors compiled and quantified the results, which, as you may

notice, are much broader and more diverse than the Modern Library's—and probably much more in line with what most readers would choose. The list is also much less controversial, which is why you may never have heard of it.

1. *The Great Gatsby* by F. Scott Fitzgerald
2. *The Catcher in the Rye* by J. D. Salinger
3. *The Grapes of Wrath* by John Steinbeck
4. *To Kill a Mockingbird* by Harper Lee
5. *The Color Purple* by Alice Walker
6. *Ulysses* by James Joyce
7. *Beloved* by Toni Morrison
8. *The Lord of the Flies* by William Golding
9. *1984* by George Orwell
10. *The Sound and the Fury* by William Faulkner
11. *Lolita* by Vladmir Nabokov
12. *Of Mice and Men* by John Steinbeck
13. *Charlotte's Web* by E. B. White
14. *A Portrait of the Artist as a Young Man* by James Joyce
15. *Catch-22* by Joseph Heller
16. *Brave New World* by Aldous Huxley
17. *Animal Farm* by George Orwell
18. *The Sun Also Rises* by Ernest Hemingway
19. *As I Lay Dying* by William Faulkner
20. *A Farewell to Arms* by Ernest Hemingway
21. *Heart of Darkness* by Joseph Conrad
22. *Winnie-the-Pooh* by A. A. Milne
23. *Their Eyes Were Watching God* by Zora Neale Hurston
24. *Invisible Man* by Ralph Ellison
25. *Song of Solomon* by Toni Morrison
26. *Gone with the Wind* by Margaret Mitchell
27. *Native Son* by Richard Wright
28. *One Flew Over the Cuckoo's Nest* by Ken Kesey
29. *Slaughterhouse-Five* by Kurt Vonnegut
30. *For Whom the Bell Tolls* by Ernest Hemingway
31. *On the Road* by Jack Kerouac
32. *The Old Man and the Sea* by Ernest Hemingway
33. *The Call of the Wild* by Jack London
34. *To the Lighthouse* by Virginia Woolf
35. *Portrait of a Lady* by Henry James
36. *Go Tell It on the Mountain* by James Baldwin
37. *The World According to Garp* by John Irving
38. *All the King's Men* by Robert Penn Warren
39. *A Room with a View* by E. M. Forster
40. *The Lord of the Rings* by J. R. R. Tolkien
41. *Schindler's List* by Thomas Keneally
42. *The Age of Innocence* by Edith Wharton
43. *The Fountainhead* by Ayn Rand
44. *Finnegans Wake* by James Joyce
45. *The Jungle* by Upton Sinclair
46. *Mrs. Dalloway* by Virginia Woolf
47. *The Wonderful Wizard of Oz* by L. Frank Baum

48. *Lady Chatterley's Lover* by D. H. Lawrence
49. *A Clockwork Orange* by Anthony Burgess
50. *The Awakening* by Kate Chopin
51. *My Antonia* by Willa Cather
52. *Howards End* by E. M. Forster
53. *In Cold Blood* by Truman Capote
54. *Franny and Zooey* by J. D. Salinger
55. *The Satanic Verses* by Salman Rushdie
56. *Jazz* by Toni Morrison
57. *Sophie's Choice* by William Styron
58. *Absalom, Absalom!* by William Faulkner
59. *A Passage to India* by E. M. Forster
60. *Ethan Frome* by Edith Wharton
61. *A Good Man Is Hard to Find* by Flannery O'Connor
62. *Tender Is the Night* by F. Scott Fitzgerald
63. *Orlando* by Virginia Woolf
64. *Sons and Lovers* by D. H. Lawrence
65. *Bonfire of the Vanities* by Tom Wolfe
66. *Cat's Cradle* by Kurt Vonnegut
67. *A Separate Peace* by John Knowles
68. *Light in August* by William Faulkner
69. *The Wings of the Dove* by Henry James
70. *Things Fall Apart* by Chinua Achebe
71. *Rebecca* by Daphne du Maurier

72. *A Hitchhiker's Guide to the Galaxy* by Douglas Adams
73. *Naked Lunch* by William S. Burroughs
74. *Brideshead Revisited* by Evelyn Waugh
75. *Women in Love* by D. H. Lawrence
76. *Look Homeward, Angel* by Thomas Wolfe
77. *In Our Time* by Ernest Hemingway
78. *The Autobiography of Alice B. Toklas* by Gertrude Stein
79. *The Maltese Falcon* by Dashiell Hammett
80. *The Naked and the Dead* by Norman Mailer
81. *Wide Sargasso Sea* by Jean Rhys
82. *White Noise* by Don DeLillo
83. *Pioneers!* by Willa Cather
84. *Tropic of Cancer* by Henry Miller
85. *The War of the Worlds* by H. G. Wells
86. *Lord Jim* by Joseph Conrad
87. *The Bostonians* by Henry James
88. *An American Tragedy* by Theodore Dreiser
89. *Death Comes for the Archbishop* by Willa Cather
90. *The Wind in the Willows* by Kenneth Grahame
91. *This Side of Paradise* by F. Scott Fitzgerald
92. *Atlas Shrugged* by Ayn Rand
93. *The French Lieutenant's Woman* by John Fowles
94. *Babbitt* by Sinclair Lewis
95. *Kim* by Rudyard Kipling
96. *The Beautiful and the Damned* by F. Scott Fitzgerald
97. *Rabbit, Run* by John Updike
98. *Where Angels Fear to Tread* by E. M. Forster
99. *Main Street* by Sinclair Lewis
100. *Midnight's Children* by Salman Rushdie

99 Novels: The Best in English Since 1939

This is the title of a wonderful book by the late Anthony Burgess. Published by Summit Books in 1984 and now out of print, the book presents Burgess's personal choices, along with a page for each novel explaining its significance and his reasons for selecting it.

"In my time," Burgess writes, "I have read a lot of novels in the way of duty; I have read a great number for pleasure as well. The 99 novels I have chosen, I have chosen with some, though not with total, confidence. I have concentrated on works which have brought something new—in technique or view of the world—to the form."

Burgess speaks with authority, but not with the lofty voice of a critic. Instead, he sounds like a very well read but unpretentious friend who is genuinely interested in sharing his discoveries with you. The book is definitely worth a trip to your local library. It's also available from out-of-print sources like Alibris (www.alibris.com) and Bibliofind (www.bibliofind.com).

New York Public Library's Books of the Century

To celebrate its 100th anniversary in 1995, the New York Public Library published a list of more than 150 books that, based on recommendations from its librarians, have "shaped and defined the 20th century." The complete list, which includes both fiction and nonfiction, along with comments on the significance of each work, is available in *The New York Public Library's Books of the Century*, edited by Elizabeth Diefendorf (Oxford University Press, 1996). You can also find it at the New York Public Library Web site (www.nypl.org/bookstore). Here are 50 of the fictional works from the list:

Age of Innocence by Edith Wharton
Atlas Shrugged by Ayn Rand
The Big Sleep by Raymond Chandler
The Bonfire of the Vanities by Tom Wolfe

Brave New World by Aldous Huxley
Carrie by Stephen King
Catch-22 by Joseph Heller
A Clockwork Orange by Anthony Burgess
The Color Purple by Alice Walker
The Day of the Locust by Nathanael West
Dracula by Bram Stoker
Dust Tracks on a Road by Zora Neale Hurston
Fahrenheit 451 by Ray Bradbury
Fictions by Jorge Luis Borges
Gone with the Wind by Margaret Mitchell
The Grapes of Wrath by John Steinbeck
The Great Gatsby by F. Scott Fitzgerald
Guerrillas by V. S. Naipaul
A Handmaid's Tale by Margaret Atwood
The Hound of the Baskervilles by Arthur Conan Doyle
In Cold Blood by Truman Capote
Invisible Man by Ralph Ellison
Kim by Rudyard Kipling
Lolita by Vladimir Nabokov
Lord Jim by Joseph Conrad
The Magic Mountain by Thomas Mann
The Metamorphosis by Franz Kafka
The Mysterious Affair at Styles by Agatha Christie
Native Son by Richard Wright
On the Road by Jack Kerouac
One Flew Over the Cuckoo's Nest by Ken Kesey
One Hundred Years of Solitude by Gabriel García
    Márquez
A Passage to India by E. M. Forster
Peter Pan in Kensington Gardens by J. M. Barrie
Peyton Place by Grace Metalious
The Portable Faulkner by William Faulkner
Portnoy's Complaint by Philip Roth
Remembrance of Things Past by Marcel Proust
Riders of the Purple Sage by Zane Grey
Song of Solomon by Toni Morrison
Stranger in a Strange Land by Robert A. Heinlein
Tarzan of the Apes by Edgar Rice Burroughs
Tender Buttons by Gertrude Stein
The Three Sisters by Anton Chekhov
The Time Machine by H. G. Wells
To the Lighthouse by Virginia Woolf
The Turn of the Screw by Henry James
Ulysses by James Joyce
Wide Sargasso Sea by Jean Rhys
The Wonderful Wizard of Oz by L. Frank Baum

The 50 Most Frequently Banned Books in the 1990s

Here's a top-titles list of a different sort—the most frequently banned or challenged books of the 1990s.

Nearly 40 years ago, parents and the powers that be were so upset over the Kingsmen's recording of "Louie, Louie" and whether its unintelligible lyrics were obscene that the FBI actually prepared a 560-page study, which federal investigators used in an unsuccessful attempt to have the record legally suppressed. In today's environment of explicit (and quite intelligible) rock and rap lyrics, and prime-time TV shows and movies laden with cartoon-like violence and sexual innuendo, the notion of banning *books* seems almost quaint. And it would be, if it weren't so serious.

This is the subject that Herbert N. Foerstel addresses in *Banned in the U.S.A.: A Reference Guide to Book Censorship in Schools and Public Libraries* (Greenwood Press, 1994). Among other things, Foerstel analyzes eight major book-banning incidents from 1976 through 1992, traces First Amendment cases and precedents in book banning in schools and public libraries, and interviews frequently banned authors. He also summarizes the challenges to each of the 50 "most banned" books listed here. As always, the parents and others challenging a given book rarely let the fact that they've never actually *read* the work stand in their way.

1. *Impressions*, edited by Jack Booth, et al.
2. *Of Mice and Men* by John Steinbeck
3. *The Catcher in the Rye* by J. D. Salinger
4. *The Adventures of Huckleberry Finn* by Mark Twain
5. *The Chocolate War* by Robert Cormier
6. *Bridge to Terabithia* by Katherine Paterson
7. *Scary Stories in the Dark* by Alvin Schwartz
8. *More Scary Stories in the Dark* by Alvin Schwartz
9. *The Witches* by Roald Dahl
10. *Daddy's Roommate* by Michael Willhoite
11. *Curses, Hexes, and Spells* by Daniel Cohen
12. *A Wrinkle in Time* by Madeleine L'Engle
13. *How to Eat Fried Worms* by Thomas Rockwell
14. *Blubber* by Judy Blume
15. *Revolting Rhymes* by Roald Dahl
16. *Halloween ABC* by Eve Merriam
17. *A Day No Pigs Would Die* by Robert Peck
18. *Heather Has Two Mommies* by Leslea Newman
19. *Christine* by Stephen King
20. *I Know Why the Caged Bird Sings* by Maya Angelou
21. *Fallen Angels* by Walter Myers

22. *The New Teenage Body Book* by Kathy McCoy and Charles Wibbelsman
23. *Little Red Riding Hood* by the Brothers Grimm
24. *The Headless Cupid* by Zilpha Snyder
25. *Night Chills* by Dean Koontz
26. *Lord of the Flies* by William Golding
27. *A Separate Peace* by John Knowles
28. *Slaughterhouse-Five* by Kurt Vonnegut
29. *The Color Purple* by Alice Walker
30. *James and the Giant Peach* by Roald Dahl
31. *The Learning Tree* by Gordon Parks
32. *The Witches of Worm* by Zilpha Snyder
33. *My Brother Sam Is Dead* by James Lincoln Collier and Christopher Collier
34. *The Grapes of Wrath* by John Steinbeck
35. *Cujo* by Stephen King
36. *The Great Gilly Hopkins* by Katherine Paterson
37. *The Figure in the Shadows* by John Bellairs
38. *On My Honor* by Marion Dane Bauer
39. *In the Night Kitchen* by Maurice Sendak
40. *Grendel* by John Gardner
41. *I Have to Go* by Robert Munsch
42. *Annie on My Mind* by Nancy Garden
43. *The Adventures of Tom Sawyer* by Mark Twain
44. *The Pigman* by Paul Zindel
45. *My House* by Nikki Giovanni
46. *Then Again, Maybe I Won't* by Judy Blume
47. *The Handmaid's Tale* by Margaret Atwood
48. *Witches, Pumpkins, and Grinning Ghosts: The Story of the Halloween Symbols* by Edna Barth
49. *One Hundred Years of Solitude* by Gabriel García Márquez
50. *Scary Stories 3: More Tales to Chill Your Bones* by Alvin Schwartz

Oprah's Book Club

Talk-show host Oprah Winfrey is not only one of the world's most powerful television executives, she's also a major force—some say *the* major force—in American book publishing. When she announces the selection for her monthly on-air book club, the "Oprah Effect" sets in: the book is catapulted onto bestseller lists, readers quickly empty the bookstore shelves, and publishers are sent into a reprint frenzy to satisfy the demand.

Winfrey is credited with bringing respected authors like Toni Morrison and Anna Quindlen to the attention of a mass audience, and for launching the careers of Wally Lamb and many other previously unknown novelists. Here are the books she has recommended during the three-plus years that her book club has been in operation (September 1996 through December 1999), presented in alphabetical order by title. For more information, including author biographies, book descriptions, and reading guides, visit the Oprah Web site at www.oprah.com and click on "Book Club."

The Best Way to Play by Bill Cosby
Black and Blue by Anna Quindlen
The Book of Ruth by Jane Hamilton
Breath, Eyes, Memory by Edwidge Danticat
The Deep End of the Ocean by Jacquelyn Mitchard
Ellen Foster by Kaye Gibbons
The Heart of a Woman by Maya Angelou
Here on Earth by Alice Hoffman
I Know This Much Is True by Wally Lamb
Jewel by Bret Lott
A Lesson Before Dying by Ernest J. Gaines
A Map of the World by Jane Hamilton
The Meanest Thing to Say by Bill Cosby
Midwives by Chris Bohjalian
Mother of Pearl by Melinda Haynes
Paradise by Toni Morrison
The Pilot's Wife by Anita Shreve
The Rapture of Canaan by Sheri Reynolds
The Reader by Bernhard Schlink
River, Cross My Heart by Breena Clarke
Song of Solomon by Toni Morrison
Songs in Ordinary Time by Mary McGarry Morris
Stones from the River by Ursula Hegi
She's Come Undone by Wally Lamb
Tara Road by Maeve Binchy
The Treasure Hunt by Bill Cosby
A Virtuous Woman by Kaye Gibbons
Vinegar Hill by A. Manette Ansay
What Looks Like Crazy on an Ordinary Day by Pearl Cleage
Where the Heart Is by Billie Letts
White Oleander by Janet Fitch

BESTSELLER LISTS

The bestseller list was introduced in 1895 by Harry Thruston Peck, editor of a literary magazine called *The Bookman*. This is the same Peck who, in 1901, wrote of Mark Twain's works, "A hundred years from now it is very likely that *The Jumping Frog* alone will be remembered." But that's another story.

Ever since that first bestseller list came into being, such lists have been a major influence on book buying. Even if you don't read the book section of a major Sunday newspaper, you can't avoid noticing a given title's bestseller status emblazoned, embossed, or "starbursted" on its cover when you pull it off the shelf.

What Is a "Bestseller?"

The term is loosely applied, to be sure, particularly by publishers' marketing and publicity departments. A "national bestseller" may have appeared only on one or two regional or industry bestseller lists. An "international bestseller" generally means a book that was a bestseller somewhere else in the world, but not in the U. S. About the only reliable indicator is that if a book appeared on the *New York Times* bestseller list, that fact will most likely be noted specifically.

What many people don't understand is that bestseller status is a measure of the *rate* of sale, not the total number of copies. In other words, these lists measure the most popular books at a given point in time. A number-one bestseller might have sold 20,000 copies in a week, or 200,000 copies. Furthermore, they are by necessity a *relative* measure. A book selling 20,000 copies in a week right before Christmas, when business is booming, may not make any bestseller lists, whereas the same sales in the middle of July could conceivably put a book at the top of the lists.

Bestseller lists are also influenced by the particular titles that are on the market at a given time. If several books by brand-name authors hit the bookstores at about the same time, they can dominate the top slots and push all the other titles down on the list. Case in point: 1999 saw fewer adult fiction bestsellers than usual, because the three Harry Potter titles held top spots for many months.

Does Bestseller Status Matter?

In general, yes. Certainly it matters to publishers, because success begets success. A book selling enough copies to make it onto a bestseller list will typically sell even *more* copies as a result of being on the list—in part because certified bestsellers receive the biggest discounts and prime display space. And it matters to authors the way an Academy Award matters to actors—at the very least it means a larger advance for their *next* work.

But should a book's bestseller status matter to readers? Here, too, the answer is "yes." Usually. Novels typically become bestsellers for one of four reasons:

- The book is by a brand-name author whose many fans will buy anything with his or her name on it.

- The book is so good and so appealing that people tell their friends about it, and sales are propelled by word-of-mouth.

Bestsellers Goin' Back in Time

Here's a bit of strange trivia. In 1901, the number-one bestseller on the *Publishers Weekly* list was *The Crisis* by Winston Churchill. Sure sounds like Sir Winston, but it's not. Sir Winston Churchill wrote a book called *World Crisis* (1923–29). But the Churchill on the 1901 bestseller list was an American, and the book he wrote was a novel.

Owen Wister's *The Virginian* displaced the Churchill book in 1902, a year that saw Conan Doyle's *The Hound of the Baskervilles* at number seven and Booth Tarkington's *The Two Vanrevels* at number eight. But Churchill came roaring back to number one in 1904 with *The Crossing*, a year when Kate Douglas Wiggin's *Rebecca of Sunnybrook Farm* took the number-eight spot. In 1905, a non-Churchill year, Edith Wharton's *The House of Mirth* finished up at number eight. But the American Churchill returned to the top spot the following year and again in 1908.

For more fascinating explorations into bestseller lists through the decades, get a copy of the *People Entertainment Almanac*, published annually by Cader Books and People Books. Or visit www.caderbooks.com/bestintro.html, where you'll find an archive of the *Publishers Weekly* bestseller lists for the entire century.

- The publishing house thinks the book is so good that it is willing to risk scarce advertising dollars to promote it.

- The book is selected by Oprah Winfrey for her book club.

Of course, brand-name authors have been known to produce substandard books that become bestsellers anyway. And publishers that have paid a lot of money for a book will usually promote it to protect their investment, regardless of its actually quality. Most of the time, however, a novel (or a work of nonfiction, for that matter) becomes a bestseller because it offers something that makes it stand out from the other 70,000 books that are published each year. A slot on the bestseller list—probably even more than favorable reviews—is the best indication there is that a given book will deliver for you. But *which* list?

Leading Lists: They're Not All the Same

At first glance, you'd think it would be easy to determine which 10 to 15 novels sold the most copies during the previous week and thus qualify for a bestseller list. But, of course, it isn't.

For starters, the book business has no standardized method for gathering sales data at the point of purchase (unlike the Soundscan system in the music business, or the universal reporting of movie grosses in the film industry). All the various lists rely on *reported sales* from a variety of retailers and/or wholesalers. But each major list uses a different mix of sources, and then weights that data in its own idiosyncratic way.

The *Washington Post*, for example, consults Barnes & Noble, Crown, Waldenbooks, and Olsson's. The *Wall Street*

Sandbagging Amazon.com

Ever the innovator, Amazon.com founder Jeff Bezos one day realized that it would be rather easy to report the current sales ranking of every book sold from his database of over two million books. And so it was done. The "Top 10,000" sellers are updated every hour, and the "Top 100,000" are recorded once a day. The rankings aren't likely to be of interest to anyone but a book's author and publisher, but they do exist—a fact that prompted reporter Jamie Malanowski to conduct a little experiment for the *New Yorker* (3/15/99).

What does it take to make a book move up in Amazon.com's ranking system? Malanowski decided to buy one copy of the same book every day for a week. The title she selected was Thomas Carlyle's *The French Revolution*, first published in 1837. (Her thought was that this book wasn't likely to be mentioned on Oprah or in Liz Smith's column, and thus wouldn't be subject to momentary spikes in popularity.) Here are the results:

Day	Amazon Ranking and Sales Activity
Monday	92,010 (Starting point. Bought copy #1.)
Tuesday	77,392 (Bought copy #2.)
Wednesday	69,967 (Bought copy #3.)
Thursday	62,741 (Bought copy #4.)
Friday	57,982 (Bought copy #5.)
Saturday	Unknown (Forgot to log on, and no book purchased.)
Sunday	54,362 (Super Bowl Sunday. Bought copy #6.)
Monday	2,923 (Note big jump! Bought copy #7.)
Tuesday	39,338 (Another big jump, in the other direction!)

Malanowski later spoke with an Amazon.com publicist and explained the test and its results. The publicist said that, although she was forbidden to disclose actual sales figures for *The French Revolution*, "at the higher numbers on the list an incremental difference can have a big impact." Indeed! As Malanowski reported in the *New Yorker*, "In the space of a week, with a mere six purchases and the help of…the year's most highly rated television extravaganza, Thomas Carlyle's thickish history jumped more than 89,000 places."

Journal contacts the first three of these and adds B. Dalton, Waldenbooks, Bookland, Books-a-Million, Books & Co., Bookstar, Bookstop, Borders, Brentano's, and several other national chains, plus Amazon.com and Barnsandnoble.com. The *New York Times* list reflects sales "at almost 4,000 bookstores, plus wholesalers serving 50,000 other retailers...statistically weighted to represent all such outlets nationwide." Yet some in the industry would say that the *Times* list has a regional flavor because books likely to be of particular interest to an Eastern audience tend to appear there first, even though the same books are available at the same time in stores across the country.

And everyone deals differently with the vast array of "nontraditional" outlets that are rapidly accounting for more and more sales—online booksellers and merchants, gift shops, mass merchandisers, and others. It used to be that the major wholesalers—like Ingram and Baker & Taylor—provided a good indication of what all these other retailers were selling, since they invariably supplied much of their inventory. But as leading merchants establish their own warehouses and supply chains, this data gets more dispersed.

Small wonder, then, that the leading bestseller lists rarely track slot-for-slot. But that hardly matters. In our Internet-enabled age, it's easy to check dozens of bestseller lists from around the country. What matters is that a given book is on one or more leading lists and therefore probably worthy of further attention.

Where to Find Bestseller Lists

Chances are, you'll find one or more of the leading bestseller lists posted at your favorite bookstore. And your local library almost certainly subscribes to the *New York Times*, the *Wall Street Journal*, and other major newspapers and magazines that carry bestseller lists. In addition, your library is also likely to offer Internet access.

If that's the case, or if you have an Internet connection at home or at the office, use the list presented here to locate your favorite bestseller list. Better yet, visit the TopBestsellers.com Web site (www.topbestsellers.com). Once there, you'll have access to a number of the leading bestseller lists. In addition, TopBestsellers.com lets you call up book reviews from various newspapers, search for bestsellers by subject, view each title's ranking by bestseller list and average score, and look at yearly summaries of bestsellers.

LEADING NEWSPAPERS AND MAGAZINES

Boston Globe
www.boston.com/goingout/books

Chicago Tribune
chicagotribune.com/leisure/books/printedition

Los Angeles Times
www.calendarlive.com/books/bestsell

New York Times
www.nytimes.com/books

Publishers Weekly
www.publishersweekly.com

San Francisco Chronicle
www.sfgate.com/eguide/books

USA Today
www.usatoday.com (click on "Books")

Wall Street Journal
interactive.wsj.com/edition/current/summaries/leisure.htm

Washington Post
www.washingtonpost.com (click on "Entertainment" and then "Books")

OTHER BESTSELLER LISTS

Amazon.com
(Covers Amazon.com sales only.)
www.amazon.com (click on "Books")

Barnesandnoble.com
(Covers sales to B&N online customers only.)
www.bn.com

Book Sense
(Bestsellers among independent booksellers, and monthly recommendations on new books by people who have actually read them!)
www.bookweb.org/booksense/bestsellers

Wordsworth
(Bestsellers among independent booksellers.)
www.wordsworth.com (click on "Indie Bestsellers")

Chronicle of Higher Education
(Bestsellers on college campuses.)
www.chronicle.com/books/bestsellers.htm

Readers' Resources

READING GROUPS

There's only one thing that comes close to the pleasure of reading a novel, and that's discussing the book with others who have also read it. In fact, one could almost say that the experience of reading a book isn't complete until you've had the opportunity to talk about it. Inevitably, the other person's reaction to various characters and interpretation of different scenes will get you thinking, reacting, and possibly seeing things in a different light. Imagine, then, how your understanding and appreciation of a book is likely to deepen when the discussion involves five or six people. Combine the discussion with a bite to eat and some socializing among friends, and you've got the makings of a very enjoyable get-together.

That's what reading groups are all about. So it's little wonder that, by some estimates, there are as many as 500,000 groups in the United States. Most consist of 10 to 15 members meeting once a month in someone's home or at a sponsoring bookstore to discuss that month's book. That works out to at least five million readers each buying as many as nine or ten books a year. (Book groups tend to meet during the school year and resume after summer vacation.) No wonder many publishers work overtime to encourage such activities!

Reading Guides

A publisher's encouragement often takes the form of "reading guides" for books that it expects to be popular with book clubs and reading groups. These publications usually include a synopsis of the book, an author biography, selected reviews, questions designed to prompt discussion among group members, and suggestions for further reading. The guides are typically offered two ways: a print version supplied in packs of 10 or 20 and made available through local bookstores or by calling the publisher, and an online version that can be downloaded free of charge at the publisher's Web site. Some publishers have even started binding the guides into paperback editions.

WHERE TO GET THE GUIDES

One way to find out if a reading guide is available for a specific book is to call your favorite bookstore. Or you could try calling the publisher or visiting its Web site using the information you'll find in the "Publisher and Author Contacts" section of this book. But you can probably save time by going instead to the **Resource Center for Book Groups** (www.readinggroupchoices.com) created and maintained by Paz & Associates, a Nashville-based consulting firm dedicated to helping independent bookstores sell more books.

When you get to the Web site, click on "Guide Directory" and then specify whether you want to search for reading guides by author or book title. The directory, which currently includes information on more than 700 reading guides, will tell you exactly what number to call or Web site to visit to get a specific guide. In some cases, all you have to do is click on a title, and you'll be taken instantly to the guide for that book, which you can then browse online or print out for later reading.

You can also order the current year's collection of 60 reading guides in a booklet called *Reading Group Choices*. The booklet sells for $4.95 for a single copy, and a mere $1.25 each for orders of ten or more. Call 800-260-8605, or order online at www.readinggroupchoices.com.

Books for Group Leaders

HOW-TO MANUALS

These books offer both step-by-step instructions for reading group leaders as well as recommended reading lists for book group discussions:

The Reading Group Handbook: Everything You Need to Know from Choosing Members to Leading Discussions by Rachel W. Jacobsohn (Hyperion, 1998). The author of this 240-page guide is the founder and director of the Chicago-based Association of Book Group Readers and Leaders. She also runs some 30 book groups in the Chicago area and conducts workshops and training sessions for would-be reading-group leaders. For a sample of her advice, look for her "Ten Tips for Starting and Running a Successful Book Club" at www.readinggroupchoices.com (click on "Group Leaders").

The Authors Speak

In 1993, while driving home from a meet-the-author event so crowded that he could get nowhere near the featured guest, David Knight had a brainstorm. Why not use the increasingly available and affordable technology of voice mail to record author messages that readers could listen to by dialing a toll-free number?

Thus was born BookTalk, a telephone hotline offering recorded messages from over 1,000 authors. Simply dial 818-788-9722 and punch in the appropriate four-digit "box number" for the author of interest. For example, the box number for Judy Blume talking about *Summer Sisters* is 4609; for Sara Paretsky talking about *Ghost Country*, 4747, for Anna Quindlen and *How Reading Changed My Life*, 4722.

Publishers pay BookTalk between $100 and $200 for each box number, which then gets included along with the BookTalk phone number in print ads for the book. But you can also dial up and simply browse BookTalk. Or you can go to www.dearbooktalk.com and search a list of over 500 titles and author box numbers.

What better way to begin a book-group meeting than to put BookTalk on speakerphone and have the group listen to the author of that month's selected book discuss it for a minute or two?

The New York Public Library Guide to Reading Groups by Rollene Saal (Crown, 1995). This slim little volume (180 pages) is packed with practical advice for starting a reading group and tips for leading stimulating discussions. The book also includes 35 annotated reading lists on topics ranging from "Old Favorites" to "Magic Realism" to "Ghosts and Ghouls."

The Book Group Book: A Thoughtful Guide to Forming and Enjoying a Stimulating Book Discussion Group, edited by Ellen Slezak (Chicago Review Press, 1995). Now in its second edition, this popular 338-page book is actually a collection of essays about setting up and running an effective book group.

WHAT-TO-READ GUIDES

These three books concentrate more on *what* to read, rather than the nuts and bolts of starting and running a reading group:

The New Lifetime Reading Plan by Clifton Fadiman and John S. Major (HarperCollins, 1997). A classic guide to world literature that's been in print for more than 40 years, this extraordinary book has always offered entertaining and informative commentary on the great works of Western civilization. But the latest edition broadens the book's scope to include writers and literary works from around the globe. And a new appendix provides short profiles of 100 important 20th-century authors, from Margaret Atwood and James Baldwin to Evelyn Waugh and Richard Wright. An excellent bibliography offers guidance on the best biographies and critical works to consider for further reading.

The Reading List, Contemporary Fiction: A Critical Guide to the Complete Works of 110 Authors, edited by David Rubel (Henry Holt, 1998). Unlike most reading list guides that organize book titles by topic, this one is organized alphabetically by author. All the authors are still alive and writing novels, short stories, or both, and each author entry includes brief descriptions and excerpts from major reviews for *every* book of fiction the author has published. Major works are identified with an asterisk, so that you can zero in on them if you're reading a particular author for the first time.

What to Read: The Essential Guide for Reading Group Members and Other Book Lovers by Mickey Pearlman (HarperCollins, 1994). Except for a brief introduction profiling ten reading groups in different parts of the country, this 228-page book is devoted exclusively to annotated book lists, organized into 33 different topics. The book descriptions are quite brief, often just a phrase or two, but the selection is both broad and deep.

Other Reading Group Resources

Association of Book Group Readers and Leaders
Founded by Rachel Jacobsohn, author of *The Reading Group Handbook* (Hyperion, 1998), this organization's mission is to promote the creation of reading groups and to help their leaders run them effectively. Membership is $18 a year and includes a subscription to the newsletter *Reverberations*, plus special guides and publisher promotional materials. For information about joining, contact ABGRL, P.O. Box 885, Highland Park, IL 60035; 847-266-0431; rachelj@interaccess.com.

Vintage Reading Group Center
For the best-organized, most comprehensive collection of reading group resources currently on the Internet, visit Random House's Vintage Reading Group Center (www.randomhouse.com/vintage/read). In addition to offering a large selection of reading-group guides for specific books (all published by Vintage and other Random House imprints, of course), the site offers lots of practical advice and information for reading group leaders. Be sure to click on the "Cheat Sheet" button to be taken to a page chock full of information about organizations, books,

newsletters, and other resources designed to help you make the most of any reading group, whether you're the leader/organizer or one of the participants.

Rachel's Compendium of Book Discussions

Another excellent collection of reading-group resources is offered by former book-club leader Rachel Jaffe at Rachel's Compendium (www.his.com/allegria/compend.html). The emphasis here is on *online* book discussions, like the "Table Talk" section of the online magazine *Salon*, as well as book-related Internet newsgroups, Web message boards, forums, and more. But if you click on "Offline Book Discussions," you'll find a nicely annotated selection of reading-group resources, including links to publisher-specific offerings, book-club how-to's, and directories of clubs in the U.S. and Canada.

Best Books for Reading Groups

Need a recommendation for the next meeting of your book discussion group? Curious to know what other groups across the country are reading? The Vintage Reading Group Center (www.randomhouse.com/vintage/read) maintains a list called "The Best Books for Reading Groups," based on a survey of hundreds of reading groups and updated periodically with suggestions from visitors to their Web site.

You'll find the current list of 50 titles, including both fiction and nonfiction, posted at the site. Books of all publishers (not just Random House imprints) are included. Here are the top 20 favorites for 1999:

1. *Memoirs of a Geisha* by Arthur Golden
2. *Midwives* by Chris Bohjalian
3. *Cold Mountain* by Charles Frazier
4. *The Reader* by Bernhard Schlink
5. *Snow Falling on Cedars* by David Guterson
6. *Angela's Ashes* by Frank McCourt
7. *Divine Secrets of the Ya-Ya Sisterhood* by Rebecca Wells
8. *The Shipping News* by E. Annie Proulx
9. *Stones from the River* by Ursula Hegi
10. *A Civil Action* by Jonathan Harr
11. *The English Patient* by Michael Ondaatje
12. *A Lesson Before Dying* by Ernest J. Gaines
13. *The Color of Water* by James McBride
14. *Corelli's Mandolin* by Louis de Bernières
15. *Angle of Repose* by Wallace Stegner
16. *A Prayer for Owen Meany* by John Irving
17. *A Thousand Acres* by Jane Smiley
18. *The God of Small Things* by Arundhati Roy
19. *Alias Grace* by Margaret Atwood
20. *American Pastoral* by Philip Roth

AUDIOBOOKS

Books have been available in cassette form since at least 1985. But in recent years, they've become more popular than ever. A 1999 survey conducted by the Audio Publishers Association (APA) found that over 20 percent of households listen to audiobooks, almost double the number that reported doing so in 1995.

Where do people listen? Most often in the car, but a growing number report listening to audiobooks when exercising, traveling on a plane, or taking mass transit. Fiction accounts for almost half of all listening time and unabridged fiction is the single most popular audiobook category, capturing about a third of the hours spent listening to books on tape.

What You Need to Know

The APA survey found that the average audiobook user has been listening for about four years. But if audiobooks are new to you, here are the some things you need to know about them:

Abridged vs. Unabridged. Works of fiction may be offered on tape (and occasionally on CD) in two versions: abridged and unabridged. The abridged versions typically consist of two cassettes, while unabridged versions include many more. (*The Hobbit* is presented on 8 tapes in unabridged form, for example, while *Moby-Dick* is presented on 15.) Many people mistakenly assume that "abridged" means 20 to 25 percent of the book has been snipped out. "Twenty to twenty-five percent of the book is what you have on your *tape*—and not a bit more," warns bestselling author Barbara Kingsolver. Subplots, colorful minor characters, metaphors, and anything else that does not contribute to "the bones of a plot, and a razor-thin modicum of style" gets left out of abridged audiobooks.

As it must. If it takes you ten hours to read a book yourself, there is no way for that experience to be duplicated on two one-hour cassette tapes. Bottom line: Abridgements may be fine for nonfiction and self-help titles. Possibly even for thrillers. But serious fiction suffers terribly.

Narrator. The voice and reading skill of the narrator are crucial to the quality of the audiobook experience. Occasionally, the author will do the reading, as is the case with Frank McCourt, who reads *Angela's Ashes* for Recorded Books, or Douglas Adams, who reads *The Hitchhiker's Guide to the Galaxy* for Dove Audio. And it's not uncommon for a famous actor to serve as narrator, particularly for abridged versions. Unabridged readings, however, are usually done by actors who specialize in this area, many of whom, like Penelope Dellaporta, Bernadette Dunne,

Frank Muller, and Nelson Runger, have developed enthusiastic followings of their own.

Renting, Buying, or Borrowing. The best way to get started with audiobooks is to investigate the collection of tapes available at your local library. Almost every library these days has a collection of "talking books," so you're sure to find some abridged or unabridged titles of interest. It's important to realize, however, that each branch in your library system may have a different audiobook collection. So if you can't find anything you like at your nearest branch, use the computerized card catalog to check for recordings located at other branches. Usually, you can ask to have such items delivered to your nearest branch and pick them up a day or two later.

Of course no library is likely to have a collection as extensive as the thousands available for rental or purchase from a major audiobook publisher. Audiobooks typically rent for $15 to $25. The rental period is 30 days, starting on the day you receive the tapes. Buying the audiobook instead is more expensive—sometimes as much as $100 or more depending on how many tapes are in the set—but you can listen to them at your leisure without worrying about a time limit. And when you're finished with the tapes, you can always pass them along to a friend or donate them to your local library.

Master Directory. For the definitive guide to what's available in audiobook format, check the reference section of your local library for a book called *Words on Cassette*, published annually by R. R. Bowker (the same company that does *Books in Print*). The latest edition lists some 67,000 audiocassettes that you can look up by title, author, reader/narrator, subject, or publisher. (It sells for $160, which is why we suggest looking for it at the library.)

Where to Get Audiobooks

Abridged versions of novels are sold in traditional and online bookstores. Unabridged versions are beginning to show up in stores, but the best sources are specialty companies that make tapes available for rental or for purchase. For the best selection of audiobook titles, both abridged and unabridged, get to know the specialty companies.

PUBLISHERS

The Audio Publishers Association maintains a comprehensive directory of audiobook publishers at its Web site (www.audiopub.org). Just click on "Listener Resources." You will then be able to look for companies offering audiobooks by mail or on the Web. As you would expect, the depth and breadth of each firm's offerings vary widely.

That's why you may want to start with the top three publishers of unabridged audiobooks:

Blackstone Audiobooks
800-729-2665
www.blackstoneaudio.com

Books On Tape
800-882-6657
www.booksontape.com

Recorded Books
800-638-1304
www.recordedbooks.com

All three do an excellent job of handling both the rental and purchase of audiobooks. Each will be happy to send you a free catalog. Our personal favorite, however, is Recorded Books. No one else in the business puts such an emphasis on the narrators, offering profiles and regular updates on the plays, movies, and TV series each has done. Four of their frequent narrators (Mark Hammer, Ron McLarty, Lynne Thigpen, and Tom Stechshulte) appear as judges on *Law and Order*, for example. So when you have a choice of sources, as is the case with works in the public domain, you may want to check Recorded Books first.

DISTRIBUTORS

The main disadvantage of dealing directly with audiobook publishers is that each company offers only its own titles. To select from the offerings of lots of audiobook publishers, try one of these online distributors, all of which offer audiotapes for sale (though not for rent):

Audiobook
www.audiobook.com

Amazon.com
www.amazon.com

BarnesandNoble.com
www.barnesandnoble.com

Of the three, AudioBook does the best job of presenting its offerings online. A subsidiary of the Audio Book Club, it claims to be "the world's largest marketer of audiobooks through the Internet and direct mail" with over two million customers.

DOWNLOADABLE FILES

Due diligence requires that we also mention the availability of "downloadable audiobooks" and other spoken-word files. Instead of buying or renting audiotapes, you pay a fee and download files from the Internet.

One of the leaders in the field is a company called Audible, Inc. (www.audible.com), located in Wayne, Pennsylvania. For the select few with an MP3 player and some extra time to spare, you can plug your device into the speaker port of a computer's sound card, and download between 2 and 28 hours of "content." Prices are up to 60 percent cheaper than the purchase of cassettes. But is it worth the hassle—particularly given the fact that the portable players hold just two to seven hours of audio? Our guess is that, for the moment, most audiobook listeners will choose instead to rent or buy audiobooks, or borrow them from the library on tape or CD.

Do-It-Yourself Audiobooks!

If you want to get audiobooks via computer, there's actually a way of doing it yourself, without paying anything for downloads. To start with, check one of vast online repositories of public-domain books: Project Gutenberg (www.gutenberg.net) is the premier source. Another good collection is available at the University of Pennsylvania's Online Books Page (digital.library.upenn.edu/books). Both sites offer comprehensive, searchable databases of thousands of "e-texts," which you can read, search, and even modify in any standard word-processing program.

Using Text-to-Speech (TTS) software, which tells your computer to read aloud any text you feed to the program, you can then use these files to create your own audiobooks. You can even select your preferred reader "voice" in most cases. No, the listening experience isn't going to compare to a commercially produced audiobook. But today's TTS software is much more humanlike than the flat, computerized voices of the past. And, you're probably not going to find audiobook editions of, say, Oscar Wilde's *A Florentine Tragedy* or Flaubert's *Salammbo*. But the full text of both works is available online.

For a very serviceable, free TTS program, go to www.readplease.com and download a copy of ReadPlease 2000.

Reviews

If you rent or buy a lot of audiobooks, you should know about *AudioFile*, a magazine that specializes in audiobook reviews. Published six times a year, the magazine provides recommendations and informed opinions on both content and performance. For a free issue, call 800-506-1212 or visit www.audiofilemagazine.com. If you like the magazine, you'll be billed $20 for a full subscription (five more issues). If not, you can simply write "cancel" on the invoice and keep the free issue.

CATALOGS AND REFERENCES

Today, book lovers and passionate readers are a recognizable niche as far as direct marketers are concerned. So it's rarely a question of finding a catalog of interest—it usually finds you. Nevertheless, there are a scant handful of catalogs that really are unique and may well merit your attention. That's what we'll tell you about here, followed by some suggestions for stocking your reference shelf.

Catalogs for Serious Readers

A Common Reader
800-832-7323
www.commonreader.com

Imagine someone who shares many of your interests and who does nothing all day but look for books of every sort that he thinks you'd like to know about. That's what this most uncommon of catalogs offers. As company founder James Mustich Jr. puts it, *A Common Reader* is "a catalog in which the discovery and delight, the amusements and satisfactions that books provide are savored and shared. Each month we put together a discriminating selection of books we've enjoyed and think you might enjoy as well. Some are best browsed, some are for study, but all belong to that class of books one is eager to pass on to a friend."

The Web site is worth a visit, but the only way to really grasp the collection is to get the free 136-page monthly catalog. Each book is presented with a first-person description that may run several hundred words. In addition to an active inventory of over 3,000 titles, there are nearly 100 "A Common Reader" (ACR) editions that bring you books that have fallen out of print or been overlooked by traditional publishers.

Bas Bleu, Bookseller by Post
800-433-1155
www.basbleu.com

Bas Bleu is French for "bluestocking," a term used to describe a literary woman that may have originated in the mid-1700s with an informal group of British ladies who preferred to replace the customary after-dinner card playing at social gatherings with something more intellectual. During the planning for one such gathering, which was to include Dr. Johnson, David Garrick, Horace Walpole, and others, the leader of the group was told by a learned man that he couldn't attend because he didn't have the requisite pair of black silk stockings. She replied that he should come in "his blue stockings"—the worsted wool stockings people used for everyday wear. Thus Bluestocking (or Bas Bleu) became the nickname for the group.

Of course, it's also possible that the group's members were aware of a Parisian club of women called "Bas Bleu" founded in 1590 for a similar purpose. What gives the name its interesting twist is that calling a woman "a bluestocking" is not a compliment. The term came to mean a woman who pursued her intellectual interests to the detriment of her other duties. So, you've got to love a mail-order house (or "bookseller by post") that selects such a name.

Bas Bleu produces a catalog of books and bookish things five times a year. "We read the books and write the reviews right here," says company president Eleanor Edmundson, "but we're a retailer, not a publisher.... Our selections are eclectic—and rarely do any of them appear on the bestseller lists." Nor are you likely to find the fiction the firm selects in the racks at the supermarket or airport shop. For travel books, Bas Bleu is more interested in the stories of gifted writers than lists of what to do and where to stay. And their children's books "celebrate imagination and humor rather than cautionary tales."

According to Edmundson, "People buy from us—at least this is *our* theory—because they feel the items we pick for our catalog match their tastes." To see for yourself, visit the company's Web site, or call their toll-free number to order a copy of the print catalog.

Easton Press Leather-Bound Books

800-211-1308

Leather-bound volumes with gold stamped covers are the ultimate book-lover's luxury. And from all reports, Easton Press does it right: acid-free archival paper, signatures that are sewn instead of glued (all glue dries out eventually), 22-karat-gold accents, gilded edges, ribbon page markers, and moiré fabric end sheets. At a typical cost of $40 or more per book, Easton Press editions aren't cheap. But they make wonderful gifts and personal treats.

Reader's Reference Books

We've never encountered a reference book that we didn't want to own. The topic hardly matters. It is the satisfaction and sense of security that comes with knowing that, should a question or query arise, there is at least the chance that the answer will lie in some book, somewhere on our shelves.

Yet, as the authors of several sourcebooks, glossaries, and other guides, discovering how reference works are created came as a revelation. Before we started doing this professionally, it never occurred to us that reference

Where to Find More Great Catalogs

Track down a copy of *The Catalog of Catalogs: The Complete Mail-Order Directory* by Edward L. Palder (Woodbine House, 1999), available from bookstores and possibly at your local library. The latest edition is over 600 pages and sells for $26. It provides contact information for some 15,000 catalogs in more than 900 subject categories—including a dozen pages of entries for book-related catalogs. You'll find sources of bookmarks and bookplates, book repair, lots of specialty book sources (dance, Civil War, mountaineering, fire fighting, parenting, etc.), used books, book-search services, and large-print and Braille editions.

books are very human creations, requiring a constant flow of decisions on what to put in and what to leave out, and on how deeply to cover a given topic.

Every reference book must provide respectable coverage of some central, essential core of information related to its major focus. But if that core is the first concentric circle produced by tossing a pebble into a pond, there's plenty of room for human decisions in the outer rings. That's why some reference works are better than others. And it is why we want to suggest several very special reference works here. Some you may want to own; some you will want to look for at the library. Our purpose here is to call them out so that you can zero in as time permits.

Benét's Reader's Encyclopedia by William Rose Benét and Bruce Murphy (HarperCollins, 1996). This is one of the greatest literary reference works of all time—a must-have book for passionate readers. At over 1,140 pages, it covers nearly every cultural or literary term that you're likely to encounter. You'll also find author biographies, depictions of major fictional characters, explanations of literary movements, and plot summaries of major books and plays. Once you've thumbed through *Benét*, you'll want a copy for your personal library. But it's also a wonderful gift book for high school and college graduations and other special occasions. It's guaranteed to expand its owner's horizons.

Brewer's Dictionary of Phrase & Fable by Ebenezer Cobham Brewer, Adrian Room, and Ivor H. Evans (HarperCollins, 2000). Since its first publication in 1870, this book has become one of the world's best-loved and most-browsed-through reference works of all time. Here you'll find the meanings of—and the stories behind—terms and phrases drawn from mythology, literature, history, folk customs, pop culture, philosophy, science, magic, and superstitions. (The book's definition of bluestocking was helpful in preparing the description of the Bas Bleu catalog for this book.) The latest edition is over 1,180 pages and contains hundreds of new entries and expanded etymologies.

Genreflecting by Diana Tixier Herald (Libraries Unlimited, 1995). Though written as a guide to help librarians recommend books to their patrons, this is a wonderful reference work for anyone interested in genre fiction. How about Westerns featuring a town sheriff or a marshal as the central character? Or a crime novel that focuses on smuggling? Science fiction stories centered on love and sex? Novels with female detectives? Or African-American sleuths? How about fantasy novels featuring dragons? This remarkable book has the answers. It covers every genre and subgenre of fiction you can think of—truly an incredible accomplishment.

Contemporary Authors. This is a publication of the Gale Group (www.gale.com), that reference-work powerhouse. The complete work covers some 100,000 modern novelists, poets, playwrights, nonfiction writers, journalists, and scriptwriters. There are over 128 printed volumes, but many libraries can give you access via CD-ROM or direct connection to the Gale online database. This is an excellent starting point for author information, since each entry provides biographical information, plus excerpts from various commentaries and reviews. The publication doesn't take a position on a given author, it simply reports—sometimes at greater length than one might want, but better more than less.

The Literary Almanac: The Best of the Printed Word, 1900 to the Present (Andrews McMeel, 1997). This slim volume (288 pages), organized chronologically by year, presents the hardcover fiction and nonfiction bestsellers, the winners of major literary awards and prizes for adult fiction and nonfiction (Nobel Prize in Literature, Pulitzer Prize, National Book Award, PEN/Faulkner Award, and Booker Prize), and the Caldecott and Newbery Medal winners (for children's literature). Also included are the names of writers who were born or died that year. Laced through this basic structure are many and wondrous eclectic delights, including capsule author biographies, photos, book jackets, quotations, and excerpts from books and reviews. Also a list of the jobs some writers held before becoming writers and an all-too-brief list of literary love affairs. Since it is organized by year, the book offers the ideal way to gain a sense of historical context. It is also catnip for trivia lovers. (Who would have guessed, for example, that Ann Beattie, Tom Clancy, Stephen King, David Mamet, Salman Rushdie, and Danielle Steel were all born in 1947?)

A Reader's Guide to Twentieth-Century Writers, edited by Peter Parker and Frank Kermode (Oxford University Press, 1996). Did you know that William Saroyan and his cousin wrote "C'mon-a My House," the song Rosemary Clooney made famous? Or that General Francis Nash, the man for whom Nashville, Tennessee, was named, was Ogden Nash's great-great-great uncle? You'll discover these and many more serious facts among the profiles of nearly 1,000 novelists, storywriters, playwrights, and poets featured in this book. Prepared by over 40 critics, biographers, and academics, the entries provide summaries of each person's life and works as well as a bibliography and a brief overall critical assessment. The entries tend to be much livelier and more entertaining than those found in similar reference works, many of which are also published by Oxford University Press.

OUT-OF-PRINT AND USED BOOKS

In the 1950s, Ohio's Stark County District Library regularly sent "Bookmobiles" to spend a few hours at local elementary schools. A third grader attending Edgefield Elementary at the time fell in love with two books: *King Arthur* (1950) by Mary MacLeod and *The Silver Horn of Robin Hood* by Donald E. Cooke (1956). It took 41 years, but copies of those two books are now in his possession.

The first was found, after years of perusing dusty shelves, in the stacks at Masons' Rare & Used Books in Chambersburg, Pennsylvania. The cost was $4.75. The second title was located in minutes via Bibliofind on the Internet and purchased from the Book Baron in Fullerton, California, for $5.00 plus shipping and handling. If memory serves, a loud "Whoop!" immediately followed the discovery of the one book in Chambersburg. But for the second book, the main reaction was a smile of satisfaction, followed by an echo of Richard Anderson as Oscar Goldman on *The Six Million Dollar Man* saying "We *have* the technology."

The Future

There are two main types of customers for out-of-print books: The collectors who, God bless 'em, are in search of treasures. And the readers who, like us, are amazed at how many times they run into the "Out of Print" screen at the Amazon.com or BarnesandNoble.com sites.

On reflection, though, it's not so surprising. Warehousing books costs money. So if a book isn't selling at least 300 to 500 copies a year, most publishers will declare it out of print and sell off any stock to a remainder house.

In the not too distant future, though, out-of-print books will no longer require hundreds of cubic feet of warehouse space. Instead, they'll be stored on just a few pennies' worth of space on a hard-disk drive and printed on demand one at a time or downloaded over the Internet. These things are already being done on a small scale and,

as of this writing, the pace of change is leaping forward. Many major publishers are endeavoring to digitize their entire backlists, and the major bookselling chains and wholesalers are implementing various print-on-demand processes and storage facilities.

But what about all those books published over the last 50 years or more? The ones with bar codes on their dust jackets or back covers can be entered quickly and easily into a used-book dealer's online database. Some books, like the two titles from the 1950s mentioned earlier, re-

E-Books

On the consumer front, a classic battle of competing technologies is shaping up in the market for "e-books"—books you can download via the Internet and read on an electronic device. The books themselves may be out-of-print titles, current bestsellers, or classic works in the public domain. Since the real money is in the electronic distribution of current titles, the competitors have focused on ways to make sure that, once purchased, the digital file that constitutes the e-book can be read by just one person at a time and that readable copies cannot be distributed to others. But they differ widely in their approaches to the e-book idea.

Some have created portable readers modeled on the Dynabook concept first proposed in 1968 by computer visionary Alan Kay. These are essentially diskless notebook computers that use touch-screen technology instead of keyboards or simple buttons to page forward and back through a book. Some plug directly into a phone jack to download content. Others use a personal computer with an Internet connection as an intermediary. At this writing, some 2,000 titles can be purchased instantly from Web sites operated by Powell's Books (www.powells.com) and BarnesandNoble.com (www.bn.com). Most of the fiction consists of inexpensive public-domain classics. Some makers of these devices, notably Nuvo Media, offer hundreds of public-domain titles in their proprietary format free of charge.

The competing approach is to develop reader-friendly software designed to display books on multipurpose devices like notebook computers, Palm Pilots, and personal digital assistants using existing display software like the Acrobat Reader.

Supporters in both camps promote the fact that their products offer at least three benefits to

consumers: they let you carry around a dozen or more books without the weight of traditional volumes, make it easy for you to annotate the text (some devices include a stylus), and offer savings of 20 to 40 percent on the purchase of new books. Those savings, however, are potential savings. Discounts are up to the publishers, who also determine which (if any) pages can be printed out. At BarnesandNoble.com recently, we found the hardcover edition of a current bestseller discounted a whopping 50 percent, while the e-book was discounted a mere 20 percent.

For more information about the field in general, visit eBookNet at www.ebooknet.com. To learn more about the leading players, visit these Web sites:

Everybook EB Dedicated Reader
www.everybook.net

Glassbook Internet Reading Software
www.glassbook.com

Librius eBook and Software
www.librius.com
www.books2read.com

NetLibrary
www.netlibrary.com

Nuvo Media Rocket eBook Reader
www.nuvomedia.com

Peanut Press
www.peanutpress.com

SoftBook Reader
www.softbook.com

Versabook Software
www.versabook.com

quire more time to enter. But then, for used-book sellers and book clerks, this is not usually a problem. Rush periods are almost always more than offset by idle time. So check the stock, guys, and start keyboarding! Many used-book dealers have already managed to enter huge portions of their stock into electronic databases and make them available online.

Getting Your Hands on Them

The existence of the Internet has dramatically increased the availability of used and out-of-print books while greatly reducing prices. In fact, according to the *Wall Street Journal* (June 18, 1999), many book collectors have seen the value of their collections plummet in recent years. One example: In 1997, a first edition of Charles Frazier's *Cold Mountain* sold for $225. A year later, thanks to the availability of many copies via the Net, the price had fallen to $112.

People are checking their attics, basements, and garages and offering what they find on the Net, usually at an auction site. Prices for even common books vary widely, and it is wise to take an amateur's rating of a book's condition as "fine" with a grain of salt. But the books are indeed available in one condition or another.

Amazon.com and BarnesandNoble.com, the two giants of online bookselling, both offer out-of-print (OOP) books. When you hit an OOP screen for a particular title, you can tell the system that you want it to query its "network of used bookstores" and notify you by e-mail when it finds the book. In our experience, both companies do a good job in this area. But you may want to take things into your own hands. Using our own OOP titles as examples, we looked at a variety of online sources and found prices for the same title, in the same condition, being offered for as little as $5 or as much as $35.

The lesson is, let Amazon.com and BarnesandNoble.com do their searches for you—it's free after all—but if you want the best price, you're going to have to search on your own. So here's what to do:

1. Take full advantage of Amazon.com (www.amazon.com) and BarnesandNoble.com (www.bn.com). As of this writing, you can go to a separate out-of-print feature on BarnesandNoble.com and conduct a search. You can't do that on Amazon.com (not yet, anyway), but you can tell the system to search its current auction and zShops offerings, which usually turns up several OOP titles. (Do a quick search and leave the focus set to "All Products.")

2. Search Alibris (www.alibris.com) and Bibliofind (www.bibliofind.com), two of the powerhouses of online used books. We searched both sites for *The Silver Horn of Robin Hood*. Alibris turned up copies at $26, $20, and $15, while the Bibliofind search located copies at $20, $15, and

$12. All were said to be in "very good" condition. The lesson is, don't take the first offer—yet another reason why you will want to be in control of the search process.

3. If you don't find the title (or the price) you're looking for at Alibris or Bibliofind, or you simply want to broaden your search before committing to a specific purchase, try Powell's Books (www.powells.com) or one of the other online sources in the following list.

Online Sources

Advanced Book Exchange
www.abebooks.com

Alibris
www.alibris.com

Amazon.com
www.amazon.com

Antiquarian Booksellers' Association of America
www.abaa.org

BarnesandNoble.com
www.bn.com

Bibliofind
www.bibliofind.com

Blake's Books
www.blakesbooks.com

Book Closeouts
www.bookcloseouts.com

Bookfinder
www.bookfinder.com

Powell's Books
www.powells.com

Rereadables
www.rereadables.com

BOOK REVIEWS

According to the U. S. Copyright Office, 68,175 new books were published in 1997, up from 62,039 the previous year. Few would disagree that numbers like that probably represent too much of a good thing. For readers, the trick has always been to identify the really good books before they get shipped back to the publisher and on to the pulping machines. And, of course, the main way to do that is to consult book reviews.

Here, too, there is an embarrassment of riches. Most major newspapers and newsmagazines regularly publish book reviews written by on-staff reviewers, or by novelists and other writers with credentials in a given field. Larger newspapers may also publish separate sections covering books each Sunday. And there are entire publications devoted to books and book reviews.

Fortunately, there is also the Internet. As we've seen elsewhere, the Net has a great deal to offer passionate readers. But nowhere is it more useful than in finding book reviews. In the past, if you saw an ad for a book that sounded interesting, you had to wait for a review to appear in your favorite newspapers and magazines. With the Internet at your disposal, you can now call up multiple book reviews within minutes of seeing an ad or hearing about a book on National Public Radio, or C-SPAN, or from a relative or friend. What's more, regardless of where you live, you can easily tap current and past reviews from all the leading big-city newspapers, the weekly newsmagazines, and respected specialty publications like *Booklist*, *Publishers Weekly*, and *Library Journal*. In some cases, you can even download and print out the first chapter of a book that's of interest.

Yahoo is the search engine best suited to locating book-review sites on the Internet. To see for yourself, go to www.yahoo.com, search for "book reviews" (be sure to use the quotation marks), and then click on "Arts>Humanities>Literature>Reviews."

For a more targeted approach, we suggest the print publications and Web sites described here. As you will discover, some are clearly far superior to others. But Web sites are constantly improving. There are literally hundreds of sources of book reviews, but we feel these are the ones to watch.

Favorite Sources

BOOK: THE MAGAZINE FOR THE READING LIFE

www.bookmagazine.com
800-317-2665

Imagine: An entire magazine devoted to author profiles and book reviews. Published six times a year, *Book* is the natural next step in the "celebrities" movement. Chefs, CEOs, entrepreneurs, and now authors. Single copies are available in the newsstand sections of most major bookstores. Subscriptions are $20 a year.

For more information, and the full text of book reviews from the magazine's current issue, visit the magazine's Web site (www.bookmagazine.com). Though it's not available yet, a searchable "archives" section is promised for the future.

BOOKLIST

www.ala.org/booklist
800-545-2422

Published for over 90 years by the American Library Association, *Booklist* publishes short (200–300 words), sharp reviews of some 7,000 books each year. Designed for busy librarians, the reviews get right to the point. Subscriptions are $85 a year for 22 issues. To subscribe, call 800-545-2422, ext. 5716. Or visit www.ala.org/booklist on the Web, where you can view a recent issue of the magazine and search for reviews and feature articles from the past five years.

BOOK TV

www.booktv.org
CSPAN-2
(8:00 A.M. Saturday to 8:00 A.M. Monday, Eastern time)

C-SPAN, the cable channel that does such a superb job of covering the House of Representatives, government, and politics, made a big hit with Booknotes, a program in which Brian Lamb, C-SPAN's versatile chairman and CEO, spends an hour interviewing a nonfiction author. (Gotta do something when Congress isn't in session!) Springboarding from that success, in 1998, Lamb introduced Book TV on C-SPAN2, the channel that televises the Senate. Book TV's motto is "all books—all weekend—every weekend." That's because it's on from 8:00 A.M. Saturday to 8:00 A.M. Monday (Eastern time).

The program focuses on nonfiction rather than fiction. However, with the firm conviction that people who read books read all kinds of books, we've felt compelled to include it here. When you visit the *Book TV* Web site (www.booktv.org), you will instantly see why. The program offers a veritable candy store for the intellect.

There are five main categories of programs: history, biography, children's books, the business of books, and encores of *Booknotes* broadcasts (including easy-to-print transcripts). Authors, agents, publishers, bookstore owners, visits to literary landmarks, round-robin discussions with book reviewers located in various cities—you'll find all that and more. And, you can view both current real-time broadcasts and previous programs online—an important point since many cable systems don't carry C-SPAN2. You can even search the *Book TV* archives to locate programs or authors of particular interest.

BOOKWIRE

www.bookwire.com

Bookwire is the enterprise of publishing reference giant R. R. Bowker. The good news is that it has a great deal to offer the book enthusiast. The bad news is that it could be better organized and provide much stronger search functions. The site offers easy access to *Publishers Weekly*, where you can read all the latest news and feature articles about the publishing industry. (*PW's* book reviews, called "Forecasts," will soon be available here as well, but only to the magazine's subscribers.) You'll also find links for *Library Journal*, *Boston Book Review*, and *Hungry Mind Review*—all good sources of book reviews. (The owners of *Hungry Mind Review* have recently sold the name, so don't be surprised if it's called something else when you visit.)

NEW YORK TIMES

www.nytimes.com/books
800-631-2580 (to order *New York Times Book Review*)

The *New York Times* is the country's de facto newspaper of record, and all indications are that it has always taken that responsibility very seriously. Combine this with the fact that New York City is the center of the book-publishing industry, and you would expect the *Times* to offer a broad selection of book reviews written by top reviewers. You would also expect the paper to make that information available on its Web site.

What you might not expect is for that Web site to be so good, so complete, and so well thought out that it would set the standard for all other book-related Web sites. But that's exactly what you'll find at www.nytimes.com/books.

For openers, you can search the *Times* database of 50,000 book reviews published since 1980. The *Times* can offer this extraordinary feature because the full text of the paper has been available online since that date. The difference is that in the pre-Internet years, you had to pay hefty fees to an online system called Lexis/Nexis in order to get access. Now the book reviews are free.

As regular readers know, the *New York Times* publishes book reviews in two venues. There are the reviews that appear in the daily paper written by staff reviewers like Christopher Lehmann-Haupt and Michiko Kakutani. And there is the *New York Times Book Review*, which is published as a stand-alone newsprint magazine each Sunday. The reviewers there tend to be authors, scholars, and academics.

Reviews from both publications are available at the Web site. So, too, are the first chapters of scores of novels and nonfiction books. (Wisely, the *Times* presents the text instantly, ready to print out from your browser, instead of forcing you to fiddle around with PDF files that must be downloaded and displayed with the Acrobat reader.)

If you don't have Web access, you might want to subscribe to the print edition of the *New York Times Book Review*. The cost is $52 for 52 weeks. Call 800-631-2580.

NEW YORK REVIEW OF BOOKS

www.nybooks.com
800-829-5088

In the words of *Esquire*, the *New York Review of Books* has established itself as "the premier literary-intellectual magazine in the English language." Founded in 1963 by Robert Silvers and Barbara Epstein (during a New York City newspaper strike that made it impossible to consult any of the papers' book reviews), this magazine is designed to offer a forum for "the most interesting and creative minds of our time" to discuss current books and issues in depth. In other words, not only will you find book reviews by important authors, you will find learned discussions of politics, economics, society and culture, and social justice. And scanning the book ads will acquaint you with the latest serious books.

An annual subscription (20 issues) is $58. Call 800-829-5088. To read current reviews and articles or search the archives dating back to 1995, go to www.nybooks.com. You'll find it a fascinating publication.

REALBOOKS

www.realbooks.com

Knight-Ridder (KR) has long been a powerhouse in newspapers and online information. Recently, it has begun to marshal its resources to provide online access to its archives of book reviews and to other features like Chapter One, which lets you view and print out the first chapter of scores of books. The company calls its Web site Real-Books, and it is well worth a visit, if only to investigate and take advantage of the Chapter One offerings.

New York Times on the Web: Featured Authors

When you visit the Books page of the *New York Times* Web site, be sure to click on "Specials/Audio." Doing so will take you to a part of the Web site offering unexpected riches. Click on "Previous Features" and then on "Authors."

This will take you to a master directory, where you'll find links for scores of authors, from Ann Beattie, Saul Bellow, and A. S. Byatt to Gore Vidal, Kurt Vonnegut, Tom Wolfe, and Virginia Woolf. Click on, say, "Don DeLillo," and here is what you will find:

• A 1997 article by DeLillo called "The Power of History" from the *Sunday New York Times Magazine.*

• A 1982 interview with the author.

• Reviews of each of his works, starting with *Americana* in 1971.

• A 30-minute interview with Terry Gross of NPR's *Fresh Air*, which you can listen to at your computer using the RealAudio player (downloadable from the *Times* site).

• A copy of the front page of the *New York Times* for October 4, 1951, the sight of which DeLillo said struck him "with the force of revelation" and inspired his novel *Underworld.*

• Readings by the author from *Mao II* (20 minutes) and *Libra* (16 minutes) that were presented at New York City's 92nd Street Y.

Other author offerings are equally rich and varied. And each reflects a spirit and an intellect dedicated to going beyond the mediocre and to using every available asset and every available feature to create a truly superb offering. Great Web sites don't just happen—they are envisioned and created by really dedicated, imaginative people. And this is a truly great site.

Reader Reviews

When a movie mogul says a new picture's "got legs," what he or she means is that it has good "word of mouth." People who have seen the movie tell their relatives and friends to go see it, and the box office just builds.

The same thing happens with books. People who love a book share their enthusiasm with their friends. Often the person who bought the book will maintain a list of friends who get to borrow it next. As frequent participants in such lists, we apologize to our fellow authors for the royalties lost. But then, having been introduced to an author by a friend, we have found ourselves buying a copy of the author's *next* title because we couldn't wait for the list to come around to us.

Our point here is to note the relevance of "reader reviews." One way to find them is to tap into Internet "newsgroups"—free-floating bulletin boards that accept messages and comments from anyone. If you want to see what's available, go to www.yahoo.com and search for "alt.books" using quotation marks as shown here. This will produce a list of alt.books newsgroups devoted to specific authors (like alt.books.dean-koontz or alt.books.anne-rice). Click on a selection, and Netscape or Explorer will launch its newsreader module. Tell the program to "get new messages" and you're off to the races.

An even better way to get the impressions of readers regarding a specific title is to search for it on Amazon.com or BarnesandNoble.com. At this writing, Amazon.com offers more reader comments on average per title. But neither of these competitors seems shy about making available all comments, whether good or bad. And both give you the opportunity to offer your own review, helping along the next browsing reader.

Amazon.com
www.amazon.com
(Search for specific author or book title.)

BarnesandNoble.com
www.bn.com
(Search for specific author or book title.)

Yahoo!
www.yahoo.com
(Search for "alt.books" to find newsgroups.)

Newspapers and Magazines

When it comes to book reviews, author interviews, and book-related stories, no one seriously contests the dominance of the *New York Times*. But several other newspapers and general-interest magazines are major contenders. And many of them are available on the Internet, although the extent of their presence varies.

At this writing, for example, the *New Yorker* Web site (www.newyorker.com) is devoid of value—you can send a letter to the editor, but you can't even view the table of contents for the latest issue, let alone search for and print a book review. Of course, like all Web offerings, that could change.

To find the Web site of your favorite book-review-carrying newspaper or magazine, go to www.yahoo.com, type the name of the publication in quotation marks in the search box, and conduct your search. (Because Yahoo's database is assembled by human beings, it's the best tool to use when looking for the Web site of a particular publication.) Here are some of the "biggies" that are worth checking:

NEWSPAPERS

Boston Globe
www.boston.com/globe/living/bookreviews

Chicago Tribune
chicagotribune.com/leisure/books

Los Angeles Times
www.calendarlive.com/books/bookreview

New York Times
www.nytimes.com/books

San Francisco Chronicle
www.sfgate.com/eguide/books

USA Today
www.usatoday.com

Wall Street Journal
www.wsj.com (subscription required)
The Friday "Weekend Journal" section typically includes several book reviews. To search for reviews in past issues, visit the Web site and click on "Table of Contents" and then "Book Reviews."

Washington Post
www.washingtonpost.com/wp-srv/style/books

NEWS MAGAZINES

Entertainment Weekly
www.ew.com

Newsweek
www.newsweek.com

People
www.people.com

Time
www.time.com

U. S. News
www.usnews.com

Special Events and Publishers

Book fairs and festivals are magic. At the national level, they pull together into one place authors, editors, critics, agents, publishers, bookstore owners, chain-store buyers, and many dedicated readers. As such, they are a lot like any other industry-specific gathering. Business is transacted and deals are made. Which, of course, is the main reason such gatherings are held in the first place.

But book fairs are different. Whether national, international, or regional, they are about ideas and culture and entertainment and possibilities. In practical terms, some new, inexpensive energy-conservation device introduced at a convention of plumbing or electrical contractors will probably have a greater total positive impact on mankind and the environment. But it's impossible to contain the enthusiasm for new ideas, new fiction, new *everything* that pervades a major book fair. Even in an age drenched in Internet connectivity and electronic media, books still hold a very special place in our lives. The feel of them, the smell of them, the sensation of turning the page and revealing new illustrations or plot twists—not only is there no frigate like a book, there is no flat-screen, hand-held computer like a book, either. Nor will there ever be.

It's a sentiment shared by millions of people, all of whom vote with their feet by attending the hundreds of conventions, fairs, and festivals held each year to celebrate (and sell) books. If you are not among them, the information presented here may reveal some unsuspected possibilities. Book fairs and festivals aren't just for publishing people. Readers are always welcome.

This section begins by focusing on the big national and international events. Not that it is likely that you will attend—though if you happen to live in a host city, you might consider stopping by. The goal here is to provide the information access points (usually a Web address) you need to get more details. So the next time you read that some new author was the sensation of BookExpo America, you'll be able to quickly find out what that means.

The second part of this section zeros in on local and regional book events. And here our assumption is that, once you know about some relatively close event, you might very well want to attend. It is a joy to report, however, that the growing enthusiasm for books and book events is such that there simply is not room to list them all. That's why you'll also find hands-on instructions for using the Internet to locate information about book-related events in your area—regardless of where you live.

The Center for the Book: Events, Fairs, and Programs

The Center for the Book in the Library of Congress was established by federal law in 1977 to stimulate public interest in books, reading, and libraries. Among other things, it maintains what is undoubtedly the most current and comprehensive list of book fairs, book events, and special reading-related programs available anywhere. Simply point your Web browser at lcweb.loc.gov/cfbook and click on "Book Fairs and Other Literary Events" to be taken to an alphabetical listing. Or click on "Book Events Calendar" to view the same information organized by date. In both cases, you'll find phone and fax numbers and clickable links to the event's Web site. This is a truly invaluable resource.

NATIONAL AND INTERNATIONAL EVENTS

BookExpo America

BookExpo America (BEA) is the largest publishing industry trade event in the United States. It is the direct descendent of the convention known as the ABA, after its sponsor, the American Booksellers Association, the leading organization of independent (non-chain) bookstore owners. The ABA was formed in 1900 and held its first convention in 1902 at the Herald Square Hotel in New York City. A total of 60 people attended, including Mark Twain, who was the featured speaker. Today, the event typically draws some 25,000 or more attendees. The convention is now run by Reed Exhibition Companies and is cosponsored by the ABA and the Association of American Publishers.

BookExpo America is usually held in late May or early June, but the host city varies. It really is a trade event, but featured guests always include celebrities with books to push and celebrity authors, so you might actually be able to get one to autograph a book for you. But you'll have to get in line with publishing professionals, who are as star-struck as anyone else. For the latest information on the next Book-Expo, call 800-840-5614 or visit bookexpo.reedexpo.com.

International Antiquarian Book Fair

Sponsored by the Antiquarian Booksellers' Association of America (ABAA), these fairs are held each year in Boston, New York City, and California (alternating between Los Angeles and San Francisco).

Unlike BookExpo America and other trade conventions, at ABAA book fairs, buying and selling actual copies of books is a major focus. You might have access to more titles in Chambersburg, Pennsylvania, and in other towns with large clusters of used-book stores. But at this book fair you have the added assurance that all dealers abide by the ethical standards established by the ABAA. You'll find a master calendar of future events at the ABAA Web site (www.abaa.org), but for details on upcoming fairs in a specific city, use the phone numbers or Web sites listed here:

Boston (November)
617-266-6540
BostonBookFair.com

New York City (April)
212-777-5218
NewYorkBookFair.com

Los Angeles (February/even years)
818-986-6165 (fax)
LosAngelesBookFair.com

San Francisco (February/odd years)
415-551-5190 (voice)
415-551-5195 (fax)
SanFranciscoBookFair.com

International Festival of Authors

For more than 20 years, Toronto has hosted this 11-day fall festival featuring some 60 authors from around the world who participate in more than 1,000 scheduled events at the city's Harbourfront Centre and other locations. The program includes all kinds of author appearances: readings, on-stage author interviews, and lectures by noted biographers of literary figures. For information, call 416-973-4760 or visit www.icomm.ca/ifoa.

Malice Domestic

Held each spring in Washington, D.C., this convention salutes "mysteries of manners"—books typified by the works of Agatha Christie, namesake for the group's annual Agatha Awards. No explicit sex. No excessive gore or violence. And an amateur detective confronting a group of characters who know each other and exist in a relatively confined setting. (The American equivalent of a British "cozy" mystery.) For information, call 301-261-5728 or visit www.erols.com/malice.

National Storytelling Festival

Sponsored by the National Storytelling Association, this three-day event has been hosted for more than 25 years by the tiny (pop. 3,500) Appalachian town of Jonesborough, Tennessee. Davy Crockett was born nearby, Daniel Boone trapped in the area's woods, and Andrew Jackson fought his first duel here. But in 1973, the town was in deep decline.

Then Jimmy Neil Smith hit upon the idea of holding an annual storytelling festival. It started slowly, but today some 12,000 people come to Jonesborough each fall to listen to more than 40 tale-tellers, raconteurs, and yarn-spinners practice their craft on stages in seven or more big tents set up around town. As the *Los Angeles Times* put it, "What New Orleans is to jazz...Jonesborough is to storytelling." For information, call 800-525-4514 or 423-753-3700, or visit the National Storytelling Association Web site at www.storynet.org/nsa/aboutnsa.htm.

Romantic Times Book Lovers Convention

Billed as a "Celebration of Romance and Suspense," this annual four-day conference for romance readers, writers, and booksellers is sponsored by *Romantic Times* magazine. The program typically includes seminars, workshops for aspiring and experienced writers, a book fair, autograph sessions with top romance authors, and nightly costume balls. The convention is held in a different city each year. For information, call 718-237-1097, or visit www.romantictimes.com and click on "Book Lovers Conventions."

World Fantasy Convention

This annual gathering of authors, editors, rare book dealers, artists, collectors, and others "interested in Light and Dark Fantasy literature and art" is limited to 850 participants. The four-day event, which is typically sold out well in advance, concludes with a banquet at which the World Fantasy Awards are presented.

Unlike *Star Trek* conventions, few members wear costumes, according to convention organizers, and "there is no gaming or masquerade." For a retrospective of past conventions dating back to 1975 and plans for upcoming events, visit www.worldfantasy.org.

World Horror Convention

One of the newer "World Conventions," this one is designed specifically for fans of horror and dark fantasy. For details on the next four-day event, usually held in May, visit the World Horror Convention Web site at www.worldhorror.org.

World Mystery Convention (Bouchercon)

The oldest and largest annual convention for mystery lovers is Bouchercon, a four-day gathering of readers, authors, critics, book dealers, publishers, editors, and agents, named in honor of the late author and critic Anthony Boucher (William Anthony Parker White). Dates and locations have been announced for the next two conventions, where the featured guests include Elmore Leonard (Bouchercon 2000) and Sue Grafton (Bouchercon 2001). For additional details, contact:

Bouchercon 2000
Denver, Colorado (Sept. 7–10, 2000)
303-444-8410
www.bouchercon2000.com

Bouchercon 2001
Washington, DC (Nov. 1–4, 2001)
info@bouchercon2001.com
www.bouchercon2001.com

World Science Fiction Convention (Worldcon)

Established by the World Science Fiction Society (WSFS), the first Worldcon was held in New York City in 1939 and attracted some 200 SF fans. More recent events have drawn as many as 7,000 participants, who vote on the annual Hugo Awards and choose the site for the next convention. For more information, visit the WSFS Web site at www.worldcon.org.

Currently scheduled Worldcons, which are always given a unique name that reflects the location of the host city, include the following:

Chicon 2000
Chicago, Illinois (Aug. 31–Sept. 4, 2000)
chi2000@chicon.org
www.chicon.org

Millennium Philcon 2001
Philadelphia, Pennsylvania (Aug. 30–Sept. 3, 2001)
phil2001@netaxs.com

ConJose 2002
San Jose, California (Aug. 29–Sept. 2, 2002)
conjose@sfsfc.org
www.sfsfc.org

REGIONAL EVENTS

As the following list confirms in small fashion, lively and popular book fairs can be found almost anywhere in the country. Even those events held in midsized cities routinely attract 20,000 to 30,000 visitors. Storytelling festivals are also growing in popularity, with some 200 cities and towns in North America hosting events of one sort or another. Here are some of the most popular local and regional events held each year in the United States and Canada.

Arizona

Arizona Book Festival
Phoenix (April)
602-257-0335 (voice)
602-257-0392 (fax)
azbookfest.org

Northern Arizona Book Festival
Flagstaff (March)
520-556-0313
multihome.www.desert.net/nabookfest

California

Latino Book Festival
Los Angeles and other locations (spring and fall)
714-973-7900
kathy@latinofestivals.com
www.latinofestivals.com

Los Angeles Times Festival of Books
Los Angeles (April)
213-237-5779
www.latimes.com/festival

Sacramento Reads!
Sacramento (September)
916-443-6223
lcweb.loc.gov/loc/cfbook/bkfair/sacram.html

San Francisco Bay Area Book Festival
San Francisco (October)
415-487-4550
www.sfbook.org/html/festival.html

Steinbeck Festival
Salinas (August)
831-753-6411
www.steinbeck.org

Canada

Banff Mountain Book Festival
Banff, Alberta (November)
403-762-6406
www.banffcentre.ab.ca/CMC
This is the only book festival in North America to feature "literature of the outdoors."

Colorado

Rocky Mountain Book Festival
Denver (October/November)
303-839-8320
www.aclin.org/~ccftb

Connecticut

Mark Twain Days
Hartford (July)
860-493-6411
www.hartnet.org/~twain/tour.htm

Florida

BookFest
Palm Beach (March)
561-471-2901
www.pbccc.org/html/body_bookfest.htm

Day of Literary Lectures/Night of Literary Feasts
Fort Lauderdale (March)
954-357-7404

Fort Lauderdale Antiquarian Book Fair
Fort Lauderdale (January)
954-357-8243
www.co.broward.fl.us/lii07800.htm

Key West Literary Seminar
Key West (January)
888-293-9291
keywestliteraryseminar.org

Miami Book Fair International
Miami (third weekend in November)
305-237-3258
www.mdcc.edu/bookfair
This annual event competes with "New York Is Book Country" for the title of biggest book fair in the United States. The weeklong celebration includes educational events during the day, author readings and lectures in the evening, and a three-day street festival featuring 250 authors and hundreds of exhibitors. Typical attendance: 250,000.

Sarasota Reading Festival
Sarasota (November)
941-957-5109
www.newscoast.com/readingfest

Times Festival of Reading
St. Petersburg (November)
800-333-7505 (ext. 4142)
727-893-8481
www.festivalofreading.com

Zora Neale Hurston Festival of the Arts and Humanities
Eatonville (last weekend in January)
407-647-3307 (voice)
407-647-3959 (fax)
zora@cs.ucf.ed
longwood.cs.ucf.edu/~zora

Illinois
Illinois Authors Book Fair
Springfield (October)
217-524-8835
www.sos.state.il.us/depts/library/programs/icb.html

Latino Book Festival
Chicago (November)
714-973-7900
kathy@latinofestivals.com
www.latinofestivals.com

Printers Row Book Fair
Chicago (May)
312-987-9896
www.printersrowbookfair.org

Kentucky
Corn Island Storytelling Festival
Louisville (third weekend in September)
502-245-0643
lcweb.loc.gov/loc/cfbook/bkfair/corn.html

Kentucky Book Fair
Frankfort (third weekend in November)
502-564-8300
www.frankfortky.org/visitor/annualevents.html

Louisiana
Tennessee Williams/New Orleans Literary Festival
New Orleans (March)
504-581-1144
twfest@gnofn.org
www.gnofn.org/~twfest

Maryland
Baltimore Book Festival
Baltimore (September)
410-752-8632
www.bop.org

How to Find Other Book Events

If you have Internet access, you can quickly and easily locate book fairs and festivals in your area by consulting the Center for the Book in the Library of Congress (lcweb.olc.gov/loc/cf-book). But you might also try using your favorite search engine. To find events in North Carolina, for example, go to Yahoo (www.yahoo.com) or AltaVista (www.altavista.com) and type the following in the search box:

+"book fair" +"north carolina"

For best results, be sure to include the plus signs and quotation marks. You might also try a similar search, substituting "festival" or "storytelling festival" for "book fair."

Massachusetts
Boston Globe Book Festival
Boston (October)
617-929-2649
lcweb.loc.gov/loc/cfbook/bkfair/bostongl.html

Harvard Square Book Festival
Cambridge (May)
781-444-0878
www.bookfestival.com

Minnesota
Spotlight on Books
Alexandria (April)
320-762-1032
lcweb.loc.gov/loc/cfbook/bkfair/spot.html

Mississippi
Faulkner and Yoknapatawpha Conference
Oxford (July)
601-232-5993
www.olemiss.edu/depts/south/conferences

Natchez Literary Celebration
Natchez (June)
601-446-1242
www.colin.cc.ms.us/nlc

Oxford Conference for the Book
Oxford (April)
601-232-5993
ann@cssc.olemiss.edu
www.olemiss.edu/depts/south

Tennessee Williams Festival
Clarksdale (October)
800-626-3764
601-627-7337
www.clarksdale.com/twilliams

Missouri
Celebration of the Book
Columbia (November/odd years)
573-751-2680
mosl.sos.state.mo.us/lib-ser/libpub/mcb/celeprog.html

St. Louis Storytelling Festival
St. Louis (May)
314-516-5036
www.umsl.edu/~conted/storyfes.htm

Nebraska
Nebraska Literature Festival
Location varies (September)
800-307-2665 (in Nebraska only)
402-471-2045 (in Lincoln and outside Nebraska)

Nevada
Great Basin Book Festival
Reno (September)
800-382-5023
775-784-6587
www.unr.edu/nhc/bookfest

New Mexico
Border Book Festival (New Mexico)
Las Cruces (March)
505-524-1499
bbf@zianet.com
www.zianet.com/bbf

Santa Fe Festival of the Book
Santa Fe (October)
505-473-7266
www.ci.santa-fe.nm.us/sfpl/festival.html

New York
New York Is Book Country
New York City (September)
212-207-7242
www.bookreporter.com/nyisbookcountry
A New York tradition since 1979, this weeklong festival culminates with a Sunday street fair on Fifth Avenue that typically draws upwards of 250,000 book lovers and readers.

Small Press Book Fair
New York City (March)
212-764-7021
http://www.smallpress.org/bkfair.htm

North Carolina
North Carolina Literary Festival
Chapel Hill (April, even years)
919-962-5665
nclitfest@irss.unc.edu
sunsite.unc.edu/litfest

Novello Festival of Reading
Charlotte (October)
704-336-2801
www.plcmc.lib.nc.us/novello

Page One Festival of Books
Cary (March)
919-460-4963
919-469-4344 (fax)

Ohio
Buckeye Book Fair
Wooster (November)
800-686-2958 (ext. 1617)
330-287-1617
bbfharris@aol.com
www.the-daily-record.com/past_issues/bookfair

Oklahoma
WinterTales Storytelling Festival
Oklahoma City (February)
405-270-4848
info@artscouncilokc.com
www.artscouncilokc.com/wintertales

Pennsylvania
Celebration of Black Writing
Philadelphia (February/Presidents Day Weekend)
215-735-9598
lcweb.loc.gov/loc/cfbook/bkfair/celblack.html

Women's Ink
Philadelphia (Fall)
215-735-9598
lcweb.loc.gov/loc/cfbook/bkfair/womens.html

South Carolina
A(ugusta) Baker's Dozen
A Celebration of Stories Festival
Columbia (April/May)
803-929-3440 (voice)
803-929-3448 (fax)
www.richland.lib.sc.us/baker.htm
The event is named in honor of Augusta Baker (1911–98), who served for many years as Coordinator of Children's Services for the New York Public Library system.

Tennessee

Chattanooga Conference on Southern Literature
Chattanooga (April, odd years)
800-267-4232
423-267-1218
423-267-1018 (fax)
artsed@bellsouth.net
www.artsedcouncil.org

Southern Festival of Books
Nashville (October)
615-320-7001
tn-humanities.org/sfbmain.htm

Texas

High Plains Book Festival
Amarillo (September)
806-378-4228
info@bookfestival.arn.net
bookfestival.arn.net
San Antonio Inter-American Book Fair and Literary Festival

San Antonio (February)
210-271-3151
lcweb.loc.gov/loc/cfbook/bkfair/sananto.html

Texas Book Festival
Austin (November)
512-477-4055
www.austin360.com/texasbookfestival

Utah

Great Salt Lake Book Festival
Salt Lake City (September)
801-359-9670

Virginia

Virginia Book Festival
Charlottesville (March)
804-924-3296
vabook@virginia.edu
www.vabook.org

Washington

Bumbershoot Literary Arts Festival
Seattle (September/Labor Day Weekend)
206-281-7788
www.bumbershoot.org

Northwest Bookfest
Seattle (November)
206-378-1883
www.speakeasy.org/nwbookfest

PUBLISHER AND AUTHOR CONTACTS

How many times have you read a book that gave you so much pleasure or touched you so deeply that you really, really wanted to express your appreciation to the author? Lot's of times, of course. But contacting an author isn't usually very easy to do. Some authors are naturally reclusive and, frankly, don't want to hear from readers, no matter how enthusiastic and full of praise. Others have made themselves available in the past, only to be taken advantage of by fans who do not seem to realize that authors don't have time to read and critique every aspiring novelist's work or advise every new writer on how to break into the business. So they deliberately make themselves scarce. Still others warmly welcome all readers and fans, gently turning aside those who make demands with a friendly form letter.

In the best of all possible worlds, every author would publish an e-mail address at the back of each book, making it possible for readers to quickly and easily send a note of appreciation, criticism, or comment. Better still, every publisher would have a Web site that included a feature specifically designed to facilitate the distribution of electronic fan mail to its authors. No postage. No paper. No hunting for the correct land address. Just dash off a quick e-mail message and move on, feeling better because you've expressed your thoughts, and knowing that you've made the author feel good in the process.

Sadly, the publishing industry being what it is, we're a long way from that happy state of affairs. Still, knowing from long personal experience how much it can mean to both writer and reader to make contact, we've done our best in this book to facilitate such communications, while simultaneously shielding authors from uninvited in-person visits and unwanted mail.

So, if you want to send a note of appreciation to an author, check the individual's write-up in this book first. In many cases, we've included a specific fan-mail address drawn from publicly available sources like *Contemporary Authors*, author-specific Web sites, and directories.

If we haven't included a fan-mail address, note the name of the author's publisher and come back here. The list that follows includes the phone numbers and Web addresses for the publishers of all the authors featured in this book. But it also contains the "author fan mail" land address for each publisher. You may or may not get a reply from your favorite author. But one thing is certain: Using the addresses specified here will speed your correspondence on its way and reduce the chances of your letter sitting on some clerk's desk for the next six months before being forwarded to the proper department. (Be warned, however, that because of changes in ownership and the vicissitudes of Manhattan real estate, some of these publishers are sure to have moved to new locations by the time you read this book. Many Random House imprints, for instance, are headed for temporary quarters in 2000 while owner Bertelsmann constructs a new building. So before writing to one of their authors, you may want to call the toll-free number or consult the Web site for the current address.)

How to Find Publishers Not Listed Here

One of the best ways to track down contact information for the 9,000-plus other book publishers is to visit the reference section of your local library, where you're almost certain to find the two-volume *Literary Market Place*. Published by R. R. Bowker and updated annually, *LMP* (as it's known in the book business) is the most comprehensive printed directory of the publishing industry, with listings organized by types of books, subject, and geography.

Alternatively, if you have access to the Internet, you might try using your favorite search engine to locate the publisher's Web site. Most book publishers these days maintain a presence on the Web to promote their current offerings and provide contact information for readers, including the preferred address to use for sending fan mail to their authors.

Alfred A. Knopf
800-733-3000
410-848-1900
www.randomhouse.com/knopf

Author Fan Mail:
(Author's Name)
c/o Promotion Dept.
Alfred A. Knopf
201 East 50th Street
New York, NY 10022

Amereon Limited
516-298-5100

Author Fan Mail::
(Author Name)
c/o Publicity Dept.
Amereon Limited
800 Wickham Avenue
Mattituck, NY 11952

Avon Books
800-762-0779
212-261-6800
www.avonbooks.com

Author Fan Mail:
(Author's Name)
c/o Publicity Dept.
Avon Books
1350 Avenue of the Americas
New York, NY 10019

Ballantine Books
800-733-3000
410-848-1900
www.randomhouse.com/BB

Author Fan Mail:
(Author's Name)
c/o Publicity Dept.
Ballantine Books
201 East 50th Street
New York, NY 10022

Bantam Books
800-323-9872
212-354-6500
www.randomhouse.com

Author Fan Mail:
(Author's Name)
c/o Bantam Books Publicity
1540 Broadway
New York, NY 10036

Carroll & Graf Publishers
212-889-8772

Author Fan Mail:
(Author's Name)
c/o Publicity Dept.
Carroll & Graf Publishers
19 West 21st Street, Suite 201
New York, NY 10010-6805

Crown
800-733-3000
410-848-1900
www.randomhouse.com

Author Fan Mail:
(Author's Name)
c/o Crown Publicity
201 East 50th Street
New York, NY 10022

Delacorte Press
800-323-9872
212-354-6500
www.randomhouse.com

Author Fan Mail:
(Author's Name)
c/o Delacorte Press Publicity
1540 Broadway
New York, NY 10036

Doubleday
800-605-3406
212-354-6500
www.randomhouse.com

Author Fan Mail:
(Author's Name)
c/o Doubleday Publicity
1540 Broadway
New York, NY 10036

Dutton
800-253-6476
212-366-2000
www.penguinputnam.com

Author Fan Mail:
(Author's Name)
c/o Dutton Publicity Dept.
375 Hudson Street
New York, NY 10014

Farrar, Straus & Giroux
888-330-8477
212-741-6900
www.fsbassociates.com/fsg

Author Fan Mail:
(Author's Name)
c/o Publicity Dept.
Farrar, Straus & Giroux
19 Union Square West
New York, NY 10003

G. P. Putnam's Sons
800-253-6476
212-366-2000
www.penguinputnam.com

Author Fan Mail:
(Author's Name)
c/o Publicity Dept.
G. P. Putnam's Sons
375 Hudson Street
New York, NY 10014

Writing to an Author

One can take or leave professional critics, but it is a rare author who deep down doesn't want to hear from readers. Writing, as has been said many times before, is a solitary occupation. All of us welcome sincere comments and reactions to what we have produced.

With that in mind, when a book has had an impact on you, when you finish the last page and say, "Wow!"—when you can't get a character out of your mind or find yourself replaying a scene's dialog in your head while you're splitting logs or mowing the lawn—resolve to write the author to convey your reaction. So few readers actually take the time to do this that your note is likely to have a significant impact.

But don't expect a response. It's nothing personal. Few authors have secretaries and publicists to handle reader correspondence. Many have classes to teach and papers to grade. Others have articles to write and interviews to do. And, oh, yes, most are spending every bit of free time on their next novel. Here are a few points to consider when preparing your letter:

1. Hold yourself to a single page. Time and talent are all an author has to sell, so you can't expect anyone who writes for a living to take the time to read a rambling, multipage letter, no matter how enthusiastic.

2. Resist the urge to ask for advice on how to get published, how to find an agent, or how to get your own novel read by an editor. *Writer's Digest* and many other magazines and books address those questions frequently.

3. Save yourself the wasted postage of sending a manuscript for an author to read. It will end up in the trash, unopened, in most cases.

4. Be aware that an author typically earns between 10 and 15 percent of the cover price on a hardback book and about 7.5 percent on a paperback edition. So the author's share of that $9.00 paperback you bought is less than 70 cents. If you borrowed the book from the library, the author earned no income from you at all. So you probably shouldn't mention it if you did.

5. Though it's no guarantee, you will increase the likelihood of getting a reply if you enclose a self-addressed stamped envelope with your letter.

Grove/Atlantic
212-614-7850

Author Fan Mail:
(Author's Name)
c/o Publicity Dept.
Grove/Atlantic
841 Broadway
New York, NY 10003

Harcourt
212-592-1000
www.harcourt.com

Author Fan Mail:
(Author's Name)
c/o Publicity Dept.
Harcourt
15 East 26th Street
New York, NY 10010

HarperCollins
212-207-7000
www.harpercollins.com

Author Fan Mail:
(Author's Name)
c/o Author Mail, 7th Floor
HarperCollins
10 East 53rd Street
New York, NY 10022

Henry Holt
212-886-9200
www.henryholt.com

Author Fan Mail:
(Author's Name)
c/o Publicity Dept.
Henry Holt
115 West 18th Street
New York, NY 10011

Houghton Mifflin
800-225-3362
617-351-5000
www.hmco.com/trade

Author Fan Mail:
(Author's Name)
c/o Trade Division
Houghton Mifflin
222 Berkeley Street
Boston, MA 02116-3764

Knopf Publishing Group
800-733-3000
410-848-1900
www.randomhouse.com/knopf

Author Fan Mail:
(Author's Name)
c/o Promotion Dept.
Knopf Publishing Group
201 East 50th Street
New York, NY 10022

Library of America
212-308-3360
www.libraryofamerica.org

Author Fan Mail:
(Author's Name)
c/o Publicity Dept.
Library of America
14 East 60th Street
New York, NY 10022

Little, Brown
212-522-8700

Author Fan Mail:
(Author's Name)
c/o Author Mail
Little, Brown and Company
1271 Avenue of the Americas
New York, NY 10020

Modern Library
800-733-3000
410-848-1900
www.randomhouse.com/modernlibrary

Author Fan Mail:
(Author's Name)
c/o Publicity Dept.
Random House
201 East 50th Street
New York, NY 10022

Oxford University Press
212-726-6000
www.oup-usa.org

Author Fan Mail (regular mail):
(Author's Name)
c/o Publicity Dept.
Oxford University Press
198 Madison Avenue
New York, NY 10016
Author Fan Mail (e-mail):
publicity@oup-usa.org

Pantheon Books
800-733-3000
410-848-1900
www.randomhouse.com/knopf/pantheon

Author Fan Mail:
(Author's Name)
c/o Promotion Dept.
Pantheon Books
201 East 50th Street
New York, NY 10022

Penguin
800-253-6476
212-366-2000
www.penguinputnam.com

Author Fan Mail:
(Author's Name)
c/o Penguin Publicity
375 Hudson Street
New York, NY 10014

Putnam
800-253-6476
212-366-2000
www.penguinputnam.com

Author Fan Mail:
(Author's Name)
c/o Putnam Publicity
375 Hudson Street
New York, NY 10014

Random House
800-733-3000
410-848-1900
www.randomhouse.com

Author Fan Mail:
(Author's Name)
c/o Publicity Dept.
Random House
201 East 50th Street
New York, NY 10022

Scholastic Press
212-343-6100
www.scholastic.com

Author Fan Mail:
(Author's Name)
c/o Scholastic Press
555 Broadway
New York, NY 10012-3999

Scribner
800-223-2348
212-698-7000
www.simonsays.com

Author Fan Mail:
(Author's Name)
c/o Scribner Publicity Dept.
1230 Avenue of the Americas
New York, NY 10020

Simon & Schuster
800-223-2348
212-698-7000
www.simonsays.com

Author Fan Mail:
(Author's Name)
c/o Publicity Dept.
Simon & Schuster
1230 Avenue of the Americas
New York, NY 10020

St. Martin's Press
212-674-5151
www.stmartins.com

Author Fan Mail:
(Author's Name)
c/o St. Martin's Press
175 Fifth Avenue
New York, NY 10010

Tor Books
212-388-0100
www.tor.com

Author Fan Mail:
(Author's Name)
c/o Tor Books
175 Fifth Avenue, 14th Floor
New York, NY 10010

University of Pennsylvania Press
800-445-9880
410-516-6998 (fax)
www.upenn.edu/pennpress

Author Fan Mail:
(Author's Name)
c/o Publicity Dept.
University of Pennsylvania Press
P.O. Box 4836
Hampden Station
Baltimore, MD 21211

Viking

800-253-6476

212-366-2000

www.penguinputnam.com

Author Fan Mail:
(Author's Name)
c/o Viking Publicity
375 Hudson Street
New York, NY 10014

Vintage

800-733-3000

410-848-1900

www.randomhouse.com/viking

Author Fan Mail:
(Author's Name)
c/o Vintage Promotion
201 East 50th Street
New York, NY 10022

William Morrow & Co.

212-261-6500

www.williammorrow.com

Author Fan Mail:
(Author's Name)
c/o William Morrow & Co.
Attn: Royalties Dept.
10 E. 53rd Street
New York, NY 10022

W. W. Norton

212-354-5500

www.wwnorton.com

Author Fan Mail:
(Author's Name)
c/o W. W. Norton
500 Fifth Avenue
New York, NY 10110

Index

Names of featured authors are shown in **boldface** type; page numbers in *italics* refer to the primary entry.